Poetics of
Breathing

SERIES EDITORS

David E. Johnson, *Comparative Literature, University at Buffalo*
Scott Michaelsen, *English, Michigan State University*

SERIES ADVISORY BOARD

Nahum D. Chandler, *African American Studies, University of California, Irvine*
Rebecca Comay, *Philosophy and Comparative Literature, University of Toronto*
Marc Crépon, *Philosophy, École Normale Supérieure, Paris*
Jonathan Culler, *Comparative Literature, Cornell University*
Johanna Drucker, *Design Media Arts and Information Studies, University of California, Los Angeles*
Christopher Fynsk, *Modern Thought, Aberdeen University*
Rodolphe Gasché, *Comparative Literature, University at Buffalo*
Martin Hägglund, *Comparative Literature, Yale University*
Carol Jacobs, *German and Comparative Literature, Yale University*
Peggy Kamuf, *French and Comparative Literature, University of Southern California*
David Marriott, *History of Consciousness, University of California, Santa Cruz*
Steven Miller, *English, University at Buffalo*
Alberto Moreiras, *Hispanic Studies, Texas A&M University*
Patrick O'Donnell, *English, Michigan State University*
Pablo Oyarzún, *Teoría del Arte, Universidad de Chile*
Scott Cutler Shershow, *English, University of California, Davis*
Henry Sussman, *German and Comparative Literature, Yale University*
Samuel Weber, *Comparative Literature, Northwestern University*
Ewa Ziarek, *Comparative Literature, University at Buffalo*

Poetics of Breathing

Modern Literature's Syncope

Stefanie Heine

Cover image: Jayne Wilton, *Drawing Breath (Child's Breath)*. Breath and light on sensitized paper. © Jayne Wilton. Used with permission.

Published by State University of New York Press, Albany

© 2021 State University of New York

All rights reserved

Printed in the United States of America

No part of this book may be used or reproduced in any manner whatsoever without written permission. No part of this book may be stored in a retrieval system or transmitted in any form or by any means including electronic, electrostatic, magnetic tape, mechanical, photocopying, recording, or otherwise without the prior permission in writing of the publisher.

For information, contact State University of New York Press, Albany, NY
www.sunypress.edu

Library of Congress Cataloging-in-Publication Data

Name: Heine, Stephanie, author.
Title: Poetics of breathing : modern literature's syncope / Stephanie Heine.
Description: Albany : State University of New York Press, 2021. | Series:
 SUNY series, literature . . . in theory | Includes bibliographical references and index.
Identifiers: LCCN 2020032402 | ISBN 9781438483573 (hardcover : alk. paper) |
 ISBN 9781438483580 (pbk. : alk. paper) | ISBN 9781438483597 (ebook)
Subjects: LCSH: Respiration in literature. | Rhythm in literature. | Literary style. | Respiration.
Classification: LCC PN56.R465 H45 2021 | DDC 809/.933561—dc23
LC record available at https://lccn.loc.gov/2020032402

10 9 8 7 6 5 4 3 2 1

As though to breathe were life!

—Alfred, Lord Tennyson, "Ulysses"

Contents

List of Illustrations		ix
Acknowledgments		xi
Preface		xv
1	Movements of Syncopnea	1
2	Composed on the Breath: Authentic Voice, Embodiment, Innovation (Jack Kerouac, Allen Ginsberg)	49
3	Generative Caesurae: Mediality, Rhythm, Affect (Robert Musil, Virginia Woolf)	117
4	Impossible Expiration: Reduction, Inanimate Voices, Persisting Bodies (Samuel Beckett, Sylvia Plath)	171
5	Breath at Point Zero: Trauma, Commemoration, Haunting (Paul Celan, Herta Müller)	241
6	Pneumatic Gender Dynamics, Queering Breath	305
Notes		329
Bibliography		381
Index		407

Illustrations

Figure 2.1 Allen Ginsberg, *Fall of America* and "Iron Horse" (draft). 69

Figure 2.2 Allen Ginsburg, "Iron Horse" (tape composition, reading, draft, and printed version in comparison). 71

Figure 2.3 Allen Ginsberg, *Fall of America* and "Iron Horse" (draft). 79

Figure 2.4 Allen Ginsberg, *Fall of America* and "Iron Horse" (draft). 80

Figure 2.5 Allen Ginsberg, "Iron Horse" (draft). 81

Figure 2.6 Allen Ginsberg, *Fall of America* and "Iron Horse" (draft). 82

Figure 2.7 Allen Ginsberg, *Fall of America* and "Iron Horse" (draft). 84

Figure 2.8 Allen Ginsberg, "Iron Horse" (draft). 84

Figure 3.1 Robert Musil, *Klagenfurter Ausgabe*, V/3/62, March 27–November 1937. 132

Figure 3.2 Robert Musil, *Klagenfurter Ausgabe*, V/3/45, August–December 1938. 132

Figure 3.3 Robert Musil, *Klagenfurter Ausgabe*, III/6/60, mid-1934–August 1935, author's translation. 134

Figure 4.1 Samuel Beckett, *Malone meurt*, MS-HRC-SB-7-4, 44r. 181

Figure 4.2 Beckett, *The Unnamable*, MS-HRC-SB-5-10, 109r. 192

Figure 4.3 Sylvia Plath, "Tulips" (prosody). 226

Figure 4.4 Sylvia Plath, "Tulips" (meter). 226

Figure 5.1 Paul Celan, "Ricercar" (draft). 274

Figure 5.2 Paul Celan, "Ricercar" (draft). 275

Acknowledgments

Working on literary breath teaches a lesson: all our writing is, to some extent, *écriture soufflée* (a concept that is, of course, itself stolen). Everything we write is inspired, taken from somewhere or someone else; we do not own the words we use, and our concepts, thoughts, and readings are, to a certain extent, always owed to others. This book is a work of inspiration and conspiration.

I am deeply indebted to Charles de Roche, John Paul Ricco, and Sandro Zanetti, who have shaped my writing, reading, and thinking over years. Without their ongoing support, encouragement, and engagement with the project on all levels, *Poetics of Breathing* would not have been possible.

For their inexhaustible help with the manuscript in its final stages I owe more than thanks to Brian Alkire—a "match struck unexpectedly in the dark"—who greatly improved the book's style, continually enhances my writing, and came up with its subtitle, and Philippe P. Haensler, who contributed a significant number of ideas and helped me to fine-tune my language and arguments.

I am grateful to the many attentive readers and listeners who made significant contributions to individual chapters and the book as a whole; above all, Felix Christen, Thomas Fries, Spencer Hawkins, Torsten Jenkel, Selmin Kara, Monika Kasper, Michael Krimper, Victor Li, Kristina Mendicino, Sergej Rickenbacher, Arthur Rose, Fabian Schwitter, Cory Stockwell, Rahel Villinger, and Martina Wernli.

The Department of Comparative Literature in Zürich has consistently been an intellectual home: I am grateful for having been part of this academic community. I owe a great deal to my friends and colleagues at the University of Zürich and Toronto, and I have benefited tremendously from the exchanges and collaborations with members of the team at the Life of

Breath research project at Durham University. The productive feedback at numerous workshops and conferences was invaluable for the book's development. I thank the Swiss National Foundation (SNF) for the fellowship at the University of Toronto and the university's Centre for Comparative Literature for hosting me.

My research benefited greatly from the help offered by the staff at the archives I visited; my special thanks go to Melissa Watterworth Batt at the Thomas J. Dodd Research Center, Joshua McKeon at the Berg Collection, and Tim Noakes at the Special Collections, Stanford University.

An earlier version of a part of the subchapter "Ebb and Flow: Breathing and Composition" was originally published in my coedited book, *Reading Breath in Literature* (2019). An earlier version of a part of the subchapter "'animi velut respirant': Rhythm" was originally published as "'animi velut respirant': Rhythm and Breathing Pauses in Ancient Rhetoric, Virginia Woolf, and Robert Musil" in *Comparative Literature*, vol. 69, no. 4, pp. 355–369; copyright 2017, University of Oregon; all rights reserved; republished by permission of the copyright holder and the present publisher, Duke University Press.

For their kind permission to reproduce or cite archival material I thank the following:

The Estate of Samuel Beckett, c/o Rosica Colin Ltd., London, for excerpts and images from Samuel Beckett's "The Unnamable," "Malone Dies," and "Souffle."

Bertrand Badiou and Suhrkamp Verlag for excerpts from Paul Celan, *Die Gedichte aus dem Nachlaß*, edited by Bertrand Badiou, Jean-Claude Rambach, and Barbara Wiedemann, comments from Barbara Wiedemann and Bertrand Badiou; copyright Suhrkamp Verlag Frankfurt am Main, 1997; all rights reserved.

The Wylie Agency and the Allen Ginsberg Estate for excerpts from the Allen Ginsberg Papers by Allen Ginsberg; copyright Allen Ginsberg, used by permission of the Wylie Agency LLC.

The Wylie Agency and the Jack Kerouac Estate for excerpts from the Jack Kerouac Papers by Jack Kerouac; copyright by Jack Kerouac, used by permission of the Wylie Agency LLC.

Österreichische Nationalbibliothek for manuscript excerpts from Robert Musil, *Der Mann ohne Eigenschaften*.

The Estate of Charles Olson and the Charles Olson Research Collection, Archives and Special Collections, University of Connecticut, for excerpts of unpublished manuscripts by the poet Charles Olson. Works by Charles Olson published during his lifetime are copyright the Estate of Charles Olson; previously unpublished works are copyright the University of Connecticut; used with permission.

The Society of Authors as the Literary Representative of the Estate of Virginia Woolf for excerpts by Virginia Woolf.

My editor at SUNY Press, Rebecca Colesworthy, has been a wonderful collaborator and support: her belief in the book project and efforts in the process of realizing it have been invaluable. I would also like to express my gratitude to James Peltz for his guidance and assistance regarding permissions; to Cathy Blackwell for her assistance in getting the manuscript ready for production; to my production editor, Jenn Bennett-Genthner; to SUNY's marketing director, Fran Keneston; and to the wonderful copy editor, Nicole Balant.

I am thankful for the generosity of those who offered their help in fields and matters that exceed my competence: Ben Akrigg (early uses of *pneuma*), Bettina Mosca-Rau (deciphering manuscripts), Brian Nevin (tape recordings), Leonard Stein (Hebrew), and Christian Zehnder (Russian).

Last but not least, special thanks go to my students at the Department for Comparative Literature in Zürich: the conversations in class are an ongoing source of inspiration. A version of this manuscript served as my qualifying work for *Habilitation* at the University of Zurich.

Preface

Lying at the heart of language, breathing escapes words. At the same time, attempts have continually been made to write about it, whether in the context of medical discourses, theology, philosophy, or literature. Entering the space of respiratory literature via its corporeal basis, I first want to listen closely to an audible breath: in an individual exhalation, captured on Jeff Buckley's studio album *Grace*, in which a breath containing the core concerns of a specifically modern literary engagement with breath can be unfolded. What has always struck me most about Jeff Buckley's performance of Leonard Cohen's "Hallelujah"—a song that by now has almost been covered too often—is a detail we can easily miss hearing.[1] In the original studio version, and only there, after a minute-long instrumental intro, one can hear Buckley exhaling before he strikes the strings of his guitar and starts singing.[2] Unleashing the song's compelling atmosphere, this seemingly peripheral element sets the tone for Buckley's cover.[3]

Buckley's audible breath anticipates the following six minutes and forty-five seconds on tape: it contains the ambivalence of the lyrics and the iridescent mood of a hymn for a world in which God has long been dead, as it shifts back and forth between intimacy and distance, triumph and defeat, challenge and resignation, love and violence, disillusion and enchantment; between physical and spiritual, religious and secular, exalted and mundane, destruction and creation.[4] Buckley's voice is piercing, every pluck of the guitar's strings a cut—subtle and low-key; his interpretation expresses maximal urgency—it is untroubled yet pressing, both vulnerable and strong. A sense of incongruity is already palpable in this preliminary exhalation.

The very fact that we are confronted with an exhalation is strange and frustrates our expectations: to be able to sing, after all, one first needs to breathe *in*, to *inhale* in preparation for the act of singing, which is a controlled exhalation: a parallel to inspiration, one model of aesthetic production, a term that points to what enabled or triggered the artistic creation. This parallel would be particularly convincing given that inspiration reverberates in the lyrics when the speaker, in a self-reflective twist, gives an account of how it came into existence, merging a biblical reference to King David's "secret chord" with the chords of "Hallelujah" that we hear at the exact moment they are named in the song.[5] If we focus on the corporeal dimension of the song's "primal scene"—primal here in a physiological sense, as breathing makes speaking and singing possible in the first place—it would be logical to hear the inhalation before the sounds carried on Buckley's exhaled breath. We might be encountering a random involuntary bodily emission, but the place where it occurs on the recording, before the song is performed, points to an inverted inspiration that disrupts conventional chronology as well as prevailing attributions of meaning.

Like any breath, the one we hear at the beginning of "Hallelujah" is difficult—maybe even impossible—to read. At the same time, there is a limited scope of plausible meanings.[6] Buckley's single exhalation at the outset can hardly be aligned with the erotically charged repeated inhalations addressed in the lyrics: "And remember when I moved in you / and a holy dove was moving too / and every breath we drew was Hallelujah." Even though the explicit reference to "breath," together with the holy dove, one of the most prominent symbols for divine inspiration in Christian iconography, may tempt us to relate the lines back to the audible respiratory sound, the latter resists being interpreted in terms of sexual pleasure, an ecstasy coinciding with spiritual experience. If one wants to adhere to this context at all, the exhalation rather sounds like a postcoital breath, indicating exhaustion—or disappointment? Could it be disappointment because the moment of fulfilment has already passed, or perhaps has never taken place?

Or is it a breath expressing hesitance? It sounds as if an enormous exertion is lying ahead, as if we could already hear the resignation in the face of an effort that will be too much, that will have been too much. Do we hear Buckley bracing himself before a task that will be too hard to accomplish, that will have been too hard to accomplish? The breath's tense would be future perfect: an expiration that inspires, a life-giving impulse that is already occupied by death, the expectation of a potential endeavor that is already frustrated but executed nevertheless. Let us keep in mind that Buckley was recording his debut album; lacking enough material of his own, he added three covers, including "Hallelujah," which was in fact the cover of a cover: Buckley's version is based on John Cale's rendition of the song on a Cohen tribute album (Light xxvii). This does not sound very "inspired" in the common present-day use of the term, as a spark initiating something original or new. It rather recalls a much older model of inspiration: the idea that artists passively voice what is breathed into them by a superior being. In the light of a music industry obsessed with authenticity and originality, Buckley's sigh before he starts playing "Hallelujah" makes sense without being decipherable.

And there might be more to it still. The strained expiration may be indicative of the fact that Buckley is about to give himself up to another voice, or other voices: Cohen's and Cale's.[7] Do we hear an anxiety of influence, an awareness that everything has already been said? Could it be unease about the challenge of living up to one's predecessors? Or the fear that such patricide may be the only way of being creative at all? Or perhaps that the love for the paragon and his music can only be disappointed in the attempt to consume and incorporate it? Do we listen to a breath carrying the burden of outdoing the adored precursors, a breath that is going to act out its French meaning, which is "to steal" or "to dispossess"?[8] In this case, Buckley's exhalation would have anticipated the enthusiastic reception of *Grace*, which was not immediate and only reached its peak after the artist's untimely death in 1997 (see Light 69, 90–91). Not until then did the only album he released become what it is now: a legend, a classic, and for numerous music magazines and critics, one of the best albums of all times. Moreover, "Hallelujah" owes much of its enormous popularity to Buckley's cover on *Grace*. First rejected by the record company and then hardly noticed when released on the album *Various Positions*, Cohen's original was everything but a success (see Light xx). Neither did Cale's cover attract much attention. It is thus no exaggeration to say that Buckley "broke" Cohen's "throne" by drawing "from [his] lips" the "Hallelujah"; it is no exaggeration to say that, with respect to "Hallelujah," Buckley "outdrew" Cohen.[9] And perhaps the sense of deprivation pervading Buckley's cover—both the atmosphere generated by the recording and its belated fame—is implicit in the future-present of the strained breath preceding it.

Maybe the exhalation that left Buckley's body to be captured beyond his lifetime on a recording medium gives a sense of how Buckley makes Cohen's song come to "itself" (a "self" that has always already been lost) by appropriating it. "Hallelujah" presents deprivation on various levels. The lyrics are all about loss and dispossession: the faith and religious feelings the song evokes as a primary source for the images it draws on have long been lost—"it's a cold and it's a broken Hallelujah." In the fictional account of its own genesis—something that by definition is before and thus beyond the song's realized state (i.e., its state in the moment we hear it)—"Hallelujah" is composed by someone who is beside himself: the "baffled king," the very king whose throne will be broken, whose words will be drawn from his lips. In other words, the song is attributed to someone who loses all that made, defined, and "identified" him. In his reference to the biblical King David, Cohen himself makes a futile attempt to unthrone someone who, in the most foundational text of Western cultural history, is presented as an unparalleled musician. As a fictional "cover" of David's psalms in a time when the majesty of gods and kings is irrecoverable, Cohen's "Hallelujah" was pervaded by deprivation before Buckley or Cale even touched it. The history of its actual composition puts the song's *own* identity into question. Cohen's exhaustive four to five years' work on it and the excess of lyrics he produced[10] make it impossible to decide what the "original" version of "Hallelujah" might be—is it what he performed on numerous occasions?[11] What he recorded for *Various Positions*? What ended up on the *Cohen Live* album?[12] What was printed in the collection of lyrics and poetry titled *Stranger Music*? Given that the song has never been identical with "itself," it may be no coincidence that "Hallelujah" became one of the most covered songs of all time.

In an installation centering on the extreme popularity of "Hallelujah" today at the exhibition dedicated to Cohen at the Musée d'Art Contemporain de Montréal in 2017–2018, we hear a (likely unintentional) echo of Buckley's breath. As the accompanying text of the still-accessible web version of the participatory work *I Heard There Was a Secret Chord* puts it: "This project lets people everywhere experience the invisible vibration uniting people from around the world currently listening to Leonard Cohen's 'Hallelujah.' Real-time user data representing these listeners is transformed into a virtual choir of humming voices that users join to hum-along" (*I Heard There Was a Secret Chord* Info.). Encountering the "virtual choir," we not only hear voices humming the melody of "Hallelujah" but also breaths. And everyone familiar with Buckley's cover cannot help but hear his exhausted exhalation with these respiratory sounds. It is precisely in this moment that the "unity" of participants highlighted by the work's official description (*I Heard There Was a Secret Chord* Info.) is shattered. Once we take the breath into account while humming along, the communal experience—which is, as the informational text suggests, a "metaphysical connection"—also becomes one of encountering and acknowledging physical separation.

Like any recorded breath, including the breaths we encounter in *I Heard There Was a Secret Chord*, Buckley's expiration is perceived as an isolated sound, alienated and separated from the body it departed from. That which, according to familiar narratives, is supposed to be a vital force attesting to his physical being (perhaps his soul) has just left him in the moment of listening to *Grace*. Hearing something that was emitted from Buckley's body evokes an intimacy that is interrupted immediately when we realize that we are faced with sound waves produced by a machine located somewhere miles away from Woodstock, New York, where *Grace* was recorded years ago. It is strange to hear the breath of a man who has been dead for more than twenty years—to hear what maintained his physical body, what granted him life, at a moment when he no longer is alive. Hearing Buckley's exhalation, we also hear his last breath. The sound entering our ears insinuates that we never own the air we breathe; that we continually depend on a physiological mechanism we cannot control; that it is an alien, inanimate substance that keeps us alive by entering and leaving our body, something we take but cannot keep, in a process of perpetual loss. It's a cold and it's a broken Hallelujah.[13]

1

Movements of Syncopnea

My reading of Buckley's breath and his rendition of Cohen's "Hallelujah" introduce the spectrum of the following study of breathing in modern literature. In the first chapter, the implications of artistic respiration observed in Buckley's exhalation are put to the test by visiting a number of critical settings in which breath has been thought and written about across the centuries. The characterizations of breathing as liminal, on the verge of semantics, primary, disrupting, relational, and non–self-identical repeatedly recur across the various contexts I investigate, thus constituting a historical-theoretical framework for my investigation of modern respiratory literature.

What I observed in Buckley's recording of "Hallelujah," that the audible breath is a marginal element tending to be unheard, pertains to breathing in general. Breath usually escapes perception and often remains unnoticed; breathed air is mostly invisible. In artistic renderings too, breath is seldom visible at first glance. That a book-length comparative study of breath in modern literature has not yet been done could be due to this fact. Another reason is certainly the hesitance and suspicion some historical accounts of breath, and the network of terms that go along with it, provoke, an issue to which I will return later in this chapter.

It has to be admitted from the outset: when one writes about breath in literature, one never writes about breath as such. Literature cannot record physiological respiration; whenever breathing enters a written literary work, it will be semanticized to occur as a word, image, metaphor, or metonymy. Consisting of arbitrary signs, literature necessarily fails to reproduce the sound or visual appearance of breath accurately. This, however, is precisely the reason why literary renderings of breath are so intriguing. Words can only hint at the phenomenon of breathing: breath necessarily escapes them; they capture its tendency to withdraw from what is visible and heard. That we never see or hear breath as such in a literary text, but only encounter indications of it that point to something else located somewhere else, increases the awareness that breath has no fixed place or mode of occurrence. Every inhalation is always on the verge of becoming an exhalation; the oxygen in our lungs is on the verge of becoming carbon dioxide outside our body; the audible sigh recedes into silence; the curling white shapes in the cold air dissolve. Literary depictions of respiration and the word "breath" may invoke a fleeting image or sound, but if we shift our attention from what we imagine back to the page or screen we're reading, we return to silent letters.

The letters of the word "breath" point, not only to a physiological process, but also to a rich and complicated etymological and cultural history. Precisely because breath challenges representation, it often marks moments when literature reflects the limits of language's meaning-bearing, referential function. An investigation of breathing in literature is bound to have a double focus: on the matter in question and on the ways in which this matter has been thought about, written about, presented, and represented. My analyses will move along points of intersection: where breathing meets something other than itself (a linguistic sign, a printed letter, a sheet of paper, an electronic display, a recorded sound, etc.), where it enters language and interrupts it, and where it is transferred between different media and materialities of literature. In other words, the way breathing has been thought about, written about, and aesthetically rendered never fully coincides with the physical phenomenon—with what we do when we inhale and exhale. At the same time, a ruptured movement, an uneven symmetry, a non–self-coincidence, and the very notion of transference are indeed characteristic of the physiological breathing process. The inhaled air is split into various constituents in the body and chemically does not coincide with what is exhaled. Our life as human beings is reliant on the continual intake of an inorganic substance that becomes part of our body, only to depart from it again, now transformed. The fact that breathing is necessary in order to live also shows that what we consider organic life depends on our bodies' alliance with inorganic substances: as breathing beings, we are never fully "ourselves." As L. O. Aranye Fradenburg puts it, "Breathing is an experience of (embodied) extimacy: the 'me'-ness of a strange element, the strangeness of what is in me" (181). With every breath we take, we find ourselves at the limit of what is deemed our own (our body, etc.) and what is deemed other (the outside world, etc.). A respiring living organism is never self-contained, the "self" of a breathing being is scattered into fragments that do not make up a coherent identity. "Catching one's breath" is catching up, for an instant, with that part of the "self" that always exceeds it. In ongoing excessive exhalations, the subject continually outbreathes itself.

The movement of breathing is a continuity of interruptions: intervals determine the alternation of inhalation and exhalation—inhaling and exhaling necessarily disrupt, or cut into, one another. A living being's breathing rhythm is never completely regular; it is continually intermitted by inhalations induced by contingent impulses and factors. While the analogy between bodily breath and breathing in words will always be slightly askew, it is precisely this incongruence that turns out to provide the most fruitful point of comparison, especially if one is concerned with modern literature, in which crises of representation and the dilemmas of rendering them have been increasingly negotiated.

In my analysis of modern literary respiration, I try to avoid two associations with which breath is often invested: a notion of organicism and a kind of re-spiritualization, which is especially perceptible in New Age discourses. In aesthetic renderings, breathing, a physiological process, something living beings are supposed to do, meets inanimate materials and media—taken seriously, the focus on breath in literature alone forbids conceiving of it in purely organic terms. My preferred method is close reading: however, the biological metaphor of an "organic unity" in literary texts, which has been promoted especially by the New Critics (and, even more so, attributed to them retrospectively)[1] is rendered inoperative for the very same reasons. A reading such as the one I did of Buckley's "Hallelujah" often shows that different elements of an aesthetic work do not relate to each other harmoniously and do not amount to a holistic "organism";[2] put more generally, a close reading of breath tends to reveal that a work's internal interrelations are fundamentally frictional. In investigating how breath is negotiated as a poetic figure and principle in twentieth- and twenty-first-century literature, my focus will be on the arrhythmias of self-reflexivity: those moments, movements, or points where texts reflect on and display their own mediality, materiality, and linguistic constitution, as well as their production and reception.

To provide a conceptual framework for poetic breathing, I will introduce a term defined by a non–self-coincidence that connects mutually interruptive meanings: *syncopnea*. "Syncopnea" does performatively what it says semantically, connecting and cutting short breath (*pnoé*) and the Greek word *syncope*, a word conjoining two contradictory elements: *coptein*, to cut off, beat, or scratch, and *syn-*, a preposition designating unity (Liddell and Scott 1940). The uses of the word "syncope" in English all designate an interruption of something continual: in medicine, fainting or a failure of the heart's action; in music, the interruption of a regular rhythm; and in phonology, the loss of a sound within a word.[3] Jean-Luc Nancy summarizes these semantic implications as follows: "A rest, a suspension, a fluttering, a stronger beat over a silence. And a loss of consciousness" (*Expectation* 113). When he first introduces the term in *The Discourse of the Syncope*, Nancy writes: "The syncope simultaneously attaches and detaches. . . . Of course, these two operations do not add up to anything, but neither do they cancel each other out. There remains the syncope itself, the same syncopated, that is to say, cut to pieces . . . *and* somehow rejoined through amputation" (10). In short, Nancy's motto is "syncope versus synthesis, or, more specifically, syncope at the heart of synthesis, smack in the middle" (*Expectation* 113). Nancy here alludes to the proximity of syncope and the heart in medical discourses.[4] The anatomical interdependence of cardiac and respiratory cycles ties the syncope to breath. Moreover, the rhythm of breathing as outlined here can as such be considered syncopal, and the pause, a constitutive element of the breathing process, always involves the risk of turning into apnea, a bodily shutdown akin to medical syncope. Nancy links breath, heart, and syncope when he addresses the constitution of the subject:

> The beat of this difference/différance does not arise in a given Subject: it exposes him to possibility, chance, and risk. It is born in the archaic pulsation around which—breathing, heart, listening, inside/outside—crystalizes, originarily, the enigma of "some one."
> Rhythm engages time with a relation to self by exposing it, in its milieu, to the suspense of the beat, to the caesura or syncope that binds and unbinds measure during this time. (55)

The breathing subject comes and continues to be in rhythms of syncopnea, "acts of inhaling and exhaling, which . . . are . . . always in dissonance with itself" (Salminen 114), and which continually endanger its status as a subject as such. Catherine Clément designates syncope as the moment when "the subject blacks out" (*Syncope* 69), when the autonomous, conscious being is overtaken by a bodily rupture: a suspended breath, for example, or "a cough, that banal everyday suffocation; banal, yes, but it is spasmodic, and as such provokes a little suspension of being. Paroxysmal, like a fit, it brings on coughing that doctors call syncopal, during which one gets ringing of the ears, vertigo, and loss of consciousness" (7). For Nancy, the syncope also marks a relation "between language and the world: . . . the space where the concept is not possible, where reference leaps, . . . where, naming fails. . . . The space where something is silent" (*Expectation* 113). Extending Clément's claim that "breathing *is* the art of rupture" (*Syncope* 13), my book focuses on how literature captures the rupture of breathing.

As a methodological consequence, I trace the tensions within syncopnea rather than attempting to establish a systematic conceptualization of the poetic implications of breath. This would be bound to fail, as breath has resisted clear-cut categorizations throughout its etymological and conceptual history. Three major implicit points of reference for such an investigation of syncopal literary breath have already been addressed: (1) the etymological history of breath and the network of terms associated with it; (2) how breath and the terms related to it have been thought about in the Western tradition; and (3) the physical, material, and kinetic features of breathing as a physiological process. Concerning the second point, my selection of the specific historical conceptions of breath discussed in this book requires a short explanation. In literature of the twentieth and twenty-first century, one can observe an emphasis on the physical qualities of breath and a stronger focus on the lungs as bodily organs and air as an inhaled and exhaled material substance. Therefore, I will primarily consider corporeal understandings of breath. The heightened focus on the physical domain in negotiations of breathing in modern literature and art is not entirely new; it rather points back to pre-Socratic and Stoic philosophy (e.g., in the notion of *pneuma* as a primary substance). In the conceptual history of breath, the Stoics highlighted its material implications before it became, with time, more spiritualized and immaterialized.

This can be illustrated with the etymological history of breath-related terms.[5] In the earliest uses of *pneuma*, in the fifth century BC, the meanings "wind" and "breath" predominated, while the word only rarely designates "spirit" (see Kirk, Raven, and Schofield 443). In Stoic philosophy, *pneuma* was the term used to refer to the corporeal world-soul (see Hahm 4). In Christian notions, especially, of *pneuma* as divine breath, over time the spiritual dimension of the word starts to prevail and to be strictly separated from the physiological act of breathing. In the Latin translation of the Old Testament, *pneuma* generally turns into *spiritus*, which still encompasses approximately the same array of meanings, while, however, increasingly stressing the incorporeal dimension of the term (Lutze 52). In the translations into Germanic languages, where no word with the same range of meanings as *pneuma* and *spiritus* exists, this tendency is reinforced: when *spiritus* is translated as "ghost," for example, it refers to a divine entity or the human's portion of eternity, an immaterial being, rather than to the mortal breathing body (60). In the New Testament, this emphasis is upheld. This development of respiratory terms probably accounts for the fact that physical breath has been sublimated rather than abjected, even though it involves waste expelled from the body. The etymology of the English word "breath" counteracts such a spiritualization, as it is derived from an Old English word that has utterly physical, palpable implications: *bræþ* or *bréþ* means "odour, smell, exhalation as of anything cooking or burning" (*Oxford English Dictionary* online). Even though, as Steven Connor argues, the airy atmosphere, "however relentlessly spiritualised it was, could never entirely free itself from the materiality of vapour or breath" ("Beckett's Atmospheres" n.p.), the spiritual overtones dominated the cultural history of breath for centuries.

This may in part account for the fact that breath tended to be considered suspicious or was even ignored for a time in twentieth-century literary criticism, with its increasing focus on the body and materiality. Over the last few years, however, breathing has been rediscovered in the humanities.[6] My book contributes a comparative study of breathing in modern literature to this recent research, focusing on how the corporeal dimensions of breath receive articulation and how the respective works display their own mediality while attending to respiratory matters. In the works I analyze, spiritual and transcendental-historical notions of breath have often been rethought in terms of movements that no longer involve metaphysical overtones: *trans*mission, *tra*versing, *trans*gressing. As I am interested in the specifically poetic implications of breath, I reconsider classical models of inspiration and the role of breathing in ancient rhetoric. To establish a theoretical and historically informed background for the close readings of specific articulations of breath in modern literature, I will trace movements of syncopnea along the following lines: liminality; generative, formative, and constitutive implications of breath; disrupted temporalities and transactuality; and precarious interdependence.

Breath and Liminality

It is hardly surprising that in Gilles Deleuze's *Essays Critical and Clinical*, a collection of texts dedicated to moments when literary language "tends toward an 'asyntactic,' 'agrammatical' limit, or . . . communicates with its own outside," breath repeatedly marks such a limit: "breath-words, the asyntactical limit toward which all language tends" (5).[7] Breath is liminal on various levels: it moves between visibility and invisibility, sound and silence, readability and obscurity.[8] Physiologically, it operates across the borders of the body, and etymologically, the meanings of oscillating terms such as *pneuma*, *psyche*, *anima*, and *spiritus* float between binary oppositions: inside and outside, material and immaterial. Holding together the various meanings with which breath has been associated, these terms have a unifying effect (*syn-*). At the same time, the etymological threads are continually cut (*coptein*). The radical difference of the meanings renders a smooth coherence among them impossible; they will always be apart, despite being contained under the same umbrella term, which interrupts the latter's self-identity: what, for example, *is pneuma*, if it is supposed to be breath *and* wind *and* spirit? Breath-related terms enact what Nancy calls "the impossibility 'itself' of the same." Following Nancy, we can argue that the "sameness" of a word like *pneuma* "*undecides itself*: it undoes itself as it constitutes itself" (*The Discourse of the Syncope* 10) through its different meanings. Over the centuries, "breath" was associated with the whole spectrum of signifieds that the terms *pneuma*, *spiritus*, and *anima* encompass. The word as we know and use it today is a multitude constituted by semantic displacement and shifted identifications.

In "La parole soufflée," Jacques Derrida negotiates the cultural and etymological implications of breath. They do not, as one might expect, serve as an example of phonocentrism and the Western metaphysics of presence. On the contrary, for Derrida, the "oversignification which overburdens the word 'souffle'" (224) demonstrates that we never own the signifiers we use when we speak. Because words always precede us and are invested with their own historicity, the idea of having our own speech turns out to be an illusion. As Derrida argues, the excess of meanings historically linked with "breath" reveal the fact that language keeps slipping from our grasp and keeps dispossessing us, forcing its own history into our mouths whenever we speak. The complexity of the etymologies of breath-related terms and their complicated relations to the ways in which breath has been conceptualized in antiquity and Christian theology cannot be unwound here; the discussion of one example, however, shall show how correlations between anatomy, philosophy, and etymology are themselves caught in a movement of syncopnea.

Anaximenes: Breath, Air, Soul, Wind

Pneuma: "wind," "breath," "breathed air," "spirit": seeing these meanings simultaneously and side by side when we open any Greek dictionary evokes the impression that *pneuma* unifies them. However, a closer look at a crucial passage in pre-Socratic philosophy shows how brittle an analogy between the various meanings of *pneuma* turns out to be. The sentence to be focused on is the first recorded equation of wind, breath, air, and spirit, or soul, in Greek; probably the first microcosm-macrocosm analogy; and possibly one of the first recorded uses of the word *pneuma* as such.[9] Anaximenes, a prominent member of the Milesian School (sixth century BC) supposedly claimed: "Just as our soul [ψυχή], . . . which is air [ἀήρ], holds us together, so wind/breath [πνεῦμα] and air [ἀήρ] surround the whole cosmos" (quoted in Kirk, Raven, and Schofield 158–59). The sentence is attributed to Anaximenes by the doxographer Aetius (first or second century BC), who adds the comment, "Air and wind/breath are used synonymously" (quoted in Kirk, Raven, and Schofield 159). Aetius's work is recorded by an unknown writer referred to as Pseudo-Plutarch (first or second century AD). The complicated transmission of the "quotation" makes it impossible to be reliably attributed to the one author Anaximenes. As with all existing fragments of early Greek philosophy, the contemporary material records were lost and multiple mouths and hands have been at work in the process of transmitting them; that the original fragments were subject to reinterpretation and adaption in this process is unquestionable. Classicists agree that the quote has not been taken over directly from Anaximenes because it contains words he could not possibly have used.[10] The passage's material history alone has some respiratory characteristics: it resonates with the dispossession Derrida associates with breath in "La parole soufflée" as well as the transmission and transformation processes of physiological breathing.

Apart from the discussions about possible sources for the specific wording, the analogy established in the uncertain quote has caused extensive debates among classicists because it does not quite add up. A contemporary reader familiar with the etymological entanglement of the words "soul," "air," "breath," and "wind" may easily interpret the analogy as follows: a life-giving principle, an airy soul, sustains human beings, just as an airy cosmic soul sustains the universe. Such a reading, however, runs the risk of projecting Stoic thought onto Anaximenes's text.[11] Classicists continue to wonder about the basis of the comparison,[12] and as Jonathan Barnes notes, "The terms of the analogy are not identical" (55). The asymmetry of the analogy becomes more obvious in a visual depiction:

| soul (ψυχή) is air (ἀήρ) | breath/wind (πνεῦμα) and air (ἀήρ) |
| holds us together | surround the whole cosmos |

Aetius's comment that "air and wind/breath are used synonymously" already smooths over an unevenness in the comparison. Many interpreters (e.g., McKirahan 146; Kirk, Raven, and Schofield 162; Guthrie 128) stress that the first part of the comparison draws on the notion of a breath-soul that keeps humans alive and departs at death, which "was already an old popular belief" in Anaximenes's times (Kirk, Raven, and Schofield 162). Such an interpretation makes perfect sense; the movement of breath (identified with the soul) from the body's inside to the outside gives some plausibility to the arrangement of the comparison as a whole: inner breath is compared to an outer breath, and the self, "our soul," to the outer world. In this reading, breath operates as mediator between the clauses; however, it turns out to be a fairly fragile one.

Apart from the fact that we cannot even be sure whether *pneuma* was the word used by Anaximenes, and if so, whether it was used in the sense of wind, breath, or both, an explicit reference to breath is absent from the first clause. The analogy would be more symmetrical if *pneuma*, a term that can refer to "inner" and "outer" breath, both wind and breathed air, figured in both clauses.[13] That the explicit reference to breath occurs in relation to the cosmos and not in relation to the human is somewhat surprising to present-day readers,[14] but in the historical context, "wind" was probably the word's primary meaning.[15] In Anaximenes's formula, notions of inside and outside disperse: air, a substance of the outer world, is equated with the soul. Designated as a constitutive part of the human, it is not clear from Anaximenes's words whether this part is inside or outside the human body, or both; whether it holds us together from outside, from inside, or by mediating between inside and outside. In the sentence, *pneuma* figures as a word whose ambiguous meanings are not reconciled, but rather cut across each other: while some of its semantic implications are associated with a physiological process of the human body, another meaning locates it on the outside—the cosmos, which is also considered a living animal by many ancient thinkers.[16]

Kirk, Raven, and Schofield note that the "possible dual application" of *pneuma* as wind and breath "*could* have led Anaximenes to the parallelism of man and the world" in the first place (160). This speculation suggests that an indifference pertaining to the *word pneuma* inspired Anaximenes's analogy, the two sides of it representing a pictorial outgrowth of the two meanings "breath" and "wind" respectively—but then, *pneuma* is only present in the second clause. The *form* in which the first recorded equation of soul, air, breath, and wind occurs is significant: it appears as a literary device, an analogy. What decisively formed the way breath has been thought and written about throughout the centuries, its identification with air, wind, and spirit, first figured in a literary use of language. While the multiple meanings of *pneuma* tend to be reconciled in the adoption of the word as a term for the all-permeating substance that holds the world together in Stoic philosophy and—in an adapted manner—in many present-day New Age accounts of breathing, the difference of the terms supposedly equated in the analogy is rendered especially perceptible by the parallel arrangement; highlighting the breaches and asymmetry of the supposed equation, it is the very form of the analogy that displays a movement of syncopnea.

Inside and Outside

Anaximenes's formula complicates the relation between inside and outside: in the analogy between the human body and the cosmos via soul, air, and *pneuma*, these localizations become uncertain. As Jean-Christophe Bailly puts it in his essay "The Slightest Breath (On Living)," the "space of breath is the coming and going through which the outside and the inside communicate" (4). This claim is not only plausible from a physiological perspective; the interferences between inside and outside also pervade the cultural history of breath, as Anaximenes's analogy showed. Nancy demonstrates how the notion of the soul represents an intervention of binary understandings of the body's exteriorities and interiorities. The intersections he traces could, from another perspective, be considered essential characteristics of a breathing body: a body determined by a continual exchange with exteriority, that extends itself to the outside. In contrast to the predominant idea that the soul is something "*other* than the body," Nancy defines it as "the body outside itself" (*Corpus* 126). For him, the soul, especially Aristotle's understanding of it, is a way to think about the body's relation to its own exteriority. Interpreting Aristotle's claim that the soul is the "*first entelechy of a natural organized body*," Nancy sums up that the soul "is not some thing but the fact that there is a body, its *existence*" (128). "The soul is the presence of the body, its position, its 'stance,' its 'sistence' as being *out-side* (ex)" (128).

> If our entire tradition has spoken . . . about the soul, it's because . . . it has thought, not in the soul alone but in the *difference* between body and soul, the difference between body and soul, the difference that the body *is* in itself, for itself—this

difference in tension, in extension, in a certain tone of the outside. And what's been thought under the name of *soul* is nothing other than the experience of the body. (134)

That the soul has continually been tied to physical breath through the words *pneuma* and *spiritus* supports Nancy's notion of the "soul as an experience of the body," which, as he claims, has been present "on the textual surface of the whole tradition" (134). What physiological breath shares with a cosmic, divine breath-soul are the implications of such a soul for the body: as Nancy's reading of the soul shows, the concept of the body derived from taking into account the particularities of a breathing body and that of a body tied to a soul are strikingly alike. In a similar vein, Nancy equates body and spirit in the context of Christianity, designating spirit as "the organ of sense," "the subtilizing of all forms of bodies—of their extension, their material division, in the distilled and revealed essence of the *sense* of the body: the spirit *is* the body of sense, or sense in body" (77). Here, the coincidence of body and spirit is explicitly linked to breath. Nancy defines Christianity as "a religion of breath," "of exhaling," "of expiration and inspiration, a general pneumatology." "The Spirit passes from Father to Son"; "the spirit's body, gathered up, concentrated in its breath, offered in sacrifice to the father it returns to by expiring, the body of the last cry, of the final sigh where everything is consumed" (77).

While Nancy's discussions of the soul primarily focus on one direction of the body's relation to an outside that is its own extension, Christian pneumatology is described as a respiratory exchange between father and son. What about the being who receives the spirit/soul/breath? Like any respiring body, it is invaded by an exteriority that becomes an integral part. This radically unsettles any fixed positions of exteriority and interiority, just as the notion of a soul/spirit as the body outside itself does. The way Nancy theorizes the biological body complements his understanding of the soul/spirit. In "The Intruder," a text centering on the heart transplant he underwent, Nancy addresses a stranger occupying the body, "a disturbance, a trouble in the midst of intimacy" (161). The intruder who is foreign precisely because it is "inside" separates the I from itself, turning it into something unfamiliar (163): "An intruder is in me and I am becoming a stranger to myself" (167). In Nancy's text, both the new transplanted heart and "his" own heart, which stopped working properly, are perceived as foreign. In other words, he focuses on what becomes *noticeable* as an intruder because its integration in the body does not run smoothly. When the organism does its most regular respiratory work, there are strangers whose invasion goes unnoticed: inhaled foreign particles enter the lungs breath by breath. "Our own breathing is . . . an Other that inhabits us," as Michel Chion puts it (334).

Life and Death, Animate and Inanimate

Throughout the centuries, the soul has been conceptualized as that which animates the body. This leads to the next cluster of binary pairs that breath continually undermines: even though the association of breath with a life force tends to predominate, on closer consideration, it becomes evident that breath is continually situated on the limit of the animate and inanimate, organic and inorganic, life and death. Elizabeth A. Povinelli condenses these respiratory intersections in one sentence: "Life and Nonlife breathe in and breathe out" (44).

The respirational intertwining of animate and inanimate can be traced back to antiquity. The Pythagorean philosopher Philolaus of Croton located breathing between what is alive and what lacks life. According to Aristotle's pupil Meno, Aristotle argued that life is characterized by warmth, that "the productive [i.e., life-giving] factor has no share in the cold," and that "our bodies are composed of the hot; for they have no share in the cold." The role attributed to breathing is quite peculiar: "immediately after its birth the living thing draws in the breath outside, which is cold; and then, as if of necessity, it expels it again. This desire for the breath outside arises in order that, as the result of the inhalation of the breath, our bodies, which are by nature too warm, may be cooled by it" (quoted in Kirk, Raven, and Schofield 341). Before a reasonable function is ascribed to it, breath figures as something other than life and the body. Philolaus deems it necessary to explain the desire to breathe, as if it were a paradoxical thing to do. The appended explanation, that breath has the function of cooling the body, which is *too* warm, is then taken up in the famous account of respiration by Aristotle. It is important that Aristotle only mentions the life-maintaining function of breath while Philolaus first presents it as life's opposite by stressing that life and the living body *have no share* in the cold. His explanation for why breathing is necessary implies that the body has to incorporate a stranger, something other than life, to maintain it.

Only full identifications of the soul or *pneuma* as life-giving instances and breath, which are very rare in antiquity, would prompt a notion of purely vital breath.[17] Most classical narratives suggest that life depends on enduring substances (the soul or *pneuma*) inhabiting the body and leaving it in the moment of death; rather than being identical with those substances, breathing is most often simply described as being, in some way or other, involved in acquiring or nourishing them. To give two examples from ancient Greek medicine: "Erasistratus believed the *pneuma* to be acquired through respiration . . . and Praxagoras believed the *pneuma* to be nourished by respiration and therefore partly acquired from the outer air" (Hahm 162). In Democritus's view, breath prevents the soul atoms from escaping and dispersing (Aristotle, *On Respiration* 437–39). The Stoic philosopher Chrysippus argues that *pneuma*, which he identifies with the soul, enables both breathing and living.[18] In all these accounts, breath, while being related to the vital instance and involved in maintaining life, is neither vivid nor vivifying per se.

The biblical image of the "breath of life," which most prominently occurs in Genesis 2.7 when God blows into "man's" nostrils in order to animate what he formed out of soil, is one of the most influential sources for the tendency to identify breath with life. In the Hebrew original, the "breath of life" is "נִשְׁמַת חַיִּים" (*nishmat ḥayyim*) (*The Interlinear Hebrew-Aramaic Old Testament*, 1:4). Whereas the animating quality of the breath itself is unclear in that scene (it is only certain that it animates man), the "breath of life" is used as a metonymy for life in the English translation of later passages in the book of Genesis (e.g., Genesis 6.17, 7.15, 7.22). It must be added that the King James Bible takes over the formulation of Genesis 2.7, "breath of life" (7, 8), whereas in the Hebrew original, various different wordings are used: in Genesis 6.17 and 7.15, "רוּחַ חַיִּים" (*ru'aḥ ḥayyim*) (*The Interlinear Hebrew-Aramaic Old Testament*, 1:15, 17), and in Genesis 7.22, "רוּחַ חַיִּים נִשְׁמַת" (*nishmat ru'aḥ ḥayyim*) (*The Interlinear Hebrew-Aramaic Old Testament* 1:17). This may not make a great semantic difference, but the linguistic coherence in the English translation helped establish a dominant metonymy that shapes the English understanding of breath to this day. The breath of God in the Bible not only has the capacity to give life; it can also effect the exact opposite—in Job 4.9 God destroys life by the very physical gesture he gave life to man in Genesis: "By the blast [*nishmat*] of God they perish, and by the breath [*ru'aḥ*] of his nostrils are they consumed" (*The Bible*, 610; *The Interlinear Hebrew-Aramaic Old Testament* 2:1329).[19] While in Genesis the breath blown into man's nostrils animates, in Job the breath blown from God's nostrils takes men's life. In the King James Bible, the proximity of the passages is less obvious because *nishmat* is translated as the "blast" of God. Along with the narrative of the creation of man in Genesis, this account of God's respirational punishment of the wicked recalls the ancient Egyptian notions of a breath of life and a breath of death that can be imparted to men by divine agencies (Piperno 33). In the Old Testament, the consequences of God's breath depend on his intentions: if his plan is to give life, it animates; if he wants to punish, it kills; if he is enraged, the breath cleaves the surface of the earth (2 Samuel 22:16). In the context of the natural world, God's breath is said to cause frost and ice (Job 27.10). In Ecclesiastes, the word "הֶבֶל" (*hevel*) (*The Interlinear Hebrew-Aramaic Old Testament*, 3:1582), which in Hebrew means "vapor" or "breath," is highly prominent: it designates ephemerality and nothingness and links breath to the futility of life. In the King James Bible, this link is subdued because *hevel* is not translated as "breath," but rather as "vanity": "vanity of vanities; all *is* vanity" (75). In contrast to the "breath of life," the breath of death, destruction, or frost and breath as ephemerality did not become dominant images in the cultural imaginary and everyday speech. The privileged association of breath with life owes more to the reception and translations of the Bible than to the biblical text itself.

Biologically speaking, breathing is without doubt a vital principle: we could not live without it. However, the idea of breath as the primary animating principle is more textually than physiologically founded: it is deeply indebted to classical and biblical sources such as those discussed here. In *Histoire du souffle*, Daniel Piperno observes that many mystifications of breath as a vital or metaphysical principle in antiquity go hand in hand with the assumption that the cessation of breathing marks death (13): in other words, the soul as a material or immaterial essence of life leaves the body with the last breath. In modern medicine, respiration no longer represents the sole factor of determining life or death: today, the cessation of the functions of the brain are equally decisive for declaring a person dead.[20]

Breathing renders the borders between animate and inanimate porous. Physiologically speaking, respiration is mechanical: a passive, monotonous process the body executes without us usually being aware of it.[21] Chion stresses that "breathing is something about which we are mostly unconscious. It is something objective and nonintentional in us" (334). As a consequence, we have to give up our status as the subjects of breathing: *we* don't breathe; rather, something in our bodies does—*it* breathes. In this sense, respiration runs counter to a notion of mental aliveness defined by active and intentional acts.[22] In spite of its autonomous functioning, it is possible to direct one's breathing: "Breathing is . . . the sole bodily process that can switch between being reflexive and unconscious to being voluntary and conscious" (334), Gorbman claims, and L. O. Aranye Fradenburg describes it as "involuntary but manipulable" (181). However, the only thing we can influence to some degree is the rhythm of breathing, the length of inhalations and exhalations—we cannot choose not to breathe, and we have little control over most processes of external respiration and none over inner, that is, cellular, respiration.

In current medical accounts of cellular respiration, what is usually associated with a life force (animation, creation, growth and thriving, etc.) collides with its very opposite: consumption, decomposition, and waste. There is a "basic chemical similarity of respiration to combustion" (Slonim 6).[23] Cellular respiration involves metabolic reactions, processes of chemical transformation in which decomposition and recomposition constantly alternate: organic matter is broken down and cell components built up, energy is released and consumed. It operates syncopically: in the course of anabolism, or synthetic metabolism, molecules are assembled, and in catabolism, or degradative metabolism, organic molecules are broken down in order to produce energy (Slonim 10). It is important that cellular respiration is determined by catabolism: breaking down glucose into carbon dioxide and water, using oxygen, and thus producing the energy necessary for a body's organic functioning. In this process, a waste that constitutes a significant part of our breathing is generated: carbon dioxide, which has to be expelled from the body by means of exhalation. In short, breathing sustains life by decomposing matter and turning it into waste.

The respirational maintenance of life implies a dependence of the body on the outside (see Salminen 113); as breathers, our bodies are unsealed. The exposure to the outside at the heart of the life-sustaining process poses a continual risk: every breath we take could infiltrate substances fatal for our body; even knowing that we are exposed to poisonous gases cannot prevent us from inhaling them—not being able to stop breathing may kill us. David Lloyd points out another crucial nexus of breath and mortality: "If every breath is the anticipation of expiration, if every anticipation is expressed in an intake, a holding of breath, is it not also the occasion of dread, of the anxiety that its movement in the rhythm of mortality itself inspires? Breath, we could say, is the intimacy of death within the subject" (188–89). Or, in Jean-Christophe Bailly's words, breath is "the tangible and intimate form of living's exteriority to itself, or its ex-timacy [*extimité*]" (5)—it is life outside itself, life touching on the inanimate, which is, in turn, constitutive of it.

As I've shown, breath itself is not devoid of life's other from a present-day physiological and chemical perspective: the respiratory process involves an assemblage of organic and inorganic matter. Breath is "vibrant matter" in Jane Bennett's terms: "a turbulent immanent field in which various and variable materialities collide, congeal, morph, evolve and disintegrate" (xi). While Bennett ascribes vitality and activity to the assemblages involving inorganic matter so as to counteract a predominant conception of matter as dull and passive,[24] *Poetics of Breathing* insists on the dullness and passivity of breath, attending to how these characteristics intersect with what is, and has been, considered active or vital. Accordingly, the book approaches breath in terms of "inanimation," as David Wills understands it, involving "*what is inanimate in animation*" and "the extent to which *the inanimate animates*" (x). Exploring "origin[s]" of life in various textual settings, Wills's *Inanimation* focuses on "constituting instance[s]" when the "inorganic 'suddenly' becomes organic" (xii). Throughout Western cultural history, breath has been situated at precisely this threshold—the biblical creation narrative being a paradigmatic example. Against the widespread tendency to move breath from such a liminal position to the domain of life and the organic because it initiates the transition from inanimate to animated according to many cultural and medical narratives, *Poetics of Breathing* elaborates on "*what is inanimate in animation*." The study of modern literary breath thus presents a counternarrative that challenges both the priorization of life and the very binary oppositions between animate and inanimate and between organic and inorganic. This endeavor is particularly facilitated by literary breath's enmeshment of respiration and language. Wills convincingly argues that lives are "inanimated by means of language . . . language itself generates and self-generates as a privileged form, perhaps *the* privileged form, of inanimate life" (xii). Starting from the premise that breath is *inanimated* by language in literary renderings, my readings focus on moments when, in turn, dead respiratory letters emit living qualities, when "*the inanimate animates*."

Breath as a Generative, Formative, and Constitutive Principle

The associations across the Western tradition of breath with a life-giving impulse are tightly linked to ideas of breathing as an animating impulse that initiates, generates, and constitutes. In numerous cultural narratives, breath plays an essential role in the creation of the cosmos, living beings, or works of art; physiological accounts not only link respiration to life but also discuss breathing as a necessary precondition for the articulation of spoken language, which is, in turn, reflected in linguistic philosophy and poetic negotiations of breath. Focusing on breath as an animating, generative force is liable to reduce it to pure life without taking into account its entanglement with the inorganic. In this respect, it is helpful to bear in mind Wills's argument that the inanimate precedes the animate: "before there is living . . . prior to knowing what living means—there is an encounter with the nonliving, with . . . the in- or non-amimate" (xii). This consequently determines an "*inanimating* logic" of "life" as such (6). In the following section, in tracing some of the narratives and discourses that treat breath as anterior or primordial, I want to explore the ways in which a respiratory threshold between inanimate anteriority and life or animated creation ruptures vitalist trends, especially with regard to literature. In his study of Paul Celan's poetics, Wills paves the way for such an approach: "Specifically, I contend that the relation between poetic expression and breathing, the play of inhalation and exhalation thanks to which we live and are able to express ourselves, in fact relies on its own (inanimate) interruption: a turning of the breath out of the breath occurs to inanimate the life that breathing sustains, and such a turning can be identified as a poetic function" (113).

Air and *Pneuma* as Primary Substances

The connotations of breath with giving or maintaining life are firmly established in our cultural memory. Less widely known is that in antiquity breath was often connected to the idea of a primary generative substance. Anaximenes, who, as we have seen, drew an analogy between soul, air, and a cosmic breath or wind, held that air was the originary substance from which everything else emerged. A number of classicists argue that this analogy might have been crucial for the choice of air as primary substance.[25] Keeping in mind the iridescence of the terms in the analogy from a present-day view allows us to rethink what has been deemed a monist worldview that reduces the multiplicity of all phenomena in the world to a single principle. Hippolytus recounts Anaximenes's theory of the animating primal material as follows:

> Anaximenes . . . said that the principle is unlimited [APEIRON] air, out of which come to be things that are coming to be, things that have come to be and things that are coming to be, and gods and divine things. The rest come to be out of the products

of this. The form of air is as follows: when it is most even, it is invisible, but it is revealed by the cold and the hot and the wet, and movement. It is always moving, for all the things that undergo change would not change unless it was moving. For when it becomes condensed and finer, it appears different. For when it is dissolved into what is finer, it comes to be fire, and on the other hand air comes to be winds when it becomes condensed. Cloud results from air through felting; and water when this happens to a greater degree. When condensed still more it becomes earth and when it reaches the absolutely densest stage it becomes stones. (Hippolytus, *Refutation*, 1.7, 1–3; quoted in McKirahan 49)

Classicists have asked what it actually was that Anaximenes understood as air (e.g., Kirk, Raven, and Schofield 146). From today's perspective, the wording of Hippolytus's account makes such a question appear redundant: the "form of air" is described as essentially changeable; it almost seems as if air *was* not something, but rather constantly *became* something else: "it comes to be fire," "winds," "clouds," "water," and even "earth and stones." Even though such a reading might not be historically defensible, I pursue it a little further so as to explore its specifically *processual* understanding of breath. Let us, for a moment, consider Anaximenes's air in terms of a Heraclitian perpetual flow. Plato disdainfully summarizes Heraclitus's thought as follows: "There is nothing which in itself is only one thing . . . the things of which we naturally say that they 'are,' are in process of coming to be, as the result of movement and change and blending with one another. We are wrong when we say there 'are,' since nothing ever is, but everything is coming to be" (Plato, *Theaetetus* 152d–e, quoted in McKirahan 142–43). As the generating principle is fundamentally characterized by *becoming*, the notion of something constituted as a *being* is dismissed as such. Moreover, it becomes difficult to differentiate the generative principle from what it constitutes.[26] When air is claimed to be accountable for things' emergence and their continual transformation, it is presented as a principle that not only generates things but also keeps determining their mutability.

The transformative movement of Anaximenes's air according to its description by Hippolytus can not only be related to the unstable terms in Anaximenes's analogy of soul, air, and cosmic breath/wind, but, by extension, also to the complex semantic network of breath-related terms. *Pneuma, anima, psyché*, and similar terms are words that constantly change their aggregate states, resisting a consistent state of being. Anaximenes's air is a primary substance that becomes all the other substances it generates. Far from the monist position usually attributed to Anaximenes, this would imply that everything is involved in an ongoing process of becoming different from itself. Stoic *pneuma*, a primary generative substance comparable to Anaximenes's air, is given the function of "holding things together and giving them unity" (Hahm 142). "According to Chrysippus the cosmos is permeated and given life by *pneuma*, the same substance that permeates a living thing and makes it alive. Just as this *pneuma* makes a man a living, organic whole, so the cosmic *pneuma* makes the cosmos a living, organic whole, with each single part grown together" (163). The idea of a harmonic unity created by an *identical* substance permeating both the cosmos and human bodies is unsettled when one considers how heterogeneously this substance is described in what itself is a highly heterogeneous corpus of transmitted pre-Socratic and Stoic texts.[27] With a view to the different material components attributed to *pneuma* (air, fire, breath, sperm, etc.) and its various subdivisions, syncopnia gives shape to the picture that emerges: that which grants unity and cohesion to the various phenomena of the world is itself a multiplicity cut into innumerable parts.[28]

Imaginations of a Primordial Wholeness of Breathing

Later philosophical negotiations of breath that draw on pre-Socratic and Stoic ideas about breath-related primary substances tend to make the material qualities and the suggested unity these substances generate appear more coherent than the ancient texts suggest. The reflections on breath of Luce Irigaray and David Michael Kleinberg-Levin reveal the risk that such tendencies could revert to what Derrida called a phonocentric "dream of a life without difference" ("La parole soufflée" 226).[29] In *The Age of Breath*, Irigaray heavily relies on classical, especially pre-Socratic, sources. She claims that cosmic breathing, or wind—what she terms the "feminine divine"—bridges the human and the cosmic world and "never separates itself from nature, but transforms it, transubstantiates it without ruining it" (7). Women's task is to reinstall a lost unity, "to reunite incessantly earth with heaven through the breath, this vehicle of the soul" (8). Vague echoes of ancient originary substances such as *pneuma* or Anaximenes's air are evoked in the speculation that cosmic air and breath may (re)constitute a lost unity. To some degree Irigaray leaves it indeterminate whether what she has in mind is a unity of identical parts, a multiplicity constituted by different parts, or a wholeness in which parts fluidly merge into one substance that may change its form and consistency. Mentioning that cosmic breath *transubstantiates* without being *separated* from what it was, that is, nature, is somewhat contradictory: even though a transubstantiated substance may remain in one piece, it is, by definition, different from it was before and separated from it in terms of consistence (or other qualities).

Despite this, Irigaray holds on to a notion of wholeness and unity that suggests self-identity. In *The Forgetting of Air in Martin Heidegger*, she identifies air with the forgotten "condition of possibility," the "groundless ground" of what *is*, of beings (5). In contrast to thinkers like Derrida or Nancy, who embrace the idea of an existence outside oneself based on a split from an "original unity" that was an illusion in the first place, Irigaray considers existence as a relation governed by mastery adopted by those who disregard the generative wholeness granted by a forgotten primary air described as "unmixed, undivided" (61). With regard to cultural history, such an undivided air represents a smoothed-over reconsideration of *pneuma*—concerning physiology, it would be unbreathable for human beings, as a continual intake of unmixed oxygen is fatal. Irigaray's motto, "I breathe, therefore, I am," which she claims is "forgotten in Being's *ek-sistence*" (163), rests on an imaginary and thoroughly textual air that itself consists of mixed constituents: Irigaray's wide range of philosophical sources, from pre-Socratic thinkers to Heidegger, including various "Eastern" approaches, as she calls them.

Similarly informed by Heideggerian terminology and pre-Socratic notions of a type of breathing that connects humans "with the ecology of a larger whole" (75), Kleinberg-Levin sketches two possibilities inherent in breathing in his book *Before the Voice of Reason: Echoes of Responsibility in Merleau-Ponty's Ecology and Levinas's Ethics*: (1) "Our condition as 'fallen,' our 'pathology' as finite, as mortal, as 'thrown' into the contingency of a groundless existence, even affects, and is manifest in, the very nature of our breathing" (78). (2) In opposition to this rather negatively charged possibility, Kleinberg-Levin proposes

> the possibility of a deeper, more primordial experience with being, an ecstatic potentiality for breathing . . . the possibility that we could enjoy a more life-enriching experience with breathing—especially in relation to the realm of nature. . . . For breathing is the gift of our original integration into the wholeness and openness of being, of nature. Could we somehow return,

hermeneutically, to the experience of a pre-ontological body of breath, an experience more primordial than the one we usually inhabit as adults, and retrieve it for present living? (78)

Following an observation Merleau-Ponty adopted from Henri Wallon, that the "body is already a respiratory body" from the moment of birth on, Kleinberg-Levin argues that the infant is situated in a state of "primordial ecstatic openness" (79). Conjoining ontogenesis and the history of philosophy, he suggests that language, in its "infanthood," acknowledges a harmonious unity comparable to the one an infant inhabits:

> The airs that we breathe, the winds that we welcome in our chest, belong to the atmosphere; they come from the harmonious sphere of elements which encompasses and embraces our earthly lives, sustaining our capacity to breathe. And with a rhythm all their own, these airs, these winds we breathe in are exhaled, returned to their source. The ancient Greek language acknowledged the soul's indebtedness to the atmosphere, giving the soul a name that identified it with its breath. (72)

> The infant's body of breath is a body without airtight defences, without fixated boundaries. Confronted by the child's experience, can we say where our breath ends and where the winds begin? Is there any point in the atmosphere that can really be a matter of indifference to our breathing? (79)

Kleinberg-Levin flirts with the analogy between a primordial state of cultural history and that of the human being. Such a search for an originary wholeness is a temptation for numerous writers who reflect on the liminality of breath and the nonsealed corporeality of respiring beings. When Kleinberg-Levin argues that "breathing is our most fundamental openness, our most fundamental experience of non-duality" (79), "non-duality" implicates nondifference, and "fundamental experience" suggests a unity tied to a primordial state that actually existed and can be regained. In this respect, the relation of breath to nature and the body lends itself to imaginations of a paradisiacal "lost" origin. What Kleinberg-Levin sketches is an openness of bodies whose boundaries dissolve, "vanquish[ed] into thin air" (72). The body's opening is an experience of sameness: it is reunited with what it was in the "beginning." The airs we inhale "are exhaled, returned to our source";

breath and air are identical, just as our respiring bodies relate again to what they used to be part of; breath by breath, they recover their "original integration into the wholeness and openness of being, of nature" (72).

In texts such as those of Irigaray and Kleinberg-Levin, the myth of a "natural" origin is constructed by reference to cultural and etymological connotations of breath. One could claim that these connotations are motivated by physiological respiration; however, we have seen that the matter is more complicated. While breathing is a "natural" process of the body, its identification with a "natural state" of primordial harmonious unity is a *narrative* entangled in a dense intertextual network. The reflections of Irigaray and Kleinberg-Levin (both drawing on Heidegger) are based on the strong claim that they have uncovered something forgotten or unnoticed: Irigaray claims that invisible air is "always there, . . . allows itself to be forgotten" (8). In *The Age of Breath* this then leads to an appeal to women to "incarnat[e] actively in herself the divinity received at birth" (4) and become even more divine "through faithfulness and attention to her own breathing" (5). Kleinberg-Levin argues that the concealed origin can be regained through "awareness" (75, 81). The two writers themselves seem to forget or overlook something: the *difference* pervading breath, not least the difference between the physiological process of respiration and the cultural and etymological histories of the term "breath." Kleinberg-Levin's demand for "awareness" and Irigaray's demand for a reincarnation of the divinity women received at birth imply the reconciliation of a supposed "natural state" with a body that has been alienated from its "true nature." By reverting to a "lost origin," a natural, precultural, and prelinguistic state, these accounts impose their own narrative on breath, which always resists the semantic impositions of meaningful speech. Paradoxically, both Irigaray and Kleinberg-Levin situate breath "before" the symbolic order of language—the fact that their recourse to an original organic unity is itself a construct generated by linguistic means in writings drawing heavily on cultural narratives and figures of speech is another blind spot.

Breath and Language

Prelinguistic Breathing

Kleinberg-Levin's observation that "our silent breathing is the necessary condition . . . for the possibility of speaking" (74) and Irigaray's claim that there is "no speech without air to convey it" (167) draw attention to a basic anatomical fact: in order to speak, we have to breathe.[30] Breathing is an essential bodily prerequisite for speech, a silent, mostly unnoticed medium of spoken words. Drawing attention to the sound or silence of breath in language points to what lies both before and at the heart of articulated, meaningful speech. Temporally, the relation of language and breath is a *synchrony* that involves syncope: breathing precedes meaningful speech and at the same time cuts into it, carrying its sounds and segmenting it with silences. When Kleinberg-Levin argues that "breathing is our most primordial articulation of the conditions necessary for speech" (76), he weaves linguistic accounts of the anatomical prerequisites of speech production into his narrative of a "lost origin": "speech is born in the 'sacrifice' of breath—its disciplined binding for the sake of a voice capable of producing recognisable and meaningful sounds" (76). Thus, the supposedly undifferentiated presemantic breath is invested with specific characteristics and integrated in a dualism: "pure," unbound breath precedes speech and is then "sacrificed" to its structure, disciplined and alienated to a "secondary" breath tainted by language.

When prelinguistic dimensions of breath are negotiated in this book, the focus is on the *tensions* and *interferences* between breathing and speaking or writing, the moments when language interferes with breath and breath with language. This is a bidirectional process: given that we necessarily breathe while we speak (i.e., that the anatomical precondition is articulated in what it constitutes), the usually silent bodily respiration can make itself heard or noticed, can interrupt the semantic and structural dimension of the language it generates and the sound it carries. Here, Kleinberg-Levin's account is to the point: "Speech requires the disciplined shaping of the breath. And yet, although speaking binds the breath, it cannot ultimately escape the rhythms that nature has made constitutive of our breathing" (74).

Breath and the Development of Speech

Another narrative in which breathing ultimately resists the idea of a prelinguistic unity is concerned with the development of speech. In psychoanalytic theories, especially by and following Jacques Lacan, the child's entry into the domain of language, the symbolic order, implies a cut: it is the final step in abolishing an undifferentiated state in which the child has no notion of subject and object, inside and outside, and dwells in a state where self and other are not separated. For Lacan, the first fissure is induced in the mirror stage, the moment when the infant recognizes his or her reflection, identifying with the image of a unified self in a narcissist gesture of alienating misrecognition. However, another separation from a "primordial unity," from the "purely semiotic," can be located at a much earlier stage. In *A Voice and Nothing More*, Mladen Dolar attempts to free the voice from its phonocentric charges by theorizing it as a venue of misrecognition preceding the mirror stage:[31] "if the voice is the first manifestation of life, is not hearing oneself, and recognizing one's own voice, thus an experience that precedes self-recognition in a mirror?" (39) The "first manifestation of life" refers to the moment of birth, accompanied by a scream—a scream that coincides with the first breath. In contrast to Kleinberg-Levin's romanticized notion of the "infant's primordial body of breath" (82) as a self-contained wholeness, the newborn infant's compulsion to breathe air can be considered an initial cut preceding the one inflicted by the mirror stage and the entry into the symbolic order.

As François-Bernard Michel writes in *Le souffle coupé: Respirer et écrire*, the first breath marks a traumatic instance of separation:[32] "respiration is thus originally linked with the traumatic separation from the mother, a possible source of pain" (188, my translation). In medical textbooks, this moment is described in a language no less drastic: "when a baby is born, the environmental change is sudden and dramatic. . . . The foetus, comfortably surrounded by, and physiologically adapted to, the liquid amniotic fluid, must begin to breathe air, exchanging O2 and CO2 with the environment" (Slonim 144). The prelinguistic birth cry usually accompanying the first breath is already a cry of "lost unity," of a being that has just experienced being exposed to and intruded by an outside that, from then on, constitutes its own extimacy. The alienation of the child through identification with the mirror image, and the further, ultimate alienation of the self from "itself" through its identification with the signifier "I" is not preceded by a nonalienated stage of prelinguistic breathing: the first breath not only marks the separation form the mother, but also from the "self." More precisely, it thwarts two fantasies: the intrauterine unity with the mother as a state beyond difference, and the idea of a self that is self-contained.

Breath, Voice, Rhythm

What still needs more elucidation with regard to the prelingual implications of breathing is its relation to voice and rhythm. Simply put, whenever there is speech, there is voice, and wherever there is voice, there is breath. Breath is a necessary precondition for voice and voice a necessary precondition for speech. There may be voice beyond or before speech, and breath beyond and before voice. Voice has been discussed in terms of what both coincides with speech and lies before and beyond it, most prominently by Dolar. Many arguments that he makes about the voice *also* pertain to breath, which partially overlaps with voice: as "zero point of vocal emission" (71), breath carries the voice. Moreover, voice and breath are situated in a comparably liminal position with regard to speaking.

Dolar's major argument is that voice is not yet meaningful speech or *logos*, but is essentially involved in generating it: "the voice is . . . the quasi-natural bearer of the production of meaning . . . , it is *what does not contribute to making sense*. It is the material element recalcitrant to meaning" (15). The voice is thus located *between* the body and language (73), between the symbolic order and the domain of the physical, material, and animalistic. In its "insignificant will to signify," "mere *vox*" coincides with breath, as Agamben suggests when mentioning the "pure breath of the voice" (*The End of the Poem* 64–65). Some articulations of voice, including screams, laughter, and musical sounds such as humming or piping, tend to be equally as nonsemantic as breath-sounds such as coughs or sighs; these sounds beyond meaningful speech "tie the human voice to an animal nature" (Dolar 23). Aristotle, whom Dolar quotes in this context, would not consider these sounds as "voice" at all: "what produces the impact must have soul in it and must be accompanied by an act of imagination, for voice is a sound with a meaning, and is not merely the result of any impact of the breath as in coughing" (Aristotle, *De amina* 420b, 28–37; qtd. in Dolar 23).[33] Aristotle excludes respiratory sounds as instances when the organs of *voice production* are heard—"voice then is the impact of the inbreathed air against the windpipe" (23)—from the *produced voice*, which goes hand in hand with meaning, intellect, and the rational soul.

Even though Dolar convincingly shows that the voice is *not only*, or *more than*, significant speech, it is important to make a distinction between breath and voice in their primary and most frequent occurrence. Considering all the articulations of the voice that we make, presymbolic sounds are rather the exception. Conversely, with regard to respiration, the production of meaningful speech is not its primary function—bringing forth voice and language are, according to medical reference books, mere "side effects." We predominantly breathe silently: the production of sound is a possibility but not a necessity. What are the implications of this in view of traditional philosophical and ontological categorizations? If I am because I think and I am human because I speak, what does breathing make me?[34]

In fact, can I even speak of an I when I think of myself as a breathing being? Or does the breather in me shatter this very I to pieces? Breath is a disturbing phenomenon—one could even speculate that the invention of the soul and its link to breath comprise an act of soothing: when sublimated as the soul, namely, that which distinguishes the human being as human, breath no longer puts the subject into question. However, once we look at it more closely, as Nancy does, for example, the soul is no less unsettling. As breathers, we are not only allied to animals but also to plants; if the uncanny nature of voice is that it makes the boundaries between the speaking human and the growling animal porous, how uncanny is breathing, which both connects me to the panting beast and to mute organisms that barely seem alive? The attempt of counteracting narratives of a harmonious, natural breath sustaining a safe human identity can be put in less gloomy terms: breath generates human-nonhuman assemblages, or multiplicities. If the voice drags the animal into speech, breathing brings along the plant, the coral, bacteria, and so on. Concerning meaningful speech, the surplus of breathing—a surplus that will keep articulating itself in spoken language, or in written language that reflects its physiological "roots"—is vaster than that of the voice. The respirational surplus expands further if we take into account the *rhythmical* constitution of breath. Rhythm not only pervades breathing humans, animals, and plants; it also involves the domain of inorganic nature: the movement of the waves, the phases of the moon, the seasons.

At the same time, rhythm is precisely the quality that breath shares with language. Breath carries the voice and punctuates it with silences: speech is voiced during exhalation, while the breath-pause and inhalation interrupt the flow of sound. In his book *On Voice in Poetry: The Work of Animation*, David Nowell Smith highlights the elements that breath imparts to voice, describing them as preconditions that are integral to language, as an "articulation that precedes language 'in' itself" (52): "Again the concern is with anteriority, but now an anteriority that lies within language before language can be posited as 'in itself.' It thus turns out that *rhythm, cadence, caesura, syncopation*, far from being exterior features to a lexico-syntactic system, become integral modes of language's bodily articulation" (66; emphasis added). What Nowell Smith claims about the voice applies to breath as well: it is "a condition of language, conditioned by language" (52). This involves a tension. As Kleinberg-Levin observes, speaking involves a "disciplined shaping of the breath." However, "the rhythms that nature has made constitutive of our breathing" (74) at the same time enter and determine language.

The biological necessity of pausing for breath at some point may interrupt a regularly outlined rhythm, for example in a poem. It is important that rhythm as such is not metrical: in Lisa Robertson's words, "Rhythm is a figured, embodied improvisation, not a measure" (15). Catherine Clément characterizes rhythm as essentially syncopal: "a fragment of the beat disappears, and of this disappearance, rhythm is born" (5).[35] Apart from the safe claim that we breathe rhythmically and not metrically (and that the physiological rhythm of respiration shares the quality of a slight irregularity with what makes up literary rhythms), one is faced with a zone of indeterminacy: most of the time, it is impossible to identify the precise spot where a natural breathing rhythm turns into a culturally manipulated one when we pronounce sentences. Moreover, the rhythm that breath introduces to language unsettles a clear distinction between the oral and the written: is the rhythmical structure of written language a trace of the fact that we have to breathe in order to speak? Or, speaking in accord with Haun Saussy, is rhythm already a form of inscription that in oral traditions enabled the memorization and reiteration of texts?[36] Is the silence of breath something that ties it more strongly to written than to spoken language? In literature, one often faces syncopal intersections of spoken and written language: breath-pauses that structure speech can find their way into print, but a one-to-one translation of breathing rhythms into writing hardly exists. Highlighted caesurae point beyond the opposition of speech and writing, to a moment when nothing is heard, the moment *before* anything is said or written. Commenting on Friedrich Hölderlin, Nancy mentions that "the rhythm of the breath responds to the interruption of sense" (*Expectation* 105). Breathing rhythms operate outside signification, but, as Kleinberg-Levin puts it, breath can "give way" to voice, and voice can give way to (meaningful) speech.

The surplus of breath with respect to the bodily, nonsemantic aspects of speech and its production always meets another surplus in language on the level of meaning: the etymological and cultural oversignification of respiratory terms. While some aspects of the voice can convincingly be discussed in terms of the presymbolic alone, a negotiation of breath and language never gets around the meanings tied to it. It is precisely this semantic dimension of breathing that leads Dolar to a reflection of the voice that at the same time highlights its materiality and resists a reduction to the corporeal, both in the sense of an empirical bodily dimension of speech and a mystified primal corporeality:

> in many languages there is an etymological link between spirit and breath . . . ; the voice carried by breath points to the soul irreducible to the body. One could use a French pun, and say that the voice is plus-de-corps: both the surplus of the body, a

bodily excess, and the no-more-body, the end of the corporeal, the spirituality of the corporeal, so that it embodies the very coincidence of the quintessential corporeality and the soul. The voice is the flesh of the soul, its ineradicable materiality, by which the soul can never be rid of the body; it depends on this inner object which is but the ineffaceable trace of externality and heterogeneity, but by virtue of which the body can also never quite simply be the body, it is a truncated body, a body cloven by the impossible rift between an interior and an exterior. The voice embodies the very impossibility of this division, and acts as its operator. (71)

It is the *semantic* connection of breathing to the soul that incites Dolar to think about voice and its physiological implications differently. As Dolar lets the soul-body binary crumble when he *thinks* and *writes* about the voice in *terms* of breath, his reflections become fruitful for a negotiation of the materiality and corporeality of speech beyond orality alone. As the written traces of "breath" enter the argument, he offers us means to consider spoken and breathed language in its written form. Based on Dolar's conclusion, we could argue that breathing embodies the very impossibility of the division of speaking and writing and acts as its operator.

Inspiration

The most well-known etymological connection of "breathing" to a notion of origin is the Latin *inspirare*, "to breathe into," and *inspiration*, which implies a life-giving spirit entering the body and triggering creative outcomes (*The Princeton Encyclopedia of Poetry and Poetics* 708). The contemporary common use of "inspiration" as an umbrella term for creative ideas and their sources has its root in this more specific meaning in antiquity and the classical models of artistic creation based on it. The classical accounts of inspiration hold that ideas emerge through a rush of breath from an external source. Poetic inspiration tends to be seen as a force from a higher power exceeding the artist's control. The reference to a superior being enabling the creation of art is responsible for the fact that inspiration is often looked upon suspiciously from a contemporary perspective and is widely considered an outdated model of aesthetic production processes. Moreover, the concept seems to embrace a notion of breath as a purely life-giving force, which we have already scrutinized.

However, a closer look at the structural implications of inspiration models shows that they are determined by syncopnea and imply a sense of unworking. In "La parole soufflée," Derrida brings these aspects of inspiration into focus. Going back to the "souffleur" in the theater and the meaning of the French verb "souffler," which, besides "blowing" and "breathing into" can refer to "stealing," Derrida argues that inspiration disempowers the author, threatening autonomy and implying a dispossession of the author's own voice. The context in which this is discussed is the writing of Antonin Artaud, who, according to Derrida, "attempted to forbid that his speech be spirited away [*soufflée*] from his body" (220). Derrida claims that Artaud counteracts the "indispensable *différance*" (221) inscribed in the notion of inspiration as well as in the word "souffle" with the idea of "a good inspiration" (224), a life breath that corresponds to the nonarbitrary, bodily "speech prior to words" demanded in *The Theatre and Its Double* (Artaud 42). Derrida's diagnosis is clear: such a conception of "good breath" is a construct symptomatic of "the dream of a life without difference" and a "metaphysics of the flesh" (226). He stresses that the transcendent implications of inspiration, outdated as they may be, unsettle the notion of an immediate, purely corporeal speech as Artaud imagines it. The spiritual or transcendental being who inspires, that is, threatens the integrity of the inspired body, is radically other to that fleshly body. It is not only foreign speech that is forced through my body in the act of inspiration that renders me passive, but speech from a foreign entity, something radically different from my fleshly body. For Derrida, the reference to a transcendental entity in models of inspiration (and, analogously, in any narrative of life being breathed into someone) recalls the fact that, just like our speech or creative output, our body does not belong to our self: "Ever since I have had a relation to my body, therefore, ever since my birth, I no longer am my body. Ever since I have had a body I am not this body, hence I do not possess it. This deprivation institutes and informs my relation to my life. My body has thus always been stolen from me" (200). Even though the evocation of a transcendental entity accentuates Derrida's point, the argument can be sustained without presupposing a spiritual being, as the discussion of Nancy's "intruder" has shown. When Nancy explicitly refers to inspiration, he does so negatively, albeit precisely at the moment when he discusses the nontranscendental originary relation to an alterity/outside: "This outside is not that of an authority or a spirit that breathes, it is the outside in which and for which responsibility has engaged itself: the outside in which there is nothing and in whose silent breast no god, no muse, no genius keeps watch over—or observes. It is this silence of the outside that holds all authority and exhales all inspiration" (*Expectation* 159). Rethinking inspiration in terms of an other/outside beyond notions of a transcendental higher being (instead of abandoning it, *exhaling* it all, as Nancy proposes), *Poetics of Breathing* embraces a conflation of inspiration and respiration that does not amount to a "metaphysics of the flesh."

In modern literature, classical ideas of how artworks come to be are frequently renegotiated when breath as an anatomical condition of possibility and unnoticed precondition of literary texts is addressed. A prominent example that anticipates more recent poetics of breathing is Walt Whitman, who equals "respiration and inspiration" in "Song of Myself" (*Leaves of Grass* 30). On reconsidering inspiration in terms of respiration, one can outline a position between two dominant, problematic poles of how aesthetic production tends to be conceived of today: (1) the passivity of merely taking over a superior, external, pregiven voice; and (2) the idea of fully internalizing the inspiring voice in the sense of an aesthetics of genius or the illusion of radical poetic autonomy, an *in*dividualization of the artist, and a self-made-work.[37] In the theory of respirational inspiration that I will outline, the way the body works is of major importance. If we attempt to think a scenario of creative initiation modeled after the physiological breathing process, inspiration necessarily becomes a matter of interdependence. Without assuming the artist's subjection to a higher or divine power, inspiration as respiration implies dependence on an outside force: in parallel to the air entering the body, creative inspiration is reliant on external influences. The relation of inspiration to what is produced is not a one-to-one equivalence. The output is created through transformational processes, exchanges, and transferences, which corresponds to the respirational gas exchange (the inhaled oxygen does not coincide with the exhaled carbon dioxide). Physiological inspiration never happens in isolation: it is followed by a pause, an expiration, another inspiration, and so on. Thus, within the framework of respirational inspiration, the creation of an aesthetic work is not accomplished by a singular initiation act, in contrast to classical models, according to which animation constitutes an isolated moment of origin. To breathe is not to be but *to become*—just as we have to keep breathing in order keep on living, the respirational-inspirational work is involved in a constant process of generation.[38]

This leads into some key assumptions and methodological premises of *Poetics of Breathing*: when it comes to a work's inspiration/respiration, the focus will not be on a singular initiation scene but rather on a continual process of generation and formation. The book thus ties in with contemporary approaches that understand poetics as processual and are mindful of the ways in which literary works reflect their own mediality and material constitution—what they are made of, how they were made, and how they keep being in the making. Strictly speaking, this means that literary texts do not reflect what they are, but how they work, what they do, what generated them, and what they are in process of becoming. Such a view unfolds inspirational-respirational multiplicities in motion, not self-contained, stable entities. Literary works always exceed the words printed on paper: they involve people who made them, other works that influenced them, historical and cultural contexts, institutions that canonize or decanonize them, recipients who will or will not read them, and so forth. The physical body of the book continues to be constituted by factors and beings outside that body, and it keeps emitting meaning, affects, and so on. *Poetics of Breathing* construes inspirational-respirational literary works as human-nonhuman assemblages whose relation to breathing bodies exceeds mere analogy.

In this context, Wills's thoughts on the connections between life and writing in *Inanimation* are instructive, especially given the strong linguistic ties between "life" and "breath," as summarized in a striking manner by Ernest Renan in *De l'origine du langage*: "In all languages breath has become synonymous with life, for which it serves as a physical sign"[39] (112; quoted in Derrida, *Heidegger: The Question of Being & History*).[40] Wills argues that "the life of a text has no clear analogical relation to how we understand organic life," and consequently asks,

> [Is] the usage of the word life as it relates to a written text metaphorical? . . . Is there simply real, literal, organic life, on the one hand, and a series of metaphorical extensions of this literality, loose figurative usages of the word, on the other? Or rather, doesn't life function through a variety of forms that never reduce to organic examples, however dominant and numerous the organic examples may be? (112)

Does "breath," "a physical sign" as Renan puts it—a word that rambles and slips, allies with other words and their meanings, attaching and detaching itself continually—engage in a movement that is itself sensory and corporeal? Is it a movement of linguistic agency that is not executed autonomously but only possible through relations, alliances with, and physical proximities to humans who speak, write, and read it? Isn't that what keeps language alive—in terms that exceed the biological? Isn't language animated thus? Or, shall we say language is *inanimated*, as the generative linguistic movement oscillates between what is considered organic and inorganic? Regarding the semantic movements and transferences of "breath" as *analogous to* the physiological processes it stands for would suggest a relation in which the "actual" respiratory body becomes figural, abstracted into language by means of comparison, metaphor, or metonymy.

As an alternative, *Poetics of Breathing* understands respiratory language as a syncopal movement of physical, sensuous signifiers on the verge of the figurative. Etymological or metaphorical transferences of meaning—meaning, the old spiritual-mental antagonist of the fleshly signifier, the sublimated part of the sign that predominated for so long—encompass material processes, concrete interactions of bodies. These are human bodies that interact with word-bodies and their signifieds—hands on pages of lexica and pens touching paper when thinking and composing manifest themselves materially in the course of etymological and philosophical investigations, the creation and reception of literature, and so forth. Paying close attention to the word "breath" and the semantic field surrounding it makes us conscious of the ways in which a signifier cannot be fully subsumed by meaning and meaning cannot be fully subsumed by the word's body. Situated between the physical and the spiritual semantically, and between the material and the immaterial physiologically, breath keeps gesturing toward an ongoing process of embodiment and disembodiment that, in a linear chronology, undermines the anteriority of either terms in these pairs.

Transactual Relationality and Interdependence

Nancy's claim that "chronology is without respiration" (qtd. in *Nancy Now* 3) raises the question of how a temporality *of respiration*, and, more specifically, of literary respiration, may be characterized.[41] My discussions of an anteriority of breathing with regard to language have suggested two things. (1) Such an anteriority implies a temporal displacement of what is assumed to be before or at the beginning: breathing as a bodily precondition for speaking constantly accompanies actual speaking; respirational inspiration does not mark an initiation moment located at one point in time but rather continues to operate. (2) The generative implications of breathing presuppose processes that are not executed autonomously but are dependent on interactions between various entities. I want to conclude the first chapter by sketching a model of respirational reception based on these two insights gained from investigating historical and contemporary negotiations of breath as a word, figure of thought, and physiological process.

The second point needs some elucidation. When we breathe, we necessarily enter into relations with the environment, the atmosphere, and other breathers. Many reflections on respiration in critical theory and philosophy take the relationality and interdependence involved in breathing as a starting point: a prominent example is Peter Sloterdijk's "Breathed Commune" in *Bubbles*. Others include Jean-Christophe Bailly, who states that "the space of breath is this coming and going through which the outside and the inside communicate. It is through this that they insufflate one another. . . . One sees respiration outside of oneself in others' bodies and in the bodies of creatures" (4) and David Michael Kleinberg-Levin, who claims that "when breathing takes place with phenomenological mindfulness, it becomes an experience of interaction, interconnectedness and interdependence" (72). To add an ecocritical perspective, Elizabeth A. Povinelli argues that "the lung seems the most appropriate organ for the Anthropogenic climate change era because it points to the openness of all beings to their surroundings. Several strands of contemporary critical theory might agree" (51). In *Receptive Bodies*, Leo Bersani presents the scenario of an infant's first cry and breath after birth as a paradigmatic example of "our earliest transactions with exteriority (inhaling and exhaling)" (86):

> With its first, exuberantly welcomed scream, the human infant announces its respiratory interdependence. Within the womb, it could rely on the mother breathing for it. Having accomplished the at once biologically and symbolically necessary severance from the mother's breathing rhythm, she is on her own, dependent on her own lungs to sustain the precarious individual life into which she has just fallen. Breathing is the tiny human's first experience of her body's inescapable receptivity: absorption and expulsion. (85)

Bersani highlights that the interdependence of a breathing body entails exposure and receptivity at the same time. Focusing more on the implications of exposure and the body's openness to the outside and the Other, Emmanuel Levinas extensively uses respiratory vocabulary in *Otherwise Than Being*:

> The animation, the very pneuma of the psyche, alterity in identity, is the identity of a body exposed to the other, becoming "for the other," the possibility of giving. (69)

> A further deep breathing even in the breath cut short by the wind of alterity. . . . To open oneself as space, to free oneself by breathing from closure in oneself already presupposes this beyond: my responsibility for the other and my aspiration by the other, the crushing charge, the beyond, of alterity. That the breathing by which entities seem to affirm themselves triumphantly in their vital space would be a consummation, a coring out of my substantiality, that in breathing I already open myself to my subjection to the whole of the invisible other . . . , is to be sure surprising. . . .

> An openness of the self to the other, which is not a conditioning or a foundation of oneself in some principle . . . , breathing is transcendence in the form of opening up. It reveals all its meaning only in the relationship with the other. . . . This pneumatism is not nonbeing; it is disinterestedness. . . . In human breathing, in its everyday equality, perhaps we have to already hear the breathlessness of an inspiration that paralyzes essence, that transpierces it with an inspiration by the other. (180–81)

Drawing on Levinas, Kleinberg-Levin notes that "breathing is already an experience of the ethical relation" (85) and Irigaray, distancing herself from Levinas, argues that the task of women is "to make divine this world—as body, as cosmos, as relation with others . . . through the breath" (*The Age of Breath* 8). There are two recent book-length studies devoted to the ethical relationality of breathing, Lenart Škof's *Breath of Proximity: Intersubjectivity, Ethics and Peace* and Magdalena Górska's dissertation, *Breathing Matters: Feminist Intersectional Politics of Vulnerability*. Ashon T. Crawley bases the major arguments of *Blackpentecostal Breath: The Aesthetics of Possibility* on a "radical sociality" granted by the "sharing of breathing, of breath, of air" (40). Against the assumption that breathers are *unified* through the intake and emission of the same (natural) substance, and, in simplified terms, an ethical appeal that we should be in solidarity, we should be united because we all breathe, as breath is what we have in common, *Poetics of Breathing* advocates for an *ethics of breathing together-apart*, as beings thrown into an atmosphere with others; others who are—to various degrees—always different from one another and cannot be held together by a substance as frail and intangible as air. In *The Use of Bodies*, Agamben claims that "what is common is never a property but only the inappropriable" (93). I argue that literary breath—syncopnea—is precisely such an inappropriable matter that fosters a communality of singular-plural beings. It is what Lisa Robertson, in another context, describes as "a worldly and abundantly shared incongruity" (64).

A respiratory take on what Nancy outlines as *Being Singular Plural* provides the framework for an ethics of breathing emerging in the syncopated relations between humans and literary texts. The reception model to be outlined rests on two presuppositions inspired by Nancy's book.[42] (1) Any relationality of breathing is based on contiguity, not connection. Breathed air "passes *between us*" (*Being Singular Plural* 5). An exhalation literally *passes*; it evaporates, the CO_2 transfuses the surrounding air; even when I inhale what you just exhaled, I take in something that already became different from what left your body. Breath is not a "connecting tissue" (5); respiratory contact is a momentary touch of bodies extended to the outside—when your exhalation touches mine; it is a touch of material substances that are not solid yet are palpable. The collision of our breath is an encounter between what we no longer own, between what is on the verge of being part of our body and departure; breathing with each other is not *in sync* but *syncopal*, a mode of being together whose "law of touching is separation" (5). (2) The touch of breath is a touch of singularity: of singularities that become their "'own' clearing," their "'own' imminence" in the touch, revealing themselves "*beside*, always beside" (7). The (mostly unpleasant) experience of accidentally or unavoidably inhaling the breath of strangers makes it abundantly clear that we take in an "other." But even the breath of the person closest to us is fundamentally other. We all breathe, but we all breathe differently: the rhythms and patterns of our breath as well as its chemical consistency are unique, like fingerprints.[43] Against the notion of an individual's singular essence, *respirational singularity* is enacted in a continual process, a process through which the organism turns into a multiplicity constantly engaging with the outside. Just as being is always "being with," breathing is always "breathing with." "There is no being I that precedes being many, being with, originary alterity," (12) "what we exist *in* it [nature, the world] in the mode of a constantly renewed singularity" (9).

Nancy does not reduce "being with" to interactions between human beings and bodies: "The ontology of being-with is an ontology of bodies, of every body, whether they be inanimate, animate, sentient, speaking, thinking"

(84). The body goes "from itself to itself; whether made of stone, wood, plastic, or flesh, a body is the sharing of and the departure from self, the departure toward self, the nearby-to-self without which the 'self' would not even be 'on its own' ['*a part soi*']" (84). Apart from exposing us to other human beings, breathing implies a most fundamental sense of shared being with animate and inanimate entities that surround us: the particles of the atmosphere and the microorganisms we constantly inhale, and so forth. Our respirational relations entail animate organisms that breathe differently and things that do not breathe at all. When we pneumatically touch another human multiplicity or the nonhumans we are in contact with through breathing, we are not connected by sameness, but rather "marking a distinction from other singularities" (32). As Nancy argues, such a contiguity of singularities constitutes the singularity of an I as such: "The singular is primarily *each* one and, therefore, also *with* and *among* all the others. The singular is a plural" (32). "The togetherness of singulars is singularity 'itself.' It 'assembles' them insofar as it spaces them; they are 'linked' insofar as they are not unified." Pneumatic singularities "are 'linked' insofar as they are not unified" (33).

A respiratory take on Nancy's notion of "being singular plural" does not shed light on the mysteries and paradoxes implied: what exactly is the I, my singularity, when it is at the same time a "not-I" constituted by others? How can we conceive of a *singularity* composed of *repeated* contacts, an "unbecoming community" (Ricco 25) of breathers?[44] And how could we imagine a "literary community" of breathers? Jacques Rancière describes the modern literary community as constituted by a "whirlwind of impersonal sensory events . . . a perpetual movement randomly assembling an infinity of atoms that get intertwined, part with one another, and get interlaced again in a perpetual vibration . . . [a] common breath" (98–99). For Rancière, the "common sense" that modern literature creates relies on movements on the molecular or atomic level that dissipate identity and calls these movements the "breath of the impersonal" (99). Such a breath is not limited to human organisms—Rancière specifically locates it in literary texts: "Literature turns the power of disidentification into the power of writing itself, the power of dissolving, for its own sake, the rigid forms of social identity and relationships to produce its own events in the breath of the sentences" (100). As a formulation that organically emerges within Rancière's text, "the *breath* of the sentences" is left uncommented on. Beyond the context of Rancière's work, one of this book's tasks is to explore what "breathing sentences," "breathing words," or "breathing letters" may imply and in what ways they might be involved in enabling "a sociality of shared-separation" (Ricco 25).

When we read literature, we always, to some degree, enter a "sociality of shared-separation." Not only do we engage and bond with entities radically unlike us, fictional characters, words, and so on. We also make contact *across* time, across the "distances of the textual condition," (7) in Peter Middleton's terms; namely, the distances between the sites of the texts' "composition and first publication" and the specific time, place, and cultural context in which we are reading them (3). We reach out or are reached out to in a transactual manner[45]—I refer to "actual" in the sense of being "in operation or existence at the time," as what is "present, current" (*Oxford English Dictionary* online). What specifically interests me in this context is the possibility that entities "rooted" in different moments in time may touch in the process of becoming "uprooted." The notion of contiguity instead of connection allows us to think of a separating touch, a touch implying distance. Along with Nancy, I consider these proximities in terms of space: breathers who touch are spatially extended bodies rendered nonidentical yet singular in the contact. What about an extension of bodies in time? In order to think about this, it is necessary to make more explicit something that is already at work in the extension of bodies in space: the body extended by breath is transferred to the outside without any tissue connecting it to an anchor point—rather, the physiological organism itself becomes a point of departure and displacement. If we imagine bodies touching across time, it has to be acknowledged that these bodies are transferred, displaced, non–self-identical. The suggested model of literary reception involves a process of transference and contiguity—a metonymical relation across space and time, which, in contrast to a metaphorical one, is not determined by similarity.

What happens between the writing body, the written body, and the reading body? As Lisa Robertson beautifully puts it, "the person and an impersonal speech test and inflect and mix into each other" in "the folded time" of reading (12). The writer and the reader are both in contact with the text but seldom with each other; moreover, the touch of the writer and that of the reader rarely occur at the same time. What is touched across time is a third instance, the text with its "impersonal speech," an entity that in strange ways represents a dissected part of the extended, transferred, and displaced bodies of writers and readers. In the "inconspicious" act of reading (Robertson 12), we engage in transactual touches: we are both in contact with the text materially in front of us and with earlier moments in time, for example, when the text was written, spoken earlier, or spoken for the first time. In his discussion of the techniques of inscription in oral traditions, Haun Saussy mentions that "rhythm is schematic and projective. It sets a pattern and supplies the elements for filling it out. The potential text and the realized are not one, and the writing on human memory is precisely a marking of potential features (goals, means, areas of indeterminacy)" (161). In other words, rhythms (that may have been determined by breathing) inscribed in memory take effect transactually: they are potentials yet to be realized and may allow for the reiteration of an oral text. Analogously, reading out loud can be the actualization of a breathing rhythm slumbering in a written text. A text's breathing rhythm always points beyond its "present" time and beyond the concrete actualization through physical respiration: the bodily breath that might have influenced the textual one is always in the past, and the fleeting moment when a text meets a reader's inhalation and exhalation is always already on its way to sink back into a state of potentiality. As the physical breaths of authors and readers never coincide, articulable textual breaths are sites of "shared-separation" in which "I . . . become foreign and unknowable to myself in accordance with reading's audacity" (Robertson 13). What Nancy claims about the temporality of poetry can be extended to the transactual rhythm of literature in general: "The present of poetry is the present divested of presence. It is not the perpetual present of discourse, always in retention and pretension between its past and its future. But a present suspended over its presentation. A breath held or a resumption of breath. Between inspiration and expiration, between first cry and last word" (*Expectation* 116). One of the most prominent images addressing a transactual relationality of reading is that of "breathing new life" into a text through the act of reading. This image, which firmly installed itself in the way we talk about literary texts, unsettles the idea of an inspirational act in the beginning of a text's existence in time, executed by a single being. Respirational inspiration, as *Poetics of Breathing* proposes, takes place instance by instance ("au coup par coup" [Nancy, *Being Singular Plural* 33]), across time, from both sides of the writer-text-readers triangle, and it is performed by multiple different agents. In order to trace the image of breathing new life into a work further, and to add some flesh to the skeleton of my suggested model, I briefly want to discuss two prominent, canonical texts that exemplify it, one from the perspective of the writer, the other from the perspective of the reader: Shakespeare's *Sonnet 81* and a passage from Georges Poulet's "Phenomenology of Reading."

As in other sonnets, the speaker/writer in *Sonnet 81* is concerned with the question of how a beloved person may be "immortalized" through writing:[46]

Or I shall live your epitaph to make,
Or you survive when I in earth am rotten.
From hence your memory death cannot take,
Although in me each part will be forgotten.
Your name from hence immortal life shall have,
Though I, once gone, to all the world must die.
The earth can yield me but a common grave
When you entombèd in men's eyes shall lie.
Your monument shall be my gentle verse,
Which eyes not yet created shall o'er-read,
And tongues to be your being shall rehearse
When all the breathers of this world are dead.
 You still shall live—such virtue hath my pen—
 Where breath most breathes, even in the mouths of men.
(*Norton Shakespeare* 1959)

As the addressee's endurance across time depends on the premise that the "you" enters "gentle verse," the question of how the beloved may transcend time is at the same time a question of how a written text may last. The sonnet suggests that the lasting existence of its subject, "you," and itself, may be provided by interactions between writing, produced by the "I," and humans who live later. Thus, two modes of reception are sketched that both involve the senses: reading silently, with the eyes ("Your monument shall be my gentle verse, / Which eyes not yet created shall o'er-read") and reading out loud, by means of tongue and breath ("And tongues to be your being shall rehearse / When all the breathers of this world are dead"). The poem highlights this differentiation rhythmically: the lines in which the oral pronunciation is addressed are written in perfectly intact iambic pentameters: "And tongues to be your being shall rehearse"; "You still shall live—such virtue hath my pen—"; "Where breath most breathes, even in the mouths of men." While these words can be smoothly articulated, our tongues tend to stumble when we pronounce the lines referring to reading with the eyes (or they are explicitly prevented from doing so by visual aids ["entombèd"]): "When you entombèd in men's eyes shall lie"; "Which eyes not yet created shall o'er-read."[47] Thus, the sonnet seems to confirm Haun Saussy's claim that the endurance of oral texts depends on rhythmical regularities that are easily inscribed in the memory. It is important to note that the sonnet presents several modes of how the text and its subject may last:

the first claim is solely that the "you" will be *remembered* once the sonnet is written: "From hence [i.e., these lines] *your memory* death cannot take." In this first step of the argument, "immortal life" is only given to "your name"—which is not given in the poem. Verse is described as a monument in which words are preserved; words on paper endure across time, but they constitute tombstones. The written words last in an inanimate way and reading with the eyes "entombs" the anonymous "you."

The "magic" of animation, what is supposed to give life to the "you" as a "being" (in contrast to the written "name" that will merely be remembered), is only granted by tongue and breath: "*tongues* to be *your being* shall rehearse." "*You still shall live* . . . Where *breath* most breathes, even in the *mouths of men*" (italics added).[48] The sonnet addresses a physical, respirational inspiration, not a spiritual one. As Catherine Bates observes, this twist and the recourse to spoken language render the whole idea of a life retained through literature fragile: "Words suddenly seem a lot less solid as they threaten to melt away or evaporate into thin air—mere speech" (345), a medium less durable than the paper words are written on. Bates argues that "such prophesies of enduring fame might fulfil themselves every time the poem is read, but they can just as equally cancel themselves out entirely. If the poem remains unread, no one will be any wiser" (346). This is exacerbated by making the "ongoing life" of the "you" and the words that preserve it dependent on mortal human breathers. As the poem seems to suggest, there may be new breathers after "all the breathers of this world are dead"—but what if we read "this world" not as this generation, but rather, from the perspective of today's breathers, as Planet Earth in an age referred to as the Anthropocene? Will there be other breathers after us, nonhuman ones maybe? Will they read Shakespeare? We don't know. These are the uncertainties pervading the sonnet's claims about the continuing of life through writing and reading.

The death of "all breathers of this world," even if we read "this world" as "this generation," which is what the speaker/writer seems to have in mind, includes the biological death of the person addressed as "you." In order to be reanimated by future breathers, the "you" has to die and to be "entombèd" in inanimate words. Let us imagine the addressee, along with Nancy, as someone who "expires not in speech but with speech" (*Expectation* 50). The scenario Shakespeare draws is very close to a literary community that has "no common space" ("Literary Communism" 73) and is always "*to come*" (71), a community based on the separation of the "one" in itself and from itself: "This 'one' who has always already been what it is but who only becomes so by expiring—death and speech together, speech and breath about to be lost in order to be found, formed . . . between the immemorial and the unarriving" (*Expectation* 51). When the breathers to come take the expired "I" into their mouths, "recitation recites this ins-ex-piration, the rise and fall, the beat, the beating of this breath" (51).

That "you still shall live" in the mouths of future breathers is only granted by a transformation of the biological, breathing body into "dead" words by means of "my pen"—a pre-Derridean assertion that writing precedes lively speech. In the course of being rendered durable through interactions of speaking and writing, the addressee's "being" undergoes constant transformations and is subject to displacements. This is also indicated by the ambivalent claim that "tongues to be your being shall rehearse." The obvious reading is that tongues to be (in the future) will rehearse the addressee's being, by reciting the poem or talking about the person addressed in the poem. But there is another possibility: "tongues to be your being" may indicate that future tongues engaging with the sonnet *become* and consequently *are* "your being." The words chosen support this reading, as they linguistically perform a merging of "tongues to *be*" and "your *being*." In this context, it has to be stressed that instead of giving the addressee's name, which would tie it to a specific person, the sonnet consistently addresses its subject with the personal pronoun "you," a shifter that can be occupied by anyone. And if we read a text, don't *we* always somehow feel addressed when we encounter a "you"?[49] The "you" in *Sonnet* 81 is caught in a transactual, respiratory relation of being singular plural.

Just as the "you" becomes a shifting entity or being, the *place* where it is supposed to be animated—"Where breath most breathes, even in the mouths of men"—is unsteady: "the mouths of men" designates a concrete, definitive anatomical location of the human body. That these mouths are invoked as a specification of "where breath most breathes," however, unsettles the seemingly clear localization. In "where breath most breathes," we enter a scenario of displacement and transference: a personification followed by a metonymy. A characteristic of the human breather, the capacity to respire, is transferred to "breath" itself, and breathing is used in the metonymical sense of "living": breath "lives" most, is most "vivid," when "in the mouths of men." The movement of transference pervading the words alternately shifts them toward and away from the organic human body, breath moves between being embodied in a human mouth, and disembodied in figural language. That the sonnet itself constitutes a place of transformation and mutability is suggested by Helen Vendler when she observes that words move into other words; the poem "toys anagrammatically with words-inside-words: *created* contains *read*, *breathers* conceals 'hearers,' and *earth* and *rehearse* contain 'hear.' Moreover, the "words *death* and *breath* differ only by their initial consonants; that is, they share more than they realize" (361). Her finding that the "central words are phonemically or graphically linked" (362) indicates that the sonnet does not present itself as a stable site: its particles—sounds and letters—move across word boundaries; the lines between what is distinguished on the semantic level, reading with the eyes and reading with the mouth, tongue and breath, are constantly crossed by the words' material constituents. What the speaker claims to have created constitutes a mutable pneumatic assemblage of a textual body relying on an interdependence between its own moving particles and the ones who engage with them in acts of reception across time. The moment when "breath most breathes," namely, when breath seemingly enters a domain of self-identity and autonomous agency, is suspended immediately once this place is identified with "the mouths of men." Neither the sonnet itself nor its linguistically entombed addressee, "you," is a living organism capable of breathing autonomously; it may only maintain a kind of "life" through later breathers providing inanimation/animation.

What about those later breathers? What happens to them when they interact with texts? A very brief look at George Poulet's "Phenomenology of Reading" gives some hints. "And so I ought not to hesitate to recognize that so long as it is animated by this vital inbreathing inspired by the act of reading, a work of literature becomes (at the expense of the reader whose own life it suspends) a sort of human being, that it is a mind conscious of itself and constituting itself in me as the subject of its own objects" (59). Through animating the text with "vital inbreathing," the reader's life is suspended, Poulet claims. This image, sketching a vampiric act of the undead text sucking the life and breath out of the human who reads it, results from an argumentation stressing the interrelationality of literary work and reader. The "openness of the book" implies that "it asks nothing better than to exist outside itself, or to let you exist in it. In short, the extraordinary fact in the case of a book is the falling away of the barrier between you and it. You are inside it; it is inside you; there is no longer either outside or inside" (54). Consequently, reading, then, "is the act in which the subjective principle which I call *I*, is modified in such a way that I no longer have the right, strictly speaking, to consider it as my *I*. I am on loan to another, and this other thinks, feels, suffers and acts within me" (57). The radical consequence of reading is that we do not stay the same; we become other than what we may have assumed to be a stable self at the moment; another being, another thing or I, *invades* us in the act of reading and becomes part of us when we enter the space of literature, which dissolves the boundaries between inside and outside, self and other. The pneumatic relations we engage in when we read—described by Poulet in terms of breathing and inspiration—are a form of "being/breathing with" in which we are constituted as other. What Poulet excludes in his reflections on reading are the material dimensions of literature: the relationality he describes is based on a shared or "common consciousness" (59) of reader and work. It is precisely this notion of breathing that can lead us toward a more corporeal conception of the interrelations and interactions determining reading. The reading child Walter Benjamin depicts in *Einbahnstrasse* gives us an idea thereof: "Sein Atem steht in der Luft der Geschehnisse und alle Figuren hauchen es an" (41); "His breath is part of the air of the events narrated, and all the participants breathe with his life [more literally translated as breathe at him]" (*One-Way Street and Other Writings* 72).

Prospect

The chapters to follow attend to the particular poetics of breathing articulated in literary texts and outlined in essays, manifestoes, interviews, and notes by Jack Kerouac, Allen Ginsberg, Robert Musil, Virginia Woolf, Samuel Beckett, Sylvia Plath, Paul Celan, and Herta Müller. The historical focus of the book is *modern* literature. By "modern" I do not refer to a (more or less) strictly defined literary period (for example "modernism") but rather to literature from the twentieth century onward.[50] It is important to stress that the book's approach is philological rather than historical: the question of why certain poetics emerged in a specific time and which particular historical factors facilitated them could be the subject for further research, but it exceeds the scope of the present book, which, as a premise, attempts to pay close attention to the literary texts themselves as well as to their intertextual entanglements.

The broader time frame, "modern literature," is inextricably linked to the book's primary interest: exploring points where the physiological process of breathing and the corporeal aspects of literature interpenetrate and interrupt each other and investigating the material conditions of literary production and reception in respiratory terms. In line with an ongoing process of secularization, twentieth- and twenty-first-century literature has tended to focus on *physical* breath. While breathing as inspiration or *pneuma* has been widely discussed and reflected on in literary works throughout the centuries in terms of a creative, spiritual, or divine power, the visceral aspects of breath and the bodily act of breathing have continually found resonance. In the twentieth century, this latter dimension is emphasized more distinctly. That the modern tendency to embrace corporeal and material dimensions of breath is not entirely new has become apparent in the glimpses at crucial respiratory moments throughout cultural and literary history that are provided in this chapter. Modern literature consciously or unconsciously recalls such moments while adapting and rewriting the transcendental-spiritual history of breath. In a literary discourse that diagnoses a crisis of representation and increasingly reflects the dilemmas of rendering meaning, breath becomes a favored site through which these concerns can be creatively negotiated.

Moreover, modern literature's heightened awareness of the sensual (e.g., acoustic, tonal, visual) aspects of words and the reversions to literature's oral origins also contribute to its embrace of the respiratory. It is important to note that this happens at a moment when literary works are primarily composed in writing and read silently. In other words, in modern literature, breath often evokes orality in written language. The book's primary concern are instances of mediated breath and respiratory intermediality; rather than focusing on oral forms of modern literature, I am interested in how breath moves between the spoken and the written, how it is mediated and transferred between different media and materialities of literature. The incongruences accompanying such transpositions and translations provide the crucial point of comparison between modern literary texts that embrace and produce a language of rupture.

The major theoretical trajectories of a poetics of breathing elaborated in this chapter—syncope, liminality, generative, formative and constitutive movements, disrupted temporalities, and transactual relationality and interdependence—are both directive for the discussion of the texts in the individual chapters and crucial for the methodological approach and structure of the book as a whole. The choice of attending in detail to select works through close readings—a practice that, metaphorically speaking, requires breathing space—instead of providing a more encompassing comparative overview of breath in modern literature is motivated by the aspiration to write and think "in empathy with [the] subject matter," as Spyros Papapetros puts it (xiii). Tracing the singularity of literary breathprints produced by the particular authors and texts that are focused on can only be achieved through microanalyses of the literary works. At the same time, the works' transactual dimension demands acknowledging the tension between close reading and distant reading; as Peter Middleton theorizes it, "the admission of the effects of temporal distance" involves "attention to the shaping densities of intervening history between composition and this act of reception" (9). Methodologically, Middleton's claim that "no criticism can simply detach a literary text from the past of its making" (5) becomes especially relevant for a book devoted to the generative and constitutive forces at work in literature. Attending to the individual works as respiratory "temporary entit[ies]" (23), I endeavored to engage in the "intimacy" of close reading (7) while at the same time incorporating what distant reading requires: "mining what is available of the aggregative textual archive that composes the textual memory" (23), especially by investigating manuscripts and drafts of the works in question in order to consult traces of the writing processes.

The implications of breathing "singular-plural" negotiated previously dissuades from the investigation of the works' unique traits in isolation. By pairing authors whose respiratory poetics are closely related but—obviously—never fully overlap, *Poetics of Breathing* presents four conversations *à travers*: between Jack Kerouac and Allen Ginsberg, Robert Musil and Virginia Woolf, Samuel Beckett and Sylvia Plath, and Paul Celan and Herta Müller. Thus, the individual chapters themselves operate in a syncopal manner, parsing intertextual connections and tensions, moments when poetics of breathing coincide and others when they diverge. Poetic kinship turned out to be more important for this book than historical contiguity, and the arrangement of the chapters follows an internal logic rather than proceeding chronologically—on transactual breathroutes, so adhering to a linear timeline was not a priority. There is a crucial reason why the book starts with a discussion of the Beat writers. In the "canon" of modern respiratory literature, the Beat and Black Mountain writers are those who most explicitly formulated a poetics of breathing in which the body is central. Inspired by Charles Olson's poetic reflections, Kerouac and Ginsberg argue that the actual breath of the author during the writing process is supposed to structure poetry and prose in order to replace inherited formal principles. The idea is one of a straightforward inscription that is at the same time an embodiment: the writers' breath is put into writing that—such are the phonocentric undercurrents—immediately maintains their living presence and carries their authentic voice. Kerouac and Ginsberg's poetic and literary writing is an ideal starting point for calling attention to the problems and inconsistencies that necessarily go hand in hand with such positions. Through investigating the authors' writing processes by examining archival material, I will show that their poetic and compositional claims were hardly ever put into practice. I will demonstrate how both Kerouac's and Ginsberg's literary texts and poetic essays or statements self-deconstruct and reveal more complex processes than what they explicitly claim.

A critical reading of Kerouac's and Ginsberg's attitude toward a "natural" body literally inspiring their texts is then followed by investigations of alternative respiratory poetics that nonetheless embrace materiality and physicality. The writers juxtaposed in the remaining chapters, Musil and Woolf, Beckett and Plath, and Celan and Müller, negotiate breath as a site of fractured corporeality, of absent presence or present absence. In their work, the relation of physiological respiration and writing presents itself as refracted, mediated, and discontinuous. The paired authors accentuate a different nexus of body, breath, and literature: in Musil's and Woolf's prose, impersonal narrative voices stage generative textual breaths detached from human characters. Beckett's and Plath's writing involves speakers that incessantly keep breathing on the verge of life and death. For Celan and Müller, breath becomes the locus for a literary commemoration of violated and annihilated bodies. By grouping the authors in this way, *Poetics of Breathing* develops a narrative trajectory: we move from Kerouac's and Ginsberg's idea that the authors' respiratory rhythms and pauses for breath are deployed in a writing practice to text-internal breath-pauses in Musil's and Woolf's highly self-reflexive works, which emphasize the acoustic dimension of the written word. Whereas in Musil and Woolf's texts, breath externalized from human bodies appears in images connected to nature, Beckett and Plath present it as machine-like and mechanical. They negotiate breathing as a minimal, repetitive, and passive process entangled in textuality and artificial speaking or sounding. From Plath's and Beckett's conjunction of breathing and barely speaking we then turn to what can barely be spoken about in Celan's and Müller's writings: the violent reduction of humans to bare life in contexts where air is unbreathable. Whereas Beckett and Plath design their texts as restricted, semianimate spaces, Celan and Müller write in reaction to traumatic, suffocating surroundings.

In *Poetics of Breathing*, each pair of authors presents a different conception of literary breath as a precondition of writing that becomes legible through oscillating rhythms of sound and silence. Kerouac and Ginsberg focus on a very concrete scenario of what precedes literary texts: the actual writing process in which the author's breath determines a work's composition. Their ideas for a new American poetry go hand in hand with a revival of orality: breath-measure takes center stage in imagined oral compositional acts that result in texts intended to be read out loud. Both Musil's and Woolf's work is concerned with almost imperceptible breath as an ontological precondition of writing: it marks form-generating intervals and pauses where musicality and rhythmicality are emitted by silent words. Beckett's and Plath's texts evoke a passive, neutral respirational ground of language. This space is articulated by speakers who dissipate into the abstraction of language without falling silent. Celan's and Müller's writings move around an empty precondition: unspeakable trauma, which renders language inoperative, cannot be remembered as event or reconstructed as narrative. From the traumatic point zero, a breath-writing situated between silence and speaking emerges.

The last chapter is dedicated to questions of gendered literary breath that emerge in the complex interplay of sex and gender in the poetic conversations of the book. The poetic-pneumatic kinships of the authors negotiated in the individual chapters are imbued with intricate gender dynamics. The tension between corporeal and textual breath is always also a tension between gendered and sexuated breath, even where sex and gender are not explicitly negotiated in the literary works. All chapters but one juxtapose a male and a female author: Virginia Woolf and Robert Musil; Sylvia Plath and Samuel Beckett; Herta Müller and Paul Celan. Concerning Kerouac and Ginsberg, another significant sexual difference is at work: both repeatedly highlight their distinct sexual orientations. Ginsberg was a prominent figure in gay activism and Kerouac staged himself as the epitome of heterosexual masculinity. A comparative look at the authors whom I've paired reveals a complex constellation that simultaneously draws on stereotypes while challenging conventional gender ascriptions. It is especially by attending to the texts' tone and cadence and the writers' respective biological sex that a respirational undercurrent running through all the chapters can be detected. How the modulations of a particularly literary breath in the texts relate to their respective authors and their gendered bodies is a question that must to some extent remain open, as the intersections between a writer's body and a written work are syncopal. In my investigation of literary breath, I repeatedly put the finger on the *cut* between the two. This is the easier part of exploring the intricate relations between writing and written respirational bodies. The concrete ways in which they come *together* and what precisely of the author's body "remains" *with* their writing—whether as exscription, trace, gap, or whatever term we choose to address it—always withdraws; it cannot be pinpointed and defies conclusive assertions. While moving along precarious breathroutes, I will nevertheless pursue a correlation between the authors' genders and textual motives, tones, and tempi throughout.[51] The writing of the women (i.e., Woolf, Plath, and Müller) tends to be what is conventionally considered more sonorous, or loud and aggressive, displaying flow and movement, whereas the writing of the men (Musil, Beckett, and Celan) take a tone that is more quiet, withdrawn, sedate, and quiescent, embracing standstill and rest. The writing of Kerouac and Ginsberg strangely correspond to this pattern: Kerouac's idea of virile spontaneous prose goes hand in hand with flow, speed, and activity, whereas Ginsberg emphasizes meditative pauses and deliberate, conscious self-examination. Rather than deriving a theory of gendered breath from the literary texts being analyzed, I remain attentive to instances where pneumatic gender constellations are interrupted, when breath at different points traverses the tendency observable with respect to the paired authors. The gender dynamics addressed in the individual chapters to a large extent remain within a binary logic (male/female). The last chapter then explores how literary movements of syncopnea unsettle gender binaries and amount to a notion of impersonal queerness and respiratory intersectionality, a breathing across organic life that gendered bodies and desires traverse.

2

Composed on the Breath

Authentic Voice, Embodiment, Innovation (Jack Kerouac, Allen Ginsberg)

> Verse now, 1950, if it is to go ahead, if it is to be of *essential* use, must, I take it, catch up and put into itself certain laws and possibilities of the breath, of the breathing of the man who writes as well as of his listenings.
>
> —Olson, "Projective Verse" 15

The opening claim of Charles Olson's influential essay "Projective Verse" responds to a set of questions that occupied two circles of avant-garde writers in the 1950s and 1960s, the Black Mountain poets and the Beat movement. How can a new literature that radically breaks with tradition be inaugurated? What basis can it have, if not tradition? The "laws and possibilities of the breath," a recourse to "natural" bodily processes,[1] promises an "emancipation of the American language of spontaneous vernacular American English from rulebound + traditional British English + socio-political prohibitions against free expression of the mind itself," as Kerouac puts it ("History of the Theory of Breath").[2] Liberating language from the shackles of the fossilized, dusty rules of meter and rhyme will vivify and renew it. A transference of the author's breathing rhythm to that of the words to be written promises an organic, embodied literature that reconciles art and life. In his discussion of breath, Olson refers to the "revolution of the ear" ("Projective Verse" 15), pointing to a revival of orality in American poetry that starts with Walt Whitman and extends to Ezra Pound and William Carlos Williams. His claims that "breath allows all the speech-force of language back in" and "speech is . . . the secret of a poem's energy" (20) can be read as a call for spoken literature, for words carried by physical breath, which are more alive than those that "print bred" (15).[3] The "new oralism" diagnosed in the 1950s and 1960s became manifest through a "boom . . . in poetry readings" (Davidson, " 'By ear, he sd': Audio-Tapes and Contemporary Criticism" xvi).[4] In Michael Davidson's words, "public reading had begun to take on definite public forms alongside other modes of public gathering—antiwar protests, civil rights marches, sit-ins and be-ins and teach-ins, music festivals" (xvi). The performative practices that started as a countercultural, "underground" movement "became mainstreamed through the Beats and their imitators," as Raphael Allison observes in *Bodies on the Line: Performance and the Sixties Poetry Reading* (xiii). Allison accurately points out that the "new orality" is characterized by a "faith in the power of 'presence,' . . . the power of poems to enact themselves and all their incongruous energies fully, faithfully, and at once" (xiii). Following what Garrett Stewart describes as the " 'phonophobia' generated in the wake of the Derridean attack" (3), such emphatic claims for "authenticity," immediacy and "self-presence" (Allison xiii) raise doubts. Focusing on the role of breath in the poetics of Olson, Ginsberg, and Kerouac enables a critique of the Beats' sometimes naïve embrace of a "new" orality without, on the other hand, resorting to a simplified notion of "phonophobia" that would be blind to the body's impacts on the production of literature. As a starting point, I explore some tensions between speaking and writing with reference to Kerouac's and Ginsberg's poetic approaches. It has to be noted that while Kerouac did refer to spoken language and the "tongue" in his comments on the new literature (e.g., "History of the Theory of Breath") and did give public readings, his overall focus was always on writing and the written text. Ginsberg's dedication to the spoken word was much stronger: he repeatedly stressed its importance in his interviews (e.g., *Spontaneous Mind* 81, 158, 272), and—as a grandfather of contemporary poetry slams—presenting his poetry orally to a live audience was a priority of his literary endeavors. The legendary reading of "Howl" at the Six Gallery is only one example.[5]

Ebb and Flow: Breathing and Composition

For a number of Beat and Black Mountain writers, what Olson designates as "speech-force" is not only to be realized in oral performances; it is also supposed to affect the words in the composition process through breath, a measure that is "arrive[ed] at . . . organically" (Ginsberg, *Spontaneous Mind* 19). Ginsberg establishes a simple compositional principle—break the line when you run out of breath: "I literally measure each line by the physical breath—each one breath statement" (*The Letters of Allen Ginsberg* 208). "So you arrange the verse line on the page according to where you have your breath stop, and the number of words within one breath, whether it's long or short, as this long breath has just become" ("Allen Ginsberg: An Interview by Gary Pacernick" 23). Similarly, Kerouac proposes that dashes should indicate the moment between inhalation and exhalation, when breath is drawn, instead of commas and colons that separate grammatical and semantic units (e.g., "Essentials of Spontaneous Prose" 57; *Selected Letters 1957–1969* 15). In these approaches, "preconceived metrical pattern[s]" are counteracted with more irregular, variable and individual structures derived from "a source deeper than the mind . . . the breathing and the belly and the lungs" (Ginsberg, *Spontaneous Mind* 19).

Ancient Origins of the Breath-Stop

What was advocated as a fresh principle for a new literature in essays, writing manuals, and oral comments of the Beat and Black Mountain writers was actually a tacit renaissance of classical thought. Research on Ginsberg's and Kerouac's respirational composition techniques tends to address their contemporary influences: in Ginsberg's case, his engagement with a westernized version of Buddhism that was en vogue in postwar America,[6] and in Kerouac's case, the references to contemporary jazz.[7] These white American writers participated in an appropriation of Asian thought and Black music that permeated the US subculture they celebrated.[8] In contrast to Buddhism and jazz, which refer to current cultural trends that are well embedded in the project of outlining a "new literature," Kerouac and Ginsberg never explicitly addressed the Western roots of their poetics of breathing.[9] The first part of this section traces the unmentioned legacy of ancient rhetoric that continually pulls the avant-gardist endeavor out of its contemporary frame.

The importance of breathing as a bodily prerequisite for oral delivery and a structuring element of speech was stressed by Aristotle, Cicero, and Quintilian. Breath played a pivotal role with regard to prose rhythm, which the rhetoricians considered more loosely measured than poetry. Prose should be structured by sequences, for example "periods," which Aristotle defines as "sentence[s] that [have] a beginning and an end in [themselves]" (*The "Art" of Rhetoric* III, IX.5, 389). In line with the compositional ideas of the Beat and Black Mountain writers, for the rhetoricians, breath marks the intervals between structural sequences. Aristotle mentions that a "period" should be delivered "in a breath . . . taken as a whole" (389), and Cicero asserts that "there should be in speeches closes [of periods] where we may take breath" (*De Oratore* 506). The period in ancient rhetoric is a clearly defined unit: a segment that represents a thought with a beginning and an end. This idea is taken up by both Ginsberg and Kerouac. Ginsberg claims that the "breath-stop and the thought-division could be the same" (*Spontaneous Mind* 359) and Kerouac observes that a jazz musician blows "a phrase on his saxophone till he runs out of breath, and when he does, his sentence, his statement's been made. . . . That's how I therefore separate my sentences, as breath separations of the mind" ("The Art of Fiction No. 41" n.p.). Confirming the assumption that a unit of breath coincides with a unit of thought or a completed statement, Kerouac and Ginsberg either consciously or unconsciously follow the rhetoricians. What they call a poetics of the body meets an old matter of controversy concerning the sound execution of artistic composition and sometimes unpredictable physical needs. The question arising with respect to both ancient rhetoric and Kerouac's and Ginsberg's poetics is: how does the necessity of drawing a breath while speaking undercut the claim to a synchronicity of breathing and thinking?[10]

The rhetoricians' reflections indicate that a seamless coincidence of sense and breath-units cannot be taken for granted. In Quintilian's detailed account of how a speech should be delivered orally, it becomes obvious that an exact concurrence of breath-pause and the completion of a period is an ideal that can only be aspired to (*Quintilian's Institutes of Oratory* 352–53).[11] The rhetoricians argue that the completion of a period should determine the moment when a breath is drawn, and not vice versa. Cicero stresses that only the "unskilful and ignorant speaker . . . measures out the periods of his speech, not with art, but with the power of his breath" (243). He argues that the breath-pause should be motivated by coherent segments of speech rather than the bodily need to inhale: "there should be in speeches closes [of periods] where we may take breath not when we are exhausted, . . . but by the rhythm of language and thoughts" (*De Oratore* 506).¹² Quintilian notes that orators can train their breath through physical exercise in order to make it more adjustable to the need of marking a period: "we ought to exercise it [the breath or breathing], that it may hold out as long as possible" (*Quintilian's Institutes of Oratory* 357).

In this respect, the position of Kerouac and Ginsberg is diametrically opposite: the physical need to draw a breath is what should determine the interval between thoughts and constitute the structural unit. Ginsberg claims that the measure of the breath-stop is "arriv[ed] at . . . organically" and rhythmical structures come from "a source deeper than the mind . . . the breathing and the belly and the lungs." Likewise, Kerouac also stresses that he separates his phrases when he "draw[s] a breath" (*Letters 1957–1969* 15) just as the saxophonist does when "he runs out of breath" ("The Art of Fiction No. 41" n.p.). However, their commitment to what Cicero designates as rude oratory does not resolve the tension between the physical need to inhale and the breath-pause's function to structure speech. The units of thoughts and statements addressed by Kerouac and Ginsberg undermine their claim of a compositional principle solely generated from the body. In the reference to the coincidence of breathing and structural units, the "nature" of their compositional theories as a *cultural* inheritance becomes apparent; the distinctly audible resonances with ancient rhetoric on their own unsettle the idea of an art that comes to be in a fully organic-corporeal manner. In the context of their writings, breath not only refers to the *body* "of the man who writes" but also to a *rhetorike techne*. What is supposed to be a reconciliation of art and life in fact turns out to be a form of discursive vitalism rooted in an older discourse that had already challenged the seamless coincidence of body and artistic composition.

In the comments about their writing process, neither Ginsberg nor Kerouac gives a clear definition of what the segments ("mind-breaks" or "thought-divisions" in Ginsberg's case, and "phrases," "sentences" or "statements" in Kerouac's) actually consist of.¹³ Whether the two writers actually did break up their lines or sentences when they had to inhale is impossible to verify from written documents.¹⁴ The difference between oral and written composition is crucial in this respect. What the ancient rhetoricians seem to have had in mind is a scenario of oral composition: orators composing their sentences as they spoke. In contrast, Ginsberg and Kerouac primarily composed in writing. An exception is Ginsberg's tape recording practice in the mid-1960s, which will be discussed in the next section. In one of his lectures, Ginsberg claims that "there seems to be some kind of correlation between the breath or halts you take while you're talking and the breath or halts you take when you're writing," but he is unable to specify the precise nature of that "correlation." When a student asks how breath-measure works during the writing process—"do you read it out loud as you're writing it down"?—Ginsberg admits, "It's an interesting thing whether it's breath or it's mind unit. I never figured that out" (*Spiritual Poetics II* n.p.). Here it becomes apparent that for Ginsberg, the breath-stop is a way to speak about and conceptualize an embodied writing process that does not necessarily correlate with the specific physiological actuality of concrete writing scenes. When writers "pronounce" the words in their head while writing, a need to inhale does not necessarily coincide with the moment at which a breath-pause would have occurred if the same sentence were spoken. In fact, we may place many more words in the span of one breath when we pronounce them in our head than when we pronounce them orally.[15] In contrast to oral composition, writing is not inevitably affected by the need to draw breath: while writing, one can inhale without inserting a pause in the sentence that is put on paper. When breath-measure is claimed to be employed in written composition, the organic foundation that it has in oral composition ceases to apply and respiration turns into an *image* of the latter. The pause markers in Ginsberg's and Kerouac's literary texts almost always seamlessly coincide with grammatical units—meaning either that the "laws . . . of the breath" were ignored in the actual writing process or that they do not result in a significantly different structure of speech than the one according to grammatical units; a healthy body may also "unconsciously" follow the control of the mind to such a degree that breathing adjusts itself to anticipated syntactic breaks, and in this case the "laws of the breath" may, unintentionally, have been the "laws of the mind."

We can thus conclude that Kerouac's and Ginsberg's reflections on breathing and writing are poetic theories rather than descriptions of actual compositional practices. As Nathaniel Mackey observes, the "'New American' poetics of breath, offering no consistent or comprehensive practicum, was primarily a figurative, theoretical discourse" (6). While it is worth considering this discourse in its own right, it is important to be aware of the ambivalent position bodily breath thus comes to occupy: celebrated as the natural source of the structure of a literary text, its actual role in the writers' compositional practices seems to be marginal. The particularities of Kerouac's and Ginsberg's poetics of breathing are elucidated in the following discussion with this in mind. The differences between the two become most prominent in their understanding of the breath-pause. Ginsberg's and

Kerouac's respective comments on the character and function of the caesura can be referred back to two seminal passages by Quintilian and Aristotle. These intertextual links pointedly reveal the trajectories of their poetic endeavors, which are pervaded by a fixation on vitalism that turns out to be more discursively than physiologically grounded.

Ginsberg and Quintilian

Ginsberg claims that the so-called natural speech pauses, which he identifies with "breath-stops," "indicate mind-breaks" (*Spontaneous Mind* 126). The "breath stop is where you stop the phrase to breathe again. Stop to *think* and breathe" (108). By claiming that "you're gonna stop and take a breath" when "you run out of thought and words" (359), he recalls Quintilian, who argues that the pause is the "point, where the mind takes a breath and recovers its energy" (*Institutio Oratia* 543). For Quintilian, the breath-pause is the moment "when the rush of words comes to a halt" (543) and the mind is relieved from its work. The pause should provide rest so that orators can assemble their mental forces anew before the next compositional effort. When claiming that the mind takes a breath, Quintilian deploys a metaphor invoking the intake of vital breath.[16] He addresses the "rush of the words" that the pause interrupts, and thus draws on a common association tied to the metaphor of "taking a breath" in the sense of relaxing: slowing down the pace of one's breathing rhythm. To do nothing except breathe suggests that one is doing almost nothing: "taking a breath" is "pausing." The image of the mind taking a breath during the pause implies that the mind has stopped doing what it usually does, namely, thinking. By claiming that the mind takes a breath in the moment of the breath-pause, Quintilian rhetorically establishes a temporal coincidence of metaphorical breath and its literal, or, strictly speaking, nonlinguistic, bodily referent.

In his remarks on the breath-pause and writing, Ginsberg employs a similar strategy of reconciling metaphorical and physiological dimensions of breathing. In the sentence "when you talk and then after a while you run out of thought and words, . . . then you're going to stop and take a breath and continue," Ginsberg synchronizes the metaphor of "taking a breath"[17] with physical inhalation. Like Quintilian, he presents the breath-pause between uttered words (literally taking a breath) as a moment of mental rest and recovery (metaphorically taking a breath) when the speaker runs "out of thought." The other implications of "taking a breath" in Quintilian's use of the metaphor, inhaling vitalizing air and doing almost nothing, are also addressed and further elaborated by Ginsberg. He states that during the pause, the writer is "waiting for the next thought to articulate itself" (*Spontaneous Mind* 126). By noting that "you're improvising and you're relying on the moment-to-moment inspiration" (411), Ginsberg proposes that physical inspiration, inhaling, coincides with inspiration in the classical sense: the generation of creative ideas. The metaphorical breath of life as a vitalizing force is thus transferred to the domain of an artistic work in progress. Drawing on his preoccupation with Buddhist thought and meditation practices, Ginsberg considers it relevant that ideas are generated where *nothing* is written or thought about. The "blank spots" or "gaps in between the thoughts" (365) that Ginsberg mentions overlap with the point where he locates the breath-stop. Out of the "unborn awareness" (365), a space of pure potentiality that opens in the moment when we do nothing but breathe, new thoughts are generated. The conflation of the "natural pause"/"breath-stop" and the "mind-break" with the emergence of new ideas—that is, inspiration—becomes most noticeable in his "Notes for *Howl*": "Ideally each line of Howl is a single breath unit . . .—that's the Measure, one physical-mental inspiration of thought contained in the elastic of a breath" (416).

Even though Ginsberg encourages his readers to take literally both the metaphor of "taking a breath" and the notion of inspiration, his theory pushes physical respiration into the background. The claim that breath is a "source deeper than the mind" becomes plausible in Ginsberg's comments on thought-generating "unborn awareness." However, reconciling breathing and inspiration in this way does not explain why the end of a thought should coincide with the need to draw a breath. The neat outline of "breath-stop = mind-break = inspiration" is an attempt to bring the body into agreement with compositional techniques, traditional ideas of how creative works are generated, and theories of thought processes. Such a carefully constructed model stands in conflict with the claim that the work of the respiratory organs, which proceeds according to its own dynamics, is supposed to determine the rhythmical structures of the poem while it is in the process of composition. The fact that respiratory rhythms are influenced by accidental external circumstances and the respective bodily condition of the breather—which, quite surprisingly for a position that supposedly foregrounds the body, Ginsberg does not address even once—counteracts the idea that "mind-breaks" should necessarily be "*identical* with natural speech pauses" (*Spontaneous Mind* 126; emphasis added). On the one hand, it is precisely the irregularity of breathing that makes it interesting for Ginsberg's polemic outline of a new poetry: he stresses that, in contrast to the "automatic and mechanic," symmetrical, and "even" measure of traditional metrical forms, the new poetry, in which "speech as breath from the body," is more variably structured (107). On the other hand, the irregularities of human breathing rhythm run counter to the smooth symmetry that Ginsberg establishes in his compositional theory. Ginsberg considers the work of the mind to be a process that is at the same time bodily and intellectual (145). His negotiations of breath-stops and mind-breaks thus challenge a simple binary between a rational, intellectual mind and an irrational, animalistic body. However, the cost of this (by all means productive) questioning of a dualism that continues to haunt the Western world is an eradication of difference: Ginsberg seals the gap between mind and body, which opens most prominently when the body speaks.

Kerouac and Aristotle

Kerouac first and foremost links breathing to a free "mindflow" and uncensored expression:

> PROCEDURE . . . sketching language is undisturbed flow from the mind of personal secret idea-words, *blowing* (as per jazz musician) on subject of image.
>
> SCOPING Not "selectivity" of expression but following free deviation (association) of mind into limitless *blow-on-subject seas of thought*, swimming in sea of English with no discipline other than rhythms of rhetorical exhalation and expostulated statement. . . .—*Blow as deep as you want*—write as deeply, fish as far down as you want.
>
> CENTER OF INTEREST . . . *blow!—now!—your* way is your only way—"good"—or "bad"—always honest ("ludicrous"), spontaneous, "confessional" interesting, because not "crafted."
> ("Essentials of Spontaneous Prose" 57–58; emphasis added)

The most obvious basis for the comparison of mindflow and breath is a term that Kerouac adopts from jazz music: "blowing." In jazz, "blowing" refers to improvisation (Witmer n.p.)—in the case of the saxophone solo Kerouac mentions in the *Paris Review* interview, such an improvisation is literally an act of blowing ("The Art of Fiction No. 41"). With respect to the breath-carried sounds produced by the saxophonist and, by analogy, by the speaker who improvises literary texts, Kerouac's image has a physiological basis. However, the suggested continuity between the flow of the mind and breathing is as rhetorically constructed as Ginsberg's equation of breath-stop and mind-break. This parallel is based on the idea that physical breathing happens unconsciously and thus escapes from the "grammatical syntactical + sociopolitical prohibitions against free expression of the mind itself" ("History of the Theory of Breath")—prohibitions the conscious mind cannot ignore.

Kerouac extends the analogy between breath and a liberated mind to language: the free flow of the mind is mirrored in the free flow of words. However, he does not go so far as to propose a purely fluid, unsegmented speech or writing. His alternative is to replace the barriers of conventional punctuation marking grammatical units with a less restraining separator, namely, breath. "No periods separating sentence-structures already arbitrarily riddled by false colons and timid usually needless commas—but the vigorous space dash separating rhetorical breathing (as jazz musician drawing breath between outblown phrases)" (57). While the ancient rhetoricians made considerable argumentative efforts to reconcile the breath-pause and grammatical units, Kerouac is eager to separate the two. In ancient rhetoric, the image of flowing water, which Kerouac invokes in the "flow" and the "seas" of language, is used in order to depict what is spoken between the pauses: Quintilian mentions "the unbroken flow of the voice . . . being carried along down the stream of oratory" (*Institutio Oratia* 541) and Cicero compares ongoing speech with "the rolling stream of a river" (*Oratory* 247). In both cases, the breath-pause is what brings that flow to a halt. Even though he takes the caesura into account, Kerouac has obvious reservations about anything that disturbs this flow.

In the unpublished essay "History of the Theory of Breath as a Separator of Statements in Spontaneous Writing," Kerouac again relates "blowing" to the jazz musician while adding references to oratory and running. In a handwritten addition, the "jazzman" is equated with a "runner or orator"; another one speaks of "jazz or a hundred yard dash or a great orator" (2). The imperative to "write excitedly, swiftly" (58) became the foundation of the most prominent Beat and Kerouac myth,[18] culminating in the repeatedly invoked scene of Kerouac taping together sheets of paper to a long scroll in order to avoid interruptions before manically typing *On the Road* in three weeks.[19] We find a remarkable echo of Aristotle in Kerouac's discussion of running, pausing, and writing. Aristotle argues that, in contrast to the style segmented by periods, colons, and commas, the loose or continuous style is "unpleasant, because it is endless, for all wish to have the end in sight" (387). He gives the following reason for the benefits of the anticipated pause: "runners, just when they have reached the goal, lose their breath and strength, whereas before, when the end is in sight, they show no signs of fatigue" (387). The advantage of the pause is that it prevents fatigue, the loss of breath, and that it impels the runner to go on. In his argument for pauses, Aristotle looks at them prospectively, as something that lies ahead. It is precisely such a prospective view that Kerouac embraces: the break no longer blocks the flow but rather generates an impetus to speed on. In a letter to his agent, Sterling Lord, he stresses that the dashes indicating the breath-pause mark something impending: "Make this clear, that my prose is a series of rhythmic expostulations of speech visually separated for the convenience of the reader's eye by dashes, by vigorous definite dashes, *which can be seen coming* as you read" (*Selected Letters 1957–1969* 11; emphasis added).[20] Kerouac also repeatedly highlights the importance of a continuity between the segments and also of looking ahead during the process of composition: in parallel to the writer of spontaneous prose, the jazz musician has to "keep track of the accidence of choruses continuity of choruses breath into the next chorus" ("History of the Theory of Breath"). By stressing the anticipatory function of the dash and its relation to speed, Kerouac highlights one direction and tempo, disregarding the flipside that Rebecca Comay discusses in *The Dash—The Other Side of Absolute Knowing*: the dash "forces an impossible double tempo in reading. You must simultaneously race ahead and hold back" (85).

For Kerouac, the pause as such—the moment when, in Aristotle's words, the runners "lose their breath and strength"—represents the most delicate point in his theory of writing. Whereas Ginsberg emphasizes the meditative potentiality of the pause as a moment of calmness and rest, Kerouac promotes the speed of flowing words.[21] Resting in the sense of slackening poses a threat to his ideal of mastering an intact, potent masculine body mirrored in the "muscle of prose" and brimming with "virility."[22] The aspired athletic speed of writing should demonstrate vigor. Kerouac claims that he wants to write "like Proust, but on the run, a Running Proust" (*Selected Letters 1940–1956* 515). "I decided to do just like he did—but fast. . . . Fast. Marcel Proust had asthma and was lying around writing and eating in bed. Once in a while he'd get up feebly, put on a coat and go down to a bar in Paris" ("Dialogues in Great Books" 192). While Kerouac models the endeavor to write a monumental cycle of novels covering his entire life on

Proust's *Recherche* (*Selected Letters 1940–1956* 515), he underestimates how many years it took Proust to do so without accomplishing the oeuvre. His wish to be a "running Proust" means not only completing his work faster but also overcoming Proust's feeble physical condition. Kerouac aspires to perform an athletic writing in contrast to an asthmatic one. His imagined literary breath is healthy, well-trained, potent. In his emphasis on speed, Kerouac ignores the fact that a strained body may be out of breath or that speaking on the run could be interrupted by gasps for air. A breath indicating the body's slackening, a breathlessness that weakens the body, or a writing shaped by asthma attacks and apnea would endanger Kerouac's poetic pursuits. The physiological foundation of writing is only desirable if the body in question is intact and disciplined into athletic strength. For Kerouac, spontaneous writing as such is a result of discipline—sticking to his own image: the runner's sprint is the immediate demonstration of what rigorous training and hardening muscles give rise to.

> The critics have failed to realize that spontaneous writing of narrative prose is infinitely more difficult than careful slow painstaking writing with opportunities to revise—Because spontaneous writing is an ordeal requiring immediate discipline—They seem to think there's no discipline involved—They don't know how horrible it is to learn immediate and swift discipline and draw your breath in pain as you do so. (*Selected Letters 1957–1969* 325)

Spontaneous prose is described as the empowering accomplishment of hard work. The aching breath recalling Shakespeare's *Hamlet* results from the exertion of a well-trained body and stands in contrast to the painful asthmatic breath exhausting a body subject to illness.[23] The reference to Proust's asthma and his debilitated physical condition shows Kerouac's longing for mastery over his body and writing alike: the healthy and strong body is a body under command. The athlete's control over his muscles creates the illusion that he is liberated from more arbitrary works of the body that may affect a person (i.e., illness). A "defective" human organism has no place in Kerouac's theory of embodied writing.

Kerouac's breath-pauses are kept remote from all associations with symptoms of the fatigued body. He describes the graphical sign marking the breath-pause and its function in the following way: "No periods separating sentence-structures already arbitrarily riddled by false colons and *timid* usually needless commas—but the *vigorous space dash* separating rhetorical breathing" ("Essentials of Spontaneous Prose" 57; emphasis added). "A sentence which after all is a rhetorical expostulation based on breathing and has to end, and I make it end with a *vigorous release sign*, i.e., the *dash*—" (*Selected Letters 1940–1956* 324; emphasis added). By repeatedly describing the dash as "vigorous" (in contrast to the "timid" commas), Kerouac injects the strength of the runner *into* the pause, the moment when his body is in danger of collapsing and his muscles are about to go limp. Associating the pause with virility motivates the choice of the dash as the sign marking it semantically and graphically: "dash," of course, refers to both a form of punctuation and the act of sprinting. Through the "dash," a sense of speed enters the pause. In the handwritten manuscripts, dashes also graphically evoke speed: the lines often look like they were *dashed off* energetically. Visually, the dash—in this case especially the printed one—establishes a proximity between the words it separates: it links them by the horizontal line almost touching their respective ends and beginnings, inviting the eye to follow. While a blank space between words encourages the eye to pause, the dash incites it to bridge the gap in a rush.[24] Moreover, in contrast to the bent commas and colons, the erect straight line of dash, which is also bigger in size, has a phallic quality.[25] When his editor at the Grove Press, Don Allen, replaced dashes with full stops and added commas in the manuscript of *The Subterraneans*, Kerouac complained about this "horrible castration job." "He has broken down the organic strength of the manuscript and it is no longer THE SUBTERRANEANS by Jack K, but some feeble something by Don Allen" (11).

This type of castration anxiety might explain why Kerouac mingles his images of breath with sexual ones in the "Essentials": "write outwards swimming in sea of language to peripheral release and exhaustion—write excitedly, swiftly, with writing-or-typing-cramps, in accordance (as from center to periphery) with laws of orgasm. . . . Come from within, out—to relaxed and said" (58). "Exhaustion," which in terms of respiration represents a threat—namely, Proust's asthmatic feebleness and Aristotle's drained runner who has lost his "breath and strength"—is redirected to the domain of sexual climax: Kerouac links the "relaxed" moment of the pause to an explosive "release" of male (creative) potency. He repeatedly writes that the dashes "release" the sentence. Apart from the sexual connotations evoked in the "Essentials," "release" also designates "liberation," the "action of freeing, or the fact of being freed." Moreover, in jazz music, "release" designates a "passage of music that serves as a *bridge* between repetitions of a main melody" (*Oxford English Dictionary* online; emphasis added). By choosing the word "release" to describe the function of the dash, Kerouac is able to connect a number of qualities that prevent the breath-pause from endangering the qualities of athletic, spontaneous writing: virility, liberation, and a sense of continuity pointing forward to the moment after the critical instant of potential slackening. The word also contains one of Kerouac's most eager wishes: making his literary achievements available to the public, *releasing* his written products, getting published, and being honored as America's healthy Proust.

Kerouac's comments on his writing processes and methods, above all the "Essentials," were the most significant elements in his attempt to create a public image of himself as a writer. The potent breathing body of the authoritative and controlling author Kerouac promotes is produced by his own words. Kerouac's literary texts evoke an impression of spontaneous, bodily, athletic writing executed by a vigorous author. The comments on the writing process and methods are designed to verify and confirm—and not least, co-create—the effect produced in the literary texts.[26] In his notes on the dash, what Kerouac expands on is as relevant as what he chooses not to address. Bearing in mind Rebecca Comay and Frank Ruda's discussion of the grammatical functions and performative impact of the dash as punctuation mark and its semantic implications (55–56), we can see that Kerouac highlights certain qualities of the dash while leaving others aside, for example "erasure," "violence, destruction," "a break, an interruption," "a detour, a hesitation" (Comay and Ruda 55). Comay and Ruda argue that the dash introduces "a moment of uncertainty in reading" (55). Against this background, Kerouac's comments on dashes and their literary use reveal an ambivalent dynamic. As if in defiance of his own stated poetics, the punctuation mark itself maintains what he attempts to overcome: the dash "dashes"—it speeds—but at the same time it "dashes"—it batters or nullifies—the virile athleticism by introducing a sense of uncertainty when, for readers, it is no longer clear whether it facilitates "flow" or inscribes hesitations, panting, stammering: "*blow!—now!—your* way is your only way—'good'—or 'bad'—always honest."

As my analysis has shown, the texts by ancient rhetoricians, Ginsberg, and Kerouac all present imaginations of the writing or speaking body. In their discussions of the role of breath in writing, especially the breath-pause, both Kerouac and Ginsberg tacitly follow the path of the rhetoricians. Starting from the same premises, their poetics ultimately diverge, however. Ginsberg's negotiation of the breath-pause amounts to a meditatively charged stasis, emphasizing the role of quiescent contemplation. In contrast, Kerouac's poetics of breathing culminates in a promotion of flow and rapid movement going hand in hand with a celebration of the potent male body that, as we have seen (and will see further in the following section), repeatedly self-deconstructs.

Smoke, Tapes, Typewriters: Respirational Writing Scenes

I now want to focus on two compositional *scenes* involving breath. One goes back to material witnesses of the creative process; the other is fictional. After investigating traces of the actual composition process documented on Ginsberg's tape recordings, I will present a very early short story by Kerouac, as yet unpublished, concerning an imaginary account of creative (type)writing. It is no coincidence that in these scenes, two of Friedrich Kittler's "ur-media" take center stage: the tape recorder and the typewriter (50). Kerouac's and Ginsberg's poetic reflections on breath promote both immediacy, a direct translation of the body to the literature produced, and a theory of embodied natural breath-writing most effectively put into practice when they either stage or prove themselves as "masters of inhuman communications technologies" (Kittler 211). As "by-products of the American Civil War," the "technologies of typewriting and sound recording" were not new (190) when Ginsberg and Kerouac used them.[27] That they had become so common by that time would, to some extent, explain the fact that neither writer tends to explicitly comment on the typewriter's or recorder's *medializing* function despite repeatedly addressing its impact on the compositional process. No longer imposing themselves on perception as shockingly modern technologies, the devices easily slip into invisibility. In Ginsberg's case, however, the tape recorder, especially his use of it during a road trip in 1965–1966, promises a resistance to newer and more technologically advanced media, as Michael Davidson argues:

> For Ginsberg the orality of the tapevoice stands in direct opposition to the reproduced heteroglossia of incorporated sound. Newsmedia, press reports, advertising, and police radio transmissions are all implicated in an information blockage against which the low-tech, Volkswagen-driven cassette recorder stands as alternative. Prophecy no longer emanates from some inner visionary moment but from a voice that has recognized its inscription within an electronic environment, a voice that has seized the means of reproduction and adapted it to oppositional ends. (*Ghostlier Demarcations* 206)

Even though Ginsberg consciously or unconsciously produces such a "prophetic" voice inscribed in electronic media, he still holds on to the notion of authentic transmission that, according to Kittler, belongs to an earlier era of media: "mechanical storage technologies for writing, images, and sound could only be developed following the collapse" of a "system" (188) guaranteeing the individual expression of a "soul" through "voice or handwriting" (9). Following Kittler's demonstration of how the writers of the nineteenth century dream of maintaining the soul in the technological-mechanical media emerging in a new system of thought that dismisses it,[28] Kerouac's and Ginsberg's poetics are exemplary for a further development: in their poetics of breathing, the body takes the place of the bygone soul. That this is, in fact, a quite straightforward substitution can be demonstrated as follows: we only need to change a few words from Kittler's comment on Nietzsche's typewriting practice in order to arrive at a most adequate description of Kerouac's and Ginsberg's poetics. "Writing in *Nietzsche* is no longer a natural extension of humans who bring forth their voice, *soul*, individuality through their *handwriting*" (*Gramophone, Film, Typewriter* 210; emphasis added). "Writing in *Kerouac and Ginsberg* is a natural extension of humans who bring forth their voice, *body*, individuality through their *breath*." "Voice," "soul," and "individuality," the humanist attributes already lost when Nietzsche buys his typewriter in 1881, return in a new pneumatic guise in the 1950s—in other words, an adapted *metaphysics* of the body emerges in the Beat context. With regard to the tape recorder, one can counter this tendency with Michael Davidson's claim that "when the complicity between presence and technology is acknowledged . . . the tape recorder ceases to be a passive receptacle for a more authentic speech and becomes an active agent in its deconstruction" (*Ghostlier Demarcations* 199). Before going into more detail, I want to add a few general comments on Kerouac's and Ginsberg's respirational poetics and the relation of each author to the technological media they use.

Ginsberg is not blind to the media with which he works. He repeatedly comments on how different writing materials and technologies (e.g., the notebook or the tape recorder) open up different compositional possibilities. He stresses that the old-school notebook, which is still easily conceivable as a "natural extension of humans," can *influence* the structure of a poem being written; just like breath: "the page determines the length of the line" (*Spontaneous Mind* 125). In contrast, as Ginsberg describes its function, the mechanical tape recorder is *at the service* of the creative product: it enables him to document his breath-stops and mind-breaks so that he can then transcribe them to the page (*Spontaneous Mind* 134–35; *Spiritual Poetics II*).

Thus, he follows a logic already formulated by Olson in a famous passage of "Projective Verse" (in this case, with respect to the typewriter): the "irony" of "the machine" that while it removes "verse from its producer . . . the voice," has "the advantage . . . that . . . it can, for a poet, indicate exactly the breath" (22).[29] This echoes a nineteenth-century fantasy that Kittler illustrates with Ernst von Wildenbruch's idea of "the phonograph as the soul's own true photograph." Olson's and Ginsberg's outlines of an immediate and exact reproduction of breath via media technology do not express a futile attempt at turning the "wheel of media technology back . . . to retrieve the soul" (83), but rather reveal the "impossible desire to reduce the real (the physiology of a voice) to the symbolic" (82).

With the legendary *On the Road* scroll, the typewriter became the most dominant image for Kerouac's motto, "write excitedly, swiftly" as seen by the wider public. It is indeed the writing tool of "increased speed" (Kittler 205), "a discursive machine-gun" (191) inexhaustibly shooting words on the page. "I'm using the typewriter now to keep up my 'diary' because my hands can't keep up now with what I want to say," Kerouac states in an unpublished "letter" to himself in 1960 ("Letters to Myself"). His extolled Underwood (see the collection of stories *Atop an Underwood*) is not only a fetish, it becomes the prosthetic steel lung carrying into effect his poetics of athletic breath and dashed blowing. As I've described, this poetics is also saturated with an aesthetics of genius, which stands in conflict with Kittler's claim that the "writing machine" marks a new era after a collapse of "the rules regulating discourses during the age of Goethe: authority and authorship, . . . the narcissism of creation" (188). In his typewriter fantasies Kerouac also celebrates the speed of writing enabled by modern technology and reactivates an old discourse, nostalgically projecting it to this medium that is no longer new. Such an endeavor must confront another issue pointed out by Kittler: "Mechanized and automatic writing refutes the phallocentrism of classical pens" (206). Kerouac does make an attempt to reverse the familiar image of a vigorously erected pen into its impotent opposite in an unpublished fragment:

> The beautiful *action* of the typewriter machine tempts you to fiddle on when you've really nothing to say and explains past failures . . . something ugly, humble, pestiferous, draggish, lumpish, loutish, callous-making like a beat old pencil does not entice you to write a damn word unless it really has to come out and always, remember, because it could never come otherwise, really giving birth in the void from the void. (Typescript fragment)

Stylized as inspiration-machine, the typewriter becomes a remedy for failure. In "Rasping Smoke in a Dry Throat," the subject of the second part of this section, the mechanical inspirator and breath, are depicted in the form of exhaled cigarette smoke and explicitly conjoined in a story about failure. Taking a closer look at actual and fictional writing scenes involving tape recorders and typewriters reveals moments when breath emerges as a resistant force that undermines the meanings the authors charge it with or challenges us to question the authors' self-presentations.

"Dynamo'd smoke-cathedrals": Ginsberg's Recorded Breath

Ginsberg's tape recordings from the mid- to late 1960s are rare examples of documented oral composition. During several road trips and train and plane rides, Ginsberg composed numerous poems, some of which were published in the collection *The Fall of America*, by speaking them into a portable Uher recorder. These tapes give us the opportunity to study the relation of physical breath to the formal structuring of language in the compositional process. Ginsberg himself explains the experiments with the tape recorder in terms of his theory of the mind- and breath-stops, for example, in a lecture in 1974:[30]

> most machines have a "stop" and a "start" button . . . , so if you're actually intending to do writing, one way is to use the automatic "control" button as the margin of your line. . . . That is, you're talking into the machine, you don't have anything to say, so you click it off. Then, when something emerges, when you notice something . . . —click! Then, when you're transcribing on a page, . . . which I've done a lot, from '65 to '70, with a Uher machine, you can use the "click" at the end of the tape line, the tape operation, as your breath stop. . . . It's the natural end of the line. (*Spiritual Poetics II*)

My analysis of the tapes, which are archived at Stanford University, reaffirmed the disconnect between Ginsberg's theoretical poetics and his compositional practice. There are, first, relatively few recordings where he makes use of the stop and start buttons during composition. The pauses in the recordings, whether indicated by clicks or longer silences, do not always coincide with the line breaks in the printed poems. In most cases, it is unlikely that the pauses indicate moments where Ginsberg ran out of breath. Instead, they may indicate points where he ran out of thought: he often speaks only two or three words, which are then followed by long intervals, which could potentially contain numerous breaths. The pronunciation of the last word before the pause is often stretched out, a sign that Ginsberg had plenty of breath left but nothing to say. Interjections like "ahem" sometimes occur during the pauses, which are cases where mind-break and breath-stop clearly diverge: while the mind is searching for words, the mouth fills the mental gap by articulating sounds through breath.

When Ginsberg retrospectively refers to the "natural" end of a line as a "breath-stop" in the lecture in retrospect, he uses the term as an *image* for the mind-break, or as a *name* for the line break in the written text. Note that in the lecture, he mentions breath in the context of transcribing the spoken poem, which has little to do with his actual breathing during composition. In Ginsberg's poetic theory, breath is primarily a means of transcription and translation.[31] "Space arrangement on the page" (line breaks, indentations as well as punctuation)[32] "indicates the breathing" (*Spontaneous Mind*). The notation then enables the author to "imitate" the process of composition while he later reads the poem out loud to an audience (*Spontaneous Mind* 126–27). What Ginsberg describes is how an effect of immediacy is created: the audience of a reading is supposed to experience the moment of spontaneous composition, the "here and now" where the author modulates spoken words by means of his breath. While breath is the ideal *image* for such a "poetics of presence, immediacy, and physical *thereness*" (Davidson 1), its physical factuality undermines the theoretical outline. A look at some of Ginsberg's actual breaths, as recorded on tape, shows how slippery and unpredictable the physiological process on which he bases much of his elaborate poetics turns out to be. In the smooth one-to-one-translation via breath that Ginsberg outlines, the movements of transference and the various media involved in the process disappear behind the alleged immediacy. By contrast, comparing Ginsberg's recorded breaths to the written and theorized ones exposes the tensions of "breath-stop syncopations" ("Fourteen Steps for Revising Poetry" 258) emerging in a clash of media and materialities.

Some passages toward the end of the first part of "Iron Horse" lend themselves especially to an investigation of pauses, clicks, breath-stops, punctuation, and line breaks in the text's various stages and forms (tape-composition, public reading, written draft, and published version).[33] "Iron Horse" is one of the few poems in which the available archival material allows us to compare the pauses during oral composition with written line breaks and then with pauses during recorded public readings. While composing the poem on a train from Santa Fe to Chicago and on a Greyhound bus in July 1966, Ginsberg frequently used the Uher's on and off buttons.[34] In contrast to the long lines of *Howl*, which Ginsberg explains by claiming that he has a "long breath," the lines in "Iron Horse" are rather short and often consist of small syntactic units. I first want to focus on a passage whose structure, discernably molded by breath on the compositional tape, is radically condensed in the typescript and printed version, so that the physical "breathing of the man who writes" vanishes without a trace. This passage is a moment where Ginsberg's compositional practice accords to some extent with his theory; however, in this case, the compositional rhythm is changed beyond recognition in the poem's final version. On the tape, we hear a multiplicity of pause markers: shorter and longer silences, clicks, and clearly audible inhalations and exhalations.

> overlooked by cranes [pause] and a high smokestack [long pause] with a broken lip [pause] in the sky [pause and click] magnetic crane [breath: inhalation and exhalation][35] dropping a pile of [short pause] iron junk [breath] into a red Burlington car [short pause] and pounding it down [breath] with its weight [exhalation] th[pause]e cap of a mansarded church overlooking behind [short pause] showing its clock ["om"] [click] the magnet lifts and drops iron filings like waterdrops [click] then pounds them down [click]

The passage is spoken very slowly and attentively, and in the frequent pauses Ginsberg seems to be steadily figuring out the next couple of words. This is certainly not a flow of words in which pauses occur because the speaker was running out of breath. As already observed, Ginsberg highlights meditative calmness when he theorizes breath. There are moments when he seems to breathe deliberately when he runs out of thought, as if to conjure up inspiration by physically breathing in. It should be noted that at this time, in the mid-1960s, Ginsberg's poetics of respirational composition is already fully fleshed out, so it is not implausible that he consciously tried to deploy his own theory. If he did so, however, it was in a modified manner: the mind-break does not naturally coincide with a breath-*stop*, but rather, the thought's *pause* is coordinated with the *act of breathing* (*not* the caesura). This can be observed when an inhalation and exhalation are clearly audible in the pause, and, above all, when Ginsberg hums a meditative "om" before starting to speak again. In the handwritten draft, the passage is more or less closely transcribed; the line breaks more or less coincide with pause markers on the tape, including the breaths. For example, "Magnetic Crane" makes up a single line and the "om" is transcribed on a line of its own (see figure 2.1).

In the typescript and the printed version, the whole passage is reduced to two lines that are significantly longer: "Under a smokestack with a broken lip / magnetic cranes drop iron scrap like waterdrops" (*Collected Poems* 447). The rhythmically irregular shredded fragments on the tape and the handwritten page are grammatically and syntactically smoothed out in the typed as well as the printed version, where they spread over two well-flowing lines of approximately the same length: ten and eleven syllables, respectively. In the course of the poem's revisions, the broken scraps Ginsberg utters undergo a process of mindful selection and are then merged into continuity. His meditative, cautiously puffed breaths, marking moments of hesitation and searching for words during the oral composition, are not indicated on the printed pages: there is no line break after "Magnetic Cranes," no "om." What becomes apparent here is that the role of breath in Ginsberg's

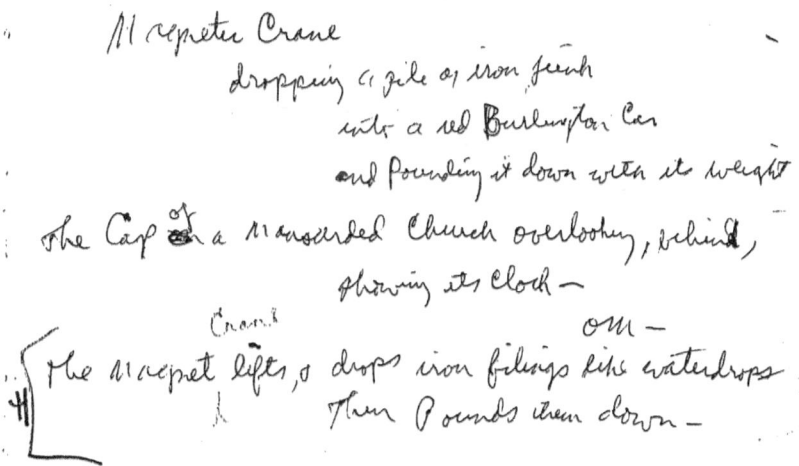

Figure 2.1. Allen Ginsberg, *Fall of America* and "Iron Horse" (draft). Allen Ginsberg Papers, Special Collections, Stanford. Copyright Allen Ginsberg. Used by permission of the Wylie Agency LLC.

actual composition process is far more complex than what he theorizes; or, put another way, that breath cannot be subsumed by a consistent poetic theory.

In most cases, we can only speculate about the actual breath-stops occurring during composition, as the clicks on the tape would conceal any actual breaths and, because the tape is switched off in the pause, we cannot hear whether Ginsberg inhaled or exhaled in the interval.[36] My next comparison of what Ginsberg calls "breath-stops" to actual breaths includes recordings of public readings. On a tape recording of a reading of "Iron Horse" at Johns Hopkins University in April 1967, Ginsberg's breaths are distinctly audible. The passage on which I focus has a clearly discernible structure. Like the repeated "who" in *Howl*, this part of "Iron Horse" has a "base" word. In "Iron Horse," "better" functions as "a base to keep measure, return and take off from again onto another streak of invention," as Ginsberg describes with respect to "who" in *Howl* ("Notes for *Howl*" 415) (see figure 2.2).

We notice at first sight that the correspondences between base word, pause, tape click, breath-stop, line break, punctuation and spacing on the page are far less exact than what Ginsberg's theory suggests.[37] Clicks or pauses in the original recording tend to be followed by the next occurrence of the base word "better," and line breaks and punctuation marks in the written versions occur where clicks or pauses can be heard on the tape. However, the concurrences are not consistent throughout. As in the "smokestack" passage analyzed earlier, one cannot discern a systematic "translation key" for the particular markers: Ginsberg often transcribes clicks or pauses as line breaks, but not in every case; the precise relation between the spacing on the page and pauses or clicks on the tape is unclear; there is no discernible correlation between the amount of white space on the page and the length of pauses on the tape;[38] and the use of punctuation marks such as commas, and dashes seems rather arbitrary, lacking a regular pattern (e.g., in accordance with certain pause markers on the tape). Overall, a number of various heterogeneous pause markers are decisive for the development of the poem's flexible, loose, and variable structure in the course of its multiple stages. The "relative measure" that Ginsberg promotes as a compositional principle does not emerge from the "intensity of the breath" alone (*Spontaneous Mind* 108);[39] rather than being rooted solely in the living body of the speaker, the irregular structural patterns are derived from a multiplicity of sources that cannot be homogenized via respirational imagery:[40] traces

Composition on tape (1:37)	Reading at Johns Hopkins (1:08)
Better a house hidden in trees (**pause** [= p])	Better a house hidden in trees
in the Mississippi bank (**click** [= c])	in the Mississippi bank (**breath** [= b])
high on a cliff protected from flood (c)	high on a cliff protected from flood (b)
Better an acre down in Big Sur (c)	Better an acre down in Big Sur
where at morning (p) one walks (p) through a path to a	where at morning one walks (p) through the path down the
cliff (p) and the ocean is revealed (p) shining bru (p)	cliff ocean revealed shining as the
blue (p) as the first day of the world (c)	first day of the world (b)
Better a farm in backlands of Oregon (c)	Better a farm in backlands of Oregon
or on the roads towards Glacier Peak (c)	or on the roads near Glacier Peak (b)
Better withdraw from the world of the Newspapers (c)	Better withdraw from the world of the Newspaper (b)
Better withdraw from the electric world (c)	Better withdraw from the electric world
Better retire before war cuts my head off (c)	Better retire before war cuts my head off
but not like Kabir (c)	but not like Kabir (b)
Better to buy a Garden of Love (c)	Better to buy a Garden of Love (b)
Better to find a wife (p)	Better to find a wife
Better to make a baby (p)	Better to make a baby (b)
Better protect the lamb in some valley (c)	Better protect the lamb in some valley (b)
Better go way from these cities filled with taxicabs and	Better go way from these cities filled with (b) taxicabs and
radios screaming of the President (c)	radios screaming of the President (b)
Better to stop smoking (c)	Better to (p) stop smoking
Better to stop jerking off in trains (c)	Better to stop jerking off in trains (b)
Better to stop seducing white bellied boys (c)	Better to stop seducing white bellied boys (b)
Better to stop publishing Prophecy (c)	Better to stop publishing Prophecy (b)
Better to meditate under a tree (c)	Better to meditate under a tree (b)
Hornets buzzing around my hair (c)	Hornets buzzing around my hair (b)
Better become a nun in the forest (c)	Better become a nun in the forest (b)
Better turn flapjacks in Omaha (c)	Better turn flapjacks in Omaha

Handwritten Draft	Printed Version
1 Better a house hidden in trees	1 Better a house hidden in trees
2 in the Mississippi bank	2 Mississippi bank
3 high on a cliff protected from flood	3 high cliff protected from flood
4 Better an acre down in Big Sur	4 Better an acre down Big Sur
5 where at morning	5 morning path, ocean shining
one walks thru a the path to a cliff	6 first day's blue world
& the ocean is revealed shining ~~blue~~	7 Better a farm in backland Oregon,
6 blue as the first day of the world	8 roads near Glacier Peak
7 Better a farm in backlands of Oregon	9 Better withdraw from the Newspaper world
8 or on the roads towards Glacier Peak	10 Better withdraw from the electric world
9 Better withdraw from the world of the Newspapers	11 Better retire before war cuts my head off,
10 Better withdraw from the electric world	12 not like Kabir—
11 Better retire before war cuts my head off,	13 Better to buy a Garden of Love
~~cuts my head off~~	14 Better protect the lamb in some valley
12 Not like Kabir—	15 Better go way from taxicab radio cities
13 Better to buy a garden of love	16 screaming President,
Better to find a wife,	17 Better to stop smoking
Better to make a baby	18 Better to stop jerking off in trains
14 Better protect the lamb in some valley	19 Better to stop seducing white bellied boys
15 Better go away from these cities filled w/	20 Better to stop publishing Prophecy—
taxicabs and radios	21 Better to meditate under a tree
16 ~~unreadable~~ screaming ~~of the~~ President,	22 Better become a nun in the forest
17 Better to stop smoking	23 Better turn flapjacks in Omaha
18 Better to stop jerking off in trains	
19 Better to stop seducing white bellied boys	
20 Better to stop publishing Prophecy—	
21 Better to meditate under a tree,	

Figure 2.2. Allen Ginsberg, "Iron Horse" (tape composition, reading, draft, and printed version in comparison). Allen Ginsberg Papers, Special Collections, Stanford. Copyright Allen Ginsberg. Used by permission of the Wylie Agency LLC.

of the compositional scene on material carriers in different media, the tape and the handwritten page.

Ginsberg's physical breath effectively disrupts the structure established in the poem when it is read aloud. The version performed at Johns Hopkins is based on the handwritten draft, in which the line breaks and the visual space arrangement already closely resemble the final version. Not surprisingly, perhaps, Ginsberg occasionally reads much more than one line in one breath[41]—his inhalations and exhalations often do not correspond either to the pause markers on the original tape or the line breaks in the draft. When he reads the line "Better an acre down in Big Sur where at morning one walks through the path down the cliff ocean revealed shining as the first day of the world" in one breath, slightly stumbling over the word "through" in the middle, one might assume that he coordinates his breath with the base word "better." However, this is inconsistent with his moments of inhalation before "high on a cliff" and "taxicabs," or when "Better withdraw from the electric world Better retire before war cuts my head off but not like Jabir" and "Better to find a wife Better to make a baby" are pronounced in one breath. It is only toward the end of the passage, where the sentences are simpler, that breaths come to correspond with the clicks on the tape and line breaks in the draft. After reading the beginning of the passage with increasing vocal agitation, using more air to pronounce longer sequences on a single breath, the slower pronunciation of shorter lines in single breaths could be explained physiologically: after exhausting himself, Ginsberg changes to a more composed measure in order to rest. One could also suspect that he vocally stages the contents of the scene: slowly, an aspired withdrawal from the sensory overflow of a war-ridden modern world is achieved and, sheltered by natural idylls, the body calms down. In this interpretation, the carefully contrived manipulation of breath amounts to a demonstration of how "natural" (here: more regular and composed) breath is recovered.

It has to be stressed that this observation about concrete breaths only applies to this one specific articulation, on April 11, 1967, in Baltimore, and cannot be generalized; in another reading of "Iron Horse" in London in 1967 (also based on the handwritten draft), the breaths occur at different moments and, again, not always in accordance with the line breaks or pause markers. Whereas clicks or recorded breaths can, in theory, be translated to line breaks that might undergo changes during revisions but are at some stage fixed on the page, the vocalized breaths turn out to vary in each individual reading of the poem.[42] While Ginsberg uses breath as an image for the transcription and translation of structural units, his actual breaths are not a consistent transferrable measure: the breath pattern of one articulation may be caught on tape, but the pattern will be different in a new vocal articulation. Out of all "relative measures," breath is the least predictable, consistent, and systematic, and it is the one that is hardest to track in the material evidence of the writing process.

In "Iron Horse," the structural function of "better" is much more pronounced in written form, where it is visually accentuated by the aligned arrangement of words on the page. The lines that do not begin with a new "better" are indented and thus look like subsidiary ones. In contrast, the clicks and pauses on the original tape do not give rise to such a hierarchy, something that makes the composition sound less rigorously structured. This becomes especially noticeable in the prepositional phrase following "Better an acre down in Big Sur," which in the printed version is highly condensed. The compositional process in this case closely resembles that of the "smokestack"-passage analyzed previously. Listening to the tape, we become witnesses to Ginsberg's mind at work and hear how he slowly and hesitantly assembles the sentence "Better an acre down in Big Sur (*c*) where at morning (*p*) one walks (*p*) through a path to a cliff (*p*) and the ocean is revealed (*p*) shining bru [*sic*] (*p*) blue (*p*) as the first day of the world (*c*)." We almost forget the poem's structure according to the base word "better"—a structure that was only introduced shortly before.[43] The "Big Sur" sentence apparently posed a challenge in the course of the poem's development: the rhythm is unspecific and the description lacks any of the astonishing unexpected images continually promoted by Ginsberg in his lectures and interviews. Reproducing the "organic time-spacing as per the mind's coming up with the phrase and the mouth pronouncing them" (*Spontaneous Mind* 135), which Ginsberg more or less does in the draft, does not seem to lead to a satisfying result: the morning walk still seems slightly stale. Ginsberg intervenes retroactively at those moments where, during composition, the mind's work was less inspired than hoped for and breath did not provide a magic solution to the problem of rhythm. "Chop it up in lines according to breath phrasing/ideas or units of thought within one breath, if any," he advises in "Fourteen Steps for Revising Poetry" (261). And chopping is what he does: the sentence is cropped to grammatically elliptical fragments, the originally rather realist description reduced to three condensed impressions. This cutting, however, is *not* executed in accordance with Ginsberg's physical breathing during the compositional process. Consider this sentence as it reads in the printed version:

>   morning path, ocean shining
>   first day's blue world
> (*Collected Poems* 446)

It does not occur on the original tape (though each individual word does). On the recording, there is unambiguously neither pause nor breath after "path"—and it's the same after "shining." In the printed version, the passage presents "rearranged lines emphasizing crude breath-stop syncopations" ("Some Metamorphoses of Personal Prosody" 258). A syncopation—in a significantly different sense in the remark just quoted—occurs in Ginsberg's revisions. In the oral composition, he cuts the "organic" ties to the breath of his own body in order to create a crisp syncopated rhythm: on the printed page, we encounter the surprise of the repeated accentual rise and fall in "ocean shining" after the pause signaled by the comma, following the indication of a dactylic pattern ("morning path"), and then, in the next line, a striking staccato sequence of stressed monosyllabic nouns ("first day's blue world").

I now want to take a look at a few more recorded breaths on the original tapes of "Iron Horse" along with the poem's content and imagery as well as Ginsberg's poetic, sociocritical, and political conceptualizations of breath. In his critiques of contemporary society, Ginsberg often sketches a grim picture of technological and industrial developments (from new media technologies to modern architecture) as symptoms of environmental and political crisis: a world of "piled blocks, streets, radios, politicians, TV stations, city halls" (*Spontaneous Mind* 109) and people exposed to "smog, noise, pollution of lakes and rivers, living in high-rise apartments and experiencing politics on TV and human relations through police-state stereotypes" (193). These images often present a binary: "*bad machinery*"—"robot standardization of American consciousness" or "greedy, defective technology" (194)—corrupting a "*good nature*" that is frequently described in respiratory terms. "Not only does smog cut off eyeball consciousness and mental awareness but it also cuts in on your breathing, poisons the body, causes suffocation, heart attacks and nervous anxiety" (192). Not surprisingly, the "machinery" is associated with the inorganic, dead, whereas "nature" is portrayed as living: "Everything's being turned into plastics and synthetics. Living forms are being turned into inorganic ones" (193); and not surprisingly, breath is situated on the organic side: Ginsberg preaches that humans have to "restore living forms to the surface of the planet—revitalize the planet's skin—without setting up a feedback that disturbs that living, breathing skin" (194).

Ginsberg expands this opposition into the domain of language and poetry: in a lecture on "Poetry, Politics and Consciousness" in 1974, he addresses the arbitrariness of language in terms of an alienating abstraction: "So a language description of an event is not identical with the event, it is an abstraction of the event" (*Allen Verbatim* 26). It is breath that allows restoring language to a state of organic self-identity in which "the words we pronounce do connect finally to our body, connect to our breathing, particularly, and breathing connects to feeling, feeling articulated in language" (28): "there's another use of [language] which is purely expressive, subjectively expressive, where the breath exhaled is a conscious articulation of feeling . . . ; therefore the spoken breath, 'Ah-om' or 'Oh' or 'Ah' or 'Uuuh,' is identical with the event that it describes because it is the event" (26). Moreover, the "natural rhythm of language" is juxtaposed with a "forced artificial bureaucratic dry rhythm affected by multiple machinery" (27–28). Ginsberg claims that most public speech passed through

> so many hands and so many machines that it no longer represents a human organism inspiring and expiring, inhaling and exhaling, rhythmically. The sentence structure no longer has any relation to any affect that could be traced along the lines of inhalation and exhalation—in other words, sad to say, the voice can finally be separated from the body. If the voice is separated from the body, it means that the rhythm will be fucked up. (28)

On the level of its contents, "Iron Horse" seems to reproduce Ginsberg's polemic tirades against the "machinery" of his times: the train itself, designated as the "Iron Horse hurrying to war" (*Collected Poems* 445), passes by an industrial "chemical landscape" (435) and "cement robots" (434) with its "engine humming" (436) and is crowded by soldiers returning from the Vietnam War. The inserted scraps of news from daily papers, TV, and the radio display a "language infiltration" (442). When we consider the poem's scene of composition, however, matters become far more complicated. Compositional technique enters the poem via explicit references to the "tape machine" (438) and "electronic clicks" (435); consisting of spontaneous observations on the train, including transcriptions of overheard dialogues and news reports, the text is as close as it gets to being "identical with the event that it describes," because it is inextricably linked to "the event" of its composition. This is precisely the point where Ginsberg's theory no longer aligns with his praxis. It is only through "multiple machinery" that a "language description of an event" can approximate the event described; words carried on a living being's breath are spoken into the tape recorder on a train, and it is only by going through "many machines" (the tape recorder and the typewriter) and "hands" (Ginsberg's when he was handling the Uher, holding the pen, hitting the keyboard of the typewriter) that the poem came to be; the traces of the many machines and hands constitute the poem in its finished version. A multiple mediation via a mix of older and newer technologies does separate the voice and the breath from the body, but, as Ginsberg would agree, this does not mean that "the rhythm will be fucked up." On the contrary, it is precisely through these "machines" that "a human organism inspiring and expiring, inhaling and exhaling" can be represented most accurately. What cannot be maintained, however, is the binary opposition between living, breathing natural organisms and inanimate machinery. A parallel argument was made by Joel Duncan with regard to Whitman, Olson, and O'Hara;[44] I will follow Duncan's line of thought in the subsequent reflections and closer analyses of Ginsberg's tape recordings. As Raphael Allison observes, Ginsberg's work with the tape recorder reveals a "paradoxical attitude toward technological mediation" (33): "what once eroded the aura of immediacy" (33), the "optimistic, celebratory swell of excitement around 'breath' and the life body" (32), "now assists it" (33).[45]

In a discussion following a public reading during his road trip in 1966, Ginsberg articulated this "paradoxical attitude" in an intriguing manner. A person in the audience raised his voice to ask what he calls a "down question"—a question reacting to what is perceived as a contradictory situation: Ginsberg lamenting the loss of "harmony" and "unity" in the contemporary world that does not resonate with nature and natural experience while recording every single word he says on a tape recorder: "What do you expect to get from that machine of yours right there?" Without hesitation, Ginsberg replied:

> I play it back and set up a feedback into my own electronic network, which disturbs the habitual programming of the roll. It feeds back, like mirror images the roll on itself, so I'm set aside from the roll and have to listen to the roll from the outside

and get separated from it. That's one use. Then there's occasional times when I get out of myself and then that's recorded there. (*Albuquerque Auto Poesy Reading at Santa Fe College*)

Ginsberg is describing a reciprocal, circular human-machine interaction in which the characteristics of both entities are neither strictly juxtaposed nor attributed positive or negative connotations. The body of the person who is speaking is not depicted in "natural" terms to begin with; on the contrary, it has its "own electronic network." It is this already machinic-organic human that intervenes in the recording machine's "habitual programming," probably implying something like the "forced artificial bureaucratic dry rhythm affected by multiple machinery." Ginsberg outlines a circuit that unsettles the self-identity of both the human and the machine: after recording an input produced by the human voice, the recorded output, a machine breath, is played back. In this process, the human and the recorder experience a moment of syncope—of cut unity, hearing "oneself" as other: the recorded voice, the output, returns to the human who created it and is now "separated" from the "roll"; a no longer purely human but at the same time not purely artificial voice becomes the input for a machine encountering its own strange mirror image. Such a scenario radically challenges the strict division of "syn" and "coptein" that Ginsberg implies when he bemoans the loss of a "common communal communistic sharing of soul among all members of the body politic" (*Allen Verbatim* 33) and the "body chant" (33) "of unison and oneness with all of nature" because "capitalism and our economic system require the excessive *chopping up* of nature into lumber" (34; emphasis added). Against such depreciating comments on the act of "chopping up," Ginsberg's compositional practice demonstrates how *coptein* turns out to be the basis of *syn*: he chops up the living breath into reproducible electronic signals, cuts these signals into lines on paper, or, in reverse, cuts out breaths, pauses, or clicks that marked split units on tape in order to create smooth, continuous lines. Paying attention to movements of syncopnea, and bearing in mind Michael Davidson's argument that "technologies of presence," like the tape recorder "will always offer a hybrid voice—a voice in the machine—that cannot speak entirely for itself, even though it posits self-presence as its ground" (*Ghostlier Demarcations* 199), I want to investigate a few examples of multimedial, hybrid breaths in "Iron Horse" involving disruptions, tensions, and interpenetrations of living organisms and machinery.

"Iron Horse" is pervaded by respirational imagery. The air predominating the poem is what Ginsberg categorizes as corrupted, full of smoke, steam, dust, and toxic gases. The way these polluting substances are presented, however, runs counter to the way in which Ginsberg condemns them in interviews and essays. In the poem's images, the opposition of destructive, deadly, inorganic airy substances and lively, natural breath crumbles. The polluting air does not indicate suffocation: on the contrary, it is *breathed* by smokestacks and chimneys. Thus, life enters the inanimate structures embodying the industrial machine; not because breath is naturally identified with life, but because Ginsberg's personifications and animalizations (e.g., the "Iron Horse")—the hybrid machine-creatures—constitute the poem's most vivid, vibrant images: "Giant fire's orange tongues & black smoke / pouring out that roof" (*Collected Poems 1947–1997* 449) or "Bright steam / muscular puffing from an old slue" (448) relate to "breathing as a baby" (432) and "puffin' / a peaceful O pipe" (436) like Milton's Satan to his God. The "dynamo'd smoke-cathedrals" (448) and "viaduct windowless industry" (447) are more alluring than the "house hidden in trees" (446) and the "farm in backland Oregon" (446). Paradoxically, and contrary to Ginsberg's argument,[46] poetically, the machinic, polluting air turns out to be more inspirational than the clean, natural one. In the poem's strongest imagery, the deadly "iron cancer on the city's throat" (449) proliferates, the figurative cells spreading wildly and the smokestack's "muscular puffing" inducing a pulsating rhythm. Thus, Ginsberg's conviction that the "ecological cancer" (*Spontaneous Mind* 191) caused by the polluted air suffocates is reversed. In "Iron Horse," the poetic devices counteract the claim that "living forms are being turned into inorganic ones; cancer has exactly the same effect. Instead of continuous spontaneous creation, there's continuous spontaneous consumption of matter reduced to dead form" (193).

In "Iron Horse," Ginsberg articulates his concern about smoking cigarettes, which he keeps associating with the ills of the modern world.[47] "Better to stop smoking" (446) is one of the suggestions for a withdrawal from the industrial war machine, and cancer, one of Ginsberg's paradigmatic images for the latter, is mentioned as a fatal effect of smoking: "I smoke too much I'll die lung cancer" (434) and "clear your throat, / lie there in the dark, / cough with cancer" (438). At one moment on the original tape recordings, we hear an actual cough—and considering Ginsberg's known personal habits, it's a cough related to smoking. In his intriguing analysis of Ginsberg's audio recordings, especially with respect to the physical "sonic environments" the recorded voice is enmeshed in on the tapes from the 1965–1966 road trip, Lytle Shaw convincingly argues that for Ginsberg, "ambient radio sound, throat gurgles, open windows, and the hum of the car" were a "threat . . . that, to be contained, needed to be translated to the more human domain of print" (*Narrowcast: Poetry and Audio Research* 70). In the following discussion, I focus on the particular way the cough we hear on the "Iron Horse" tape, a sound that was only accidentally recorded, is translated into writing. Even though we can argue with Shaw that the cough poses a threat—not only as a random noise but also in its relation to smoking—containment does not capture the intricate process of transcription it seems to trigger. Tracing the development of the passage around the cough on the tape, we can observe how a smoke-image is generated in a movement of transformation. The oral composition was triggered by sights passing by as the train entered Chicago and it can be assumed that Ginsberg was recording what he saw at the very moment: "The first [p] aged brick apartment houses [p] with their [hesitation] grey [hesitation] back [hesitation] porches [the air after the bilabial stop "p" is audibly pushed, then the word is followed by a breath] stairways [breath] liquor signs painted ancient [cough] belfried church with cross atop [c]." The handwritten draft shows that Ginsberg listened closely to the tape when he transcribed it; in this case, the respiratory sounds are very accurately incorporated on the page: line breaks follow breaths and the moment where he coughed is marked by a dash (see figure 2.3).

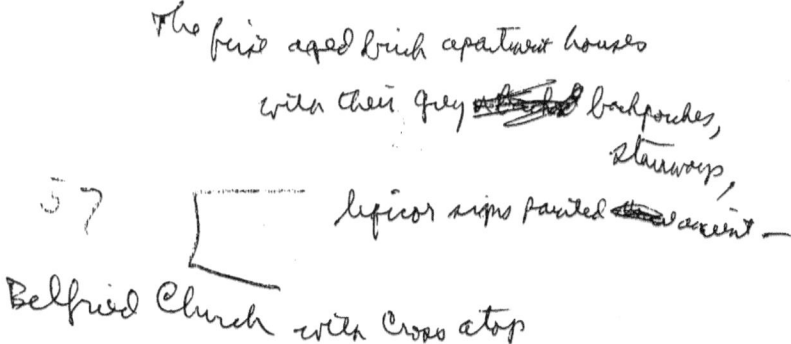

Figure 2.3. Allen Ginsberg, *Fall of America* and "Iron Horse" (draft). Allen Ginsberg Papers, Special Collections, Stanford. Copyright Allen Ginsberg. Used by permission of the Wylie Agency LLC.

80   Poetics of Breathing

Both on the tape and in the draft, Ginsberg continues as follows—there are no audible breaths and the transcription follows the nonrespirational pause markers less strictly (see figure 2.4):

> passed on the second story by the Avis truck [c]
> elevated up [p] on the superhighway [c]
> checkaboard red white [p] on the tanks [c]
> granite aches [b] on the old red houses [c]
> confronting [c] dynamo'd [c] smokecathedralfactories [c]

In the typescript and the published version, this passage is heavily revised and rearranged: much is deleted and condensed; even the order of the lines is changed (see figure 2.5).[48]

> Church spires lifted gray
>   hazy towers downtown
> a belfried cross beneath
>   dynamo'd smoke-cathedrals,

The "belfried church with cross atop," followed by the cough on the tape is—literally—*turned* into a "belfried cross beneath" and immediately followed by "dynamo'd smoke-cathedrals"—the lines occurring between the two images in the earliest versions are erased. In contrast to other physical breaths audible on Ginsberg's tapes, the cough that involuntarily interrupted the composition leaves traces throughout the drafts right up to the final version: the line break

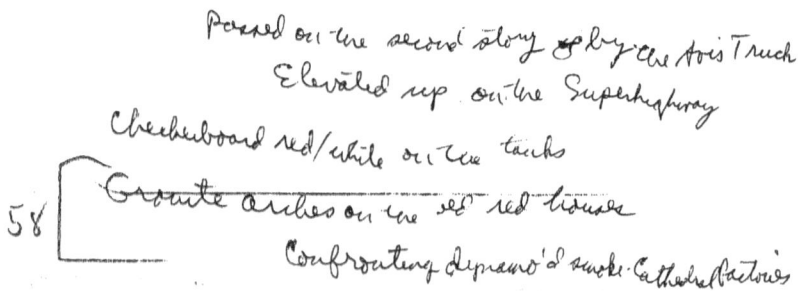

Figure 2.4. Allen Ginsberg, *Fall of America* and "Iron Horse" (draft). Allen Ginsberg Papers, Special Collections, Stanford. Copyright Allen Ginsberg. Used by permission of the Wylie Agency LLC.

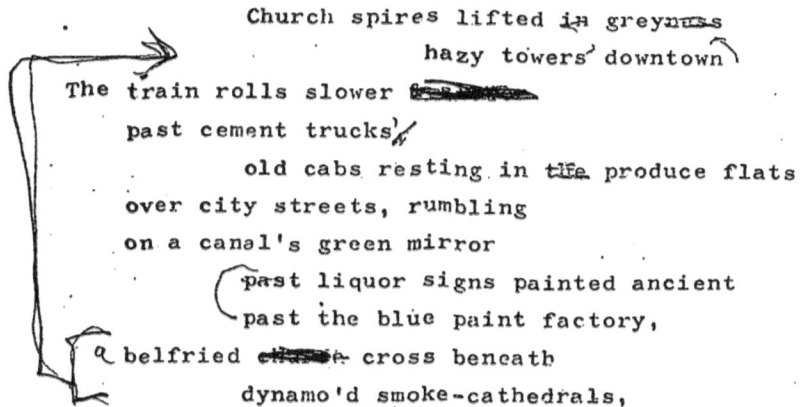

Figure 2.5. Allen Ginsberg, "Iron Horse" (draft). Allen Ginsberg Papers, Special Collections, Stanford. Copyright Allen Ginsberg. Used by permission of the Wylie Agency LLC.

after "belfried cross beneath" still reminds one of the place it occurred, and the "*smoke*-cathedrals" recall its origin. Through Ginsberg's semantic and syntactical revisions, the two images, now pulled together, conjoin various moments of the compositional process. When he notes down visual perceptions, scraps of the industrial landscape, and thus also transcribes how his mind works, Ginsberg exemplifies his own description of the act of composition: "You observe your own mind during the time of composition and write down whatever goes through the ticker tape of mentality" (*Spontaneous Mind* 259). Ginsberg often contrasts the hyperconsciousness of "writing down your thought forms as they occur" (31) to the evocation of the unconscious in automatic writing. What does enter the compositional process *un*consciously in the passage in question is the work of the body, which invades the tape recording and is paid tribute to in the course of the poem's development.

Changes made during the revision process are essential. A faithful description of the industrial landscape becomes an atmospheric impression: it is the *air* of the scenery, rather than its visual particulars, that is the subject of *re*-capturing. The two conjoined images are instances of a transformed compositional process: the body is inscribed in them through a cough. How this inscription occurs is a major part of the creative process: Ginsberg very deliberately puts two lines together, one contiguous to the cough because of the moment it occurred in the composition (belfried cross/church), the other semantically through the cough's cause (dynamo'd *smoke*-cathedrals).

The *conjunction* of these two lines is a good example of Ginsberg's ideal of the creative image: "you get two images which the mind connects in a flash." This "visceral thing" causes "an electrochemical reaction on the body" (31). Referencing Artaud, Ginsberg claims that words "when introduced into the nervous system" have the capacity to change "the molecular composition of the nerve cells or something like that" (32). Rather than only being destructive, the smoke-caused cough becomes a dynamo that generates a current between electronic signals, words, secular-sacral industrial buildings, and biological processes of organic bodies.

To conclude, I want to focus on two moments where physical breath lacking any smoke traces—the ones Ginsberg celebrates as natural and vital for composition—meet industrial breath in words. On the tape recordings, the industrial and "natural" human breaths intermingle in more than simply a metaphorical way. In a passage assumed to have been altered into the final version, we hear Ginsberg inhaling while articulating an image of nonhuman respiration on his breath: "bright steam [*b*] muscular [c] puffing [c] from an old slue [c] Meadowgold Butter besmeared with coal dust [*b*]." In the handwritten transcription, the audible breaths are transcribed as line breaks, although not all clicks are considered (see figure 2.6).

> Bright steam
> muscular puffing from an old slue
> Meadowgold Butter besmeared with coal dust

The curved stroke in the draft indicates that Ginsberg considered merging the lines but finally decided on maintaining the line break where industrial

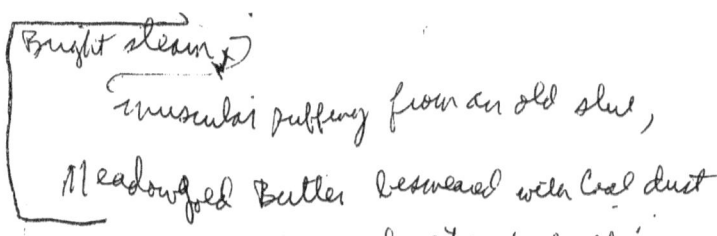

Figure 2.6. Allen Ginsberg, *Fall of America* and "Iron Horse" (draft). Allen Ginsberg Papers, Special Collections, Stanford. Copyright Allen Ginsberg. Used by permission of the Wylie Agency LLC.

steam met his physical breath—a sediment in black pigment on the page, not unlike the coal dust on the "Meadowgold Butter" sign Ginsberg saw when entering the train station in Chicago. Ginsberg's bodily breath is conjoined with a machine breath in a passage that almost directly follows the one just investigated: "under the cave [c] of smoky arches [c] leaving over the rail yard [c] inching to the platform [*b*] with the *groan of wheels* against [c] whitened rail [c] buildings all black around" (emphasis added). This passage is especially interesting in light of Ginsberg's comments on sounds coinciding with their "own Idea" in sighs (*Allen Verbatim* 26). He claims that "the sound of the sigh—well it isn't the entire sigh because there's also the breath moving—the sound of the sigh is identical with what it means, unlike most other statements, or unlike other sounds" (27). The identity of sound and meaning is explained as follows: "the words we pronounce do connect finally to our body, connect to our breathing, particularly, and breathing connects to feeling, feeling articulated in language" (28). However, in the moment when Ginsberg's breathing sound gives way to a spoken "groan of wheels," there is no identity of sound, body (or emitting entity), and feeling. The image of the groaning wheel is based on the transference of a respirational sound associated with a certain kind of feeling (despair, pain, etc.) to the train, an object without emotions. The sound of Ginsberg's own breath is in turn not emotionally charged: we hear an unmarked, regular inhalation. Attributing respirational activity to inanimate entities in images like the slue's "muscular puffing" or the "groan of wheels" in combination with audible breaths on the tapes accounts for a syncopal transmission of "breath moving" across materials and semantic fields—breath is thus involved in *motion*, rather than being identical with *emotion*: the breath of a human body runs into the images without reaching a full identification, and in the images themselves, industrial machinery and organic respiration meet but do not entirely coincide.

The development of the passage around the groaning wheels from tape to print reveals further interrupted transmissions of "moving breath" (see figures 2.7 and 2.8).

> the groan of iron tons inching against
>   whitened rail,
>   giant train so slowly moved
>   a man can touch the wheels

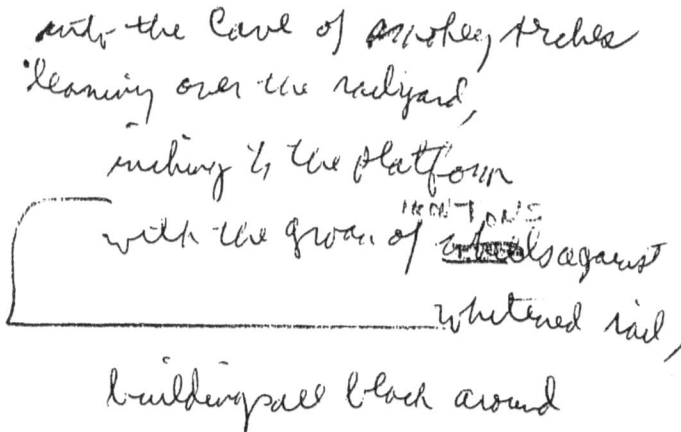

Figure 2.7. Allen Ginsberg, *Fall of America* and "Iron Horse" (draft). Allen Ginsberg Papers, Special Collections, Stanford; copyright Allen Ginsberg. Used by permission of the Wylie Agency LLC.

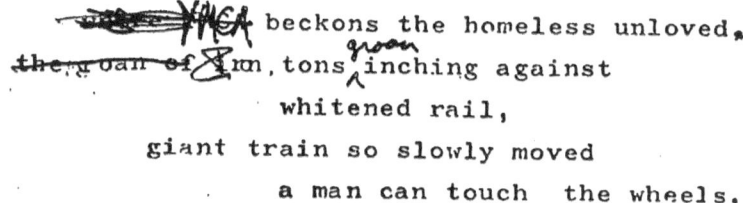

Figure 2.8. Allen Ginsberg, "Iron Horse" (draft). Allen Ginsberg Papers, Special Collections, Stanford. Copyright Allen Ginsberg. Used by permission of the Wylie Agency LLC.

In the handwritten draft, Ginsberg replaces "wheels" with "IRON TONS," making more palpable the physical qualities of the inorganic material of the object uttering the groan. In the typescript, the groan no longer occurs in the form of a prepositional phrase ("*with* the groan of . . .") and thus becomes more autonomous. In the variant crossed out in the typescript but which then becomes the final version, the groan is the subject of the sentence: "the groan of iron tons inching against / whitened rail." In contrast, in the handwritten revisions on the typescript, "groan" is added again after having been deleted and becomes a verb: "iron tons groan inching against / whitened rail." Throughout the poem's various stages, the groan moves not only between the physical and the figural as well as organic and inorganic articulators but also across word classes and grammatical relations. What we encounter is the motility of a wandering breath that never quite remains itself: a breath whose mutability undermines any notion of self-identity.

A closer look at Ginsberg's compositional processes shows that the manifold transferences and transformations of multiple elements (e.g., various pause markers, words) across various media throughout his creative practice is much closer to the bodily process of respiration—gas exchanges in the body, the irregular rhythms of inhalation and exhalation—than to his theoretical conception of breath and its role in writing, suggesting symmetries and one-to-one translations that are more machinic than organic.

"Rasping Smoke in a Dry Throat": Kerouac's Typewriter Fantasies

In 1940, when Kerouac was eighteen years old and far from fame, he wrote two short stories about writing: one, "A Play I Want to Write," is included in the collection *Atop an Underwood: Early Stories and Other Writings*; the other, "Rasping Smoke in a Dry Throat" is still unpublished. Both texts have a similar outline: the narrator, clearly designed to resemble the author Kerouac, describes how he is about to write a successful play. In the stories focusing on the circumstances in which those plays are to emerge, the "great plays" themselves represent a prospective *gap*; while the narrator fantasizes about how successful and financially rewarding his literary work will be in "A Play I Want to Write," "I will bet a quarter million dollars and pull in the Pulitzer Prize and the Nobel Literature Price for $50.000" (*Atop an Underwood*, 29), its content remains absent because it is not yet written (either by the narrator or by the author himself). It is no coincidence that in both stories, the narrator uses a typewriter, which Kerouac stylizes as a tool that creates literature ex nihilo: "The beautiful *action* of the typewriter machine tempts you to fiddle on when you've really nothing to say . . . really giving birth in the void from the void." Especially at this early stage in Kerouac's career, the typewriter fantasy might be invested with what Marshall McLuhan will later diagnose as "the entirely new attitude to the written and printed word" caused by the typewriter: "The typewriter fuses composition and publication" (*Understanding Media* 260). Thinking along these lines, we could argue that Kerouac, who at this moment is not yet published himself and hungry for success, has his young narrators choose the typewriter as their favored tool because it promises to create great literature automatically and publish it instantly.

The stories also outline other preconditions for success. In "A Play I Want to Write," which is more explicit and straightforward about these requirements (and the fantasy of future fame), we read the following: "The setting for this play will soon hit me in the face. I am waiting for this moment this summer when I shall be sitting or walking, but all the same breathing, and suddenly I will start with a jump and say: What a setting for a play!" The prospective play emerges from "a spontaneous burst of passion which I will develop all of a sudden, then I shall rush to my typewriter and begin to extract pages from the book [a "looseleaf" notebook described earlier in the text] and begin writing" (*Atop an Underwood* 28). Retrospectively, one clearly recognizes Kerouac's accounts of how *On the Road* and *The Subterraneans* came to be in this brief sketch of a creative moment. It is striking to see how early the idea of spontaneous writing preoccupied Kerouac, and that, somewhat paradoxically, he reproduced a very old idea of his (with a long literary tradition) when he proclaimed his revolutionary "new" way of writing in the context of *On the Road*[49] and developed his poetics of breath upon being asked to explain his method after supposedly having dashed down *The Subterraneans* in three days.

In the early stories, the product of the inspirational scenes is absent. Projecting creative output into the future produces an ambivalent setting. While anticipated fame and wealth presupposes that inspiration was fruitful, it is at the same time exposed as fantasy: one triggered by the fear that inspiration, which has not yet come to the narrator at the moment he is writing the story, may not occur, or be unproductive. That inspiration is related to respiration is already hinted at when the narrator in "A Play I want to Write" stresses that the "spontaneous burst of passion" happens while he is "sitting or walking, *but all the same breathing*" (emphasis added). Apart from this rather odd reference to breath, both stories describe how the narrator fuels creative inspiration with nicotine: "When I shall have finished it [the play], and have had smoked about two packs of cigarettes which I don't inhale but just smoke because they help me write, then I shall read it to myself" (28–29). Throughout Kerouac's juvenilia, a cliché image of phallic, empowering smoking recurs: there is the cool macho-trucker, "smoking knowingly," living a desired life—"women and drink and trucks and to hell with anything else"—"He bought the pack of cigarettes, letting his last cigarette butt hang from his twisted mouth and spiral smoke up to his scowling eyes" ("New York Nite Club" 62). And there is the eponymous cigar in a short play, where "the audience should be supplied with good fat five-cent cigars. The women should at least light them and hold them in their hands; but the men *must* smoke them. It is essential" ("There's Something about a Cigar" 66). This play itself features Nick, a "cigar-smoking poet" (67) distributing his gendered fetish among a group of guys who then puff away to the echoing mantra, "There's something about a cigar." The cigar gives "courage" to the flaneur in New York who was "shy of the world"; first and foremost, however, smoking promises an attitude of cool indifference to the "wicked world", the "tremendous muffled roar" of "time march[ing] on," a the sound of a memento mori that is supposed to accompany the whole play,[50] Nick's inability to "express himself" and the potential failure of the play itself. In a self-reflexive comment, the author-narrator notes "I'm sure no one will like this play . . . but what the hell do I care. I can always light up a cigar and smoke it and say: 'So what'" (69–71). So what—the asemantic and transitory implications of breath are invoked when the futility of smoking is stylized as a nonchalant reaction to a vain world. Despite what at first seem to be contrary implications, the image of the cigar (as well as other references to smoking in Kerouac's early work) in some respects functions analogously to the phallic dash marking virile breath: in both cases, Kerouac implies that certain practices of breathing ward off vulnerability and failure; in both cases, his texts at the same time reveal a flip side of the gesture of mastery that is presented.

"Rasping Smoke in a Dry Throat" meshes with yet complicates Kerouac's staging of smoking in his early work. When Kerouac put together his own archive in the mid-1960s, he seemed content with his early accomplishment and introduced the story with the comment "JACK KEROUAC AGE 18!" He also situates the text in a line of literary development, as an early step toward his later "revolutionary" style by adding the notes "First lines of 'modernistic' period" and "a moment of new + ecstatic light, as I remember." He thus suggests that the text itself represents what it outlines as a potential of the play that is about to be written: the narrator muses that writers can make a "bright" "spark" through their literary products that, fleeting as it may be, can nevertheless counteract "our smallness" in a "waning world." Smoking has an ambivalent relation to this spark. On the one hand, the quick consumption of the cigarette, the dissolving exhaled smoke, and the futility of the world are presented as equivalents: "The waning cigarette and the waning world the waning civilization and the dwindling smoke." On the other hand, the text draws parallels between smoking and literary creation: "the smoke finding its way to the ceiling and absolving into the air, like the spark I mean the spark we have made"—our lives may fade away with the earth, which is itself no more than "a spark of light in the span of eternity." "So what!" we may add, or rather: we smoke and produce our literary counterspark. The choice of the word "absolving" is indicative of an ambivalence that pervades the text and cannot be erased by Kerouac's confident remarks after the fact—a confidence suggesting that "Rasping Smoke in a Dry Throat" is itself the literary spark, "a moment of new + ecstatic light." Was, as the narrator of the story relates, the "perfect English I learned this year from the Dean" really good enough to create "one of the brightest [sparks]"? Did young Kerouac, for whom English was sometimes a challenge—"Se dur pour mue parle l'Angla parse je toujour parle le Francais Canadien" (Typescript fragment)—confuse "absolve" and "dissolve"? Or did he deliberately choose a word whose Latin roots refer to "finish, complete, to bring to perfection" (*Oxford English Dictionary* online)? Was the idiosyncratic use of "absolving" a "first line" of Kerouac's "modernistic period," an act of "setting" himself "free" from conventional language—or simply a mistake?

Speculations and problematic conflations of author and narrator aside: in the story, the respirational movement of smoking and literary production go hand in hand. The story's first words are "Rasping smoke in a dry throat. Smoke in the room . . . smoke finding its way out of the window"; then—and here respiration meets media technology—there is also "smoke over the typewriter." Like the smoke "finding its way out of the window," the literary spark leaves the author's body and is externalized via typewriter to make its way out into the world. More specific links between smoking and writing can be discovered when we look more closely at Kerouac's descriptions and the words he uses: "Rasping smoke in a dry throat" points to the scratchy feeling of inhalations or exhalations while smoking. However, "rasp" also means to "*inscribe* by scraping or scratching" (*Oxford English Dictionary* online; emphasis added). The smoke "rasps" in the throat, it scrapes against soft tissue—the friction may produce a spark, but the smoke may also keep scratching when it finds its way out. It may leave a more lasting mark before it dissolves into the air. The "smoke over the typewriter" thus implies a physical proximity between exhalation and inscription. Both tobacco residue and the typewriter leave black marks. There may even be a material continuity of tar and the ink on the typewriter ribbon, if that ink were carbon based. In any case, when the narrator claims that he is "one of the grimy coal-shovelers, supplying the fuel" for the "spark," he imagines a carbon-based inspiration that will enable the production of great literature. If the burning coal produces a spark, so might the burning cigarette—the narrator may thus, via smoking, turn from coal-supplier to spark-producer. In contrast to "A Play I Want to Write," a text staging fantasies of success in which smoking supports productive writing, "Rasping Smoke in a Dry Throat" creates a dense net of analogies and parallels (e.g., between typewriting, smoking, and coal mining) that does not add up to a clear picture or message. It is left open whether the smoke will leave lasting traces (in the form of a literary accomplishment) or simply fade away; it is not clear whether "rasping" primarily consumes and merely produces waste material or whether that very material is the source for a literary creation, the "coal" for the spark; and it is uncertain, too, whether a "spark which lasts one second and dies out" is even produced at all. In the text, the exhaled breath is ambiguous—it *alludes* without becoming a fixed image with a stable meaning. Even the written breath itself, sedimented in black ink on the typed page, is unstable. It winds its way through the text as an imperfect refrain that does not constitute a symmetrical narrative arrangement: "Rasping smoke in a dry throat" is the opening sentence, it does not occur in the second paragraph, then concludes the third paragraph, disappears again, and finally introduces the sixth and last paragraph in a variant formulation, "Rasping smoke (more rasping, much more in the ash tray) in a dry throat," an uneven parallel between the first and the last paragraph.

The indeterminate status of exhaled smoke becomes especially noticeable when one takes a closer look at its relation to the "spark," which exceeds the simile, "smoke is finding its way to the ceiling and absolving into the air, like the spark does I mean the spark we make." While the narrator claims that the spark "lasts one second and dies out," the semantic implications of "spark" as "vital or animating principle," "a trace of life or vitality" (*Oxford English Dictionary* online) inscribe a counterforce. Smoking bears similarly contradictory connotations: the exhaled smoke itself is transient, but, according to "A Play I Want to Write," smoking also entails a vital force, a life-giving, inspirational breath that helps us write. Besides sharing oscillating ascriptions of vitality and futility—the biblical breath of life meets *hevel*, the breath of ephemerality and nothingness—spark and smoke further coalesce in the proverb, "The smith always has a spark in his throat." The meaning of the historical slang expression, to "have a constant thirst" (Partridge 1120), echoes in the "dry throat" and it is a short path from the "grimy coal-shovelers supplying the fuel" to the blacksmith's anvil emitting sparks. The origin of the saying is not clear. From a medical perspective, the smith's permanent thirst may point to a symptom of metal flume fever, which can be caused by the inhalation of toxic fumes during metalwork (Kaye, Young, and O'Sullivan 269). Thus, the sentence "rasping smoke in a dry throat" latently undermines a fantasy of literary production that the text evokes, at least to some degree (especially if we read it alongside "A Play I Want to Write"). On the surface, the text is concerned with the transitoriness of spark and smoke, that is, the possibility that creative output may not last. Another danger arises with the echoing proverb and its link to smoking. Listening to its reverberation in the repeated sentence "rasping smoke in a dry throat," the text becomes infused with combusted substances that potentially put the body at risk. The way the spark is produced may be damaging and inspiration may be life threatening. The act of creation may be destructive and debilitating for the body of the creator. Kerouac knew that smoking is bad for health and potentially fatal. In his attempt to write a variation of Whitman's *Leaves of Grass*, also in 1940, Kerouac celebrates "delicate nicotine" and the "heaven of sweet smoke," and then notes, "They tell me that life will be shortened, and I listen attentively," only to once more express a 'so what' attitude with the lines "light my pipe / Without any regard for their solemn warnings" ("I Know I Am August" 43). This is a clash between the two forms of Kerouac's respiratory pursuit of literary mastery: the nicotine-induced posture of indifference in "There's Something about a Cigar" is a shield against vulnerability; at the same time, this attitude is a reaction to the dangers of this very breathing practice for the virile, healthy, athletic body.

Another ambivalence about smoking appears in "Rasping Smoke in a Dry Throat" in a moment of potential self-criticism. In the text, a body that could be kept healthy is deliberately emaciated. The narrator's throat is dry due to a lack of food and drink; the potentially damaging rasping smoke becomes a substitute for bodily nourishment. It is important that the narrator at the same time repeatedly admits that food and drink are available to him: "An empty stomach with food in the fridge isn't empty," "there's water in the faucet." These are hints at what he reveals in the last paragraph: "I wish some time I was poor and alone so I could write better but I know I am a fortunate ~~bum~~ . . . with good fortune strewn all over my face which is ugly to the eyes of the beings who caused the longest and brightest spark." Later in his career, Kerouac would consistently cultivate the public image of an underdog; in this early text, however, the author-narrator admits a degree of privilege. The image of smoky breath now reveals a self-critical dimension: "grime" replaces the "good fortune" strewn over the narrator's face. In the chain of connotations established, smoking becomes the (metaphorical) ground with which the narrator can reach into the domains of coal shoveling and metalwork. Through smoking, the narrator imitates the respirational circumstances of the coal- or metalworker involuntarily exposed to toxic fumes—in order to "write better" (and thus to become more privileged, famous, and wealthy—as stressed in "A Play I

Want to Write"). While the cigarette is the necessary basis of the privileged kid's analogy, "rasping smoke" at the same time exposes its inappropriateness.

Anxiety—Ecstasy: Inspiration

"I don't inhale": Kerouac's Repression

While Kerouac playfully alludes to inspiration in his early stories when he lets his author-narrators claim that smoking helps them write, these texts already anticipate the inspiration anxiety pervading Kerouac's later work, especially his theories of breathing and composition. Physiological inspiration—in the sense of inhalation—is conspicuously bracketed throughout Kerouac's work; whenever relations between breathing and writing are addressed, the focus is on exhalation, breathing *out*. In the early texts, the figural inspiration smoking fuels is limited to physical expiration. "Rasping Smoke in a Dry Throat" lets the reader follow the exhaled smoke as it moves through the room and "find[s] its way out the window." The starting point of the smoke's movement is inside the narrator's body, his throat—smoke is not shown entering the body. In "A Play I Want to Write," the narrator explicitly stresses: "[I] had smoked about two packs of cigarettes *which I don't inhale* but just smoke because they help me write" (emphasis added). "Just smoking" thus implies that the external substance is prevented from entering the body as much as possible. The sentence from the early text points to what Kerouac later expands on in "Essentials of Spontaneous Prose," where breathing as "blowing" is limited to exhalation. Kerouac sketches a respirational process in which inhaling is avoided and the substances entering the body from outside are left unmentioned;[51] he creates the impression that a breath solely generated in one's own body enables literary creations: "tap from yourself the song of yourself, *blow!—now!—your* way is your only way." In this model, the focus on a particular respiratory phase is used to rewrite the classical notion of inspiration—or, rather, to outline a theory of literary initiation in which physiological exhalation replaces both figural and bodily inspiration so that the creative air emerges in the "self" rather than being infused by an external agent.

Kerouac expressed his reservations about inspiration early on. In 1943, in an attempt to figure out how a "new literary form" might be achieved, Kerouac notes: "A novelist needs experience, insight, craftsmanship, understanding and organizational genius. Poetic inspiration is only secondary." He further explains: "craftsmanship requires years of developing, . . . ; organizational genius is partly a gift, partly an outgrowth of craftsmanship. Poetic inspiration is a gift" ("Supreme Reality"). Even though these reflections about a possible "new literary form" are substantially different from Kerouac's later notion of "spontaneous" writing, inspiration is already considered "secondary" because it is not something the writer achieves autonomously; while craftsmanship, experience, and so forth can be *developed* by the writer himself, inspiration is imparted from outside, it is a "gift." A self-made writer is not, according to Kerouac, reliant on gifts—one of his earliest premises; later, the idea of craftsmanship (i.e., that writing skills are generated slowly) is replaced by the fantasy of the work as immediate creation. In 1950, he noted: "No one has to look for 'inspiration.' You only have to admit to yourself, 'I have made this thought because it was there in my mind, and that is the truth of my mind *at this moment!*' The moment is in the writing" ("Writing for Yourself"). The rush of creative energy granted by inspiration—as opposed to slowly-acquired craftsmanship—is recuperated and turned inward. In "Essentials of Spontaneous Prose," Kerouac adds the last twist to this theory by introducing the notion of breath. Bodily breath replaces the gift of inspiration; the innate creative power that is explosively set free in the writing process comes as naturally and instantaneously as breathing—a type of breathing without inhaling.

Kerouac's deployment of the image of breath represents a shift it from its traditional location in both figural and literal accounts of inspiration, where it is the origin, the initiating moment that *precedes* creative production as such. In "Essentials," breath appears where writing is *in progress*—where words are spontaneously structured in accordance with respiration: "Not 'selectivity' of expression but following free deviation (association) of mind into limitless blow-on-subject seas of thought, swimming in sea of English with no discipline other than rhythms of rhetorical exhalation." As the free flow of exhalations in "Essentials" is embedded in a sexual register, the exhaled creative product amounts to ejaculation: "Blow as deep as you want—write as deeply, fish as far down as you want, satisfy yourself first." "Admit in own uninhibited interesting necessary and so 'modern' language what conscious art would censor, and write excitedly, swiftly, with writing or typing cramps, in accordance (as from center to periphery) with laws of orgasm, Reich's 'beclouding of consciousness.' Come from within, out to relaxed and said" (57–58). In the parallel of ejaculation and literary creation, Kerouac imagines a scenario of male childbirth that coincides with orgasm. Sexual procreation poses the same "problem" as inspiration: something is *conceived from outside*. In Kerouac's outline, the substance generating the fetus, usually entering the woman's body from another one, is maintained in a single male body, who creates the product instantaneously in the moment of climax. By letting conception and birth coincide and the two bodies involved in procreation collapse into one, Kerouac attempts to circumvent the external force or body that enables creation.

One of the sources of the virility that Kerouac invokes is Wilhelm Reich's concept of "sex economy." Kerouac explicitly refers to Reich when he mentions the "laws of orgasm," which are compared to the "discipline" of "rhetorical exhalation." He does not, however, mention Reich's idea of unrestricted flow in terms of exhalation and orgasm in *The Function of the Orgasm*. Reich's idea of "sex economy" complements Kerouac's poetics of athletic breathing, the vigorous dash as release sign coinciding with the runner's spurt. For Reich, sexual climax ultimately does not lead to exhaustion but rather grants the "efficient circulation of energy in the human organism" (181). According to the principle of "sex-economy," "psychic health depends on orgiastic potency" (7). The healthy psyche is invigorated by a free flow of "vital energies" (7) and endangered when this flow is interrupted: the "damming up of biological energy" (6) through moralistic "regulation" (181) implies a "suppression of natural life" (7).[52] Reich's stress on "establishing free-flowing energy and, in conjunction with it, genital potency" (170–71) meets its poetic equivalent in Kerouac's theory of spontaneous prose. The idea of "sex *economy*" allows turning what is potentially precarious—the loss of control—into something productive and liberating: "*Orgiastic potency is the capacity to surrender to the flow of biological energy, free of any inhibitions; the capacity to discharge completely the dammed-up sexual excitation through involuntary, pleasurable convulsions of the body*" (102). In the moment of orgasm, surrender becomes a means for freedom and the uncontrolled body provides pleasure and potency. Kerouac translates Reich's depiction of sexual climax, the "flowing of the electrical charge of the organism toward the periphery" (52), into a scene of literary composition: "from center to periphery" = "Come from within, out—to relaxed and said." Here, Kerouac is drawing on a passage in which Reich discusses the climactic "phase of involuntary muscle contractions" (more precisely, "the ejaculatory muscle contractions in the man" [106]). Reich notes that at "this point, consciousness becomes more or less clouded" (105). While Kerouac quotes from this passage, it is worth noting that there is no reference to Reich's following description of the climax: "The increase of the excitation can no longer be controlled; rather it grips the entire personality and causes an acceleration of pulse and deep exhalation" (105). The deep exhalation during the climax of the "orgiastically gratifying sexual act" (102) mentioned by Reich ties in with the echoes of Aristotle in Kerouac's theory of writing: the "pleasant" style in which the "end in sight," the anticipated breath-pause, ensures that rhetorical runners do not "lose their breath and strength" (387). Rather than referring to Reich's orgiastic "exhalation," Kerouac deploys what he called the "trademark" of his writing, the "vigorous release sign, i.e., the dash—" (*Selected Letters 1957–1969* 324): "write outwards swimming in sea of language to peripheral release and exhaustion—" (58). Obviously, the dash marks climactic "rhetorical exhalation" in "Come from within, out—to relaxed and said"—a moment to which I will return.

In *The Function of the Orgasm*, the "outwards" movement, "from center toward the periphery" has a counterpart: "*sexuality could be nothing other than the biological function of expansion 'out of the self' from the center toward the periphery. In turn, anxiety could be nothing but the reversed direction, i.e., from the periphery to the center, back into the self*" (266–67). Both movements find expression in the body: "The sexually aroused penis expands. In anxiety, it shrivels" (267); "respiration" is "a condition of continuous oscillation, in which the organism is continually alternating between parasympathetic expansion (exhalation) and sympathetic contraction (inhalation)" (266). Kerouac reproduces this parallel between breathing and the sexual act in his "Essentials," focusing on the "state of pleasurable expansion" and omitting the "state of anxious contraction" (295). In this respect it is worthwhile to look more closely at Reich's discussion of breath. Exhalation is his favored respiratory mode while inhalation is associated with a risk: for Reich, "respiratory disturbances in neuroses" become manifest when "you will not exhale fully"(306); "There is not a single neurotic person who is capable of breathing out deeply and evenly" (333). "In a state of fright, one involuntarily breathes in; we are reminded of the involuntary inhalation which takes place in drowning and actually causes death" (307). Despite this bias in favor of exhalation, Reich ultimately stresses the importance of the complete respirational process. In his account of internal respiration, Reich particularly addresses the importance of the intake of oxygen in order to produce "vital energy":

> Simple deliberation indicated that biologically, respiration has the function of introducing oxygen into the organism and of removing carbon dioxide. The oxygen of the introduced air brings about the combustion of the digested foodstuffs. Chemically speaking, combustion means everything which takes place

in the fusion of substances with oxygen. This process generates energy. Without oxygen, there is no combustion and, therefore, no production of energy. In the organism, energy is produced through the combustion of foodstuffs. In that way, heat and kinetic energy are generated. Bioelectricity is also produced in this process of combustion. (309)

The depiction of the chemical aspects of respiration amounts to an argument against "respiratory inhibition." In this case, respiratory disturbance pertains to both inhaling and exhaling. Blocking full inbreaths and outbreaths goes hand in hand with "suppressing feeling and sexual arousal" (307); importantly, "feeling" here also contains anxiety: "In reduced respiration, less oxygen is introduced, actually only as much as is necessary for the preservation of life. With less energy in the organism, the vegetative excitations are less intense and, therefore, easier to control. Viewed biologically, the inhibition of respiration in neurotics has the function of reducing the production of energy in the organism and, hence, of reducing the production of anxiety" (309). Reduced respiration, which in the quotation refers to reduced inhalation ("less oxygen is introduced"), is considered a defense mechanism against anxiety. If respiratory inhibition promises an "overcoming of emotionality altogether, pleasure as well as suffering" (358), the liberation of breath, in turn, is supposed to grant orgiastic bliss while at the same time breaking the protective shield against anxiety. Reich dismissively recalls the "Yoga breathing exercise" with its aim "to combat affective impulses" and "obtain peace" (357). "Eliminating the conditions of anxiety" (359) is unnecessary in the context of Reich's theory, which assumes a well-balanced *economy* of emotions once the "natural energy" is allowed to flow. Kerouac's translation of Reich's claim that "the most important means of freeing the orgasm reflex is a *breathing technique*" (333) into a writing method, and his use of Reichian ideas and terminology in his manifesto, can be described as symptomatic in Reich's terms. In contrast to the "Yogas," Kerouac embraces the liberating flow—but he shares the latter's aim of "eliminating conditions of anxiety." In an attempt to avoid the "state of anxious contraction," the shriveled penis, Kerouac ends up promoting a model of "reduced respiration"—a respiration without inspiration. In his references to Reich in "Essentials," and elsewhere in his writing, Kerouac deliberately makes an analogy between the "prohibitions" imposed on literary language, which uses only a minimum of its "potential power," and "oppressions" of "intimate sexual relations" ("History of the Theory of Breath"). Free-flowing breath, free-flowing language, and free, emancipated sexuality are supposed to go hand in hand. Lacking inspiration however, Kerouac's "liberated" breath turns out to be a closet: the body that does not inhale (which, in Kerouac's poetics also means that it is not penetrated) becomes a suffocating site that is not free of homophobic and misogynist impulses.

Kerouac's complicated relation to inspiration includes one of its figural meanings: literary influence. In the promotion of a spontaneous writing generated from his own body alone, he embraces the idea of a self-made writer or autonomous poetic genius. To an author who claims that he exclusively draws his subject matter from his personal life, attributes his style to his bodily functions and who radicalizes the equation of writing and life in the motto "my art *is* life" ("The Repetoire [*sic*] of Modern Ideas"; emphasis added), is *my* life, the thought that one's creation may go back to a source other than the self poses an existential danger exceeding mere anxiety of influence. In the "Essentials," the fantasy of an autocreation cut from tradition is exposed in the moment when it is most prominently evoked: "tap from yourself the song of yourself, *blow!—now!—your* way is your only way." By mentioning the "song of yourself," Kerouac draws on another voice, a literary predecessor, precisely at the point where autoinspiration and immediacy are claimed. The celebrated "now" of spontaneous creation points back to roughly one hundred years earlier, and the "song of yourself" is tapped from Whitman. Paradoxically, Kerouac seems to disregard external influence in *what* he is saying (*your*—and not Whitman's—way is your only way), while at the same time reproducing Whitman's words.

Kerouac's inspiration anxiety is most intense when it comes to "his" theory of breathing and writing itself. We see this in the way he integrates Reich in his essay. There is, as mentioned, no explicit reference to Reich's extensive discussions of breathing—when reading "Essentials," we do not get the impression that Reich wrote about breath at all. Instead of referring to Reich's climactic "deep exhalation," Kerouac draws a dash—inscribes the mark of his own hand, the so-called trademark of his own genuine style. Even though the dash has been used since the Middle Ages, initially to indicate a "final pause" (Houston 147), Kerouac claims it for himself: "others have tried to imitate it but they don't know how" (*Selected Letters 1957–1969* 324). Given that the dash is supposed to mark the point where a "rhetorical expostulation based on breathing" ends (324), this is a surprising statement, which is somewhat at odds with Kerouac's poetics of individual self-expression. How could Kerouac judge other writers' breathing, and what is there to "know" about the length of an individual's breath? An unpublished essay from 1962, "History of the Theory of Breath as a Separator of Statements in Spontaneous Writing" (notably, the title is immediately followed by the words "By Jack Kerouac"), is revealing in this respect: the accusation that others do not know how to apply Kerouac's theory is tightly linked to the assumption that this theory was taken away from him. Thus, Kerouac anticipates Derrida's observation that "souffler" also refers to stealing and inspiration undermines the idea of one's "own" voice, a voice that is always already stolen. In "History of the Theory of Breath," Kerouac attacks Ginsberg on two bases: the first imputation is that Ginsberg, "like 99.9% of American poets . . . doesn't understand breath and phrasing."[53] Then, he accuses Ginsberg of plagiarism. He juxtaposes sentences from "Essentials," which, as he stresses, was written in 1953, and "Notes Written on Finally Recording Howl," from 1959, to prove that Ginsberg stole his theory. After having shown the parallels between his text and Ginsberg's, Kerouac states: "No mention of my understanding of breath, or the fact that I applied it to my own poetry" and "my prose and my original theory on prose merge with 'his' theory on poetry . . . it's the same theory, cunningly bunted but too late and fouled back." Obviously, there is a tension between Kerouac's assumption that Ginsberg does not understand "breath-measure" and applies it incorrectly, and the claim that "it's the *same* theory." In a handwritten comment, Kerouac adds: "I set this down selfishly for my own sake, almost maliciously, but it's true. Ideas are universal but never universally invented." It is worth noting here that Kerouac denies any influence from Olson, whose "Projective Verse" was written three years earlier than the "Essentials." In the *Paris Review* interview, he stresses: "I formulated the theory of breath as measure, in prose and verse, never mind what Olson, Charles Olson says, I formulated that theory in 1953" ("The Art of Fiction No. 41").

The question of who "invented" the theory of breath-measure was discussed in the first section of the chapter: it undoubtedly goes back to antiquity. We could still ask who it was that rediscovered it in the 1950s in America. However, writing an accurate "History of the Theory of Breath" in the context of the Beat and Black Mountain schools would be impossible: the writers in question all knew, or at least knew of, each other, and many oral exchanges were not recorded. We would have to turn back time and both listen in and ask the writers about who directly influenced whom and who read whom or heard of what—but even in that scenario, we could not be sure which claims to trust. An investigation of the archival and published records available suggests the following genealogy: Charles Olson's "Projective Verse," published in 1950, is the first explicit record of breath-measure as a compositional tool.[54] Olson extensively discussed the idea that breath may be essential for a new formal structuring of poetry in letters to Frances Boldereff and Robert Creeley around the time he wrote "Projective Verse."[55] Chronologically, Kerouac's "Essentials of Spontaneous Prose," written in 1953, is the next text in line. In Kerouac's archive there is no earlier account of breath-measure. Ginsberg's first recorded references to the structural function of breath in poetry appear after he wrote "Howl," in response to questions about the composition of the poem, for example, in his famous letters to Richard Eberhart in 1956 ("lines" as "one speech-breath-thought" unit, *The Letters of Allen Ginsberg* 135) and John Hollander in 1958, and the "Notes on Howl" in 1959.[56]

Ginsberg never ceased to emphasize Kerouac's influence. Given what Ginsberg stressed in the Eberhart letter, it seems redundant that Kerouac felt the need to defend his "invention": "Kerouac invented and initiated my practice of speech-flow prosody" (*The Letters of Allen Ginsberg* 137). The extent to which Ginsberg reinforces Kerouac's self-image becomes especially obvious in a recorded discussion during a poetry class he gave at the University of Wyoming in 1971. When Ginsberg explicates both Olson's "Projective Verse" and Kerouac's "Essentials" in the context of breath-measure, a student asks whether Kerouac was "first." Ginsberg admits that he wasn't. The student then refers to the *Paris Review* interview where Kerouac suggests ignoring what "Olson says" ("The Art of Fiction No. 41"). Ginsberg attempts to mitigate Kerouac's insistence on being the initiator of breath-measure by justifying his desire to stand out: "Yeah, I think [he did claim to have come up with the idea of breath-measure first in the interview]. But he was drunk. That is, Kerouac was bein [sic] sick of bein [sic] lumped as a literary poet together with a bunch of other literary poets working in a 'projective' verse form" (*Allen Verbatim* 163). In the course of his argument, Ginsberg gets entangled in a contradiction that is of extreme significance for the notion of breath-measure. Ginsberg attempts to debunk the critics' claim that "among other people practicing projective verse is Jack Kerouac" by emphasizing that Olson and Kerouac were not "mutually influenced": "I don't think Kerouac even saw that [the "Projective Verse" essay]. Though Kerouac was writing spontaneous poetries around 1950 also. So there was like almost a synchronism—everybody began writing open form" (163). While this argument is designed to save Kerouac's idea of autocreation despite the fact that he was not the inventor of breath-measure, the suggestion that the invention was made by "everybody" simultaneously raises the question of its singularity. How individual can the idea of breath-measure be if "everybody" came up with it in the late 1950s? One could claim that breath-measure is always singular because everyone breathes differently, has a singular breath. But that does not seem to be the only point of the discourse around it. In fact, it is a point that does not even get much attention. In contrast, actual physical breath in its particularity rather seems to be pushed into the background in favor of an *image* or *idea* of breath that becomes synonymous with "open form," spontaneous uninhibited writing and orality. Ginsberg's elaborations above are a good example: he seamlessly moves from "the breath of the poet" to verses "written to be pronounced" (162) and "open form" (163), as if he were using interchangeable terms. This tendency is predominant in most discussions of breath-measure by various authors at the time—regardless of whether the issue at stake was poetry or prose, in written or spoken form.[57] Submerged in this larger image-complex, breath becomes a synonym for the voice and orality, and the word's figural meanings become more dominant than the physiological process designated. The paradox of this process is that the figural meaning evoked designates precisely what breath loses through its metaphorization: individuality and singularity.

I want to conclude this discussion with two different accounts of breath and voice by Kerouac and Amiri Baraka. Kerouac struggled to find a method of writing throughout the 1940s—he made many attempts and abandoned many; none was published or led to a successful text. The extent of self-doubt becomes painfully visible in a comment in the back of a notebook from 1944 where he reflects on his writing:

> I'm filled with great doubt. What's the principle behind all this? Art is not enough? Or I am not enough of an artist? Outcries can't satisfy, tonight. . . . / The new vision, I told Lucien, is in art: of that I was so gloriously certain. Now I don't know. Without art, voyez, I am not able to live. Without art, I am not John Kerouac—I am only Jack the Ripper. I seek *identity*.

It is only in 1950 that Kerouac claims to have found identity by discovering his "own voice." The crucial event was a letter he received from Neal Cassady, written in a way Kerouac then wishes to reproduce. Writing to Ginsberg, he mentions that Cassady's famous "Joan Anderson" letter "was the basis of my idea about prose" (*Selected Letters 1940–1956* 464). Kerouac's immediate reaction to Cassady himself in 1950 highlights the priority of voice—his own voice, to be precise: "Well, since Mexico, I've been trying to find my voice. For a long time it sounded false. . . . My important recent discovery and revelation is that the voice is all. . . . You, man, must write exactly as everything rushes into your head, and AT ONCE" (233).[58] After having written *On the Road* and *The Subterraneans* in Cassady style—or at least in a way that made the novels appear to have been created in a rush, all at once—Kerouac makes another, this time successful attempt at formulating a method of writing. And it is only there, in the "Essentials," that breath becomes part of the vocabulary Kerouac uses to talk about writing, as an extension of the metaphor of the "own voice." While the talk about "my voice" was still closely linked to the "voice" that inspired him—Cassady's—"my theory of breath" is the accomplishment Kerouac fully claims for himself.

A quite different conjunction of breath and voice is described by Amiri Baraka, who, then known as LeRoi Jones, was very actively involved in the Beat and Black Mountain movement and first published Olson's "Projective Verse." In 1960, he describes his writing style in line with the theory of breath-measure that "everybody" employed—notably, breath and voice are used synonymously:

> I'm certain that a great deal of my natural voice rhythm dominates the line. For instance, my breathing—when I have to stop to inhale or exhale—dictates where I have to break the line in most cases. . . . Mostly it's the *rhythms* of speech that I utilize, trying to get closer to the way I sound *peculiarly*, as opposed to somebody else. (*Conversations with Amiri Baraka* 7)

After 1965, when he distanced himself from the Beat and Black Mountain poets, it seems as if Baraka noticed that the theory of the breath-stop was precisely what did not make his writing sound peculiar, "as opposed to someone else," but, on the contrary, inscribed his black voice in a white discourse.[59] As he claims, "at that time, for me to say ['This is what I am saying'] . . . would have come out as Creeley-Olson" (108). When he describes his emancipation from "people whose work I was around, people like Charles Olson and Allen Ginsberg" (101), he again refers to his "own voice": "What I was doing was trying to break away from European influences and the strong influences of many white poets who had affected my work" (92). "I was trying to find a voice, my own, and I needed to oppose myself to the European influence" (93). From that point on, breath, in contrast to voice, is no longer highlighted by Baraka.[60] "Breaking away from white forms" (92) may have implied breaking away from a specific idea of breath-measure, which, with its root in Greek and Roman antiquity is a "European form" (93). Baraka thus decouples a particular way of thinking about breath and writing from the more general idea of "voice," as a way to address his emancipation. As Baraka claims, "it began to be my own kind of *sound*, my own voice" in his 1965 novel *System of Dante's Hell* (*Conversations with Amiri Baraka* 108): "Now, Creeley, Olson, et al. were themselves post-bourgeois/academic poets, and that was valuable for me. But they were also, in some ways, an *extension* of Western art, and so I tried to get away from them in *System*" (110). For Kerouac, integrating breath into his theory about writing brings the development of his "own" voice to completion. In contrast, when Baraka describes the emergence of his own authentic black voice, breath leaves his vocabulary along with the "*extension* of Western art" (110).

"Scored in Broken Breaths": Ginsberg's "Power" of Inspirational Weakness

While the question of one's *own* voice is central to Kerouac's poetics of breath, which consequently eludes notions of inspiration, Ginsberg came up with an idiosyncratic theory of inspiration that focuses on how other voices penetrate one's own body in the early 1980s. Developed rather spontaneously in the course of a lecture in 1980, this theory remains fragmentary, although it represents a decisive expansion of his previous thoughts on breath, not least because it strongly focuses on reception rather than composition, especially on reading poems out loud. The starting point is his old suggestion to take inspiration literally: "spirit means breathing—'*spiritus*'—Latin—breathing—inspiration means breathing" (*Expansive Poetics*).[61] The basic idea is that "the breath of the poet ideally is reproduced by the breathing of the reader" (*Allen Verbatim* 162). Ginsberg is expanding here on thoughts that had already been formulated by Olson and Kerouac, which he reinterprets in terms of breath: "A poem is energy transferred from where the poet got it (he will have some several causations), by way of the poem itself to, all the way over to, the reader" (Olson, "Projective Verse" 16).[62] "Blow as deep as you want—write as deeply, fish as far down as you want, satisfy yourself first, then reader cannot fail to receive telepathic shock and meaning-excitement by same laws operating in his own human mind" (Kerouac, "Essentials of Spontaneous Prose" 57). Reading a poem out loud—Ginsberg's favorite example is Shelley's "Ode to the West Wind"—is supposed to "reproduce within our bodies this [i.e., the author's] experience of inspiration" (*Expansive Poetics*). For Ginsberg, what inspiration creates is not a new work of literature, but rather the perpetuation of an existing one. By "transmitting the same breath from the poet to the reader," the poem that is read endures over time: "the poet makes a little machine which you can then insert in the body of a reader hundreds of years later; and if he breathes according to the instructions of the commas . . . , he can then reduplicate that very same delicate breath" ("Basic Poetics #15").

Some details of this theory are questionable: it has already been discussed that punctuation marks and actual breath during composition hardly coincide, and materially, poet and reader clearly do not share the "same" breath.[63] It is nevertheless worthwhile to look further into Ginsberg's notion of inspirational transmission. How can the "little machine" be understood, and what precisely in a poem is it that enables "transferrable breath"? Commenting on "Ode to the West Wind," Ginsberg makes a suggestion: what endures is "cadence" or "rhythm."

> Once he's [Shelley] created this rhythm it's going to be heard forever, people are going to recognize it. . . . And that, in this way, his very breath, the cadences of his breath, or the sequences of his breathing, is going to become historically immortal. So Shelley's own body, or a piece of Shelley's body, is going out into the world to persist in other people's bodies. So he created a machine which, when introduced into our bodies, will recreate itself over and over again. . . . So he's really projected a piece of his body out permanently. (*Expansive Poetics*)

The idea presented is not one of a *pneuma*-like substance that remains over time. Neither are the printed words as such considered the "permanent" aspect of a poem. Rather, Ginsberg outlines a transactual process: a *rhythm*, created by a human being, a human body that breathes rhythmically, is externalized, inscribed in the poem (a "piece" of Shelley's body is going out into the world) and via written words becomes retrievable by human bodies that live later. The rhythm can be "re-created" when it is "introduced into our bodies." What Ginsberg describes as an "immortal," homogenous breath shared by author and reader, is based on cuts and ruptures on various levels: the "same" breath that unites is generated through "measured verse" ("Basic Poetics #15"), that is, breath divided into sequences; it also presumes a body shattered to pieces that detach, disseminate, and transubstantiate. Moreover, the transferability of breath, which, according to Ginsberg, makes it lasting, is reliant on a transferability of the *word* or *concept* of breath to heterogeneous domains: the body and prosody, the literal and figural breath-measures. By claiming that Shelley "project[s] a piece of his body out permanently," Ginsberg projects his own theory of breath-writing onto Shelley—he seems to take it for granted that Shelley structured his poetry according to breath-measure without investigating Shelley's writing practices. And he projects Olson's terminology and his own interpretation of Olson's "Projective Verse" onto Shelley. What Ginsberg claims about Shelley, that he "unloosens the body, unleashed the breath" ("Basic Poetics #15"), also pertains to the way his own theory works. Identified with rhythm, breath wanders across conceptual domains, is moved across bodies torn from their biological rootedness: via breath-writing (whether literally or figuratively), the poet's human body is transferred to the poem, a "part" of it detaches itself through the writing, becomes machine, and then again enters human bodies; breath-rhythm moves between the individual (the particular body of writer and reader) and universal (the "rhythm . . . people are going to . . . recognize"). Concerning the latter, Ginsberg mentions an "archetypal basic rhythm relating to the human body that . . . becomes permanently a part of the physiology of the race or the memory of the race or touches on some basic breathing rhythm of the race so that it can outlast the more fragile metallic construction of buildings, pyramids" ("Basic Poetics #14"). If we take a look at how Ginsberg developed his theory, which can be nicely traced in tape recordings and transcriptions of two lectures he gave at the Naropa Institute in 1980, we can observe how a respiratory vocabulary is unleashed hand in hand with a respirational bodily experience.

One of the basic triggers for Ginsberg's reflection on inspiration as a phenomenon of reception that makes literature durable was his discussion of "As You Came from the Holy Land," a sixteenth-century poem attributed to Sir Walter Raleigh. Ginsberg's classes often consisted of reading poems aloud with his students, discussing them, and adding his own comments. He starts his class on February 28 by recounting how he tried to figure out the proper rhythm of "As You Came from the Holy Land" in preparation for the session the night before. "At 3 am" it finally "became a solid sound sculpture" when he found an appropriate way of pronouncing it. In the process of repeatedly reading the poem out loud, in search of its proper rhythm, the printed words turned into an "air" or "breath sculpture" (Basic Poetics #14); the convincing articulation of words that "ride out on the breath" ("Basic Poetics #15") obviously had an effect on Ginsberg: something was triggered by the visceral experience of reading. When he presents the poem in class, he keeps coming back to a passage that he calls a "pretty thing," and that, as we can hear on the recording, always makes him chuckle with delight as he reads it:

> As ye came from the holy land
>   Of Walsinghame,
> Met you not with my true love
>   By the way as you came?
>   (qtd. in Zukofsky 68)

The poem is structured according to the ballad stanza, but its rhythm is irregular, deviating from the traditional alternation of four- and three-stress lines. Ginsberg's revelation is reading the last line as an anapest with a caesura in the middle of the line: "by the *way* | as you *came*." Implementing the "little caesura" ("Basic Poetics #15") remodulates the breath into a "funny rhythmic continuum" and an "archetypal rhythm," which is "almost like a waltz" ("Basic Poetics #14"), is revealed in the act of reading. During the instance of pronunciation, the specific molding of the air in the phonetic apparatus and the way the words sound when they come out of the mouth incites an immediate, almost involuntary reaction (of recognition and almost childlike delight), the trace of which can be heard on tape in Ginsberg's repeated chuckle.

After sharing his pleasurable finding, Ginsberg mentions that he read the poem from his edition of Louis Zukofsky's *A Test of Poetry*, an annotated anthology of poetry that became a popular reference book in postwar America. He then goes on by commenting on the anthology, which juxtaposes poetry across various literary periods, "to show the continuum through millennia of a certain rhythm" ("Basic Poetics #14"), and discusses a few of Zukofsky's own comments by flipping through the book, including the motto, "Condensation is more than half of composition. The rest is proper breathing space" (81). After that, Ginsberg continues the class by reading various poems. In Samuel Daniel's "Let Others Sing of Knights and Paladins," he stumbles on the line "authentic shall my verse in time to come," which reminds him of similar prophesies about the durability of poetry: Shakespeare's "Sonnet 65" ("in black ink my love may still shine bright"), Shelley's "Ode to the West Wind" ("scatter . . . my words among mankind") and his own "Plutonian Ode" ("My breath near deathless ever at your side"). These prophecies "of the immortality of the verse or the poet's spirit" encourage him to bring in his idea that inspiration is breath, which then leads to a first formulation of the theory summarized previously, including a further reference to a comment in Zukofsky's *A Test of Poetry*:

> so that if someone took the poem or line, or set of lines, and then repeated it in their own bodies, "as you came by the way," a certain delicacy lightness and delicacy of emotion, or opening, or feeling, or relationship, "as you came by the way," is reproduced by the body that reproduces the lines and so it catalyzes the same emotions. . . . Zukofsky says "objectified emotion endures," not just emotion but emotion when it's put into an object, when it is objectified on the outside in a rhythm, I guess. When the emotion is objectified outside as a rhythm. . . . I haven't thought all this out before it has just been occurring to me like a further extension of thoughts that I had before, somewhat catalyzed by . . . digging the "as ye came from the holy land of Willingham": realizing how that particular rhythm is endured from the 16th century to now and is still available; if you pay close attention to the words you can still figure out that precise delicate or some variety of that precise delicate very real measure of the breath and the measure of feeling. ("Basic Poetics #14")

What he will later repeat as a theory of inspiration and "immortal breath" came to be as "words rid[ing] out on the breath" ("Basic Poetics #15") in two senses: the reflection was initiated by Ginsberg's pronunciation of the ballad line on his breath. In a moment when this respiratory articulation produced a particular affecting rhythm, the inspirational spark triggered a theory of inspiration sourced in the mouth, in the act of speaking and breathing. In the course of the class, Ginsberg then lets his words "ride out on the breath," get loose in a chain of associations provoked by various, mostly random instances: he ties his bodily reading experience to the word "breathing," which comes up accidentally in the book he read the poem from (in Zukofsky's sentence, "Condensation is more than half of composition. The rest is proper breathing space"), then integrates it into his previous compositional theories about breath, his conjunction of inspiration and respiration, and finally adds a further idea of Zukofsky's ("objectified emotion endures") when he, again, accidentally, comes across Daniel's prophetic line, "authentic shall my verse in time to come."

Ginsberg's idea of an inspiration that grants poetry a transactual quality presupposes the interaction and interdependence of bodies that radically open up—inspiration requires "unlock[ing] the doors of the body for the wind to blow through." The author's body "unloosens" and "vanishes into the air" ("Basic Poetics #15") to then slumber in a poem in the form of a rhythm that can be reactivated by a reader's body. The "opening" of both parts implies a physical transformation. The author's body is shattered to pieces that almost dematerialize, and, as Ginsberg stresses, reading a poem rhythmically "actually will alter your metabolism":

> it'll alter your breathing and you'll get high. In other words, for instance, if you pronounce some of *my* poetry aloud, or of you pronounce Hart Crane's "Atlantis" aloud, or of you pronounce Poe's "Bells" or "The Raven" aloud, or Shelley's "Ode to the West Wind," or some passages of Dante aloud, doing the right breathing, you can get high—the breathing—like the lines are built to get you high. It's like taking a pill. ("Buddhism and Breathing")

Ginsberg repeatedly stresses that "Ode to the West Wind"—which he assumes to be "scored in broken breaths" (*Allen Verbatim* 162)—"scheduled the breathing so that you hyperventilate" ("Basic Poetics #15"). Even though the effects are described in positive terms, his reference to the biologically accurate fact that changing the way you breathe has immediate effects on your body implies that reading out loud involves a physical intrusion. It implies exposing your body to a breathing rhythm dictated from outside.

In a lecture given in Belgrade in October 1980, which has been neglected in Ginsberg scholarship and is not included in any collection of his works,[64] Ginsberg expands on the thought that we expose our body to the outside when we breathe. Stressing the vulnerability of the respiring organism, the reflections in *Power and Weakness of Poetry* give Ginsberg's theory of "immortal breath" a new twist. He starts the speech by reproducing the breath-inspiration equation, stressing what might have struck one as an air of grandeur accompanying his idea of "immortal breath": "Power of poetry is in breath we breathe: breath is in english from latin spiritus or in-'spiration.' So power is breath." He then adds a further, contrary aspect to the equation: "weakness is: human breathing with lungs." The "weakness" implied by a breathing body exposed to the outside is analogized with an individual's exposure to state violence: "So the body of poet is vulnerable, open. Open to invasion of police, of torture, of intimidation." Ginsberg situates the vulnerability of the respiring body in various domains: "the poet is defenseless. . . . Defenseless against illness, defenseless against the wars of the world, and defenseless against death and the destruction of his ambition, and fixation, and obsession." It is at this point that Ginsberg makes the first argumentative step in resolving the seeming contradiction of "breath is power and breath is weakness":

> This weakness *is* intelligence because the poet is open to messages from outside, including pain. . . . So poet is sensitive to intelligence coming to him from outside, from outside his own ego. He hears something else outside his own self—this is different from power of the state or nation, and also different from the monolithic chauvinism . . . of the human species itself, which in our century has destroyed many species of sentient beings.

In Ginsberg's interpretation, intelligence means "taking in": the vulnerable, breathing body is helplessly exposed to the outside and also necessarily absorbs it. This is what opposes the inspired one to a "monolithic chauvinism" that indulges in a myth of self-sufficiency, repels the outside and reacts to it with violence and destruction. For Ginsberg, openness and vulnerability enable a respirational poetic resistance: the body that takes in also "sends out."

> So the poet's weakness is his power which he sends on the sound vibrations of his breath. All he needs is his own "soft machine," his own body, to broadcast. . . . As the poet Sappho twenty six hundred years ago broadcast cadences, rhythms, which continue for millennia. . . . Breath-rhythm has longer life than the civilization that surrounded her. . . . So, Jean Arthur Rimbaud, William Blake, Walt Whitman, have voices that last longer than their police, than their state, their culture, and their own egos. . . . In that sense the poet's weakness, his openness, is his power.

Ginsberg's idea of a poetic, respirational counterpower is more hopeful than heroic. The "immortal breath" is far from hubris: it is not a means for poets to overcome mortality through their work or fame. That "an airy breath, just an empty airy breath measured properly . . . will outlast the Empire State Building, giant battleships" ("Basic Poetics #15") and "metallic construction of buildings, pyramids, sphinxes, bombs, Plutonium" ("Basic Poetics #14") does not imply that this breath exceeds the things listed by superior strength or potency. On the contrary, the "soft machine" functions according to an opposite logic to symbols of power and thus resists the "civilization that surrounded" it. Nowhere does Ginsberg's poetics of breathing diverge more radically from Kerouac's than in these later thoughts on inspiration. The presupposed breathing and writing body could not be more different: Kerouac's virile, healthy, phallic creator sealed from the outside and Ginsberg's open, vulnerable one, which is "defenseless against illness" and alternates between receiving[65] and pouring out. When Ginsberg outlines the sketch of a respirational writer who "is sensitive" to forces "outside his own ego" and defenseless against "the destruction of his ambition," he counteracts an image with which Kerouac flirted: the "monolithic chauvinism" of a self-made genius.

A Silent Propellant: Charles Olson

"Projective Verse" has been a continual background presence in this chapter and its influence on the authors discussed is undeniable. It would be wrong, however, to assume that Olson's poetics of breathing is equivalent to either Kerouac's or Ginsberg's. The critical perspectives of an embodied respirational poetics and its "hyper-masculinist" implications (Mossin 22) that I have presented in my readings of Kerouac and Ginsberg could be extended to Olson.[66] What I want to do in the final part of the chapter, however, is to offer a different view, one that takes into account aspects of Olson's poetics that complicate the relations between a respirational human body and the literary work in progress as Kerouac and Ginsberg theorize it. Olson's respirational poetics is more fragmented and dispersed than Ginsberg's and Kerouac's. Whereas Kerouac's reflections on "blowing" are basically limited to one text, "Essentials," and its recapitulation in other writings and Ginsberg was eager to come up with coherent conceptualizations of breathing with regard to composition and reading out loud, Olson's remarks on breath are quite unsystematically scattered across his published and unpublished writings. From 1946 onward breath keeps appearing, disappearing, and reappearing in Olson's attempts to sketch a new poetics, whether in the context of accomplished texts or scribbled notes. The numerous instances where breath enters Olson's oeuvre cannot be boiled down to a consistent theory. His respiratory references, sometimes inserted in essays, sometimes occurring as loose notes, are richly suggestive—"that valley of the breath, the lungs, that exit of it the throat"

("The Cave"), "I need not add the pressure of death, when one practices a trade of the breath like verse" (*Charles Olson and Frances Boldereff* 203), "all the conditions atoms and breath can create by act and multiplication" ("Mouths Biting Empty Air")—and not seldom contradictory: "sound-breath particles" (Pun as the True Meaning as Well as of Rhyme), "the muscle that speech takes, . . . breath" ("II/A Long Time to Fill the Wells"), "breath allows *all* the speech-force of language back in" ("Projective Verse" 20), "voice (as of vowels) as distinguished from breath (as of f, s, sh etc.)" ("Notes on Language"), "BREATH (as not sound)" ("Notes on Language"), "The language is not speech alone / but *ear* / And breath" ("Quantity in Verse and Shakespeare's Late Work"). These tensions cannot be resolved—having a closer look at the draft versions of "Projective Verse," however, shows that respiratory tensions are precisely what distinguishes Olson's poetics from Kerouac's and Ginsberg's phonocentric embrace of breath.

What was ultimately published as "Projective Verse" can be traced to a rather large corpus of drafts: a first version, which Olson shared with Frances Boldereff and Robert Creeley in letters, was written in February 1950.[67] According to what Olson writes to Boldereff, he performed some major revisions in early July after the essay came back from *Poetry NY* and the editor was "hen-shit about it, asking rewrite" (*Charles Olson and Frances Boldereff* 395).[68] Apart from the first draft and two later versions that are much closer to the printed one (presumably the revisions done in July), the archive at the University of Connecticut contains multiple attempts at the essay's opening, which were probably written after the first version and before the longer revised drafts. The final version is the result of a process of adding and deleting, stitching together and moving around material from the early drafts as well as citations from other texts. While the resulting fragmentary character of the essay goes hand in hand with Olson's resistance to argumentative logic and clear categorization, some passages in the early versions in which he more explicitly elucidates his starting points are revealing for the role breath plays in the context of projective verse. From these earlier versions, it becomes quite clear that for Olson, the implications of composition and its relation to orality are substantially different from what Ginsberg and Kerouac have in mind when they address the writing process.[69] In the very first draft, Olson explains that the choice of the name "projective verse" allows him to distance himself from certain notions of the "aural" and "oral": "Why the tag 'projective'? (1) 'Aural' won't do, for any verse worth the name is aural; (2) 'oral' is merely the mouthing of speech, has to do with 'rhetoric' at its worst and, at its best, does not hint at the larger physiology of speech" ("Projective Verse: Early Drafts" February–July 1950). Without reducing the importance of the ear and mouth, the "larger physiology of speech" seems to imply a *connection between* the two that exceeds the act of delivering spoken words through the mouth or receiving them by ear. In one of the attempted openings to the essay, Olson writes:

> Projective verse is that verse which, by a shift of the base of poetics, acknowledges that verse comes from speech and goes, after its making, in the direction of speech. This is not, it is necessary to say, a matter of recitation. It as a matter, rather, of a recognition on the part of a the [sic] poet of the role that the voice plays as a silent propellant in composition itself. ("Projective Verse: Early Drafts")

Thus, projective verse designates a *direction toward* speech, toward the ear and the mouth; "speech force" is not understood as actualized speech. The widely discussed "*kinetics*," "energy," or "force" ("Projective Verse," e.g., 16, 20) of projective verse, what drives composition, is described as a "*silent* propellant" (emphasis added). Here it is important to draw attention to a shift of terms in the course of the drafts: in the later versions, "breath" frequently replaces "voice."[70] The famous "laws and possibilities of the breath" (15) and "pressures of" the poet's "breath" (17) were originally "laws" and "pressures" of the "voice" ("Projective Verse: Early Drafts").[71] In contrast to the conflation of terms discussed earlier in the chapter in examining discourses in which breath and voice are used as synonyms to address orality in general, Olson's exchange of the terms in the opening of "Projective Verse" is an attempt to be more precise and concise. In the printed version, the many passages where Olson discusses his choice of "projective verse" as an alternative for "oral" and "aural" and the implications of composition's "silent propellant" are condensed in the statement, "Verse now, if it is to be of *essential* use, must catch up and put into itself certain laws and possibilities of the breath, of the breathing of the man who writes as well as of his listenings" (15). A passage that anticipates the transition from the paradox of a silent voice toward breath is (probably) the latest version of the opening, before the revisions of the whole text.[72] There, the first sentence still contains the "advantages of the human voice which are still neglected." These advantages are then elucidated as follows: "a recognition on the part of the poet of the role that the voice plays as a silent propellant in composition itself. What I am suggesting is, that we need a more conscious and deliberate admission of the part that a poeT's [*sic*] own breathing takes in his work as well as his hearing" ("Projective Verse: Early Drafts"). In Olson's poetics, there are two major reasons why the implications of "voice as a silent propellant" can be encapsulated in the single word "breath."

First, Olson stresses the *silence* of breath in his discussions of prosody: "BREATH (as not sound [*sic*])" ("Notes on Language") is negotiated in terms of percussion and beat. In unpublished notes for his essay on quantity in Shakespeare's late plays, Olson gives a very precise definition of what he means by breath with respect to prosody:[73]

> It would actually be quite possible to graph prosody: quantity would lie out on a horizontal, accent on the vertical, and breath be the "spaces" or "rests" cutting across both, "stoppings" of the forward and the rising-falling motions of the words. The breath of prosody is, indeed, the silences or interruptions of sound as quantity is the voicing of them and accent the explosion of then, the force of the utterance. (*Shakespeare Essays: Notes and Fragments*)

I want to highlight three points: first, Olson writes about the "the breath of prosody" here, implying that language itself has a respirational rhythm. Hand in hand with this, "Projective Verse" addresses the breath of a poem's line: "the line *its* metric and its ending—where *its* breathing, shall come to, termination"—the possessive pronoun here tends to be overlooked because the sentence starts with: "And the line comes (I swear it) from the breath, from the breathing of the man who writes" (19; emphasis added). The *shift* from the writer's to the line's breath is barely noticed in Olson's critical reception. However, it is precisely in this transformation of breath where Olson performatively stages what is most central in his poetics, the "*kinetics* of the thing" ("Projective Verse" 16). Second: in a scenario of oral pronunciation, what Olson designates as breath here would be a short, almost silent moment, when only respiration can be heard. There is no indication that this has anything to do with the breath-pause of the person who speaks. In contrast to Ginsberg and Kerouac, Olson never mentions a coincidence of breath-unit and sense-unit.[74] Referencing Shakespeare, Olson speaks of a *breath in writing*—a breath that is not necessarily in accordance with a human's physiological respiration. One could argue that Olson thus merely uses breath as a technical term for the pause. However, the interstices produced by what is designated as breath introduces a rhythmical organization—a movement that is not dissimilar to human breathing. Third:

breath is described as what happens *between* the vertical and horizontal axes of prosody, what "cuts across" accent and quantity, what interrupts sound and thus constitutes rhythm. In other words, Olson sketches a movement of syncopnea. When he mentions the importance of the "breath of the man who writes" in "Projective Verse," these points should be taken into consideration. In particular, the "silence" that breath implies for Olson and his suggestion that breath is related to, but not identical with, speaking aloud can easily escape notice in the final version of "Projective Verse." The only explicit hint at silent voicing remaining in the published text is the statement that the spaces a poet notates with the typewriter "indicate how he would want any reader, silently or otherwise, to voice his work" (22).[75] Compared to earlier versions, the silent propellant—which, I argue, is condensed in the word "breath"—has indeed become inconspicuous.

Second, breath functions as a *propellant* when Olson describes it as something that acts projectively. The most explicit articulation of this was formulated long after "Projective Verse," in 1958: "It is from the breath that speech comes" ("II/A Long Time to Fill the Wells"). In "Projective Verse," the comments gesturing in this direction are quite conflicting: the projective poet will reach "down through the workings of his own throat, to that place where the breath comes from . . . , where the coincidence is [or, as the first draft puts it: "coincidentally"], all act springs" (26). That the origin of breath is located in a specific body part here shows that Olson is not always fully consistent when he grapples with ways of describing the space where "all act springs" as projective: strictly speaking, the notion of the projective as such precludes the specification of a fixed place of origin (i.e., "the throat," or, as other passages suggest, breath):[76] to do so would be analogous to opening the box in which Schrödinger's cat lingers in a state of indeterminacy. Projective verse implies a direction toward points in space and time that are suspended as fixed points precisely because they lie either ahead or beyond in the projective moment as such—as soon as they were "reached," we could no longer speak of them in terms of the projective. This makes plausible Olson's rejection of "oral" and "aural" as tags and preference for the term "projective verse," which reflects a literature that "comes from" and "goes" in "the direction of speech." Before coming back to this passage and the possible implications of "coincidence" in composition, we will see that breath is associated with the place where "all act springs." That this "place" is necessarily suspended in the context of projective poetry has consequences for the question of where and how the "breathing of the man who writes" can be situated.

It is precisely in this respect that Olson's poetics of breath differs most prominently from Kerouac's and Ginsberg's approaches, in which the writer's body is considered a cause for a straightforward transference of human breath to words. The predominance of phrases like "the breathing of the man who writes" in the final version of "Projective Verse" has, not surprisingly, invited readers to interpret Olson's poetics in exactly this way. Such readings, however, do not take into account other claims Olson makes about projective verse. I have already tried to show that breath rather indicates a directional movement (toward hearing and speaking, for example) than a cause in the sense of a singular, fixed point of origin or destination. There are numerous passages in "Projective Verse" that sketch a radically *processual* scenario of composition.

> The objects which occur at every given moment of composition (of recognition, we can call it) are, can be, must be treated exactly as they occur therein and not by any ideas or preconceptions from outside the poem, must be handled as a series of objects in field in such a way that a series of tensions (which they also are) are made to *hold*, and to hold exactly inside the content and the context of the poem which has forced itself, through the poet and them, into being. / Because breath allows *all* the speech-force of language back in. (20)

In the moment of composition, a moment when projective verse takes place, *everything* becomes cause: "objects which occur at every given moment of composition" (including elements of the author's body and the poem under hand) become a "series of tensions," in which there is no temporal or spatial precedence: "all act springs" "where the coincidence is," namely, the coincidence of all objects/tensions involved: this is what "field composition" implies. What seems like a loosely inserted sentence, "Because breath allows *all* the speech force of language back in," makes perfect sense here if we read it as the silent propellant at work when things come together (coincide) in the field of composition, namely, literally in the act of putting together. Olson stresses that mobility, energy, or force "happen[] *between* things" (*Selected Letters* 141).[77] In a letter to Robert Creeley, he explicitly links such a movement "between things" to rhythm and breath:

> And so much the fact of rhythm, that, in speech is silence which is the interstice, the space. . . . Or what we call the breath, the breathing, there—the taking of breath, like they say, how, this is allowing in the factor which the word silence is altogether inadequate to characterize, it is so fat and moving a thing, even

though it only shows the top of its head in speech. (*Charles Olson & Robert Creeley: The Complete Correspondence* 10: 107)

What "only shows the top of its head in speech" is at work during composition, when the "poem" "creates its own" "form" (*The Principle of Measure in Composition by Field: Projective Verse II* 17),[78] when "form literally is born in writing" (*Form, no more than means, is caused*), when rhythm in the pre-Socratic sense of "the form in the instant it is assumed by what is moving, mobile and fluid, the form of that which does not have organic consistency" (Benveniste 285) occurs, when elements "strike against and pile up one upon the other, or go and stay apart, or fuse and cease to be themselves, any and all the conditions atoms and breath can create by act and multiplication" ("Mouths Biting Empty Air"). The latter quote is taken from a very early text, "Mouths Biting Empty Air," written in 1956, which Olson integrates in "Projective Verse": a major part of the discussion of syllables ("Projective Verse" 18) is copied word by word from it.[79] The comments on breath in "Mouths Biting Empty Air" show that, for Olson, a respirational act of creation is not a one-to-one translation: the items that "strike against," "pile one upon the other" or "fuse" in this process "*cease to be themselves.*"[80] This implies that "the breath of the man who writes," the breath in the moment of writing, does not coincide with a respirational movement independent from or preceding this moment. What Olson has in mind neither amounts to adapting writing to human respiration, nor to adapting breath to a given rhythm of language.

In this respect, it is important to note that Olson stresses both the particularity of human breathing patterns and the rhythm of specific languages:[81] in a draft for "Projective Verse," he mentions "the rhythms . . . personal to the composer" ("Projective Verse: Early Draft"), which is later replaced by the "breathing of the man who writes," and in an unpublished essay from the mid-1950s he defines rhythm as follows: "rhythm is surely what meter measures, but it measures what the language does by its own nature; and (2), what the particular man's language does" ("A New Short Ars Poetica"). That language itself is rhythmically structured and specific languages have their particular rhythmic patterns is stressed in a passage from Edward Sapir's book *Language: An Introduction to the Study of Speech*, which Olson quotes repeatedly:[82] "Since every language has its distinctive peculiarities, the innate formal limitations—and possibilities—of one literature are never quite the same as those of another" (237). For Sapir, this has consequences for the production of literature: even though he claims that "[a]rt is so personal an expression that we do not like to feel that it is bound to predetermined form of any sort" (236), the fact that different languages have different "rhythmic systems" (246)[83] means that there is "some limitation . . . to this freedom, some resistance of the medium" (236). The "obedience" ("Projective Verse" 18) of the poet to prosodic elements of language which Olson repeatedly highlights[84] implies taking account of both the inherent rhythms of language as well as the writer's own breath. This obedience, however, does not refer to a rhythmical pattern occurring before the composition (in the human body, or in the words of the given language), but to what happens in the instant these two preexisting rhythms meet in the moment of writing: "That's rhythm, when he [the writer] writes the thing. He is merely obeying like an animal does" ("Form, No More Than Means, Is Caused"). The writer obeys by drawing all attention to the clash of his or her own breath and the prosodic particularities of the words at hand, by recording and "declaring" how "the shaping takes place, each moment of the going" ("Projective Verse" 19). In this way, "a poet stays in the poem, and goes by breath, not by inherited form" (388).[85] When Olson mentions that "BREATH" implies "hammering out the INform" (*Charles Olson & Robert Creeley: The Complete Correspondence* 1: 50) this involves "the necessity on a man today to use hinself [sic] as an instrument in whih [sic] the larger physiology of the human voice is as existential to his work as the physiology of the ear" ("Projective Verse: Early Drafts"). In the process of composition, the writer's body is changed: it becomes an instrument of writing, instrumentalized for the poem, while the language of the poem turns into a body that hosts the "man who writes." In this sense, the larger physiology of speech, which as "sub-sonic or meta-speech" contains "voice/breath . . . elements" (*Quantity in Verse and Shakespeare's Late Work*), involves a conjunction of the breath of language and breath of the human who writes, a movement in which breath is "cutting across both." Projective verse can be considered, to think with Agamben, a "form-of-life" where the use of bodies "modulates itself in a rhythm" (*The Use of Bodies* 173). From this perspective, the "zone of indifference between one's own body and the body of another" (22), the body of language, is "discontinuous" and implies "a state of *imbalance* or asymmetry." "In other words it [the poem] can only be *alive* if it is *out* of the balance it is seeking to reach" (Olson, "Verse [notes]").[86]

3

Generative Caesurae

Mediality, Rhythm, Affect
(Robert Musil, Virginia Woolf)

Charles Olson's reflections on breathing reveal a certain continuity between the disparate literary climates of postwar America and European modernism: despite all "*imbalance* or asymmetry," Olson's notion of breath as a "silent propellant" of writing leads right to the heart of the three critical respiratory scenes in this chapter, from Robert Musil's "Atemzüge eines Sommertags" ("Breaths of a Summer's Day"), Virginia Woolf's short story "The Lady in the Looking-Glass: A Reflection," and the middle part of Woolf's novel *To the Lighthouse*. All three texts concern *intervals*: moments when the narrative pauses or ceases, becomes still—empty spaces filled by breath, which comes to have a constitutive function in each of them.

Until his death in 1942, Robert Musil continually returned to work on a text titled "Breaths of a Summer's Day." Like the entire epochal novel *The Man without Qualities*, the planned chapter remained a fragment even though a clean copy of the draft exists. The major part of the chapter is dedicated to a conversation between the novel's protagonist, Ulrich, and his sister Agathe. Not unrelated to the erotic tension between the two, the conversation pivots on what Ulrich designates as two ways of being passionate, "the appetitive, and, as its counterpart, the nonappetitive" (1331). What subliminally accompanies the discussion of these concepts and triggered it in the first place is a scene Agathe and Ulrich observe in silence—a stream of blossoms carried by a "breath" (1327): "the conversation—which had issued from a dream of nature, the sight of the parade of blossoms that still seemed to be drifting through the middle of their minds with a peculiar uneventfulness—... was under the influence of this idea and dominated by the surreptitious notion of a "happening without anything happening" (1332). In the last version of the draft, the passage recounting "the parade of blossoms" is placed at the very beginning of the chapter. The few sentences preceding the description of the wind-carried blossoms indicate that the "natural spectacle" is happening in a temporal gap or interval: "The sun, *meanwhile*, had risen higher.... Not even the cessation of the conversation had accomplished this ["change" of the "circumstances" entering the siblings' "consciousness"]; it was *left hanging*, without a trace of rift" (1327; emphasis added). In this moment no event takes place, and thus no content can be narrated. The words involved in the "happening" of this narrative standstill are the following:

> A noiseless, streaming snowfall of lusterless blossoms, emanating from a group of trees whose flowering was done, hovered through the sunshine, and the breath that bore it was so gentle that no leaf stirred. (1327)

> Ein geräuschloser Strom glanzlosen Blütenschnees schwebte, von einer abgeblühten Baumgruppe kommend, durch den Sonnenschein; und der Atem, der ihn trug, war so sanft, daß sich kein Blatt regte. (*Der Mann ohne Eigenschaften* 1232)

Breath appears in a strikingly similar way in two passages by Virginia Woolf. "The Lady in the Looking-Glass" begins after Isabella Tyson, who will become the main character of the text, has left her house. The focus from the beginning is on the "happenings without anything happening" in the deserted room she has left behind. Marked by the same word used in the English translation of Musil's chapter, a liminal state is described: "*Meanwhile*, since all the doors and windows were open in the heat, there was a perpetual sighing and ceasing sound, the voice of the transient and the perishing, it seemed, coming and going like human breath, while in the looking-glass things had ceased to breathe and lay still in the trance of immortality" (63–64; emphasis added). "Time Passes," the middle section of *To the Lighthouse*, which is conceived of as an interval between the preceding and following part of the novel where the narrative content is reduced to a minimum, also centers on an abandoned house. As Jacques Rancière stresses, "The only characters playing in the house are little airs" (103). "Time Passes" moves the novel's plot into square brackets, focusing on the "events of that impersonal life of airs" (103): "airs that breathe" (*To the Lighthouse* 138) or "clammy breaths" (150), "detached from the body of the wind" (138). "So with the house empty and the doors locked and the mattresses rolled round, those stray airs, advance guards of great armies, blustered in, brushed bare boards, nibbled and fanned, met nothing in bedroom or drawing-room that wholly resisted them" (140). In a different context yet conceptually in line with these breath-infused narrative pauses, Andreas Gelhard, Ulf Schmidt, and Tanja Schultz theorize the notion of "standstill" in respiratory terms: the suspension of immobilizing/standing still corresponds to an active-passive breathturn, the silent caesura between inhaling and exhaling." They argue that "the notion of 'immobilizing', or 'standing still' is suspended between active and passive . . . because the absence or intermission of a happening at the same time enables it. Immobilizing or standing still creates what stands and endures, . . . it can appear as a condition of possibility" (8; my translation).[1] Along these lines, the liminal standstills in Musil's and Woolf's texts make apparent what enables them by staging breaths that are transparent in regard to literature's mediality and materiality. They thus tie the semantic, etymological, and physiological implications of breath on the level of representation to what goes beyond it and facilitates literary rendering as such: the medialization of literary language, its acoustic and rhythmic dimensions, and the writing process. This chapter moves between Woolf's and Musil's texts, attending to those moments at which literary texts reflect their own literary-linguistic constitution. In contrast to the Beats' attempt to embed breath in a poetics of presence and immediacy grounded in the writer's body, the modernist's attention to breath is text-internal and highlights the corporeal aspects of language as well as its mediation. In other words, respiratory images in Musil and Woolf coincide with self-reflexive textual gestures. In the three passages that I compare, these gestures are tied to the domain of nature that emanates vibrating intensities. In Musil's *The Man without Qualities*, breathing then becomes a movement through which such intensities of literary language are transposed to an impersonal erotic force between the characters' open "receptive bodies": the interplay between the textual and the respirational "affectively energize[s] a nonhuman . . . intimacy" (Bersani 80), which is the main focus of the chapter's last section.

"Animi velut respirant": Rhythm

We breathe in rhythms: in and out, again and again. In modernist texts such as Musil's and Woolf's, this physiological fact is inextricably linked to poetic questions that are negotiated in the literary works themselves. The vital, organic implications of pulsating breath go hand in hand with a processual conception of literature and language. In his very short reading of "Breaths of a Summer's Day,"[2] Christiaan Hart Nibbrig claims that the text makes *rhythm* perceivable (107). He emphasizes that rhythm is not something given that can then be represented. Rather, it is considered a movement of language that produces and defines its own temporal quality. The rhythmical movement of language keeps being *in process*, nascent, so to speak. For Hart Nibbrig, rhythm is a movement of self-disruption, which he calls the "breathing of texts" (96): "texts breathe in the way they interrupt themselves and thus move on" (107; my translation).

Flow and Segmentation

Before I look at how texts *move on* or sketch scenarios of how they might move on, I want to call to mind what Woolf has to say about how her texts *came to be*. Even before she famously claimed that she was writing *The Waves* "to a rhythm not to a plot" (*The Diary of Virginia Woolf* 3: 316), she highlighted the importance of rhythm for her creative process when commenting on the composition of *To the Lighthouse* in a letter to Vita Sackville-West:

> Style is a very simple matter, it's all about rhythm. Once you get that, you can't use the wrong words. But on the other hand here I am sitting after half the morning, crammed with ideas, and visions, and so on, and I can't dislodge them, for lack of the right rhythm. Now this is very profound, what rhythm is, and goes far deeper than words. A sight, an emotion creates this wave in the mind, long before it makes words to fit it; and in writing . . . one has to recapture this, and set this working [which has nothing apparently to do with words] and then, as it breaks and tumbles in the mind, it makes the words fit it. (*Letters of Virginia Woolf* 3: 247)[3]

Rhythm thus plays various roles in Woolf's writing process: it is an initial trigger for writing—a "wave in the mind" that has to be "recaptured" in the composition process in order to "dislodge" ideas and visions for the text in progress. Moreover, it is the governing principle of the actual arrangement of words: the right rhythm "makes the words fit it." Rhythm is thus a crucial element on three different levels. (1) On a *generative* level, rhythm is a domain of potentiality: constitutive for their emergence, it goes "much deeper" than the words to be articulated and is located "before" the actual writing process.[4] (2) The writing process as such, in which the words are structured, is a *formative* movement. In contrast to the pure potentiality of the generative level, the formative one is characterized by processuality: the words are in the process of assuming a realized form. (3) Finally, the *actualized* level refers to the written text and the way words appear on the page.

To uncover the intertextual network surrounding rhythm and writing that connects Woolf's and Musil's modernist approaches to antiquity—the very theories of respirational rhythm that resonate in Kerouac and Ginsberg—it is essential to pinpoint and define the nodes where the textual threads to be pursued intersect. Émile Benveniste's essay "The Notion of 'Rhythm' in its Linguistic Expression" addresses the presumed derivation of the word "rhythm" from ῥεῖ, "to flow," and the assumption that it originally referred to the movement of waves (281–88), which Woolf's depiction of rhythm as a "wave in the mind" invokes. Against this "simplistic picture that a superficial etymology used to suggest" (287), Benveniste argues that in pre-Socratic philosophy ῥυθμός originally meant "form": "the form in the instant it is assumed by what is moving, mobile and fluid, the form of that which does not have organic consistency"—an "improvised, momentary, changeable" form. In contrast, Plato supposedly introduced the still-dominant notion of rhythm as form in the sense of "arrangement," "constituted by an ordered sequence" of movements that are "broken . . . into alternating intervals" (281–87).[5] The notions of rhythmical *flow* and *segmentation* echo in Woolf's claim that rhythm "breaks and tumbles."[6] In Benveniste's etymological study, formative and generative movements are related to flow and segmentation in a different manner respectively. The claim that the flowing form does not yet have an "organic consistency" suggests that it can be located on a generative level. The further characterization as a "form in the instant it is assumed" reveals a transition to the formative level. In contrast, rhythmical form as an "ordered sequence of slow and rapid movements" (287) implies a transition from the formative level to the actualized one: a measure that is applied to movement, resulting in the realization of a measured, regulated rhythm.

The rhythmical force that Woolf describes is consistent with the pre-Socratic idea of a generative-formative flow in Benveniste's sense: rhythm eludes the writer's intention and control. Moreover, in contrast to the idea of a fixed formal principle for the writing process, as predefined by the author or a literary tradition, rhythm, as Woolf characterizes it, seems to have a life of its own, exerting its formative power in a flowing, moving manner. Especially in the modernist context, rhythm is often related to a preconscious, prelinguistic domain and has repeatedly been discussed with regard to origins (Konersmann and Westerkamp 8). At first sight, classical conceptions of rhythm seem to stand in contrast to the modernist ones. Aristotle, Cicero, and Quintilian all discussed rhythm as an essential principle for the composition of prose texts. This involves various ways of breaking up elements of speech like words and sentences into clearly defined units, which is precisely what Benveniste designates as the later meaning of rhythmical form as segmentation. The rhythmical form pursued by the rhetoricians is located between the formative and the actualized levels: rhetoric as a compositional technique teaches how words should be arranged in order to produce the desired outcome of a well-measured text.

Woolf's and Musil's modernist positions resonate both with aspects of the pre-Platonic and the later rhetorical notions of rhythm, while at the same time incorporating them into a contemporary context. As to the latter, it has been broadly discussed that rhythm became an influential term around and after 1900, especially in the arts.[7] The numerous studies of rhythm and modernism especially focus on the following aspects: rhythm is investigated in terms of movement, and, hand in hand with this, is considered a basis of a poetics of movement. The close proximity of rhythm and the body, its heartbeat and breath, for example, became of major interest, inviting literary writers and scholars alike to concentrate on sensual aspects of writing rather than representation and meaning (Konersmann and Westerkamp 9–10). The awareness that rhythm is determined by repetition and variation, and consequently has a freer structure than signatures of meter and measure, was relevant to many writers striving for a more lively, animated literature (9, 11–12). While Musil's and Woolf's texts can be situated in these frameworks, at the same time they display a remarkable awareness of the technical implications of rhythm with respect to language. By reading the texts closely as well as consulting the material traces of Woolf's and Musil's writing process in drafts and manuscripts, I attempt to show how the composition and generation of literature are reflected in organic and structural-technical terms alike. How is breathing related to all this? In the modernist and ancient texts being investigated, the breathing pause marks the point where the two conceptions pointed out by Benveniste—rhythm as continual flow and rhythm as segmentation, or, in Woolf's words, its tumbling and its breaking-meet.[8]

The Breathing Pause in Ancient Rhetoric Revisited

Ancient rhetoricians developed various rules for breaking up prose into sequences. Cicero's use of the image of a flowing stream versus falling water drops to distinguish between rude and refined oratory represents a hierarchization of the opposing meanings of rhythm Benveniste uncovered.[9] The prose rhythm demanded by the ancient rhetoricians is generally determined by intervals. As already pointed out in the previous chapter, the most crucial structural interval is closely linked to breath: according to the rhetoricians, breathing pauses are supposed to cut speech into well-measured units. The unresolved conflict concerning the coincidence of thought-unit and breath-unit (which, as we have seen, continues to influence poetics in the 1950s and 1960s) leads Cicero to a forcibly constructed argument that beauty coincides with natural utility: "But as in most things, so in language, Nature herself has wonderfully contrived, that what carries the greatest utility, should have at the same time either the most dignity, or, as it often happens, the most beauty" (III, XLV, 244). Thus,

> the stoppage of the breath, and the confined play of the lungs, introduced periods and the pointing of the words. This invention gives such gratification, that, if unlimited powers of breath were granted to a person, yet we could not wish him to speak without stopping; for the invention of stops is pleasing to the ears of mankind, and not only tolerable, but easy, to the lungs. (III, XLVI, 245)

Avoiding such strained arguments, Quintilian admits that in practice, the breathing pause is more variable than in theory (XI 3, 33–39). The physical dimension of breathing, which is by no means ignored in the ancient texts, unsettles the compositional ideals they present. Bodily breath indicates a point where the theories no longer add up neatly. At the same time, breath has a special status precisely because it is discussed in the context of composition and is not merely treated as one of the anatomical prerequisites for speech. Whereas the throat or saliva, for example, are only peripherally touched on, breath is regarded as a constitutive factor for the structuring of speech. In the ancient texts, the period is not only a grammatical unit, but also a unit of meaning. The rhetoricians' strong focus on the unit of thought may give the impression that ancient rhetoric contrasts with the modernist emphasis of the senses and nonsemantic aspects of language.

Another close look at a passage of Quintilian discussed alongside Ginsberg's poetics in the last chapter shows that breathing pauses, thought units, and the sensual, oral perception of speech intersect when rhythm is discussed. The "presence" of rhythm is

> most necessary and apparent at the conclusion of the period, firstly because every group of connected thoughts has its natural limit and demands a reasonable interval to divide it from the commencement of what is to follow: [sic] secondly because the ear, after following the unbroken flow of the voice and being carried along down the stream of oratory, finds its best opportunity of forming a sound judgment on what is heard, when the rush of words comes to a halt. (IX, IV, 61, 541)

Although the breathing pause is the moment completed thoughts can be processed semantically, it is a *sensory organ*, the *ear* rather than the mind, that makes that "judgment." The pause is thus the "best opportunity" to consider sense in two senses: meaning and sense perception. In the English translation, this ambiguity is intensified by the expression "sound judgment" ("aures . . . magnis iudicant"), which implies that the ears make a reasonable judgment; at the same time, we also hear that the ear judges the words' *sound*-dimension. In the following sentence, a most striking linkage of body and mind occurs; Quintilian describes the pause as "this point, where the mind takes breath and recovers its energy" (IX, IV, 62, 543)—"*animi velut respirant ac reficiuntur*" (542). The actions of mind and body are thus inverted: while the ear metaphorically starts to "think," to make a "judgment" during the interval, the mind engages in a physical process: it "takes breath." On a metaphorical level, the implication is rather straightforward: during the pause, the mind takes a break in order to recover its strength. However, on a more literal level, the passage presents an excessive repetition that seems to hollow out any meaning. There is a duplication of breath on two levels: first, *animus* means mind, but at the same time recalls *anima*, which also designates breath. Second, the pause is the moment when the speaker is supposed to take a breath as well as the moment when the mind takes a breath—the moment the breath takes a breath takes a breath. In the pause, the "stream of oratory" is interrupted, only to drag us into a vortex of meanings that, for an instant, leaves us hearing nothing but rushing letters. If, in order not to get lost in the whirl, we grab for the meaning Quintilian offers us in the first place, we realize that the point where (meaningful) speech and thought is reanimated and restored (*reficere*), the point *between* thoughts and units of completed speech-sequences, is an asignificant, sensual stream of air (*respiratus*). Such an amorphous, ungraspable stream—and this takes us back to Benveniste and right into the heart of the modernist texts—is the source of form being generated, namely, in Quintilian's words, the point where the "presence" of rhythm is "most necessary and apparent." The "stream of oratory" addressed by Quintilian is located on the actualized level; however, in his reflections on the incision between segments, a formative-generative notion of rhythmical flow enters the moment of the pause.

Text-Internal Generative Caesurae

I will now return to the passages from Musil and Woolf that I presented at the beginning of the chapter. In contrast to the breathing pauses of ancient rhetoric, Woolf's and Musil's narrative pauses are not *between* words but instead are intervals *filled* with words.[10] In fact, the words in these liminal textual spaces that disrupt the semantic and diegetic level themselves become liminal entities: while they still mean something, their acoustic materiality is foregrounded. In Giorgio Agamben's terms, this may be the point "where language stops," not in the sense that "the unsayable occurs, but rather where the matter of words begins" ("The Idea of Matter" 37), the point where language starts to *reflect on itself*. In commenting on the phenomenon of caesura in poetry, Agamben notes: "For the poet, the element that arrests the metrical impetus of the voice, the caesura of verse, is thought" (*The Idea of Prose* 43). The thought mentioned here is—like Quintilian's *animus*—hollowed of any content and located on the generative level: "The rhythmic transport that gives the verse its impetus is empty, is only the transport of itself. And it is the emptiness which, as *pure word*, the caesura—for a little—thinks, holds in suspense, while for an instant the horse of poetry is stopped" (44). In Musil's and Woolf's texts, breath coincides with narrative caesurae in which a "rhythmic transport" indeed creates the texts' "impetus." The parade of blossoms in Musil's "Breaths of a Summer's Day" marks a pause between Agathe's and Ulrich's exchange of thoughts. It is mentioned that the siblings' conversation "*issued from* a dream of nature: the sight of the parade of blossoms" (1332; emphasis added). Thus, a caesura—the eponymous breaths of a summer's day—figures de facto at the center of the conversation: the breath-carried blossoms allowed it to emerge ("das Gespräch, *hervorgegangen* aus"; 1237; emphasis added) and keep determining its trajectory. What is addressed on the diegetic level coincides with the composition of the chapter on the formative level: already in a note to the chapter from 1938, Musil mentions that "the whole [chapter] is a continuation of the breaths = movement of the beginning and in accord/ in unity with it"[11] (V, 3, 110; my translation). The interval marked by the breaths is thus seen as a formative rhythm, a "movement of the beginning" that defines and is contained in what is to follow.

Precisely because of their narrative depletion, Woolf's and Musil's respiratory intervals are sites of heightened linguistic intensity.

> Ein geräu*sch*loser *S*trom glanzlosen Blüten*sch*nees *sch*webte, von einer abgeblühten Baumgruppe kommend, durch den Sonnen-*sch*ein; und der Atem, der ihn trug, war so sanft, daß sich kein Blatt regte. (Musil, *Der Mann ohne Eigenschaften* 1232)

> A noi*s*eless, *s*treaming *s*nowfall of lu*s*treless blo*ss*oms, emanating from a group of trees whose flowering was done, hovered through the *s*un*sh*ine, and the breath that bore it was so gentle that no leaf stirred. (Musil, *The Man without Qualities* 1327, emphasis added)

> *Meanwhile*, *s*ince all the door*s* and window*s* were open in the heat, there wa*s* a perpetual *s*ighing and *c*easing *s*ound, the voi*c*e of the tran*s*ient and the peri*sh*ing, it *s*eemed, coming and going like human breath, while in the looking-gla*ss* things had *c*eased to breathe and lay still in the trance of immortality. (Woolf, "The Lady in the Looking-Glass" 63–64, emphasis added)

> So with the hou*s*e empty and the door*s* locked and the mattre*ss*es *r*olled *r*ound, those *s*tray airs, advance guards of great armies, *b*lustered in, *b*ru*sh*ed *b*are *b*oards, nibbled and fanned, met nothing in bedroom or drawing-room that wholly resisted them. (Woolf, *To the Lighthouse* 140, emphasis added)

In all three scenes, breath is detached from a human body, externalized—one is tempted to say, transferred to nature. At the same time, the textual breaths remember their own etymology: *anima*: air, a current of air, a breeze, wind; *anima*: breath; *anima*: mind. We encounter a point of emptiness where, following Agamben, the caesura as *pure word* thinks; a point where words reflect their own mediality:[12] breath transferred, carried over to sounds of an empty house, to nibbling animals (*meta-pherein*), breath carrying blossoms, the word "breath" carrying its past and present networks of meanings, including cultural attributions of meaning connected to *pneuma*. In Musil's and Woolf's intervals, one can thus observe an agglomeration and overlap of different semantic connotations around the word "breath" that are very similar to Quintilian's description of the pause—"*animi velut respirant ac reficiuntur*"—where a generative rhythm surfaces.

While Quintilian has a physical breathing pause during oral delivery in mind, Musil's and Woolf's collocations of breath and intervals *evoke orality* in *written texts*: we encounter a striking accumulation of sound continuities, and especially an insistent repetition of s- and sch- sounds in the sentences around the breaths in *all* these passages—which, amazingly, is not even lost in translation in Musil's case. On the diegetic level, Musil and Woolf present a different picture of notions of flow, motionlessness, and sound. Musil stresses that the "snowfall of . . . blossoms" is "noiseless," and that movement is arrested: "no leaf stirred." Hand in hand with the narrative pause the scene represents, time stands still. At the same time, and somewhat paradoxically, the blossoms are "streaming." In contrast, Woolf's scenes are defined by swift movement and sound: within the narrative pause, where nothing happens in terms of the text's plot, lively activities are going on. In "Time Passes," which unlike "Breaths of a Summer's Day" focuses on the *swift passage* of time, the airs circulate in an agile manner. Their invasive "brushing," "nibbling," and "fanning" characterizes them as "streaming" breaths, even though Woolf does not spell out the connection as explicitly as Musil does. Moreover, Woolf's breaths produce sounds: they "bluster," sigh (139), and even speak (138). Similarly, the "sighing and ceasing sound," "coming and going like human breath" in "The Lady in the Looking-Glass," involves movement and noise. In this passage, a lack of motion and silence stand in counterpoint to one another: "in the looking-glass things had ceased to breathe and lay still." Woolf thus shows a view that *shifts* from sonorous swaying to stillness and immobility. While both Musil's and Woolf's respiratory intervals evoke sound through the highlighted tonal patterns in their silent letters, the dissimilar acoustic and dynamic qualities described are mirrored in their rhythm and pace:

> So with the house empty and the doors locked and the mattresses rolled round, those stray airs, advance guards of great armies, blustered in, brushed bare boards, nibbled and fanned, met nothing in bedroom or drawing-room that wholly resisted them. (Woolf, *To the Lighthouse* 140)

> Ein geräuschloser Strom glanzlosen Blütenschnees schwebte, von einer abgeblühten Baumgruppe kommend, durch den Sonnenschein; und der Atem, der ihn trug, war so sanft, daß sich kein Blatt regte. (Musil, *Der Mann ohne Eigenschaften* 1232)

Woolf's sentence moves fleet-footedly in a musical flow to be read in one breath. Musil's shorter one is more heavily punctuated, inviting readers to pause frequently and take a breath—a moment of silence—in the middle, after the semicolon. While the accumulation of verbs "blustered in, brushed bare boards, nibbled and fanned, met nothing" suggests speedy forward motion, the inserted participle clause "von einer abgeblühten Baumgruppe kommend" interrupts the syntactic flow and points backward. Woolf and Musil thus create respectively distinct tones. The different emphases concerning rest/flow and silence/sound, which are presented by the female and male author through ungendered narrative voices, correspond to the tendency observed in Kerouac's and Ginsberg's writing. For the time being, I will leave it at that; the emerging trajectory of pneumatic gender constellations will receive further attention in my discussions of Plath/Beckett and Müller/Celan.

Even though Woolf's and Musil's literary treatments of silence/sound and movement/standstill in some respects differ significantly, the undeniable formal similarities in this respect require further attention. The sound continuities highlight the written words' tonality and create a flow of sibilants. Consequently, a sense of orality and sound emerges in the printed letters, whose material manifestation (print on paper) at first glance lets them appear quiet and immobile. Insisting on stillness and silence, Musil's soundless and immobile breath-carried blossoms are indicative of this tension. In "Time Passes," the breaths' movements and sounds go hand in hand with the acoustic flow created, while in "The Lady in the Looking-Glass," the juxtaposition of such a scenario with one involving immobility and silence points to the incongruent relation between sound and movement invoked in and by words that are set in silent print. These specific constellations furthermore anticipate a moment when print may be animated and turned into sound: the highlighted acoustic qualities of the words invite possible readers to put them into their mouths and exhale them as breath-carried sounds. In that case, the very words that refer to breaths detached from human beings in all texts would enter a human body again. However, we tend to read prose quietly and only "pronounce" the words in our mind.[13] Rather than presenting a scenario of actual, physical pronunciation, Musil's and Woolf's texts stage a liminal moment, a moment in between: on the page, the words are not yet orally articulated—they sound silently. The passages highlight a *potential* pronounceability—textual breaths may, at some point, coincide with physical breath.[14] By maintaining a potential that is not yet realized, a generative moment is evoked in the actualized texts in the form of an acoustic flow.

In Musil's text, a generative moment is also addressed in semantic terms. "Breaths of a Summer's Day" stages a strange moment in which speaking and signifying are only anticipated (the conversation is not yet "hervorgebracht") in words that are already formulated and carry meaning (we can perfectly read the letters describing the breaths of a summer's day). The temporal oscillation and momentary disruption of time (a simultaneity of *not yet* and *already*) evoked by Musil is taken up, and, not quite accurately, one may say, put into words by Agathe, who tries to give expression to what she experienced while watching the blossoms: "Time stood still, a thousand years weighted as lightly as the opening and closing of an eye" (1328). In "Breaths of a Summer's Day," everything that performatively takes place in the scene where "nothing happens" gains explicit articulation afterward. The text explicitly states that time is suspended and boundaries dissolved: "Spring and fall, speech and nature's silence, and the magic of life and death too, mingled in this picture" (1327). The text clearly distinguishes between *presenting* a "picture" of "silence" and what is subsequently *recounted* in language, the comments on the scene and the conversation it generates.[15] According to Musil's dramaturgy, we are supposed to assume that we first encounter a scene *before* language, and then one *in* language. After we *see* or *experience* a scene designed as an immediate event presented by an extradiegetic voice, we *read* the extradiegetic narrator's comments on it, the thoughts it triggers in Agathe, and her conversation with Ulrich. Unlike the visually perceived parade of blossoms, these later scenarios are all characterized by their discursivity, their rootedness in language: they are explicitly written, thought about, and spoken about.

The schism between these two modes—presentation versus representation—is addressed in the text itself, which describes the intrusion of words into the silent scene as a splitting:[16] the first sentence Agathe utters after the siblings watch the blossoms "cut[]" the cloudy silence "apart ["Diese Worte . . . zerteilten," *Der Mann ohne Eigenschaften* 1235]."[17] Agathe realizes the radical difference between the observed generative scene and the thoughts triggered by it:

> So her thoughts were still under the spell of the procession of flowers and death; they were, however, no longer moving with it to its rhythms of mute solemnity; Agathe was "thinking flittingly," as it might be called in contrast to the frame of mind in which life lasts "a thousand years" without a beating. This difference between two frames of mind was quite clear to her.[18] (1329–30)

Agathe's thoughts, the comments of the extradiegetic narrator, and Ulrich's and Agathe's conversation articulate a system of differences and oppositions: two frames of mind, two ways of being passionate, and so on. Even the retrospective comments on the procession of flowers are presented as being already located in a system of differences that has to rely on oppositions in order to refer to a state in which binaries are supposed to be dissolved: "Spring and fall, speech and nature's silence, and the magic of life and death too, mingled in this picture" (1327).[19] The determinative differences *within* this binary system are suspended in another "frame of mind." This state of nondifference *generates* the articulation of differences. In Agathe's reflection, this generative frame of mind is characterized by a "rhythm" according to which her thoughts move, whereas the frame of mind following it, which was brought forth by the generative frame, causes her thoughts to sway "back and forth."[20]

Agathe's distinction between the two frames of mind coincides with the two senses of rhythm pointed out by Benveniste: the continual, flowing, "streaming," formative movement of the blossoms goes hand in hand with the pre-Socratic sense of ῥυθμός, whereas thinking "to and fro" implies a measured sequence, a movement between two different loci or qualities that characterizes the later idea of ῥυθμός, which is defined by "distinctive proportions of elements" (373). The scene, presenting what is later referred to as a condition without difference, is itself an incision. That the liminal state cuts into something that preceded it is more obvious in earlier drafts of the passage (draft 61 [V, 3, 43] and its variant versions [August–December 1938]), where the chapter starts with Ulrich's and Agathe's conversation before being interrupted by the "dream of nature." The earlier versions thus emphasize something that should not be overlooked: the scene does not depict a mystical, unbroken, integral origin that stands at the beginning. Rather, the procession of blossoms occurs at a "cessation of the conversation." That no rift is noticeable at the moment when the conversation is "left hanging" ("[das Gespräch] war hängengeblieben, ohne einen Riß verspüren zu lassen"; emphasis added) does not mean that there is no breach. The pause, in which a streaming continuity takes place, is per se an instant that segments and cuts into pieces. Whereas Aristotle, Cicero, and Quintilian stress that the pause interrupts the stream of oratory and thus constitutes prose rhythm, in Musil's chapter the stream as generative rhythm seems to be shifted into the pause itself with the breath-carried blossoms. A closer look at Quintilian's discussion of the pause has shown that an overlap between ῥυθμός as continuous flow and as segmentation is already anticipated in the ancient text. In "Breaths of a Summer's Day," the staging of a prelinguistic state paradoxically highlights the scene's linguistic constitution. While "breath" may evoke an animistic vital principle that "magically" or "mystically" generates language (e.g., the words uttered in the remaining chapter by Ulrich and Agathe), at the same time it undermines this assumption by revealing its own nature as a word—a word that has, throughout its history, been associated with animation, but also equally with inanimate substances such as air or wind.

Formative Rhythm in Musil's and Woolf's Writing Process

Musil's deliberate method of composition—comparable in its obsessiveness to the sometimes excessively complex compositional rules established by the classical rhetoricians—can be especially well demonstrated by the sentence that most emphasizes the continuous flow. In "Ein geräu*sch*loser *S*trom glanzlosen Blüten*sch*nees *sch*webte," signifiers and referents almost seamlessly resonate when pronounced orally: the described flow carried by air coincides with the air-stream carrying the swooshing sibilants. This effect is produced by a methodical arrangement of words. A few excerpts from early drafts show how Musil tried out numerous words—"hellgrau" (light gray), "leicht" (light), "blass" (pale), "lichtgrau" (light gray), "licht" (light), "hell" (bright), "durchsichtig" (transparent), "gewichtlos" (weightless)—over a long period of time before he came up with the most harmonious and dense formulation. The sound continuity would not be as accentuated had he used any of the other words he took into consideration.[21] Let us have a closer look at the individual text-stages (see figures 3.1 and 3.2):

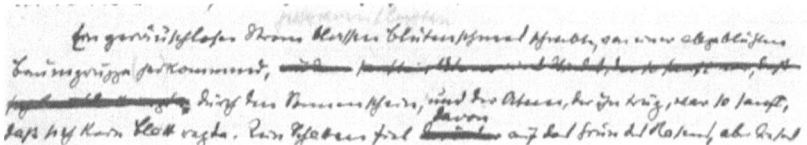

Figure 3.1: Robert Musil, *Klagenfurter Ausgabe*, V/3/62, March 27–November 1937. Copyright Österreichische Nationalbibliothek. Used by permission.

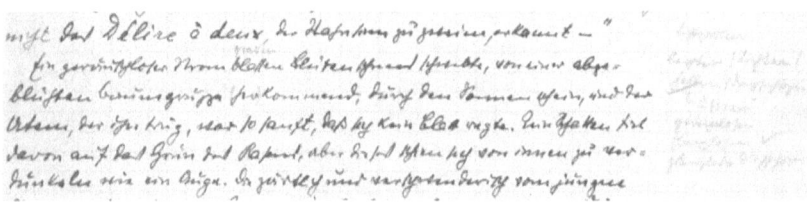

Figure 3.2: Robert Musil, *Klagenfurter Ausgabe*, V/3/45, August–December 1938. Copyright Österreichische Nationalbibliothek. Used by permission.

Ein geräuschloser Strom blassen (hellgrauen / leichten) Blütenschnees schwebte, von einer abgeblühten Baumgruppe (her)kommend, ~~mit dem sanften Atem eines Windes, der so sanft war, daß kein Blatt regte~~, durch den Sonnenschein, und der Atem, der ihn trug, war so sanft, daß sich kein Blatt regte.

Ein geräuschloser Strom blassen (grauen) Blütenschnees schwebte von einer abgeblühten Baumgruppe (her) kommend durch den Sonnenschein und der Atem der ihn trug war so sanft daß sich kein Blatt regte.	lichtgrauen leichten / lichten ~~hellen~~ / durchsichtigen ^{L} = tönend gewichtlosen glanzlosen ✓ glanzlos = durchsichtigen

Ein geräuschloser Strom glanzlos-durchsichtigen Blütenschnees schwebte, von einer abgeblühten Baumgruppe kommend, durch den Sonnenschein, und der Atem, der ihn trug, war so sanft, daß sich kein Blatt regte. (Draft, end of 1938 [*Der Mann ohne Eigenschaften* 1326])

The semicolon before the breath is mentioned (this *is* lost in translation),[22] as it appears in the printed version, was only added in the last drafts in 1941.

> Ein geräuschloser Strom glanzlosen Blütenschnees schwebte, von einer abgeblühten Baumgruppe kommend, durch den Sonnenschein; und der Atem, der ihn trug, war so sanft, daß sich kein Blatt regte. (emphasis added)

This shows once more how meticulously Musil perfected the passage. The semicolon marks a pause; we are, very much in line with ancient rhetoric, supposed to take a short break where a grammatical unit is completed, in order to inhale precisely at the moment when the word "breath" is mentioned—another instance where a concurrence of signifier and referent is evoked. Here, we witness another movement of syncopnea, a continuity (between signifier and referent) determined by an interruption (the pause suggested by the semicolon).

Musil's selection from an array of words he writes next to each other in a row in draft V, 3, 45 to create acoustic harmony is also a syncopal movement. In the spacing of the draft, a rupture becomes *visible*: when reworking the passage (the use of a different pen suggests that the alternatives to "blassen" were added later) Musil first substitutes a word he seems dissatisfied with (as in the earlier draft; V, 3, 62). He then adds a list of alternative words, one below the other, at the margin. The result is a textbook-illustration of Roman Jakobson's "poetic function": Musil chooses from a range of words those that create a contiguous sequence determined by tonal similarities: "Equivalence is promoted to the constitutive device of the sequence" (Jakobson 71). The harmonious similarities created by the poetic function are based on combining two "axes": the "axis of selection" and the "axis of combination" (71). Even though they are combined and intersect in the poetic use of language (*syn*), the division between the two axes—the split of language into two parts (*coptein*)—is what makes the poetic function possible in the first place. To borrow Cicero's image, the continual vertical stream in Musil's draft breaks up into "falling drops of water"—what enables the flowing stream in the final version is a selection of distinct drops.

In a very early note to the "garden chapter," incisions likewise dominate visually (through the spatial arrangement of the page) as well as syntactically and semantically (see figure 3.3):

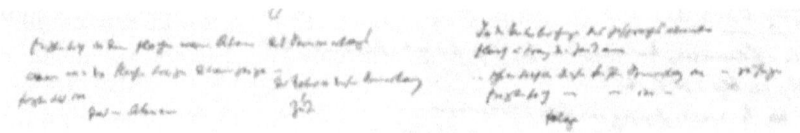

Figure 3.3. Robert Musil, *Klagenfurter Ausgabe*, III/6/60, mid-1934–August 1935, author's translation. Copyright Österreichische Nationalbibliothek. Used by permission.

fügte sich in den flachen warmen Atem des Sommertags		In den Unterbrechungen des Gesprächs atmete
warm wie die flachen trägen Atemzüge –		flach u träg die Zeit an
fügte sich in	der Natur an diesem Sommertag	. . . schien sich an diesen heißen Sommertag in – zu fügen
das – Atmen	Zeit	fügte sich – – in –
		Folge

placed itself in the flat warm breaths of the summer day		In the interruptions of the conversation breathed
warm like the flat idle breaths		flatly a. idly the time at
placed itself in	of nature on this summer day	. . . seemed to place itself — at this hot summer day
the – breath	time	placed itself – – in –
		succession

A heavy repetition of the verb "*fügen*" ("placing," "joining") occurs at the very spot where Musil uses the space of the page to experiment with the placement of words and tests how some motivic strands may be joined together. It should be called to mind that *compositio* in ancient rhetoric has been translated as "Wortfügung" in German. In order to join them together in a harmonious, fluent manner, Musil first cuts the sentences and words apart, dissecting them into smaller pieces that can then be arranged. Considering Musil's writing process, a flowing and continuous rhythm turns out to be the result of a careful arrangement of "distinctive proportions of elements" (Benveniste 285).

Woolf's passages from "The Lady in the Looking-Glass" and *To the Lighthouse* also present a harmonious acoustic flow. As in Musil's passage, the coincidence of breath being mentioned on the diegetic level and the accumulation of sibilants potentially pronounced and carried on a stream of air leaving the readers' lungs points to a close correspondence between signifiers and signifieds that is confirmed by the words' arrangement. A comparison of the typescript and the printed version of the sentence about the nibbling airs in "Time Passes" shows that this arrangement is also a result of a painstaking composition process on Woolf's part. In the printed version, we read: "*S*o with the hou*s*e empty and the door*s* locked and the mattre*ss*es *r*olled *r*ound, tho*s*e *s*tray air*s*, advan*c*e guard*s* of great armie*s*, *b*lustered in, *b*rushed *b*are *b*oards, nibbled and fanned, met nothing in bedroom or drawing-room that wholly resisted them" (140). Alliterations and other tonal continuities, as well as rhythmization, are stronger than in the typescript version of the same sentence: "the stray airs, spies, advance guards of great armies, blustered in, brushed bare mattresses and, as they nibbled and moistened and fanned this way and that, met nothing that wholly resisted them" (6). Some alliterations are added in the printed version, like "rolled round," and some words are exchanged for others for alliteration's sake: "brushed bare mattresses" turns into "brushed bare boards." In this particular instance, the text evokes an overlap between what is said and how it is said, especially if we read it out loud: the combination of sibilants (the s-sounds) phonetically indicates a free airflow, rhotic consonants (r-sounds) imply a partly obstructed airflow, and bilabial stops (b-sounds) effect an obstruction of the airflow. Thus, the acoustic rendering parallels what happens in speech production (i.e., when the words are pronounced) to the airs' movement on the diegetic level, as they flow through the house and brush against obstacles. Whereas in the typescript, "blustered in, brushed bare mattresses and, as they nibbled and moistened and fanned this way and that" is rhythmically unmarked, the much more concentrated "blustered in, brushed bare boards, nibbled and fanned" in the printed version highlights the quick pace of a repeated pattern of stressed and unstressed syllables.

Respiratory Composition

As discussed earlier, Woolf emphasizes the importance of rhythm for composition when she states that recapturing the rhythm that "breaks and tumbles in the mind . . . makes the words fit it." Although Woolf and Musil did not follow strict compositional rules such as those formulated by the classical rhetoricians, they did painstakingly fine-tune their texts. As a result of the revisions and condensations, the words' acoustic dimension often appears more prominent. This becomes particularly noticeable in the passages representing a narrative pause. In other words, the texts' composition becomes most transparent at points where we are told the least. In ancient rhetoric as well as in the modernist texts, intervals are crucial for compositional structure and organization. This also pertains to the narrative level: the thematic elements dominating the pauses (the shadows and lights and the sighing and ceasing sounds in "The Lady in the Looking-Glass," the airs that breathe in "Time Passes," and the breath-carried blossoms in "Breaths of a Summer's Day") are echoes of particular words or motives in the remaining parts of the texts that keep returning to them, which leads to an organization according to rhythmical patterns. While Aristotle, Cicero, and Quintilian discuss breathing in the context of a speech's oral delivery, the speaker's body, and composition, breath occurs in Woolf's and Musil's texts when the body of the text—in this case, its acoustic dimension—is highlighted, which is in turn effected by especially careful composition. In the three modernist texts discussed here, orality thus shifts to the level of composition: a skillful arrangement of words emphasizes the letters' tonal nature, leading to a harmonious flow of sounds carried on a continuous air-stream. But this is only half the story: because Woolf's and Musil's texts appear to us in print, we first (and foremost) read rather than speak them. This means that we see the sibilants that create a continuous sound pattern as individual letters separated from each other spatially: on the page, there is a small incision, a white space, after each letter and a larger one after each word. From this perspective, it becomes more obvious that in order to create a tonal continuity, words have to be cut into their smallest elements; the letters have to be isolated and divorced from the context of the word as a whole. Thus, language is dissected into smaller units than in the context of ancient rhetoric and we are faced with an atomization of words. This is an encounter with rhythmical stream in its particularly modernist form, which recalls the disassembled colors and fragmented brushstrokes that create a current of paint on impressionist canvases and the "incessant shower of innumerable atoms" *composing* life itself (Woolf, "Modern Fiction" 160). It is worth noting that in Benveniste's explorations of the "original" meaning of rhythm, he specifically mentions Heraclitus and Democritus, both of whom assumed that the world consists of atoms. In Musil's and Woolf's texts, a form-generating, mutable, flowing stream of particles—a modernist version of generative soul atoms engaging in a respirational movement—is staged by deliberately shredding language into its smallest pieces.[23]

On a less microscopic level, the generative impact of respiratory rhythm for composition can be traced by attending to the textual history of "The Lady in the Looking-Glass." In order to do so, a few words on the structure of the short story as a whole are necessary. The text's focus moves from the empty room to the eponymous "lady," Isabella Tyson; in this process, attributes of the room are shifted to the depictions of Isabella, who "sigh[ed]" (66) and "stood perfectly still" (68). The text's most prominent formal feature is the series of parallels between the empty house and the woman. They become most explicit when the "lights and shadows" that "came pirouetting across the floor, stepping delicately with high-lifted feet and spread tails and pecking allusive beaks" and the "obscure flushes and darkenings too, as if a cuttlefish had suddenly suffused the air with purple" (63) are echoed in a simile: "Her mind was like her room, in which lights advanced and retreated, came pirouetting and stepping delicately, spread their tails, pecked their way; and then her whole being was suffused, like the room again, with a cloud of some profound knowledge" (67). In the earliest typescript, dated May 28, 1929,[24] the description of the house is already outlined in great detail, while the passages featuring Isabella Tyson are more loosely drafted and occupy much less space than in the second typescript or the printed version. The parallels and repetitions that define the structure of the printed story are not yet elaborated in the first typescript. Only in the second version, which is almost identical to the printed one, are passages from the description of the empty room transferred to the reflections on Isabella Tyson. With this textual history in mind, one can observe that the structure of the narrative around the human character emerges from a respirational rhythm pervading the narrative pause: the not-yet-human, the pure movement of "*mortal breath* coming and going" (first typescript 2; emphasis added) in the first version anticipates a textual organization determined by parallels and comparisons, which is entailed in the printed version's simile "coming and going *like human breath*" (printed version 64; emphasis added)—a simile that in the final version of the text anticipates the analogies later drawn between Isabella and the room.

A similar shift from indeterminate breath to human breath accompanying the transition from the generative/formative to the actualized level can be observed in another passage of the story and its genetic history. The first typescript features a parallel between Woolf's notion of a "profound" rhythm as that which goes "far deeper than words" and breathing. Isabella Tyson's "profounder state of being" is "difficult to turn to words," the narrative voice states; on the typescript page, we can see traces of how Woolf herself tried to find words to describe this "all important, unconscious" profounder state: she scribbled "the state that in the mind what breathing is / in the body" between the typed sentences (4). In the course of its composition, breath thus first enters the passage between the lines. While we can semantically tie it to the description of Isabella's "state of being," breathing is spatially detached—visually it stands on its own. The difficulty of turning Isabella's still indeterminate state into words on the diegetic level coincides with a search for words in Woolf's writing process. This search for a rhythm that "makes the words fit" a state that, in turn, corresponds to the "profound" prelinguistic quality of generative rhythm itself, is manifested in the words "the state that in the mind what breathing is / in the body": located between the accomplished typed sentences, they bear witness to the writing in process and oscillate between what is said in the text and the author's compositional activity. In other words, breathing first occurs in the text as formative/generative rhythm. Only in the second typescript and the printed version it is firmly embedded in a comparison indicating a concrete, fixed, actualized *state* with regard to Isabella Tyson, now defined as "happiness or unhappiness": "It was her profounder state of being that one wanted to catch and turn to words, the state that is to the mind what breathing is to the body, what one calls happiness or unhappiness" (66). The earliest typescript mentions that "the looking glass at once began to draw her [Isabella] in to *compose* her to immortalize her" (5). The explicit reference to composition during the act of composition, which disappears in the printed version, self-reflexively points to the idea that in the later, *composed* state, Isabella will be immobilized along with what is represented in the story. If we merely focus on what is represented and told on the diegetic level, "things" will have "ceased" to breathe in the actualized text. By paying attention to the rhythm *of* composition, however, we notice how the generative/formative rhythm of the "mortal breath coming and going" continues to pervade the text in its printed form.

"Through the Middle": Respiratory Mediality

As the title "The Lady in the Looking-Glass: A Reflection" suggests, a mirror takes center stage in the text: generating mediated images and mediating between inside and outside as well as between the house and Isabella, it becomes a site where literary mediation reflects itself. Analogously, breath appears in Woolf's and Musil's texts as a figuration of the medial,[25] especially the medium of language. As already stressed, the three passages discussed in detail are liminal, in-between, *intermediate*; following theorists who draw attention to the fact that the Latin word *medium* means "middle" and "interval" (e.g., Münker and Roesler 8), I propose that the scenes are located *in media*. Precisely because the narrative content is reduced in these intervals, that which carries the story and itself usually remains unnoticed, the medium of language and mediality as such, become visible. The coincidence of respiratory images and reflections of mediality in Woolf's and Musil's texts is a constellation of parallels on various levels:[26] both breathing and mediality are essentially *liminal*, or *in between*, and both tend to be *invisible* or *unnoticed*. In these respects, breathing correlates with the way media work. One can also observe more direct points of contact between breath and media. In Stoic philosophy, *pneuma* mediates between the gods and humans, inorganic and organic nature (Weinkauf 107). Similarly, God acts through *pneuma* in the Christian tradition (Dünzl 318). In various ancient and Christian models of inspiration, human beings become the medium of a divine agent through which their creative output emerges (Greene et al. 708). Apart from these cultural attributions of meaning, physiological breath functions as *medium for spoken words*. Along with the sounds, exhaled air also carries and transfers the words' meanings—which quite literally leads to the metaphorical. *Meta-pherein* means "carrying over": metaphors are engaged in an act of transferring, just like media and exhaled air. In Musil's and Woolf's liminal intervals, the medial qualities of breathing draw attention to the linguistic mediality of the texts themselves. The texts' recourse to the natural media of breath, air, and wind may be interpreted as an attempt to recover a notion of organicism in an industrialized world where technical media become ever more present. However, Musil's and Woolf's texts defy the idea of a purely natural-organic medium by tying the breaths strongly to linguistic processes as well as to printed and spoken words. The pneumatic mediality they invoke is defined by a movement between the natural/living world and that of the inorganic/artificial.

Mediality and Invisibility

The scenes surrounding the breaths in these texts are situated on the border of what is visible and perceivable. Musil's passage describes something that can barely be sensed: the stream of blossoms is "noiseless," and the blossoms themselves, which in the last draft are described as "glanzlos/lustreless" were "durchsichtig/transparent" in an earlier version of the chapter[27]; they are carried by a translucent breath and "cast no shadow" (1327). Hart Nibbrig mentions that what is at stake is hearing silence and seeing light and air (104). The middle part of *To the Lighthouse* is introduced by comments of the characters on the difficulty to see when dusk is falling: " 'It's almost too dark to see,' said Andrew, coming up from the beach. 'One can hardly tell which is the sea and which is the land,' said Prue" (137). Visibility decreases to an impenetrable darkness when the family and their guests left the house:

> So with the lamps all put out, the moon sunk, and a thin rain drumming on the roof a downpouring of immense darkness began. Nothing, it seemed, could survive the flood, the profusion

of darkness which, creeping in at keyholes and crevices, stole round window blinds, came into bedrooms, swallowed up here a jug and basin, there a bowl of red and yellow dahlias, there the sharp edges and firm bulk of a chest of drawers. Not only was furniture confounded; there was scarcely anything left of body or mind by which one could say, "This is he" or "This is she." (137)

In the opening scenario of "Time Passes," things become radically imperceptible—they are devoured by darkness. Judging from the following sentences, one may assume that the "happenings without anything happening" determining the whole chapter, especially the airs' doings, are not even *fully imaginable* because they withdraw from perception: "Nothing stirred in the drawing-room or in the dining-room or on the staircase. Only through the rusty hinges and swollen sea-moistened woodwork certain airs, detached from the body of the wind (the house was ramshackle after all) crept round corners and ventured indoors. *Almost one might imagine them*, as they entered the drawing-room" (138; emphasis added). When placed at the beginning of "Time Passes," the state of being on the verge of the perceptible marks the space in which imagination as such operates, where imaginability—the imagination of what is then described as the liminal happenings of "Time Passes"—is generated.

The setting of "The Lady in the Looking-Glass" is similar; even before the invisible breaths are mentioned, we observe something that is usually invisible:

> The house was empty, and one felt, since one was the only person in the drawing-room, like one of those naturalists who, covered with grass and leaves, lie watching the shyest animals—badgers, otters, kingfishers—moving about freely, themselves unseen. The room that afternoon was full of such shy creatures, lights and shadows, curtains blowing, petals falling—things that never happen, so it seems, if someone is looking. (63)

By addressing the unseen and unnoticed on the diegetic level, the texts point to a withdrawal that conditions their own mediality. Especially in the context of recent German media theory advocated by scholars like Sybille Krämer and Dieter Mersch, mediality has been investigated in terms of withdrawal and present absence.[28] The medium, it is claimed, is absorbed by the message to the degree that it vanishes. Musil himself addresses how air and water escape perception when they function as "messengers": "air and water, of which one never thinks? Otherwise colourless, good-natured messengers" (1453). This goes hand in hand with Krämer's argument that the medium itself disappears in the act of mediating ("Medien, Boten, Spuren" 72).[29] As Mersch puts it: "Media forfeit their own appearance by letting *something* appear. Their presence has the format of an absence."[30] And further: "No mediation can mediate its own condition or for that matter its materiality and structure—this is the culmination of the medial paradox" (208).

Mersch does not go into detail when it comes to the medium's "materiality" and "structure." In fact, the process and structure of mediation as well as the material dimension of specific media have to be distinguished with respect to mediality's invisibility. The process of mediation becomes invisible due to *transparency*: in its mediating function, the medium tends to be a transparent screen for what it mediates (Krämer, "Medien, Boten, Spuren" 68). The materiality of concrete media (e.g., the pages of a book, a canvas, a screen) are not as such transparent nor invisible (although it might go unnoticed). Mersch's somewhat indeterminate comment that "no mediation can mediate its own . . . materiality" may suggest that a medium's material constitutes an *obscure* point that resists being mediated itself. He argues that a medium's mediality can "reveal itself" ("Tertium datur" 210)—not as something mediated or represented, but in a performative manner, as an event, in Musil's terms as "a happening without anything happening."

> No medium can communicate its own mediality because the form of the message cannot itself be the content of the message. The resulting basis for a negative media theory is that the structure of the medial cannot be that which is mediated—it *shows itself*. All attempts of formulating a negative media theory are grounded in daring the impossible and teasing *showing itself* out of mediation and making the medial within the medial visible. (210)

I tentatively reformulate what Mersch expresses in terms of a Heideggerian ontological difference (the Being of beings cannot itself be a being) in simpler terms: the "form" or "structure" of the "medial" has a different nature and function than the mediated content or "message." That the message's form/structure cannot be encountered in terms of its content because the two are ontologically different does not necessarily imply an incompatibility—it rather marks a rupture. The postulation of the medium's ultimate disappearance in its mediating function is an overstatement, as Mersch's own explorations show. We can grasp something of the medial when we look in the right place and from the right angle.[31] As Mersch suggests, mediality shows itself in art, especially when one focuses on "ruptures and dysfunctionalities" (212), for example, moments when representation is disrupted and nothing seems to be narrated or shown any more.[32]

Thinking with Mersch, Musil's and Woolf's narrative interruptions "permit *effects of media reflection*" (217).[33] In the passages discussed, breath becomes a *Schnittstelle* (German for interface, consisting of the words "cut" [Schnitt] and "place" [Stelle]): where overlapping, cutting into each other, and disruption take place simultaneously. Within the texts' narrative pauses, breath occurs on the level of "content." The etymological, cultural-historical, and referential-semantic implications of breath (pointing to the physiological respiration process) already lead us into the domain of mediality. This is when a moment of syncopnea occurs: two levels come together precisely at the point where they are cut apart. We encounter a shift from referencing and evoking mediality to mediality showing *itself*. Breath is thus located between the transparent and the obscure: its material constitution in the real world is transparent. In Woolf's and Musil's texts, the word referring to the airy substance turns into a site where the mediality of language becomes transparent. In precisely this moment, when the materiality of the letters takes center stage, that meaning is obscured—for a moment, we only see words emitting sounds; taken in by the sibilants that we silently hear, the content being conveyed evades us. Breath's liminality is further stressed in the passages discussed here as it is enmeshed in invisibility on the diegetic level and thus lets mediality reveal itself. The fundamental withdrawal of mediality as Mersch theorizes it coincides with a sensual palpability: physiological breath is invisible and corporeal at the same time, and in Musil's and Woolf's work, such respirational qualities are transferred from the domain of breathing bodies to the textual surfaces on which the materiality of language is highlighted.

By insisting on the formulation that mediality "shows itself," Mersch mitigates the role of those who look and perceive (including he himself, who obviously is someone who observes the "effects of media reflection" in the works he investigates). Both Krämer and Mersch to some extent undermine the idea that media primarily or exclusively involve relations to viewers, listeners, or readers; that they mediate *something* to *someone*. What becomes visible about mediality in an artistic work always depends on how we look and what we focus on. A change of perspective can, for example, make the medium's material perceptible, whereas it may go unnoticed when we concentrate on what is being represented. We may notice the page and the printed letters in Musil's and Woolf's texts if we turn away from what is said—or, in our case, if we pay attention to what is said and take the hint: Musil and Woolf describe scenarios of near-imperceptibility and present breath as an invisible medium. They thus *invite* readers to turn their attention from these represented scenarios of invisible mediality to the medial processes that condition them.

Mediation, Representation, Processual Figurative Language

Mersch argues that, on the one hand, "media forfeit their own appearance by letting *something* appear," and, on the other, that the invisible "shows itself" in a performative way when *nothing* (or very little) is brought to appearance. I will expand on this differentiation through a closer look at "The Lady in the Looking-Glass: A Reflection." In the title, "reflection" is ambiguous: the text offers a reflection on Isabella Tyson, focuses on the reflections of the looking glass in her house, and thus reflects its own medial constitution. This ambiguity of "reflection" opens a play of mirroring back and forth that does not result in conveying a clear mirror image—a literary portrait of Isabella Tyson, for example. Before the text turns to Isabella Tyson, the deserted room is at center stage. In this scene, the mirror petrifies what it displays: "the looking-glass reflected the hall table, the sunflowers, the garden path so accurately and so fixedly" that the image becomes "all stillness" (61). The things reflected in the empty room are *trans*fixed, deanimated, and struck by a paradoxical *moment* of eternity, a "trance" that is *trans*itional in its timelessness: "in the looking-glass things had ceased to breathe and lay still in the trance of immortality" (64). In this scenario, the narrative is brought to a halt and immobilized. However, the focus is not solely on the mirror image. What we see is a "strange contrast": the immobile mirror image, where "things had ceased to breathe" versus strangely animated shadows and lights in the living room where "nothing stayed the same for two seconds together," pervaded by the "voice of the transient and the perishing . . . coming and going like human breath." "One could not help looking from one to the other," the narrative voice utters, bringing us, the readers, into the position of the anonymous observer, "one." We are invited to look to and fro in sync with the "coming and going" of "human breath," from "all changing here" to "all stillness there" (63).

What do we see? We see two different kinds of mediation, I suggest. On the one hand, we have the mirror surface as a medium that *represents* what is reflected, lets *something* appear: the image of the hall tables and the sunflowers, for example. On the other hand, a *pneumatic mediality* is displayed: we face several phenomena that are carried, moved, and transmitted by air: "lights and shadows, curtains blowing, petals falling" (62) as well as the "sighing and ceasing *sound* . . . coming and going like human breath" (64; emphasis added). The medium of air does not give an image of something else; rather, what is carried on air is depicted in the process of being *caught* in its movement, assuming new forms. The text presents events that go unnoticed, "things that never happen, so it seems, if someone is looking." In contrast to the mirror image, we do not see what is mediated; we see what is usually withdrawn and can only be perceived processually: the "happening" of mediation "showing itself." At precisely the point where mediation via air is mentioned, the medium of the text itself, language, is highlighted. Here it is essential to quote the passage on the "things that never happen . . . if someone is looking" as a whole:

> The house was empty, and one felt, since one was the only person in the drawing-room, like one of those naturalists who, covered with grass and leaves, lie watching the shyest animals—badgers, otters, kingfishers—moving about freely, themselves unseen. The room that afternoon was full of such shy creatures, lights and shadows, curtains blowing, petals falling—things that never happen, so it seems, if someone is looking. The quiet old country room with its rugs and stone chimney pieces, its sunken book-cases and red and gold lacquer cabinets, was full of such nocturnal creatures. They came pirouetting across the floor, stepping delicately with high-lifted feet and spread tails and pecking allusive beaks as if they had been cranes or flocks of elegant flamingoes whose pink was faded, or peacocks whose trains were veined with silver. And there were obscure flushes and darkenings too, as if a cuttlefish had suddenly suffused the air with purple; and the room had its passions and rages and envies and sorrows coming over it and touting it, like a human being. (63)

The passage starts with a simile: "one felt . . . like one of those naturalists"; the images introduced as part of that simile, the "shyest animals—badgers, otters, kingfishers," soon start to move "about freely" far beyond the framework of a comparison. The description of the lights and shadows as shy creatures that pirouette, step with high-lifted feet, spread tails, peck allusive beaks, etc. exceeds the model of "something standing for something else"; what we see is language in the act of transmitting meanings across words: *metapherein* in a literal sense. Among other media theorists,[34] Krämer explicitly links transmission and mediality (Krämer, "Medien, Boten, Spuren" 78); the circulation[35] of meaning put in motion by the transmissions from one metaphoric attribution to the next in the passage demonstrates how the medium of language produces meaning by showing figurative language in the process of figuration. Breath also emerges in a simile: "the voice of the intransient . . . coming and going *like* human breath" (Woolf, "The Lady in the Looking-Glass" 63–64, emphasis added).

In the first typescript it becomes apparent that breath is not merely used as an image for a human being but rather engages in a movement of its own: the doors and windows produce an impersonal voice "of the mortal breath coming and going" (2). Such an impersonal breath can be identified with the movement of figurative language itself, a movement which can also be discerned in "Time Passes," where the "airs that breathe" are personified and animalified. Throughout "Time Passes," a mix of human and animal attributes is transferred to the airs: they breathe, nibble (150), fan (140), snuffle (141), have "feather-light fingers and the light persistency of feathers" (138), they "fold their garments," look (138), blow (139), and speak (141). These exuberant attributes make the airs somewhat hard to imagine. One could argue that life is breathed into the "dead" letters precisely because they escape clear depiction, triggering our imagination. The word-airs are thus animated by the transferred, metaphorical meanings. They literally *become* what they signify: airs that breathe. As words, the airs also behave in alignment with what they signify in a different respect: they are described as invisible agents in permanent movement, stealthily slipping through hinges and woodwork and penetrating and pervading the house, which makes them hard to grasp on the level of what is signified. Their disembodiment on the descriptive level thus not only opens up a form of embodiment through personification (or rather animalization) but also an embodiment of meaning in the words themselves. Mediated meaning undergoes embodiment. In Spyros Papapetro's words, one could argue that in Woolf's texts, "animism becomes animalism, and animation leads to animalization" (223). The respiratory animalization of language in Woolf's passage articulates itself by meanings being carried across words. In Musil's text, an analogous movement occurs on a floral level: a breath *carries* a stream of blossoms. In all of these examples, words demonstrate a movement of *meta-pherein* that does not result in a stable image.

To complete my argument, I now return to "The Lady in the Looking-Glass." It has been observed that two kinds of mediality are juxtaposed in the passage focusing on the empty house: one in which something is represented (the mirror reflecting images) and one in which mediality primarily presents itself in making its mode of mediation transparent. This happens at a moment when almost nothing is told, and importantly, nothing is told about Isabella Tyson. While both models of mediality are presented simultaneously in this scenario, a couple of corresponding passages follow each other once Isabella Tyson takes center stage. To repeat, Isabella Tyson's thoughts, again, are rendered as follows: "Without making any thought precise . . . she was filled with thoughts. Her mind was like her room, in which lights advanced and retreated, came pirouetting and stepping delicately, spread their tails, pecked their way" (67). First, the occurrences in the room are presented in their own right and the extended simile displayed a transfer of meaning as a process of *meta-pherein*; later, they serve as an image for what is going on in Isabella Tyson's mind. At precisely this instant, Isabella Tyson is reflected in the mirror and the invisible happenings are erased: Isabella "had no thoughts." When they function as an image for something else, namely Isabella Tyson's thoughts, the movements of the shy creatures are arrested and the transfer of meanings is terminated. Mediality stops "showing itself"; instead, it shows the image of what is mediated. And, in an amazing twist of the text, this represented image is extinguished once it threatens to take over. In the significant short moment when Isabella Tyson is seen as a reflection in the looking glass, she is erased—and with it, the preceding meditations about her: "Here was the woman herself. She stood naked in that pitiless light. And there was nothing. Isabella was perfectly empty."[36]

Reading this scene with Mersch in mind, one could argue that a medium attempting to mediate its own mediality will end up representing nothing—that in this paradoxical process, the represented image has to be erased. However, the poetic reflections in Woolf's story counteract the assumption that the medium becomes invisible behind what it mediates when representation is efficient, when the illusion of the represented image works. One is rather reminded that mediality is what makes represented images possible in the first place, and that the images would vanish if the work of mediation were eliminated. Once Isabella Tyson becomes the main focus, the text is mostly concerned with imagining her inner life. In contrast, when the human character is not the main focus—and I want to stress that this pertains to all the passages discussed in this chapter[37]—it displays its own literary procedures. It is important that breath appears in precisely these contexts: it has moved from the human/narrative domain and only relates back to them through a figurative language that starts to reflect on its own respirational-medial processes. The many similes connecting the room and the invisible happenings in the room to human observers (e.g., "the room had its passions and rages and envies and sorrows coming over it and touting it, like a human being," "sounds . . . coming and going like human breath") do not tell us anything about Isabella Tyson. Instead, they show something: an agency of the inanimate, a livingness or animation of lifeless words in the transfer of their meaning.

Mediating Textual Airs

Turning from "The Lady in the Looking-Glass" to the breathing airs in "Time Passes," my focus—part of the larger question of how language as a medium presents itself—will now shift from figurative language in process to the text's writing process.[38] The "airs that breathe" both mediate between the various drafts, containing traces of the text's material history, and between the fictional narration and Woolf's writing process.[39] In "Time Passes," we observe how the holiday house abandoned by the family and guests who inhabit it in parts I and III is devoured by nature and decays to "rack and ruin" (150), until it is finally restored again by a cleaning lady, Mrs. McNab, and her helpers. The airs pervading the house are in an ambiguous relation to these counteracting agencies. Clearly, they are part of the destructive natural forces. Emerging when the house starts falling apart and apparently contributing to its decay by blowing sand and "nibbling," the airs are presented as a force of unworking. When Mrs. McNab temporarily gives up her task of reverting nature's work, it is said that "the trifling airs, nibbling, the clammy breaths, fumbling, seemed to have triumphed" (150). However, in contrast to the animals and plants occupying the house, whose destructive impact is more conspicuous, the airs are primarily described as an external, roving presence, something that is persistently *there*, moving about, exploring.

When Mrs. McNab and her helpers come back to finally restore the house, the airs are no longer mentioned. Have they disappeared with the other natural forces? If we look closely, it becomes evident that they have not. The way the cleaning women move around the house, "stooping, rising, groaning, singing," their "lapp[ing] and slamm[ing], upstairs now,

now down in the cellars" (152), is strikingly similar to the way in which the airs "crept" around "corners," "entered the drawing-room," "mounted the staircase and nosed round bedroom doors" (138). Going back to earlier passages about Mrs. McNab, one can observe a strange correlation between her and the airs, even in the words used to describe them: they both "sigh" (139, 149) and "rub" (138, 142) and they both ask "How long shall/would they/it endure?"[40] Certain words and attributes are thus transferred from the airs to Mrs. McNab. Keeping in mind that the airs themselves appear as personifications (along with transferred meanings), we now see that the words and attributes transferred from the airs to Mrs. McNab gain embodiment in a human character. This transmission is similar to what we saw in "The Lady in the Looking Glass," where movements of light and air, described as acting "like a human," are transferred to the protagonist. However, the airs in "Time Passes" are not arrested in a representational image but rather incorporated in a human character whose work resembles the work of the text itself, as will be seen later. The personified airs give an answer to their repeated question of what will endure: "*we* remain" (141; emphasis added). This turns out to come true: *they* remain, not as airs, but as mediators between the forces of nature and civilization on the diegetic level and as mediators of signifiers and meaning on a linguistic level. Not only as figurations but also as agents of mediation, the airs or breaths move and transmit between culture/nature, inside/outside, human/inanimate, embodied/disembodied. Operating in a subliminal, semidormant way rather than actively, they display a paradoxically persistent force of unworking at the basis of how the text "works."

Keeping this in mind, I want to consider the drafts of "Time Passes." Three preliminary versions of *To the Lighthouse* have been recorded: the initial holograph draft, an intermediate typescript, and the proofs.[41] To investigate the role of the airs in and between these documents, a few remarks on Woolf's writing process and the development of "Time Passes" are necessary. What Woolf mentions about her plans for *The Waves* is a very adequate description of her writing processes in general: "what I want now to do is to saturate every atom. I mean to eliminate all the waste, deadness, superfluity" (*The Diary of Virginia Woolf* 3: 209). Her revisions in *To the Lighthouse* are characterized mostly by reducing, deleting, tightening, and condensing. In her diary, Woolf comments on writing "Time Passes," mentioning that she is "flown with words" but the text "needs compressing" (76). After having composed the first holograph draft in a process of consistently writing about two pages a day over the period of almost a month, that is, after systematically producing written material, the text is radically reduced in the typescript and even more so in the printed version.[42] Many passages are either fully deleted or compressed and little is added. The structure of the chapter as a whole and the array of the scenes already given in the manuscript, however, remain almost unchanged. When revising the drafts, Woolf is involved in a laborious and time-consuming process of removing surplus material. A correlative of this intertwining of writing and eliminating what is written, of construction and deconstruction, can be found in the fictional processes described in "Time Passes." The development of nature proliferating, the airs' corrosive interventions, and the cleaners' cultivating obliteration and tidying of nature's sprawls can be read in parallel to Woolf's writing and editing process, where productive and destructive forces are interwoven: by deleting increasing amounts of her written material, Woof destroys parts of the text she created. If we look at pages of the holograph draft, the deletions evoke the impression of a text that is decomposing. At the same time, the destruction of parts of the writing in the drafts is what grants the emergence and creation of the text in its final form. Mrs. McNab's "incorrigible hope" (*To the Lighthouse* 143) in the light of her almost unmanageable task can be read as a reference to Woolf's editing process: the corrections themselves rest on something "incorrigible," the hope that they will at some stage lead to a finished text.

The airs function as traces of the material history of the text and as markers through which the distinct properties of the material carriers become perceptible. The different text-stages of "Time Passes" reflect the material particularity of the respective version, manuscript, typescript, or published book, as well as the process of writing and revising. In the holograph draft and the typescript, the airs relate more strongly to the writing process itself than in the printed version. In the draft, we find a sentence on the airs that performatively contradicts what it says: "how they [the gray airs of midnight] had no power to smooth, to ~~obliterate, to destroy~~, touch or destroy" (Draft of "Time Passes" 155). While it is affirmed that the airs have no power to obliterate or destroy on the diegetic level, the words "obliterate" and "destroy" are cancelled at precisely this spot on the text's surface. Thus, a curious effect is produced for the readers: it seems as if the airs actually do have the power to obliterate. In the draft, the word "obliterate," and along with it "destroy," most directly relates to the writing process: it does what it says and is literally obliterated in the process of a revision. In the printed version (and the typescript),[43] the word "obliterated" disappears: "one might say to those . . . fumbling airs that breathe . . . , here you can neither touch nor destroy" (*To the Lighthouse* 138). Thus, what self-referentially points to the process of editing in the draft, is eliminated in the printed version. Moreover, the performative contradiction of the airs' incapacity to destroy disappears along with the interruption the readers are faced with, as we are suddenly distracted from *what* is said when our eyes meet the obliterated "obliterate" in the draft. In the draft, the presence of "~~obliterate~~" makes the airs' undoings transparent to the writing process. In contrast, the attributes "touch or destroy" as they appear in the printed version *can* be related to Woolf's revisions, but their seamless integration into the fictional narration does not immediately direct the reader's attention to the writing process. Still, with the draft in mind, "destroy" can be identified as a trace of the eliminated self-reflexive "to ~~obliterate, to destroy~~."

Further, in the holograph draft and the typescript, the airs are described as agents that move about with beady eyes: they are repeatedly called "spies" (Draft 157; Typescript of "Time Passes" 4, 6). In the printed book, the word "spy" only occurs once, where it does not explicitly refer to the airs: "And now in the heat of summer the wind sent its spies about the house again" (*To the Lighthouse* 144).[44] In contrast, the identification of the airs as spies occurs in various passages of the holograph draft and the typescript that "survived" in the printed version in a different wording[45]—avoiding the characterization of the airs as spies in the printed version thus seems to be a deliberate decision. In the holograph draft, the air-spies are described as a "stealthy patrol" (156), "prying & peering" (155). The spies' militant surveillance corresponds to Woolf's process of reviewing and inspecting her drafts as a prerequisite for her relentless corrections and deletions.[46] Whereas the airs can thus be read as embodiments of the editing process in the holograph draft and the typescript, this self-reflexive gesture is subdued in the printed version. In a later passage of the holograph draft, the disappearance of the reference to the writing process seems to be anticipated in the following sentence: "as if some insidious jaw *concealing its operations* had finally bitten through some tie & loosened the shawls hold upon the skull" (161; emphasis added). The insidious jaw clearly belongs to the airs, as the "soft jaws of the clammy sea air" are mentioned earlier and the airs continually try to loosen the shawl in the course of the text. This sentence is deleted in the typescript and the printed version. If we read the airs' operations in parallel to the editing process, the passage thus foresees what is going to happen in the further history of the text: the unconcealed self-reflexive references to the reviewing process in the drafts are hidden in the printed version. The operations of the airs, that is, invisible substances embodying mediality (i.e., embodying something that usually remains unseen), are thus rendered invisible in the course of the writing process.

Despite these invisibilizations on multiple levels, the airs themselves do not disappear in the published text; rather, precisely because the explicit references are cut, they can be read as *traces* of the writing process. When we read the airs as traces, they become mediators rendering something visible that usually remains unseen,[47] by embodying a medium that effects the presence of an absence (Krämer, "Medien, Boten, Spuren" 85). Moreover, the airs' diegetic claim that "we remain" once more confirms itself. As words, as images, the airs survive Woolf's deletions and they are still present in *To the Lighthouse*. Their semivisible insistence that tends to shift into a presence of absence exceeds *To the Lighthouse*; the airs do not only move between the stages of "Time Passes," but also traverse the borders of the text and enter "The Lady in the Looking-Glass," where words imbued with their resonance appear in an early typescript version, only to disappear again in the printed short story. An echo of a passage featuring the airs in "Time Passes" can be found in the first typescript of "The Lady in the Looking-Glass" when the "bare boards" that the airs brushed in *To the Lighthouse* surface in a description of the empty room: "And the shabby beautiful old country room with its bowls and rugs and bare boards" (1).

Looking back at the drafts of *To the Lighthouse*, we can see how the airs function as mediators between the text's various stages held on different material carriers: the holograph draft, written with a pen on now yellowed paper; the typescript whose thin paper is now torn and wrinkled at the edges; and the many copies of the book, which now exists in numerous editions. Like breaths pervading these text-stages, the airs draw attention to the novel's material history and emergence, thus keeping the reminiscence of the writing process alive. The airs also especially seem to bear witness to the particular texture of the respective material properties of holograph draft, typescript, and print edition. In the holograph draft—and only in the holograph draft—it is mentioned that the "light airs" "seemed to come from some wandering taper,[48] which is moved uncertainly by a wavering hand" (157)—a self-reflexive reference to the act of writing with a pen, which is exactly Woolf did at the moment she put down the sentence. While the airs' handwritten constitution is materially manifested in the manuscript, the reference to the "wavering hand" no longer appears in the typescript and the printed versions. The material dimension of writing is much more overtly perceptible if we look at manuscripts where we can see the lines of the pen the writer held in hand on the paper she touched. When we see Woolf's personal handwriting, we automatically focus on the shapes of the letters and the flow of the lines constituting the words. As Woolf's handwriting is not immediately decipherable for someone unfamiliar with it, the meaning of the words is withheld for a moment and we first concentrate on their visual appearance. This is different in the printed book where the letters, set up in a uniform type, appear in an unobtrusive, perfectly readable manner.

The words' materiality is nevertheless highlighted in the printed version on a different level—as in the manuscript, this occurs in a description of the airs we are already familiar with. "*S*o with the hou*s*e empty and the door*s* locked and the mattre*ss*es *r*olled *r*ound, tho*s*e *s*tray air*s*, advan*c*e guard*s* of great armie*s*, *b*lustered in, *b*rushed *b*are *b*oards, nibbled and fanned, met nothing in bedroom or drawing-room that wholly resisted them" (140). As I have already discussed in detail, the sound and rhythm of the words in the printed version is more strongly foregrounded than in the typescript. The emphasized materiality of words in this passage is acoustic: to best perceive the language's material qualities here, we would have to articulate them with our mouths and let them be carried on our breath. The "airs"—as signifiers—would then meet the air that physically leaves our bodies. In this case, we, the readers, would function as a medium through which the words are animated for the few seconds they are voiced. As long as such a possible "animation" is in the mode of potentiality, the words persist in their inanimate slumber like the disembodied airs who, constantly on the verge of "ceasing" and "disappearing" (138), "iterate and reiterate" their refrain of "we remain" (141).

"What then is the medium through wh. we regard human beings?" Woolf asks in the outline of *To the Lighthouse* (Outline for "To the Lighthouse" n.p.). Instead of trying to answer this question, I would rather ask about the *relation between* the medium and human beings. It has been observed that the airs are connected to the human being who comes back to the deserted house, Mrs. McNab, and that this connection is established through linguistic processes of transferring meaning. The question of the human also comes up when we investigate how the airs function as markers of the texts' respective materiality. In the passage I just discussed, Woolf's handwriting becomes central in the manuscript, while the readers' capacity to potentially voice the words is crucial in the printed version. The airs on the page thus mediate between the pencil in Woolf's hand and the words in our mouths. Throughout the respective versions of "Time Passes," the airs operate as mediators between writing and reading—that is, between human beings who are most probably separated by time and space. The acoustic dimension of the written words is not only highlighted in these sentences of "Time Passes," but also in the "The Lady in the Looking-Glass," where the "*s*ighing and *c*ea*s*ing sound, the voi*c*e of the tran*s*ient and the peri*sh*ing" is mentioned, and in Musil's "noi*s*eless, *s*treaming *s*nowfall of lu*s*treles*s* blos-*s*oms / Ein geräu*sch*loser *S*trom glan*z*losen Blüten*sch*nees *sch*webte." In the passages that turn away from human characters, being uttered by impersonal narrative voices, a notion of *per-sonare* is staged: the sibilants *sound through* the words, and, if we take the hint, the sounds will be carried through our bodies on the breath that functions as physical medium of spoken words.

Focusing on contiguities of breath and mediality in terms of their liminality has shown that the moments when Musil's and Woolf's texts reflect their own medium are by no means gestures of aestheticist withdrawal. The turn to "themselves," to their own medium and mediality via respirational imagery, is, at the same time, an opening toward the instances between which the medium is located. Breath becomes a textual site that initiates a syncopal movement between what is mediated to whom and provokes leaps between different levels of mediation and material carriers. The self-reflexive twists in which mediality becomes pneumatically perceivable are moments of highlighted permeability: analogous to, yet not identical with, a body's respirational process, the texts alternately turn inward and outward. In the remaining parts of the chapter, I continue tracing such movements of syncopnea beyond the specific focus on mediality, attending to other moments in which self-reflexivity shatters any notion of closure or withdrawal. In a next step, a closer look at Musil's "Breaths of a Summer's Day" will reveal how the poetic breaths disrupt the closure suggested by the concept of the "Other Condition." Then, I use a comparative reading of "Breaths of a Summer's Day" and the intertextually linked passages around Ulrich's and Agathe's "Journey to Italy" to discuss a literary breath involved in circulations of transhuman erotic affects and intensities.

Beyond the Other Condition

"Breaths of a Summer's Day" has primarily been discussed by literary schol-ars in the context of the so-called "Other Condition"[49] and a secularized form of mysticism.[50] This stands to reason not least because Musil himself suggests that "perhaps, the utopia of the Other Condition" is "the basic theme of the whole second volume" of *The Man without Qualities* (1749). The "Galley Chapters" and the clean copies of some further chapter sketches, of which "Breaths of a Summer's Day" is a part, immediately continue the published second part of *The Man without Qualities*. "Breaths of a Summer's Day" is located in the context of a group of chapters in line with the so-called "Holy Discourse" chapters of the novel's second part. In the second "Holy Discourse" chapter, Agathe and Ulrich, who "happened upon a path that had much in common with the business of those possessed by God, but . . . walked upon it as people of this world, and pursued it as such," discuss a condition in which "everything somehow flows over into you, all boundaries gone." In this condition, characterized by "stillness and clarity," "everything enters into a new relationship with everything else"; "It is something infinitely serene and all-encompassing." In describing what matches a conception of *unio mystica*,[51] Agathe utters a sentence marking a direct connection to "Breaths of a Summer's Day": "It's all like a tall tree on which not a leaf is stirring" (826–28).

The "Other Condition" is a term more frequently used in the sketches for *The Man without Qualities* than in the chapters involving Agathe's and Ulrich's conversations. It has been thoroughly theorized by Musil in an essay written before the novel, "Toward a New Aesthetic" (1925). Here, Musil distinguishes between two states of mind, the common one, which is determined by rational thinking, measuring, causality, and so forth (198–99), and the "other" one, in which

> there is neither measure nor precision, neither purpose nor cause: good and evil simply fall away . . . and in place of all these relations enters a secret rising and ebbing of our being with that of things and other people. . . . It is in this condition that the image of each object becomes not a practical goal, but a wordless experience; and the descriptions . . . of the symbolic face of things and their awakening in the stillness of the image belong without a doubt in this context. (199)

The parallels to the description of the "happening without anything happening" in "Breaths of a Summer's Day" are obvious—but one should not disregard the deviations; for example, as the analysis of the writing process with respect to rhythm has shown, the scene around the blossoms does not lack "measure" and "precision" at all. What Musil calls the "Other Condition" does not fully coincide with how he presents it in his literary texts (or with what scholars designate presentations of it). It has often been claimed that the stream of the blossoms is an articulation of the Other Condition,[52] and many Musil scholars stress the importance of a self-reflexive language approaching the unspeakable in the context of the Other Condition and mysticism.[53] Repeatedly, language has been considered the realization of the Other Condition in the novel.[54]

It seems compelling to discuss breath in these contexts: the dissolution of boundaries, the collision of the physical, sensual, and something quasi-transcendental in a secularized context, the unspeakable, invisible, unrepresentable, seemingly immediate that paradoxically, nevertheless, or precisely for that reason, is articulated in language—all these aspects of the Other Condition can be integrated in the cultural and etymological narratives of breath. It also ties in neatly with my framework of breath in literature. However, the breaths of a summer's day resist such conceptualizations. When one looks at the passage from a slightly different angle, one notices how Musil's own figures of thought and the terms and theoretical reflections he offers us in *The Man without Qualities* and beyond collapse to some degree. Especially in the moments when Musil conceptualizes what cannot be conceptualized, when he spells out how conceptual boundaries dissolve, he deploys the dichotomizations that are supposedly overcome or suspended. This is particularly noticeable when it comes to the notion of the Other Condition, which, as a term, is constructed within the framework of an opposition: the normal condition versus the Other Condition. Embedded in a language of duality, the term "Other Condition" fails to do justice to what it supposedly designates from the outset.

When it comes to relating the breaths of a summer's day to the concept, the implications of "Condition" are similarly problematic as those of "Other." The peculiar temporality of the respirational scene cannot be subsumed under the term *condition*. The breath-carried blossoms pass by in a fleeting moment that does not evaporate into thin air after its occurrence.[55] On the contrary, it persists: the scene sets the mood of the conversation and Agathe's and Ulrich's reflections keep coming back to it; it keeps puncturing the subsequent narrative. The transience of breath undermines the assumption that Agathe's and Ulrich's ecstatic experiences represent a lasting condition. In yet another scene where inside and outside seem to collide, an "impression" is said to "hover between the internal and the external, the way a held breath hovers between inhalation and exhalation" (1183). This comparison to breath suggests that the *moment* when boundaries are transgressed or suspended is bound to pass. Some kind of fatal *jouissance* implying a total dissolution of boundaries and differences may well be on the horizon of Ulrich's and Agathe's experiment of sibling love. At the same time, the passages where breath comes into play in this context represent momentary breaches, transgressions, and suspensions that render boundaries porous. The seeming "timelessness" of these moments turns out to be a disruption of ordinary, chronological time. In terms of breath—the breaths of a summer's day, for example—the boundary between inside and outside is breached, which undermines the assumption of a clear-cut dichotomy of inside/outside as such. However, this does not imply that inside or outside are erased or fuse into an all-encompassing unity—just as little as inhalation and exhalation merge when we breathe.

The references to breath in contexts evoking the Other Condition alert us to two problematic implications of the latter: that it is constructed in terms of a dichotomy (the normal versus the Other Condition) *and* that the implications of one part of this pair suggest that all differences are erased: "all boundaries *gone*" (827).[56] Concerning the stream of blossoms, further problems arise: even though affinities between the Other Condition and the "dream of nature" can be observed, they do not overlap completely. The investigation of rhythm showed that the continuous flow, the seeming dissolution of fixed boundaries, is only one aspect of the "happening without anything happening" in "Breaths of a Summer's Day." What we face in the passage is not a *reconciliation* of dichotomies or *merging* of difference despite the fact that clashing elements collide (snow and blossoms, movement and stasis, etc.). Rather, the flow displays a multitude of small, dissected particles that keep being arranged and rearranged in a continuity determined by interruptions. On the diegetic level, singular elements, the blossoms, are caught in a stream of air. On the level of the signifiers, individual letters constitute a tonal current.

In many readings, the breaths of a summer's day are treated as an image, or metaphor, for the Other Condition—in fact, the Other Condition is mostly discussed in relation to image, symbol, allegory, or metaphor ("Gleichnis")[57]—and again it is Musil himself who hands these terms to critics.[58] The cluster of terms around the German "Gleichnis," intensely reflected by Ulrich in *The Man without Qualities*, suggest that something stands for something else. Along the same line, one could argue (and critics have done so) that the breaths stand for the Other Condition, the immediate moment, the *unio mystica*. Do they? I suggest they do not. I intend not to read the passage of the blossoms as a metaphor, allegory, or symbol for something else, but rather as a moment when language for a moment stops *representing* in order to reflect its own medium, materiality, and the mechanisms of producing meaning. Rather than illustrating the siblings' state of mind, the blossoms emanate a vibratory intensity of their own (both on the level of the signifiers and the signified), which cuts into Agathe's and Ulrich's reflections.[59] The scene presents itself as an instance of syncopnea: there is a relation between the siblings' conversation and the breaths interrupting it, but it is not one of equivalence. Before Agathe voices her thoughts and continues the conversation, she is literally inspired by the scene: taking "a deep breath," she starts speaking the words that broke up, "zerteilten," the "cloudy weight of silence" (1130). The breaths of a summer's day, transferred to Agathe, transfused into her body, are *with* her and *cut* apart the silence through the words she utters. Stating that the characters experience the Other Condition, a *unio mystica*, or the Millennium, through the natural scene, ignores the peculiarity of the passage: that something is "happening without anything happening" *in* the stream of "lustreless blossoms" carried by a "breath," that this happening is detached from the novel's protagonists and not in sync with their reflections. In this vein, Hart Nibbrig argues that the passage is neither uttered by the characters, nor by the narrator, but rather by a voice independent from them: the voice of the text itself (104).

The breaths of a summer's day are qualitatively—one could even say ontologically—different from the conversation that follows and clearly touches on what Musil conceptualizes in "Toward a New Aesthetic." Recounting the scene in words used by Agathe, Ulrich, the narrator, or Musil only demonstrates the failure of these as *terms*. The endlessness of the conversations seemingly centering around something Ulrich and Agathe cannot quite get at is symptomatic of this. Musil's unremitting work on "Breaths of a Summer's Day" demonstrates how the attempt to conceptualize something that thwarts conceptualization continually escapes the closure promised. Concerning the writing process, "Breaths of a Summer's Day" was Musil's most obsessive chapter; he continued working on the conversation part for years, up until his death.[60] While the conversation about the mystics, the borders between inside and outside, the Millennium, and the two ways of being passionate—the conversation in the language of binaries—becomes infinite as Musil continually rewrites it, the passage about the breath-carried blossoms is left untouched in the later versions of the chapter.[61] Thus, what is referred to as the conversation's trigger in Musil's text, at a certain point keeps hovering inertly over the remaining chapter in progress, much like the blossoms described in it. That the passage is pervaded by paradoxes on multiple levels, as observed, does not keep it from being plainly *there* (in stark contrast to the utopic, impossible spaces of the Other Condition, the *unio mystica*, or the Millennium). There is nothing impossible about the scene of the blossoms, it is right in front of our eyes and right in front of Ulrich's and Agathe's eyes—self-evidently like the way we breathe. Breath may be unnoticed, but it is not non-experienceable and not at all necessarily mystical. Even though it may be invisible and unrepresentable, it moreover does not imply an impossibility when it comes to language—on the contrary, breathing is always copresent when we speak. Breath generates spoken language, like the "dream of nature" that generates the conversation as something both before and in language.

Here I want to come back to the question of self-reflexivity. In her article on Musil and modernist mysticism, Martina Wagner-Egelhaaf rightly stresses the passage's particularly modernist self-reflexivity, claiming that signs become autonomous, referring only to themselves (198). This statement is exemplary for a tendency of criticism highlighting how modernist works tend to refer to their own language or linguistic constitution. Accusations regarding modernism's assumed air of an *art pour l'art* are supported by claims like those of Wagner-Egelhaaf, who suggests that Musil's writing celebrates a self-enclosed textual space that feeds on itself and has no outside.[62] One of the major aims of this chapter is to show how some justified reproaches to modernist literature may be based on assumptions about self-reflexivity that disregard the complexities of the literary texts themselves. In this respect, a closer look at Musil's notion of the Other Condition, which, in its reception by literary scholarship, has been deemed a site of textual self-reflexivity, is very revealing. Wagner-Egelhaaf links the closure of literary self-reflexivity to the purely immediate experience of a mystical union and a state without difference. However, my readings in this chapter aim to demonstrate that in opposition to self-contained bubbles, the respiratory self-reflexive gestures in Woolf and Musil's texts open them up, effect as many joints as cuts or disruptions, and time and again reveal that the texts are not identical with themselves.

A flipside of the dreamy, utopian Other Condition has been uncovered both by Musil himself and some Musil scholars. In his very late drafts and notes for *The Man without Qualities*, Musil observes a "deep link between the love story and the war" (1752); he notes that "pseudorealities lead to war. The Parallel Campaign leads to war!," mentions the "religious element in the outbreak of the war," and then adds that "deed, emotion, and Other Condition join as one" (1755). Indeed, it is plausible to establish a parallel between Ulrich and Agathe's withdrawal from the world in the course of their experiment of sibling love, which in some passages is described as a love between twins, between two that are identical, and the fatal political obliviousness in the self-contained world of Diotima's salon, where the Parallel

Campaign is forged. In his essay "Anderer Zustand / Ausnahmezustand," Hans-Georg Pott regards utopian ideas as a seed of terror (142). He argues that, when put into practice politically, anachronistic and restorative ideas of unity belong to a complex of devastating utopias that were jointly responsible for World War I and the Nazi state (144). Although he concedes that the intention behind the experiment of the Other Condition and sibling love is designed to oppose war and terror, he still sees some uncomfortable traits of the precise opposite rooted in the endeavor. In contrast to the problematic self-enclosure both of a certain conception of self-reflexive language and the Other Condition, the scene of the blossoms, in which dichotomies do not merge to oneness but shimmering particles for a moment hover in a liminal state determined by syncope rather than unity, presents a radical opening, especially when one does not only consider the breaths an image, and even less as metaphor or analogy, but in terms of sound. As we have seen, the sound continuities in the scene expose the words' mediality and materiality and point to the writing process and textual reception, the possibility of a text's oral pronunciation. This is a self-reflexive gesture. By referring to "itself," or rather to processes that determine it, the text becomes permeable to something that exceeds its current constitution (e.g., as a book): it becomes permeable to "itself" in another form (e.g., the drafts, the change of medium when someone pronounces them on their breath), as other. The writing process in which the sound continuity was composed precedes the letters on the page, so by highlighting them, the text points to a *before* that is also an outside. In order to become spoken sounds, the written letters depend on entering a body that is fundamentally different from their own corporeality, their material manifestation as print on paper.

To take one of Ulrich's sentences slightly out of context: "the spoken word loses its self-sense and acquires a neighboring-sense" (1179; my translation).[63] In the sentence surrounding and embedding the stream of blossoms, the words' selves are given up in favor of a tonal proximity or a neighborhood that exceeds the boundaries of single words, as the reading eye is invited to follow the repeated sounds indicated by the letters. Thus, words open up to other words; they become tonally porous. Their porousness would culminate if the words were literally carried on a human's breath, that is, when the externalized breath of a summer day were incorporated by someone external to the text, only to be expelled into the air again. However, we are faced with a celebration of the "sense of possibility" rather than realizations. Thus, the liminality of the breaths of a summer's day is stressed: they remain in a state of unpronounced vocality; as signifiers and on the diegetic level, they are suspended in a rhythm determined by discontinuous externalizations of the internal and internalization of the external, of embodiment and disembodiment, of encounters between animate and inanimate bodies that clash and interpenetrate. This finds expression in a sentence Agathe whimsically addresses to Ulrich—and here a completely different kind of collapse of self is articulated, which runs counter to the grave mystical unity of an Other Condition: "Sometimes you feel your breath blow back from your veil still hot, like a pair of strange lips: that's how it sometimes seems to me—call it illusion or reality—that I'm you!" (1201)

Affect

The erotic connotations of breath in *The Man without Qualities* are framed by Ulrich's and Agathe's experiment of sibling love. However, the kind of affect at stake, which exceeds Ulrich's two categories of passion, detaches from the characters of the novel and amounts to an eroticism beyond heterosexual desire and human passions as such.[64] What Agathe describes is remarkable: divided from the body that emitted it, the exhaled breath ricochets and returns to the mouth it just left. The breath reencounters the lips it departed from as something alien and strange, resulting in an erotic touch, or kiss, by an inorganic substance. The breath itself is compared to lips—the body part it just emerged from, which only stresses the strange inversion presented here: the gaseous lips disconnected from a human body are ontologically different from it, amorously caressing the human lips as Other.

Even though Agathe tells Ulrich that in this moment it seems that "I'm you," it is clear that what is at stake here is not two persons merging into one, but rather a brief touch, in Nancy's terms, a joyous cutting across of the Other.[65] The breath, which Agathe seems to associate with the "you," is something that departed from her own body but has never been an integral part of it, something that is not even alive and only appears vital because of the warmth it still carries from the passage through the organs of a living being. It is possible to figuratively identify "you" with Ulrich, which gives the relation between Agathe and Ulrich a new twist. Far from being "Siamese twins" (976), that is, far from being similar if not identical beings—Ulrich considers their love "self-love" (975)—in this image, they would be radically different from each other: what they would be *to* each other is an alterity in Levinas's sense. Their love would not be a stable, lasting (Other) condition, but rather a moment when two distinct beings collide and momentarily touch.

In other words, it is a love that, following Nancy, "comes *across* and never simply *comes* to its place or term, that it comes across itself and overtakes itself, being the finite touch of the infinite crossing of the other" ("Shattered Love" 102). "I'm you" would then not indicate a unity but—again drawing on Nancy—suggest that encountering the other, crossing paths, touching, being exposed, and rendered vulnerable, constitutes the subject as such: "Love represents *I* to itself broken . . . he, the subject, was touched, broken into, in his subjectivity, and he *is* from then on, from the time of love, opened by the slice, broken and fractured, even if only slightly. . . . From then on, *I* is *constituted broken*" (96). In other words, "the syncope of the subject, in the crossing of the other, affirms an absolute *self*" (107). The rupturing touch of the other simultaneously lets the self emerge shattered: the blown back breath is a cut which at the same time joins and constitutes a broken subject ("I'm you"). This is one reading of Agathe's utterance. However, it is equally plausible to refrain from identifying the breath with Ulrich and consider the scene an erotic encounter beyond the human.

In the course of another conversation between Ulrich and Agathe, Ulrich encourages us to do so in designating "I" and "you"—the very words Agathe uses when she concludes "that's how it sometimes seems to me . . . that *I'm you*!" (emphasis added)—as nonhuman *objects*.

> No, the object is not a means for us. It is a detail, the little nail, a smile, a curly hair of our third sister. "I" and "you" are only objects too. But we are objects that are engaged in exchanging signals with each other, that is what gives us the miraculous: something is flowing back and forth between us, I cannot look at your eyes as if at some dead object, we are burning at both ends. But if I want to do something for your sake, the thing is not a dead object either. I love it, that means that something is happening between me and it; I don't want to exaggerate, I have no intention of maintaining that the object is alive like me (and has feeling and talks with me), but it does live with me, we always stand in some relationship to each other. (1431)

Ulrich describes humans—compounds of tissue, water,[66] gases, acids, minerals—as objects among others:[67] a nail, a hair, etc. The focus on what goes on between objects or bodies unties the ascriptions "life/organic" and "dead/inorganic" from their conventional anchorage. That "signals" are exchanged, "something is flowing back and forth" and "happening between" them, that they "stand in some relationship to each other," unsettles a clear distinction between dead and living objects. What Ulrich reflects here anticipates Nancy's thoughts on how sense "happens" between bodies, be they animate or inanimate, marking the relation with the outside, other human bodies or things.[68] In Ulrich's sensual gaze, Agathe's eyes and the "little nail" are equally suspended between being animate and inanimate. The vitality of objects Ulrich encounters does not result from a projection of his feeling for Agathe to the object he relates to; he also stresses that he does not want to impose the quality of being alive as a human on the object and does not violate its singularity as being something ontologically different. What makes the relation to another human, Agathe, and things like the nail or hair comparable, is that they "*live with*" Ulrich (emphasis added). In many Ulrich-Agathe passages, the affective relation to another person crosses over to such a more encompassing affective "being with": "And the whispering with one's companion is full of a quite unknown sensuality, which is not the sensuality of an individual human being but of all that is earthly, of all that penetrates perception and sensation, the suddenly revealed tenderness of the world that incessantly touches all our senses and is touched by them" (1180). In other words, "they thought that they, and things as well, were no longer mutually displacing and repelling hermetic bodies, but opened and allied forms" (1456).

Journey to Italy: "It was their breathing"

Agathe's utterance discussed in the beginning of this section presents the breathing body as the epitome of a nonrepelling body open to the outside; breath is a space that invites an interrelation between animate and inanimate matter in *The Man without Qualities*. I want to expand on this by reading the breath-carried blossoms along with two related passages in a much earlier set of drafted chapters, dating back to 1924–25[69]—the quotation in the previous section is from one of these chapters, compiled under the title "Ulrich-Agathe Journey." The so-called "journey to paradise" centers on one major topic: the consummation of incest. Ulrich and Agathe travel to Italy, "traversing the scale of the sexual with variations" (VII, 9, 156; my translation). Musil first planned these chapters as a possible ending and then discarded them (Fanta, annotation in *Klagenfurter Ausgabe* n.p.). In his final plans for the novel, incest is not consummated; rather, Ulrich's and Agathe's experiment of sibling love is acted out in their conversations.[70] In retrospect, one is confronted with a twisted structure: the physical realization of Ulrich's and Agathe's desire is written out in the early chapters on the journey, but it remains a mere potentiality in the final plans of the novel. When comparing the chapters on the journey to the chapters on the conversations, one is thus constantly faced with strange traces of a paradoxical and temporally dislocated actualized potential. Walter Fanta suggests that especially in "Breaths of a Summer's Day," the last remainder of Ulrich's and Agathe's desire is sublimated in the conversation and the incest enters the text as an imaginary happening. He points out how the chairs that Agathe and Ulrich abandoned "like stranded boats" (1327) in "Breaths of a Summer's Day" recall the "boats" "on a narrow stretch of coast" (1450) in Italy (Fanta, annotation in *Klagenfurter Ausgabe*). Both boats open the scene for the respective chapters, or, in the case of the journey, the chapter complex as a whole. Another textual remainder is the word "Atemzüge"[71] in the second chapter of the journey, which starts with the comment that Ancona "was firmly fixed in their memory" (1451).[72] It almost seems as if such a memory exceeds the memory of the characters and is fixed textually in a later chapter, "Breaths of a Summer's Day," where the happenings in Italy never happened. The memory is retained in the word "Atemzüge," which will then constitute the title of the later chapter; like the breaths in Woolf's "Time Passes" that mediate between the various stages of the drafts and figure as the remaining traces of the writing process, Musil's "Atemzüge" mediate between a rejected draft and one that was supposed to be part of the novel to come. That the breaths in the late chapter, in which the incest is not consummated, carry traces of the earlier passages, goes hand in hand with the fact that the yet-unpronounced letters only evoke sound silently in "Breaths of a Summer's Day."

The passage where the breaths occur in the journey chapter parallels the one on the parade of blossoms. Ulrich and Agathe arrive in Ancona "dead-tired and in need of sleep" (1451):

> When they had gone to sleep it seemed to them that the white curtains in front of the windows were constantly lifting and sinking in an enchanted currant of refreshing air; it was their breathing. (1451)

> Wenn sie eingeschlafen waren schien ihnen jedesmal, daß die weißen Gardinen vor den Fenstern in einem bezaubernden Strömen erquickender Luft sich hoben und senkten; das waren ihre Atemzüge. (*Der Mann ohne Eigenschaften* 1652)

As in "Breaths of a Summer's Day," and with the same effect, Musil places a semicolon before the mention of breath; in both passages, breath is externalized and described as an air-stream that lifts and moves something.[73] In "Breaths of a Summer's Day," breath occurs when the conversation is stuck, the parade of blossoms is deemed a "dream of nature" and Ulrich and Agathe are in a dreamy state; in the journey chapter, they "rested, dreamed" (1451). The position of the narrator is strange: described is what Ulrich and Agathe perceive when they are asleep, the movement of the externalized breaths a perception of someone unconscious. Alternatively, one may assume that an anonymous narrative voice enters the sleepers while the breaths leave their bodies to be transferred to the curtains lifted by air—only to recount that transference. It is important to note that this scene happens before any sexual encounter takes place. In this state before the incest "happened," the ecstasy strived for is already preempted. Ecstasy happens literally, as a displacement: "their breaths" move in the same rhythm. What is separated from Ulrich and Agathe is caught in the same stream and for a moment collides. One could either argue that Ulrich and Agathe step outside their bodies and then unite (which would correspond to *unio mystica* or ecstasy in a mystical sense), or that desire and passion themselves detach from the characters with their breath and the erotic encounter does not happen between Ulrich and Agathe, but rather in the rhythmical movement of the stream, the touch of air and curtain-cloth, the gaseous textile embrace, and the intertwining of inorganic materials. The passage allows both readings—and here we have to stick with the German, or slightly adapt the English translation. The second part of the sentence in German, "das waren ihre Atemzüge" more adequately corresponds to "those were their breaths" (my translation). At first glance, "*ihre* Atemzüge" ("*their* breaths") seems to refer to Ulrich and Agathe, but grammatically it is equally possible that "ihre" refers to the curtains and streams—that the movement of the wind-carried curtains is not an image for Ulrich's and Agathe's breaths, but rather for the joyous breath of curtain and air.

My argument here ties in with a resistance to reading the breaths of a summer's day as an image for Ulrich's and Agathe's endeavors. Indeed, I want to stress that the breath-carried blossoms are charged with an eroticism that is more than a stand-in for what is going on between Agathe and Ulrich.[74] A draft for the chapter from 1942 supports this assumption: Musil mentions the "silent *passion* of the parade of blossoms" (V, 5, 229; my translation; emphasis added) and the "noiseless stream. The *arousing* sight of the garden" (V, 5, 228; my translation; emphasis added). The breaths in the room in Ancona and the garden are, in Deleuze's and Guattari's terms "a bloc of sensation, that is to say, a compound of percepts and affects." "Percepts are no longer perceptions; they are independent of a state of those who experience them." This goes hand in hand with the odd narrative perspective in both scenes, which becomes especially clear in the journey scene: that which "appears to" Ulrich and Agathe while they sleep is not a dream, but neither can it be a perception in a conventional sense—rather, we are confronted with a "percept." Analogously, one can observe a transition from Ulrich's and Agathe's emotions to affects: "Affects are no longer feelings or affections; they go beyond the strength of those who undergo them. Sensations, percepts and affects are *beings* whose validity lies in themselves and exceeds any lived. They could be said to exist in the absence of man" (164). I do not want to make a teleological argument here, contending that the erotic relation between humans is overcome in another scenario of inorganic affects. What interests me more are the ways in which human and inhuman passions interpenetrate each other in the transition from affections and perceptions to affects and percepts and vice versa.

Opened and Allied Forms

I finally want to turn to the passage where this impersonal pneumatic eroticism reaches its climax: "the miracle happened to these bodies. Ulrich was suddenly part of Agathe, or she of him" and the siblings finally experience what "they had been preparing themselves for this every day for weeks" (1456). This encounter is determined by an utter inertia that functions as an impetus. The peak of intensity is triggered by a suspension, a standstill,[75] a pause comparable to the "happening without anything happening" when Ulrich's and Agathe's conversation comes to a halt in "Breaths of a Summer's Day," and the lifted curtains while they "rested" in Ancona. In this scene, what is carried by the air (or by a breath) is Agathe's body itself:

> Her body was light and fleet, it seemed to her that she was floating in the air. A great, miraculous impetus had seized her heart, with such rapidity that she almost thought she felt the gentle jolt. At this moment brother and sister looked at each other confounded. . . . No thoughts stirred in them . . . ; all words had receded far away, the will lifeless; everything that stirs in the individual was rolled up inertly, like leaves in a burning calm. But this deathlike impotence did not weigh them down; it was as if the lid of a sarcophagus had been rolled off them. Whatever was to be heard during the night sobbed without

sound or measure, whatever they looked at was without form or mood and yet contained within itself the joyous delight of all forms and moods. . . . They saw without light and heard without sound. . . . They thought that they, and things as well, were no longer mutually displacing and repelling hermetic bodies, but opened and allied forms. (1456)

Their bodies did not move and were not altered, and yet a sensual happiness flowed through them, the like of which they had never experienced. . . . Wherever they touched each other, whether on their hips, their hands, or a strand of hair, they interpenetrated one another.

They were both convinced at this moment that they were no longer subject to the distinctions of humankind. They had overcome the stage of desire, which expends its energy on an action and a brief intensification, and their fulfillment impinged on them not only in specific places but in all the places of their bodies, as fire does not become less when other fires kindle from it. They were submerged in this fire that fills up everything; swimming in it as in a sea of desire, and flying in it as in a heaven of rapture. (1457)

The parallels to the stream of blossoms, right up to identical and echoing words (no thoughts stirred/no leaf stirred, "schwebte" [floated]/"regte" [stirred]) are obvious. Ulrich and Agathe are inert "like leaves in a burning calm" and the noiseless blossoms casting no shadows in "Breaths of a Summer's Day" are something that can only be perceived by someone who, like Agathe and Ulrich, "saw without light and heard without sound." Ulrich's and Agathe's bodies assume qualities of lifeless things; erogenous zones randomly wander across their motionless bodies that are more inanimate than animate. They open to a more extensive permeability: every touch is an interpenetration. What became of Ulrich's and Agathe's human bodies and now rather resembles the assemblage of blossoms is suffused and caught in a stream. The description of this stream evokes the Stoic's fiery *pneuma*, which has part in everything and permeates all; however, in Musil's account, the "fire that fills up everything" is not life-giving, but rather induces a death-like state. In the passage, we encounter a rhizomatic bodily pleasure disrupting a notion of sex teleologically directed toward climax and reduced to more or less rigidly defined erogenous zones or penetrable body parts. The "miracle" presented suggests that bodily sensations depart from their designated places and pulverize to become part of a fiery substance, a fluid rhythm within a moment of standstill.

What is later called "fire," what surrounds Ulrich and Agathe before their sensations disassemble and their bodies become porous to a degree that it is hard tell what is inside and what is outside, is described as follows: "Whatever was to be heard during the night sobbed without sound or measure, whatever they looked at was without form or mood and yet contained within itself the joyous delight of all forms and moods." This scenario brings us back to the notion of rhythm as a generative principle: a flow in which *form* is in process of being assumed—when it is not yet articulated as fixed measure, but already contained in the precondition that generates it. The surroundings in which Ulrich and Agathe are disseminated thus open what is represented to the textual rhythm itself. That Ulrich's and Agathe's bodies become inert as well as thing-like, and the categories of animate and inanimate themselves become fluid and permeable, encourages another leap away from the diegetic level: Ulrich's and Agathe's moment of ecstasy can be read in analogy to the encounter between human, animate readers and inanimate printed things on paper. Affects or blocks of sensations embodied in the inert words of the suspended scenes may function here as "impetuses" to "seize" *us*. The wandering of erogenous sensitivity across Ulrich's and Agathe's bodies, which open up precisely at the moment when they and "things" become "allied forms" resembles the wandering of attention across the immobile pulp and print of a book in our hands. The page, the words, and our fingers or eyes may interpenetrate wherever they touch—touch in a way Whitman described it years before *The Man without Qualities* was written:

> This is no book,
> Who touches this, touches a man,
> (Is it night? Are we here alone?)
> It is I you hold, and who holds you,
> I spring from the pages into your arms—decease calls me forth.
>
> O how your fingers drowse me!
> Your breath falls around me like dew—your pulse lulls the
>   tympans of my ears,
> I feel immerged from head to foot,
> Delicious—enough (*Leaves of Grass* 455)

Following the Italian philosopher Mario Perniola, we might experience a "sex appeal of the inorganic" when we read these lines, or passages like

Musil's. When he discusses the sex appeal of the inorganic in the context of literature, Perniola focuses on "an opaque, autonomous language, whose essential aspect is self-referentiality" (121), which goes hand in hand with the highly self-referential narrative pause in "Breaths of a Summer's Day." While Perniola rejects the desexualized nature of a certain kind of "pure," self-enclosed language, he advocates for an attraction to what he terms as "inclusive metawriting":

> Perhaps the attraction exercised by metaliterary devices depends precisely on the impression that by their means writing acquires a kind of autonomous sensibility with respect to the writer and the reader. Now inorganic sexuality resembles this kind of sentient book which receives and makes room for all languages, enters into them and bends them by making them reflect themselves. Inclusive metawriting is revealed, thus, as a metasexuality without either subject or form, in which the single body is changed in the extension of another's body. It acknowledges and transforms everything by removing materials from whatever context and suspending them in a field crossed by continuous tensions. (126)

A moment in "which the single body is changed in the extension of another's body," a literal interpenetration between the body of the reader and the body of words,[76] takes place when we read aloud, which brings me back to the stream of sibilants in "Breaths of a Summer's Day." The fluid current of blossoms that anticipates being carried by externalized breath produces free-floating affects no longer bound to a specific subject in the text; it breeds a language in which organic and inorganic particles couple and decouple—on the diegetic level, the blossoms and the air, and beyond them, the sounds, emanate from the letters even when we read silently. If I read the words out loud and "consummate" the potentiality the text creates by its tonal continuities, disembodied breath is blown back to me, my mouth, "like a pair of strange lips," and the sound vibrations carried on it penetrate my ear. It may seem to me "—call it illusion or reality—" that for a moment I coincide with, *am*, the words entering my body with this kiss. Hand in hand with Alexander Honold's claim that texts themselves cannot sing (188), I want to stress that texts themselves cannot breathe—not only in order to stick to facts, but, more importantly, because claiming otherwise would disrespect their nature as inorganic things, or, in David Wills's terms, their inanimation: the "life" of "words . . . no longer seems to derive from the breathing voice that emits them but instead comes from the animation of inanimate marks, from something that pulsates otherwise" (Wills 116). We can still speak of breathing words in a nonmetaphorical manner, as literary writing at least occasionally forms "human-non-human assemblages" and thus turns into "vibrant matter"—or, moving from Bennett to Perniola, quite to the contrary, evokes a "sex appeal of the inorganic."[77]

4

Impossible Expiration

Reduction, Inanimate Voices, Persisting Bodies (Samuel Beckett, Sylvia Plath)

In Sylvia Plath's and Samuel Beckett's writing, breath marks intersections between the organic and inorganic, presenting speakers or voices whose respiration persists while they move beyond life. In contrast to Musil's and Woolf's breaths of the natural world, which engage in vital activities independently of human bodies and literary characters, Beckett's and Plath's texts continually focus on the agents who speak, utter, or write while their speaking or sounding slips into the impersonal, where it is accompanied by a minimal, repetitive, and passive process of breathing.[1] Let me begin by discussing two exemplary instances. As their title suggests, the prose miniatures collected in Beckett's *Texts for Nothing* revolve around a lacuna: set in a placeless place and uttered by a subjectless subject, they perform "lessening" on all levels. In the very first text, a speaker who considers "turn[ing] away from the body" utters: "And what I'm doing, all important, breathing in and out and saying, with words like smoke, I can't go, I can't stay" (75–77). A similar perpetuation of breath in an indeterminate zone between departing and abiding is postulated in Plath's "Suicide off Egg Rock." The poem focuses on a man who is about to drown himself. The "man in despair" (*The Letters of Sylvia Plath* 2: 306) uncannily assimilates to the bleak surroundings and has already become inanimate when he walks into the water; however, the attempted suicide is bound to fail because his body is "a machine to breathe and beat *forever*" (Plath, *The Collected Poems*

115; emphasis added).[2] In both texts, breathing persists while the agency and sense perception of the speaker (in Beckett) or body spoken about (in Plath) dwindle. Beckett's speaker is "all deaf" and admits, "I can do nothing any more," "there's no more to see, I've seen it all, till my eyes are blear," "my feet dragged me out . . . , I let go their ways and drag me here, that's what possessed me to come" (*Texts for Nothing* 75–77). The subject of Plath's poem is "smoldered stone-deaf, blindfold, / His body beached with the sea's garbage" (*The Collected Poems* 115).

Both breathers succumb to a hostile and extreme environment until there is not much left of them: the "sun's corrosive / Ray" "shrank" Plath's "he," while Beckett's "I," "like buried in snow," notes that "the cold is eating me" (*Texts for Nothing* 77). The surroundings that erode the texts' subjects to a point where they are reduced to mere breathing are themselves sparse. In Plath's poem, "ochreous salt flats" and an industrial landscape form the background; the sea, a sandspit, and an egg-shaped barren rock are seen in the distance (*The Collected Poems* 115). In the first *Text for Nothing*, "quag" and "heath" cover the "flat top" of a "hill," overlooking "the distant sea in hammered lead" and "the city in its haze" (75–76). In both texts, these landscapes recede into colorlessness. Plath's visual and audible fade-to-white, "Everything glittered like blank paper," "He heard when he walked into the water / The forgetful surf *creaming* on those ledges" (*The Collected Poems* 115; emphasis added), correlates to Beckett's "mist that blotted out everything" accompanied by an acoustic fade-to-black: "All is noise, unending suck of black sopping peat" (*Texts for Nothing* 75–77). Both texts address what they are made of, "words," and in both cases literature's creative products turn out to be unreadable indexes of decomposition. Beckett's I breathes and speaks with "words like smoke" and in "Suicide off Egg Rock," the paper is blank because "the words of his book wormed off the pages" (*The Collected Poems* 115)—an image that grows out of the flies invading a fish carcass described in the lines immediately before. Along with the subjects and landscapes, these words wane: they move away, dissipate, worm off. At the same time, smoke and worms are *remainders* of combustion and decay—material remains move on after another substance has disintegrated.

The way breath is handled in both texts ties in with such processes of decomposition that do not terminate; breath is the recalcitrant persistence of material always on the move. In Beckett's respiratory "words like smoke," this connection is made explicit; in "Suicide off Egg Rock," the words worming off the pages also clearly correlate with the "machine to breathe and beat forever." Both images present organic-inorganic assemblages—the body-machine and the book-organism—which relentlessly keep going. Movements that determine the biochemical respiration process, a continual production of waste, consumption, decomposition, and transformation of substances, constitute both texts' poetic core, pervading the writing on various levels. Beckett and Plath address disintegration, decay, and fading, but nothing disappears without a trace; in contrast to what Beckett's title suggests, there is no reduction to *nothing*. Instead of an immaterial, purified emptiness, vanishing and decomposition bring along surplus material, waste, or organisms that feed on what decays;[3] materials and substances are neither maintained nor fully eliminated—they "can't go" and "can't stay." In Plath's poem, images of organic and inorganic dissolution, perishability, proliferation, and persistence interlace: the grilled meat of hotdogs "drizzled," "gas tanks," and factory stacks" are described as "that landscape / Of imperfections his bowels are part of"—a parallel of industrial waste and human excrement—"spindrift" and a flock of gulls disperse, the man smolders, his body moves with "the sea's garbage," simulating it, while "flies fil[e] . . . through a dead skates' eyehole" and the words writhe off the pages. The sun's annihilating power is resisted by "Egg Rock," whose name combines fertility and birth as well as inanimate barren material: "Everything shrank in the sun's corrosive / Ray but Egg Rock on the blue wastage" (115). In the first *Text for Nothing*, the speaker describes its "haggard vulture face," assuming that "perhaps it's carrion time." It is almost submerged in the residues of decaying organic matter, "hummus" (77–78), and peat.

The I claims that it keeps speaking after having died a number of deaths already: "I've given myself up for dead all over the place, of hunger, of old age, murdered, drowned." Throughout these decreases, the respirational process has not terminated; in fact it seems to involve an involuntary revitalizing mechanism that refuses the I a proper death: "breathing your last to put new life in you" (78). Plath also outlines an insistence of breath beyond death: as pointed out, the body of the subject in "Suicide off Egg Rock" is described as "A machine to breathe and beat forever." The poem strongly suggests that a clear-cut death is improbable: we are urged to assume that the breath will go on *forever*, that the machinic body will keep running, no matter what the subject has in mind. If we consider further texts by Plath, these hints are corroborated. Failed suicide attempts are a recurring motif, most famously presented as a spectacle of resurrection in "Lady Lazarus": "Dying / Is an art, like everything else. / I do it exceptionally well" (*The*

Collected Poems 245). The most concrete literary intertext of "Suicide off Egg Rock" can be found in Plath's novel *The Bell Jar*, when the protagonist Esther visits Lynn Beach in Massachusetts (i.e., the clearly recognizable setting of the poem), following a suicide attempt. She tries to drown herself, only to realize that her "body had all sorts of little tricks . . . which would save it, whereas if I had the whole say, I would be dead in a flash" (153).[4]

Breath defies the will and escapes one's control. Against her intent, Esther's body keeps coming up for air: "I dived, and dived again, and each time popped up like a cork." Despite the respiratory strain, her body is sufficiently saturated with air to stay buoyant: "I was panting, as after strenuous exertion, but floating without effort." The incessant air supply assimilates inorganic matter: "The grey rock mocked me, bobbing on the water easy as a lifebuoy" (154). When Plath describes her own attempt to drown herself in a letter, which both "Suicide off Egg Rock" and the passage in *The Bell Jar* recall, she mentions the overwhelming "urge to life, mere physical life. The body is amazingly stubborn when it comes to sacrificing itself to the annihilating directions of the mind" (*The Letters of Sylvia Plath* 1: 656). In "Suicide off Egg Rock," the *life force*, the body's resistance to the death wish—a seemingly biological-organic will to life that has its own agency—is presented as inorganic, passive, and purposeless: "A machine to breathe and beat forever." In contrast to the description in the letter, this is no longer a revolt against the mind or a fight for survival but rather has become a dull persistence to no specific end.

In "Suicide off Egg Rock," the breathing-and-beating machine perpetuates existence in a repetitive, mechanical, numbing rhythm. Hinting at the processes of the cardiovascular system, Plath writes: "And his blood beating the old tattoo / I am, I am, I am" (*The Collected Poems* 115). The military term "tattoo" that introduces the regular iambs of the repeated "I am" recalls the old disciplines of poetry disseminating a sepulchral air. The iambic mill then resounds in "machine to breathe and beat forever." In Plath's work, this machine indeed keeps breathing and beating as a language automaton when Esther in *The Bell Jar* notes: "As I paddled on, my heartbeat boomed like a dull motor in my ears. / I am I am I am" (152). Through this linguistic recycling, a nonanimate waste-life beats on.[5] The echo of "I am I am I am" keeps reverberating in Plath's literary work after her suicide in 1963. This is especially worth highlighting as her texts continue to be read as confessional, as documents of her life, tied to her personal experience. In the case of these scenes in "Suicide off Egg Rock" and *The Bell Jar*, making such a connection is encouraged by the references to her own suicide attempt as described in the letter. Nevertheless, the literary accounts are already decoupled from Plath's life, not only because they are attributed to literary characters but also because of their specific verbalization. The dull motor of "I am I am I am" is a language-machine that severs the I from the person uttering it, undermining the living, mortal body.[6]

The deanimating force of language is also highlighted by the I in Beckett's *Texts for Nothing*, which is highly conscious of its own linguistic constitution. As Elliot Krieger observes, "The 'I' that speaks throughout the Texts is not a person, but is the text itself, the black words printed on the white page. All human referents are consciously delimited as outside- or, in the words of the text, as 'above'-the narrative." Krieger stresses that the sentence, "And what I'm doing, all important, breathing in and out and saying, with words like smoke, I can't go, I can't stay . . . is not an inarticulate cry of human despair; it is a reflection of language on its own nature" (987–88).[7] The I is indeed locked in a textual space and condemned to stay in a state between life and death: the printed letter will persevere as long as the book endures. As a word-thing, the I is not alive like a human being; neither can it be considered dead, because it continues speaking and being read. This transitional state is reinforced by the nature of I as a shifter: it is impossible for the I to remain in one determined place. In this liminal condition, the speaker's activity is reduced to a minimal perpetuation of its existence as a speaker in a text, which is precisely what the reference to respiration in *Texts for Nothing* highlights: the speaker's breathing is neither a vitalizing organic act nor an animating metaphysical one. The inanimate speaker's exhalation creates "words like smoke"—literally, particulate linguistic matter, shredded residues from the novel Beckett wrote before; with the statement "I can't go, I can't stay,"[8] scattered ashes of the most famous words of *The Unnamable*, "I can't go on" (134), fume into the *Texts for Nothing*. Beside the semantic resonances between "I can't go, I can't stay" (*Texts for Nothing*) and "I can't go on, I'll go on" (*The Unnamable* 134) as well as their shared parallelism, the *Texts for Nothing* reproduce linguistic material that already recurs throughout *The Unnamable*.[9]

Analogously, Plath's "I am I am I am" is both a recurring textual remnant and an impersonal utterance, affirming the insistence of a being that both is and is not: it is present as a sign, while, on paper, the uttering body may be, and often is, absent. Thus, in Plath's texts, the I's challenge the conflation of her life with her writing. "I am I am I am" is always already a pulse from beyond the grave. Plath addressed the complicated relation of her body to her writing on February 1, 1959, in a journal entry on the writing process of "Suicide off Egg Rock": "I began a poem on 'Suicide Off Egg Rock' but set up such a strict verse form that all power was lost: my nose so close I couldn't see what I was doing. An anesthetizing of feeling. . . . To forget myself for the work, instead of nudging the work to be my reason for being and my self" (*The Journals of Sylvia Plath* 469). This reflection on the author's relation to the work in progress is intricate. What Plath underlines is that excessive physical proximity—keeping her nose too close—impaired the first version of the poem, which she then revised. A few weeks later, on February 28, Plath reports her satisfaction with a new version:[10] "Yet I have written two good poems, better in their way, particularly the last, than any I have written: Point Shirley, and Suicide Off Egg Rock" (472). In Plath's earlier journal entry, the explicit criticism concerns the verse form—not being able to see what she was doing because she was too close—resulted in a strict form damaging the poem's "power." The new version of the poem, which she finds better than anything she has written so far, thus presumably has a more adequate form, closer to or even identical with the free verse of the published version of "Suicide off Egg Rock."

The *emotional* distance Plath mentions in the earlier journal entry, "an anesthetizing of feeling," is still a topic in the later one from February 29: "Why can't I bring love back into my poems: start even with persona, if I am afraid" (472). While Plath did not seem to consider this kind of distancing a fault of the poem itself, the remark is still ambivalent. In a similar vein, it is unclear whether the line "To forget myself for the work, instead of nudging the work to be my reason for being and my self" is a mere observation, a regretful thought, or a guideline she formulates for her writing. In any case, Plath observes that "Suicide off Egg Rock," even though—or precisely because?—its first version is the result of her body being too close, amounts to oblivion, an annihilation of the self, as opposed to a self-realization through writing or a writing that provides "reason for being and my self." In the poem, the tension between self-erasure, self-expression, and bodily impact is most tangible in "I am, I am, I am," words pronouncing a self that undoes itself by its very affirmation, a body that lives on without really living. Here, "the strict verse" is maintained. It persists as a remnant of the "weak" first version of the poem; the breath of nostrils clinging to the page too tightly prevents the writer's self from controlling her words, and it imparts an anesthetized inspiration.

Beckett: "Dull with breath. Endless breath. Endless ending breath"

"L'air qui respire à travers mon cahier"

The sphere of Beckett's writing is pervaded by an ambivalent inspirational air, a "sterile prolixity," as Blanchot calls it, which, "at the same time and from the same point of view [means] lack of inspiration—creative force and aridity intimately confounded" (*The Space of Literature* 177).[11] Blanchot's idiosyncratic conception of inspiration, which shares a lot with Beckett's literary "inspirational" breaths, starts from the premise we are familiar with from classical accounts: inspiration constitutes the "origin" of artistic works; however, moving "toward the origin of the work" (174) implies approaching a domain where the work's achievement or realization is utterly put at risk. The artist becomes drawn to the space of the neutral, "where nothing is made of being, and in which nothing is accomplished" (46). This is the space of *désoeuvrement*, unworking, where *being* reigns and not *beings*—to put it in terms of ontological difference—and where the work lingers in a precarious potentiality. Submerged in this domain, rendered passive and disempowered, the artist no longer cares about pushing the work into the world of "beings." Inspiration is both arid and creative because it is at the same time what makes the work possible and what might keep it from ever being called into existence. "Not wanting to betray what inspires it, [the artist] seeks to reconcile the irreconcilable and to find the work where he must expose himself to the essential lack of work, the essential inertia [désoeuvrement]" (185). This ambivalence lies at the heart of Blanchot's claim that "The leap is inspiration's form or movement" (177).

A moment of inspirational syncopnea, at which creation and deprivation cut into each other, can be pinpointed in *Malone Dies* when the eponymous narrator describes how he writes the very text constituting the novel. "But my fingers too write in other latitudes and the air that breathes through my pages and turns them without my knowing, when I doze off, so that the subject falls far from the verb and the object lands somewhere in the void, is not the air of this second-last abode, and a mercy it is" (321). *Where* does this scene—*my* entry point into Beckett's literary space because it contains, in a nutshell, the trajectory of his poetics of breath—take place? The fingers write "in *other* latitudes," the air is *not* "of this second-last abode," that is, not the world of the living, which was addressed earlier when Malone mentions, "I was still alive and breathing in and out the air of earth" (320). It is, rather, the space where Blanchot will later situate the unnamable, the space where someone "fallen out of the world" is "hovering between being and nothingness, henceforth as incapable of dying as of being born," and caught in the movement of unworking, which, paradoxically, makes the creation of a work possible; it requires a proximity to "excess of impotence, sterile prolixity, a spring, a source that somehow must be dried up in order to become a *resource*" ("Where Now? Who Now?" 116). Impotence enters the scene where the words keep falling from the writer's hand while he dozes off and loses control over where they land on pages moved by breathing air. It is not even *his* breath that turns the pages of the notebook, but the one of an alien air, an air that is not from the lived-in-world, acting "without" his "knowing." Even though there is no explicit hint that the respiratory movement of the air is "incessant, . . . *interminable*" (113) in the short passage of *Malone Dies*, readers familiar with Beckett's work will immediately make that assumption. As Steven Connor observes, Beckett's "[b]reathing is endless intermission"; every breath is already "expecting to be its next" ("Beckett's Atmospheres" n.p.), including the "last" one: "it's over and done with the puffing and panting" (Beckett, *Texts for Nothing* 103) only means that "the breath [will] fail better still" (112), "the head . . . stops breathing, then pants on worse than ever" (75).[12] The impersonal breathing air in Malone's writing scene is "a spring, a source" of unending "sterile prolixity," it is inspirational in the Blanchotian sense. "Inspiration's primary characteristic is to be inexhaustible": beginning and ending are categories foreign to its domain; the "beginning" of a particular work may stem from it, but at this later moment it has already passed over into the world of beings. "This is a harrowing experience, which can only be pursued under the veil of failure." "Failure threatens" because the work "pushes the artist . . . away from itself and its realization. This experience has become so grave that the artist pursues it endlessly" (*The Space of Literature* 181–86).

In the aftermath of Blanchot's essay on *The Unnamable*, "Where Now? Who Now?," scholars repeatedly observed that such lines of thought resonate with Beckett's texts and poetics.[13] That inspiration and breath have received little attention in these studies may be due to the fact that the former is only mentioned *ex negativo* in Blanchot's essay on Beckett. The speaker in *The Unnamable* is not "someone driven by the noble compulsion many feel entitled to call inspiration . . . expressing what is new and important" ("Where Now? Who Now?" 111), Blanchot claims, without referring to his own diametrically opposite notion of the term, rigorously discussed in three essays published in the same year as "Where Now? Who Now?"[14] In

Beckett's work, breathing, speaking, and writing are closely related, if not at times parallelized to the degree that they appear to be interchangeable. However, a focus on breath is precisely that which, apart from the obvious parallels between Blanchot and Beckett, reveals moments in which such resonances become dissonant. Juxtaposed with Beckett's panting speakers, Blanchot's notion of inspiration is barely related to breathing. In contrast to Beckett's spaces, pervaded by various forms of bodily and figural breath, Blanchot's inspiration almost seems to be oblivious to both its physiological and etymological roots. If we look and listen into the inspirational spaces Blanchot sketches, there is not the slightest breath.[15]

In the following discussion, I want to explore what a comparison to the Beckettian version of this space, saturated with respirational imagery, leads to. Here we come back to Malone's writing scene, which shall be juxtaposed with one of the most prominent examples Blanchot gives for inspiration: automatic writing. Against common understandings of it, automatic writing, for Blanchot, is all but easy: it is "an extreme demand" for writers to expose themselves to "the insecurity of the inaccessible" (*The Space of Literature* 177–78). In "Inspiration, Lack of Inspiration," Blanchot describes automatic writing with the same two adjectives as he characterizes the "neutral voice" invading the unnamable's speech: "interminable" and "incessant" (*The Space of Literature* 26; "Where Now? Who Now?" 113). "What approaches" in "inspiration or automatic writing" "is the neutral, indistinct word which is speaking's being, la parole désoeuvrée" (*The Space of Literature* 181, 190). When Malone's "fingers . . . write in other latitudes" while he dozes off, it is precisely such a language of unworking that is taking over. The moment the two writing scenes most distinctly touch is when Blanchot addresses the writing hand. Automatic writing "puts the hand that writes in contact with some original; it made of this active hand a sovereign passivity, no longer a means of livelihood, an instrument, a servile tool, but an independent power, over which no one had authority any more, which belonged to no one and which could not, which knew not how to do anything—but write: a dead hand" (179). This "dead hand" is the subject of a further writing scene, described in "The Essential Solitude," another text first published in the same year as the ones discussed here so far. There, the "sick" or "dead" hand is one that "keeps on writing" because it is, like Malone's fingers, "writing in other latitudes": it is a "shadow of a hand," echoing the "shadow mouth" that authors are obliged to listen to when they write automatically according to André Breton (cited by Blanchot in "Inspiration, Lack of Inspiration"). It can't let go of the pen it holds, because "what it holds belongs to the domain of shadows . . . the fundamental passivity" (25).

In Malone's writing scene, two shadow forces are at work (or, rather *au désoeuvrement*) in this other abode: the fingers and the breathing air. Like Blanchot's shadow hand or Breton's shadow mouth, the air has its own agency that escapes the writer's control. But it also has its own breath. In contrast to Malone's fingers, that, analogous to the dead hand and the shadow mouth, are—at least within the figural depiction—still connected to the writer's body, the breath is completely detached and impersonal. Both Blanchot's and Breton's depictions to some extent correspond to customary notions of inspiration: the force from without enters and directs the writer's body. Traditional images, like God leading the pen, are variations of the scene, which draw on the etymological roots of "inspiration": a creative force being breathed into the artist. As Breton's writer listens to what the shadow *mouth* says, inspiration is mediated by breath even though no air is infused to the body. In the image of Blanchot's shadow hand, the breath has disappeared. Malone's writing scene makes breath most explicitly present, but—while obviously recalling them—it does not function like classical inspiration models. Inspirational breath moves the pages of the notebook rather than entering and manipulating the writer's body. In contrast to classical inspiration scenes, in which the inspiring force takes control over the writers' movements and their own rhythms vanish through the occupation, Beckett describes two independent movements that are not in sync: the words falling from the writer's fingers and the pages turned by the breathing air.

This is a movement of syncopnea par excellence: the writer is unconscious (subject to syncope in the medical sense), and the words that fall in random places appear on the pages cut from one another, disconnected.[16] Whereas the flow of writing is not interrupted, the rhythm of the resulting text is disturbed because the moving pages prevent that flow from being manifested in the words on paper. The words, dropping continually from Malone's fingers, are disjointed as the breathing air keeps turning the pages. According to the description, the words are syntactically connected while they emerge but appear severed form one another in the notebook—as if the detached breath had left its mark on the page. Beckett describes a musical syncopation transferred to syntax. Due to the discordant movements, grammatical functions are misplaced; subject, verb, and object do not occur where they are supposed to: "the subject falls far from the verb and the object lands somewhere in the void." The whole extremely convoluted sentence in which the writing scene is depicted demonstrates what it is said to effect—this involves a jump from the scene's content to how it is formulated: "But my fingers too write in other latitudes and *the air* that breathes through my pages and turns them without my knowing, when I doze off, so that the subject falls far from the verb and the object lands somewhere in the void, *is* not the air of this second-last abode, and a mercy it is" (321; emphasis added). The subject of the second noun phrase, "the air," has fallen far from its verb, "is"; an object is nowhere to be found. Beckett thus *syn*chronizes the writing process described and the sentence produced. Readers almost get the impression that Malone's strange way of writing immediately manifests itself on paper where subject and verb are *cut* from each other and regular syntax is *disrupted*. That Beckett creates the impression of a coincidence of the described writing scene and the text in which it occurs is as such a further syncopal movement. The unification of the text and its origin as Malone sketches it starts to crumble once we try to imagine another origin, namely, how Beckett wrote it. The suspended verb appears to be the result of a highly conscious attempt to create the effect of random placement depicted in the passage.[17]

A look at the handwritten draft of original French version of *Malone Dies* allows for a less speculative consideration of Beckett's writing process. The passage's textual genesis reveals further instances of syncopnea (see figure 4.1).

respire à travers
Mais mes doigts aussi écrivent sous d'autres latitudes, et l'air qui ~~caresse mon~~ cahier et en tourne les pages à mon insu, quand je m'assoupis, de sorte que le sujet s'éloigne du verbe et que le complément se pose tout seul quelque part dans le vide, cet air n'est pas celui de cette avant-dernière demeure, et c'est bien ainsi. (*Malone meurt* MS-HRC-SB-7-4, 44r)[18]

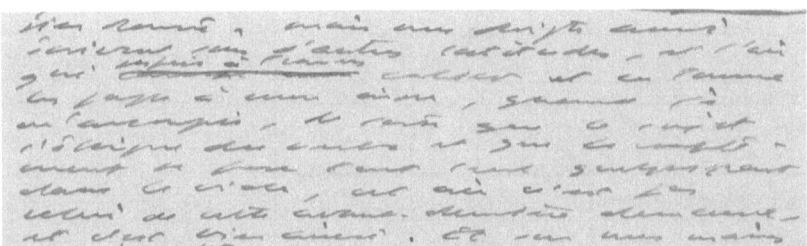

Figure 4.1: Samuel Beckett, *Malone meurt*, MS-HRC-SB-7-4, 44r. Samuel Beckett Papers at the Harry Ransom Center, University of Texas at Austin. Used by permission of the Estate of Samuel Beckett, c/o Rosica Colin Ltd., London.

Except for one significant interruption, the passage appears to have been written in one sitting.[19] If we compare the visual appearance of the draft to the depicted writing scene in terms of movement, the cursive handwriting in Beckett's notebook rather resembles the flow of the breathing air than the dropping of words from the fingers: the words are written in connected lines, one fluidly leading to the next. It is therefore striking that the single point where flow is disturbed occurs right after the word air, when the breath moving the air is introduced. In fact, the breath *is* the interruption: "respire à travers" is written above the deleted "caresse mon." For readers who now see the manuscript, the words stand right at the stumbling block of the deleted line. The words "respire à travers" mark a moment of hesitation; they occur precisely where a stroke *runs across* and *through the middle* of "caresse mon." The canceling, cutting line (*koptein*) visually coincides with (*syn*) the meaning of the words taking its place: it *is* "à travers."

In the moment when Beckett's writing scene literally becomes an inspirational one, that is, the moment when breathing is introduced in favor of caressing, it diverges most prominently from Blanchot's account of automatic writing. For Blanchot, inspiration "is the approach of the uninterrupted" (*The Space of Literature* 181) and the dead hand "keeps on writing" incessantly. In "The Essential Solitude," Blanchot also mentions the "other hand," which counteracts the "dead" one, driven by an "imperious command," the demand of inspiration. While the dead hand passively moves, the "other hand" is "capable of intervening at the right moment to seize the pencil and put it aside" and has "the power to stop writing, to interrupt what is being written" (25). The imperative Kerouac formulates for his hyperactive spontaneous prose also applies to Blanchot's conception of automatic writing: "no revisions." While Beckett evokes the "sovereign passivity" of the dead hand and describes a writing process determined by an "independent power, over which no one had authority any more" (*The Space of Literature* 179), the inspirational force is the result of an "other hand": the hand of the actual author, Beckett, who stops the flow of writing—in Blanchot's words: who grabs the pencil from the dead hand, the very hand he writes about—and intervenes. The air that "breathes" is the result of a revision. Whereas for Kerouac, mastery is enacted by a flowing/blowing that shuts out inspiration, Blanchot claims that "mastery always characterizes the other hand," stopping the dead one (25). Is Beckett's autonomous blowing of the air, the air that supposedly renders the writer powerless, in fact the act of his own hand's mastery? The revision certainly is the conscious act of a writer exerting his competence. In the manuscript, however, there is an instance where the writing on the page stages itself as something that slips from the author's grasp. In my discussion of this instance, I want to pay attention to an overlap between the two writing scenes that meet on the same material carrier: the fictional one—featuring Malone and his notebook—and Beckett's actual writing process, traces of which are preserved in the manuscript.[20] If we look at the correction closely, we notice that it results in an agrammatical sentence:

> respire à travers
> l'air qui ~~caresse mon~~ cahier

"Mon" is crossed out along with "caresse": the canceling line got out of hand. In this moment of the text's genetic history, before the word is reinserted again in the final version, "l'air qui respire" seems to have taken on a life of its own and Beckett's autonomy is momentarily blown away. The deletion deprives the writing subject of owning the notebook he's writing on: "*mon* cahier" turns into "cahier." In Beckett's creative process, the breathing air coincides with an anonymizing force that undermines the author's authority. It is significant that "mon" read backward is "nom." When "mon" is deleted, the notebook in which *Malone meurt* is written ceases to be attributable to a proper name, it is no longer Malone's or Beckett's,[21] momentarily enters the neutral space of inspiration and is seized by the dead hand, or, rather, the shadow breath, "which belonged to no one" (179).

As I have shown in the discussion of Woolf's drafts, revisions per se involve a notion of unworking: in moments when the work is not yet accomplished, composition is accompanied by decomposition, and the writer is faced with what Blanchot describes as the "powerlessness inherent in starting over—this sterile prolixity . . . which never is the work, but ruins it and in it restores the unending lack of work [le désoeuvrement sans fin]" (*The Space of Literature* 37; *L'Espace littéraire* 29). In a similar line, Dirk Van Hulle and Shane Weller consider Beckett's revisions in *The Unnamable* a process of "self-decomposition" (*The Making of Samuel Beckett's L'Innommable* 191).[22] They take the idea of linguistic self-decomposition from Fritz Mauthner, whose language criticism amounting to a demand to reach *beyond* language Beckett famously reproduced when defining the highest goal of a writer in 1937. Drawing on Mauthner, Beckett advocates for a "Literatur des Unworts," a literature of the "unword" (*Disjecta* 54). Van Hulle and Weller observe a "process of 'unwording'" (191) in Beckett's writing and translation process, which is manifested both in the drafts and in the resulting final versions. Following Bruno Clément's work on *The Unnamable*, they especially highlight how epanorthosis, "the rhetorical use of self-correction and word replacement" (103), produces "material traces of the writing process" (28): a "manuscript effect" in the final texts, which creates "the impression of a work in progress that is also a work in *regress*" (163).

The replacement of "caresse" with "respire" is an instance when progress and regress, creation and "decreation" traverse. As a result of Beckett's intervention, "l'air qui caresse mon cahier" is discarded. Thus, "caresse" also follows the meaning of its anagram "écrases," "you annihilate" or "smash." This intricate dynamic of annihilation is only revealed if we look to and fro between manuscript and final version: "caresse" and the anagram that anticipates its disappearance are visible in the draft alone; at the same time, the performative gesture of "écrases" only manifests itself in retrospect, in the final version where the word no longer appears. Van Hulle and Weller make the "hypothesis that the final text [of *L'Innommable/The Unnamable*] was meant to be transparent about its genesis" (28). With regard to "caresse," the final version of *Malone Dies*, considered on its own, is *not* transparent about its genesis: any trace of the word is obliterated, "écrasé." Moreover, the writing scene in *Malone meurt/Malone Dies* imagines a genesis of the text we're reading that does not coincide with Beckett's writing process, namely, it is not transparent about it. We have to look at the first French manuscript in order to get an insight into the "un-creative" process through which inspirational breath enters the text in the course of decomposition.

What about the words substituted by breathing? In the context of a loving touch, "caresse," the air would have been in close proximity to the fingers from which the words fall; the continuity between the two movements being described would have been stronger. When "caresse" is replaced by "respire," the image of the air is cut from the fingers but made more coherent in itself: breath and air belong to the same lexical field, they are etymological relatives. However, "l'air qui respire à travers" is not as smooth as it may seem at first—something is "travers," in the sense of askew. The most straightforward image would be "air that is breathed," not "air that breathes"; or, if we go along with the personification, "air that blows." In this context, the French word Beckett chooses is surprising: it is "respirer" rather than "souffler." With its root in the Latin *sufflare*," the verb "souffler" corresponds to the English "blowing" and by tendency designates exhalation or the air pushed out. It is also saturated with figural meanings: the biblical and classical images of inspiration or breath of life are expressed by it as well as connotations to wind, and movement caused by it (Littré 4: 1195–97).

Rather than opting for the word that would in many respects tie in neatly with the image, Beckett decides in favor of the more literal, medical term "respire," which is commonly used for the physiological breathing process. Beckett generally avoids the word "respiration" in English and translates both "souffler" and "respire" as "breath." In his French usage, where he does make the distinction, he tends to stick to the connotations suggested by dictionaries: "respire" is used when physiological breath is addressed. While "souffler" sometimes also occurs in this sense, Beckett consistently chooses it when he employs breath in a figural way. Thus, following Beckett's logic, the choice of "respire à travers" rather than "souffle à travers" is significant. If we take Beckett's choice seriously, "l'air qui respire à travers mon cahier" to some extent resists being read figurally. Even though a whole number of figural meanings and etymological relatives of breath are evoked—the wind, the inspirational blow, the animating principle—"respire" recalls the physiological. As much as "l'air qui respire" resembles Musil's breaths of a summer's day and Woolf's "airs that breathe"—being equally detached from a human body and similarly characterized by both a flowing and an interrupted rhythm—there are significant differences: in Musil's and Woolf's passages, the airs are located in the natural, vegetative world; in *Malone Dies*, it is not "of this second-last abode" at all. Neither, however, is it purely textual: through "respire," a body insists—and, in contrast to Musil's and Woolf's breaths, it is not the acoustic body of words that makes itself perceptible. Even though "l'air qui respire à travers mon cahier" has a fairly regular rhythm, there is no particular emphasis on the material (e.g., sonic or visual) dimensions of language. The same goes for "the air that breathes through my pages."

So what kind of body is drawn in the passage? And what about the relation of the speaker to that body? The context of the writing scene is relevant in this respect. Malone does what Beckett's speakers often do: addressing the body only to notice that it wanes and becomes inaccessible. The writing fingers and breathing air are embedded in a sequence of body parts that Malone calls "extremities"—stretching the anatomical term to designate the most remote points of the body, parts parting, literally syncopating. Immediately before Malone reflects on the writing fingers, he mentions the feet: feet that feel infinitely far away, in fact, are no longer felt at all: "Strange, I don't feel my feet any more . . . , and a mercy it is. And I feel they are beyond the range of a the most powerful telescope." After the fingers, the penis is described analogously: "Now my sex, I mean the tube itself, . . . I do not expect to see my sex again" (321). The "extremities" are presented as "parts to recede, in their respective directions"—in fact, they have already de-parted; they act like breath, like the air that is a component of the organism and then moves off.

It is no coincidence that in Malone's depiction of the "extremities," the writing scene is exactly in the *middle*: feet—fingers/breathing air—penis.[23] Breath is the dividing-unifying *center*—the "ga(s)p"[24]—in a space that may best be conceived of through Nancy's notion of "exscription." Thinking with Nancy, Beckett sketches a scene of "original separation" in which a "speech-subject," or writing subject, "expires . . . with speech"—"speech [or writing] and breath about to be lost in order to be found, formed in the hyphen between the immemorial and the unarriving" (Nancy, *Expectation* 51).[25] Nancy is interested in the moment when bodies pass into writing. When he thinks about how "exscription passes through writing," he suggests that "we have to write from a body that we neither have nor are, but where being is exscribed" (*Corpus* 19). For Nancy, being and body intersect in the "ex" of existence that pervades the movement of exscription: "The body *is* the being of existence." Existence has no essence "but only ex-ists" (15); "The body's neither substance, phenomenon, flesh, nor signification. Just being-excribed" (19). Drawing on Blanchot's dead hand, he goes on to argue: "If I write, this strange hand has already slipped into my writing hand. . . . Hence the impossibility of writing 'to' the body, or of writing 'the' body without ruptures, reversals, discontinuities or trivialities, contradictions, and displacements of discourse within itself" (19). In contrast to "inscribing," suggesting that bodies are supposed "to be woven into letters" (11), exscribing is "addressed to the body-outside . . . as I try to write it, right alongside this outside, or as this outside" (19). Such a body "is self in departure, insofar as it parts—displaces itself right here from the *here*" (33); such is the re-spiring body: spirited away over and over again. In *Malone Dies*, "l'air qui respire" marks the process of the body's exscription. We almost hear an echo of Beckett's writing scene in *Corpus*, when Nancy writes, "We have to throw ourselves across this 'subject' [au travers de ce 'sujet']" of the body (21). The ruptures and displacements in the writing scene could, in Nancy's words, be described as what exscription of the body causes: the text's "*proper* movement" (11), the movement of syncopnea.

The writing body "that we neither have or are," a body outside itself, is still, in a peculiar and nonpossessive way, our body—Malone still talks of "*my* feet," "*my* fingers," "*my* sex." The ex-scribed extremities "rejoin[] through amputation": "The syncope simultaneously attaches and detaches" (Nancy, *The Discourse of the Syncope* 10). Malone writes a body that is already unreachable, a body on the verge of being gone and simultaneously recalled through—à travers—the writing that exscribes it in a re-spirational movement. "*My feet*," "*my fingers*," "*my sex*"—who is speaking here? Who is the I that still considers the body his own, while at the same time stressing that speaker and body drift apart? In *Malone Dies*, the title gives an answer, the speaker has a name. As we know, it becomes more complicated in *The Unnamable*, where the question "who now?" is explicitly posed in the opening. In the writing scene discussed here, Malone already anticipates the unnamable. When the I addresses its own fading—"I doze off"—we can no longer be sure that it is still I that speaks. In fact, we are inclined to assume with Blanchot that in the space of inspiration "I can do nothing and 'I' never speak" (*The Space of Literature* 179). What are we left with? "My fingers write"—fingers drifting into "other latitudes," the I who claims to own them is dozing off. Not much left to grasp. We are told about the consequence, though: "the subject falls far from the verb and the object lands somewhere in the void." What is said about the grammatical subject also pertains to the subject of writing: it falls (asleep); parts of the body, "my fingers," do what is said of the "object," they detach and "land[] somewhere in the void," "write in other latitudes." In the sentence, the grammatical subject that does what the sentence says, the air occurs with two verbs that were often (albeit not quite accurately) linked to etymological speculations: being and breathing. In Beckett's text, there is, at first glance, a significant distinction between being and breathing. The verbs function differently; the subject that breathes is not identical with the subject that is. First, breathing is transitive whereas being is intransitive. The air acts on an object: it breathes through the pages. Second, being only occurs in the negative: "the air . . . is not." The being of the air (in this moment, the being of the grammatical subject), in the sense of existence, is syntactically suspended and syncopated. And it is the air's breathing that—on the level of content—effects this suspension: we are told that subject and verb are torn apart because the air breathes through the pages; the proposition "through," "à travers," indicates the direction, the movement of how breathing syncopates being. The impersonal air, already detached from the I, breathes physically, is on its way toward a partition—a syntactical disruption that binds it to its second verb, which at the same time marks its cut from the ontic domain, the moment when it passes into a "is not," a neutral "there is." This is what happens to the subject of writing and speaking in Beckett's scene. In his reflections on Descartes, Nancy argues that the body should not be considered "the property of a subject, or of an ego, but that it *is* the 'Subject'" (*Corpus* 131). "The body is the ego that senses itself to be other than the ego. We could say it by using all the figures of the self's interiority facing exteriority . . . the inside, which senses it is outside. / That's what the body is" (131). In *Malone Dies* the respiring air "is" such a body, precisely in the leap of the "subject," performed by the syntactical displacement, the words "is not."

Such a movement of syncopnea is not exclusive to *Malone Dies*: it breathes through many of Beckett's texts. One of them is *The Unnamable*, where Malone's writing scene is echoed: "I don't feel a mouth on me, I don't feel the jostle of words in my mouth . . . I don't feel that either, the words falling you don't know where, you don't know whence, drops of silence through the silence, I don't feel it, I don't feel a mouth on me" (99). Here, the scenario in which words fall at random is not one of writing, but of mute speaking, of silent recitation: "when you say a poem you like . . . for yourself . . . without the least sound" (99). In other words, in the resonance of the passage from *Malone Dies*, the scene of written literary production moves to one of oral reception. More precisely: of negated oral reception, or speaking, in which the mouth as such is only a recalled body part, and no longer a present one analogous to Malone's extremities. The mouth, "this jetty that says 'I,'" as Nancy describes it in *Ego Sum*, is staged as a "place/nonplace" of uttering (*Ego Sum* 111). In *The Unnamable*, the mouth is exscribed, the concrete place from which someone who is right here says "I" has become a nonplace, a word that is negated, that the I, another word, denies to feel or have. The awareness of the text that it deals with "mouth" as a word becomes explicit in the original French, where the passage reads "je ne me sens pas une bouche, je ne sens pas les mots se bousculer dans ma bouche" (*L'Innommable* 159). Here, the "jostle of the words" is, literally, a jostle of repeated letters: bouche/bousculer/bouche. The banality that the written letter I has no mouth points to the less banal spacing involved when a body utters "I," which Nancy describes as follows: "*ego* makes or makes itself into *exteriority*, spacing of places, distancing and strangeness that make up a place, . . . spatiality of a true *outline* in which, and only in which, *ego* may come forth, trace itself out, and think itself" (*Ego Sum* 112). The mouth, as "the opening of *Ego*" (112), is that outline, the place through which I utters itself and, as Nancy stresses, "through which breath flows, and with breath sound" (xi). The unnamable says something similar abut a mouth that is not yet there but only anticipated: "I have no mouth, and what about it, I'll grow one, . . . the air will gush into me, and out a second later, howling" (*The Unnamable* 101).

"I'm the partition"

Is the displaced, exscribed mouth that does not produce sound in the passage echoing Malone's writing scene breathing? In *The Unnamable*, the "words falling, you don't know where, you don't know whence" certainly call to mind the air that breathes through the pages, the air that is not from this penultimate abode in *Malone Dies*. In the most Nancean part of the whole reflection on the absent mouth, breath enters the textual stage, but, in contrast to Malone's writing scene, it does so in a figural sense:[26]

> without a mouth I'll have said it, I'll have said it inside me, then *in the same breath* outside me, perhaps that's what I feel, an outside and an inside and me in the middle, perhaps that's what I am, the thing that divides the world into two, on the one side the outside, on the other the inside, that can be as thin as foil, I'm neither one side or the other, I'm in the middle, I'm the partition. (*The Unnamable* 100; emphasis added)

Like "l'air qui respire à travers," this figural breath syncopates. As an idiom, "in the same breath" corresponds to what the French original says, "puis aussitôt" (*L'Innommable* 160), immediately after, almost at the same time. As often in the idiom's use, what happens almost at the same time is opposed: "I'll have said it inside me / outside me." The conceptual-semantic cut between inside/outside is conjoined by "the same breath." And here the figural recalls the physiological: when I speak, what I say is literally in and on the same breath "inside me" and "outside me." The words I say are carried outside with the very same breath that I had inside my body. It is precisely this syncopnea in speaking that the I affirms and then considers to identify with—"perhaps that's what I feel," "perhaps that's what I am." The speaking and writing I is "neither one side or the other" but "in the middle": it coincides with cutting and binding breath, occupying precisely the same liminal space as breath—in *Malone Dies* between the other waning extremities, in *The Unnamable* "inside me, then in the same breath outside me." The only thing that "I" can *be* is the breaking involved in saying, or writing "I am," *ego sum*, or, in Beckett's terms "I'm"—the utterance which involves a linguistic syncope, the I's "being" affirmed only to be cut. For Nancy, this is where the body is located: "there is this *limit*, this edge, . . . , this extremity, this outline, . . . which can be withdrawn . . . , and pulled into the nonextension of a point or self-center, simultaneously distending or extending itself through passages and partitions . . . this limit *is the body*" (*Corpus* 23). In a later passage, Nancy refers back to this sentence when he addresses the exscribed body: "a body is always what writing *exscribes*. . . . What's exscribed *remains* this other *edge* that inscription, through signifying on an edge, obstinately continues to indicate as its own-other edge. Thus, for every writing, a body is the own-other edge" (87).

What follows in *Corpus* most concretely recalls a passage in *The Unnamable*: "a body . . . is therefore also the tracing, and the trace. . . . In all writing a body is the letter, yet never the letter, or else, more remotely, more deconstructed than any literality, it's a 'letricity' no longer meant to be read. What in a writing, and properly so, is not to be read—that's what a body is" (87). In "I'm the partition," the words do what they say. The *letters* "I'm" *are* the partition (or, initially, as the first typescript puts it, are "i̶n̶ the partition" MS-HRC-SB-5-10, 97r):[27] the apostrophe crops the "am" to a single letter and, in the same breath, ties it closer to the I. Moreover, on the page, I looks like a vertical divider. In the moment it catches the *eye*, I is a partition—it oscillates between being a vertical stroke that seems to divide words from each other and being a sound-pattern connecting and dividing the two words "I" and "eye." Importantly, we only "hear" the homonymy in the silent written words because we re-call how they sound when carried out of the mouth on the breath. When it silently speaks to the eye, I becomes a trace of(f) the breathing body. In this moment, the I—speaking with Nancy, the letter as body—ceases to be a letter: as a vertical dividing line, it no longer signifies. I draws the line between meaningful sign and dividing stroke. Nancy locates exscription and the "body of literature" precisely at this point:

> It will be writing, if "writing" indicates the very thing *that swerves from signification* and which, therefore, *is exscribed*. Exscription is produced in the loosening of unsignifying spacing: it detaches words from their senses, always again and again, abandoning them to their extension. A word, so long as it's not absorbed without remainder into a sense, *remains* essentially extended *between* other words, stretching to touch them, though not merging with them: and that's language as *body*. (*Corpus* 71)

In this passage of *The Unnamable*, the I is not only exscribed and "swerves from signification" in the formulation "I am the partition"; it constitutes "unsignifying spacing" in the sentence's textual environment. When we look at the page, the obsessively repeated I's stand out:

> I don't know what it is, I don't know what I feel, tell me what I feel and I'll tell you who I am, they'll tell me who I am, I won't understand, but the thing will be said, they'll have said who I am, and I'll have heard, without an ear I'll have heard, and I'll have said it, without a mouth I'll have said it, I'll have said it inside me, then in the same breath outside me, perhaps that's what I feel, an outside and an inside and me in the middle, perhaps that's what I am, the thing that divides the world in two, on the one side the outside, on the other the inside, that can be as thin as foil, I'm neither one side nor the other, I'm in the middle, I'm the partition, I've two surfaces and no thickness, perhaps that's what I feel, myself vibrating, I'm the tympanum, on the one hand the mind, on the other the world, I don't belong to either. (*The Unnamable* 99–100)

Let us, as an experiment, take "I'm the partition" literally. Considered as actual partitions on the printed page, "I" and "I'll" segment the text into sections that are neither semantically nor syntactically organized—for example:

> I don't know what
> I feel, tell me what
> I feel and
> I'll tell you who
> I am, they'll tell me who
> I am,
> I won't understand, but the thing will be said, they'll have said who
> I am, and
> I'll have heard, without and ear

In the text's genetic history, there was one visually unrecoverable moment where such a "loosening of unsignifying spacing" even more strongly imposed itself. As Van Hulle and Weller point out, seven pages in the first English typescript—including the passage discussed here—are "completely unpunctuated" (*The Making of Samuel Beckett's L'Innommable* 247). It is uncertain whether this was an intentional experiment or a "mechanical failure in the typewriter" (247). What we can observe quite clearly is that Beckett seemed to have left spaces where the commas, which he then added by hand later, would have been (see figure 4.2).

If we imagine the page before the punctuation was added, the I's appearance as dividing lines is even stronger; they look like Beckett's overdimensional penciled commas turned vertical—they look as if they may *function* like commas. Each I becomes a letter that spaces, "a word, [that] so long as it's not absorbed without remainder into a sense, *remains* essentially extended *between* other words." On Beckett's page, the spaces, commas, I's, and I'lls enact a play of syncopation: irregular pausing/speeding, contraction/expansion. "I'll" contains this play in itself: the lls visually reproduce the I—letters turn into a sequence of strokes—the apostrophe looks like a cut version of I, l or Beckett's large penciled commas, the linguistic syncope effects a contraction that acoustically accelerates the flow of speech. It is no coincidence that in this moment *will* is literally cut back—the certain, predictable future crumbles along with the determination and intentionality of a speaker who finds himself reduced to a rhythmical-respirational patterning that starts to prevail over meaningful language.

"I'm the partition," being outside and inside "in the same breath," recalls the syncopnea of "l'air qui respire à travers mon cahier" in Malone's writing scene, which is echoed shortly before the formulation occurs in the "words falling, you don't know where, you don't know whence." In the passage of *The Unnamable*, I constitutes a breathing space of the exscribed body, the body departed through writing. In "I'll have said it inside me, then

```
I must feel something, yes, I feel something, they say I
feel something, I don't know what it is, I don't know what I
feel, tell me what I feel, I'll tell you who I am, they'll tell
me who I am, I won't understand, but the thing will be said,
they will have said who I am, and I'll have heard, without an
ear I'll have heard, and I'll have said it, without a mouth
I'll have said it, I'll have heard it inside me, then in the
same breath outside me, perhaps that's what I feel, that
there is an outside and an inside and I in the middle, perhaps
that's what I am, the thing that divides the world in two,
```

Figure 4.2. Beckett, *The Unnamable*, MS-HRC-SB-5-10, 109r. Samuel Beckett Papers at the Harry Ransom Center, University of Texas at Austin. Used by permission of the Estate of Samuel Beckett, c/o Rosica Colin Ltd., London.

in the same breath outside me" breath occupies the same syncopal space as I in "I'm in the middle. I'm the partition": between, at the breaking point, rejoining through amputation. The typographic stumbling of the I into an unsignifying space, a divider, its faltering between sign and stroke, is an instant of syncopnea that can be related back to the link that is often established between breath and punctuation. As we have seen in the preceding chapters, breath has continually been thought as a structural element of language since the time of the rhetoricians. Moreover, as Agamben puts it, there is a "constant relation between punctuation and breathing that appears from the very first treatises on punctuation and that takes the form of a necessary interruption of meaning" (*Potentialities* 223). Thus, the I's can be considered a respirational punctuation that *exscribes* "an asyntactical and, more generally, asemantic element" (223). This would be an inorganic breathing body of language, in contrast to what Kerouac imagines as embodied punctuation: dashes *inscribing* the organic body of the writer. It would be a respirational punctuation that does (unlike Kerouac's dashes, which in fact reproduce conventional forms) silently and subliminally generate alternative structures and resists grammar and syntax.[28]

Van Hulle and Weller convincingly suggest that the temporary "disappearance of the commas" in the passage of *The Unnamable* anticipates "the entirely unpunctuated nature of the novel *Comment c'est / How It Is*" (247). In the ongoing paragraphs of *How It Is*, the at times heavily repeated words have a similar effect as the I's in the passage of *The Unnamable*: they punctuate the text and interrupt the flow by referring the readers back to earlier occurrences, having the effect of a stuttering echo. Like irregular derelict refrains, the repeated words introduce some structure to the text in addition to the spaces between the paragraphs. The most paradoxical of these refrains is "when the panting stops" / "quand ça cesse de haleter" (*How It Is*; *Comment c'est*).[29] Repeated over and over again, the "panting" does not stop but rather semantically underlines the breathless drive of the text. However, at the same time, "when the panting stops" formally marks an interruption, a punctuation.[30] Such an ambiguity is characteristic of Beckett's literary breath. It goes on when it is supposed to stop and still interrupts. Cessation and the incessant overlap.

In *The Unnamable*, failing breath marks the ultimate decrease of the speaker, the last thing to fade after the departure of the "figures" who invade it, entangling the I, the you, and the he in whirl of personal pronouns, initiating a short-lived ending:

> No one left. . . . It's I . . . who am talking about me. *Then the breath fails, the end begins, you go silent, it's the end, short-lived, you begin again,* . . . there is someone there, someone talking to you, about you, about him, then a second, then a third, then the second again, then all three together, these figures just to give you an idea, talking to you, about you, about them, all I have to do is listen, then they depart, one by one, and the voice goes on, it's not theirs, they were never there, there was never anybody, but you, never anybody but you, talking to you about you, *the breath fails, it's nearly the end, the breath stops, it's the end, short-lived,* . . . *it begins again.* (112; emphasis added)[31]

Not only is the "failed" failure of breath, the short-lived end, implying that "it begins again," enacted performatively by the repetition of almost the exact same words ("the breath fails," "it's the end, short lived," "you/it begin/s again." The repetition moreover leads to a profusion of words that matches up to the excessive number of "figures" invading the speaker: when the pack of voices is gone, the speaker announces its reduction to the most minimal physical act, breathing, and the cessation thereof, in superfluous language. In its repetitiveness, this language is poor at precisely the moment it is abundant; there's too much and too little at the same time. As will be shown in the next section, to "make abundant use of the principle of parsimony" (*The Unnamable* 107), as the unnamable proclaims, is a major precept of Beckett's poetics of breathing.[32]

"Stuffed full of these groans that choke"

A close look at the profusion of breaths pervading Beckett's oeuvre challenges a line of Beckett reception that tends to predominantly focus on the "principle of parsimony." This was encouraged by the author's minimal comments on his own work. In comparing his writing to that of James Joyce, Beckett claims: "I realised that my own way was in impoverishment, in lack of knowledge and in taking away, in subtracting rather than adding" (Beckett qtd. in Knowlson 352). In an interview with Israel Schenker in 1956, Beckett describes *The Unnamable* as and endpoint of ultimate reduction: "In the last book, *L'Innommable*, there's complete disintegration. No 'I', no 'have', no 'being.' No nominative, no accusative, no verb. There's no way to go on" (xvii). What sounds like an appropriate description of the novel's content is completely counterfactual if we look at the text-surface: as we have seen, "I's" are excessive, and there are plenty of "haves," "ams," nominatives, accusatives, and verbs. Beckett's comment on *The Unnamable* frames the novel as "grand apnoea" (*Texts for Nothing* 114)—a formulation that only appears later in *Texts for Nothing*, the work that immediately follows after the "short-lived" end from which there's supposedly "no way to go on." The speaker in *Texts for Nothing* then states that such a final breath can only be "pant[ed] towards" (114) but never reached *as* endpoint. Against Beckett's own stress on parsimony, "*panting* towards the grand apnoea," a sentence that contains his respiratory imagery in a nutshell, expresses abundance and impoverishment at the same time: the exhausting and exhausted breath is not minimal and inconspicuous, but rather, on the contrary, profuse and loud. While breath in Beckett usually indicates lessening—a reduction of the speakers, a movement toward silence, nothingness, death—breathlessness articulates itself as excessive panting. Breath impoverishes the ones who speak but is itself saturated: it is heavy, noisy, hypervisible and expressed in avalanches of words that evoke an overabundance of meanings imbued with the rich etymological history of breath-related terms.

One might assume that the short play *Breath* works differently. Described as a "culmination of Beckett's late 'style'" (Goudouna 2), *Breath* attests to his tendency toward increasing formal reduction, moving roughly speaking from novels to prose miniatures and plays that tend to get shorter. It is a play stripped to the bones: employing the "classic Aristotelian form . . . in its complete reduction" (24), *Breath* solely consists of three stage directions for a disembodied, precisely timed, recorded sequence of *birth cry, inspiration, silence, expiration, birth cry*. In her book *Beckett's Breath: Anti-Theatricality and the Visual Arts*, Sozita Goudouna investigates the piece as a "minimalist challenge to the theatre" (5). She also claims that it is a realization of "Beckett's aspiration to find a means to transform language into a kind of erasure to find a means to 'literature's end'" (23) and "almost reaches 'the point zero of language'" (55). When we see it on stage, the play indeed does away with words and the speaker is abandoned. Instead, we hear a single respirational cycle and two cries, mechanically reproduced from a recording.[33] In contrast to the staging of utter depletion in the performance, the stage directions, especially their concrete wording, echo a number of Beckett's earlier works and lead right into an intertextual thicket. The many cries and breaths pervading his prose and plays are recalled, and the "miscellaneous rubbish" the stage is supposed to be "littered with" is a reverberation of the "miscellaneous rubbish" Vladimir's pockets are "bursting with" in *Waiting for Godot* (15) as well as an exact repetition of words that occur in *Molloy*: "At the end there were two recesses . . . opposite each other littered with miscellaneous rubbish and with excrements" (78). To add a further intertextual reference, Beckett himself pointed out that the play is "not unconnected with" the French maxime "On entre, on crie / Et c'est la vie. / On crie, on sort, / Et c'est la mort" (Beckett qtd. in Knowlson 566).

From an intertextual perspective, *Breath* nonverbally stages a vertiginous exchange and transmission of words. In *The Unnamable*, we can find an anticipation of the stage directions of *Breath* in a passage concerned with glutted, overspilling speech and breath. The explicit resonances with *Breath* only become apparent if we look at the drafts, the *passage* from the French to the English text. In the printed English version, we read:

> I am alive. Warmth, ease, conviction, the right manner, as if it were my own voice, pronouncing my own words, words pronouncing me alive, since that's how they want me to be, I don't know why, with their billions of quick, their trillions of dead, that's not enough for them, I too must contribute my little convulsion, mewl, howl, gasp, and rattle, loving my neighbour and blessed with reason. But what is the right manner, I don't know. It is they who dictate this torrent of balls, they who stuffed me full of these groans that choke me. And out it pours all unchanged. (*The Unnamable* 48–49)[34]

In the original French text, the series of convulsed asemantic respiratory sounds is: "vagir, chialer, ricaner et râler" (*L'Innommable* 81). On the left blank page of the notebook in which the draft of the English translation is written, Beckett scribbled the English words he then uses in a vertical list beginning with the first one of French original, "vagir."

vagir
mewl
howl
gasp
rattle
(*The Unnamable* MS-HRC-SB-5-9-2, 05v)

This is a movement parallel to the one in *Breath*, from birth cry to death rattle. The most conspicuous word in the stage directions of the play is the specification of the cry as an infant's "vagitus" (*Breath* 9), or "vagissement"

(*Souffle* 137) in the French translation.[35] Along with the intersection of notions of life and death in the passage of *The Unnamable* where audible breathing is so dominant, the occurrence of "vagir" is consequently a significant resonance with *Breath*. The trajectory from birth to death, "vagir" to "rattle," is not apparent from either the final French or the English version of *The Unnamable*: the French "râler" is as little associated with a last breath as the English "mewl" with a birth cry. In other words, the succession from first to last breath is a transitional moment in the textual genesis of *The Unnamable*. This brief emergence of a respiratory sequence, the narrative of a life *en miniature*, does not mark the endpoint of a teleological movement; neither does the play *Breath*, which is anticipated in this *passage* (in both senses), represent Beckett's aesthetic fulfillment or the final destination of his poetics of breathing. If we contextualize *Breath* in terms of Beckett's literary development, namely, as a writing that radicalizes reduction and moves toward formal abstraction and subtraction of content, it is indeed point zero. However, tracing a context of respiratory intertexts that point to each other *reciprocally*, that is, from earlier writing forward to later writing and from later writing back to earlier writing, reveals a different picture. In the passage of *The Unnamable*, the speaker is not reduced; on the contrary, the issue is the "billions" and "trillions" of voices, sounds, and words that constantly invade it. The apertures of the respiratory body amount to torrential influx and pouring outflow: "I too must contribute my little convulsion, mewl, howl, gasp, and rattle. . . . It is they who dictate this torrent of balls, they who stuffed me full of these groans that choke me. And out it pours all unchanged" (48–49). In the French published versions, the verb used in order to express the stuffing is "farcir": "ce murmure qui m'étrangle, c'est eux qui m'en ont farci" (*L'Innommable* 81). Once more, an echo of *Breath* emerges between the French and English versions: in contrast to the English translation, there is no respiration in the French sentence—"murmure" becomes "groans"—the subtitle Beckett considered for *Breath/Souffle* in the French translation, "*Farce* en 5 actes" ("Souffle" Manuscript 1227/7/2/1; "Souffle" Typescript 1227/7/2/3; emphasis added) recalls "farcir." Through this circulation of the word "farce," its meaning of "stuffing" also touches on *Breath*, where the obvious implication is "interlude" or "dramatic work . . . excit[ing] laughter" (*Oxford English Dictionary* online). With it, a notion of overabundance, being "stuffed with groans" enters the play reduced to an interlude, to a minimal physiological act.

In the passage of *The Unnamable*, there is something redundant about the list of respirational utterances whose point seems to be expressing an excess rather than specific qualities of sound.[36] Beckett's translation suggests that he was not too interested in the particular nuances of the audible breaths. For example, "ricaner," sneering or giggling, becomes "gasp." In the handwritten draft of the English translation, the surplus manifested in these words is further stressed by their duplication. Except for the initial "vagir," the list on the left-hand side of the notebook is reproduced horizontally on the right-hand side in the running text. The arrangement on the left-hand side recalls the list of words in Musil's draft of the sentence describing the breaths of a summer's day. However, Beckett's writing practice is completely different—he does not select the most suitable word from the list, but rather uses them all. The speaker's description of how what was stuffed into it is exhaled again also aptly applies to that specific moment of the writing process: "out it pours all unchanged." The function of Musil's list is to perfect the respiratory image and its deliberate silent sounding. Beckett's list is all about breathing profusely and at random. In harsh contrast to Musil's transparent and silent current, Beckett's breaths have a thickness: the "groans" saturated with all the invading voices and sounds are so dense that they suffocate the speaker, who is not able to process them but can only belch out what was forcibly crammed into him.

In the first manuscript of the English translation, this is explicitly marked as an inspiration scene.

> It was they who ~~taught me~~ *inspired* this torrent of balls and glutted me *with* these groans that choke me. And out it pours all unchanged. (*The Unnamable* MS-HRC-SB-5-9-2, 06r)

This oral inspiration scene confirms how Blanchot characterizes the unnamable's speech: it represents an "excess of impotence" and "sterile prolixity." In the draft, Blanchot's description of inspiration as "sterile prolixity" finds a most literal and embodied expression: the abundance of breaths forced into the speaker spills over and out without anything new being created. *The Unnamable* dispels the traditionally positive connotations of inspiration: it is choking, induces surfeit rather than elation, the input is expelled unchanged—it is literally superfluous. Inspiration is not staged as a "drama of . . . theft" (Derrida, "La parole soufflée" 220) and dispossession, but as one of being possessed by other words, voices, and breaths. That "inspired" is turned into "dictate" in the revision of the draft does not mean that breathing and speaking are equated in the passage—the description of different respirational sounds is so palpable that it is hard to identify them with "words," or just read them as metaphors for uttering language orally.

Rather, what Beckett highlights is that both breathing and speaking are not the subject's own and not integral to it. Thus, the phonocentric narrative is counteracted. Neither spoken language and voice, nor breathing can restore a lost presence or identity—one's "own voice" always presents itself in the mode of "as if" ("as if it were my own voice, pronouncing my own words"). Breath is not a gateway to a more authentic life or mode of writing but subject to mechanisms akin to those making language an alienating, distancing, splitting, and mediating force; therefore, it cannot recuperate a more lively, original form of language.

With regard to such passages, one realizes that Beckett's early embrace of Mauthner, the ambition to reach beyond language and pursue a "Literatur des Unworts" (literature of the unword), does not represent a solution of the dilemma of writing. Even if "jene fürchterlich willkürliche Materialität der Wortfläche" ("the dreadfully arbitrary materiality of the word-surface"; *Disjecta* 53) is dissolved, there is little relief in prelinguistic breath when it manifests as strained, repetitive, congested howling, gasping, and rattling. Moreover, the passage twists Mauthner's claim that "every word is *impregnated* with its own history, every single word carries in itself an endless development from metaphor to metaphor" (115; my translation; my emphasis).[37] Beckett does stage what Derrida calls the "oversignification which overburdens the word . . . souffle" (224), but the bodily image he ties it to, suffocation, runs counter to Mauthner's notion of impregnation. The rich history a word carries along with it, which for Mauthner implies fertility, turns into a fatal overkill in Beckett's text. Beckett exhibits breath's etymological and metaphorical past precisely at the moment when he turns inspiration into "these groans that choke me." In a similar move, he alludes to the biblical breath of life by transforming the phrase "pronouncing someone dead" to "words pronouncing me alive": the life-giving act becomes violent, imbued with fatality. Breath and words are presented as invaders acting on the body; glutted with preexisting meanings, the word "breath" imposes these on any subject into whose mouth it is put. Even though Beckett effects a resistance to the entrenched connotations by his counterintuitive formulations, they at the same time highlight a persistent inevitability and sense of deadlock. As a recurring motif in Beckett's writing, life and death are entangled to a degree that one necessarily contains the other.

"With breath in his nostrils, it only remains for him to suffocate"

By embedding breath in an intricate constellation of birth and death, Beckett draws on one of his well-known sources, Otto Rank's *The Trauma of Birth*.

In his attempt to uncover a "biological foundation" (43) of the unconscious, Rank traces the source of anxiety back to a feeling of suffocation that accompanies the "primal trauma" (8) when the infant is ripped out of a state of "*intrauterine primal pleasure*" (17): "We shall take as our guiding principle Freud's statement that all anxiety goes back originally to the anxiety at birth (dyspnoea)" (11). In his "Psychology Notes" from the 1930s, Beckett sums up Rank's argument as follows, reproducing the original text almost word by word: "Just as all anxiety goes back to anxiety at birth (dyspnoea), so every pleasure has as its final aim the reestablishment of the primal intrauterine pleasure."[38] Angela Moorjani points out that Rank is a revealing reference with respect to the "fizzled births-into-deaths" in Beckett's works (173). Supporting Moorjani's claim, Graley Herren adds a convincing argumentation in his article "A Womb with a View": "Beckett utterly rejects [Rank's] idealized depiction of intrauterine life. On those several occasions when he confided his memories before birth, he consistently recalled the womb as a chamber of horrors" (242). These "memories" are, of course, themselves narratives, created either by Beckett about himself or by people who knew him. Peggy Guggenheim, for example, recounts: "Ever since his birth he had retained a terrible memory of life in his mother's womb. He was constantly suffering from this and had awful crises, when he felt he was suffocating" (*Out of This Century* 205). In Guggenheim's report, Beckett situates the source of a symptomatic feeling of suffocation in the intrauterine state whereas Rank claims that "all neurotic disturbances of breathing (asthma) . . . repeat the feeling of suffocation *at birth*" (51; emphasis added). In such accounts, the Rankian scenario is recalled and adapted in a way that goes hand in hand with Beckett's fictional references to it.

What Beckett takes over from Rank is the conjunction of birth and suffocation, and consequently, a shortcut between birth and death. However, in Beckett's depictions the relations between birth and suffocation are significantly different from the way they are theorized by Rank. Rank does not elaborate on the "dyspnea" at birth, apart from the claim that it is the first *anxiety* occurring right at the traumatic moment of separation from the mother. A comment on the infantile "identification of death with the return to the mother" (27), which was not included in the English translation, provides more insight into respirational anxiety: the infant "wishes to go back to a place where there were no interferences from outside yet."[39] The baby's first breath outside the mother's womb is a drastic "interference from outside." The outside air has to be taken in in order to be able to live—death could be the desired state because breathing stops. When death and birth meet in connection with breath in Beckett's writing, the implications are different. It has already been pointed out that in Beckett's literary work, the "grand apnoea" is an illusion—the panting will never stop. As Malone puts it in an allusion to Rank's description of the desperate birth cry: "To have vagitated and not be bloody well able to rattle" (*Malone Dies* 341). In the French original of *The Unnamable*, the Rankian scene of natal suffocation is rewritten in such a way that the "last" breath coincides with birth: "Et naîtrai enfin dans un dernier soupir, ou dans un de ces hoquets qui déparent hélas trop souvent la solennité du trépas" (*L'Innommable* 93).[40] The last breath is thus revoked as a *last* one that could be strived after in the quest to return to a primordial state.[41] Moreover, death is not a repose: the "solemnity of passing" is disturbed by strained involuntary respiration, the "hiccups." In other words, in Beckett's writing, breath unsettles both the idea of an intrauterine paradise and a regained peacefulness in death. Beckett's literary breathing upsets the idea of a state of untorn harmonic unity. It syncopates, not by marking the cut from a lost synthesis (Rank), but rather by tying together what is imagined as an ideal of primordial unity and the state of separation following it, thus pointing back at the continual interruptions that have always already been at work.

In a discussion of Beckett's literary adaptations of Rank's theory, the question of language must not be neglected. It is important to notice that in *The Trauma of Birth*, the mechanisms of the *psyche* are founded in a loss of *breath*. Beckett's literary allusions to the trauma of birth highlight the *tension* between the physiological and the etymological, linguistic or figural breath that Rank evokes in an argument for what he considers the strictly "biological" root of "the whole development of mankind" (*The Trauma of Birth* xi), including the development of language and memory. In the following, I want to elucidate this claim by first going back to *The Unnamable*, and then offering a close reading of *Breath*. As Beckett studies have repeatedly pointed out, one outline of the speaker in *The Unnamable* is thoroughly linguistic (see Van Hulle and Weller 190): "I'm in words, made of words" (*The Unnamable* 104). This linguistic constitution of the speaker is touched upon in a passage where the I proposes replacing the first person with the third person, "he."

> Words, he says he knows they are words. But how can he know, who has never heard anything else. Not to mention other things. . . . For example, to begin with, his breathing. There he is now with breath in his nostrils, it only remains for him

to suffocate. . . . More lies, he doesn't breathe yet, he'll never breathe. Then what is this faint noise, as of air stealthily stirred, recalling the breath of life, to those whom it corrodes? (70)[42]

Both surrounded and imbued with words to a degree that he becomes indistinguishable from them, the speaker tries to turn to "other things": "For example, . . . his breathing." However, there is no escape from the immersion in words. The turn to "breathing" turns out to be an evocation of textual references rather than a return to a prelinguistic bodily process. "There he is now with breath in his nostrils, it only remains for him to suffocate" refers to two pieces of *writing*, *The Trauma of Birth* and the Bible.[43] Thus, it is not surprising that the speaker realizes: "More lies, he doesn't breathe yet, he'll never breathe," that is, he'll never breathe physically as long as he is a speaker in a literary text, a cluster of letters enmeshed in a literary world. The bodily residue that is then mentioned, "this faint noise," seems to resist the total prevalence of language for an instant only to be embedded in a figure of speech, the simile "as of air stealthily stirred" and then "recalling" the biblical metonymy, "the breath of life" that in further reference to Rank "corrodes."

The biblical breath in the nostrils is explicitly mentioned in *The Trauma of Birth*. Rank considers the Genesis story an example of "heroic compensation"; it is one of the "deliverance myths" that represent "a direct reversal of the real occurrence." Rank argues that the "motive lying at the bottom of the entire myth formation" is "to make of no effect the primal trauma" (113). In other words, myths are a strategy to master the trauma of birth, to create narratives in which birth is free of anxiety. The Bible offers a "phantastic reproduction of the primal situation": "The breathing of breath into the nostrils . . . refers to the accompanying dyspnoea of the newly born" (108–13). In the biblical story, the newly created human does not experience suffocation but is *given* breath. In his reference to the breath in the nostrils, Beckett's afterthought "it only remains for him to suffocate" smashes the consoling implications Rank attributes to the biblical scene and thwarts the idea of "heroic compensation." Beckett's cynical take on the "breath of life" points beyond the narrative content of the story told in Genesis. Bearing this in mind, we can trace a mechanism of *substitution* and *displacement* pervading Rank's theory. For Rank, myths such as the creation of men in Genesis *replace* the experience at birth and cover up its traumatic impact in order to make it more bearable. Such narratives created by men operate in a way similar to childhood memories. Rank claims that "all memories of infancy must, to a certain extent, be considered 'cover-memories'" because "the 'primal scene' can never be remembered" (*The Trauma of Birth* 8). What is translated as "cover-memories" refers to Freud's "Deckerinnerungen," that is, an observed predominance of "unimportant" or "accidental" childhood memories. Freud explains them as follows: "The indifferent childhood memories owe their existence to a process of displacement. . . . They represent the substitute for other really significant impressions, whose reproduction is hindered by some resistance" (*Psychopathology of Everyday Life* 57–58). In Rank's theory, the breath into the nostrils functions like a *Deckerinnerung*—not because something unimportant is remembered instead of something essential and more troubling, but due to a process of displacement. The narrative of the invigorating infusion of a life-giving breath substitutes a feeling of suffocation that cannot be remembered. When Beckett embeds the biblical "breath of life" in a passage that also alludes to Rank, he hints at an immemorial foundation of that very metonymy.[44] By adding that the breath of life "corrodes," Beckett uncovers the trauma of separation for which the vital breath substitutes, one could argue with Rank. However, if we take the process of displacement seriously, we have to consider the possibility—or probability—that the trauma of birth as Rank sketches it is yet another cover, a narrative that substitutes something subject to censorship. A basic contradiction in Rank's book is his detailed description of the trauma of birth, which, as he claims, "can never be remembered" (8).

That Beckett was suspicious of the elaborations Rank provides in the outline of the primal trauma, especially its consequences for the development of language, becomes apparent in a handwritten comment in his "Psychology Notes" on Rank's elucidation of how anxiety leads to "symbol formation" (*The Trauma of Birth* 50). Rank argues as follows:

> The first reaction after birth is the cry which, by violently abolishing the difficulty of breathing, may presumably relieve a certain amount of anxiety. The same cry is then repeated as a desire for the mother, whence the formation of the lips, practiced by the infant at the breast, leads as a motive to the formation of the universal syllable *ma*. This enables us to grasp the formation of sound from symbol *in statu nascendi*; for the lips formed for sucking represent the first substitution of the mother by a, so to say, autoplastic attempt. Should the desire which causes the sucking formation of the lips be ungratified, then again is released the first painful cry of anxiety which signalized the separation from the mother. (102)

Beckett summarizes: "shape of lips at the breast lead to formation of universal human syllable *ma*," and, in a handwritten note, adds "Macché!" ("Psychology Notes"). This smart and funny comment reveals Beckett's reservations concerning such organic theories of language formation. The single word "Macché" in itself contains a complex linguistic counterscenario to Rank's smooth and strictly causal argumentation: the "universal" syllable enters a multilingual vortex that resists a unified translation. The Italian "macché" scrutinizes Rank's claim: "Certainly not," "you must be joking"! The word contains Rank's "ma," the syllable and the mother it *substitutes*, which is followed by "ché," meaning "What?" (what kind of mother?), recalling the Gaelic *c'è*, meaning "Who?" (*Gaelic Dictionary* 196) The mother as tangible origin of all trauma is thus called into question, a question that will later introduce the indeterminate space of *The Unnamable*: "Who now?"

This short digression helps to pinpoint what the "breath of life" in this passage implies. Rather than *covering* the feeling of suffocation at birth, "the breath of life" displays the mechanism of displacement it is involved in as a linguistic expression entangled in an intertextual net. When physiological breath enters language, it is shifted into the domain of inorganic signs. This involves a harsh caesura, contrasting with Rank's theory of an organically motivated "symbol formation" that goes back to the child's gradual autoplastic adaptation. In Beckett's linguistic reflection, the rupture is not compensated but rather exposed. The passage of *The Unnamable*, "recalling the breath of life," suggests that breath is suffocated into the domain of words: the speaker who claims that he breathes in a literary text lies; his organic breath is beyond the words that constitute his linguistic world. Perhaps that is why the final "grand apnoea" can never take place in Beckett's texts; some kind of suffocation has already happened, as a precondition of writing. Following this line of reading, the "breath of life" in *The Unnamable* also points to the displacement at work in the metonymy of "breath" standing for "life": the equation of breath and life involves a shift, putting both "breath" and "life" out of place—at least of a place that would be biologically, organically rooted.

Also drawing on Rank's *Trauma of Birth*, Beckett's play *Breath* stages tensions between the organic and the inorganic, the lively and the machinic, the physiological and the linguistic. As Herren observes, *Breath* commemorates the Rankian "vagitus of the newborn taking its first breath" (243)[45]—the "faint brief cry" in the stage directions is specified as "Instant of recorded vagitus" (*Breath* 9). It immediately becomes apparent that the allusion to Rank's "*biological* basis" (*The Trauma of Birth* xiv) of the unconscious is undermined. Organic bodies are completely absent from the play: as Goudouna observes, both "the subject and the performer" are eradicated (9). Artificially produced breath, specified as "amplified recording," is embedded in symmetrically arranged, mechanically precise stage directions: "Faint brief cry and immediately inspiration and slow increase of light together reaching maximum together in about 10 seconds"; "Expiration and slow decrease of light together reaching minimum together . . . in about 10 seconds and immediately cry as before" (*Breath* 9). David Lloyd argues "breathing thus signifies here . . . the insistent moment of inanimation in the animate. The exhausted traces of the breath . . . continue to bear witness to the vestiges of the life of which they are the relicts" (189). That the sounds of breath and the cry are *recorded* heightens the impression of the impersonal and anonymous. What we hear is a machine-breath and a machine-cry. *Breath* is a "technicule" (Goudouna 13) that puts its artificiality and aesthetic form on display: the symmetrical arrangement and exact timing hardly correspond with a living body's much more irregular physiological processes (see Arthur Rose, "Combat Breathing" 128). At the same time, the play obviously invites being read as an allegory of life and death.

In this respect, another passage from Rank's *Trauma of Birth* that Beckett reproduces in his "Psychology Notes" is revealing. Even though the play itself does without words, this intertext shows the extent to which the linguistic dimension of breath still affects it. In commenting on Parmenides's "logical abstractions of 'being' and 'not being,'" Rank refers to the questionable etymological connection of breathing and being: "He spun these out of the originally quite real and human facts of being and not being, which in their anthropomorphic application to the world can yet be traced linguistically: for 'esse means at the bottom: to breathe!'" (*The Trauma of Birth* 171). Beckett notes: "Esse means to breathe!" ("Psychology Notes"). When he "described the play *Breath* as . . . a whole play, and life" (Beckett qtd. in Connor, "Was That a Point?" 276),[46] the supposed etymological chain of "breathing-living-being" is evoked.[47] If we read the play as an allusion to Rank's text, an inversion can be observed. The mechanical, perfectly symmetrical, disembodied breath rather presents itself as a "logical abstraction"[48] than a "quite real and human fact[]." In the play, breath hints at the idea of an "anthropomorphic application" and at the same time constitutes a "farcical" embodiment of the linguistic connotations breath is saturated with that can be traced back to a concrete intertext (i.e., Rank). The abstract form of the play detaches it from a biological, physiological origin. This is a twisted echo of Rank's reflections on form and content in the preface of *The Trauma of Birth*: "the deepest biological content [i.e., the birth trauma] . . . remains tangible as manifest form even in the highest intellectual accomplishments. . . . The chief purpose of this work is to draw attention to this *biologically based law of the form which determines the content*" (xiv–xv). For Rank, the "mental productions of mankind" and the "deepest biological layer of the Unconscious . . . correspond with, and harmoniously supplement each other" (xiv), which he then describes as a correlation of form and content. The content of *Breath* explicitly refers to Rank's biological basis, the birth trauma, by staging a vagitus and breath, and Beckett offers an interpretation of the content in biological terms: "a whole life." The "law" of its "form," however, operates abiologically.

It is important to acknowledge that the almost perfect symmetry staged by *Breath* only applies to the English original.[49] To begin with, the French translation from 1971 does not exactly correspond to the English original. The numerical arrangement of the stage directions is different: while in the English version, "CURTAIN," symmetrically arranged in the beginning and end, bracketing the three stage directions, is not numbered, the French lists "Noir" as "1" and "5" (*Souffle* 136). In contrast to the numbering of the stage directions from "1" to "3" in the English version, evoking the three-part Aristotelian structure (beginning, middle, and end), the French drafts spell out "Farce en 5 actes" ("Souffle" Manuscript 1227/7/2/1). Moreover, in the French version, one can detect a significant disruption of the symmetrical arrangement itself—and it is the breath that plays the most crucial role here. In the English original, the directions for the cry are "Instant of recorded vagitus. Important that two cries be identical, switching on and off strictly synchronized light and breath." The ones for the breath are simply "amplified recording" (*Breath* 9). In the French translation, there is a striking addition; the cries and the breaths are contrasted with one another: "Essentiel que les deux cris soient *identiques*"—"Essentiel que les deux phases inspiration-expiration soient bien *différenciées*" ("It is essential that the two phases inspiration-expiration are well differentiated"; *Souffle* 137; emphasis added). Beckett presents the two sentences in a parallel manner in French, in contrast to the English version, where the corresponding explication of the breath concerning identity/difference is lacking. At the same time, the "essential" clarification that the breaths should be different from each other shatters the symmetrical structure of the play as a whole. The variant breaths are the only instances deviating from the exact repetition the play stages ("Curtain"; "hold about 5 seconds"; "cry"; "increase/decrease of light in 10 seconds"). While the cry is completely mechanized (recorded, identically repeated), the breath of the French translation, incorporated as it is in this machinic setting, recuperates some traits of the physiological process, in which no "movement inhalation-exhalation" is identical.

This is even more accentuated in a handwritten draft of the French translation where the noun preceding "inspiration-expiration" is, tentatively, "mouvement" instead of "phases" ("Souffle" Manuscript 1227/7/2/1). Whereas the term "phases" underlines inorganic and repetitive qualities, the much more open and variable "mouvement" resonates with a dissimilarity of two individual breaths that is closer to what we do when we actually breathe. Littré only has two definitions for "phase": (1) "Diverse appearances of the moon and some planets according to which they receive the light of the sun." (2) "Successive changes that can be observed in certain things" (Littré 3: 1095; my translation). The first and most dominant definition of planetary phases designates a regular succession of repeated, clearly determinable states. If we understand inhalation and exhalation in *Breath* as *phases*, their being "well differentiated" could imply a generalized pattern analogous to the full moon versus crescent moon, for example. In that sense, differentiated phases are quite removed from the idea of individual physiological rhythms, in which each inhalation and exhalation is variable. Moreover, Littré's first definition of "phase," which resonates in *Breath*, moves the expirations and inspirations out of the human domain into the cosmic, the removed world of inanimate celestial bodies. The etymology of "phase" given by Littré, "Φάσις, action de briller" ("shining"; 1095) and the stress on the moon's or planet's alternations of illumination goes hand in hand with the strictly synchronized light in Beckett's play. Thus, depersonalization still predominates over breath in the final version of the French translation.

Only when visiting the archive in Reading to view the drafts of *Souffle* did I find something that unsettles the depersonalized air of Beckett's *Breath*: the *handwritten word "mouvement,"* following two deleted attempts to specify "inspiration-expiration." It seems no coincidence that this word only appears in Beckett's manuscript, bearing the mark of his hand's movements in the very moment of writing—writing, a cultural technique that involves disciplining the hand into certain moves but at the same time maintains traces of a breather's individual bodily rhythm. Semantically, "mouvement" has a much broader variety of meanings than "phase": it can refer to celestial bodies, but Littré also defines it, among others, as *"terme de musique," "terme de peinture et de sculpture," "terme d'architecture," "terme[] de literature," "terme de mécanique,"* or *"terme de physiologie"* (Littré 3: 656–58). In other words, "mouvement" is a very open term that can be applied in various domains that the play *Breath* invokes: the aesthetic, mechanical, and organic-physiological. In the final version, the latter is only hinted at to be abandoned by the inhalation, exhalation, and cry. In the manuscript, where the movement is not yet defined as a strictly periodic one, a recurring sequence (phase) of expiration-inspiration potentially still encompasses "les mouvements involontaires, mouvements appartenant à la vie organique" ("involuntary movements pertaining to organic life"; Littré 3: 657; my translation). The first definition of "mouvement" Littré lists is: "Action par laquelle un corps ou quelqu'une de ses parties passe d'un lieu à un autre, d'une place à une autre" ("Action through which a body or one of its parts pass from one place to another"; 656; my translation). Such a movement is characteristic for breathing, which is constantly passing from one place to another. In Beckett's manuscript, "mouvement" itself is involved in such a dynamic: the word already seems to be moving toward the inorganic/abstract/machinic, passing into "phase." The very *movement* that "inhalation-exhalation" engages in within and across the various versions of *Breath/Souffle* reveals a residue of something that is not assimilable to either abstract formal symmetry, to the mechanic inanimateness of technical reproduction, or to the organic nature of a living body.

Plath: "And still the lungs won't fill"

"My god the iron lung"

Movements between the organic and the inorganic determine Plath's respirational images. In the poem "Paralytic," the "machine to breathe and beat forever" from "Suicide off Egg Rock" assumes a most literal form. In one of the last texts she wrote, on January 29, 1963, Plath focuses on a man in hospital who is kept alive by artificial respiration: "My god the iron lung / That loves me, pumps / My two / dust bags in and out" ("Paralytic," *The Collected Poems* 266). Echoing Beckett's characters whose "extremities" wane and whose speaking organs are negated, Plath's I states "No fingers to grip, no tongue" (266). We are faced with the very paradox Beckett counters with the question "Who now?" Who is speaking, if the I obviously cannot? The patient[50] is deprived, not only of his speaking organs, but also of the body parts that would allow him to handle a writing instrument ("No fingers to grip, no tongue"). Moreover, the preceding line, "my mind a rock" (266), also forbids reading the poem as the record of a thought process or interior monologue. Through its depiction of the breathing apparatus, "Paralytic" implicitly reflects its own mute and mindless articulation. Whatever writes or speaks seems to function like the iron lung that breathes for the patient: it performs what the I's body is no longer able to do. In combination with the most banal "explanation" that it was Sylvia Plath who composed the poem, that she did the speaking and writing, this implication yields a remarkable constellation: confounded with the articulating instance in the poem, Plath, whose writing was insistently conflated with her life by critics who considered her texts to be testimonies of her psychological and bodily condition, becomes an artificial inspirator. In the spirit of Beckett's "recalling the breath of life, to those whom it corrodes," "Paralytic" subverts the biblical image of vitalizing inspiration. The body being sustained by the godly iron lung is inanimate: the "mind" is "a rock" and the "starched" breast has become part of the hospital sheets (266).

The poem contains some technical particulars of historical iron lungs. The Children's Hospital in Boston, where Plath grew up, is famous for its use of the first version of an iron lung, which was developed by and named after the Harvard doctor Philip Drinker, on an eight-year-old girl suffering from polio-induced paralysis (Drinker and Shaw 245; Rothman et al.). It is reported that the prototype of the machine consisted of an "iron cylinder and a couple of the new-fangled vacuum cleaners that were becoming so popular in homes across America in the 1920s" (Ciment 280). In the moment the poem displays them as "dust bags," the organic lungs thus coincide with the "iron lung." The patient, whose organs are identical with the machine's components, becomes a cyborg. Along with its protagonist, the poem presents *itself* as a breathing machine. Its radical enjambment, the extremely short lines often breaking long and elaborate sentences into agrammatical scraps, imitates how the respirator impairs speech. When they introduced their newly developed apparatus in a scientific article, Philip Drinker and Louis Agassiz Shaw addressed the "effect of the pressure changes upon speech" and observed that the function of talking "is cut off abruptly by inspiration" (238). The respirator's specific impacts on speech were presented to a broad public in a video from 1956, promoting the March of Dimes. One can see how the journalist Drew Pearson, "reporting from inside an iron lung" struggles to speak, making unusual breath-pauses in the middle of sentences. The way Pearson describes his experience in the iron lung in his column *Washington Merry-Go-Round* at times literally resonates with Plath's poem:

> I found myself locked in . . . hands unable to touch my head. . . .
> A body that breathes whether you want it or not. . . . It's an
> eerie sound, that breathing, like the wash of waves on the shore,
> a steady pounding of the air, pounding in, sucking out, forcing
> your lungs to expand and contract . . . in and out . . . all night
> long. . . . You don't argue with an iron lung. It's the boss. It
> does the breathing. (Pearson n.p.)

Even though in the poem, the patient lacks the organs that would permit him to produce oral language, "Paralytic" stages a speech syncopated by artificially inflated lungs through its line breaks while recurring iambic and trochaic patterns reproduce the monotonous rhythm of the mechanical respirator.

> It happens. Will it go on?—
> My mind a rock,
> No fingers to grip, no tongue,
> My god the iron lung
>
> That loves me, pumps
> My two
> Dust bags in and out,
> Will not
> Let me relapse
> While the day outside glides by like ticker tape
> (*The Collected Poems* 266)

The respiratory state sketched in the poem conjoins and adapts two psychoanalytic scenes: the Rankian trauma of birth and the Freudian death drive.[51] The breathing machine vaults the patient into a scenario in which the world of the living is left behind in favor of a precondition with both traits of a state before birth and after death. Recalling Rank, the poem presupposes an experience of suffocation that causes a return to a quasi-intrauterine state. The mechanical respirator, "the iron lung / That loves me," is a womb-like space. Patients are placed into the cylinder up to the head, the maternal machine encloses their bodies and does the breathing for them. Tracy Brain who discusses the "primary bodily relation of the infant with the mother" in "Paralytic" notes that "elements of technology and infancy" are indicated in a dictionary entry on "iron lung" that Plath underlined in her copy of *Webster's*: "A *device for artificial respiration in which rhythmic alternations in the air pressure in a chamber surrounding a patient's chest force air in and out of the lungs*. It is of special value when the nerves governing the chest muscles fail to function because of *infantile paralysis*" (qtd. in Brain 120; emphasis in original). When Plath wrote "Paralytic," iron lungs were still strongly associated with polio. It was during outbreaks in the 1940s and 1950s that they became a common sight in hospitals (see Rothman et al.). This concrete medical-historical context tying the poem's evocations of a fetal state to infantile paralysis thwarts a straightforward Rankian reading of "Paralytic" as a "womb phantasy" (*The Trauma of Birth* 5), an imagination of "the pleasurable primal state" (176). The poem can hardly be considered an attempted "*mastery* of the birth trauma" (5; emphasis added). The passivity of the patient is overarching; he has lost control over body and mind alike and has fully surrendered to a "god" that cannot breathe life into him even though it keeps ventilating his lungs.

Another Rankian topos resonating in "Paralytic" is the trauma of separation and the urge for reunion it triggers. The patient is presented as inseparable from and at times identical with the womb-like space enclosing him; however, this maternal space is utterly inorganic. The return to an inorganic state evokes the text Rank continually attempts to reinterpret: Freud's *Beyond the Pleasure Principle*. The lines "Dead egg, I lie / Whole" (266) link the "return" to "a lost union" (Rank *The Trauma of Birth* 173)[52] alluded to with an image that conflates birth and death (recalling Plath's poem about Egg Rock).[53] This would, theoretically, go hand in hand with Rank's postulation of an infantile "identification of death with the return to the mother" (27). What becomes questionable with respect to the poem is Rank's insistence on "the *libidinal foundation* for this fundamental striving, the return into the primal state" (176; emphasis added), which is ultimately an attempt to take over Freudian ideas and terms while refuting the latter's assumption of a death drive: "what biologically seems to us the impulse to death, strives again to establish nothing else than the already experienced condition before birth and the 'compulsion to repetition' arises from the unquenchable character of this longing" (Rank 196). In a gesture that is itself regressive, Rank disclaims Freud's speculation that there might be a drive beyond the pleasure principle; instead, he declares a respiratory trauma is key to the human psyche: "the primal anxiety-effect at birth, which remains operative through life, right up to the final separation from the outer world (gradually become a second mother) at death, is from the very beginning . . . an expression of the new-born child's physiological injuries (dyspnoea—constriction—anxiety)" (187). Plath's "Paralytic" offers a deeply ambivalent and complex negotiation of a respiratory scenario that recalls the Freudian death drive and resists the Rankian "biological reduction."

The patient's description of his respiratory environment expresses an ambivalence concerning the desired return to a "primal state," which Rank, hand in hand with Freud, deems is "actually no longer attainable" (187): "My god the iron lung . . . / Will not / let me relapse" (266). In the context of the poem, the most common meaning of "relapse," the "recurrence of an illness after an interval of recovery," does not seem accurate, as the patient is far from recuperation. In this medical sense, the iron lung merely prevents his condition from degenerating, or, quite simply, from dying. From a Freudian perspective, the broader meaning of relapse, "to revert (to a previous state . . .)" (*Oxford English Dictionary* online), complicates the matter: the previous state strived for is thus deathlike. Freud argues that "inanimate things existed before living ones," and, due to an urge to "to restore the inanimate state" (*Beyond the Pleasure Principle* 49), "the aim of all life is death" (32). From this angle, the iron lung's prevention of death indicates that it *prohibits* the restoration of a former state. The strophic arrangement of the poem and the line breaks display an ambiguity with regard to "relapse":

> My god the iron lung
>
> That loves me, pumps
> My two
> Dust bags in and out,
> Will not
>
> Let me relapse

Isolated from the sentence it is grammatically part of, "Let me relapse" articulates a demand that is denied by the work of the iron lung. When read as an individual line, "Will not" points to what Freud calls "the expression of the inertia inherent in organic life" (30), an abandonment of will to the passivity of the inorganic. When we read the poem out loud, the differences between what the iron lung does and the implicit wish expressed by the patient literally depend on respiration: if we make the breath-pause accord to the grammatical unit of sense, the iron lung will not let the two dust bags relapse. If we pause between stanzas and thus breathe according to the syncopated rhythm, mimicking the impaired speech of someone locked in an iron lung, the will negates itself and "Let me relapse" becomes an urge. In the latter case, organic breath is intricately entangled with machinic respiration. On the diegetic level, the words isolated by the breath-pause act in the service of the death drive and against the iron lung's inanimate preservation of the biological body. On the formal level, the reader's breath surrenders to the forced ventilation of the iron lung the poem's line breaks assimilate.

That the patient in "Paralytic" has moved beyond the pleasure principle is quite plainly stated: he abandoned libidinous drives, "all / wants, desire / falling from me like rings" (*The Collected Poems* 267). His everyday life slips into oblivion; the "wife" and "daughters," reduced to a flattened photographic image, become as anonymous as the hospital staff (266).[54] The poem describes a withdrawal from "a whole world I cannot touch" (266), the sonic and visual environment is subdued and diminished: sounds have the qualities "soft" and "still," the daughters "whisper," and "the day outside glides by like ticker tape" (266). In Freud's words, the I recedes from "the pressure of external disturbing forces" (*Beyond the Pleasure Principle* 30) and submits itself to "a function whose business it is to free the mental apparatus entirely from excitation or to keep the amount of excitation in it constant or to keep it as low as possible." According to Freud, "the function thus described would be concerned with the most universal endeavour of all living substance namely to return to the quiescence of the inorganic world" (56).

In the lines "Dead egg, I lie / Whole / On a whole world I cannot touch," the resonances between "Paralytic" and *Beyond the Pleasure Principle* reach their peak. In one of his famous "far-fetched speculation[s]," concerned with the constitution and development of the mental apparatus, the system of Perception-Consciousness, Freud comes up with a peculiar illustrative scenario in which the death drive's striving for "quiescence" and a reduction of external stimuli is first sketched. "Let us picture a living organism in its most simplified possible form as an undifferentiated vesicle of a substance that is susceptible to stimulation." He then describes the modification this organism undergoes "as a result of the ceaseless impact of external stimuli on the surface of the vesicle" (18–20) as follows:

> This little fragment of living substance is suspended in the middle of an external world charged with the most powerful energies; and it would be killed by the stimulation emanating from these if it were not provided with a protective shield against stimuli. It acquires the shield in this way: its outermost surface ceases to have the structure proper to living matter, becomes to some degree inorganic and thenceforward functions as a special envelope or membrane resistant to stimuli. (21)

In "Paralytic," the human in the iron lung regresses to "an organism in its most simplified possible form," akin to the "undifferentiated vesicle" when it is described as "Dead egg / Whole." The poem outlines various ways in which a "protective shield against stimuli" becomes an inorganic envelope of the patient's body: the breathing apparatus's metal case as such resembles the shield, which in further descriptions assumes various other material constitutions. In the lines "Eyes, nose, ears, / A clear / Cellophane I cannot crack" (266), the body's orifices morph into an impenetrable plastic envelope. It is significant that these body parts are all sensory organs, which, according to Freud, are nothing but remnants of the protective shield in "highly developed organisms," where the "receptive cortical layer of the former vesicle has long been withdrawn into the depths of the interior of the body, though portions of it have been left behind on the surface. . . . These are the sense organs . . . which also include special arrangements for further protection against excessive amounts of stimulation" (*Beyond the Pleasure Principle* 21–22). In "Paralytic," the sense organs develop backward and become an inorganic membrane. An even earlier state the patient reverts to is hinted at by the "dead egg," where the "outermost surface" is a mineral shell and the prenatal assumes traits of the preorganic.

On the basis of the respiratory environment generated by the iron lung, the poem imagines an organism, or inorganism, that keeps the interferences of the external world, which breathing continually exposes us to, to a bare minimum: from a breathing mediated and regulated by the apparatus, the speaker moves to an almost completely sealed state. It is striking, though, that there is a significant difference between the image of the cellophane and that of the dead egg. Whereas the described airtight cellophane can only lead to suffocation, the linguistic presentation of the dead egg does not indicate a termination of respiratory openness.

> Dead egg, I lie
> Whole
> On a whole world I cannot touch

Plath's textual staging of the "dead egg" condition suggests porousness: "Whole" is a homophone of "hole." The image recalling Freud's vesicle goes hand in hand with an acoustically undifferentiated state in which the self-contained, unified inanimate organism becomes all opening. The opening is underlined by the word's most dominant phoneme, oʊ, which in its graphic form as a letter—o—mutely coincides with "hole" and visually becomes a zero (0) point, which is a redefined inorganic primal state. An interplay between acoustic and visual reading effects that signifier and signified cohere and "Whole" *is* what it says, paradoxically, by being other than itself at the same time.[55] In the word "whole," visual, auditory, and semantic qualities become permeable. The letter "o" depicts both the cyclical self-enclosed unity of "whole" and the permeability of "hole." It has the shape of an egg, being defined by a protective shell, and it largely consists of a gaping puncture. The protective shield is pierced, which is precisely what Freud defines as trauma: "We describe as 'traumatic' any excitations from outside which are powerful enough to break through the protective shield" (*Beyond the Pleasure Principle* 23). In the lines depicting a state of wholeness, Plath keeps pace with Freud's steps on his oddest tracks of speculation, moving from the limit of representation and biological plausibility to the limit of the conceivable. She presents the flipside of an impermeable enclosure: a being that is all-breath, which resists being imaginable because its respiratory exchange with the outside is total: whole = hole. As consequently as this thought follows what the poem sketches, "I think, the moment has come for breaking off" (52)—for me, at this point, just as it did for Freud at a particular moment in *Beyond the Pleasure Principle*.

I will, however, continue with the passage that urged Freud to write this sentence. In his attempt to derive the sex drives from the death drive, Freud, in a first step, goes back to Plato's *Symposium* and recounts the myth of originally unified beings that were split and then strive to return to their former state through copulation. In a second step, he transfers his interpretation of the myth to his speculations about the origins of organic matter: "that living substance at the time of its coming to life was torn apart into small particles, which have ever since endeavoured to reunite through the sexual instincts." What Freud has in mind is a development from unicellular to multicellular organisms. "Shall we follow the hint given us by the poet-philosopher, and venture upon the hypothesis that . . . these splintered fragments of living substance . . . attained a multicellular condition and finally transferred the instinct for reuniting, in the most highly concentrated form, to the germ-cells?—But here, I think, the moment has come for breaking off" (51–52). "Paralytic" enters such murky territory, articulating reservations in the lines "Dead egg, I lie / Whole." While the dead egg, read as an unfertilized one, is a unicellular organism, the "regained" wholeness is presented as an ambivalent one. "I lie" on the one hand suggests that the patient rests in its primordial state; on the other hand, the double meaning of "lie" also uncovers the possibility that reaching such a state is a deceit.[56] Thus, the ultimate *syn*, a condition of "original" indivisible wholeness, is split into two contradictory assertions.

On the linguistic level, the poem stages a transition from a unicellular to a multicellular constitution, or from protists to germ-cells, in "Whole / On a whole world I cannot touch." The letter "o," "the pure O of undifferentiated voicing," as Jonathan Culler calls it in his essay on apostrophe ("Apostrophe" 63), a smallest particle of language that visually resembles the unicellular organism, is securely embedded in the word "whole" and represents its acoustic nucleus. The domination of "o" as a sound when the word is carried by breath persists when we read silently. Thus, the letter "o," visually coinciding with a hole, takes in the word *as a whole*. After the line-break, the linguistic protist "o" splits from its vesicle (Whole / On) and becomes reproductive in the course of the line, coalescing with other words: "On a whole world I cannot touch." The "splintered fragment[]" attains "a multicellular condition" driven by the "instinct for reuniting." Freud integrates his idea of repetition compulsion into his wildest speculation: "The sphere of embryonic developmental processes is no doubt extremely rich in such phenomena of repetition; the two germ-cells that are involved in sexual reproduction and their life history are themselves only repetitions of the beginnings of organic life" (50). Repetition compulsion essentially involves a repetition of the original trauma of separation and animation. Transferred to the poem, the "o," already entailing the trauma in its self-enclosed shape punctured by a gaping void, assumes a fertilized state by being compulsively repeated.

That "Paralytic" displays this process through the "o," of all letters, brings us to Freud's very first and most well-known illustration of repetition compulsion, a linguistic scenario in which breath has a latent presence. The little boy playing the "fort-da" game re-enacts the traumatic absence of his mother by making a wooden reel on a string disappear and reappear behind his cot. The mother is not only substituted for by the objects the boy throws away and recovers (he tosses more than the famous reel), but, significantly, also by the uttered words accompanying their disappearance and reappearance. While throwing the objects away, "he gave vent to a loud, long-drawn-out 'o-o-o-o'" (8). This utterance, which Freud identifies as the German word "fort" ("gone"), is also an unwitting citation of one of the most famous transcriptions of an audible expiration, Hamlet's last breath: "The rest is silence. O, o, o, o. Dyes" (First Folio V. ii, 789).[57] Through the unconscious quote, Freud's primal scene of repetition compulsion encompasses a textual trauma of (re-)animation: the written reproduction of the child's compulsive utterance contains a last breath resurrected, a literary last breath which, in being reiterated, prevents proper death. Hamlet's dying sigh is perpetuated in the child's ongoing "o-o-o-o." In "Paralytic," words get caught in an impersonal, non-intentional repetition compulsion when this textual breath, in tandem with the artificial respiration of the iron lung, surreptitiously recurs in "O*n* a wh*o*le w*o*rld I cann*o*t t*o*uch."

Freud describes the inextricable relation and interplay between life and death drives within an organism as "Zauderrhythmus" (43), "a faltering rhythm" (my translation).[58] In this moment, one can observe a coincidence between the theory developed (together with the phenomena described, observed, analyzed), and the way his own writing conveys its contents: *Beyond the Pleasure Principle* "rushes," halts, and "jerks back" (35) in a syncopated rhythm. Freud's writing fluctuates between "flying" and "limping" (58), he keeps interrupting his dashing associative vortex, reminding of his reflections' speculative and hypothetical nature, only to keep pursuing them to the oddest ends; "breaking off" at moments when the assumptions appear to be too devious is the "starting-point for fresh investigations" (57). Freud jumps between different fields—philosophy, literature, metaphysics, biology, psychoanalysis—and freely transfers ideas from one to the other. Consequently, *Beyond the Pleasure Principle* does not come to rest. Rather than presenting a coherent theory, it is punctuated by hesitations, open questions and inconsistencies. My reading of Plath's "Paralytic" with Freud's text follows the latter's "faltering rhythm." Therefore I pursued the poem's ambivalences and its pulls in different, at times opposing directions, stretching them further, perhaps beyond their breaking point, embarking on the domain of "far-fetched-speculation" (18), staggering through intertextual shrubbery, no longer safe from slipping on branches and going astray.

It is by taking these uncertain paths, along with a "faltering rhythm," that I can belatedly formulate a more precise thesis for the texts discussed in this chapter: in Plath's and Beckett's writing, respiration is a repetition compulsion;[59] a syncopating beat of breath persists in these textual spaces because it operates beyond the principle of life. The texts negotiate the way in which the verbalization of breath creates a tension between the deanimation of organic bodies and the animation of inorganic matter. They stage various ways in which inanimate materials take over, perpetuating the respirational habit[60] of organic bodies and continually haunted by a vegetative memory of breathing.[61] Such a textual compulsion to breathe can be subsumed neither by the notion of a drive for life nor the physiological function of a living being, and at the same time it maintains traits of living organisms. While a precondition or former state is often linked to breath in Beckett's and Plath's texts, its nature remains more undefined or ambivalent than in the psychoanalytic works they evoke. Plath's and Beckett's literary concerns with organic/inorganic crossbreeding go hand in hand with locating breath at the transitional zone where the precondition passes over into a later state or a later state closely approximates a former one. When urges to keep on breathing, even without a biological body, are articulated in Plath's and Beckett's work, we encounter the faltering rhythm *of* and *within* movements of respirational repetition compulsion rather than one between two dualistically opposed drives.

"The vivid tulips eat my oxygen"

Freud described the theory presented in *Beyond the Pleasure Principle* as a "pre-eminently dualistic view of instinctual life." He outlined an interaction between drives "operating in contrary directions" (43) in contrast to the hitherto assumed monistic predominance of the pleasure principle. The tensions I traced in "Paralytic" by reading it with Freud's death drive reveal a tendency that is characteristic of Plath's poetic concern with breath in general. Across Plath's literary work, breath is consistently situated in a field of conflicting forces. In multiple instances, her texts juxtapose different respiratory modes that, at first sight, seem to constitute a dualism. One of the most praised poems during her lifetime, "Tulips,"[62] demonstrates this most distinctly. "Tulips" is, in many ways, "Paralytic's" textual sister: apart from the significant difference that the hospitalized protagonist is sketched as a woman,[63] the setting, mood and condition of the speaker are almost identical. The suggestion of a death drive taking over is even more pronounced than in "Paralytic." Having "given [her] name and [her] day-clothes up to the nurses / And [her] history to the anaesthetists and [her] body to the surgeons," the patient "let things slip" and is swabbed "clear of [her] loving associations." She becomes "utterly empty," devoid of desire, is "pure" like a "nun" (*The Collected Poems* 160–61), and her "body is a pebble" embedded in "numbness." The state of "lying by myself quietly" is described as a desirable dazing "peacefulness": "How free it is" (160–61). The patient is disturbed by a bouquet of tulips that violently reintroduces life into the quiescent, nearly inanimate condition. In the "white," "quiet" "snowed-in" world, the unwanted flowers are "too excitable," "too red," "hurt[ing]" and "[u]psetting" her "with their sudden tongues and their color." They are considered a menacing presence the patient wishes to be protected from: "The tulips should be behind bars like dangerous animals"; "They are opening like the mouth of some great African cat" (160–62). What particularly threatens the "quiet" space are the organs of speech the flowers are armed with: the carnivorous "mouth" and "sudden tongues" (161). With the tulips and their oral features, a different, more animated, audible mode of respiration enters the hospital room and starts interfering with the patient's breath.

At this point, it is worth focusing on the acoustic scene in "Paralytic": in the later poem, sound keeps pervading a writing that proclaims orality's abandonment when vivid speech is drowned by dull rhyme in the lines "No fingers to grip, no tongue, / My god the iron lung" (emphasis added). In "Tulips," the patient is wrapped in a lull of aɪ-sounds that the word "quiet" and the whiteness seem to emit. While the patients' soundscape in "Tulips" and "Paralytic" is thus very much alike, the earlier poem introduces another acoustic quality. The tulips' breath is perceived as a sonic intrusion: "Even through the gift paper I could hear them breathe" (161). Then the flowers' clamorous presence stirs an air that until they arrived was barely moved by the speaker's monotonous respiration:

> Before they came the air was calm enough,
> Coming and going, breath by breath, without any fuss.
> Then the tulips filled it up with a loud noise.
> Now the air snags and eddies round them (161)

The calm air is recalled in "Paralytic." Even though there is no hint that the patient in "Tulips" is ventilated, the mode of respiration is identical with that inside the iron lung. Like in "Paralytic," the I in in "Tulips" breathes passively. In contrast to the flowers that do things with air—they "*filled* it up with a loud noise" and "*eat* my oxygen" (161; emphasis added)—the hospitalized patient is acted upon by the air. The air determines her respirational rhythm, which is as mechanically regular as the one imparted by the iron lung pumping the "dust bags *in and out*": "*coming and going, breath by breath*, without any fuss" (emphasis added). In this respirational mode, the I not only stops being active, it stops being a subject as such. "Paralytic" radicalizes what is already gestured toward in "Tulips": the I ceases to be a grammatical agent in the poem. Apart from the negated action "A clear / Cellophane I cannot crack," the only verbs taking "I" as a subject are "I lie" and "I smile," which both point to passivity and submission.[64] Moreover, in these instances the I acoustically dissolves in the lull of aɪ that will then predominate the sonic atmosphere of both "Paralytic" and "Tulips" when the focus is on the calm respiratory state. To cite only a selection: "I smile" ("Paralytic" 267), "I lie," "My mind," "white tight" (266); "lying by myself quietly," "the light lies on these white walls," "like an eye" ("Tulips" 160). Submerged in a repetitive sonic undercurrent, the I ceases being an entity and *i*dentity of its own.

"Tulips" sketches a different scenario of how the state of indifference is punctuated than "Paralytic." Whereas in "Paralytic," the shelter of the iron lung opens up when "whole" collapses into "hole," creating an ambivalence between respiratory nirvana and traumatic gasp, "Tulips" presents two diverging modes of breathing that intermingle once the protective shield is pierced. When the patient hears how the flowers breathe "through the gift paper" (161), she witnesses the penetration of a sealed membrane closely resembling the "cellophane I cannot crack." From that moment on, what appeared to be two independent antagonistic respiratory forces are blending. Cracking the protective shield not only means that the lively air upsets the rhythm of the deadly calm one. More important, the solid opposition of the two modes of being—white, quiet numbness versus red, loud animation—crumbles once the latter is no longer kept apart (behind the gift paper, or bars, like a dangerous animal). As soon as the lively air is no longer contained, it seeps into the previous atmosphere and the distinctive qualities of both start to diffuse so that neither the death wish nor the drive for life remain intact. In contrast to what might be expected, the tulips do not forcefully animate the patient. Instead, their vividness is suffocating and their liveliness drowns her: "The vivid tulips eat my oxygen"; "they weigh me down"; "A dozen red lead sinkers round my neck" (161). A look at the handwritten draft of the poem,[65] especially at passages Plath deleted and changed, shows how a clear-cut distinction between the two antagonizing principles is deliberately abandoned. In the draft, Plath tentatively sketches two separate individuals that relate to their self in an opposing manner: the patient gives it up, watches its identity recede, while the egoistical tulips are obsessed with it. Similarly, in the draft, the calm air appears in relation to a self. In the published version, Plath renounces all attempts at explicitly negotiating the two modes of being and breathing in terms of identity, self, and ego. What she demonstrates instead is how both cease to be self-contained forces or entities when they collide.

In the course of the poem in its final printed version, images that were neatly juxtaposed in the first stanzas are completely mixed up. In the very moment the gift paper becomes porous, an image is transferred from the patient to the flowers: being muffled in whiteness.[66] The patient describes an environment that at first contrasts with the tulips: "The tulips are too *excitable*, it is winter here. Look how white everything is, how snowed-in" (160). Let us recall how Freud defines trauma in *Beyond the Pleasure Principle*: "We describe as 'traumatic' any *excitations* from outside which are powerful enough to break through the protective shield" (23; emphasis added). Precisely at the moment when the protective shield is pierced in the poem, the tulips themselves are wrapped in white (and its dominant diphthong, aɪ): "Even through the gift paper I could hear them breathe / L*i*ghtly, through their wh*i*te swaddlings, l*i*ke an awful baby." The sonic lull that distinctly characterized the patient's undisturbed state thus finds its way into the description, pervading their respiration. When the tulips' breath is set free, "the air snags and eddies round them the way a river / Snags and eddies round a sunken rust-red engine." The tulips' bright color has faded to rust-red and they assimilate a metaphor the speaker uses when describing herself as a "thirty-year-old cargo boat." Thus, the flowers shift from being "vivid" to being drowned as well as inanimate, and the comparison to an "engine" moves them in the proximity of mechanical breath. In the draft of "Tulips," Plath stressed the intensity of the flowers' redness in the stanza preceding the description of the modes of respiration and the image of the "rust-red engine" but decided to delete the indications that the tulips are brightening and bleed. In other words, she decides against highlighting the *contrast* between the tulips and the patient established in the beginning of the poem. In the lines immediately following the description of the penetrated gift paper and the transference of "being wrapped in whiteness" to the flowers, their color bleeds into the speaker's domain: "Their redness talks to my wound, it corresponds." The traumatic punctuation of the shield literally becomes a wound, an opening that prevents the neat distinction of the flowers and the patient. It is thus consequential that Plath discarded the line in the draft in which the tulips are said to bleed, namely, where redness and blood are contained within the domain of the flowers, and opts for a blood transfusion instead. In the last stanza, this image complex is taken up once more: "They [the tulips] are opening like the mouth of some great African cat, / And I am aware of my heart: it opens and closes / Its bowl of red blooms out of sheer love of me" (161–62). Here, the dangerous opening of the mouth—recalling the pierced shield and the wound—corresponds to the speaker's heart. In the depiction, the heart (1) echoes the regular movement of the calm breath "coming and going" as well as the iron lung "that loves me" in "Paralytic" when it "opens and closes . . . out of sheer love of me" and (2) it *becomes* tulip: with "its bowls of red blooms" the flower-heart breathes mechanically.

The inversion created in the poem in a first step slowly begins to diffuse. At the outset, associations connected with human and vegetative existence are turned around. The plants breathe vividly and are characterized by active, "voluntary movement" whereas the human is "monotonous, dull; inactive, unchallenging" and close to "lacking consciousness," almost "devoid of sensation and thought" ("vegetative"; *Oxford English Dictionary* online). The way Plath presents human breath and the respiration of plants also recalls Aristotle's discussion of the respective beings' souls. Paying attention to the Aristotelian echoes in the poem reveals how the initial redefinitions of human and vegetative existence start shifting without restoring the conventional ascriptions. Aristotle starts his reflections in *De Anima* by presenting existing theories of the soul. Recounting the atomists' take, he states, "There are some who maintain that the soul is pre-eminently and primarily the cause of movement." As this presupposes that the soul is "itself in motion," "Democritus affirms the soul to be a sort of fire or heat" (*De Anima* 1: 2, 404a, 11). Both qualities, mobility and warmth, are associated with the tulips in Plath's poem: they stir the air and emanate heat: "The walls, also, seem to be warming themselves" (*The Collected Poems* 162). In his own analysis, Aristotle famously distinguishes various parts of the soul. "The part of the soul in which even plants share" (*De Anima* 2: 2, 413b, 55) solely exists with the "nutritive faculty," lacking the "sensitive" (ch. 3, 415a, 61), and the "reasoning faculty" (ch. 3, 415a, 63). The nutritive faculty consists of growth, reproduction and nutriment. Nutriment implies an ability of "causing motion and being moved" (ch. 4, 416b, 69), which also means having vital heat. "Now it is necessary that all food should be capable of digestion, and digestion is promoted by heat; this explains why every animate thing has warmth" (71). Thus, the tulips' warm and mobile breath is neatly in line with Aristotle's definition of the "nutritive soul" (63). Immobile in a snowed-in world, the speaker lacks even these most basic characteristics of the "soul of plant" (ch. 3, 415a, 61) while also being reduced to the nutritive faculty: her fundamental vital functions are upheld, the capability of sensation and intellect fades away. Agamben, who takes Aristotle's separation of "nutritive or vegetative life" (*The Use of Bodies* 129) as a starting point for his analysis of *bios* and *zoe* (e.g., *Potentialities* 231), gives an example of bare life that recalls the patients in "Tulips" and, especially, "Paralytic": "Karen Quinlan, the American girl who went into deep coma and was kept alive for years by means of artificial respiration and nutrition" (*Homo Sacer* 163–64).

Attributing the vital faculties that Aristotle distinguishes to the agents and patients in Plath's poem ultimately throws the Aristotelian system into disarray when questions of speech are addressed in "Tulips." The flowers outgrow the mute vegetative kingdom in which the human patient is firmly locked. From an Aristotelian perspective, their oral utterances are not those of speaking beings but animal growls: their vocal organs resemble the "mouth of a great African cat," and they produce "noise" rather than voice. Let us recall Aristotle's widely debated passage on the voice:

> it is not every sound made by an animal that is voice. Noise can be produced even with the tongue or as in coughing: but it is necessary for voice that the part which strikes should be animate and that some mental image should be present. For voice is certainly a sound which has significance and is not like a cough, the noise of air respired. (*De Anima* 2: 8, 420b, 89)

The extent to which the poem echoes this passage is remarkable. The tulips have "sudden tongues" and their audible breath fills up the air with "loud noise" that is not characterized as meaningful. In contrast to this according to Aristotle nonanimate noise, the hospitalized human produces signifying speech: her first person account results in a perfectly readable poem. Plath interrupts Aristotle's theory of voice in the process of evoking it. In contrast to Aristotle's "soul which animates the vocal organs" (ch. 8, 420b, 89) by endowing "significance," Plath ties animation to the vocal organs as such. The flowers' vividness is inextricably linked to their capacity to produce oral sounds whose vibrations vitalize an air machinically moved by silent respiration. The emphasized quietness of the I's world is compared to "the dead . . . Shutting their mouths" (*The Collected Poems* 161)—and we remember that the inanimate patient in "Paralytic" has "no tongue." In the draft for "Tulips," Plath considered that "the dead would talk like this, if they came back" but then deletes the sentence and thus refrains from designating the patient's nonoral and mute mode of language production as *talking*. By letting the mute, dead, meaningful words of a human turned vegetative and the vivid oral noise of plants turned animal collide, the poem not only resists the Aristotelian outline but also a more general binary opposition between lively speech and dead letters.

Plath produced "Tulips" both as a written and spoken text. Not only does the printed poem highlight oral aspects with its at times almost excessive sound continuities. And not only is it part of those later poems about which Plath claims that "they are written for the ear, not the eye: they are poems written out loud" (*Ariel* 195). "I've got to say them . . . I say them aloud" (Orr 170). "Tulips" was in a more concrete sense written to be read out loud: Plath was "commissioned to write [it] . . . for a summer festival of poetry" (*The Letters of Sylvia Plath* 2: 577) at Mermaid Theatre in London in July 1961. When we listen to the recording of her performance by the British Library[67] today, Plath's voice reaches us from beyond the grave. Plath was highly aware of this uncanny effect audio recordings can have. In her diary she comments on listening to a recording of Gene Derwood in January 1958:

> His [Oscar Williams's] dead poetess-wife's face looms pale, high cheekboned, with lowered eyes, out of the shiny record-cover. . . . For what reason? To haunt us with her live words, her live voice, her live face, she who lies somewhere rotten, unstitching stitch by stitch? He sends . . . her words, to us. So, *blown ghost*, she comes to our tea, more substantial than many inarticulate mortals. That is strange: the deadness of a stranger who is somehow never dead—the knife of death unfelt, the immortals hover in our heads. (*The Journals of Sylvia Plath* 314–15; emphasis added)

When the ghostly sound vibrations of a deceased woman's voice infuse the air, the dividing line between life and death seems momentarily blown away. Both the celebrations of her later embrace of lively orality and the haunting effect of her recordings—especially in respiratory terms—quickly leads into the territory of Plath myths. Alfred Alvarez, who repeatedly stressed the oral quality of the *Ariel* poems, famously stylizes her as a "literary dragon who in the last months of her life breathed a burning river of bale across the literary landscape" ("The Blood Jet Is Poetry" n.p.); Gail Crowther and Peter Steinberg describe "her breathing, the audible manifestation of her life" "captured by the microphones" as "most haunting" (*These Ghostly Archives* 138); Wen Stephensen claims that "in the 1962 recordings . . . she lives the poems, and the intensity is almost unbearable" (qtd. in Moses 92).[68] When one by all means wants to connect Plath's oral turn to her life, a much less uncannily fascinating factor should be considered: recordings turned out to be essential for Plath financially and the BBC was the closest thing she had to a steady source of income.[69] Especially after her separation from Ted Hughes, when Plath was alone with her two children and increasingly worried about how to assure her livelihood, recording poetry and "doing odd jobs on the BBC" (*The Letters of Sylvia Plath* 2: 951) became crucial. The oral focus of her late poems, which she stressed particularly in BBC contexts,[70] is at least partially motivated by the professional life and the respite from financial concerns and domestic tedium that the recording jobs promised.[71]

Let me return to "Tulips." The zone of indetermination in the poem—where two modes of breath conflate and attributes of animation and lifelessness are set loose—expands if we take its multimedial constitution into account. In her reading of "Tulips,"[72] Plath's voice—described by Kate Moses as "a plurality" (93)—is anything but consistent: switching from a high-pitched, frisky, light, vivacious, fleet-footed dance to a deep, gloomy, menacing, foreboding tone in which long-drawn words are given weight, it moves back and forth between creating a lively atmosphere and creating a deadly one.[73] Even though the ascending and descending pitches correspond to motives in the poem, Plath does not vocally impersonate the two forces it depicts: her voice never falls into to a monotonous rhythm and never becomes obtrusively loud or piercing. Neither do the variations between her dominant vocal modes match the passages where either tulips or the patient are focused on. From the beginning, her voice enacts what the poem performs after the separating membrane is penetrated. It literally blows out a system of differences, just as the two modes of breath in the poem do. Plath's recital matches most what the poem says in the line "Coming and going, breath by breath, without any fuss." Plath creates a regular, undulating rhythm by pausing after each comma, stressing the respective first word, letting the two following ones abate. She thus speaks in agreement with the line's content (i.e., monotonous breath) but imposes a regularity that is not mirrored in its linguistic outline. The line is not composed according to a regular meter; if we divide it into the three parts Plath pronounces in a similar way, we see that the arrangement of syllables and their prosodic stresses (2) does not correspond to the symmetry she calls forth in her performance (1) (see figure 4.3).

In Plath's performance, the "delivery instance" (Jakobson 79) ensures that "two rhythms are in some manner running at once" (Gerard Manly Hopkins qtd. in Jakobson 80).[74] Or, put in another way, Plath's modulated breath is not in sync with the words on the page. There is also another notable breath-related tension between content, meter/rhythm, and Plath's reading. In the loosely structured poem, there are three lines that stand out as the only instances of iambic pentameter (see figure 4.4).

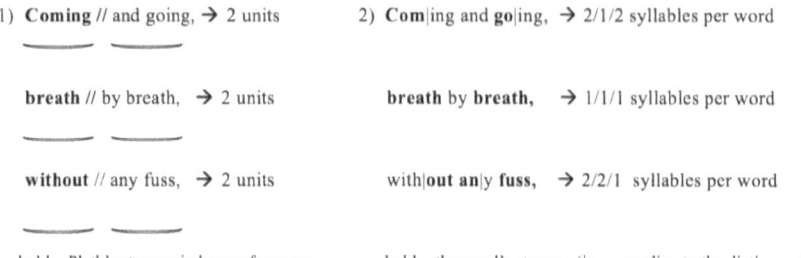

Figure 4.3. Sylvia Plath, "Tulips" (prosody). Author provided.

— / — / — / — / — /
A dozen red lead sinkers round my neck (stanza 6, line 7)
— / — / — / — / — /
The vivid tulips eat my oxygen (stanza 7, line 7)
— / — / — / — / — /
Before they came the air was calm enough (stanza 8, line 1)

Figure 4.4. Sylvia Plath, "Tulips" (meter). Author provided.

All the other lines in the poem are longer, between seventeen to eleven syllables, and mostly resist scansion. The tulips' deadening effect of suffocating and drowning in these regularly patterned lines goes hand in hand with Plath's increasing concern about the stifling impact of regular forms. In 1959, she notes in her journal: "my main flaw is a machinelike syllabic death-blow" (*The Journals of Sylvia Plath* 492).[75] "Tulips" continually approximates a syllabic structure while at the same time undermining it: throughout, a similar number of syllables per line occurs but the count never becomes fully consistent. In the three lines that have exactly ten syllables, an unstressed syllable is followed by a stressed one; thus, the most traditional English meter is reproduced and the poem's freer rhythms are tied back to the "machinelike death-blow" and the "old tattoo." The correspondence of the deadening form with the lines' content is first disrupted when the tulips are said to be "vivid," and then, more extensively, in the line "Before they came the air was calm enough."

When Plath pits lifeless "bound verse" against vivid free verse, she broadly echoes avant-garde concerns about traditional forms. The negative connotation of measured poetry becomes more pronounced in Plath's later poetic comments. Earlier in her career, when she tells her mother of her studies at the University of Cambridge in a letter from 1957, she evaluates strict form differently: "I took 'Stylization' and, I think, wrote a very clever essay ostensibly in praise of style in all its forms, as a religious devotee of style, defining it as that order, line, form & rhythm in everything from the sonnet to the whalebone corset which renders the unruly natural world of Becoming bearable" (*The Letters of Sylvia Plath* 2: 143). By stressing that measured forms make the ever-mobile stream of "Becoming *bearable*," Plath suggests that they have a soothing effect. Whether the "*calm* air" in "Tulips," which is embedded in a regular pattern of stressed and unstressed syllables that can be scanned as iambic pentameter, represents a desired quiescent state or the despised "death-blow" of the stuffy old form, is left undecided. The poem remains ambiguous: while the calm air, which is merely moved by the patient's regular breath is said to be *disturbed* by the "vivid" tulips, the monotonous beat of the lines addressing this process contradicts what they say. In her oral performance, Plath upsets any notion of steady measure in these passages of the poem: the lines lending themselves to be recognized as iambic pentameters on the page are spoken in an irregular rhythm. For example, in "A *dozen red lead sink*ers *round* my *neck*," she stresses three syllables in a row, and in "Be*fore* they *came* the *air* was *calm*-en*ough*" she counterpoints calmness and constant measure with swift movement, increasing the pace in the end by taking no pause between "calm" and "enough." The way patterns are destabilized in these respirational lines is paradigmatic for the poem as a whole. Dissecting the words on the paper—counting syllables and stresses, tracking down sound continuities, and so on—shows how Plath dissolves forms and structures in the process of establishing them: they fall apart before they become fully recognizable, while the sense of an underlying pattern remains. A tension between the "bound" and the free-flowing also prevails in her acoustic performance: despite all variations, it sounds highly controlled. Kate Moses cites Cynthia Ozick, who describes Plath's early recordings as "burnished, precise, almost inhumanly perfected" (Ozick qtd. in Moses 92) and herself notes that Plath almost creates "a dissection of the words and phrases in the . . . slow, stilted formality of her delivery" (96). That at the same time neither her voice nor the rhythm is steady amounts to a "disturbance of sound" (Alvarez qtd. in Moses 93).

Cold Breath

A large number of Plath's free verse poems look and sound like ruins of some established form, remainders of a rhyme scheme or meter at times still being perceptible. Warm vital breath is evoked as a faint trace of a firmly-established traditional idea (fiery pneuma etc.), often only through a more idiosyncratic contrasting notion of cold inanimate breath, which we have encountered in "Paralytic" and "Tulips." A comparative look at this respirational mode across Plath's work reveals a cluster of traits that repeatedly occur in combination: the breath I will, following Plath, call "cold" (in opposition to the warm *pneuma*) is characterized by lifelessness, sterility, whiteness, frozenness, petrification, paralysis, numbness, anesthesia, oblivion, stasis, and monotony.[76] In "A Birthday Present," "The diaphanous satins of a January window" are "white as babies' bedding and glittering with dead breath. O ivory!" and the fatal yet desired unspecified gift "breathes from my sheets, the cold dead center" (*The Collected Poems* 206–7). The "ghost flower" in "Polly's Tree" is "flat as paper and / of a color / vaporish as frost-breath" (128). A similar vegetative breath pervades "The Sleepers": "Among petals pale as death / . . . They sleep on, mouth to mouth. / A white mist is going up. / The small green nostrils breathe" (123). In the recently discovered unpublished poem "To a Refractory Santa Claus" the speaker imagines a warm climate "where teeth / Don't chatter, where breath / Never puts on the white disguise / Of freezer air" (*These Ghostly Archives* 43). "Private Ground," first titled "In Frost Time," presents a winter setting in which a "handyman," alive "with smoking breath" drains "goldfish ponds" that "collapse like lungs," depriving the stranded baby carps of their vital respiratory environment (*The Collected Poems* 130). "The Munich Mannequins" starts with the lines "Perfection is terrible, it cannot have children. / Cold as snow breath, it tamps the womb" (262). In "Barren Woman," the sterile I, "empty," "blank-faced and mum as a nurse" finds herself in a petrified museal space in which "marble lilies / Exhale their pallor like scent" (157). One of the speakers in "Three Women" "saw death in the bare trees, a deprivation" and is "so white, suddenly." Observing how "the white sky empties of its promise," she notes "Again, this is a death. Is it the air, / The particles of destruction I suck up? Am I a pulse / That wanes and wanes, facing the cold angel?" (177). These variations of the recurring motif of cold breath are especially susceptible to blurring when meeting its traditional counterpart, warm breath, as we saw with "Tulips."

In the Sylvia Plath collection at the Lilly Library, warm breath and breathless perfection, lifelessness and sterility, are assembled in one concrete place: a sheet of paper. On the verso of a typescript of the poem "Stillborn," we can find the handwritten draft of a poem Plath never completed or published.[77] Against the respirational framework outlined here, the two pieces of writing converse if we read them together. "Stillborn" starts with a "sad" self-"diagnosis," "These poems do not live," which is repeated toward the end: "they are dead, and their mother near dead with distraction." Identifying the speaker as "mother," Plath merges poetic creation and childbirth. The "mother" specifies her offspring's lifelessness further: "they stupidly stare, and do not speak of her"; "They smile and smile and smile and smile at me." The muteness and immobility is already implied in the title, "Stillborn," which designates a baby born dead, but also encompasses "still" in the sense of silent and motionless. The latter is stressed in the line "they missed out on walking about like people." Another characteristic of the infant poems that are born without coming alive is formal perfection: "They are proper in shape and number and every part." Two lines later, this trait is put on relentless display: "They smile and smile and smile and smile at me," an immaculate iambic pentameter embellished with smooth assonances—not surprisingly, of aɪ-sounds—is a mockery of accomplished form, exhibiting the merciless gestural reaction to what it does in what it says. Lifeless monotony is depicted as a lack of breath: "And still the lungs won't fill and the heart won't start." Whereas Plath's cold breath complicates the dominant cultural opposition of breath = life and nonbreath = death by tying breath to death, "Stillborn" seems to be more conventional when it reproduces the nonbreath = death formula. The lifeless poems share a number of characteristics with the cold breath that often pervades Plath's texts—but in "Stillborn" they go hand in hand with nonrespiring entities. However, the line "And still the lungs won't fill and the heart won't start" unsettles the traditional view it at first glance seems to confirm. In contrast to the repetitive and rigid pattern of "smile and smile and smile and smile" (which immediately precedes), "And still the lungs won't fill and the heart won't start" displays a more vivid rhythm and variable internal rhyme, amounting to a performative contradiction.[78] The words claiming that the poem does not breathe counteract the stillness and immobility the speaker attributes to them. Once more, we can observe a respirational resistance to a distribution of animate and inanimate traits that is in line with the domains and conceptual fields they are traditionally situated in.

Bearing this in mind, let us turn the page. "The breath of my body steams up to me, I am warm."[79] In the next line of the draft, which Plath then crossed out as a whole and to my knowledge abandoned, the speaker adds that this condition is not death. Throughout the poem, which is not fully fleshed out, warm breath is contrasted with death, which is repeatedly described as cold. The speaker draws a somewhat surprising conclusion from this familiar pairing: if death were warm, she would not mind it. In contrast to "Stillborn," it is not the life-giving capacity of breath that is desired, but its thermal quality. While this tentative and ultimately abandoned attempt at a poem does not lend itself to an expansive reading, it is nevertheless worthwhile to observe how Plath experimented with yet another constellation of attributes of notions of breath, both animate and inanimate. In the draft, the traditional notion of warm breath as sign of life gives rise to the idea of an acceptable "warm death." Moreover, the last couple of fragmentary lines, in which some elements of the hospital poems "Tulips" and "Paralytic" echo, link whiteness both to the warming sun of a new morning, and to living—a kind of tedious living that recalls the vegetative mode of merely being kept alive through cold breath.

That this draft ended up being written on the same sheet of paper as "Stillborn" may have been accidental. However, the constellation results in an intricate respiratory assemblage where traits of breath, life and death break loose from the places they occupied in different textual contexts: the cultural history of breath and Plath's work.

"Blown askew": Ecstatic Breath, Shattered Selves, Pneumatic Potentiality

In Plath's novel *The Bell Jar*, yet another, completely different, scenario is sketched, employing the recurring respirational motifs and their usual companions. The episode in question is set on Mount Pisgah, near the Ray Brook sanatorium, where the protagonist, Esther Greenwood, visits her boyfriend, Buddy, who is suffering from tuberculosis. Buddy compensates for his emasculated, feeble condition by teaching Esther how to ski and commanding her every move. After following his amateurish instruction "obediently" (91) for half an hour, Esther breaks free—and her escape not only rejects Buddy's patriarchal mastery but also subverts his tubercular condition, which he describes as follows: "TB is like a bomb in your lung. . . . You just lie very quietly hoping it won't go off" (84). When Buddy coerces her to ascend a hill despite a complete lack of the skills that would allow her to ski down safely, Esther first keeps doing what she is told. That she not only surrenders to the male order but also to the rope of the ski tow—that she gives in completely—involuntarily makes her disregard Buddy's direction to go only half-way up the mountain: "the rope dragged me . . . I didn't want to make trouble, so I hung quietly on." On the hilltop, passive submission turns into a respiratory revelation that was already anticipated earlier when

Esther notes "The cold air punished my lungs and sinuses to a visionary clearness." On the hilltop, the "interior voice" of reason "nagging me not to be a fool" is abandoned and the cold air takes possession of Esther's body. First, the "grey eye of the sky looked back at me, its mist-shrouded sun focusing all the white and silent distances." Then, the white, cold scenery enters Esther's mind: "The thought that I might kill myself formed in my mind coolly."[80] The mental formation immediately turns into an impulse: "I dug the spikes of my pole and pushed myself into a flight I knew I couldn't stop by skill or any belated access of will. . . . I aimed straight down" (90–93). It is during the suicidal flight that another involuntary intake of cold air physically infuses her with the white surrounding landscape, culminating in a rush of *jouissance*:

> A keen wind that had been hiding itself struck me full in the mouth. . . . I was descending, but the white sun rose no higher. It hung over the suspended waves of the hills, an insentient pivot. . . . A small, answering point in my own body flew toward it. I felt my lungs inflate with the inrush of scenery— air, mountains, trees, people. I thought, "This is what it is to be happy." (93)

This act of transgression shatters boundaries: the external air enters Esther's body, she darts outside herself and the scenery breaks in—into what? Where is "she" located when outside herself, while the outside pervades her inside? In a scene in which ecstasy and internalization collide, the categories "inside" and "outside" are suspended. In the same vein, the direction of the "straight line" becomes undeterminable. Her dash is simultaneously described as "flight" (escape and volitation) and "descending," and it has two endpoints. The poem rewrites the trajectory of Freud's death drive as a two-directional speeding toward different inanimate aims: the "insentient" white pivot of the sun, above, and beneath, "the still, bright point at the end of [the hill], the pebble at the bottom of the well, the white, sweet baby cradled in its mother's belly" (93). As so often in Plath's respirational images, the boundaries between her texts become porous. The intrauterine state that is at the same time described as a "still . . . pebble" reminds one of the hospital poems "Tulips" and "Paralytic," and the flight into the sun recalls the famous end of "Ariel," which stages an ecstatic fusion exceeding the diegetic level: the letter I visually resembles an arrow dashing upwards that then acoustically merges with its aim, the "Eye":

And I
Am the arrow,

The dew that flies
Suicidal, at one with the drive
Into the red

Eye, the cauldron of morning
(*The Collected Poems* 239–40)

The whole scenario of "Ariel," which consists of an out-of-control horseback ride, is mirrored in the scene of *The Bell Jar*. Plath makes this parallel explicit in her diary with respect to an epiphany on a bolting horse that became the center of the poem "Whiteness I Remember," chromatically in line with the snowy surroundings of the skiing episode. Right after having recounted her real-life version of the scene "on the top of the ski slope" (*The Journals of Sylvia Plath* 220) without making any respirational references, she gives the "runaway ride" (403) as another example "of the few times in my life I have felt I was all alive": "Then there was the time . . . when the horse galloped into the street-crossing and the stirrups came off leaving me hanging around his neck, *jarred breathless*, thinking in an ecstasy: is this the way the end will be?" (220; emphasis added) With the loss of control over the defiant horse and the vertiginous state this causes, notions of life and death once more start going adrift: feeling "all alive" coincides with "breathlessness" and an imagination of death.

Esther's flight in *The Bell Jar* could be considered an escapist fantasy that is shattered as soon as she is literally thrown back into reality. Esther's breakout results in broken bones and, thinking with Sara Ahmed, her "feminist snap" (187) leads right into the next trap. After her breakout, Esther, coming to herself, observes how the "old world sprang back into position," "piece by piece" (*The Bell Jar* 93) while her fractured body is back in Buddy's hands, who with a "satisfied expression" and a "final smile" says: "Your leg is broken in two places. You'll be stuck in a cast for months" (94). The dynamic of this scene is recalled when the novel's central respiratory image takes effect and Esther's mental breakdown—in many respects presented as an involuntary gesture of breaking loose, of evading the restrictive patriarchal system—vaults her into the bell jar's "stifling distortions" (230), a closed environment in which "circulating air" (206) is kept out. Inside the bell jar, with the outer world being completely shut off, Esther is "stewing in [her] own sour air" (178). "To the person in the bell jar, blank and stopped as a dead baby, the world itself is the bad dream" (227). At first sight, one might assume that the bell jar corresponds to the respiratory atmosphere sketched in the hospital poems "Tulips" and "Paralytic" while the mountain air represents a contrast: the former setting is an enclosed, man-made space determined by stillness, the latter an open natural environment inciting velocity. Within the novel, such a juxtaposition seems to be confirmed: the environment of the bell jar is diametrically opposed to the one on the mountain where an inrush of fresh air sets Esther in motion. Even though one is associated with happiness and the other with depression, the two settings do not represent a vivid and a deathly atmosphere respectively. The fresh mountain air, evoking a cosmic pneuma, infuses Esther with a fatal rather than a vital spark. It does not bestow the health it is supposed to bring to the tubercular patients in the sanatorium. That *both* kinds of air display traits of the death drive, which also pervade the hospital poems, thwarts a clear dividing line between the two environments in *The Bell Jar* as well as between the stifling bell jar/hospital versus natural mountain air. Concerning the bell jar, the comparison to the "dead baby" and the protective shield tie in with the allusions to the death drive in the hospital poems, but the latter spheres are much more permeable. The implications of cold air in the skiing scene and its intertexts also differ significantly from the hospital poems, even though they are accompanied by the same images (the intrauterine state, whiteness, etc.).

Plath thus presents different figurations of the death drive: apathetic peacefulness ("Tulips" and "Paralytic"), total seclusion (the bell jar), and ecstatic thrills (the skiing scene). In the respective texts, these scenarios differ in terms of desirability: the respiratory mode in hospital is pleasurable, the one on the mountain ecstatic, and the one in the bell jar detested. Juxtaposing natural and artificial air in terms of positive and negative connotations would be inaccurate, as both the hospital and the mountain atmosphere are objects of longing. To complicate matters further, in the description of the most prominent first manifestation of the mental breakdown, the skiing scene is transformed into a writing scene calling to mind Malone's. The mountain's "plane of whiteness" (93) is now a white page on which letters moved by air start descending uncontrollably: "But when I took up my pen, my hand made big, jerky letters . . . and the lines *sloped* down the page from left to right almost diagonally, as if they were loops of string lying on the paper, and someone had come along and *blown them askew*" (125; emphasis added). What made Esther feel thrilled in the mountains now causes despair and the blow shattering the symbolic order leads right into the bell jar. This scene is paradigmatic of Plath's breath-writing insofar as respirational words are constantly "blown . . . askew" within and across her texts, thus upsetting the conceptual frameworks they are situated in.

Looking at a sketch of the bell jar in Plath's diary, we can observe a further circulation of attributes, image-complexes, and thematic clusters. In a diary entry from July 1952, Plath reflects on the consequences of a "depressing sinus infection" (*The Journals of Sylvia Plath* 118) that makes her unable to breathe well. Following her doctor's order to take a break from her holiday job as a waitress in West Harwich, she returns home and decides not to go back to work. "And then I began to understand the difference between death-or-sickness-in life versus Life. When sick . . . I wanted to withdraw from all the painful reminders of vitality—to hide away alone in a peaceful stagnant pool, and not be like a crippled stick entangled near the bank of a jubilantly roaring river, torn at continually by the noisy current." Back home and back to writing, away from the "current" of her work at the Belmont hotel, she realizes that "life was not to be sitting in hot amorphic leisure in my backyard idly writing or not-writing, as the spirit moved me. It was, instead, running madly, in a crowded schedule, in a squirrel cage of busy people." In the same breath, the "air of back-home" becomes "strange" and "thin" and the attributes assigned to work and home start turning. When Plath notices that "soporific idling and luxurious relaxing" lacks the "exact routine" and "schedule" of working life, her images become contradictory: devoid of the rigid pattern of the "noisy current," the "stagnant pool" is a "whirlpool." She then depicts what "getting shed of a routine" "feels like": "It is like lifting a bell jar off a securely clockwork-like functioning community, and seeing all the little busy people stop, gasp, blow up and float in the inrush, (or rather outrush,) of the ratified scheduled atmosphere—poor little frightened people, flailing impotent arms in the aimless air" (118). In contrast to Esther, for whom the lifting of the bell jar indicates the return to mental health, regaining mastery over herself, and who "felt surprisingly at peace" when "open to the circulating air" (206), the people depicted in the diary are helplessly exposed to a random current and "blown . . . askew" like the words on the page that marked Esther's breakdown.

Plath's respiratory images do not lend themselves to a narrative of possible escape and liberation, a context in which breath is often embedded in by feminist and postcolonial theorists, pitting deathly suppression and suffocation against free breath and worthy life.[81] As we have seen, the assignment of qualities and states to respiratory conditions in Plath's writing is utterly unstable in the first place: they shift within her texts and across them. Then, when characters and speakers (whether fictional or not) move from one respiratory mode into another, as in the *Bell Jar* and the diary entry, there is no progress in the sense that eliminating suffocating conditions would enable liberated breath (or regress, if we turn the sequence around). In Plath's prose, exiting one respiratory atmosphere leads into a new unpredictable environment involving new dangers and risks. The breathing conditions Plath presents do not fit into either of the roles predominately attributed to her in the history of feminist reception: the "heroine" (Egeland 89) striking fiercely against the patriarchy with poems like "Daddy" and "Lady Lazarus," the "martyr" (90), or the victim helplessly exposed to her sociopolitical surroundings. Her breathers represent neither affirmative empowerment nor resignation beyond hope[82] in the light of a system that cannot be overthrown or escaped. There is a point to this lack of conclusiveness that goes beyond the argument that Plath's writing reflects the complexity, messiness, and intricate entanglements of her personal, social, political, and cultural environment.

Plath's engagement with breath persistently refuses to reproduce the systems she writes in and against—be they poetic (including her experiments with traditional forms and her takes on orality), cultural (including her responses to traditional notions of breath), or sociopolitical. Let me give one last example from *The Bell Jar*. Before being infected with tuberculosis, Buddy alleges that Esther's breathlessness has mental causes: "He was very proud of his perfect health and was always telling me it was psychosomatic when my sinuses blocked up and I couldn't breathe" (68). His belief is that a determined mind has a healthier body. Later, we get to know that he had that idea from his father, who "thought that all sickness was sickness of the will" (87). What Plath presents as a male inheritance will a few years later find its most prominent literary expression in Thomas Bernhard's *Breath: A Decision*, where the narrator, prompted by his grandfather's claim that a strong mind or soul can save a debilitated body (45), manages to escape death by controlling his breath, by an effort of will, the decision to keep on breathing (18).[83] Esther's resistance to the masculine order Buddy wants to impose on her by teaching her how to ski (i.e., to control her by instructing her how to exert mastery over her body and movements) is to abandon the notion of will as such, rather than counteracting it with her own. Esther gives herself over to the air, lets it in, and lets herself go with a flow that wrecks all features of masculine willpower, including the will to life. The *hap*piness she feels is not only about straying from the path Buddy designed for her.[84] It is the jouissance of momentarily blowing the patriarchal system (resting on will, activity, intentionality, mastery) along with the subject it wants to produce. In this short moment, the role designed for her—being submissive—assumes a subversive form and ultimately reverses an image tied to stereotypical fixed binary gender roles earlier in the novel. In this case, we are dealing with something Buddy inherits from a woman who internalized a male order that locks women into a subordinate position. Esther recounts how Buddy keeps repeating his mother's sayings, "What a man wants is a mate and what a woman wants is infinite security" and "What a man is is an arrow into the future and what a woman is is the place the arrow shoots off from" (67). On the mountain, Esther becomes the arrow, darting infinitely away from security, toward no future. The atmosphere on the mountain is one of potentiality in Agamben's sense, namely, one that cannot be contained in the "Aristotelian apparatus potential/act" and becomes inoperative. The twist of the arrow in this inappropriable air is exemplary for Plath's respiratory images that, speaking with Agamben, by "rendering inoperative the works of language, the arts, politics . . . open . . . to a new possible use" (*The Use of Bodies* 93–94).

Thus, Plath's literary breath thwarts one of the most dominant ideas in the reception of her work and life alike: that of the divided self.[85] The self split into a "real" and "false" one[86] structurally mirrors the stereotypical binaries outlined in Buddy's mother's sayings. Attaining a "real" stable identity merely implies attaining a "truer" version of "what a woman *is*" or "what a man *is*." The essentialism of true or false self is dangerously close to the definition of right or wrong behavior regarding clichéd gender roles.[87] Plath's writing persistently undermines such rigid patterns and makes self-images lose their contours when the linguistic breaths or airs unleash a circulation of attributes and, instead of "heal[ing] the fracture" (Perloff, " 'A Ritual for Being Born Twice' " 509), they yield a syncopal, faltering rhythm.[88]

> Last Words
> . . .
> My mirror is clouding over—
> A few more breaths, and it will reflect nothing at all.
> The flowers and the faces whiten to a sheet.
>
> I do not trust the spirit. It escapes like steam
> (*The Collected Poems* 152)

Gendering

Gender is central to Plath's respiratory poetics, as the discussion of feminist impulses, especially in *The Bell Jar*, has shown. Even though they are often marked as male, Beckett's speakers often seem to have entered a domain beyond gender difference. Concerning the trajectory observed in the pairings of authors in the previous chapters, which feature a tendency to embrace either movement and sound (Kerouac and Woolf) or stillness and immobility (Ginsberg and Musil), further pneumatic gender relations can be detected in Beckett's and Plath's work. They both present neutral spaces in which immobilized speakers evoke a passivity that both points to a respirational ground of language and veers toward a state of rest and peacefulness. Despite this shared layout in the respirational texts at the center of the book, the writers' respective overall reception suggests a significantly different tone: Plath's fierce, violent energy and Beckett's withdrawal, exhaustion, and quietism (e.g., Nixon; Feldman; Ackerley). Such generalized characterizations have to be differentiated with respect to specific texts. I thus want to present a few representative voices on works discussed in this chapter. Concerning *Texts for Nothing*, Stanley Gontarski and Chris Ackerley claim, "The tone is gentle, repetition creating cadence, sustained with a lilting rhythm that signals the slow entropic decline of one caught between telling and listening" (290). Arguing that in Beckett's "post-war work," the "turmoil in the minds of his narrators is typically transmitted in an unwavering, steady-handed, quiet prose, strikingly at peace with itself," Rónán McDonald claims that "the language" in "the trilogy" "is smoother and more tranquil" (89) than in his earlier work.

The poetic voice of Plath's later work, especially *Ariel*, was initially described as one in sharp contrast to these comments on Beckett's prose from roughly ten years earlier. In his foreword to the collection, Robert Lowell famously stated, "These poems are playing Russian roulette with six cartridges in the cylinder" (viii). Conflating author and work in a way that became symptomatic for Plath criticism, he claims: "Dangerous, more powerful than man, machinelike from hard training, she herself is a little like a racehorse, galloping relentlessly with risked, outstretched neck, death hurdle after death hurdle topped" (x). Likewise, Alvarez portrays the author of *Ariel* as a "literary dragon who . . . breathed a burning river of bale across the literary landscape." It is significant that these sketches of Beckett as a contemplative ascetic and Plath as a fierce extremist whose "words were hard and small like missiles, . . . flung with flat force" (Alvarez n.p.) are characterizations of a male and female author by male critics.[89] We are faced with attempts to outline the respective works that are entangled in gendered author images from gendered perspectives.

Looking back on the texts explored in the chapter, another factor has to be taken into consideration when it comes to gendered tones: within the literary texts written by a man and a woman respectively, we are dealing with gendered speakers. Even though in *Malone Dies*, *The Unnamable*, and *Texts for Nothing*, characters are pervaded by a neutral narrative voice into which they often seem to dissolve completely, they are, whenever their bodies are focused on, marked as male. In contrast, the play *Breath* does not have a speaker at all; the stage directions do not give any specifics about the potential gendering of the breath and cry-sounds that are machinic rather than human. Concerning Plath's respirational scenes,[90] "Suicide off Egg Rock" and "Paralytic" are explicitly spoken from a man's perspective whereas the I in "Tulips" and the narrator Esther in *The Bell Jar* are feminine. This turns out to be significant, especially if we compare the skiing episode in *The Bell Jar* to "Paralytic" and read them with Beckett's prose texts. Even though the patient in "Paralytic" and Esther both give themselves over to a passive mode, the qualities of their passivity are radically different: immobile resignation on the one hand, and a dashing ecstatic flight on the other. This adds to the gender pattern emerging: Plath's female protagonist ties in with Woolf's speedy prose and the dominant views on Plath's writing style, whereas her male paralytic patient, who has "no tongue." is in line with Musil's silent, motionless scene, Beckett's quiet, calm prose, and his still, male speakers.

However, this pattern dissolves as it emerges once we take into account more factors, in particular the role of breath. In the scene of the *Bell Jar*, breath figures in the mode of speed and energy: the wind that "struck" Esther "full in the mouth" forcefully fuels her flight and the "inrush" blows up the boundaries between inside and outside. In contrast, the respiratory movement in "Paralytic" is described as monotonous and the iron lung confines the patient to a state of inertia and speechlessness. Prosodically, the poem mirrors qualities of the artificial respiration it depicts while it also, in some respects, acts against them. The sentences are cut into short lines, which results in an interrupted rhythm, which is at times dull and mechanical. Simultaneously, the enjambment connects the lines, urging the reading eye or pronouncing mouth to speed across the breaks and move in the musical flow generated by the poem's continuous sound patterns. Concerning musicality, "Paralytic" is well embedded in what has been identified as the *Ariel* poems' distinctive acoustic quality. A striking richness of internal rhymes and assonances is characteristic of all of Plath's poems that are discussed in the chapter. Thus, this richness accompanies the breaths described as a respirational undertone that could be realized as sounding words carried on the breath of someone who pronounces them. This undertone traverses gender boundaries and persists no matter whether the speakers are marked male or female. Rather than trying to ask whether this might be an inscription or trace of Plath's feminine voice, it is worth noting that in these instances, a textual and impersonal breath sounds through the variously gendered speakers in a movement that may best be described as *trans*, in a double sense. Similarly, cold and warm breath and the immobile, lifeless, and quiet versus loud and vivid respiratory images that Plath recurrently sketches do not only bleed into each other within and across her texts, but also resist being assigned to a specific gender.

In the selection of Beckett's respiratory texts, one can also find instances that disrupt the gender pattern that is outlined. The mute speaking, silence, and stillness articulated in what can be summarized as Beckett's "quiet breath" is sometimes counteracted by a respiratory physicality and materiality that is all but inconspicuous.[91] While the "quiet breath" goes hand in hand with the poetics most often associated with Beckett and invites being read as an image for his (male) aesthetic asceticism, the "mewl, howl, gasp, and rattle," noisy panting, and profuse "groans that choke" pervade such metaphorical or conceptual conjunctions as obtrusive matter. Breath consistently enters Beckett's texts in the mode of the neutral, but through it the engines of unworking make themselves heard and reveal how they *move*. In this sense, the "*mouvement* inspiration-expiration" (emphasis added), which is discarded in the French manuscript of *Breath*, subliminally continues to be *au désoeuvrement*—taking effect *à travers* Beckett's texts (in both directions chronologically) and, as in Plath's work, *à travers* the gender trajectory that gradually becomes discernible.

5

Breath at Point Zero

Trauma, Commemoration, Haunting (Paul Celan, Herta Müller)

> Absolute zero is that which cannot be expressed. And we agree, absolute zero and I, that absolute zero itself is beyond discussion, except in the most roundabout way.
>
> —Müller, *The Hunger Angel*

> It, the language remained, not lost, yes in spite of everything. But it had to pass through its answerlessness, pass through frightful muting [durch furchtbares Verstummen], pass through the thousand darknesses of deathbringing speech. It passed through and gave back no words for what happened.
>
> —Celan, "Speech on the Occasion of Receiving the Literature Prize of the Free Hanseatic City of Bremen"

Paul Celan's poetry and Herta Müller's novel *Atemschaukel* pivot on cultural and individual World War II traumata: in Celan's case the Shoah and in Müller's the Soviet penal camps.[1] Whereas Plath's holocaust imagery,[2] which is often criticized for being incorrectly used as an analogy for personal suffering, is not concerned with commemoration as such, Celan and Müller write from an ineffable point zero, finding themselves faced with the paradoxical endeavor of addressing traumatic caesurae that "give no words for what happened." A fundamental premise for both authors is that a representational depiction of the atrocities would run counter to the very speech-shattering impact of the holocaust and the penal camps because it would suggest that these traumata can be contained by language. The ethics of approaching these historical caesurae linguistically lies rather in the creation of a language that is itself shattered and punctuated by silence.[3] The liminal, invisible, and usually silent occurrence of breath facilitates the creation of spaces in which the traumatic past is *articulated* without being spoken away. While narratives of traumatic memory may be essential for recovery,[4] Müller's and Celan's texts do not aim at possible healing through scriptotherapy. They instead follow an ethics of persistent commemoration in line with what Judith Kasper outlines in her book on traumatized space: in acting as a *pharmakon*, writing "does not aim to overcome the trauma" but rather inscribes the "displacements, deferrals and differences concerning the traumatic, which withdraws from representation . . . and does not stop to insist" (*Der traumatisierte Raum* 39; my translation). Moreover, Müller and Celan negotiate how traumatized voices are themselves cut off and silenced through writing. In the literary texts and poetic reflections of both writers, breath marks moments when representation and narrative are interrupted and the notion of a traumatic "subject" as such is unsettled by words and processes of verbalization. Through syncopated instances of inspiration, breathing pauses and expiration, their ethics and poetics opens up to questions of how historical caesurae can be written at all, how text-internal commemoration may take place, and how readers may engage with an inaccessible past.

Celan: "Pneumatisch berührbar"

"Es verschlägt ihm—und auch uns—den Atem und das Wort": Breath in Celan's Notes, Essays, and Speeches

Celan theorizes about breath in his *Meridian* speech.[5] At first sight, it appears in the context of a dualism, the juxtaposition of art and poetry. Situated in the domain of poetry, breath represents a countermovement to art, which Celan sketches as a lifeless, mechanical construct that is indebted to rigid formal rules, an automaton, or a Medusa's head that petrifies the natural and vital into stillness. Breath is thus negotiated within an aesthetic-cultural framework that, as we have seen, prevailed in the respiratory poetics developed in the

1950s and 1960s on both sides of the Atlantic. When writers negotiate the literature to be developed in opposition to old forms, they often do so in terms of oral versus written language and the living (new) versus the dead (old). With its cultural history, breath becomes a favored image in this respect. As the previous chapters show, however, breath tends to undermine the cultural attributions assigned to it. In the analysis of writers of the Beat Generation, I showed that attempts to stylize breath as the natural, bodily, and vivid basis of avant-garde literature are thwarted despite the writer's own intentions. In Beckett's writing, the silent, mechanical, and nonvital become a signature trait to which both breath and the body are inextricably linked. Thus, the dominant cultural narratives surrounding respiration are unsettled. Plath's ambivalent and unstable positioning of breath in contexts of the animate and inanimate has similar consequences. Her respirational constellations particularly resonate with Celan's treatment of breath in the "Meridian" speech, in which fertility and childbirth, petrification, and the mechanical figure prominently. On the surface, it initially seems as if Celan's setup is more conventional, as it situates breath in the context of the natural, organic, and lively. He describes art in its traditional forms—once more, the iamb appears as their epitome—as barren *artificiality*: "Art, you will remember, is a puppet-like, iambically five-footed . . . childless being" (*The Meridian* 2). Citing Büchner, to whom the speech is dedicated, Celan replicates a *discourse* about art that ties it to inanimate "automatons": "Nothing but art and mechanics, nothing but cardboard and watch springs!" (2) Another image for art, also provided by Büchner, is the deanimating "Medusa's head." The desire to "grasp the natural as the natural with the help of art" implies "stepping beyond what is human" (5)—freezing the living mortal into a permanent image. Celan then appeals to the "poet of the creature" who proposes a "truly radical calling into question of art . . . to which all of today's poetry has to return" (5).

As Celan stresses, the ethical demand of a poetry embracing the natural, human, and mortal, as exemplified by Büchner, arises in a specifically contemporary respirational condition: "That I worry these [questions of poetry and art] with such stubbornness today probably is in the air—*the air we have to breathe today*" (5; emphasis added). Alluding to the aftermath of the poisonous gas that the inmates of the concentration camps were forced to inhale, Celan also responds to Adorno's claim that writing poetry after Auschwitz is barbaric. As a consequence, writers felt obliged to deal with the question of what literature after the Shoah should look like and how it could be justified. Celan explicitly comments on Adorno's statement as follows: "No poem after Auschwitz (Adorno): / What kind of idea of poetry is implied here? The conceit of one who dares to contemplate and sing Auschwitz from a nightingale's or thrush's point of view hypothetically or speculatively" (*Mikrolithen* 122; my translation). What Celan suggests as an alternative to lyrical sugarcoating is a move away from artistry/art, toward a poetry dedicated to the breathing human: "No artist / the word *Atemwende* (breathturn) in *The Meridian*—a way of speaking against art and *for* the human" (122; my translation). Such a notion of creaturely, human poetry is expanded on in further passages where breath is mentioned in *The Meridian*.

When Celan introduces an alternative to art, breath appears as the interruption of a dominant discourse. In his attempt at "taking leave of . . . the man preoccupied by art, the artist" (*The Meridian* 6), Celan focuses on a scene in *Dantons Tod* and Lucile, who "doesn't really listen" "whenever there is talk about art." Lucile's perception of language is sensual: she sees and hears it. What she perceives is not the content of speech, but its material, physical aspects and a pneumatic relation or "direction" that springs from them: "language and shape . . . , breath, that is, direction and destiny."[6] For Lucile, "who is blind to art . . . , language is something person-like and tangible." In Celan's reading, she finally utters a "counterword" both against the cruelties of the French Revolution and against art: "Long live the king." For Celan, this liberating exclamation accounts for the presence of the human and finds its pneumatic equivalent in Büchner's *Lenz*. When Lenz "counters" art with "what is natural and creaturely," the juxtaposition of art and poetry becomes unstable. Celan's famous "breathturn" marks precisely the moment when the art/poetry dualism becomes questionable. Lenz's encounter with poetry is an experience of "perhaps self-created . . . distance or strangeness" (3–7). When he wants to walk on his head, having the sky as an abyss beneath him, his breath is cut short:

> Lenz—or rather Büchner—has here gone a step further than Lucile. His "Long live the king" is no longer a word, it is a terrifying falling silent, it takes away his—and our—breath and words. (7)

> Lenz—das heißt Büchner—ist hier einen Schritt weiter gegangen als Lucile. Sein "Es lebe der König" ist kein Wort mehr, es ist ein furchtbares Verstummen, es verschlägt ihm—und auch uns—den Atem und das Wort. (*Der Meridian* 7)

Directly afterward, we find Celan's probably most-quoted breath passage: "Poetry: that can mean Atemwende, a breathturn. Who knows, perhaps poetry travels this route—also the route of art—for the sake of such a breathturn?" (*The Meridian* 7). Lucile's utterance and the moment when Lenz falls silent and sees the sky as an abyss are designated as breathturns; instances when art turns into poetry, provided that "the strange" (das Fremde) is faced. Celan describes "the strange" as both the abyss that silences Lenz *and* art's characteristics as a Medusa's head and automaton. He raises the question whether Lenz, when facing the strangeness, "set[s] himself free as an—estranged—I?" (7), which recalls the claim, "Art creates I-distance" (6). The breathturn thus combines traits of art *and* poetry, complicating their differentiation. Celan highlights this ambivalence rather than trying to resolve it and presents a series of open questions in lieu of assertions.

> Who knows, perhaps poetry travels this route—also the route of art—for the sake of such a breathturn? Perhaps it will succeed, as the strange, I mean the abyss *and* the Medusa's head, the abyss and the automatons, seem to lie in one direction—perhaps it will succeed here to differentiate between strange and strange, perhaps it is exactly here that the Medusa's head shrinks, perhaps it is exactly here that the automatons break down—for this single moment? Perhaps here, with the I—the estranged I set free *here* and *in this manner*—perhaps a further Other is set free? (7)

The possibility of two kinds of strangeness, the one of art and the one of poetry, is, in a further speculation at the very end of *The Meridian*, again dismissed: "Art—thus also the Medusa's head, the mechanism, the automatons, the uncanny are so difficult to separate out and which in the final analysis is perhaps only one strangeness—art lives on" (11).

In *The Meridian*, breath is presented as interruption that resists closure and triggers questions. While the routes and directions it opens remain uncertain, the movement of breath is consistently sketched as a turning point. David Wills theorizes this very moment as a constitutive origin. When commenting on the cut-off breath taken away from Lenz, he argues that "we should understand that interruption of the breath, its violent othering, to function as the originary strangeness, the very caesura or cut that constitutes poetry, the *poietic* or *physical* uncanniness that is in operation at the pneumatic origin itself" (143). It is important that such an origin at the same time implies commemoration. In the context of Lenz's falling silent and his cut-off breath, the holocaust and its fatal air sound through without being explicitly mentioned: the formulation "furchtbares Verstummen" repeats words from Celan's *Bremer Rede*:[7] "But it [the German language after the Shoah] had to pass through its answerlessness, pass through frightful muting [durch furchtbares Verstummen], pass through the thousand darknesses of deathbringing speech" (395). In Büchner's text, Lenz's speechlessness is connected to the date "20. Jänner," recalling the Nazis' consideration of a "final solution of the Jewish question." For Celan, January 20 becomes the most eminent date of silent commemoration in poetry: "We write, in falling-, yes nearly fallen silent and speech-less way, i.e., with all the due clarity experienced from inside and outside and therefore in this or that shape perhaps still to be reckoned with, again and again the 'Lenz'ian 20th January, *this* 20th January" (*The Meridian* 59); "*this* 20th January, to which since then so much iciness has added itself" (68).[8] The encounter with the "strange" or the Other, which a poem anticipates in a "breath pause,"[9] is not limited to commemorating the unspeakable atrocities of the holocaust. Turning to the past is only one direction; the poem also speaks toward a "Gegenüber," a perceiving "you"—a possible interlocutor in what is called a "desperate conversation"—desperate maybe because both what is said and whom it is said to are precarious: it is neither granted that anything is said, nor that there will be a "Gegenüber" at all.

Celan describes the poem's relation to an uncertain "Gegenüber" with various images. In the *Bremer Rede*, the poem's "direction" toward something "standing open, occupiable, perhaps toward an addressable Thou" ("Speech on the Occasion of Receiving the Literature Prize" 398) and its dialogic nature are compared to a message in a bottle, an image Celan takes over from Osip Mandelstam's text "Vom Gegenüber."[10] That the poem's temporal dimension thus opens toward the future, that it reaches beyond the moment when it was produced and may undergo actualizations by future readers—the ones who may pick up the message in a bottle—is described as "hindurchgreifen durch die Zeit" (*Gesammelte Werke* 3:186);[11] the poem "seeks to reach [literally: grasp] through time" ("Speech on the Occasion" 396). This recalls Celan's definition of the poem as a handshake in a letter to Hans Bender: "I cannot see any basic difference between a handshake and a poem" ("Letter to Hans Bender" 26).[12] While the message in a bottle suggests a temporal and spatial separation between addresser and addressee and their contact happens via a third object—nota bene, an inanimate one—the handshake implies a direct contact between two bodies at the same time and place. In *The Meridian* and the preliminary notes and drafts, Celan outlines a third, pneumatic model of reception: "here, on breathroutes, the poem comes, the poem it is *there*, pneumatic: for everyone" (108); "The poem remains . . . *pneumatically* touchable" (108). After taking a look at some sources of Celan's poetics of breathing, I will propose four different outlines of such a pneumatic model, following different breathroutes adumbrated by Celan.

Backgrounds of Celan's Poetics of Breathing

In his use of respiratory images, Celan both takes up and challenges various conceptualizations of breath. The reflections in *The Meridian* as well as in the notes and drafts often contain interpretations and renegotiations of philosophical and theological discussions of breath with which Celan was familiar. Marks and notes in books of his personal library show that he read about the atomist theory, that soul-atoms are inhaled and exhaled, which is supposed to maintain life,[13] and that he knew about the implications of breath in Hinduism, where *ātman* designates a person's essence, their "true self," which is expelled into the elements of the world after death.[14] We hear muffled echoes of these different historical conceptualizations in Celan's notes when he plays with the idea that breath exceeds the human breathers and contains something of them that stays in the poem: "The poem remains . . . *pneumatically* touchable" (108). "The poem: the trace of our breath in language / the aura [Hauch] of our mortality" (115); "You are, when your breath marbles it, given over to your poem [Du bist, wenn dein Atem es durchwächst, deinem Gedicht mitgegeben]" (117). As the formulation "pneumatic touchability" suggests, implications of *pneuma* in antiquity and their later theological adaptions, contribute to Celan's idea of a respirational relationality.[15]

In his outline of a poetry that reaches beyond itself both spatially and temporally, Celan recontextualizes the transcendent qualities breath has been invested with throughout its cultural history: the poem's "breath" and "direction" transcend in a more literal than spiritual sense.[16] In one note for *The Meridian*, Celan explicitly links "direction" (graphically rendered by arrows) to a theological take on breath in the sense of animation: "wherefrom ← ensouling / whereto → death/God" (109). That he fails to adopt the idea of an immortal divine spirit exceeding a human's body in his poetics becomes apparent in the sentence "The poem: the trace of our breath in language / the aura [Hauch] of our mortality" (115) and in the following note: "The language of the poem is personal mortal language, like the call of 'Lucile' / What in the poem is mortal, its breath, is what actually remains; fate [Schicksal] can be read from the poem—as language is here that which has been promised one [am Gedicht ist . . . Sprache . . . das einem Zugesprochene Schicksal ablesbar]" (111). Paradoxically, what "remains" of the poem is what is "mortal" about it. Identifying the mortal part of language with breath is plausible on two levels. (1) Etymologically, by resonances of the Hebrew *hevel*, associating "breath" with ephemerality and (2) due to material and physiological characteristics: breath as a physiological process of mortal humans consisting of a transitory and fleeting airy substance. Celan stresses that breath, the individual trace of the mortal in a poem, is designated as that which remains being "zugesprochen" (spoken in the direction) to someone; the capacity of breath to "remain" seems to combine linguistic-physiological accounts of speech-production with the relationality implied by ancient ideas of a connecting *pneuma*.

Gesturing toward another direction of poetry, Celan notes that Jewish identity and history are a pneumatic matters: "Of course, there is a thematic aspect to Jewishness [Selbstverständlich hat das Jüdische einen thematischen Aspekt]. But I think that the thematic alone is not enough to define Jewishness. Jewishness is a pneumatic matter, so to speak" (*Mikrolithen* 217; my translation). "What is lived—the Jewishness lived by the Jew—shows itself pneumatically in the interval (units of breath [Atemeinheiten], yes, they exist!)" (*Mikrolithen* 31; my translation). Celan's notion of a pneumatic Jewishness and his remarks on pneumatic versus thematic ways of defining Jewishness go hand in hand with his way of approaching the most traumatic chapter of Jewish history, the Shoah, in his poetry.[17] Breath or the "pneumatic" lend themselves as terms in this respect, as they imply something present but nevertheless invisible, a relation that is there even though it might be unseen. In an unsent letter to Norbert Koch in 1962, Celan remarks that due to "recent experiences," including the holocaust, one has to perceive, write, and see differently and that consequently "the poem, more inevitably than before, is a pneumatic matter" (*Mikrolithen* 338; my translation).[18] An explicitly critical attitude to approaches that pin down what they refer to and thus temporally and spatially fix them on a page is expressed in a letter to Siegfried Lenz. Celan links "thematic" commemoration to "artistry," which, in his view, constitutes irresponsible works (338). In the letter, Celan continues as follows: "We are not witnesses through a topic, but through the *pneuma* that verifies that topic [sondern durch das dieses Thema bewahrheitende *Pneuma*]" (338; my translation). Against its surface meaning, "bewahrheiten" (verifying) implies making the subject in question "wahrnehmbar" (perceivable), "pneumatically touchable," for future readers, as opposed to having only been thematically dealt and done with by the author. The ancient and theological notions of *pneuma*, as something that is not visible or graspable but has the capacity to exceed and transcend both spatially and temporally, and thus morph into an ethics of writing: in Celan's sense, *pneuma* allows poetry to carry the silenced voice of witnesses and to act as a bearer of a particular Jewish memory.

The use of the word "pneumatic" in the context of Jewishness also points to another tradition Celan renegotiated in his reflections on breath: Jewish theology and mysticism. Celan especially studied the writings of Martin Buber, whose dialogism was influential for his notion of poetry.[19] The cola ("Kolen"), that is, breath-units ("Atemeinheiten"), that Celan keeps mentioning refer back to Buber's translation of the Hebrew bible together with Franz Rosenzweig.[20] Buber's translation project aimed at an acoustic understanding of the Bible, its "fundamental orality" (*Die Schriftwerke* 21);[21] for him, breathing pauses are important in the "recreation" of spoken language because they account for a "more natural" oral punctuation than meter. Buber relates the "natural" quality ascribed to oral language, which, following Rosenzweig, is structured according to breath, "the natural segmenting of speech" ("Scripture and Word" 43), to a human being's uniqueness: "Revelation is accomplished in the human body and the human voice, i.e., in *this* body and *this* voice, in the mystery of their uniqueness" ("On Word Choice in Translating the Bible" 74). It can be assumed that Celan's way of relating breath to voice and a human's singularity in the notes and drafts for *The Meridian* goes back to Buber and Rosenzweig. In the introductory comments to their translation, Buber refers back to the rhetoricians' idea that breathing pauses structure speech:

> Of course, to some degree this also pertains to all true poetry. . . . Thus, a metrical structure can be developed . . . , but it has to be noted that colometry, that is, segmentation into units [cola] that are units of breath and units of sense at the same time, is more original than metre. Rosenzweig accurately designated "the fundamental principle of natural, oral punctuation" as the act of breathing. (*Die Schriftwerke* 20–21; my translation)

Buber's "Kolen," "Atemeinheiten," and "Sinneinheiten" are modeled after the cola of ancient rhetoric:

> Each unit wants to be divided into natural speech-units, dictated by the laws of breathing and delineated according to meaning: the so-called cola (hence the word *colometry* to describe the typographical patterns). Each unit wants to be an easily speakable, easily perceptible and thus rhythmically ordered unity—as indeed all early oral tradition works toward what is easily speakable and easily perceptible, and thus works by the formation of rhythms. ("From the Beginnings of Our Bible Translation" 179)

When Celan integrates terms that Buber uses in his own texts, he invests them with different meaning. While Buber is interested in the structuring of speech and the accomplishment of completed units that are "easily perceptible and thus rhythmically ordered," the way in which Celan deploys the term "cola" suggests almost the contrary:

> Only when you go with your |most personal| pain to the crooked-nosed, hunchbacked and yiddy |and goitery| dead of Treblinka, Auschwitz and elsewhere, will you also meet the eye and |then| its |its Eidos: the| almond. Not the motif, but pause and interval, but the mute breath-auras, but the cola guarantee |in the poem| the truth of such an encounter. (*The Meridian* 128)[22]

> And then when you stand with your *thinking in* falling silent thinking in the pause which reminds you of your heart, and don't speak of it ~~any more~~. And ~~only later~~, speak, ~~after a while~~ |later,| of *yourself.* ~~In the~~ |In this "later," in ~~the~~ there| remembered pauses, in the cola and mora, your word speaks; the poem today—it is a breathturn |crest-times |and soul-turn||, that's how you recognize it |—be aware of it.—| (127; be aware of it, nimm es wahr = literally, perceive it)

In Celan's writing, breathing pauses, intervals, and cola are instances where order breaks down,[23] where what is not usually seen or thought of pierces through and results in an imperative to perceive; "nimm es wahr" refers to an imperative to perceive what is *least easy* to perceive, even unbearable. Celan's breathturn is located at the point where a "motif" or subject is abandoned and—as the quote performatively displays—shattered words no longer "cohere into a unity of meaning" (Buber, "On Translating the Praisings" 91). Precisely at this point, literature opens to an encounter in which commemoration takes place. In contrast to Buber's and Rosenzweig's endeavor to evoke orality by structuring their translation according to breath-units, this quotation shows that Celan emphasizes the pause's coincidence with a speaking that falls apart and falls silent. At the same time, Celan reflects on spoken language and "the presence of a voice" in the poem in his notes and drafts for *The Meridian*. A rejected beginning to the planned speech suggests that the poem's approach "on breathroutes" quite literally implies sounds modulated by the tongue and carried on the air that passed through our lungs:[24] " 'What's on the lung, put on the tongue.' My mother used to say. The poem, even if it doesn't ~~exactly~~ always resemble that which comes on doves' feet, still comes on breathroutes—and, if it wants to remain the poem, will never take different routes" (51).

Outline 1: Continuous Breathroutes

While some references to orality, to supposedly vivid speech uttered by the creaturely human body, remain in *The Meridian*, they are no longer explicitly connected to breath: the poem is said to "speak" and it is mentioned that language becomes "stimmhaft," voiceful, during encounters, which are described as "*routes of a voice* to a perceiving you" (11; emphasis added). The rejected beginning as well as other notes still play with a conception of orality grounded in the physiological: they invite the interpretation that breath acts as a medium of the voice in question whose "routes" are "breathroutes." However, it is precisely such an explicit connection of voice or speaking, routes, and breath that is later renounced in *The Meridian*.

There is a related thematic complex that is strongly linked to breath in the drafts and notes but then appears isolated from it in *The Meridian*: the singularity of a living human being, especially the writer. In the speech, Celan describes the poem as "a self-realization of language through radical individuation; i.e., the single, unrepeatable speaking of an individual" (117); "The poem is lonely and en route. Its author remains added to it. [Wer es schreibt, bleibt ihm mitgegeben]" (9). While breath is mentioned in connection to *reception* in *The Meridian* (Lucile perceives a speech that has direction and breath) and the *poem itself* (poetry is tentatively defined as breathturn), it is not addressed when Celan turns to the *writer*, whose singularity is (in ways that are no further commented on) supposedly inscribed into the poem. By contrast, in the notes and drafts, breath plays a prominent role in precisely this context:[25] "Language's sensuality, its falling under the senses is the secret of the presencing of language as a voice (person) [der

Gegenwart einer Stimme (Person)]" (114); "sense-, i.e., *breath-enlived* [sinn-d.h. *atembelebt*]" (120); "the poem: the trace of our breath in language / the aura [Hauch] of our mortality" (115). "You are, when your breath marbles it, given over to your poem [Du bist, wenn dein Atem es durchwächst, deinem Gedicht mitgegeben]" (117). If, for a moment, we ignore the fact that Celan established a direct link between breath from both the presence of a voice, the writer, and the poem's routes in *The Meridian* speech and instead consider the notes as "explanatory" additions, we can derive a more or less coherent pneumatic reception model.[26] The formulation, "breath, that is, direction and destiny," which is not expanded on further in *The Meridian* itself, can be elucidated by the drafts. When he reflects that poems still write the 20th of January, Celan notes, "The strange [das Fremde] is the horizon of the poem; ~~the~~ in the breath-carried conversation with the other ~~is the~~ this *direction* gives the sense [den Sinn]; the sense-enlivening, breath-carried [das Sinnbelebende, Atemgetragene]" (119; translation modified). This suggests that the poem's direction toward the Other is carried by breath—on "breathroutes." The outline of a pneumatic poetics could be sketched as follows: breath mediates and connects the unspeakable past and the precarious interlocutor via poem: "the route of poetry: the breathroute" (40); "here, on breathroutes, the poem comes, the poem it is *there*, pneumatic: for everyone" (108); "The poem remains . . . *pneumatically* touchable" (108). The writer's mortal breath "grows through" the poem and maintains his or her trace in the words. In these sensual traces, the "presence of a voice," become perceivable—breathable or touchable—for another mortal who encounters the poem later—not as inanimate art but as animated poetry in the breathturn. To pursue Celan's more syncopated breathroutes, I abandon this tentative, rather phonocentric outline.

Outline 2: Interrupted Breathroutes

The fact that Celan chose to sever the link between breath and the author's voice in *The Meridian* undermines this outline.[27] These textual changes should be conceived of, I argue, as a *breathturn* in their abandonment of respiratory imagery in thematic clusters around the author's singularity and orality. First let us look at the passage where Celan literally cut out "breath" by removing pneumatic imagery: the moment when Lenz falls silent. This account of breath being "taken away" appears as a trace of the notes where breath occurs in connection to voice and routes as well as the author's

"Mitgegebenheit" (being given) to the poem. A strange detail in the scene presents the author as "mitgegeben":

> Lenz—das heißt Büchner—ist hier einen Schritt weiter gegangen als Lucile. Sein "Es lebe der König" ist kein Wort mehr, es ist ein furchtbares Verstummen, es verschlägt ihm—und auch uns—den Atem und das Wort. (7)

> Lenz—or rather Büchner—has here gone a step further than Lucile. His "Long live the king" is no longer a word, it is a terrifying falling silent, it takes away his—and our—breath and words. (7)

"Lenz—das heißt Büchner"—what is this supposed to mean? "Sein" and "ihm" suddenly become ambivalent points of reference: they could imply Lenz or Büchner. It is not only Lenz who dreadfully falls silent, whose breath and words are taken away, but also Büchner's—and "our[s]." Here, the pneumatic relation between author, text (fictional character), and reader presents itself as a (breath)route interrupted by apnea.

Some notes and drafts of the speech reveal the syncopated relation between poem and author. Celan repeatedly writes that the poem is "simultaneously voiced and voiceless" (34, 55). In one note, he further specifies the medium of literary silence and voice: the poem is "a speech-art that has to be heard in the written, i.e., silent" (107). Celan thus reproduces—and, as we will see in the following discussion, reevaluates—an old discontent with *writing*: whenever a human being writes, his or her actual, living, audible voice is silenced. Writing cannot avoid acting as a Medusa's head: words carried on the breath are petrified into print, inanimate letters on a page are bereft of bodily breath and organic life. What, then, *remains* of the author in a poem? How can the poem still be "stimmhaft"? The following note suggests a possible answer: "To write poems so that they remain attuned, even there if not to our talking, then to our silence, to our keeping-silent-with-the-named [Mit-dem-Genannten-Mitschweigen]; so that we only silence ourselves before a foreign You as consonants [als Mitlaute ein fremdestes Du anschweigen]—and give it a chance" (146). Paradoxically, it is the silence, the author's falling silent, that makes him or her perceivable;[28] perceivable as a *consonant* (Mitlaut), that is, by syncopnea: a speech sound produced by interrupted airflow, a mute letter referring to such a sound, or, literally, "sounding with." Precisely in not pretending to breathe or speak, the poem keeps being "gestimmt" (tuned) toward the authors' falling silent as well as toward the unspeakable traumata potentially drawn on. This is how we may understand Celan's claim that the "strange" encompasses the "abyss *and* the Medusa's head," and that the two "seem to lie in one direction" (7). The very process of writing, of "*sich*-mitteilen,"[29] implies splitting *oneself* into writing: the body's vital parts are cut off by the silent letters, the writer's voice turns into a *persona*,[30] something sounding through, sounding through silently, as *Mitlaut*, consonant. The poem's "pneumatic" relationality, its potential to provoke an encounter, seems to be based on this caesura, pointing to a silencing that recalls the one who was silenced and calls upon someone who may reach out to it in a later time. "In every poem language waits as voice / the poem's voiceless-voicefulness— / → to invoke [Anrufen]; always still an invocation [Anrufen] (there too where it is a silent gaze; the poem . . . the *silent consonant* of the named [der *stumme Mitlaut* am Genannten]" (145). This note suggests that the poem's quality of being "voiceless-voiceful" lies in its tendency to silently wait for or invoke someone like Lucile who sees and perceives a muteness (note that art does not "speak" to Lucile—she does not understand what is said) in a moment that is called a breathturn.

A further note indicates that the poem's "voice" might not only consist in *one* voice, but possibly in two (or more) voices that do not meet, but rather miss each other: "All that has been transmitted is only there once, as voice; its reappearance, its respective present is a becoming-voiced of what has stepped back and is stored in the voiceless; decisive for its new appearance is the new voice" (118; translation modified). The "new voice" may belong to a recipient, someone like Lucile; at this moment the silent poem whose author receded into mute letters becomes "stimmhaft" again, but not through a revitalization of the author's voice. The "new voice"—possibly the voice of the "Du"—does not breathe new life into the poem; rather, it is itself left speech- and breathless: "*there too it still gives you a chance / to it faces you with silence: / maybe here we can remember the medusa-likeness* of poetry . . . ; it faces you with silence; it takes your—*false*—breath away; you have to come to a breathturn [du stehst an der Atemwende]" (123). The poem, which always also has a share in art, does to the recipient what it did to the author, it acts as a Medusa and petrifies to stillness. In this sense, writing takes away breath and words: Büchner's, Lenz's, and ours. Our breath, as readers, is taken away when facing a poem in Celan's sense—when encountering erratic language blocks that do not breathe and speak but rather confront us in silence. At the breathturn, precisely where breath is taken away (a violent act that in *The Meridian* itself figures as a trace of how Celan cut the link of breath and a singular human's speech), we may, paradoxically, confront the mortal, the creaturely—that which has fallen silent and thus gives us a *chance*: to perceive the silencing, the muted *con-sonare*, the poem's interrupted breath, direction, and destiny:³¹

> Only when with your most own pain you'll have been with the crooked-nosed and yiddy and goitery dead of Auschwitz and Treblinka and elsewhere, will you also meet the eye and the almond. And then you stand with your ~~thinking in~~ falling silent thinking in the pause which reminds you of your heart, and don't speak of it ~~any more~~. And then when you stand with your *thinking in* falling silent thinking in the pause which reminds you of your heart, and don't speak of it ~~any more~~. And ~~only later~~, speak, ~~after a while~~ |later,| of *yourself*. ~~In the~~ |In this "later," in ~~the~~ there| remembered pauses, in the cola and mora, your word speaks; the poem today—it is a breathturn |crest-times |and soul-turn||, that's how you recognize it |—be aware of it.—| [nimm es wahr]. (127)

The breathturn, in line with the "new," second voice that meets the poem, implies a turn from one body's breath to another's, for example, from Büchner's breath to Lenz's and to mine. At first sight, the word "breathroute" may invoke the idea of a path along which a breath can wander or suggest that breath itself moves like a continuous path. However, the breathroute turns out to be interrupted, not least by Celan himself, who chooses not to use the word in *The Meridian*. The breathroute dissolves into various invisible paths of breath that intersect and cut into each other.³² At the intersections, someone's breath may, for a moment, touch on a point where that of someone else has been taken away.

INSPIRATION—CONSPIRATION

In *The Meridian*, the passage introducing the breathturn contains inspired words taken from another mouth. On the one hand, a sentence in Buber's *Ich und Du* is recalled: "bis der große Schauder kommt, und das Atemanhalten im Dunkel, und das bereitende Schweigen" (*Ich und Du* 140–41); "till there comes the great shudder, the holding of the breath in the dark, and the preparing silence" (*I and Thou* 119). Celan cites this passage in a note, along with a quote from *Lenz* that is taken over in *The Meridian*.[33] The wording "es verschlägt ihm—und auch uns—den Atem und das Wort" is taken from Heidegger.[34] The Heideggerian context becomes quite obvious when Celan notes "it takes your—*false*—breath away; you have come / to the breathturn" (123)[35] and "an erratic language-block; it [the poem] faces you with silence. It throws your *idle talk [Gerede]* back at you until your breath . . . turns" (97; emphasis added; translation modified).[36] For Heidegger, the moment when breath and words are taken away designates a rupture of inauthentic existence and the idle talk of the "they." Consequently, the false breath and the "Gerede" can be read as purely *artistic* speaking, the language of an art devoid of poetry as well as a way of speaking inappropriately about the holocaust—that is, *talking about* it thematically, as a motif, instead of letting it resonate pneumatically in dreadful silences.

The "false" breath can also be considered in terms of an imitated, inspired breath. A copied and artificial breath taken away from someone, the word "Atem" taken over from Heidegger, literally stands at the breathturn. In his copy of Emanuel Swedenborg's *Homo Maximus*, Celan marked the following passage, which quite drastically depicts inspiration as an intrusion of foreign breaths:[37]

> Once, before I went to sleep, it was predicted that several people conspired against me with the aim of killing me by means of suffocation; but I did not mind their threats because I was protected by the Lord; therefore I fell asleep unworried. However, because I woke up at midnight, I distinctly felt that I did not breathe by myself, but through heaven; the breath was not mine, but I breathed nevertheless. I could also feel the ensoulment or the breath of ghosts [die Beseelung oder das Atmen der Geister] on numerous other occasions when they breathed in me, and my breath was nevertheless there at the same time, different from theirs. (*La Bibliothèque philosophique* 121–22; my translation)

The scene Swedenborg describes contains two allusions to breath and its deprivation: the short narrative's starting point is a prediction that several people con*spire* against the speaker, planning to choke him. A threat that his breath will be "verschlagen" (taken away, but also beaten up) leads to con-spiration in the literal sense of breathing-with. The violence inherent in conspiration remains present here, when the singular breath is usurped and interpenetrated by others. In presenting a movement of syncopnea in which the pneumatic becomes conspirational, the passage constitutes a structural analogy to Celan's outline of poetry: at the basis, there is suffocation—the unspeakable past, which leads to a deadly conspiracy with language; considered in parallel with the drowsy body of Swedenborg's speaker, the body of a mute, unconscious, still text is taken and breathed by others. It is a site of familiar and foreign voices, where breaths from the living and the dead conspire—they breathe together-apart.

Breath in Celan's Poetry and Translations

In the following discussion, I want to trace such conspirative movements in Celan's poetry, focusing on the several versions of Celan's unpublished poem "Ricercar" and his translation of Mandelstam's "Дано мнѣ тѣло" ("Man gab mir einen Körper"). In both drawing on Celan's poetic reflections and expanding them, the two clusters of texts present themselves as interrupted breathroutes leading toward and away from each other. In "Ricercar" and "Man gab mir einen Körper," breath is inextricably linked with hands. What might sound like a strange anatomical-physiological pair turns out to be closely related in Celan's writing. Breath is only one central image complex in the poetics Celan outlines; another such complex is clustered around hands, grasping, and touching. It is also significant that Celan uses breath and hands, respectively, in two tentative definitions of poetry: "I cannot see any basic difference between a handshake and a poem"; "poetry, that can mean a breathturn." The similar contexts in which references to breath and hands appear in the notes and drafts for *The Meridian* are remarkable. Hands—very much in the sense of the poem as a handshake—are mentioned when the encounter between strangers enabled by the poem is described: "The poem gives itself to you, into the hand of the one who therefore stands in the secret of the encounter—in what a hand does it give itself thus! It gives itself into your hand that the strangest illuminates [die von Fremdesten leuchtende] as into your own hand!" (78; translation modified). "On the hands on which it had to walk, the poem comes to you, puts itself *into your hand*. [Auf den Händen, auf denen es zu gehen hat, kommt das Gedicht zu dir, gibt es sich dir *in die Hand*]" (139). The last sentence recalls two references to breath most literally: "das Gedicht kommt auf Atemwegen [here, on breathroutes, the poem comes]" (108) and "d[ie] Luft, die wir zu Atmen haben [the air we have to breathe today]" (5). Hands also appear when the singularity of a mortal human is addressed: "Handwerk—Hände der einmaligen, (der) sterblichen Seelenmonade Mensch. / Handiwork—hands of the one-time, the mortal soul-monad man" (113).[38]

In these passages, breath and hands seem to be used as interchangeable images. It is striking that hands, like breath, disappear in the context of mortality and singularity in the speech itself. What remains in *The Meridian* of the numerous references to hands in the notes is a quote from one of Celan's own poems, "Stimmen" ("*Come to us on your hands. / Whoever is alone with the lamp, / has only his hand to read from*" [11]) and the "imprecise because fidgety finger on the map" that finds the meridian. In the finished speech, the abandoned breathroute becomes a hand route: "Come to us on your hands" is tied to the question "does one take such routes with the poems?" and the restless fingers on the map find the meridian, which "connects and leads, like the poem, to an encounter" (11–12).[39]

In the literary texts discussed here, one of Celan's central routes leads *between* the hands and the breath. The exchange of pneumatic and manual images throughout Celan's work culminates in the note "The poem remains . . . *pneumatically* touchable." "Touchable" recalls the handshake and the idea that the poem gives itself into the hands of a "you." It is precisely the conjunction of hands and *breath* that allows for holding on to the idea of a poem's touchability without assuming a direct physical contact between author and reader, for example (which the image of the handshake suggests to some degree).

The touch Celan invokes resonates with what Nancy describes in *Corpus*—an encounter between strangers, a contact that is already disrupted when someone addresses him- or herself to another in writing because it implies giving oneself up to a foreign outside. In the act of addressing, the writer becomes a stranger to him or herself, like Lenz, who "set[s] himself free as an—estranged—I":

> "Writing" means: not the monstration, the demonstration, of a signification but a gesture toward *touching* upon *sense*. A touching, a tact, like an address: a writer doesn't touch by grasping, by taking in hand (from *begreifen* = seizing, taking over, German for "conceiving") but touches by way of addressing himself, sending himself *to* the touch of something outside, hidden, displaced, spaced. His very touch, certainly *his* touch, is in principle withdrawn, spaced, displaced. It *is*: may the foreign contact draw near, with the foreigner remaining foreign in that contact (remaining

a stranger *to* contact *in* contact: that's the whole point about touching, the touch of bodies). (*Corpus* 17–19)[40]

Here, Nancy dismisses manual touching in the sense of "grasping." In another context, and more in line with Celan, he describes a touch of hands that are not present in the same place, hands that cannot shake but rather meet in an "infinitely indirect, deferred" manner: the "page itself is a touching (of my hand while it writes, and your hands while they hold the book)" (51). In *The Meridian* and the notes and drafts for the speech, the different roles that hands and breath may play in such temporally and spatially displaced literary touches remain vague. It is in the literary texts themselves that we find more specific details.[41]

"Das Glas der Ewigkeit—behaucht: Mein Atem, meine Wärme drauf": Celan's Mandelstam Translation

Celan's intensive engagement with the Jewish writer Mandelstam, who died in a Siberian prison camp, was his most explicit poetic work of commemoration.[42] Celan translated a number of Mandelstam's poems in 1958–1959 and prepared an essay on his poetry at approximately the same time he was working on *The Meridian*.[43] There are a number of overlaps between *The Meridian* and the essay on Mandelstam, and in some cases it is difficult to assign the preliminary notes to one or the other text. A note that clearly constitutes a draft for the Mandelstam essay and yet intersects with other notes on hands and mortality in *The Meridian* notes establishes a connection between the hand and inscription: "More than a few of these poems have the character of an inscription—the trembling of the mortal hand. Mandelstam's poem carries its hope with it in this "petrification," this hope for the—near or distant—eye" (72; translation modified). According to this note, the shaking hand of the mortal is "inscribed" in the poem and petrified; the poem becomes an epitaph in which mortality manifests itself *in* petrification, which is where hope lies—the hope that a later mortal eye will see it. Here, an alternative to Medusa's gaze is sketched: in Celan's reading, the petrification process in Mandelstam's poetry does not result in an immortalized image depicting nature or life;[44] it rather inscribes mortality. A pneumatic equivalent to such a petrified mortal hand can be found in "Weggebeizt," a poem from the collection *Atemwende*, in the form of congealed breath, an "Atemkristall":[45]

Tief	Deep
in der Zeitenschrunde,	in the crevasse,
beim	by
Wabeneis	honeycomb-ice
wartet, ein Atemkristall,	there waits, a Breathcrystal,
dein unumstößliches Zeugnis.	your unannullable witness.
(*Gesammelte Werke* 2: 31)	(*Selected Poems and Prose of Paul Celan* 247)

The poetic implications of the "Breathcrystal" are, in many respects, analogous to the ones sketched out in the note on Mandelstam's poetry: "Atemkristall" can be read as an ossification of the mortal being's expiration, assuming the form of an inscription that then becomes the testimony of disappearance. The petrified exhalation works like the word that names it, "Atemkristall": it is potentially touchable for someone who reads the poem, a near or distant eye, another mortal who might breathe on it and add new extensions to the crystalline structure. Thus, "dein" becomes ambiguous: depending on which angle of the "crevasse of time" one is looking from, it could refer to the writer or the reader, who invisibly coinscribes him- or herself into the poem's words.[46] Reading the Mandelstam note and the poem side by side, breath and hands, once more intertwined, are both markers of a mortal's touch inscribed in poetry. Another note connected to Mandelstam's poetry in the vicinity of *The Meridian* states the following: "The stone is the other, the not-human [das Außermenschliche], with its silence it gives speech direction and space [gibt er dem Sprechen Richtung und Raum]" (98; translation modified). "Richtung und Raum" echoes "Atem, das heißt Richtung und Schicksal [breath, that is, direction ad destiny]."[47] Here, breath and the inanimate stone seem to become replaceable images: both give speech direction. This is particularly striking when we bear in mind that in *The Meridian*, and even more so in some of the notes, breath is closely linked to the human, living, and creaturely, whereas art, the petrified result of Medusa's gaze, is "a stepping beyond the human." When we juxtapose these two notes, the silence of breath and the silence of the stone both figure as forms of the strange, which, as Celan suggests, are no longer clearly attributable to either the inanimate space of art or the creaturely organic domain of poetry. Put differently: in those moments when breath and stone poetically couple in Celan's work, the boundary between art and poetry becomes especially porous.

Celan's translation of Mandelstam's poem "Дано мнѣ тѣло" takes up the idea of the movement of a hand or a breath being ossified into writing, into a silent stone-like formation, and then "giving way" a "breathing space" where encounters may happen, and presents a more palpable and detailed sketch of the relations between such a "breathing space" and inscription.

> Das Glas der Ewigkeit—behaucht: На стекла вечности уже легло
>   The glass of eternity—breathed upon
> Mein Atem, meine Wärme drauf.   Мое дыхание, мое тепло.
>   My breath, my warmth on it.
>
> Die Zeichnung auf dem Glas, die Schrift: Запечатлеется на нем узор,
>   The drawing on the glass, the writing:
> Du liest sie nicht, erkennst sie nicht.   Неузнаваемый с недавних пор.
>   You do not read it, do not recognize it.
>
> Die Trübung, mag sie bald vergehn.   Пускай мгновения стекает муть—
>   The mist, may it fade soon.
> Es bleibt die zarte Zeichnung stehn.   Узора милаго не зачеркнуть.
>   The delicate drawing remains.[48]
> (Celan, *Gesammelte Werke* 5: 53)   (Celan, *Gesammelte Werke* 5: 52)

In his translation, Celan added two elements that differ significantly from Mandelstam's poem: neither an addressee, "Du" (you), nor "Schrift" (writing) appears in the original. Precisely these elements show that Celan embeds the poem in his own poetic reflections. While the topos of inscribing one's mortal body into art and of leaving (or not leaving) something for posterity through art is clearly addressed in Mandelstam's poem, by adding "Schrift" and "Du," Celan marks it with his own "handwriting," thus integrating it into his theory of poetry or, alternatively, inscribing this theory into the poem. By equating the drawing with writing, the shaking hand of the mortal enters the poem. An undated note shows that the poet's connection to "Glas" (glass), "Hauch" (breath),[49] "Schrift" (writing), and "Zeichnung" (drawing) were of particular concern to Celan in the course of this translation of "Дано мнѣ тѣло":

> Mandelstam:
> Glass, breath, writing
> Drawing [Zeichnung]
> Writing   Both from the poet?
> (*Mikrolithen* 127; my translation;)

"Zeichnung" is a rather free translation of the word "uzor,"[50] which usually means "pattern." In Celan's hands, the automated, repetitive, rigid pattern turns into "drawing," a much freer and more open pictorial inscription associated with individual style or expression. Celan then identifies the drawing, which is produced by a pencil in the artist's hand and indicates singularity, with "Schrift," which for him mutes and petrifies the mortal into stillness. The idea of "Schrift" was probably informed by the verb "zapechatljaetsja" (imprint, engrave) in Mandelstam's poem, indicating that the pattern is imprinted on the glass. In his translation, Celan implicitly takes up what he outlines as the poles between art's Medusa's head and the singularity of poetry in *The Meridian* and lets them coincide. When mentioning the words "Zeichnung" and "Schrift" in the note, Celan adds the question "beides vom Dichter? [both from the poet?]" and thus links them to his concern about how the poet may be *exscribed*, rather than inscribed, in the poem and how something of the poet may nevertheless remain "mitgegeben" (given with, or given over to)—given over from a body that is giving itself up to writing, via hands or breath that already became their own shadow.

In this respect, Mandelstam's voice persists in Celan's translation: "drawing," which Celan equates with writing in his translation (and which also implies the hand that wrote/drew) and breath are differentiated. The breath implies a direct physical contact of the living human with the "glass of eternity"—the material carrier, the medium of the work. The warm breath, blown onto the glass, condenses on the surface, becoming a visible blur that is bound to disappear. In contrast to Celan's "Atemkristall," this breath, which is materially caught on a surface, is said neither to last nor to wait. Set in glacial scenery, the "Atemkristall" can be read as frozen breath crystallized on a surface, which means it would also disappear if the conditions changed. However, in contrast to the blurry condensation in Mandelstam's poem, which continually changes its form in the process of diminishing, the "Breathcrystal" is fixed in relative stillness and thus is more comparable to the drawing/writing than to the "Hauch." What remains and stands still ("bleibt stehen") in "Дано мнѣ тѣло" is the drawing, or writing. In Mandelstam's poem and Celan's translation, this immobile writing or drawing retains a quality of the breath whose own trace has disappeared from the surface:[51] it is opaque like the expiration's "Trübung." Consequently, the writing that has assumed a respirational trait is not read and not recognized by the "you." Such writing does not immortalize the human who exscribes him- or herself and whose bodily traces vanish. Once mortality is breathed onto the glass of eternity, this glass is blown.[52] What remains is a petrified murkiness that cannot be deciphered and, precisely for that reason, bears witness to loss.

Outline 3: The Pneumatically Touchable Poem I

The poem itself does says nothing more. Keeping Celan's poetic reflections in mind—and the fact that Mandelstam's poem went through Celan's hands—the indiscernible writing/drawing that nevertheless still stands, is precisely the point where the mortal has disappeared and where *encounter* becomes possible. In adding the image of the "Hauch," we could imagine a breathing space in the sense of a surface on which the exhaled warm air of the author has vanished for good but that may be breathed on again by a recipient, resulting in a respirational touch whose traces remain invisible (analogous to my reading of "Atemkristall"). In our school bus, in winter, we used to pass time by blowing on the windowpane and scribbling something onto the fleeting canvas of condensation. Once it dried, what was written or drawn would disappear—but it would reemerge as soon as the surface was blown on again. Blowing on a window, expecting to find something that others may have sketched, was even more exciting than producing our own ephemeral inscriptions. Mandelstam's outline of a pattern that is impressed yet unperceivable is at least comparable to such a scenario: a transfigured Freudian *Wunderblock* bearing invisible, unreadable (and maybe forgotten) traces of memories on a surface that no longer holds the breath of the human who had them.

On a less speculative note, Celan read Whitman's "So Long" and quotes the sentence "Camarado, wer dies berührt, . . ." after the remark "Im Gedicht (geschieht) nicht Mitteilen, sondern *Sich*mitteilen [In the poem what happens is not communication but self-communication]" (132). Shortly after writing the lines "Camerado! This is no book; / Who touches this, touches a man," Whitman adds, "O how your fingers drowse me. / Your breath falls around me like dew" (*Leaves of Grass* 455). When the fingers of the reader touch the page and the reader's breath falls over what is written, the petrified words, which remain where the body of the living, singular human who wrote has disappeared, enter a new constellation.[53] They are in the hands of another human who handles them, fogged by that person's breath, which momentarily adds new contours to the whole assemblage of the poem. The encounters that the poem enables are, according to Celan, an integral part of it; the singularity of the poem and its creaturely character may reveal itself in these short moments of reception, the moments when a breathing space is touched on, when the breath of readers, humans foreign to the text that is foreign to them, start to conspire. In translating "Дано мнѣ тѣло," Celan himself engaged in such a "conspirational" move, touching

Mandelstam's poem manually and pneumatically, interweaving it with the textual threads of his own reflections on hands and breath.

What is outlined here is the work of *my* hands: intervening with Celan's translation, tying it to his poetics and Whitman's poem. My reading also involves conspiration and acts of cutting breath. The knots I make between loose textual threads and the contours I draw (contours of syncopnea—my argument turns back on itself at this point) momentarily close what Celan deliberately leaves open. In his poetic reflections and poems, the encounter enabled by pneumatic touchability is always left indeterminate; for academic interlocutors, this leads to a dilemma. Through my attempts at outlining a model of pneumatic touchability—and despite offering more than one, thus leaving multiple breathroutes open—I necessarily impose some closure. Addressing this dilemma does not resolve it; in fact, attempting to resolve it might be the ultimate violation of the text. I thus go on.

"HAUCHSCHRIFT, HANDSCHRIFT": "RICERCAR"

Following the routes of pneumatic touchability in Celan's poetry leads me to a poem that was planned for the collection dedicated to Mandelstam, *Die Niemandsrose*, but eventually not included: "Ricercar." The poem, which was written shortly after Celan held the *Meridian* speech, ties in with both the thoughts for the speech and his translation of Mandelstam's "Дано мнѣ тѣло." At the outset, a few words about the several recorded versions of "Ricercar" are necessary; designating it as "one" poem, as the preceding sentence might suggest, would be wrong. The two reconstructed versions printed in *Die Gedichte aus dem Nachlaß* are based on several typescripts. Two (A and B)[54] are dated 5/21/1961; typescript A includes minor handwritten revisions, and typescript B is an almost clean copy that constitutes the reading-text of the version titled "Ricercar."[55] There are two further typescripts (C and D) and a copy (E) with mayor revisions (*Die Gedichte aus dem Nachlaß* 368–69); there are three copies of C and two copies of D; E is a further copy of D. Copy E constitutes the untitled text reproduced in *Die Gedichte aus dem Nachlaß* and includes handwritten additions that are transcribed as the second part of the third, indented, stanza; these additions are dated 6/29/1962.

1) RICERCAR   RICERCAR[56]
Es geht,   It goes[57]
was durch die Hände dir ging,   what went through your hands

den Weg deiner Hände, den Nacht-,	the route of your hands, the night-,
den Schicksalsweg geht es.	the destiny-route it goes.

Doch: eine Zeile, einmal über ein Blatt gehaucht, auf dem gestern ertrunkenen Tisch—:	But: a line, once breathed over a page, on the table drowned yesterday—:

Über, *über Nacht, über Nacht, da werden,* *da werden* *die Tage* *weiß.*	*Over* *over night, over night, the days* *turn* *the days turn* *white.*

Der auf den Händen ging, die dies schrieben: er, der die Nesselschrift las, der Unverstandene, nur er, versteht auch die anderen. (*Die Gedichte aus dem Nachlaß* 55)	He who went on his hands that wrote this: he, who read the nettle-writing, the misunderstood, only he, understands the others.

2) Es geht, was durch die Hände dir ging, den Weg deiner Hände, den Nacht-, den Schicksalsweg geht es. Es geht seiner Wege.	It goes, what went through your hands the routes of your hands, the night-, the destiny-route it goes. It goes its ways.

Die Zeile, einmal über ein Blatt gehaucht, auf dem schwimmenden Tisch:	The line, breathed over a page once, on the swimming table:

Über Nacht, über Nacht, da werden, da werden die Tage, da werden	Over night, over night, the days turn, the days turn

die Tage	turn
weiß.	white.
Kola—Atem-	cola—breath-
Meere. Dorthin	seas. Thither
taucht der Sinn, taucht der Uhrzeiger, zu	the sense dives, the clockhand dives, to
den Namen.	the names.
Auch unter	Beneath you
dir, vom Maulwurf auf-	too, earth, churned
geworfene Erde, hat	up by mole, the
das Herz eine Uhr.	heart has a clock.
Hauchschrift, Handschrift.	Breathwriting, handwriting.
Der auf den Händen ging, die	He who went on the hands that
es schrieben, er,	wrote it, he,
der die Nesselschrift las, der	who read the nettle-writing, who
weiterlas, der Un-	read on, the un-
gelesene, Un-	read, the mis-
verstandene, er	understood, he
schrieb:	wrote:
an die Atem-, die Ich-	to the breath-, the I-
Diebe.	thieves.

(*Die Gedichte aus dem Nachlaß* 311)

While Mandelstam's poem relates to Celan's poetics on the basis of the scenario being depicted, "Ricercar" explicitly names some cues that invite a reading of the poem alongside the thoughts pursued in *The Meridian* and the notes and drafts: "Hände" (hands), "Schicksal" (destiny), "Weg" (route), "Atem" (breath), "Kola" (cola), "Sinn" (sense). The poem's words are designed to perform breathturns in both versions individually as well as between the two versions. As such, the constellation of "Дано мнѣ тѣло" and Celan's translation represent a scenario that can be read hand in hand with Celan's notes on the possible reception of poetry. In the case of "Ricercar," it is rather the poem's material history that accounts for a peculiar reception situation: the fact that it was written with the intention of being published in a collection of poems, was then rejected and left unpublished, before finally ending up being published nevertheless, posthumously, in Celan's *Collected Works* and the *Historisch-Kritische Ausgabe*.

In this respect, the poem's title is significant. "Ricercar" is derived from the Italian verb *ricercare* ("to seek" or "pursue," going back to the Latin, "to seek again"). In contrast to the poems Celan destroyed, the unpublished poems of his estate were well preserved and ready to be found by those who searched for them (see *Die Gedichte aus dem Nachlaß* blurb). "Ricercar" is also a technical term in music. Celan's poem alludes to a striking number of implications "ricercar" has had in the context of music history and translates them into another medium, *into* a constellation of *words*.[58] Rather than transposing musicality by means of tonality or sound, "Ricercar" silently alludes to the musical genre and the uses of the word in music history. The only line where the acoustic dimension of the words is highlighted by alliteration is "Hauchschrift, Handschrift." These words *refer* to writing and thus point to their written rather than spoken quality. Acoustically, they bear only a faint sound: the repeated puff of the "H" is, phonetically speaking, a voiceless aspiration. "Ricercar" is a poem on the threshold of silence: it was left unpublished by the author and was not meant to be encountered by a public. Dwelling unnoticed in the archive, however, the work always bore within it the potential for later discovery and exposure to the eyes and voices of readers and critics—a possibility the poem itself seems to reflexively anticipate.

PRELIMINARITY

In its musical uses from the sixteenth century onward, *ricercare* refers to a kind of preliminarity, a prelude, attempt, exercise or exploration in which a composer "seems to search or look out for the strains and touches of harmony, which he is to use in the regular piece to be played afterwards" (Burney qtd. in Scholes 876). The fact that Celan chose not to publish it in *Die Niemandsrose* lends the typescripts he left behind a preliminary quality; it's unprinted and thus provisional. The line "Hauchschrift, Handschrift" (breathwriting, handwriting) gestures, moreover, toward a preliminary stage in the writing process. Celan almost always wrote the first drafts of his poems by hand while the second stage of his writing process mainly consisted of typescripts (Zanetti 211). From the perspective of the "completed" printed text, the handwriting represents a provisional stage. As a practice used for early text stages, handwriting marks a transitional phase and thus becomes comparable to Mandelstam's vanishing breath blown onto the glass—what is written by hand seems as fleeting as what is written by breath. However, in contrast to Mandelstam's poem, in which the traces of the breath on the glass surface evaporate, handwritten manuscripts are often preserved and remain accessible as traces of the early stages of the writing process, which is true in the case of Celan, who meticulously archived his own writing.

No handwritten manuscripts of "Ricercar" survive—all archived versions of the poem are typescripts. Handwriting is notably absent from a poem that explicitly concerns it, the only exceptions being some minor corrections and the additions in typescript E, where a major part of the third stanza in the second version is added. While it is unclear whether there was a handwritten first draft, it is significant that all the records of the poem that Celan left behind, "Hauchschrift, Handschrift," are rendered in print. For readers with access to the poem—either in the posthumous publication or by viewing the typescripts at the Literaturarchiv Marbach—"Handschrift" does not appear as handwriting. The printed word only indicates an absence of the actual trace of Celan's hand on the page of the typescripts. On those pages, the actual "Handschrift" is only invoked as an *absence* and thus semantically coincides with the invisible "Hauchschrift." It is a vestige of something that may have been found in a preliminary version but was either not recorded or disappeared, or perhaps it was never there in the first place.

Ricercare was also a term used for the musicians' experimentation with and testing of their instrument before an actual performance (Wolff 1). In "Ricercar," Celan continues experimenting with ideas and terms he used in the *Bremer Rede* and in *The Meridian* (including the notes and drafts) as well as with linguistic material taken from earlier literary texts. Routes, hands, and breath are images Celan kept returning to in his poetic reflections, as explored previously. More specifically, "Schicksalsweg [destiny-route]" is a combination of two formulations Celan used in *The Meridian* and the notes: "Atem, das heißt Richtung und Schicksal [breath, that is, direction and destiny]" and "Atemweg [breathroute]". "Kola," a word adopted from Martin Buber, occurs in the notes for *The Meridian* in connection to the breathing pause. A link between "Sinn" (sense) and "Uhrzeiger" (clockhand) was first established in the *Bremer Rede*: "And if I inquire into its sense [Sinn], I believe I must tell myself that this question involves the question of the clockhand's direction [Uhrzeigersinn]" ("Speech on the Occasion" 396; translation modified). "[D]er auf den Händen ging [who goes/walks on hands]" alludes both to Lenz and the poem "Stimmen" (Voices), which Celan quotes in *The Meridian*: "Komm auf den Händen zu uns. / Wer mit der Lampe allein ist, / hat nur die Hand, draus zu lessen [Come on hands to us. / Whoever is alone with the lamp / has only his hand to read from]" (89). In "Stimmen," these lines are immediately preceded by "*Stimmen* vom Nesselweg her [*Voices* from the nettle path]" (*Gesammelte Werke* 1: 147; *Selected Poems and Prose of Paul Celan* 89), which resonates in "der die Nessenschrift las" (who read the nettle-writing) in "Ricercar." Moreover, the poem "Stimmen" already contains other word-material that Celan uses in "Ricercar": "Herz" (heart), "Atme" (breathe) and "heranschwimmt" (swim toward), and "Nacht" (night)[59] (*Gesammelte Werke* 1: 147). Apart from these clear references to earlier texts, "Ricercar" also contains more extensive self-citations. The sentence "über Nacht werden die Tage weiß [over night the days turn white]" already occurred in one of Celan's aphorisms. The last lines of the earlier version, "der Un- / verstandene, nur er / versteht auch die anderen" takes up the aphorism "Nur der Unverstandene versteht die anderern [only the misunderstood understands the others]" (*Mikrolithen* 25; my translation). These references and self-citations indicate that Celan used his own words as experimental material in the framework of poems in progress. The poem becomes a stage for *ricercar*, for exercise and experimentation with poetic ideas and recycled word-material.

REPETITION, VARIATION, CITATION

In cannibalizing old material, Celan's "Ricercar" recalls another dimension of the musical term: "imitative ricercar" was a type of instrumental music in the sixteenth and seventeenth centuries characterized by repetition and variation, the "imitative treatment of one or more themes" (*Harvard Dictionary of Music* 732). In a letter to Walter Jens, Celan himself suggested considering his self-citations (in the context of the letter, "Aschenblume" echoing "Aschenkraut") as ricercars: "In the musical sense, I would maybe describe it as a 'ricercar'—the anamnesis in your sense would probably be more emphasized" (*Die Gedichte* 924–25; my translation).[60] The mention of anamnesis is significant here: for Celan, taking up his own material in the manner of a musical ricercar involves commemoration. The word "Ricercar" precedes one of the already quoted notes for *The Meridian*, containing one of Celan's most explicit references to the concentration camps:

> Ricercar --- z.B.
> |Your| reversal—what is that? O̶n̶l̶y̶ w̶h̶e̶n̶ Is it the word of the almond-eyed beauty, that I hear you repeat, varied most opportunistically? Only when with your most own pain you'll

have been with the crooked-nosed and yiddy and goitery dead of Auschwitz and Treblinka and elsewhere, will you also meet the eye and the almond. And then you stand with your ~~thinking in~~ falling silent thinking in the pause which reminds you of your heart, and don't speak of it ~~any more~~. And ~~only later,~~ speak, ~~after a while~~ |later,| of *yourself*. ~~In the~~ |In this "later," in ~~the~~ there| remembered pauses, in the cola and mora, your word speaks; the poem today—it is a breathturn |crest-times |and soul-turn||, that's how you recognize it |—be aware of it.—| [nimm es wahr]. (*The Meridian* 127)

The note about writing of unspeakable deaths in the concentration camps itself stammers, as the deletions and repetitions of variant formulations interrupt fluent rhythm and grammatical coherence. The sentences in which the interval and breathturn are mentioned are punctured by caesurae; they break down and the words diverge.[61] As Judith Kasper notes in another context, using Celan's terminology: the breathturn takes the breath away and shatters language ("Damit bedingt die Atempause zugleich ein Verschlagen des Atems und des Wortes" [125]). In Celan's note, repetition and variation, practices dominant in "Ricercar," are first associated with the "word of the almond-eyed beauty"[62]—which can be considered a subdued approach to the Other or the strange that makes it digestible by imbuing it with exotic appeal—something akin to the false breath that has to be taken away.

However, Celan presents another version of variation and repetition when reflecting on an alternative way of encountering the Other in the form of the Jews killed in the concentration camps. In one of his aphorisms, Celan juxtaposes the "word of the almond-eyed beauty," in this context probably alluding to Anne Frank, "the beautiful diary-keeping Jewish girl,"[63] with the "hunched, stuttering, limping Jew who was gassed." He continues by repeating not only the words he just used, but also words occurring in the note cited previously: "He, the Jew is your brother, be aware of him and turn back [nimm ihn wahr und kehre um]—to yourself, you hunched, stuttering, limping—you royal creature" (*Mikrolithen* 34; my translation). "You" and the gassed Jew cut across in the breathturn, in the course of a verbal repetition.[64] It would be negligent to read the repetitions and variations in *The Meridian* note as a mere protocol of how Celan worked on his formulations. The note as such is a continually self-interrupting space of a syncopal writing. Its recurring words—sometimes crossed out and sometimes in brackets—fracture the sentences *in* the note and thus commemorate the bodies of violated Jews, the stuttering of voices who were robbed of their breath.

Self-citations transfigured by variation and repetition like those in "Ricercar" also become occasions for commemoration;[65] apart from the author remembering his own writing, or the reader remembering the author's earlier writing, they often involve a more forceful invasion of memory. In her article on Jorge Semprún's Baudelaire citations in his accounts of the concentration camp at Buchenwald, Kasper notes that citations always cut into the textual fabric they coconstitute, inflicting lesions ("Kata/strophisches Lesen. Baudelaire in Buchenwald" 118).[66] Arno Barnert, who investigates Celan's citational practices in this book *Mit dem fremden Wort: Poetisches Zitieren bei Paul Celan*, argues as follows: "The intriguing aspect of quoting is that it opens up more or less visible intervals and breaches, both within the quoted text and between it and the text in which the quote occurs" (11; my translation). Drawing an analogy to the physiological movement of breath, Barnert understands quoting as a breathturn:

> Such a breathturn is no metaphysical, abstract event; considering quotes in a poem, it becomes immediately evident: initially, quoting implies "breathing in" something other, an artificial-mechanic intake of foreign word-material; thereby, the quoting *I* can be alienated and may get entangled in an unfathomable state of obliviousness. This alienation does not have to last though; an "expiration," an utterance gently transferring the foreign material into something of one's own is always possible. (100; my translation)

In "Ricercar," the self-citations are incisions in which breath is taken away; where the singularity of "Die Zeile, / einmal über ein Blatt gehaucht [the line, / breathed over a page once]" is destroyed because it occurs for the second, or third, or fourth time. It is no coincidence that the lines following the colon, that is, the lines that could actually be designated by the breathed word "Zeile," are the words quoted from the aphorisms. Moreover, the aphorism directly following "Über Nacht werden die Tage weiß" is "Ein schweres Wort, das hingehaucht sein will [a heavy word wanting to be breathed down]" *Mikrolithen* 21; my translation); "Die Zeile, einmal / über ein Blatt gehaucht" thus itself recalls words written earlier by Celan;

in the second and third typescripts, it also recalls the earlier version of "Ricercar" already containing this line, in contrast to the other references to breath, including "Hauchschrift, Handschrift," which were only added in typescript C. Upon rereading the line "Zeile, einmal / über ein Blatt gehaucht," the writing may no longer appear as one's own but rather as something foreign; the "Atem-" and "Ich-Diebe" (the breath- and I-thieves) have already done their work through language. The marks of the author's singular body have disappeared into the written words, which are part of a universal sign system—they can refer to the hand or breath of the writer, but the indexical tie is cut once a line is breathed onto a page. Whoever breathes and writes always addresses oneself to the breath- and I-thieves ("er / atmete, er / schrieb: / an die Atem-, die Ich-/ Diebe"). What is apparently individual, the "Hauch"—maybe forming a unique ephemeral shape like the one on the glass in "Дано мнѣ тѣло"—is already transferred to a repeatable medium; "Hauchschrift" and "Handschrift" can only appear as words pointing to the absence of a physically breathed writing or handwriting. The lack of proximity between an actual hand and breath on the page we see, in the medium of mass-produced printed letters, is precisely where the fleetingness of a "Hauch" becomes most perceptible: "wahrnehmbar."

That the poem was not published but rather archived was only a momentary delay and interruption to a process of thievish inspiration by readers (e.g., readers like me who try to interweave threads of the poem's citations) who can only overwrite the author's voice. The dedication to the breath- and I-thieves as well as the line "er / atmete, er / schrieb [he breathed, he wrote]" first appear in typescript D. Typescript C has different implications: "der Un- / Verstandene, er / Verstand sie, die Atem-, die Ich- / Diebe" (the misunderstood, he understood them, the breath-, the I-thieves). "Understanding" the breath- and I-thieves in typescript D turns into giving oneself over to those that will steal the one who "breathed and wrote" in typescript E. The act of someone *addressing* the poem to someone else is rendered in the past tense and is a moment in the written poem where the I and the breath are already stolen. The very same "he" who writes to the breath- and I-thieves is also described as a reader: "er, / der die Nesselschrift las, der / weiterlas" (he, who read the nettle-writing, who read on). Given that "Nesselschrift" is a reference to one of Celan's earlier poems, "Stimmen," the reading performed by "he" can be understood as rereading one's own words. Upon rereading one's earlier text, one's own reencountered words—the words that have gone through one's own hands—go their own ways.

The first line of "Ricercar" can be read in that direction: "Es geht / was durch die Hände dir ging / . . . Es geht seiner Wege [It goes, what went through your hands, it goes its ways]." Taking up these words again—words in which one's own breath has been choked—results in a scene that recalls Swedenborg's inspiration: the breathing of a foreign ghostly breath—an inspiration coinciding with theft of the breath and the self.

In a note on *The Meridian*, Celan mentions that "citations are . . . foreign bodies as such [Fremdkörper schlechthin]" (*The Meridian* 156). Self-citations are no exception: one's own words are reencountered as strangers; the reappropriated words appear as foreign bodies, an alienated *Hauch-* or *Handschrift* in print. In *The Meridian*, Celan uses the word "herausgreifen" (to pick out—but importantly in German "greifen" means to grasp, e.g., with one's hands) in the context of quoting: "ich habe hier nur zwei Sätze herausgegriffen [here I have picked out only two sentences]" (4)—quoting is handling inspired words. Celan observes "I had . . . encountered myself" (11) after he quotes his own poem, including the line "*Come to us on your hands*," which was written, as he notes, from the direction of "his" January 20. Remembrance in quoting then raises the following question: "Does one take . . . such routes with the poems? [Geht man also . . . geht man mit Gedichten solche Wege?] Are these routes only re-routes, detours from you to you?" (11). Encountering "oneself" turns into a detour from "you to you." The detour implies a turn—a breathturn: from "I" to "you" ("I had . . . encountered myself" → "detours from you to you") and from coming to going: "*Komm* auf den Händen zu uns" → "*Geht* man also" (emphasis added). This breathturn is echoed in "Ricercar." Alluding to the line "Komm auf den Händen zu uns [Come on hands to us]" in *Stimmen*, which is quoted in *The Meridian*, "Ricercar" starts with "Es geht, / was durch die Hände dir ging" (It goes, what went through your hands). "Es geht seiner Wege" (it goes its ways) recalls the "Um-wege, Umwege von dir zu dir" (detours from you to you), and "Der auf den Händen ging" (who walked on his hands) is "Komm auf den Händen zu uns" (Come on hands to us) turned around. On the breathroutes between *The Meridian* and "Ricercar" inverted walkers on hands come and go; they become perceivable as a succession of breath*turns*. The syncopal breathturns staged in the poem between words and parts of words, and beyond the printed page between the poem and its readers, once more brings us back to the musical ricercar: from 1540 on, it designated a way of composing determined by counterpoint (Scholes 876), that is, countervoices juxtaposed against each other.

HANDWRITTEN BREATH-SEAS

In all versions of "Ricercar," some of the linguistic counterpoints are marked graphically: the middle passages are indented or italicized. The most palpable counterpositioning occurs in typescript E, the model for the second text printed in *Die Gedichte aus dem Nachlaß* (see figure 5.1):

> *Kola—atem-*
> *meere. Dorthin*
>
> Hauchschrift, Handschrift.
> Der auf den Händen ging, die
> es schrieben, er,
> er die Nesselschrift las, der
> weiterlas, der Un-
>
> *taucht der Sinn, taucht der Uhrzeiger, zu*
> *~~zu~~ den Namen!*
> *≠ Auch unter*
> *dir, vom Maulwurf auf-*
> *geworfene Erde, hat*
> *das Herz eine Uhr*[67]

Not only are the parts of the stanzas literally juxtaposed; they also appear in different forms: typed and handwritten. Moreover, there may be a temporal gap between the undated typescript and the handwritten addition dated 6/26/62, that is, more than a year after the first version of the poem. In typescript E, the printed line "Hauchschrift, Handschrift" is surrounded by what it refers to: handwritten words, including "atem." Visually, the cursive handwriting, which has a more fluid appearance than the printed letters, streams around the printed lines. The appearance of the fluid mass of letters corresponds to their semantic reference: seas. The handwritten passage addresses domains that are located underneath: a space beneath the surface of

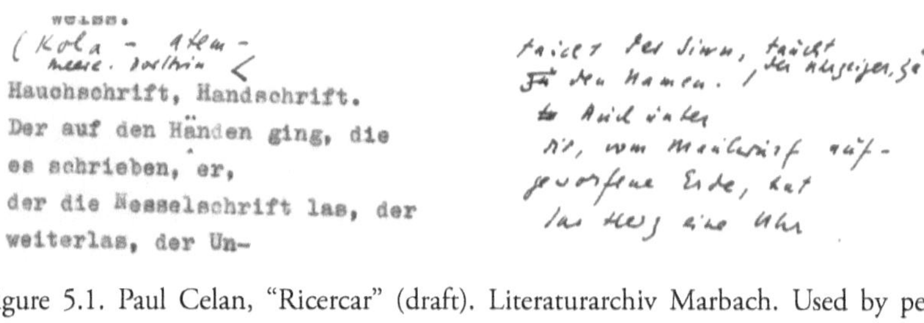
Hauchschrift, Handschrift.
Der auf den Händen ging, die
es schrieben, er,
der die Nesselschrift las, der
weiterlas, der Un-

Figure 5.1. Paul Celan, "Ricercar" (draft). Literaturarchiv Marbach. Used by permission of Bertrand Badiou and Suhrkamp Verlag.

the water that is where "sense" and "clockhand" dive and a domain beneath the earth. What is semantically situated underneath is written by hand, forming a kind of subtext on the surface of the page and an undercurrent of the poem articulating core threads of Celan's poetics (see figure 5.2).

> *Kola—atem-*
> *mere. Dorthin*   *taucht der Sinn, der Uhrzeiger, zu*
>   *zu den Namen!*
> Hauchschrift, Handschrift

The words added later in handwriting designate something prior to what follows in the poem: in contrast to the present tense of "taucht," all subsequent actions ascribed to the "he" are written in the past tense. Whereas the opening and closing passages of the poem can be read as retrospective reflections on its own genesis, the middle passage instead stages a simultaneity of reading and the creation of what is read. Both the handwriting itself and the reference to "Kola" point to the act of composition. In "Ricercar," Celan's use of the words "Kola," "Atem," and "Sinn" is yet another way of destabilizing Buber and the rhetorician's breath and sense unit. On the page, such a unit is already torn apart graphically: the word "Kola" erratically stands on its own without being grammatically embedded. "Atem" is located between dashes that at first sight seem to isolate the word; on a second glance, though, the second dash appears as a hyphen connecting the word to "meere" in the next line, resulting in the cut "Atemmeere" (breath-seas). Consequently, the lines can be read as a *reformulation* of Buber's formula "Kola = Atemeinheiten": "Kola = Atemmeere." "Sinn" is torn away from "atem-/meere" more drastically by the placement of the added lines on the right hand side of the page. "Dorthin" indicates a direction. Visually, it points out where, across a long gap of white space, the sentence continues and grammatical cohesion can be regained. Like "atem-/meere," "Dorthin" displays a syncopal movement of severed unity.

Figure 5.2. Paul Celan, "Ricercar" (draft). Literaturarchiv Marbach. Used by permission of Bertrand Badiou and Suhrkamp Verlag.

Linking the word "Sinn" with the deictic "Dorthin" and thus indicating the direction results in a doubling: etymologically, "Sinn" *is* "direction."[68] "Sinn" as interrupted direction brings us back to a note for *The Meridian*: "The strange [das Fremde] is the horizon of the poem; t̶h̶e̶ in the breath-carried conversation with the other . . . this <u>direction</u> gives the <u>sense</u> [den Sinn]; the sense-enlivening, breath-carried" (119; translation modified). The constellation formed by "Atem" and "Sinn" in Celan's writing clashes with Buber's symmetrical identification of the two terms (Atemeinheit = Sinneinheit). While "Sinn" in the sense of a direction remains closely linked to breath, the direction is interrupted by intervals in which breath is cut short by breathturns. In "Ricercar," "Sinn" dives across the chasm of the blank page, into a breath-sea, a word which is cut apart and thus presents a space where meaning is suspended. The image of breath-seas as such is a strange one: while "Meeresatem" (sea-breath) could plausibly evoke a similarity between the rhythmical movement of the sea and the breathing body, seas of breath are less immediately accessible to the imagination. Instead of offering a facile metaphor,[69] Celan confronts us with a formation of words in which straightforward meaning is interrupted. In "Ricercar," "sense" is both visually and semantically located in this indeterminate space.

Outline 4: The Pneumatically Touchable Poem II

As Sandro Zanetti stresses, Celan's use of "sense" is comparable to Nancy's use of the term (63). Along with Nancy's conception of "sense," I want to come back to the question of singularity and the encounter with an Other the poem opens onto. Celan's idea that the horizon of "das Fremde" lends direction and sense to the breath-carried conversation with the Other is very close to Nancy's argument that "there is no sense except in relation to some 'outside' or 'elsewhere'" (*The Sense of the World* 7). Sense is what happens between entities that touch; it touches on unknown domains. Each constitution of sense in the instance of touch is singular; it does not coincide with a given meaning. Rather, "sense comes before all significations, prevents and over-takes them, even as it makes them possible, forming the opening of the general signifyingness [or significance: *signifiance*] (or the opening of the world) in which and according to which it is first of all possible for significations to produce themselves" (10).

The way in which Nancy situates sense before the constitution of meaning goes hand in hand with the setting of sense in "Ricercar." In the poem, sense dives into an "outside" or "elsewhere," the handwritten (i.e., preliminary as such) "atem-meer," in which an interrupted meaning is only generated in a liminal space, the line break.[70] Sense is also said to dive toward "names"—that is, words that designate one specific thing or person in their singularity and very often do not have a meaning.[71] Celan stresses the connection of names and singularity in a note for *The Meridian*: "In the single and finite the ~~poe~~ word becomes name (Im Einmaligen und Endlichen wird das ~~Gedich~~ Wort zum Namen)" (75). By linking "Name" not only to uniqueness, but also to finitude or mortality, Celan establishes a proximity between breath and names. In "Ricercar," unnamed names are located *in* the "atem-meer."

With Nancy's reflections on sense and singularity in mind, I will now sketch a variant of the pneumatic production and reception model derived from Celan's Mandelstam translation (refer back to "Outline 3"). For Nancy, sense is determined by a multiplicity of singularities: "Sense is the singularity of all the singular ones" (*The Sense of the World* 68). He refers to Celan's "auseinandergeschrieben [written apart]"[72]—a word that most accurately describes the spatial displacements of "atem-meere" and "Dorthin . . . taucht der Sinn"—in the context of "being-exposed-of-the-ones-to-the-others": "being inscribes/excribes [*sic*] the one of/in the other as the unique being of every one. All of sense passes this way . . . : all of sense is along the edge of the being 'with'" (71). For Nancy, singularity is partaking—splitting oneself through and into others: "l'unicité singulière est ce qui le partage et ce qu'il partage avec la totalité de la multiplicité singulière" (*Le Sens du monde* 117). Partaking, in turn, is also inseparable from sense and the aesthetic: "The sensible or the aesthetic is the outside-of-itself through which and *as* which there is the relation to itself of a sense in general, or through which there is the *toward* of sense" (*The Sense of the World* 129). Going back to Celan, the exscription dividing the speaker or writer from itself, the act of addressing itself to the breath- and I-thieves, is precisely the moment when sense articulates its direction. In this moment, the I is constituted as such; there is no I prior to its thieves, no pneumatically touchable poem before the loss of breath. It is in instances of syncope—the intervals between the printed "Hauchschrift, Handschrift" and the handwritten passages around it, the spatial gaps between "atem-meere" and "Dorthin . . . taucht der Sinn"—that sense "comes to presence" "by the possibility of being touched" (128), which means becoming pneumatically touchable.

As contemporary readers, we can physically touch Celan's handwriting, for example if we have typescript E of "Ricercar" in front of us. But we can also touch on sense: we can sense the interrupted direction leading toward the now absent hand that held the pen and we can sense how words, detached from the writer and themselves cut apart, create a space where meaning is interrupted and only in *process* of coming to be. According to Nancy, the singular is "being-as-act or being-in-action. . . . Actuality *tout court*: nothing more and nothing less" (72).[73] Such a definition of singularity may fall short in the reception of Celan's poetry. The moments in reading when sense coincides with singularity put singularity at risk. For example, my reading of the numerous divisions and interruptions in "Ricercar" is the result of a momentary contact: my contact with Celan's text. It is singular in the sense that it occurred in one specific moment of time, between the multiplicity that is me and the multiplicity that is the poem. This is a somewhat banal observation—it holds for every act of reading and says nothing about the text in its particularity or readers in theirs. I obviously, however, consulted the poem repeatedly, over a longer period of time. Does this thwart the notion of a singular encounter with a singular text, or, may it, in Nancy's terms, involve a singular-plural "being-as-act or being in-action" that evolves in the act of repeated reading?[74] To what extent *this* reading, the reading *I* present here, is singular at all remains an open question. When it succeeds in being faithful to what Celan wrote, it rephrases something that is already there or something that lies at hand. Whenever it does not, I add something to it and jeopardize its singularity. And I added a great deal: insights of former readers and broader theoretical reflections, including Nancy's ideas about touching and sense. As they open up toward actualities of reading, of sense taking place, of touches between reading eyes and printed hands and breaths, Celan's poems become transactual "*Sinnbewegungen* auf ein Unbekanntes zu [sense-movements toward something unknown]" (119), "atem-meere," "Atemwenden." However, when such a breathturn occurs in reading, the unknown is often linked to what is known or already written—reading as scholars always involves the risk of smothering the breathing space opened up by literature, which is a space of pneumatic encounter.

Müller: "Die Atemschaukel überschlägt sich"

The writing project that resulted in the novel *Atemschaukel* began with a double silence. Herta Müller was exposed to a suffocating lack of speaking about the massive deportation to Soviet prison penal camps after World War II in her hometown in the Banat.[75] In 2002, she finally found someone who shared his memories of the penal camps and could provide her with material for her long-planned novel: the writer Oskar Pastior, a member of the literary group Oulipo and author of numerous poetry collections. Pastior died unexpectedly while he and Müller were in the process of putting his memories into writing. At this point, the inspirational voice was cut off and Müller had to finish the planned collaborative novel on her own. From this moment on, Müller's text was dedicated to the silenced voice of someone whose language had already been shattered by the traumatic experience in the camps, as she stresses ("Lebensangst und Worthunger" 12, 15). In the novel, breath, or more precisely the neologism "Atemschaukel" (breath-swing), marks a space between silence and disrupted language. In one of her rare comments on the word, Müller remarks the following:

> Death has no word-costume. There is no word that could make it comprehensible. "Atemschaukel" is a word behind Oskar Pastior's death. This word too is a pantomime; in this pantomime, something Pastior and I never spoke about most noticeably swings: the difference between death and loss. What balances in the breath-swing is what I had to learn from Oskar Pastior's disappearance: one cannot speak with death. But with loss one has to. ("Immer derselbe Schnee" 145)[76]

Müller deliberately avoids addressing "Atemschaukel," the word that is also the novel's title,[77] in terms of its *meaning*, offering no interpretation or deciphering.[78] By leaving the semantic level indeterminate, Müller's comments draw a connection between the word "Atemschaukel" and the characteristics of bodily breath, its invisibility and asemantic nature. According to Müller, "Atemschaukel" is caught in a movement within which what was left unspoken by she herself and by Pastior "swings." The word rotates between silence and speaking: between death, which withdraws from words, and loss, which demands them. Far from forcing the unspeakable into language, the word "Atemschaukel" hovers in the air, mediating between a caesura and the necessity of addressing the deprivation caused by it. In the quoted interview, Müller relates the swaying movement around a traumatic chasm performed by "Atemschaukel" to Oskar Pastior's death and the interruption of the writing process that it caused.[79] In the novel, an equivalent movement is described with regard to addressing the unspeakable: "Der Nullpunkt ist das Unsagbare. Wir sind uns einig, der Nullpunkt und ich, dass man über ihn selbst nicht sprechen kann, höchstens drumherum" (*Atemschaukel* 249). "Absolute zero is that which cannot be expressed. And we agree, absolute zero and I, that absolute zero itself is beyond discussion, except in the most roundabout way" (*The Hunger Angel* 238).[80] The moment in the novel when point zero is identified with the unspeakable, which only allows talking or writing *around* it, correlates with Müller's descriptions of the situation preceding her work on the book and the writing process itself: the silence about deportation in her hometown and the silence induced by Pastior's death. In the interview, the word swings beyond the novel's narration: it both exerts its movement within the accomplished text and points to a preliminary moment when the relation between the two authors was disrupted by death during the writing process.

Breath-Rifts: The Production of Atemschaukel

In her account of the writing process,[81] Müller suggests numerous parallels between the approach to the unspeakable emerging in the act of recounting Pastior's recollection and what happens in *Atemschaukel*. The novel's protagonist Leo Auberg, who is modeled after Pastior, plans to write down his experiences in the camp after he returned home. In an attempt to avoid writing the polished story of a "false witness" (271), he remembers how he burst into tears on the way home from the camp while one of his fellow sufferers noted: "Look how he's bawling, he's falling apart." Leo recounts: "I thought about this sentence a lot. Then I wrote it down on an empty page. And the next day I scratched it out. The day after that I wrote it down again underneath. Scratched it out again, wrote it down again. When the page was full I tore it out. That's memory" (270). In contrast to Leo's attempts to write down his memories of the camp, which result in torn out pages covered with scratched out words, *Atemschaukel* itself is an accomplished and highly successful novel. However, in a parallel to Leo's attempt, its composition was determined by various acts of writing and deleting, speaking and silencing. In interviews, Müller repeatedly describes her work with Pastior as a long process of her asking questions, Pastior sharing his camp memories, reading out loud what they noted down, typing, retyping, and revising (see *Mein Vaterland* 198–200; "Immer derselbe Schnee," 129). The writing scene Müller depicts invites a comparison with Leo's attempts to commit his memories to paper: remembering, writing, reconsidering, deleting, and so on. What Müller has never mentioned in interviews this far is that some passages of the novel are based on Pastior's notebooks from 1955 and that she and Pastior published a shorter prose piece together in 2005, "Von Hungerengel eins zwei drei," which already contains central pieces of the novel.

When comparing the novel to the co-authored "Vom Hungerengel eins zwei drei," one observation stands out: in contrast to the many scenes, formulations, and words that end up being adopted in *Atemschaukel*, neither the word "Atemschaukel" nor any other references to breathing occur in "Von Hungerengel eins zwei drei."[82] Respiratory images also fail to play a central role in Pastior's notebooks. Celan chose not to incorporate most of the respiratory references in the notes and drafts into the final version of the *Meridian* speech, while Müller adds breath at a critical moment: it enters the novel-in-process as a dominant image after Pastior's voice fell silent. Müller's own silence about the novel's textual precursors in which breath was absent points to a partial suffocation of inspirational sources. She withholds any reference to Pastior's notebooks and "Vom Hungerengel eins zwei drei," two textual sources from which some passages are taken over without many changes. Yet on many occasions Müller addresses her repeated cutting of Pastior's voice in the writing process. She stresses the importance of departing from Pastior's memories of the camp, of fictionalizing and transforming them. To avoid the risk of writing a polished or sentimental camp narrative, Müller claims that it was necessary to create "a connection between my outside view and his inside view. . . . Because Pastior had to leave the camp again and again and I had to enter the camp" (*Mein Vaterland* 209).[83] By fictionally extending biographical material, Müller decoupled Pastior's memories from his person.

In an interview with Michael Lentz, Müller described Pastior's experience of the camp as a "fall from civilisation and out of the world," a "blow on the head," a "rift running through the middle of a person" ("Lebensangst und Worthunger" 17).[84] By tearing memories from Pastior during the writing process, Müller reproduces a rupture that, according to her interpretation of his narrative, essentially defines the shattering impact of the camp on the deported. The "rift running through a person" echoes a central passage of a lecture on poetics Müller held in Paderborn in 1989/90 ("Der Teufel sitzt im Spiegel" 77). In these reflections, which are not explicitly related to the camps but also concerned with a writing triggered by trauma and fear, breathing plays a central role.[85] Breath as such is the expression of a rift: "We breathe in 'breaths' [Atemzüge]. We eat in 'bites.' We talk in 'words.' We take hold of objects in 'grasps.' We walk in steps. . . . Everything is pervaded by a rift" (77).[86] In contrast to the deceptive unitary image produced by the eyes, Müller wants to make the rift perceivable:

> If one wants to capture these successions and all these rifts in writing, one has to shred what assembles in the process of writing

> forth a thought. One tears at the net of sentences until they
> become transparent, until the rifts show through in the sentence
> and the sequence of sentences in the text. Until the mute sen-
> tences between the written sentences expose their silence. Until,
> while writing, one senses that the text finally breathes, that the
> sentence finally is as it sees itself. (81)

For Müller, texts start to breathe once they are fissured and become brittle. These early reflections on writing reveal a continuity with *Atemschaukel*'s genesis—a compositional process determined by syncopnea. Müller links this "rift through the person" to both the experience of the prison camps and the physiological breathing process. This rift corresponds in a disrupted way to her own writing process: tearing Pastior's memories from him by fictionalizing them, introducing more references to breath after Pastior died, and linking the word "Atemschaukel" to his death. The word "Atemschaukel" reveals a series of violent ruptures and a process of uncanny transference: the silence surrounding Pastior's death, the transformation of his memories in the novel's production process, the act of cutting his memories from his person, and the movement of these verbalized memories once detached. Beyond Pastior's memories, his notes, Müller's notes, and the novel all involve breaches which "Atemschaukel" simultaneously reveals and swings across.

Phobic Animation: Poetic Implications of Breathing Words

In Müller's account, breaches are consciously imposed on the writing-in-process so that it may "breathe" and act on its own beyond the author's control: "the sentence finally is *as it sees itself*." For Müller, a text's "breathing" implies its development of an autonomous "life" and the animation of its words. When she discusses the poetic processes in *Atemschaukel*, Müller suggests that the animism she ascribes to words, their capacity to act independently, requires that they detach themselves from factual reality:

> Die erfundenen Wörter holen Luft. . . . Sie schnappen sich das, was sie brauchen. Und was sie nicht zulassen, das lehnen sie ab. . . . Sie brauchen das Wechselspiel und nutzen das Anbinden ans Reale, um sich loszumachen.
>
> The invented words gasp for air. . . . They grab what they need. And what they don't approve they reject. . . . They need inter-

action and make use of the tie to the real in order to detach themselves. ("Gelber Mais und keine Zeit" 136)

While Pastior and Müller were still working together on the novel, Pastior came to feel betrayed by Müller's invention of Leo as a fictional character and that an "I-person started to do with his memories whatever he wanted" (*Mein Vaterland* 209).[87] This betrayal is essential for Müller's poetics of breathing. Inducing cuts and ruptures not only makes silence perceivable, it also implies a gesture of detaching and loosening words from "the real," which allows them to undergo processes of transformation beyond the author's control and develop what Müller calls "vagrant qualities" ("vagabundierende Eigenschaften"). By displaying "vagrant qualities" in a process where "everything becomes something different" ("Immer derselbe Schnee" 96), words, for Müller, reenact the movement of verbalization: things are transformed when they are put into words. In the case of *Atemschaukel*, the act of becoming different, of being involved in a continual process of transformation and change, is not only related to the transference of things, thoughts, and memories to words, but also to the extreme situation of the camps as described in the novel. For Leo, the camp and the memories it produced constitute a radical unsettling: nothing remains in its place. In the camp, things and words begin to ramble. In some cases, this is a source of consolation. For example, a piece of wire and some threads of wool morph into a Christmas tree (137). The poetic qualities of words create a space of dignity and beauty in an utterly hostile place where human beings are reduced to bare life. However, the uncontrollable wandering of things and words can also turn into "phobic animation,"[88] a scenario in which the atrocities of the camp unpredictably and violently hit the novel's protagonist, who is helplessly exposed to these attacks. For example, hunger, personified as "Hungerengel" (hunger angel) becomes a being who acts independently, governing every aspect of Leo's daily life like a sometimes benevolent, soothing, and compliant but other times a relentless, cruel, and murderous autocrat.

The poetic transference of signifiers across different words often results in painful associations pervading Leo's language, leading to a linguistic repertoire in which no word is innocent and free from suffering. The name for a specific kind of Ukrainian coal, "Hasoweh," is dear to Leo because, when this is read as a German word, it assumes a meaning unrelated to the coal, which is a major constituent of the work that threatens to cause death by exhaustion on a daily basis: "Hasoweh" "klingt wie ein verwundeter Hase [that sounds like a hare in pain]"[89] (*Atemschaukel* 124; *The Hunger Angel*

114). The bittersweet beauty of this shift of meaning across languages collapses into blunt pain when Leo attributes it to the "heartbreaking sound" (122) uttered by dying steppe-dogs (prairie dogs)—especially the steppe-dog Leo one day strikes dead for no particular reason. Here, the transference of words is physically reenacted when Leo handles the rodent with his shovel as he does the coal, resulting in a death cry. In this moment, Leo realizes how the brutalization and cruelty of the camp infect him, and shortly after, "Hasoweh" turns into Leo's wail of homesickness (125). "Hasoweh" also recalls the German word "Halsweh" (sore throat); it thus incorporates the pain inflicted on the deported by a language used to subject them, a language of respiratory congestion: "The Russian commands sound like . . . a constant clearing of the throat—coughing, sneezing, nose blowing, hacking up mucus" (23). The most gruesome echo of "Hasoweh" resounds in Leo's observation that a hare appears in the face of a person who is about to die of hunger (111): "Father, the white hare is hunting us down, chasing us out of life. He's growing in the hollows of more and more cheeks. He hasn't crawled out of my face yet, he's just been looking at my flesh from the inside, because it is also his. Hasoweh" (220; translation modified). The roaming of words which seem to have a life of their own also has the effect that the camp does not stay in the past after Leo returns home, but starts to haunt him in the present: "There are words that do whatever they want with me. They're completely different from me and they think differently than what they really are. . . . There are words that have me as their target, that seem to be created solely for my re-deportation [Rückfall ins Lager]" (*The Hunger Angel* 221; *Atemschaukel* 232). The major difference between the camp and home is that at home "nothing could be anything other than itself" (254), whereas in the hunger-driven camp, everything is continually becoming other than itself.

Presenting a mutability of words in *Atemschaukel* therefore implies doing justice to the experience of the camps—conveying an "accurate" impression of pain and suffering that escapes realist depiction. In accordance with Müller's theory of writing, fabulated language becomes "valid" in *Atemschaukel* because it is appropriate: "A sequence of words turns into invented truth. Everything is still artificially constructed, the unreal becomes valid in the text through its accurate language" (*Mein Vaterland* 197).[90] In "Immer derselbe Schnee und immer derselbe Onkel," Müller admits that such an accuracy of depicting the matter in question and a precision with respect to perceptions, which, paradoxically, is based on detachment from factual reality, has its price:

I don't trust language. I know best from my own experience that in order to become precise, language has to take something that it does not own. I don't know why language-images are so thievish, why the most valid comparison robs qualities it has no right to appropriate. Surprise only emerges through invention, and it becomes evident again and again that a proximity to reality only starts with the invented surprise in a sentence. Only when one perception robs another one, an object robs and uses the material of another one—only when what is mutually exclusive in reality becomes plausible in a sentence, the sentence can prevail against reality as an autonomous reality which was put into words but is word-valid [als eigene, wie ins Wort geratene, aber wortgültige Realität]. (98–99)

In *Atemschaukel*, Müller creates the effect of a *parole soufflée*: words steal attributes from others, creating a breathing language that conveys the "word-valid" reality of the camps. "Hasoweh," for example, plunders meanings from both Ukrainian and German, combining them to a shatteringly plausible compound of pain. Müller moreover tears Pastior's memories from his person in an act of thievish inspiration: in her own words, the novel's language is based on "stolen life" (*Mein Vaterland* 195). The violence accompanying the process of breathing words that develop an autonomous life can thus also be revealed in the way Müller derives the language of *Atemschaukel* from Oskar Pastior's memories. The "invented words gasp[ing] for air" point to a fundamental rift between life and language. In her *Paris Review* interview, Müller notes: "Language is so different from life. How am I supposed to fit the one into the other? How can I bring them together? There's no such thing as one-to-one correspondence" (n.p.).

In Müller's writing and poetics, breath, life, and death traverse without corresponding. In an autobiographical comment, she conjoins breath and death in what at first seems a soothing image that relapses to the fear and uncertainty that let the image emerge. When remembering how she reflected on mortality as a child, Müller mentions: "I thought that all breaths one draws are counted. I thought that they string like beads and form a necklace. And when the breath-necklace has a length reaching from mouth to graveyard, one dies. Because breath is invisible, no person knows the length of their breath-necklace. That is why no person knows when they die, not about themselves or about others (*Mein Vaterland* 12). She then goes on to admit that the attempt to measure life-time to get a grip of time and mortality results in "calculations without result" that only "increased the fear" of death (*Mein Vaterland* 12). In *Atemschaukel*, a swaying between control and loss of control, balance and loss of balance is addressed when Leo attempts to discipline his body to reach an equilibrium of inhaling and exhaling during the roll call: "I practiced forgetting myself during roll call and attempted not to separate breathing in and breathing out [das Ein- und Ausatmen nicht voneinander zu trennen]" (*The Hunger Angel* 20; translation modified; *Atemschaukel* 27). Not only does this wish to reach a radical balance, to reduce his bodily efforts to a minimum in order to save the vitally important energy, fail: "My bones were heavy as lead, breathing in and out at the same time did not work" (170). If the ultimate economization of the respiratory process were to succeed, it would be fatal: an identity of inhalation and exhalation means to breathe no more, that is, to die.

Between Balance and Delirium: Movements of "Atemschaukel" in the Novel

In Müller's writing, breath constantly swings between measured control and its dark, uncontainable flipside. In the novel *Atemschaukel*, the word "Atemschaukel" itself undergoes constant transformation. It does not stand for something: it does not *stand*—and much less so *for something*. "Atemschaukel," in Müller's terms an invented word gasping for air, performatively displays the fissure of a breath-rift, the straying movement of words torn from a fixed anchorage, the transformation of perceptions and qualities snatched from the place they came from, colliding in new constellations. A double movement between "Schaukel" and "Atem" incessantly pervades the compound. The movement of a hanging seat back and forth corresponds to the continuous repetition of balanced inhalations and exhalations Leo keeps referring to. In other respects, however, "Atem" and "Schaukel" form a less symmetrical constellation. First, their reference is different: the domain of "Atem" is the human body, "Schaukel" leads us into the field of playgrounds, fairs, or the circus; "Atem" is a process, "Schaukel" an object. Second, the tonal and visual appearance of the words is not alike: there are no similarities at all between ATEM and SCHAUKEL—they share only a single letter. The relation between "Atem" and "Schaukel" is, as such, syncopal: the rhythmical movement connects them, while other characteristics cut the compound apart. The internal tension caused by the various associations going along with both words and the tonal and visual dissonance let "Atem" and "Schaukel" both meet and rub against each other, setting the compound itself in motion: reeling from a regular back and forth into a more irregular, uncontrolled swing, "Atemschaukel" is a word whose meanings and properties keep straying.

"Atemschaukel" often interacts with rambling camp things, above all the hunger angel and the "Herzschaufel" (heart-shovel, e.g., 72). The technical term "heart-shovel" designates a particular tool used in the camps; it is Leo's ambivalent ally in his depleting work in the coalmines. "Ich halte die Balance, die Herzschaufel wird zur Schaukel in meiner Hand, wie die Atemschaukel in der Brust. [I keep the balance, the heart-shovel becomes a swing in my hand, like the breath-swing in the chest]" (*Atemschaukel* 82; *The Hunger Angel* 72; translation modified).[91] Here, we encounter an uncannily harmonious symmetry. For Leo, shoveling coal is a sequence of movements that can be perfected: executed well, it is "beautiful as a tango, a series of ever-changing acute angles against a constant rhythm" (74). In this sentence, the dance of shoveling is mirrored linguistically. The swing of the "Herzschaufel" in Leo's hand corresponds to the movement of the "Atemschaukel" in his chest, which in this instance can be read as a metaphor for the lungs. In the depictions of Leo's shoveling, which are based on Pastior's painful "pantomimic" demonstration of the movements still "inscribed in his body" (*Mein Vaterland* 206), the proximities of hands and breath traced in Celan's writing resonate: a pneumatic touchability is articulated when past and present are linked in the hand-breath constellation of both Pastior and Leo's shoveling. The parallelism in the cited passage is constituted by the coincidence of the heart and the breath-swing at the same anatomical location (the chest), the acoustic continuity between "Schaufel" and "Schaukel," and the quasi-symmetrical arrangement of "Herzschaufel," "Schaukel," "Atemschaukel." The balanced comparison is expressed in a parallel syntactic construction, respectively starting with a compound and ending with a word designating a body part.

In the course of the novel, "Atemschaukel" performs a rhythm shifting between the measured, metrical-symmetrical back and forth of a swing or up and down of a seesaw and the vertiginous circling of a "Schaukelrad," or Russian swing. In other words, it displays movements of all the apparatuses that according to the *Grimm Wörterbuch* can be referred to by the word "Schaukel" (online). Leo's comparison of shoveling to "Artistik" (*Atemschaukel* 83), circus arts, recalls a specific popular use of the Russian swing. In the process of innovating the Soviet circus, the Soviet corps of engineers developed "a giant acrobat-propelling swing" (Wall 33) based on the Russian swing, or качели, which can both move back and forth and rotate 360 degrees. Usually, the circus acrobats use the pendular movement of the swing to build up momentum for aerobatic jumps. Leo's precarious balancing acts mirror the synergy of the Russian swing's regular movement and the hazardous jumps the acrobats perform on it. In the context of circus arts, the swing may easily spin over accidentally due to the demanding use the acrobats make of it. Moreover, there is always a risk that the aesthetic perfection of the acrobats' performance gets out of control and aerial flips turn into a dizzy, fatal whirl. When transferred to the situation of the camp, the precariousness of the acrobats' art is increased to a macabre extreme. Leo's shoveling dance is performed on the verge of an abyss; his balance is soon disrupted and tumbles into a delirious stagger:

> I'm on the verge of breaking down, my throat swells. The hunger angel climbs to the roof of my mouth and clings onto my palate. He is its scale. He puts on my eyes and the heart-shovel goes dizzy, the coal starts to blur. He wears my cheeks over his chin. He sets my breath to swinging. The breath-swing is a delirium—and what a delirium. [Er lässt meinen Atem schaukeln. Die Atemschaukel ist ein Delirium und was für eins]. (*The Hunger Angel* 77; translation modified; *Atemschaukel* 87)

While the movement of heart-shovel and breath-swing is still described as parallel, it goes out of control. The beauty of the dance is now pervaded by another balance, the hunger angel's merciless scale teetering on the brink of life and death. Despite the neat balance getting out of hand, the word "Atemschaukel" still appears to be a readable one: in the passage "breath-swing" simply seems to be a metaphor for being out of breath, physically at the limit. "Breath-swing" immediately follows and echoes the "swinging breath" and, being designated as a "delirium," it is in continuity with the vertiginous movement the hunger angel causes.

In the further course of the novel, however, the breath-swing's delirium throws such equivalences off track. In the camp, Leo observes that there is relief in death: dying means

> that the tangled nest in the head, the dizzy swing in the breath, the rhythm-crazed pump in the breast, the empty waiting room in the stomach were finally leaving one in peace. (*The Hunger Angel* 243; translation modified)

dass im Kopf das starre Nest, im Atem die schwindlige Schaukel
in der Brust die taktversessene Pumpe, im Bauch der leere War-
tesaal endlich Ruhe geben. (*Atemschaukel* 247)

At first sight, the parallel arrangement of "head and tangled nest," "breath and dizzy swing," "breast and rhythm-crazed pump," and "belly and empty waiting room" recalls the equivalences established in the two preceding passages. Various precarious states of bodily deprivation are described in poetic images. However, in this passage, something is awry in the depiction of breath to the extent that the image starts to crumble. Whereas the rigid nest in head (= petrified brain), the pump in the breast (= monotonously beating heart), and the waiting room in the stomach (= hunger) can be resolved as metaphors, the swing in the breath disrupts this list, which could easily have been completed in a coherent manner, by, for example referring to "the dizzy swing in the lungs."[92] The "swing in the breath" stands out: as breath, in contrast to head, breast, and stomach, does not designate a specific part of the body, the "swing" is cut from a clearly determinable anatomical anchor point. When the dizzy swing, itself caught in movement, is situated *in* a physiological activity, *in* the breath passing various organs and transgressing the borders of the body, the image is thrown into a vertiginous whirl. Even if we read "the dizzy swing in the breath" as a metaphor of breathlessness, the vehicle ultimately steers the constellation of words toward collapse: the more closely we look at the image, the more it swings from our grasp. In the sentence, "The hunger angel leans to one side as he walks with open eyes. He staggers around in small circles and balances on the breath-swing [Er taumelt enge Kreise und balanciert auf der Atemschaukel]" (*The Hunger Angel* 133; translation modified; *Atemschaukel* 144), "Atemschaukel" is presented as an autonomous thing with which the "hunger angel" interacts. The "images" or personifications of Leo's physical condition are presented as externalized entities that act independently and no longer remain attached to the body they supposedly characterize. In such moments, "Atemschaukel" not only moves away from the protagonist and his strained respiration but from metaphorical rootedness as such.

The rambling qualities of the word "Atemschaukel" become especially significant when Leo returns from the camp. The camp haunts Leo after his deportation.

> Occasionally the objects from the camp attack me, not one at a time, but in a pack. . . . I am pursued by objects that may have

had nothing to do with me. They want to deport me during the night, fetch me home to the camp. Because they come in a pack, there isn't room enough in my head. I feel pressure in my stomach rising to the roof of my mouth. The breath-swing teeters over, I have to pant. [Die Atemschaukel überschlägt sich, ich muss hecheln.] . . . When the objects gang up on me at night, choking me, I fling open the window and hold my head out in the fresh air. . . . My breath again finds its rhythm. I swallow the cold air until I'm no longer in the camp. Then I close the window and lie back down. The bedding knows nothing and warms me. The air in the room looks at me and smells of warm flour. (26–27; translation modified)

In this occurrence of "Atemschaukel" (the first time the word appears in the novel), remotely recalling Swedenborg's nocturnal conspiration-suffocation scene discussed in the section on Celan, its metaphorical qualities still seem intact: the breath-swing's tipping over apparently points to Leo's breathlessness when faced with the "things from the camp," which choke him and want to drag him back into the nightmare he seemingly escaped from. Even though it can turn into uncontrolled panting, breath also seems to have the capacity to heal and restore: inhaling fresh, cold air releases the throat from the suffocating grasp of the invading camp objects and returns Leo to his bedroom at home. This, however, is only a very temporary reprieve—the reacquired breath-balance is unsettled in the moment the exhaled air "looks at" Leo and turns out to be an entity as autonomous and unpredictable as the "objects from the camp." The expelled air looking back calls to mind the moment when Leo observes the following about people on the street in his hometown: "Shreds of breath were swinging from the mouths of the passersby [Den Passanten schaukelten die Atemfetzen aus dem Mund] and revealed: the home-sated all make their life, but it flies away" (*Atemschaukel* 285; translation modified). In the detached, exhaled breath, the breath-swing continues its delirious ramble: parallel to the shreds of breath swinging from the mouths of passersby, the life that the staring breath pretends to "have" and give back to Leo only implies its flying away. Smelling "of warm flour," the air brings the traumatic space back into the room that has just been freed from it: flour is what was notoriously lacking in the camp. Rather than invoking a reassuring feeling of finally being surrounded by flour, its imagined scent evokes camp hallucinations: besides recalling the general wishful thinking about flour, the flour-infused air also invokes a nightmarish daydream in which Leo observes a frightening transformation after a commander hands him a paper sack: "Cement again, I think. But one corner of the sack is torn and it's leaking white flour. . . . Then I understand, the white flour is blasting powder" (194–95; translation modified). By pointing back to a moment when cement becomes flour and then blasting powder, the staring exhalation triggers a transformational movement, an explosion of sense in which the consoling liberation from suffocation reverts to choking inhalation. Consequently, another situation in the camp seeps in: "You breathe in and swallow more dust than air" (113). The various kinds of dust (cement, coal, red brick) Leo was forced to inhale during his shoveling-work is not only damaging for the lungs but also "treacherous" (28) because of its uncontrollable straying: "it flies into the air, crawls on the ground, sticks to the skin" and can be "grasped nowhere" (29). "Atemschaukel" behaves like the treacherous dust, capriciously rambling, invading the body, withdrawing from our grasp.

In the passage discussed above, Leo's relapse to the camp is attributed to camp things that attack him. Such an attack is most vividly depicted in the following:

> The clock ticked away beside the wardrobe. The pendulum flew, shovelling our time in between the furniture: from the wardrobe to the window, from the table to the sofa, from the stove to the push chair, from the day into the evening. On the wall, the ticking was my breath-swing, in my breast it was my heart-shovel, which I missed very much. [An der Wand war das Ticken meine Atemschaukel, in meiner Brust war es die Herzschaufel. Sie fehlte mir sehr]. (*The Hunger Angel* 253; *Atemschaukel* 265)

Here, things from the camp stray all the way to Leo's home: "Atemschaukel" and "Herzschaufel" invade his family house and mingle with familiar and familial objects (the clock, the wardrobe, the window, the table, the sofa), turning his home (*Heim*) into a space of the uncanny (*das Unheimliche*). Beyond what is suggested on the diegetic level, the linguistic nature of the camp's haunting becomes obvious here. The camp things are not only articulated through language; "Atemschaukel" and "Herzschaufel" are word-things that behave exactly like the described things from the camps: they invade the text's narrative of a time after the camp and sneak between the words used to describe Leo's home, which thus becomes unsettled. With "An der Wand war das Ticken meine Atemschaukel, in meiner Brust war es die

Herzschaufel," a whole sentence from the camp invades the time "after." In a twisted manner, the words used in the context of coal shoveling during the cold Ukrainian winter, "Ich halte die Balance, die Herzschaufel wird zur Schaukel in meiner Hand, wie die Atemschaukel in der Brust" (82), are dragged into a cozy Romanian living room. The balance presented in the camp sentence drastically flips: while the syntax of "An der Wand war das Ticken meine Atemschaukel, in meiner Brust war es die Herzschaufel" echoes the parallel structure of "Ich halte die Balance, die Herzschaufel wird zur Schaukel in meiner Hand, wie die Atemschaukel in der Brust," the breath-swing is now externalized—breath is torn from its proper anatomical place in the breast and transferred to the clock on the wall. In turn, the heart-shovel literally gets out of hand and invades the breast: a metaphorical reconciliation of heart-shovel and breast is interrupted because the technical term designates a tool that received its name due to its shape, recalling the visually symbolized heart devoid of its anatomical or metaphorical/symbolic connotations. Recalling the steppe-dog split by Leo's shovel, the image prompts a literal reading and evokes a slashed breast fatally invaded by a foreign object. The scene shifts from presenting a metaphorical image based on the transference of the clock's balanced, metrical ticking to Leo's body to a vertiginous, violent roving of unhinged things. Hand in hand with this, the linear time indicated by the clock on the wall gets out of joint: once the balanced movement of the clock's pendulum coincides with the analogously balanced movement of a well-guided shovel, chronology becomes unsettled. The shoveling brings back the camp and the traumatic past penetrates the present.[93]

In her accounts of working with Pastior, Müller repeatedly tells of how he physically demonstrated the movements of shoveling. Through the narration of these performances in interviews and essays, especially a comment in *Mein Vaterland*, Müller creates a link to the role shoveling plays in *Atemschaukel*, above all in the passage just discussed: "I had to watch how Oskar Pastior was dragged back into the camp and encountered his former self; in his own room on the carpet he was in two places at the same time now—brought back to the camp in his head and before my very eyes as a pantomime" (206). In Müller's description of Pastior's "pantomime" and in the Herzschaufel's work that enters Leo's living room, time is loosened and things are moved between past and present through the act of shoveling.

In the novel, the word "Herzschaufel" as such motivates the transport of the past in the present. As a word that was actually used in the camps, it functions like a thing literally dug out from the adamant Ukrainian earth[94] and transposed to a text that was written much later. Müller describes such "camp words" as important elements in the process of extracting Pastior's memories in order to write the novel (e.g., "Lebensangst und Worthunger" 46). Müller suggests that the camp words do not represent the camp but rather incorporate something of it. Cut off from the past and carried into the presence of the novel, the camp words are given a breathing space to let their vagrant qualities ramble. It is important that Müller mentions that "Atemschaukel" is not a camp word. In an interview, she states: "This word comes from Pastior but it has nothing to do with the camp" (my translation; *Profil* n.p.). Displaced and decontextualized, "Atemschaukel" performatively enacts the way in which camp words function in the novel. On the diegetic level, both the camp words and "Atemschaukel" move between past and present. Beyond that, Müller claims that the camp words are transported from a past outside the novel into the novel itself. In analogy to the acrobats who use a Russian swing as a springboard for their jumps, "Atemschaukel" and the pack of camp words with which it interacts leap beyond the pages of the book. In the case of "Atemschaukel," such a leap is performed not only between the novel and the camp; the word demonstrates the work of unhinging and loosening on further levels. "Atemschaukel" mediates between the way in which the transport from past to present is articulated in the text and the way in which Müller reflects on this in her epitexts. It furthermore forms a link between Müller's conception of the relations of past and present and her notion of animated words. The word itself functions as a meta-term for the crucial processes in *Atemschaukel* and the way in which they relate to Müller's meta-texts, while at the same time demonstrating these processes on the novel's diegetic level. As Müller stages the word, it appears as a creature of inanimation,[95] a spawn of violent crossings of life and language, acting like that which she designates as "Dinge, die ohne zu leben untot sind [Things that are undead without being alive]" (*Atemschaukel* 249; *The Hunger Angel* 238; translation modified).

"Dinge, die ohne zu leben untot sind": Haunting the Readers

"Atemschaukel" makes another leap worth paying attention to: the word swings between the novel and its readers. The analogy Müller makes between interactions of past and present in the novel and its production can be extended to what happens in the reading process. The loose camp words haunt Leo, but they also have the capacity to haunt those who encounter them while reading. *We* too are faced with these words; words that, detached from their concrete spatial and temporal reference points, stir up time: that they can carry the camp into Leo's present also means that they might carry it into the present of the readers. In her poetic reflections, Müller prompts such a reading. When discussing how words develop straying qualities and turn into animated breathing things, she delineates two "conversations" that produce such qualities and are essential to the writing process. A conversation with "the real objects of life" is followed by a second conversation in which the first conversation is verbalized and put on a page. In the transition from the first "conversation" to the second, words detach from reality and start to wander. It is important that Müller observes that the straying of the words *during* the writing process comes to a halt when they are arrested on a page: "When the sentence is put on paper and is accomplished, it is dead. It only turns into the two conversations again when it is read. [Aber wenn der Satz fertig auf dem Papier steht, ist er tot. Er wird erst wieder zu den beiden Gesprächen, wenn er gelesen wird]" ("Immer derselbe Schnee" 135). The written words only regain their capacity to "gasp for air" during the reading process. What is outlined here is different from models of readers animating words, for example by investing them with "new life" through their imagination and fresh interpretations. That the written sentences and words once again *become* the conversations defining the writing process suggests that they are retransformed into a state in which they exercise control over those engaging with them: gasping for air, being animated, means that the words "grab what they need" and "dictate what is bound to happen" ("Immer derselbe Schnee" 136).

Müller's dramatic image of tyrannical words in the writing process can be read as a way to express the fact that during composition, the writer not only relies on what is produced in her brain or imagination but also follows patterns internal to language; for example, in organizing words according their acoustic qualities, "one follows their sound, a precise mathematics" ("Lebensangst und Worthunger" 34). The "inner life of texts" implies that sentences generate their own laws, resulting in a logic that requires choosing some words rather than others because sound and rhythm demands it (34). Müller describes her revisions as working on the "breath of the sentences" (*Mein Vaterland* 197). For Müller, following text-internal inspiration requires that she reads the sentences out loud to herself again and again ("Lebensangst und Worthunger" 34; *Paris Review* interview n.p.) during the revision phase. While clearly employing prevalent connections of breath, orality, and animation or life, Müller uncovers a violent flipside. The aesthetically perfected, well-sounding text results in a "beauty that hurts" (*Mein Vaterland*

198); this pain not only concerns the tension between the words' beauty and the violence and misery they refer to. As Müller stresses, the "obsessive search for word, cadence and sound" also implies a "ruthlessness" (195): a theft, a detachment from reality demanded in the process of creating poetic language. Moreover, in Müller's theory, the words and sentences that are generated turn into unpredictable word-things that act like those that attack Leo in *Atemschaukel*. The animated words' relation to the past is also addressed in Müller's comments on the writing process: "During the writing process, past experiences look at me again with a different gaze. A glassy, unnatural gaze. As if they would know me outrageously well on the one hand, and on the other not at all. What took place happens again during writing. Thus, no past experience is ever finished" (196). Looking at the past again through writing means "to endure it once more" (196). When Müller claims that the dead words on a page transmute and morph into the animated breathing beings they were during the writing process, this also suggests that a traumatic past—even if it is a past the readers have not lived through—comes back to life and starts to haunt our present. Words like "Hungerengel," "Hasoweh," "Herzschaufel," and "Atemschaukel" may snap at the readers. This is what we—like the writer who has to go through the past again in the process of putting it into words—have to bear and endure when we read *Atemschaukel*.

When asked whether she believes in magic qualities of words, Müller replies, "There's something to them for sure. Otherwise they would leave you alone" (*Lebensangst und Worthunger* 51). She considers words relentless: "I think words are capable of anything. They can bully and protect, they can occupy you and empty you" (51). If words with straying qualities form threatening images, they do not console but rather haunt, and they "never break" ("Immer derselbe Schnee" 97). In *Atemschaukel*, it is precisely the fact that the words do not console but haunt us with the unspeakable that accounts for the novel's ethical stance. In Celan's terms, we are faced with the Other as Other (*The Meridian* 104). The words' unpredictability, cruelty, and insistence give them the capacity to act on the readers, resulting in a negotiation of a traumatic past that exceeds compassionate commemoration. The illusion of comprehending or having received an insight into the camps is blasted by a poetic language moving away from realist rendering and the fact that Leo is presented as an unreliable witness when his attempts to record his camp experience are described. In contrast to Leo's erased sentences, which constitute what he calls "memory," the words pervading the novel *Atemschaukel* have indelible qualities: they don't break to pieces or disappear; rather, they burn themselves into the readers' minds in order to haunt them. *Atemschaukel* thus forbids forgetting and attempts to present a scenario in which it is impossible to archive the camp in a place where it is safely stored and at distance, a past that remains in the past. The past as such is presented as not fully accessible and not fully renderable; Müller's stories about her work with Pastior highlight the fact that the past presented in the novel is not a fully authentic one, that memories were detached from the person to whom they belong and transformed by fabulation—that what we encounter in *Atemschaukel* is also based on acts of rendering silent.

On their own, the camp words would imply a kind of authenticity. The past they transport to the readers' present remains intact: Müller suggests that the very words we have in front of us were actually part of the camp. While the camp words detach from the past and jump into the present, "Atemschaukel" reveals that—to use the image of the Russian swing—the very ground from which such leaps are performed is unsteady; it might change into thin air. Even though "Atemschaukel" functions like a camp word in the novel, straying uncontrollably and conspiring with the pack of "things from the camp" haunting Leo, it also points to the mechanism necessary to create such a scenario, which in Leo's case is a traumatic symptom but in the reader's case opens the possibility of entering into an ethical relation to the past. As a fictional camp word that mingles with "real" ones in the novel, "Atemschaukel" uncovers the theft, silencing, and rift on which animated words are based, and which enable the creation of a plausible "word-valid reality" according to Müller's theory.

In Müller's discussion of breath in her metatexts, established connotations of breath and invisibility and its liminal position between life and death are invoked: the breath of the text is said to mark a rift in which silence becomes perceivable, and, in the way they are presented, words gasping for air act like "things that are undead without being alive" (238; translation modified). In contrast to "Atem," "Schaukel" is not discussed by Müller in the context of her poetics. The etymology of the word reveals an aspect that is crucial for the poetics of *Atemschaukel*. "Schaukel" goes back to the Old High German word "schock" or "schoken," which designates a swinging, oscillating movement but also a toss (Wurf), thrust, stroke (Stoß), or tremor, concussion (Erschütterung)—the German "Schock" and the synonymous English "shock" have the same roots (Grimm online). In the novel, the word "Atemschaukel" indeed causes strokes and tremors: it thrusts itself into Leo's life after the camp and causes concussions; it pushes into my present, transporting the shock of an uncertain, silenced, transmuted past I did not experience. The word is involved in a violent textual breathing process: it forcefully enters spaces and bodies, becomes part of them and departs in a transformed manner. "Atemschaukel" acts like the exhalation Müller describes in "Der Teufel sitzt im Spiegel": "When I see my breath, outside in the cold air, it is a distorted, white ghost that crawls back into my face before it disappears" (78)—except that it does not disappear.

Trauma, Breath, Loss

Trauma theory has become an established field covering a wide range of attempts to conceptualize the relation between traumatic experience and writing.[96] Trauma theorists such as Cathy Caruth, Shoshana Felman, and Dominick LaCapra have investigated how personal and collective traumata can be put into words and how texts can give testimony to traumatic historical caesurae. The question of how trauma can be written ethically assumes various shapings and colorings. To delineate two strands, and only roughly so: for scriptotherapeutical approaches, ethical trauma writing is supposed to facilitate healing; it often involves an aesthetic control or narrative framing of trauma's shattering force (Henke 25).[97] On the contrary, however, approaches like Caruth's are not primarily concerned with a traumatized person's recovery through writing but rather with "truthful" testimony. As the incomprehensibility of trauma can only be done justice to through ruptures and gaps, the ethical stance may, according to Caruth, precisely lie in resisting a healing closure (see Caruth 151–56). Celan's and Müller's texts operate along the lines of the second tendency. However, especially in their negotiations of breath, both writers' works draw attention to an issue that passes unheeded in the two tendencies outlined. Celan's "Atemwende" implies that the author's voice is silenced in writing, that physiological breath and wounded bodies are cut into words, and that what remains "mitgegeben" of the writer may only be a trace of being muted. Müller's *Atemschaukel* is based on traumatic memories that are detached from the body they pervade, and then transformed in the act of textualization and metaphorization. Thus, Celan's and Müller's texts display how the speaking voice may be dispossessed in the process of a verbalization of trauma, which adds a new twist to Caruth's claim that trauma is the "force of an experience that is not yet fully owned" (150).

Caruth primarily focuses on the fundamental structure of a "traumatic event" and the processes of belatedness and symptomatic repetition accompanying it. For her, the danger of speech is "that it understands too much" and mistranslates trauma into a coherence and understanding, which in scriptotherapy is considered a path toward healing: "the transformation of the trauma into a narrative memory that allows the story to be verbalized and communicated, to be integrated into one's own and others' knowledge of the past, may lose both the precision and the force that characterizes traumatic recall" (Caruth 153). Focusing on the process of textualization shows that what might be lost is not limited to the "the event's essential incomprehensibility, the force of its affront to understanding" (154), as Caruth observes. A further loss addressed in Celan's and Müller's negotiations of breath concerns the traumatized subject, which is exposed to the risk of disappearing in its own words and in the resulting literary text. The problem of verbalization is thus not solved by a "faithful" recounting that articulates the fissures and gaps involved in trauma, as Caruth suggests. An erasure of the subject through writing undermines its healing aspect but it also unsettles the notion of the traumatic event's "truth," even if that truth lies in its "incomprehensibility." When Caruth suggests that the "truly historical transmission" is determined by ruptures and gaps, she does not address a fundamental rupture that may endanger authentic rendering of trauma as such: if rendering *itself* corrupts the source voicing traumatic "truth," this truth is called into question. In Celan's and Müller's writings, the subject can no longer be taken for granted: the "transmission of a gap" in the context of a "traumatic history" beyond the "pathology of individual suffering" (156) is also the transmission of the gap caused by the possible loss of a traumatized subject in writing.

The questions raised by Celan's and Müller's texts are of fundamental importance to trauma theory: if the traumatized subject may be lost in words, what remains of trauma? How can literature still constitute a testimony to a traumatic past? Celan's and Müller's texts bear witness not only to the wounds and losses induced by trauma, but also to the loss of the subject and of truthful rendering. Celan, who chooses not to address the holocaust in thematic terms, aspires to a "pneumatic" writing that opens to readers in the silences and breaches, which point to the absence of the author's living breath. Müller does address the traumatic experience of the camps, but *Atemschaukel* and her comments on it simultaneously reflect the painful implications of writing traumatic history, especially when performed by a second generation. On the diegetic level, a process of repetition compulsion is staged: for Leo, the camp symptomatically returns in "flashbacks" and traumatic "recalls" (Caruth 153) unmitigated by processes of "working through" (LaCapra 66). In Caruth's terms, trauma articulates itself in its authentic incomprehensibility: Leo's attempt to give a faithful account of the camp experience results in deleted sentences. However, the word "Atemschaukel" disrupts the story told by recalling Pastior's falling silent at the basis of it. For readers, "Atemschaukel" thwarts the fluent transmission of traumatic memory: the *fictional* camp word disturbs the idea of an authentic transportation of traumatic experience's shattering "truth" suggested by the "real" camp words. What Müller's novel performs is a discharge of traumatic affects: affects detached from the traumatized subject confront the readers. The word "Atemschaukel" shows that camp words fail to incorporate the past fully and thus enact a fictional transmission of traumatic gaps they cannot carry over. The reception scenario anticipated by the novel and Müller's poetics does not impose this repetition compulsion on the readers; it uncovers a process of repetition compulsion that is inauthentic.

Celan's and Müller's implication of the readers is relentless. For LaCapra, the impossibility of identifying with a victim through an artwork or literary text causes an "appropriate" reaction: "empathic unsettlement," which in his account represents the right balance between "harmonizing events" (78) and a harmful persistence of "acting out" instead of "working through":

> It is dubious to identify with the victims to the point of making oneself a surrogate victim who has a right to the victim's voice or subject position. . . . The role of empathy and emphatic unsettlement in the attentive secondary witness does not entail this identity [of victim and secondary witness]; it involves a kind of virtual experience through which one puts oneself in the other's position while recognizing the difference of that position and hence not taking the other's place. (78)

Müller's and Celan's texts preclude LaCapra's reassuring positioning of the ideal reader, who is just enough affected to care and emphasize yet not enough to become caught by repetition compulsion or a false identification with a victim's position they have no right to occupy. In Müller's and Celan's work, the "position" of the traumatized victim is already unsettled: its status is unclear, partly silenced, and, in Müller's case, cooccupied by another voice. The victim's "right" to their own "voice or subject position" is already violated in and by the literary texts. Accordingly, the readers' position in the context of Celan's and Müller's work is not free from violence. In Celan's case, time and again we are made aware of the fact that we fail to do justice to his texts when we read them: we impose meaning and words on silences and mend wounds that are meant to be left open—the open encounter that in Celan's poetics of "Atemwende" is presented as a source of hope is most often disappointed when it is realized; we easily become coconspirators forcing an alien breath into the poems' silent pauses. Müller sets her inanimate breathing words loose on the reader and their attacks are as disturbing as their inability to properly transport the traumatic past. The ethics of both literary approaches to a traumatic past may lie precisely in such unconsoling articulations of syncopnea.

Respiratory Gender-Turns

In terms of tone and pace, Celan's and Müller's accounts of silence in writing diverge: the role attributed to and played by breath is significantly different. Recalling the gender trajectory pursued in the previous chapters (stillness and immobility versus sound and movement), one could claim that Müller's silence screams in an agitated whirl of mutable words whereas Celan's punctuates "erratic language-block[s]." Celan's literary work is an attempt of realizing what he outlines as a poetry that is still possible after the Shoah; namely, he does not "sing Auschwitz from a nightingale's or thrush's point of view." This reaction to Adorno primarily plays on a conventional association of poetry with the beautiful or idyllic; however, Celan also expresses an increasing skepticism toward musicality, not least after the success of "Todesfuge," his most well-known early "holocaust poem." Celan's later work to some extent counters the poetics of "Todesfuge," which is both arranged according to musical structures and accentuates the words' sounds. "Ricercar" is a good illustration of this shift, invoking a musical form without specifically highlighting the tonal and acoustic dimensions of language. Its "Hauchschrift," like the fading breath on the "glass of eternity" in Celan's translation of Mandelstam's "Дано мнѣ тѣло," amounts to "*mute* breath-auras" (emphasis added). As discussed, the image-complex around stones, crystals and petrification express an emphasis on the poems' immobile, mute, written character. Poems such as "Ricercar" or "Weggebeizt" do appear like "erratic language-block[s]; . . . fac[ing] you with silence." While Celan describes breath as "pause and interval" and consistently associates it with silence, he does not sketch it as motionless. His famous term, "breath*turn*" implies movement; likewise, breath is described as "direction," thus always already pointing beyond itself, being en route. Celan—somewhat surprisingly—embeds two of his major references to breath in *definitions*: "breath, that is, direction and destiny," "the poem today—it is a breathturn." Both fail to reveal the stable "essential nature of a thing" (*Oxford English Dictionary* online); rather, the boundaries supposed to be drawn by a definition are blown and rendered mobile. The respiratory movement embraced in Celan's poetics is continually tied to stasis: it is only in moments of contemplation and rest that the turn of breath may occur: "when you *stand* with your *thinking in falling silent thinking in the pause* . . . the poem today—it is a breathturn" (*The Meridian* 127; emphasis added).

Inquiring into possible coincidences between the quiet reflexivity of Celan's writing and the gendering of poetic speakers is almost impossible, as most of his poems are not articulated through an explicitly gendered voice. In "Ricercar," however, masculine pronouns and articles are used for the writer:

Der auf den Händen ging, die es schrieben, *er*, *der* die Nesselschrift las, *der* weiterlas, *der* Un- gelesene, Un- verstandene, *er* schrieb:	He who went on the hands that wrote it, he, who read the nettle-writing, who read on, the un- read, the mis- understood, he wrote:

One can only speculate whether Celan is gesturing toward himself as a writer, using the generic masculine form of German, or reproducing an androcentric view identifying artists as male. In the present discussion, trying to resolve this question does not lead very far and is best left open. More crucial is that the addressed "Du" (You) consistently remains ungendered. As Celan's poetics repeatedly suggest, the shifter can be a placeholder for both the poem's writer/speaker and its recipients. "Du" is not only open to be occupied ("etwas Offenstehendes, Besetzbares" ("Speech on the Occasion" 186) but essentially unknown, an Other or stranger the poem moves toward. The second person pronoun marks the site of a possible but not certain encounter with the poem, in Agamben's terms, a "potential that . . . holds its own impotential or potential not-to firm" (*The Use of Bodies* 276). Given that the encounter is unpredictable, uncertain and in a subjunctive mood, the specific parties involved cannot be defined in positive terms and thus also elude predetermined gendering. The crux of the "Du's" radical openness and *Besetzbarkeit* (occupiability) may be that the *realization* of a specific encounter (e.g., between reader and poem) matters less than the sense of inoperativity pervading the poem through the potential/nonpotential it hosts. It is important that Celan situates breath precisely in this space where the poem—through the addressed "Du" and an anticipated encounter with either past or future—becomes indeterminable: "The poem remains . . . *pneumatically* touchable"; in the "remembered pauses, in the cola and mora, your word speaks; the poem today—it is a breathturn" (*The Meridian* 127).

As has been noted, the most prominent characteristic of Müller's "Atemschaukel" is that it does not stand for something and does not stand still: along with the unhinged pack of linguistic "camp things," "Atemschaukel" turns Leo's world into a frantic dizziness, unsettling the relation between past and present. It is the trigger and carrier of violent transformations and transferences both within the book and beyond its boundaries, confounding moments of the production and reception process in an erratic whirl. With its "phobic animation," the wandering word produces a disrupted, panting text. "The breath-swing is a delirium," setting loose straying qualities, sweeping things away from where they are rooted. Müller claims that "Atemschaukel" emerged from Oskar Pastior's falling silent. In the novel, the word unleashing the attack of "things from the camp" represents a sonic intrusion when it merges with the ticking of the clock in Leo's home. In another "redeportation" scene, when flour invokes blasting powder, the breath-swing's uncanny transformation is a loud explosion of sense. Acoustically, "Atem*sch*aukel" itself contains some of the most predominant, smothering sounds of the camp. It echoes the language of the oppressors: "The Russian commands sound like . . . a gnashing and sputtering collection of ch, sh, tsch, shch" (23). In its subjugating use in the camp, Russian becomes a language of obstructed airways: "After a while the commands just sound like a constant clearing of the throat—coughing, sneezing, nose blowing, hacking up mucus" (23). Thus, the word "Atemschaukel" semantically points to the literally and metaphorically suffocating conditions of the camp, and sonically incorporates them in the grating, rasping *sch* and *k*. Moreover, "Atemschaukel's" companions are at times associated with violent noise. For example, "Hasoweh" echoes in the scream of a steppe-dog Leo strikes dead and later in his homesick wail.

From the perspective of gender and sexuality, it is crucial to note that in *Atemschaukel*, we first encounter the "straying qualities" of words that develop a life of their own in the very beginning of the novel when Leo pursues his queer desire before he is deported to the camp. What is later most prominently displayed by the word "Atemschaukel," a linguistic movement in which "everything becomes something different," already haunts Leo while he secretly has rendezvous in a park and a bathhouse. The men he meets in the park cautiously use code names like "THE SWALLOW," "HARE," "ORIOLE," "CAT," or "GULL"—a linguistic shift that goes hand in hand with the movement of cruising: "The park was a wild animal crossing, I let myself be passed from one man to the next" (2). And the roaming does not stop there: for Leo, words start to transform and unexpectedly snap at him, exactly like the animated camp words later:

> My father was an art teacher. With the Neptune Baths inside my head, whenever he used the word WATERCOLOUR I'd flinch as though he'd kicked me. The words knew how far I'd already gone. At the dinner table my mother said: Don't stab the potato with your fork because it will fall apart, use your spoon, the fork is for meat. My temples were throbbing. Why is she saying meat when she's talking about forks and potatoes. What kind of meat does she mean. I was my own thief, the words came out of nowhere and caught me. (4)

The language of the camp is also a language of prohibited homosexuality. "Atemschaukel" is inscribed with queer desire and cuts across gendered bodies and sexual identities: Herta Müller, the woman who "invents" and stages it as a site where her poetics are most prominently displayed, and Oskar Pastior, whose sexual orientation (at least marginally) enters the novel via Leo, the fictional character derived from his "stolen life"—a life "taken" in the course of a writing process where inspiration coincided with theft.

6

Pneumatic Gender Dynamics, Queering Breath

"Syncope versus synthesis, or, more specifically, syncope at the heart of synthesis, a smack in the middle" (Nancy, *Expectation* 113): in a book that has repeatedly stressed the interruptive, syncopating impulses of breath in modern literature and poetics, any attempt at final closure would be a smothering gesture. In lieu of a conclusion, I now want to more closely attend to a number of *traversions* of sex, gender, and breath, as well as drawing attention to *intersections* of breath.

In this book, I have outlined a certain tendency observable in the pairings of male and female authors: distinctive modulations of movement and sound form a pneumatic pattern that is, time and again, *traversed* by particular articulations of breath, which is frequently a textual breath that resists attribution to a specific gender. One may read the women's respiratory tones as emancipatory and subversive, ranging from sonorously musical to aggressively loud and from animatedly flowing to bold driving, Woolf's, Plath's, and Müller's breath-writing *moves out of* the domain of passivity to which women's voices and bodies have been forcibly relegated over decades of male-dominated literary history. In contrast, in their tendency to embrace the sedate, still, and static, Musil, Beckett, and Celan *move into* this "passive" domain. This again aligns with another cluster of historical clichés that juxtaposes the female hysteric with the sober, austere male voice of reason. Kerouac is the writer who at first sight seems to most plainly exemplify the inherited image of traditional masculinity. In *Poetics of Breathing*, however, this image undergoes a shift once he is surrounded by male writers pursuing a poetics of quiet breath and women writers whose respirational texts speed and flow. In their respirational texts, the authors I've focused on in *Poetics of Breathing* both challenge *and* confirm normative gender patterns. The incongruities and contradictions of these patterns, and their presence and subversions in the texts, reveal that the stereotypes at work are not as consistent as one might expect: fictional and nonfictional bodies and voices move in and out of patterns that are consequently destabilized. The constructedness and arbitrariness of gender clichés becomes apparent, which—and this is the most important point—also exposes them as nonbinding. When the individual occurrences of literary breath resist fitting the pneumatic gender scheme and instead cut through it, *syn* meets *koptein*.

My investigations of literary breath show that respiration is never a purely "natural" phenomenon that is unaffected by its cultural and discursive contexts: as Jean-Thomas Tremblay so accurately put it, "No one is ever *just breathing*" (96). Literary breath presents itself entangled in cultural and etymological histories and intertextual networks, where it is saturated with narratives and meanings that it keeps interrupting and resisting. My readings paid attention to the rhythmic entanglements and to medial qualities shared by physiological breath and language. By highlighting these moments where breath and language intersect as well as pointing out cultural contexts and intertexts, I have tried to avoid biological fallacies and phonocentric traps without neglecting the physiology of living bodies and respiratory corporeality of inanimate matter. Hence, alarm bells were ringing when I addressed the authors' sex and sexual orientation while it was obvious that ignoring it would represent a symptomatic gap. My explorations of corporeal and literary syncopnea are situated in a field of tension that the sex/gender distinction shares: the boundary is hardly clear-cut: organic bodies and culturally shaped identities continually intersect. Claiming that the linguistic entanglements of breath play into discursively coconstituted genders is as plausible as it is unproblematic. In contrast, the interferences of sexed and respiring bodies, inclinations, desires, and so on are harder to grasp and resist being assignable to a stable location, whether biology, physiology, language, social norms, or cultural inscriptions.

Gendered framings of breath dwell on the boundary between bodies and the cultural narratives ascribed to them. While breath per se has no sex, its rhythms and sounds are characteristic articulations of gendered bodies. Specific breathing practices and timbres are situated in gendered frameworks, where they often highlight the most blunt stereotypes: think, for example, of hypermasculine promotions of breath control like that of Wim Hof's,[1] or, on screen, the panting of male action heroes and feminine sensual sighs or pornographic moans. Breath has been gendered through linguistic practices (fictional and nonfictional narratives, discourses ranging from medicine to philosophy), and, not least, theorized in the field of gender studies: it repeatedly appears in feminist criticism.[2] In these contexts, breath is treated as a corporeal, ephemeral matter or fluid image that challenges inherited (male) discourses, with their tendency to create rigid thought-patterns as well as closed, homogenous systems. In dedicating the next two subchapters to feminist respiratory theory so as to open a perspective of gendered literary breath beyond the specific works discussed in *Poetics of Breathing*, I work my way back from more recent criticism to a feminist classic, Hélène Cixous's "The Laugh of the Medusa."

Breath and Intersectionality

In Magdalena Górska's recent work, breath has become a major focus of intersectional feminist criticism. As she puts it in *Breathing Matters*, "Through breathing engagements, I came to an understanding of feminism (always nonreductive and multiple) as a philosophical, activist, political and ethical practice of intersectional social justice that consists of individual and collective, mundane and organized work" (32). Górska analyzes "how quotidian practices of breathing are not only individual but also structural political matters" (36). Along with the corporeal and material specificities that reveal the power structures acting on respiring subjects, breath also assumes the role of a discursive agent in Górska's work. Breath is described as both the *material* through which power structures become *readable* as well as the *physiological force* potentially resisting them. The strained breaths of panic attacks or dusty lungs are more than "just responses to or manifestations of social conditions"; they are "a material enactment of and challenge to contemporary power relations that are enacted individually and structurally. These kinds of breath transform dynamics of living by enacting a break and necessitating change" ("Feminist Politics of Breathing" 253).[3] The resistant potential of strained breath does not lie in the bodily experience of suffocation. Only because the specific articulations of breath make the power relations they incorporate legible as "suffocating" (*Breathing Matters* 181)—both in the literal and figural sense—do they "open potentialities of being otherwise" ("Feminist Politics of Breathing" 253). These intricate respiratory entanglements may best be called *corpolinguistic*. While it no longer makes sense to isolate the respiring body from its involvements in language once we consider breathing a corpolinguistic process, it is nevertheless crucial to look closely at the points where such intersections can be identified. What feminist thinkers like Górska and her predecessors (e.g., Sara Ahmed and Christina Sharpe) presume is a dynamic interaction between discursive and corporeal processes that coconstitute a person's or group's respective respiratory condition in their specific social and historical context.

Górska describes the "materially-discursive" (*Breathing Matters* 59) entanglements as follows:

> By working with breath as a force that is common to all living and breathing . . . beings yet differential in its enactments, I propose a rethinking of politics in which corpomaterial actions matter—politics not based on universalizing, homogenizing, or essentializing understandings of embodiment or subjectivity but conceptualized and enacted intersectionally in their specific situatedness and dispersal in the individual and structural dynamics. . . . Considering such simultaneously common and differential enactments of breathing it is, hence, necessary to work with a nonreductive understanding of it—one that does not reduce breathing into one homogenized narrative, one particular enactment, or one form of politics or ethics. ("Feminist Politics of Breathing" 248)

The individual interactions of bodies with politics through a physiological process that is necessarily embedded in an environment fraught with power structures, as well as the fact that we all breathe—that is, we all engage in "corpomaterial actions" saturated with the air of politics—are the basis for what breath promises to perform as a discursive image: for antiessentialism, nonreductiveness, heterogeneity, and so forth. In the same vein, translating the material-physiological qualities of respiration into philosophical and theoretical terms, Górska argues that "in its diversity and in the flow of its worldly circulation, breath challenges binary logics that constitute contemporary notions of human subjectivity" ("Feminist Politics of Breathing" 250). Based on its physiological characteristics, breath thus becomes *a sign for* intersectional feminism; namely, for a "feminist scholarship" that challenges "contemporary Western mainstream humanism" as well as "white male supremacy" and is therefore concerned with a multiplicity of marginalized groups ("othered" as women, LGTBQ, black or brown, disabled, etc.); a feminism that "does not signify a unitary position but allows for an articulation of feminist debates as diverse, full of contradictions and openness" (*Breathing Matters* 32). When breath is conceptually linked with intersectional feminism and diversity, it also becomes a *matter to be fought for*. Breath not only functions as an image for intersectional approaches, but also for what they are aspiring to achieve politically. Echoing Christina Sharpe, Sara Ahmed, and Judith Butler,[4] Górska argues for "breathable" conditions for minorities who are subject to suffocation.[5] Both the notions of "breathable life" and "suffocation" fluctuate between the literal and the figural: actual experiences of suffocation like Eric Garner's violent death in a police chokehold or a coal worker's damaged lungs provide metaphors for suppressed minority lives; breathable life is the extension of this kind of metaphor and the factual relief from suffocation. In other words, breath is a corpolinguistic force that can lead to "breathable life." All of these shifting movements meet in the following passage:

> I therefore understand breathing as a force that not only materializes, recognizes, and manifests social power relations but also forces social and environmental transformation. In this approach, breath in its trans-corporeal and lively and deadly operations becomes not only a symbolic but also a literal enactment of the struggle for breathable life—a struggle that . . . takes place in quotidian practices of living and is inherently intersectional and posthumanist, in which the notion of humanness relies not on impermeable boundaries but rather on respiratory co-becoming. ("Feminist Politics of Breathing" 253)

In Górska's approach, the boundaries between physiology and her theorization of breath itself become permeable. The terms she employs in her thinking and writing are performative rather than descriptive: "intersectionality is, therefore, not merely a tool that shows the intersections of categories. It is, instead, something that can become an apparatus . . . of agential analysis of intra-active and differential relationalities: relationalities of bodies, subjectivities, environments, cultures, social power relations. . . . Such an approach also problematizes the idea of stable boundaries, both bodily and conceptual" (*Breathing Matters* 183). "Intersectionality" here corresponds with how "breath" is conceived of. As determined and teleological as the fight for a "breathable life" may sound, the role of breath in this line of thinking is not only that of a productive image or metaphor. Breath syncopates—

inter-sects—and undoes: stable boundaries, rigid power structures, and so on. If we follow this trajectory, we might ask to what degree breath as a destabilizing corpolinguistic force traverses Górska's own argument. One question that arises is what the identification of physical breath with feminist intersectionality may imply for the privileged breather. The aspects of respiratory physiology that lend themselves to an ethics of openness and diversity are shared by every being with lungs, regardless of their gender, ethnicity, or class. Does intersectionality enter the white male's body when he breathes, just because his respiratory organs do what they do? Does he either have to become oblivious of his breath or gain mastery over it in order to handle and subdue its subversive, queering force? It becomes clear that within Górska's corpolinguistic respiratory framework, different notions of breath start to diverge at the very moment they are claimed to coincide: even though the physiology of breathing lends itself to a structural analogy with the political notion of diversity, and so on, the two strands divide in the argument that we have a breath to fight for, whether literally or metaphorically. The ideal of a breathable life—again, in both the figural and literal sense—is always interrupted by the syncopated rhythm of breathing as such. Yet, as feminist theorists like Górska show, this very interruption is not evenly distributed, such that some social subjects are able to breathe more easily than others. In the following, I want to show how literature and writing enable us to develop a notion of respiratory intersectionality that opens "political potentialities" ("Feminist Politics of Breathing" 253) that reach beyond the idea of "breathable life."

Respirational *écriture féminine*

Hélène Cixous, whose name repeatedly appears alongside the most famous respirational feminist thinker, Luce Irigaray, shares the latter's criticism of a hitherto predominantly male constitution of the subject position of "woman" and the demand to redefine it on her own terms.[6] As is well known, Cixous is particularly interested in a new kind of *writing—écriture féminine*—that does justice to and incorporates women's bodies and thus shatters a language shaped by the "phallocentric tradition" ("The Laugh of the Medusa" 879). Like Irigaray, Cixous describes women as being nonuniform, nonhomogenous, and uncontainable (876). However, for Cixous, the liberation and articulation of such feminine qualities does not move toward an overcoming of language and (Western) culture.[7] On the contrary, she argues that "writing is precisely *the very possibility of change*, the space that can serve as a springboard for subversive thought, the precursory movement of a transformation of social and cultural structures" (879). In contrast to Irigaray, who associates breath with woman's prediscursive nature, Cixous stages an intricate play of intertextual resonances wherein the respirational force of the body slides between linguistic ambiguities. At first sight, and when considered in isolation, the explicit references to breathing in "The Laugh of the Medusa" sound familiar. Demanding that women write themselves out of suppression, censorship and deadness "individually" (880), Cixous claims that

> by writing herself, woman will return to the body which has been more than confiscated from her, which has been turned into . . . the ailing or *dead* figure, which so often turns out to be . . . the cause and location of *inhibitions*. *Censor* the body and you *censor breath* and speech at the same time. / Write *your self*. Your body must be heard. Only then will the immense resources of the *unconscious* spring forth. . . . We must kill the false woman who is preventing the live one from breathing. Inscribe the breath of the whole woman. (880; emphasis added)

The topos of freeing the breath both anticipates the feminist voices discussed in this chapter and reiterates the specifically male discourse and poetics of the second chapter: the role attributed to breath by postwar American avant-garde writers like Olson, Kerouac, and Ginsberg and their common influential source, Whitman. That "inscrib[ing] the breath" is equaled with "writ[ing] yourself" and supposed to be a "return to the body" echoes both Whitman's "Song of Yourself" and Kerouac's "Essentials of Spontaneous Prose," which in turn alludes to Whitman: "tap from yourself the song of yourself, blow!—now!—your way is your only way."

The extent to which Cixous and Kerouac use similar images and generate parallel arguments in the course of demanding a new way of writing is striking—especially given that one is embedded in a self-consciously hypermasculine endeavor and the other is making a plea for a specifically feminine writing. That Kerouac did not call his spontaneous prose "masculine" does not mean it is ungendered. On the contrary: the nonnecessity of explicitly gendering it while at the same time, as a matter of course, equating literary output with ejaculation is a paradigmatic demonstration of phallocentrism. Cixous, conversely, does not hesitate to explicitly gender the desired new form of writing as "woman's writing." She does not, however, fall into the trap of reverting either to a biologism or a gender binary, a point to which I will return after examining the parallels between Kerouac and Cixous.

Let us return to Kerouac's *Essentials*, as juxtaposed with the passage just cited from "The Laugh of the Medusa": his suggestion to avoid a "language being *dead*" (see "the ailing or *dead* figure" that the body becomes in Cixous) is "allowing *subconscious* to admit in *own uninhibited* . . . language what conscious art would *censor*" (see the body as "location of *inhibitions. Censor the body and you censor breath* and speech at the same time. / Write *your self*. Your body must be heard. Only then will the immense resources of the *unconscious* spring forth" in Cixous; emphasis added). For both Kerouac and Cixous, a central quality of the writing and bodies resisting censorship and inhibition is their quality of flow and overflow.[8] Unhindered flux generates a language that undoes traditional structures. Cixous demands that "[w]omen must write through their bodies, they must invent the impregnable language that will wreck partitions, classes, and rhetorics, regulations and codes" and "sweep[] away syntax" ("The Laugh of the Medusa" 886). In "History of the Theory of Breath," Kerouac analogously calls for the "full flow of language without rules that block . . . such as grammatical restrictions sentence structure, versifying prosodical rules." During a talk in 2007, Cixous expressed another striking resonance with Kerouac's poetics of breath: commenting on her writing practice, she mentions that "I write without interruption, as if I were a runner, a marathon runner" (Cixous, "Hélène Cixous at the NYS Writers Institute" 1: 39).

Kerouac's and Cixous's approaches diverge, unsurprisingly of course, on many levels—the *context* of Cixous's feminist project alone inscribes a significant difference. I want to take another Kerouacian echo as a starting point to demonstrate how Cixous's references to breath in particular subvert the masculine respirational poetics it invokes. Kerouac's suggestion to break with conventional syntax and punctuation by "the vigorous space dash separating rhetorical breathing" is, as I have examined in depth, both phallic and riddled with castration anxiety. I have also pointed out the ableist implications of the desired athletic, spontaneous writing that Kerouac compares to a "hundred-yard dash" and the rigorous mastery of the body that it presupposes. Cixous's translators not only make abundant use of dashes, they also use the word "dash" at a significant moment in the text. In the course of my (at first glance improbable) comparison of Kerouac and Cixous, it is remarkable that in "The Laugh of the Medusa," "dashing" appears in a passage that is explicitly directed against the kind of "glorious phallic monosexuality" (884) embodied by Kerouac's poetics, and addresses some characteristics that apply to it most accurately: "Let's leave it to the worriers, to *masculine anxiety* and its *obsession with how to dominate* the way things work. . . . For us the point is not to take possession in order to internalize or manipulate, but rather to *dash through* and to 'fly'" (887; emphasis added). Cixous's original expression, "traverser d'un trait, et 'voler'" (*Le Rire de la Méduse* 58) encompasses both the visual appearance (traversing line) and speedy movement of the dash (flying). Feminine writing "dashes" like Kerouac's spontaneous prose, but it does so in order to counter qualities embraced by and symptomatic of Kerouac's poetics. In a parallel reading, Kerouac's phallic dash is dashed, traversed by "The Laugh of the Medusa." In the process of listening to the resonances between Kerouac and Cixous, the dash is a point of collision: where two conflicting poetics (accidentally or not) clash and break.[9]

Given the strong argumentative and terminological similarities to Kerouac's poetics of breathing, it is curiously appropriate that Cixous starts to outline a strategy of "tak[ing] possession" in the very sentence that in French evokes and in English names the dash, which is the self-appointed "trademark" of Kerouac's writing. In "The Laugh of the Medusa" and beyond, Cixous's *écriture féminine* not only consists in writing woman's body and "inscrib[ing]" her "style" (882) but also in an appropriation of male discourse. It is in this respect that Cixous's endeavor diverges most prominently from both the Irigarayan argument in favor of a body beyond or before language and the Beats' embodied poetics—and, importantly, without abandoning the strong emphasis on the corporeal.[10] Whereas breath becomes a preferred image for unmediated bodily presence and articulation for the Beats, for Cixous it plays an important role both when she drafts attempts at "seiz[ing]" the "discourse of man" (887) and when she performs these seizures through her writing. Explaining this requires a short detour. In the statement, "For us the point is not to take possession in order to internalize or manipulate, but rather to dash through and to 'fly,'" the last word, in the French original "voler," is of major importance. As Cixous stresses in the passage to follow, "voler" has a double meaning: "to fly" and "to steal."

> Flying is woman's gesture—flying in language and making it fly. We have all learned the art of flying and its numerous techniques; for centuries we've been able to possess anything only by flying; we've lived in flight, stealing away, finding, when desired, narrow passageways, hidden crossovers. It's no accident that *voler* has a

double meaning, that it plays on each of them and thus throws off the agents of sense. It's no accident: women take after birds and robbers. (887)

The figure of woman as Cixous sketches her shares the airy medium she moves in with breath. The semantic movement of "voler" is akin to "souffler": both words have a double meaning, one of which is "stealing." In a conversation with Derrida, Cixous addresses the ambivalence of "souffler" while commenting on their shared approaches and influences on each other: "I saw myself clearly in your incredible text on Artaud, *La parole soufflé* [sic], in this bivalence of the *soufflé*: a word whispered/given by someone else, and a word stolen, whisked away. We both let the word take its flight: this release of the word like the release of a bird or a breath: let go something that will have made a crossing" ("From Word to Life" 2).
Cixous allows her own vocabulary from "The Laugh of the Medusa" to flow into her recapitulation of Derrida's *La parole soufflée*: "We both let the word take its *flight*: this release of the word like the release of a *bird* or a breath" (emphasis added). The image complex she creates around "voler" is thus integrated into a respirational one. Immediately before this passage, Cixous describes her own writing practice in terms of breathing:

> I have this need to let myself be haunted by voices coming from elsewhere that resonate through me. I want to have voices. As a result I am at the mercy of their inspiration [*insufflement*]. They can fail me. I master nothing, I submit to the oracles. This risk is the condition of my creative energy and of my discoveries. It can happen that I run out of breath [*souffle*], that something loses steam [*s'ensouffle*]. (2)

Anticipating the explicit reference to the influence of Derrida's *La parole soufflée*, what Cixous adds when playing with respirational words is a *work ethic* that embraces potential failure or exhaustion and rejects empowerment. She thus echoes "The Laugh of the Medusa," where women's writing is said to be determined by "a fragility, a vulnerability" (886).

Here we can return to Kerouac's poetics of breathing, which vehemently rejects inspiration, attempts to seal itself off from other voices while undermining notions of vulnerability, weakness, and failure. Reverberating Kerouacian ideas and terminology, "The Laugh of the Medusa" takes the male voice into possession, steals it, and at the same time channels into its own concerns. Reading the evocation of breath in "The Laugh of the Medusa" and the specification of "voler" as woman's articulation together with Cixous's comments in the conversation with Derrida shows that she approaches a respirational poetics that, by definition, cannot be her own. The very claim that the stolen inspirational voices also imply a dispossession, that they disempower and let words take flight, prevents the appropriated male discourse from merely being replicated—in other words, the power structures are not inverted but rather subverted. By recalling Kerouac's breath, Cixous's writing lets it "take its flight" and "jumbl[es] the order of space, . . . disorient[s] it, . . . dislocat[es] things and values, break[s] them all up, empt[ies] structures, and turn[s] propriety upside down" ("The Laugh of the Medusa" 887). At the same time, in a feminist text, the echo of a poetics so heavily charged with masculinity poses a risk of failure. In her play with masculine undertones, readers can easily be misled. We might get the impression that Cixous simply reverses a "power relation" established in male discourse, "the opposition activity/passivity" (887): once her voice takes flight, woman rises from passivity. However, rushing between positions that were coded as feminine and masculine, Cixous's text flies in the sense of "changer souvent, rapidement, ne pas s'attacher" (Littré 4: 2535) and performatively affirms her claim that it "is impossible to *define* a feminine practice of writing . . . , for this practice can never be theorized, enclosed, coded" (883). Thus, the breath "liberated" in woman's writing remains inappropriable—it could take off at any moment. Or, in Irigaray's words, "this matter escapes mastery" (*The Forgetting of Air in Martin Heidegger* 12).

One might consequently ask to what extent such a form of respirational writing can still be ascribed to a conception of "women" that Cixous explicitly contrasts to "men."[11] What at first sight might sound like a rather conventional gender binarism is interrogated in "The Laugh of the Medusa." It is important that Cixous stresses that "sexual *opposition*" is a "historico-cultural limit" that "has always worked for man's profit" and is itself the product of a discourse dominated by men (883; emphasis added). Her insistence on sexual *difference* is essential in the endeavor of bringing to mind and rewriting that history. For Cixous, using the signifier "woman," which within the male discourse is locked in a binary opposition, is an attempt to "cut through" (886) phallocentric language, to subvert it from within: "If woman has always functioned 'within' the discourse of men, a signifier that has always referred back to the opposite signifier . . . it is time for her to dislocate this 'within,' to explode it" (887). This implies rupturing the concept of "woman" as such by situating her in the "in-between" that exceeds binarity, shifting her toward "bisexuality." Against a notion of "bisexuality" that Cixous calls "classic," which clings to the "fantasy of a 'total' being" that experiences "difference" as "an operation incurring loss," she argues for an "*other bisexuality* on which every subject not enclosed in the false theater of phallocentric representationalism has founded his/her erotic universe" (884). This other bisexuality is non-classifiable as a whole; it rather articulates itself in different forms in singular bodies that in turn "multipl[y] . . . the effects of the inscription of desire." Consequently, Cixous's elucidation remains open: "Bisexuality, that is: each one's location in self (*repérage en soi*) of the presence—variously manifest and insistent according to each person, male or female—of both sexes, nonexclusion either of the difference or of one sex." A most striking and often overlooked argument in Cixous's text is that this fluid bisexuality *coincides* with a feminine subject position without necessarily, essentially, or permanently being tied to it: "Now it happens that at present, for historico-cultural reasons, it is women who are opening up to and benefiting from this vatic bisexuality which doesn't annul differences but stirs them up" (883–84). *At present,* that which most radically unsettles, agitates, and undermines sexual difference(s) without annulling them are queer bodies and desires. This goes hand in hand with Cixous's recent claim that today, in the early twenty-first century, Medusa's offspring are queer ("Medusas 'Changeance' " 184).

In Cixous's 1975 text, "haunted" as it is "by voices coming from elsewhere that resonate through," queerness can by no means only be located in the future as a site of "other bisexuality." The most clearly audible echo in her claim, "Censor the body and you censor breath and speech at the same time. / Write your self. Your body must be heard" is Walt Whitman's "Song of Myself,"[12] in which a "vatic bisexuality" was invoked in respiratory images long before Cixous lived. The "breather" of Whitman's poem, singing "My respiration and inspiration, the beating of my heart, the passing of blood and air through my lungs" (*Leaves of Grass* 24), presents itself as a permeable body driven by homoerotic fantasies—a body that, as manly as it writes itself, turns increasingly androgynous and demonstrates a "multiplication of the effects of the inscription of desire" ("The Laugh of the Medusa" 884). The singularity that speaks in the first person famously contains multitudes; "Song of Myself" is weaved of a vast number of voices uttered through a body that infinitely opens, transforms, disseminates.[13] Whitman's poetic negotiations of breath echo, on the one hand, his ideology of manly health but on the other ultimately present a prophetic vision of queerness and a nonuniform, heterogeneous "self" (see "Circulating Multitudes" 221) that resonates in Cixous when she writes "our blood flows and we extend ourselves without ever reaching an end . . . we inspire ourselves and we expire without running out of breath, we are everywhere!" (878).

Breathing à *travers*

Those moments where a respirational force traverses, on a textual level, either the gender pattern I presented or the gendered characters or poetics outlined by the authors are, in a literal sense, "queer." Syncopnea as I have theorized it—the interrupting and noncontainable intervention of literary breath—overlaps with etymologies of "queer." Eve Kosofsky Sedgwick writes: "Queer is a continuing moment, movement, motive—recurrent, eddying, *troublant*. The word "queer" itself means *across*—it comes from the Indo-European root *twerkw*, which also yields the German *quer* (transverse), Latin *torquere* (to twist), and English *athwart*" (*Tendencies* xii). Further, breath became a matter of interest for the feminist critics discussed here because it resists conceptualization and signification—in the same vein as "queer" for Sedgwick implies "the open mesh of possibilities, gaps, overlaps, dissonances and resonances, lapses and excesses of meaning when the constituent elements of anyone's gender, of anyone's sexuality aren't made (or *can't be made*) to signify monolithically" (8). While a movement *across* and the irreducibility of queer breath to a single meaning will be the basis of my theorization of queer literary breath, I want to distance myself from a third premise Sedgwick stresses, namely, that "'queer' seems to hinge . . . radically and explicitly on a person's undertaking particular, performative acts of self-perception and filiation. . . . A hypothesis worth making explicit: that there are important senses in which 'queer' can signify only *when attached to the first person*" (9). I want to argue that an exclusive emphasis on the first person and on the valorization of the subject by "performance acts of self-perception and filiation" to some extent curtail the social-political relevance of "queer." Queer breath has a potential to gesture beyond the accustomed politics of identity; it encourages a scrutinization of the very notions of "identity" and "subjectivity," which have become problematic and even pernicious as important pillars on which neoliberal gender normative discourses rest.[14] Literary breath—*queer syncopnea*—decouples itself from the first person, and from *any person*, by sounding through and traversing bodies, moving between and among gendered human bodies, gendered speech or writing, and the sonic or graphical corporeality of language.

What lies at the heart of a poetics of breathing in terms of gender and sexuality is *impersonal queerness*.

In *Receptive Bodies*, Leo Bersani theorizes breathing as the "experience" of the "body's inescapable receptivity: absorption and expulsion" (85). Inhaling and exhaling are "transactions with exteriority" (86). Considered a "force . . . independent of [the] body's gendered and sexual identity" (70),[15] breathing is an impersonalizing, queer movement constituting a corporeality that constantly interacts with the outside. Commenting on the acoustics of breath, Michel Chion notes: "The sound of breathing is also impersonal. . . . It is an ambiguous sound in several respects, between masculine and feminine, mechanical and living, involuntary and voluntary, unconscious and conscious, self and other" (334). This claim about physiological breath also holds for written literary respiration—perhaps even to a greater degree. Any transposition of breath into writing necessarily involves depersonalization, a transition from the living to the inanimate, from self to other. What still breathes in a text, through its tone, sounds, rhythms, and pauses, and through the semantic flight of respiratory images, is not only detached from an author's body, but also from the author's "voluntary," "conscious" intentions. In the moment when it passes into writing, breath most distinctly concurs with the physiological respirational rhythms that always displace bodies outside themselves. When *cut* from the writer's body, literary breath is right *with* it—a queer impersonal syncopnea traversing the author's sex and gender.

The *specific* loci where respiring body and text meet are in most cases impossible to locate; as literary scholars, we have to dwell on what David Novell Smith calls "the point at which the body-language nexus is itself articulated," which is a "vibratory nexus" that "exceeds and precedes the distinction between subject and object, constituting a mesh of relation." The fact that the "body which articulates language, and which is articulated in language" largely remains inaccessible to us (e.g., in the case of the author's body) is far from being a cause for regret. A focus on textual moments involving vibrations that "always exceed the actual entities that emit them" allows us to pinpoint how "vibrating entities are always entities out of phase with themselves" (62). *Poetics of Breathing* has explored precisely such moments: Musil's and Woolf's breathing pauses (the "breaths of a summer's day," the "stray airs"), Beckett's "respire[r] à travers," Plath's "blown . . . askew" letters, Celan's "Atemwende," Müller's "Atemschaukel," Kerouac's dash, Ginsberg's ecstatic inspiration, and Olson's "silent propellant." These are sites of intersectionality; approaching intersectionality in this literal sense, and hand in hand with intertextuality, adds to its utility in criticism today. An intersectionality of respiratory movements that are "out of phase with themselves" elucidates nonmeetings as much as encounters. More often than not, the authors' poetics, compositional efforts, and bodily involvements intersect with text-immanent and intertextual processes without coinciding. Pervaded by *syncopassive* forces, textual breaths often unsettle or unwork the deliberate poetics authors invest them with—*and* the poetics and contexts in which readers try to situate them. Textual breaths thus retain a certain indeterminacy—an indeterminacy essentially characteristic of corporeal breath—throughout their semanticization and contextualization.

When literary breaths traverse what they are inscribed with or embedded in and withdraw from straightforward readings, they insist on maintaining a certain degree of neutrality. Such a neutrality at first sight seems detached from gender and sexuality. However, as John Paul Ricco's work demonstrates, the neuter turns out to be the central mood of a queer ethics. Opposed to what Cixous calls the "neuter" of a "classic" bisexuality and which she rejects as the fantasy of a " 'total' being" *threatened* by the "loss" incurred through "difference" (883–84), the respiratory neutrality encountered in the texts discussed here *embraces* loss: the loss of that which escapes with breath, when we write it just as when we exhale. This goes hand in hand with Ricco's outline of queer neutrality, shared separation, and incommensurability in *The Decision between Us*. Drawing on Derrida's "Geschlecht: Sexual Difference, Ontological Difference," he argues that "due to the . . . withdrawal and retreat of bodies, including the traces and traits of identity—we encounter the exigency that states: name no one man and no one woman. This is what it would mean to free sex and sexuality, and perhaps even 'sexual difference,' from binary logic" (116–17). The neutral "refuses to belong to the category of subject as much as it does to that of object," as Blanchot claims (in "René Char and the Thought of the Neutral"; qtd. in Ricco 62). It constitutes a space of "incommensurability . . . which exists outside the measure of any binary set of terms" (117). Summarizing Blanchot's and Barthes's use of the term, Ricco stresses that "the neutral is that which interrupts and displaces" (62), and it does so in its impersonality or anonymity.

In my close readings, I have embraced forces of the neutral by highlighting how breath is involved in impersonal textual or linguistic movements: pauses, gaps, line breaks, syntactic interruptions, silent yet sonic vibrations of letters on a page, graphical incisions, punctuation, rhythm, prosody, semantic whirls, metaphoric and metonymic shifts, intermedial transferences, intertextual entanglements, deletions, and revisions and transitions between text-stages in writing or translation processes. In such instances, "traces and traits of identity" do, in fact, withdraw: the writers' bodies and intentions are submerged in domains that generate their own dynamics; dynamics in which reference—either to the things or the ideas words semantically indicate or to the person who wrote them—is no longer at the center, if not momentarily left behind. What predominates instead are gestures of exscription: "what must write itself alone, straight out of the always uncertain thought of language" (Nancy, "Exscription" 64). As Nancy stresses, exscription "is to be exposed, to expose oneself to . . . not-having." "Not having" here refers to the "infinite retreat of meaning" (64) that he keeps highlighting in connection with exscription. With regard to the textual breaths explored in this book, exscription points equally to a writing that cannot be owned or claimed as property, as "mine": that I produced it does not mean it belongs to me, speaks of me, coincides with me, or incorporates me.

A turn beyond identity as it is performed by exscribed breaths parallels the passages in my work where queer desire is explicitly addressed. Leo's cruising in *Atemschaukel* and the moments when Agathe's and Ulrich's erotic encounters in *The Man without Qualities* become nonhuman affects, go hand in hand with a loss of identity. In *Atemschaukel*, the repressive totalitarian regime forces the men pursuing gay desire to conceal their identity and meet anonymously. Consequently, their encounters get caught up in what Müller describes as the core movement of her literary language: "everything becomes something different." Through the code names, the cruising sites become a "wild animal crossing": Leo is not only "passed from one man to the next," he is passed between animals, plants and inanimate objects when his partners become "THE ORIOLE," "THE HARE," "THE FIR," "THE THREAD," "THE CAP," or "THE PEARL" (2). In the same manner—which turns out to be characteristic for the breath-swing's uncanny transformations—words evoking his secret desire for Leo cease to be identical with themselves through metonymic shifts: "watercolour" slips into Neptune Bath, the forked-through potatoes turn into meat and then penetrate flesh. The union that Musil's incestuous siblings Ulrich and Agathe experience not only breaches heterosexual norms, it shatters their selves. When Agathe, kissed by the air she exhaled, feels that "I'm you," "I" as well as "you" can no longer be understood as signs for two human individuals: the caress of an alien inanimate substance blends into the lovers' desire and radically shatters their identity (I am I / you are you). Moreover, "I am you" no longer indicates "I am another person" (i.e., "you") but "I and you are Other."

An erotically charged intermingling of the animate and inanimate is also linguistically performed through the impersonal affects coinciding with the breath-carried blossoms. The overlap of inertia and intensity explicitly links the breaths of a summer's day to Agathe's and Ulrich's sexual epiphanies. At the same time, the breaths are instances where "an opaque, autonomous language" (Perniola 121) boost the "sex appeal of the inorganic."

Forces of literary breath undermining identity coincide with queer desire in an early poem by Ginsberg, "Love Poem on Theme by Whitman" (*Collected Poems* 123). Invoking a section from "Song of Myself," the polyerotic scene in which a group of bathing men indulges in the caress of an "unseen hand" (36), the poem sketches a sexual encounter involving someone who is simultaneously physically present and absent. While the "identity of the sexed subject who speaks . . . is elusive," as Tony Trigilio notes, its body is clearly marked as male. When the speaker joins a couple in consummating their marriage, "homoerotic desire irrupts within hegemonic heterosexuality" (48–49). The queering of the straight sex scene goes hand in hand with the anonymization of the bodies involved. Strikingly, the transition from distinct bodies, identified as "I," "the bridegroom," and "the bride," to a mesh of aroused organs, passionate touches, and erogenous zones happens precisely at the moment of breath's entry into the scene:

> I'll go into the bedroom silently and lie down between the bridegroom and the bride,
> . . .
> bury my face in their shoulders and breasts, *breathing their skin*,
> and stroke and kiss neck and mouth . . .
> bodies locked shuddering naked, hot hips and buttocks screwed into each other
> and eyes, eyes glinting and charming, widening into looks and abandon,
> moans of movement, voices, hands in air, hands between thighs,
> hands in moisture on softened hips, throbbing contraction of bellies
> (Ginsberg, *Collected Poems* 123; emphasis added)

Something remarkable takes place when skin, the body's outer limit, meets breath, the process that keeps crossing or transgressing bodily boundaries, both internal and external: the skin that *is breathed* itself turns pneumatic and the membrane separating bodies from each other becomes permeable.

"Breathing their skin" is the last act in which the bodies are attributable to a distinct person: before, it is clear who does what to whom: "*I'll* . . . bury *my* face in *their* shoulder and breast"; after "breathing their skin," "possessive pronouns recede into an ecstatic, polysexual wrangle" (48), as Trigilio puts it. The line immediately following is infused with the mood introduced by the phrase "breathing their skin"—the grammatical continuous tense anticipates a pneumatic continuum: the indeterminacy of "breathing their skin" (what precisely does that mean, after all?—reading it as "inhaling the scent of their skin" is already a hermeneutic intervention) is passed on to "neck" and "mouth," the first two in a whirl of body parts that no longer belong to anyone in particular. In a parallel movement, not only body parts but also word classes withdraw from being clearly assignable. "Stroke and kiss neck and mouth" could either indicate neck and mouth being kissed and stroked, or a verbal rush of oral caresses: both "neck" and "mouth" also work as verbs that signify kissing. The drift over and across anonymous sites of pleasure goes on "till the white come flow in the swirling sheets / and the bride cry for forgiveness, and the groom be covered with tears of passion and compassion, / and I rise up from the bed" (*Collected Poems* 123): the erotic play becomes teleological and gendered through male orgasm, and the ecstatic bodies are split into three personae again. In contrast to the isolation of bodies distinguished by their (gender) identities and roles, "I," "bride," and "groom," the passage in which organs are ownerless becomes an entanglement that is also mirrored on the textual level. The "moans of movement" are enacted in language through sounds that fluidly cross word-borders. And it is again the breath that sets a *flow* in motion: "*br*easts, *br*eathing," "*h*ot *h*ips," "*eyes, eyes,*" "glint*ing* and charm*ing,* widen*ing,*" "*m*oans of *m*ovement," "*h*ands in air, *h*ands between thighs / *h*ands in moisture on softened *h*ips." The repetition of "eyes" and "hands" turns the words into pulsing beats and recurring "hips" clasp a torrent of words sonically "screwed into" each other.

> hot *hips* and buttocks screwed into each other
> and eyes, eyes glinting and charming, widening into looks and
>   abandon,
> moans of movement, voices, hands in air, hands between thighs,
> hands in moisture on softened *hips*, throbbing contraction of
>   bellies

By "drawing together"[16] lines eight and eleven, "hot hips" and "softened hips" anticipate the "throbbing contraction" of a pleasure that traverses the bridal couple's heteronormative bond.

"To conclude—I announce what comes after me"

In the poem that inspired Ginsberg's pneumatic queering, the passage evoked in "Love Poem on Theme by Whitman" is textually "screwed into" two other sections of the 1860 edition of *Leaves of Grass*, which present an erotic "breathing across."[17] A group of bathers is caressed by a present-absent feminine figure:

> Where are you off to, lady? for I see you,
> You splash in the water there, yet stay stock still in your room.
> Dancing and laughing along the beach came the twenty-ninth bather,
> The rest did not see her, but she saw them and loved them.
> The beards of the young men glisten'd with wet, it ran from their long hair,
> Little streams pass'd all over their bodies.
> An unseen hand also pass'd over their bodies,
> It descended tremblingly from their temples and ribs.
> The young men float on their backs, their white bellies bulge to the sun, they do not ask who seizes fast to them,
> They do not know who puffs and declines with pendant and bending arch (35–36)

This passage is anticipated in the initial lines of *Leaves of Grass*, the section called "Walt Whitman" in the 1860 edition, which was later changed into "Song of Myself":

> The smoke of my own breath,
> Echoes, ripples, buzzed whispers, love-root, silk-thread, crotch and vine,
> My respiration and inspiration, . . .
> The sound of the belched words of my voice, words loosed to the eddies of the wind,
> A few light kisses, a few embraces, a reaching around of arms (24)

In this version, the departing breath not only carries and disseminates the speaker's words, "loosing" them to the wind—it also caresses. In the later passage, the invisible lover mingling with the bathers is initially given a concrete body and identified as a woman who is longingly watching the men swimming. As in Ginsberg's poem, her body is anonymized and deindividualized in the moment bodies start to touch: "An unseen hand . . . passed over" the bathers' "bodies" and "descended tremblingly from their temples and ribs" (36). Here, the invisible, breathed "kisses" and "embraces" from the poem's beginning enter the scene. Recalling the earlier passage, loving touches can detach from a body and become autonomous, their respiratory nature accounting for their invisibility. When the "lady['s]" (35) body becomes pneumatic, it is also infused with the breath of the first-person speaker in the beginning. This "I," who famously "celebrate[s] myself" in the first line (23), can very quickly no longer be smoothly identified with the eponymous "Walt Whitman": within a few lines, the poem disperses with the smoke of breath into a multiplicity of organic and inorganic matter and immaterial phenomena: "Echoes, ripples, buzzed whispers, love-root, silk-thread, crotch and vine." "Speaking" the poem, the I is also a neutral, anonymous textual voice, whom the bathers encounter in the caress as a *shifter* on amorous sideways, straying from its linguistic domain. While the "lady," "Walt Whitman," and "I" are still present in the pneumatic touch, their individual identities, along with their gendering, dissolve and become unidentifiable: the bathers "do not ask who / seizes fast to them, / They do not know who puffs and declines with pendant and bending arch" (36). Why, we might ask, does this not disturb the scene? One answer lies in the last lines of the 1960 edition of *Leaves of Grass*: "Delicious—enough" (455).

The passage preceding this line stages a *respiration à travers le livre* saturated with touches recalling the "caresse" Beckett abandons in favor of breath in his manuscript of *Malone Meurt*. The erotic moments of the respirational scene at the start of *Leaves of Grass* and the bathers passage become an imagined scene of literary reception that I have already cited twice: in connection with Musil's sensual breaths and Celan's explicit reference in his notes for the *Meridian* speech. These passages in *Leaves of Grass* offer an intertextual context that allows us to get a more precise idea of the encounter this passage sketches. Revisiting the passage adds a further trait to the tentative model of respirational literary reception presented in the first chapter: literary *trans*actual touches across time can be queer gestures. Almost at the very end of the 1860 version of *Leaves of Grass* we read:

> My songs cease—I abandon them,
> From behind the screen where I hid I advance personally solely
>   to you.
> This is no book,

> Who touches this, touches a man,
> (Is it night? Are we here alone?)
> It is I you hold, and who holds you,
> I spring from the pages into your arms—decease calls me forth.
> O how your fingers drowse me!
> Your breath falls around me like dew—your pulse lulls the tympans of my ears,
> I feel immerged from head to foot,
> Delicious—enough (455)

This recalls the scene of the bathers and the "few light kisses, . . . few embraces, . . . reaching around of arms" of the departing breath in "Song of Myself." The "I" is present and absent at the same time—"no longer visible" (455)—as it claims, like the pneumatic caresses anticipating the "invisible hand" that descends on the bodies in the water. The speaker introduces the passage as a "farewell"—in later editions, "So Long" is the last poem in a section titled "Songs of Parting." Parting is indeed an essential part of the encounter depicted: the "songs," the very songs it claims to sing in the poem, have been "abandon[ed]" by an "I" that, in contrast to what we might first assume, does not leave behind its literary existence in favor of full bodily presence: the "man" held in the arms of the addressee (I, you, anyone reading the lines) is "call[ed] forth" by "decease," already gone, like the song sung and the book that for an instant ceases to be a book. With the abandonment of the song, self-reflexively alluding to the "song of myself," the self as such dwindles. "I advance personally solely to you" does not prefigure a meeting between two individuals but a singular experience of shared separation, a union in parting—that is, a syncope: the I loses everything that defines it as a literary I: "spring[ing] from the pages," it leaves behind the status of either fictional persona or letter, and the "decease" calling it forth cuts the reference to and possible identification with the organic body of an author-speaker. As in the bathing scene and in Ginsberg's poem, the bodies immersed in surges of arousal, lulled out of consciousness, become indeterminate. The "withdrawal . . . of . . . traces and traits of identity" (Ricco 116) opens to a confluence of ecstatic bodies—caressed bodies that are 'écrasé', exscribed, exposed. Whitman's text performs what Lisa Robertson describes as the erotics of reading: a "passive poetics of reception" (61), "an affective convention for the shadowed interchange among strangers" (13), a "replete nilling" (61). In the 1860 edition, the bodies' syncopnea, a unifying partition, a dispersion coinciding with immersion, is typographically marked by dashes:[18] "My songs cease—I abandon them"; "I spring from the pages into your arms—decease calls me forth"; "Your breath falls around me like dew—your pulse lulls the tympans of my ears." In these moments, the dash literally "queers," it *cuts across and breathes through*, "simultaneously retrospective and prospective" (Comay and Ruda 55),[19] as "a *line* of force lodged within a desiring body, yet ontologically independent of that body's gendered and sexual identity" (Bersani 70; emphasis added), at the same joining and separating an I that no longer sings itself, and a you that could be anyone.[20] "Delicious—enough."

Notwithstanding the stress on departing and "farewell," the erotic reading scene in Whitman's "So Long" is also an emphatic gesture of living on, continuing to be, persisting in time. The mode of ongoingness it sketches is neither subsumable to the idea of readers breathing new life into a poem nor does it function according to the model of biological reproduction. Whitman's passage, a paradigmatic imagining of how literary reception and literature's persistence throughout time *could* work pneumatically, is as far from a notion of survival as it is from heterosexual procreation. It gestures toward queer negativity as Lee Edelman theorizes it: refusing "every substantialization of identity" and all forms of "affirmation," "the queer comes to figure the bar to every *realization* of futurity" (*No Future* 4; emphasis added) and "induces a peculiar and disturbing relation to survival" ("Against Survival" 149).[21] I choose this moment to add a few *prospective* comments, not as an attempt to counter Edelman's argument, but, on the contrary, to continue thinking along its lines in terms of literary *trans*actuality. His provocative title *No Future* is itself a gesture of "queer resistance" to the "reproductive futurism" dominating the political sphere, manifested in the figure of "the Child" (*No Future* 2). Literature can neither affirm its future reception, nor produce children. At the same time, it keeps being concerned about its potential to last. It is precisely at this point that imaginations of literary durability in respiratory terms become especially relevant. As a "*pulsive* force" that cannot be translated "into some determinate stance or 'position'" or immured "in some stable and positive *form*" (4; emphasis added), literary breath shares defining traits with "queer negativity." In literature, breathing performs a nonfertile "ongoing" that does not aim at the realization of a specific design for life or survival. The tenuous breathroutes potentially opened by a text cannot be cast into a solid form. This is true for the most straightforward kind of respiratory reception, namely, reading literary texts out loud: the words modulated by breath dissolve into thin air before they can assume a stable form.

My analysis of Ginsberg's audio recordings shows that even if oral performances are documented on media that render them more durable, breath slips away from being captured both materially and conceptually. Given that breath is not conflated with the soul or life-giving pneuma, respiratory reception no longer lends itself to fantasies of immortality and does not promise a continuation of organic life. The authors discussed in this book all, in one way or another, outline a potential literary-respiratory futurity: through models of reception sketched in poetic comments (Celan's pneumatic touchability; Ginsberg's both powerful and weak inspiration; Olson's projective verse) or implicitly evoked in their texts (Müller's haunting, animated camp words; invitations to read out loud through an emphasis on sound, especially in Musil, Woolf and Plath), and through the texts' presentation of a lasting temporality or ongoingness that at the same time refers to themselves as texts (Woolf's and Musil's generative breathing pauses that, in their fleetingness, keep invoking the texts they appear in; Kerouac's self-deconstructing smoke-fueled fantasies of literary success; Plath's stillborn poem-children coinciding with "machine[s] that breathe . . . forever"; Beckett's speakers who can't stop talking and pant on). The works thus anticipate a form of respirational futurity that interrupts the dominant heteronormative appeal of securing the future through biological procreation. By staging scenarios of going on differently, *breathing on* beyond organic life, literary texts like the ones which formed the subject of this book imply a notion of "giving life"—*animation*—which does not coincide with giving birth. Such queer impulses encountered in canonical literature written by authors who (with the exception of Ginsberg) neither identify as queer nor primarily focus on LGBTQ topics can be traced back to the most foundational Western text promoting "spiritualization through marriage to reproductive futurism" (*No Future* 27).[22]

Here at the end, let me turn to the first breath in Genesis and revisit the arche-scene that so heavily contributed to the persistent identification of breath and life in Western culture: "And the Lord God formed man *of* the dust of the ground, and breathed into his nostrils the breath of life; and man became a living soul" (*The Bible* 2). Crucially, this animation takes place *before* and as a *prerequisite for* human procreation, namely, initiating life by heterosexual coupling and reproduction through children. It also takes place before the human so created is embedded in a gender *binary*: the creature formed is clearly gendered, identified as a man, but as the opposite sex does not exist yet, the differential term and body against which "maleness" could be defined is lacking. Now for the animation scene: it is striking how nonfiguratively, how literally and physically, the act of imparting the breath of life is described—a description that, as we have seen, subsequently led to the historically most dominant respirational metonymy. Imagine the scene: mouth on nose, "bodies locked" (Ginsberg, "Love Poem on Theme by Whitman"), breath flowing from one into the other. The way in which sexual acts and organs are evoked is anything but subtle: contact of orifices, exchange of fluids between bodies. As a site of sexual-erotic allusions, this animation scene is hybrid and promiscuous; attributes associated with specific gendered body parts and interactions begin to fluctuate. The nose is not an organ that marks sexual difference; at the same time, by combining phallic shape and vaginal opening, it unites major traits of those two that fundamentally give shape to and define it. Breathing—an act that, like the nose, is shared by both sexes (and bodies that do not conform to either)—oscillates between and moves across various sexuations: masculine insemination in a heterosexual act, and homoerotic touches, either of two vaginal orifices or two phallic extensions. Both bodies involved are gendered male but at the moment they erotically cut across each other, neither is human: the respirational intercourse takes place between a god and an amalgam of shaped inanimate material. In the Bible, this queer *pre*-creation leads the way to *pro*-creation. But perhaps this foundational scene has wandered off into a literary afterlife that—as evidenced in the texts discussed in *Poetics of Breathing*—does not exhaust itself in the metonymy of life-giving breath, but instead resurfaces in movements of syncopnea and gestures of queering that dash toward an indeterminate future and that may best find expression when lacerated by punctuation: im/potentiality—no? future?

Notes

Notes to the Preface

1. The history of the song's vibrant reception is reconstructed in Allan Light's book *The Holy or the Broken. Leonard Cohen, Jeff Buckley & the Unlikely Ascent of "Hallelujah."*

2. A discussion of this guitar intro, which deserves to be considered in its own right, can be found in Light's book (65).

3. The recording of this inadvertent sound may have been accidental, but the decision not to cut it in the editing process was deliberate. The recordings underwent a thorough editing process: "Buckley returned to the song again and again in the studio; by some accounts, he recorded more than twenty takes of 'Hallelujah' over the course of the sessions. . . . The final recording is actually a composite created from multiple takes" (Light 64).

4. Buckley's cover is based on that of John Cale, who did not stick to the lyrics of the version Cohen recorded for *Various Positions*, but rather chose and compiled passages from the excessive textual variants and sketched stanzas (in the four or five years Cohen worked on the song, he supposedly wrote eighty stanzas [Light 3]) to highlight this ambivalence to the extreme. Cale had all the textual material Cohen produced at his disposal before recording his version of Hallelujah: "In different tellings, Cale has said that Cohen faxed him fifteen verses or, truer to the author's account of the song's initial length, fifteen pages full of verses" (45).

5. All lyrics from Hallelujah reproduced here are cited from Jeff Buckley's album *Grace*.

6. Steve Berkowitz, the executive producer who attended the recording of *Grace*, explains the exhalation in the context of the recording sessions: he "noted that the breath came from Buckley's exhaustion after playing for several hours, not because he was just sitting down and starting cold" (Berkowitz qtd. in Light 65). The comment that we hear an exhausted exhalation is an ideal starting point for my reading. In contrast to Berkowitz's witness account, my position, my specula-

tions, and my argument are based on what I hear now, more than twenty years after *Grace* was recorded.

7. It does not seem at random that Rufus Wainwright refers to "Hallelujah," which he also famously covered, when mentioning that artists and performers have to stand back behind their own songs, which "have their own life," and finally to detach from them (Light xxix). The thought of self-abandonment is already present in the song itself: "Leonard Cohen said that the song represented absolute surrender in a situation you cannot fix or dominate" (Light xxv).

8. In the case of "Hallelujah," dispossession is real. As Alan Light puts it: "Many latter-day 'Hallelujah' fans, though, actually have no idea that it's a Leonard Cohen song; they assume that it was written by Jeff Buckley" (xxiii). In Glen Hansard's words: "Leonard penned it, but Jeff owned it" (Hansard qtd. in Light 67).

9. "And she broke your throne and she cut your hair / And from your lips she drew the Hallelujah"; "But all I've ever learned from love / Was how to shoot somebody who outdrew ya."

10. The history of "Hallelujah" as Cohen tells it is a history of failure—continual failure that produces an excess of words: "I've got the melody, and it's a guitar tune . . . and I have tried year after year to find the right words. . . . The song bothers me so much that I've actually started a journal chronicling my failures to address this obsessive concern with this melody" (Cohen qtd. in Light 4).

11. See Light: "To complicate things [the hesitant reception of the song upon its release] even further, Cohen began changing and reworking the song in concert" (xx–xxi).

12. The version appearing on *Cohen Live* is a second recording of "Hallelujah" from 1988. According to Light, the song "had been transformed almost completely" (38).

13. Both Jeff Buckley and Rufus Wainwright mention that to them, Hallelujah has an existential dimension, that it embodies life: "It's a hymn to being alive. . . . It's a hymn to love lost. Even the pain of existence, which ties you to being human, should receive an amen—or a hallelujah" (Buckley qtd. in Light 66–67); "it's this unifying expression of human existence, in a weird way—hallelujah—it's just life, in a sense" (Wainwright qtd. in Light xxx).

Notes to Chapter 1

1. See the chapter "New Criticism and the Concept of Organic Form" in Donald Wesling's *The Chances of Rhyme: Device and Modernity*.

2. See Jonathan Culler, "The Closeness of Close Reading," 22–23.

3. A compelling depiction of the semantic implications of syncope can be found in Catherine Clément's book *Syncope: The Philosophy of Rupture*, 4–7. Clément ultimately stresses the bodily and visceral implications of syncope, the "mother of

dissonance" (5), which "deprives the body of its obedience to the mind" (7), and its importance for the sensory dimension of art.

4. Another passage where Nancy associates syncope with the heart is the following: "This is the syncope of identity in singularity. A syncope: the step marked, in a suspense, from the other to me, neither confusion nor fading, clarity itself, the beating of the heart, the cadence and the cut of another heart within it" ("Shattered Love" 106).

5. The Greek terms *pneuma/pnoé* and *psyché*, as well as the Latin terms *anima* and *spiritus* mean "wind," "breath," "mind," "spirit," and "soul" at the same time. Similarly, the Hebrew word *ruach* means wind, spirit, and breath. The tension between the corporeal and the spiritual have shaped a semantics of breathing that has been defining for artistic articulations throughout the centuries up to now.

6. For example, by Steven Connor, Ashon Crawley, Christina Sharpe, Fred Moten, Lenart Škof, Petri Berndtson, Franco "Bifo" Berardi, Magdalena Górska, Davina Quinlivian, Jean-Thomas Tremblay, and the research team of *Life of Breath*, an interdisciplinary research project at Durham University and the University of Bristol. In the course of writing this book, I increasingly found myself in a research community that, despite very heterogeneous approaches, backgrounds, and foci, shares a new interest in breath in the humanities. For an overview of current research on breath in the humanities, see Arthur Rose's introduction to the edited volume *Reading Breath in Literature*.

7. Deleuze discovers such agrammatical, asyntactical, and inarticulate moments in the writing of Herman Melville (especially Bartleby's "formula," "I would prefer not to"), Louis Wolfson, Antonin Artaud, and Gherasim Luca, referring to them as "breaths or pure intensities that mark a limit of language" (112). For more references to breath in this context see pp. 16, 68, 69, and 71.

8. David Lloyd beautifully sums up the panoply of respiratory liminality in "Breath Crystals: A Vestigial Poetics of Breath in Beckett, Celan, and Arikha": "The rhythm of breathing . . . oscillates between the animate and the inanimate, in-spiration and ex-piration, marking the ambiguous borderline between spirit and body in a physical motion that signifies animation, the possession of spirit, and animality, the corporeality of the mere mortal creature. Breathing does not demarcate the difference between the animal and human endowed with soul or spirit, pneuma or anima, but embodies the indeterminate threshold between them, the zone of indistinction between human and animal, spirit and mere body, mere life" (188). All of these sites will be attended to in the course of the book.

9. Kirk, Raven, and Schofield mention "that Anaximenes' is the first extant use of the word πνεῦμα, which became common (for breath and for gust of wind) with the tragedians" (160). This cannot be verified, as the quote ascribed to Anaximenes was transmitted and written down much later; some scholars even assume that the word *pneuma* was not used by Anaximenes at all but has been put in his mouth retrospectively.

10. See, for example, Kirk, Raven, and Schofield 159.

11. Some scholars suspect that πνεῦμα might have been a word not used by Anaximenes himself, but ended up in the text due to a projection of Stoic ideas to Anaximenes: "πνεῦμα, . . . comes under suspicion of having a Stoic flavour" (Guthrie 131).

12. See, for example, Kirk, Raven, and Schofield 160.

13. Depending on the work that is consulted, *pneuma* is translated either only as "breath" (McKirahan 54; Wright 109; Barnes 55; Wöhrle 15; Guthrie 131), only as "wind" (Nahm 43), or as both (Kirk, Raven, and Schofield 158). Limiting oneself to one of the meanings alone would change possible interpretations considerably. Silvia Benso's intriguing reading of the passage in "The Breathing of Air: Presocratic Echoes in Levinas" is overshadowed by the fact that she only considers the meaning of breath (13–16).

14. Kirk, Raven, and Schofield claim that "one suspects that πνεῦμα, not ἀήρ, originally stood in the first clause" (162). Even though they do not give a reason for this assumption, the biological proximity of breath and the human body or the proximity between the soul and pneuma in the spiritual sense, which was especially highlighted in the Christian tradition, may have been the deciding factor for that claim.

15. The first records of the word *pneuma* appear in the fifth century. In the writings of the tragedians and historians, the meaning of "wind" predominates, but it is occasionally used in the sense of "breath" and very rarely in the sense of "spirit." I want to thank Ben Akrigg from the Department of Classics at the University of Toronto for his most generous and kind help with reconstructing the early uses of *pneuma*.

16. We can only speculate whether the double meaning of *pneuma* may have contributed to this idea or vice versa.

17. Zeno's position as reproduced by Edward Vernon Arnold is one of these rare examples: "'Soul is breath,' he taught, and 'soul is body'" (Arnold 69).

18. See Chrysippus: "We breathe and live by one and the same thing. We breathe by the natural pneuma (naturalis spiritus); therefore we live by the same pneuma. Moreover, we live by the soul. Therefore, the natural pneuma is the soul" (qtd. in Hahm 792). It is important to note that "the word for breath has been corrupted in the MS [manuscript]" (Hahm 163).

19. It is striking that the very conception of an immaterial life-principle or soul is unsettled by the very palpable description of God physically breathing life into man's nostrils in order to animate him.

20. See, for example, the 1981 US Uniform Determination of Death Act (UDDA).

21. This has already been negotiated by some thinkers of the past, as Piperno notes: respiration is considered a passive process by Plato (127) and Cicero (169);

Galen describes breathing as a mechanic phenomenon (194).

22. This would in fact go hand in hand with vibrant matter: when Bennett outlines how these assemblages work, she stresses that their agency is not inherently linked to will or intentionality (28–29). However, the insistence on describing the assemblages' self-organizing tendencies as "agency" implies a disregard for a possible value of passivity as such.

23. In chemical theories of the eighteenth century, the parallel between breathing and combustion was described through analogies of breathing and fire. In this context, Antoine Lavoisier and Armand Séguin describe respiration in terms of consumption rather than vitalization: "respiration is but a slow combustion of carbon and of hydrogen, similar in all points to that taking place in a lamp or a burning candle, and that, from this point of view, animals which breathe are really combustible bodies which burn and are consumed" (Lavoisier and Séguin 35; translation qtd. in Dejours, *Respiration* 5).

24. Bennett embraces the tendency to consider movement as a core criterion, if not a definition, of life. The motility of breath, which, like the soul in Spyros Papapetros's words "is always migrating, moving, shifting" (17), might have been an additional crucial reason why it has continually been identified with the life force.

25. For example: "his perception that air is the cosmic equivalent of the life-soul in man goes far beyond that attitude; it must, in fact, have been an important motif for his choice of air as the originative substance" (Kirk, Raven, and Schofield 161); "In making air his selection, an air in perpetual motion, Anaximenes also was respecting an age-old and still flourishing popular belief which associated, and in fact identified, breath and life" (Guthrie 123).

26. Wöhrle gives an overview of the debate on whether Anaximenes considered air the basis of the mutable things, or what the mutable things actually are (*Anaximenes aus Milet* 20). The emphasis on the perpetual movement of air and the presentation of the things air constitutes as its own different aggregate states invites to suggest "both at the same time."

27. The use of the term *pneuma* by the Stoics themselves is not entirely clear. As Michael J. White observes, "the relation between pneuma and the "creative fire" remains obscure. It may be that, as Lapidge has suggested, the former actually replaced the latter as an account of the active principle or aspect" (273). In a footnote to the passage he adds that Michael Lapidge argues that the term *pneuma* was only introduced by Chrysippus and abandoned some distinctions ("between archê and stoicheion, and . . . between pur technikon and pur atechnon") suggested by earlier Stoic texts (White 273).

28. The air or breath-related primary substances introduced by ancient philosophers tend to be very heterogeneous. Like Anaximenes, Diogenes of Apollonia chose air as the originary substance and suggests "it is a multiform—hotter and colder, drier and wetter, more stable and possessing a sharper movement, and unlimitedly many

other alterations are in it, both of flavor and of color" (Simplicius, *Commentary on Aristotle's Physics* 151.28–153.17; qtd. in McKirahan 345). In all these cases, there is a tension between the insistence on one singular primary substance and the claim that this substance is, contains, or becomes other ones.

29. I refer to the chapter "The Song of the Winds" in Kleinberg-Levin's *Before the Voice of Reason: Echoes of Responsibility in Merleau-Ponty's Ecology and Levinas's Ethics*.

30. For example, "The egressive pulmonic airstream is the basis of speech in all languages" (Dellwo, Huckvale, and Ashby 12).

31. "So if, for Derrida, the essence of the voice lies in auto-affection and self-transparency, as opposed to the trace, the rest, the alterity, and so on, for Lacan this is where the problem starts" (42).

32. This is also observed by Irigaray in *The Forgetting of Air in Martin Heidegger*. Irigaray ascribes the experience of a separation tied to the first breath to a male perspective (77), the perspective that is oblivious of the female generative principle and of air as a generative substance. In contrast, and from another perspective, the assumption that "a living body . . . draws its life from fluid matter" (83) leads Irigaray to the following claim: "No gap, breach, spacing, or distancing is possible between the living organism and the blood that has always already nourished it, including with oxygen. Nor is there any more of a gap between it and the ambient air it continually breathes once born. . . . No interval, no interstice, between it and that from which it derives its most originary form of subsistence. Were there in these circumstances any such distance, any void, the living organism would die" (84).

33. It is interesting to observe how theorists of the voice fundamentally differ in how they conceive of the soul's relation to breath. Whereas Aristotle opposes the soul and breath, Roland Barthes puts them in close proximity. In contrast to Aristotle, who mentions breath in the context of the material dimension of speech production, Barthes sets breath against the "grain" of the voice, its materiality. When commenting on Dietrich Fischer-Dieskau's singing, Barthes claims that it is the soul that accompanies his song, not the body: "all the more so since the whole of musical pedagogy teaches not the culture of the 'grain' of the voice but the emotive modes of its delivery; the myth of respiration. How many singing teachers have we not heard prophesying that the art of vocal music rested entirely on the mastery, the correct discipline of breathing! The breath is the pneuma, the soul swelling or breaking, and any exclusive art of breathing is likely to be a secretly mystical art. . . . The lung, a stupid organ (lights for cats!), swells but gets no erection; it is in the throat, place where the phonic metal hardens and is segmented, in the mask that significance explodes, bringing not the soul but jouissance" ("The Grain of the Voice" 506).

34. In a letter to Henricus Reneri from 1638, Descartes plays with his famous formula, "I am thinking, therefore I exist," varying it to "I am breathing, therefore I exist," which, as he claims, "proves nothing" (*The Philosophical Writings of Descartes*

3: 98). It proves nothing because existence as such would have to been proven first. Derrida famously discusses this passage in "Violence and Metaphysics" and later in "The Animal That Therefore I Am."

35. Lisa Robertson's conception of rhythm strongly resonates with Clément's in this respect—even though the context is a different one, namely, the recording of city "noise" for a sound project, her reflections are most suitable for describing breathing rhythms: "Enjambment is the counter-semiotic pause within the rhythmic gesture." "This arrhythmia, this enjambment, is what one is—discordant temporality." "It knows that the temporal unit is sprung on the refusal of the regularization of time, which must remain situated in the body, as the body's specificity, its revolt" (61).

36. In *The Ethnography of Rhythm: Orality and Its Technologies*, Saussy argues that "oral tradition is not the antithesis of writing, but a particular kind of writing, an inscription on other human minds." The fact that texts were transmitted and repeated runs counter to the assumption that speech is transient—it involves some kind of inscription that makes it last. What distinguishes oral traditions from "written" ones are different techniques and mediality and material carriers, namely, the human body, ears, mouth, and eyes versus wax, parchment, papyrus, and so forth. Rhythm is considered as one of the most prominent techniques of memory inscription (157).

37. Sanchiño Martínez and Schlesier, for example, ask: "Is using the concept of inspiration connected to a subversive objective of undermining the idea of autonomy and subjectivity?" (44; my translation).

38. There are a number of philological and linguistic speculations about a possible (but questionable) etymological connection between the words "breathing" and "being." Derrida discusses these theories with respect to Ernest Renan (*De l'origine du langage*) and Friedrich Nietzsche (*Die Philosophie im tragischen Zeitalter der Griechen*) in "Violence and Metaphysics" as well as in the early lectures from 1964, which are collected in *Heidegger: The Question of Being & History*: "Renan and Nietzsche, for example, refer to respiration as the etymological origin of the word Being" ("Violence and Metaphysics" 173). A further influential example, not discussed by Derrida, is Ernest Fenollosa ("The Chinese Written Character as a Medium for Poetry"), who also asserts that "being" is etymologically rooted in "breathing"; the hypothesis thus persistently exceeds different languages and linguistic communities. Renan is concerned with the French verb *être*, Fenollosa with the English verb *to be*, and Nietzsche with the Latin verb *esse*. All arguments are based on Indo-European roots, which points to a fundamental paradox: the roots, and thus the proposed origin of the verbs signifying "being," go back to a reconstructed language.

39. The observation that similar clusters of terms meaning life, breath, wind, spirit, and so forth exist in various languages (including Sanskrit, Hebrew, Arabic, Chinese, Greek, and Latin) has been considered in numerous ways by scholars across various disciplines. An example is Jan Söffner's small book *Metaphern und*

Morphomata.

40. As Geoffrey Bennington, the translator of Derrida's *Heidegger: The Question of Being & History*, provides English translations of passages from Renan's *De l'origine du langage*, I quote the sentence from there.

41. Originally from "Espace contre temps," in *Le poids d'un pensée, l'approche.*

42. In *Being Singular Plural*, breath is not addressed; the passages I quote in the following paragraph are unrelated to breathing in Nancy's book.

43. A research group at the university ETH Zürich recently confirmed that "each individual bears a unique breathprint" by measuring biochemical information of breath (Martinez-Lozano Sinues, Kohler, and Zenobi 4). With respect to tidal volume, respiratory frequency and airflow shape, Dejours et al. had already proposed a "personalité ventilatoire" in 1961 ("Étude de la diversité des régimes ventilatoires chez l'homme," abstract). A study from 1989 came to the further conclusion that "the individuality of breathing pattern is maintained over a long period despite changes in smoking habit, weight, mild respiratory diseases, and other changes" (Benchetrit et al. 199).

44. See Ricco, *The Decision between Us*, chapter 6.

45. See Heine and Zanetti, eds., *Transaktualität: Ästhetische Dauerhaftigkeit und Flüchtigkeit.*

46. In a similar context, breath also occurs in Sonnet 18: "When in eternal lines to time thou grow'st. / So long as men can breathe or eyes can see, / So long lives this and this gives life to thee" (*The Norton Shakespeare* 1929).

47. In the lines "When you entombèd in men's eyes shall lie" and "Which eyes not yet created shall o'er-read," the sonnet's formal regularity can be maintained, but not without a certain degree of manipulation: if we pronounce the usually nonsyllabic ending of "entombèd," the meter is regular, and only the syncopated "o'er-read" accounts for the ten syllables required for the iambic meter.

48. This movement between a "memorial" and a "biological" mode of "existence" in the "argumentative structure" of the sonnet has been traced by Helen Vendler in *The Art of Shakespeare's Sonnets* (361–62).

49. For a discussion of the complexities involved in lyric "you" addresses, see, for example, Waters 7–15.

50. Even though contemporary literature is not the primary focus—a majority of the works I discuss were written in the 1950s and 1960s—the analysis of Herta Müller's breath-writing shows that the respiratory poetics I am interested in continue to be pursued.

51. When attending to the interplay between prosodic and semantic factors at work in the texts, one notices that the selected works in which breath is negotiated themselves exhibit respirational qualities: a tendency to stress either pause or movement, silence or sound. As all texts are, in one way or another, concerned with the tension between these pairs, all qualities figure into each one; there are, however, clearly discernible emphases that I want to sketch out.

Notes to Chapter 2

1. See, for example, Eric Mortenson's contribution to the *Cambridge Companion to the Beats* 87.
2. As a majority of Kerouac's, Ginsberg's, and Olson's unpublished archival material (notes, drafts, essays, lectures, audiotapes, etc.) is not paginated, I cite it by title only throughout this chapter.
3. Even though Olson has often been read in terms of orality, one should use some caution when doing so. As Raphael Allison notes in his book *Bodies on the Line: Performance and the Sixties Poetry Reading*, "competing with Olson's emphasis on the breath, graphic text itself was to him of equal value" (68).
4. For a very nuanced overview and discussion of the "new oral impulse" in the 1950s and 1960s in America, see Michael Davidson's chapter, "Technologies of Presence: Orality and the Tapevoice of Contemporary Poetics" in *Ghostlier Demarcations*.
5. For a discussion of a couple of Ginsberg's readings, see pp. 1–7 of Allison's *Bodies on the Line: Performance and the Sixties Poetry Reading*.
6. For a discussion of Ginsberg's reflections of breath, poetry, and Buddhism, see Tony Trigilio's book *Allen Ginsberg's Buddhist Poetics*, especially pp. 131–39.
7. For an overview of the influence of Buddhism and jazz on the Beat movement, see the following two contributions to the *Cambridge Companion to the Beats*: John Whalen-Bridge, "Buddhism and the Beats," and Michael Hrebeniak, "Jazz and the Beat Generation."
8. Fred Moten calls Ginsberg's jazz-references a "fetishistic attempt" at the "sociopoetics of the howl," the "jazz howl of the misfortunate negro that will have been upheld by whites" and that can be interpreted "as an expression of inert authenticity" (191).
9. Given that, to my knowledge, there is no recorded evidence that they read the rhetoricians, it is impossible to tell whether Kerouac and Ginsberg based their ideas on a direct reception of ancient rhetoric or were familiar with their ideas only through secondary sources.
10. Regarding the empirical perspective on this matter, a study conducted at Northeastern University by François Grosjean and Maryann Collins from 1979 approaching the question, "What is the relationship between linguistic structure and breathing?" (100) concludes that breath-pauses "occur mainly at major constituent breaks" (110). "The need to breathe (at least at slow and normal rates) is not in control of pausing but . . . on the contrary, breathing adjusts itself to pause patterns" (109). Only when the participants of the study were asked to speak very fast, their breath-pauses did not coincide with syntactic breaks: at faster rates "the physiological need to breathe forces the speaker to stop in order to inhale," disregarding syntactic units (112). This study is based on the speaking of healthy participants, who were

asked to read a text in which punctuation marks indicated where the syntactic units are. Its results cannot be transferred seamlessly to the scenario of oral composition the rhetoricians and Beat and Black Mountain writers have in mind. However, it is revealing that breath-pauses and syntactic units seem to co-occur smoothly, but only as long as the body is under control, and that the physiological need to inhale tends to interrupt the syntax once the circumstances of the bodily condition change.

11. Also in the passages on composition, there are uncertainties about the moment when a breath is required because a thought is completed at the moment when the orator should actually take a breath: "Who, for example can doubt that there is but one thought in the following passage and that it should be pronounced without a halt of breath? Still, the groups formed by the first two words, the next three, and then again by the next two and three, have each their own special rhythm and cause a slight check in our breathing" (IX, IV.68, 545).

12. The editor's comment on this passage shows that the rhetoricians' attempts to reconcile the completion of the period with the need to inhale leads to inconsistencies: "There is no real, though an apparent inconsistency: the periods must furnish opportunity for taking breath, but must not be determined solely by the need for this" (III, XLIV, 506).

13. Even though the examples Ginsberg uses as illustrations in numerous interviews, and line-breaks or sentence segmentations in Ginsberg's and Kerouac's literary texts give some indication of these units, a precise explication is still lacking.

14. Investigating the breath-stops in their oral deliveries, in contrast, is possible in the cases where recordings were made. In Ginsberg's recordings of "Howl," for example, one can observe that the moments when he inhales and pauses do not always coincide with the line breaks. Even though Ginsberg stresses that he imitates the compositional process in his readings (*Spontaneous Mind* 126), the readings as such do not constitute valid data for an investigation of the composition process. The only thing one might infer from Ginsberg's "Howl" readings is that the moments when he has to inhale before the line ends show how his breath may not be as long as he claims in the "Notes for Howl"—even though he himself addresses this fact and attributes it to his exhaustion at the moment when he was reading (416). Concerning the noncoincidence of line breaks and breaths in Ginsberg's readings, see also Patrick Dunn's discussion in " 'What If I Sang': The Intonation of Allen Ginsberg's Performances" (90).

15. This may explain Ginsberg's long lines in "Howl," which he cannot pronounce in one breath.

16. The use of the Latin term *respiro*, the verb used by Quintilian, already included the figurative meaning of breathing as resting: "to fetch one's breath again, to recover breath; to recover, revive, be relieved or refreshed after any thing difficult (as labor, care, etc.)" (*A Latin Dictionary* online).

17. In the *Oxford English Dictionary*, "to take breath" is defined as a figurative use of the "power of breathing, free or easy breathing": "to breathe freely, to recover free breathing, as by pausing after exertion" (*Oxford English Dictionary* online).

18. Kerouac himself spent considerable efforts to create and maintain that myth, which for him goes hand in hand with having found his own style and "voice," most prominently expressed in "Essentials." Significantly, "Essentials" constitute an instruction to imitate, circulate and popularize the style Kerouac discovered for himself.

19. It has long been noticed that this is not an accurate description of how *On the Road* came to be, and that Kerouac spent years taking notes and designing drafts for the novel. (See, for example, Brinkley xxv.)

20. Kerouac only highlights one direction and tempo suggested by the dash. As Rebecca Comay observes, the dash generally "forces an impossible double tempo in reading. You must simultaneously race ahead and hold back" (85).

21. Even though Ginsberg occasionally also refers to speed, for example by referring to the next line to be written or read as "next spurt" (*Spontaneous Mind* 125), this is never at the center of his reflections—he rather seems to be echoing Kerouac's ideas of "athletic speech" (114) in these instances.

22. These keywords are written on an undated scrap of paper on which Kerouac lists characteristics of prose as it should be (echoing "Essentials": "Time is of the essence so no conceivable addition can improve muscle of prose") as well as an assessment of his present writing: "Virility of 1951 intact" ("Various Notes, Fragments and Scraps").

23. "Draw your breath in pain" is an implicit citation from *Hamlet*. Kerouac was well aware of Hamlet's last words: he quotes "Absent thee from felicity awhile," the line preceding "And in this harsh world draw thy breath in pain," in a letter to Ginsberg written in 1947 (*Selected Letters 1940–1956* 122). Moreover, in a letter to Neal Cassady in 1950, Kerouac makes an explicit reference to Hamlet, precisely when he "discovers" the strenuousness of writing spontaneously in one's own voice: "My important recent discovery and revelation is that the voice is all. Can you tell me Shakespeare's voice per se?—Who speaks when Hamlet speaks? HAMLET, not Will Shakespeare. . . . You, man, must write exactly as everything rushes in your head, and AT ONCE. The pain of writing is just that" (233). It is important to note that these earliest thoughts on spontaneous prose, in which breath is not mentioned, are inspired by Hamlet's last sigh.

24. See Comay and Ruda 55–56.

25. It is no coincidence that in the Middle Ages pen strokes marking the final pause were called "virgulae," a slang term for "penis" (Houston 147).

26. For a more detailed analysis of how the "Essentials of Spontaneous Prose" themselves represent a deliberate attempt to create an effect of spontaneity that first had to be carefully prepared see my article "First Thought, Best Thought. Improvisation bei Jack Kerouac und Allen Ginsberg." A look at Kerouac's manuscripts and drafts shows that the methods and techniques he proposes in his writing manuals and comments have never been consequently applied in his actual writing processes. I investigated a large group of materials at the Berg Collection of English and American Literature, among them drafts for *The Subterraneans*, *On the Road*, and *Visions of Gerard*. A detailed discussion of these findings, however, exceeds

the scope of this book. Generally, it is worth noting that Kerouac made extensive use of "timid commas" and hardly used the dashes in a consequential manner (to replace commas, colons, or full stops); most of the time, one can find a mixture of dashes, commas and full stops. I want to give only one example that demonstrates how Kerouac retrospectively—and against his imperative "no revisions" ("Essentials of Spontaneous Prose" 57)—aligned his texts to his own writing instructions: in order to highlight that he replaces full stops by dashes, he consequently capitalizes lowercased words succeeding a dash in the setting copy of *Visions of Gerard*.

27. Tape technology, "replacing gramophones" was fairly new and Ginsberg made poetic use of "sound reproduction revolutionized by magnetic tape" (Kittler 108).

28. To give only one example: Kittler discusses how Ernst von Wildenbruch refers "to the phonograph as the soul's own true photograph" (83).

29. For an intriguing reading of this passage that both embraces and undermines the idea of a "pneumatological primacy of speech" see Rose, "Introduction: Reading Breath in Literature" 9.

30. "A short fragment of longer trans-American voyage poetries is therefore composed directly on tape by voice, and then transcribed to page: page arrangements notates the thought-stops, breath-stops, runs of inspiration, changes of mind, startings and stoppings of the car" ("Some Metamorphoses of Personal Prosody" 260); see also the comments on composition of "Wichita Vortex Sutra" in *Spontaneous Mind* 134–35.

31. "I have adapted, for myself, the single breath-unit as the measure of how much material I can handle-notate-compose at one continuous stroke. I learned much from Kerouac. / The rhythm of this transcription becomes in this case the guiding rhythm of the poem when read aloud" ("How *Kaddish* Happened" 256).

32. See the lecture "Basic Poetics #14": "And any really good poem, poet, will make use of punctuation for that purpose, to indicate breathing. It's not just there to be performing to the rules of grammar like you learned in High School, it's there for a purpose, it's there to mark the breaths. And we're in the hands of a great poet, it's there for marking breath. In the hands of a pettifogging academic poet who does not speak his poetry aloud it might have nothing to do with breath, it might have to do with conception, mental image, but not to do with breath."

33. For the present discussion I did not consider the typescript, as the slight variations are not relevant for pinpointing the changes across the poem's various articulations.

34. I want to thank Brian Nevin from Recording Arts Canada for helping me to identify the clicks on the tapes.

35. Here, inhalation and exhalation are clearly audible. Whenever I note "breath" in my transcriptions, it cannot be clearly recognized whether what one hears is an inhalation or exhalation.

36. In general, instances of audible breath on the tapes are rare. Background noises, from a car, for example, are generally too loud to make out inhalations or

exhalations. Even in quieter environments like a train or room, it is often impossible to hear the breaths.

37. Transcribing pauses is more problematic than transcribing clicks or breaths as they occur in significantly different lengths. What I marked as pauses here are clearly discernible longer silences, as opposed to little breaks in the flow of speech.

38. See Olson: "If a contemporary poet leaves a space as long as the phrase before it, he means that space to be held by the breath, and equal length of time" ("Projective Verse" 22).

39. The term "relative measure" was adopted from William Carlos William (Ginsberg, *Spontaneous Mind* 109).

40. This goes hand in hand with Ginsberg's advice to his students in a discussion: he encourages them to experiment and to structure the line "according to some apprehensible or logical measure" (*Spiritual Poetics II*; emphasis added) which is not defined in advance.

41. Not surprisingly, he speaks the poem much faster during the reading than he did while composing it: despite the time cut when he turned the tape off, on the original recording the passage is 30 seconds longer than on the recording of the reading. In contrast to "Howl," where one line tends to be too long to be pronounced on a single breath, the lines of "Iron Horse" are often quite short for a full exhalation.

42. As Nathaniel Mackey observes, "the breathing of the poet changes from occasion to occasion" (5).

43. That we lose track of the base word on the tape is, at least in part, due to the fact that we hear linearly, one speech sequence after another. In contrast, we see the written page, where "better" is visually emphasized as a whole.

44. In his article "Frank O'Hara Drives Charles Olson's Car," Duncan convincingly argues that "the machine, in its danger, provides access to the 'now' of expression. The machine becomes the poet's ability rather than the enforcement of an external constraint" (83). What Duncan claims about Olson's compositional technique with the typewriter also applies to Ginsberg's tape recording: "Olson's line management conceives the typewriter as providing for the writer's physical immediacy" (80). "The typewriter is meant to animate [his breath] on the page" (83). For a detailed discussion of Walt Whitman, Charles Olson and Frank O'Hara, see Duncan's doctoral dissertation, "The Song in the Machine: Organic Forms of American Poetry."

45. See also Shaw 44–47, 56–57.

46. That is, the argument presented both in the poem itself and its paratexts. In "Iron Horse," Ginsberg's standpoint is most explicitly stated in the following passage: "Why do I fear these lights? / & smoking chimneys' Industry? / Why see them less godly / than forest treetrunks / & sunset orange moons? / . . . Because these electric structures rear tin machines / that will kill Bolivian marchers / or flagellate Vietnam adolescents' thighs—/ Because my countrymen make this structure

to make War / Because this smoke over Toledo's advertised in the Toledo Blade / as energy burning to destroy China" (453).

47. Ginsberg makes a clear distinction between particular kinds of smoking: while he condemns cigarettes (which he smoked himself and considered a vice), smoking marijuana and opium are situated in the field of "natural" pleasures: in "Iron Horse," for instance, puffing "a peaceful O pipe" is a recommendation for anti–war machine preoccupations.

48. While deletions and condensations happen frequently, especially in what appears to be spontaneous descriptions of scenery, Ginsberg hardly ever rearranges the order of the lines in the course of his revisions.

49. One could read this early text as prophetic, but it is at least equally plausible that Kerouac deliberately reproduced these old ideas when promoting *On the Road* and *The Subterraneans* in order to let the juvenilia appear as self-fulfilling prophecies.

50. "The doors in the back of the stage should be open to let the sound of Time in on the customers" (67).

51. On a similar note, Kerouac stresses the act of exhaling while the organ through which the air is emitted is hardly mentioned (e.g., in "Essentials of Spontaneous Prose," the mouth is not referred to at all). Whereas Kerouac seems to embrace what Nancy calls an "origin without orifice" (". . . would have to be a novel . . ." 60), Ginsberg does not cease to stress the importance of the mouth throughout his work. The title of a series of lectures, "Mind, Mouth, and Page" and the definition "poetry is mouth consciousness" (*Naropa Workshop*) are only two examples.

52. The biopolitical implications of Kerouac's notion of virile free-flowing writing have already been discussed: the "natural" breath that is supposed to structure language is the breath of a healthy, athletic body. Reich's unrestricted energy is based on a strict differentiation of "natural" and "unnatural," that is, "perverse" drives. While Reich argues that perversions only emerge when the "natural" sexual drives are suppressed by rigid morals, the very distinction between "healthy" and "unhealthy" sexual practices is based on biased cultural notions of what is considered "normal" and "deviant."

53. Even though Kerouac's explanations of what exactly it is that Ginsberg and 99.9 percent of American poets get wrong about "breath and phrasing in jazz improvisation" remain vague, the major critique seems to be that Ginsberg, according to Kerouac, limits the theory of breath to "the glowing all-inclusive term prosody," which "applied to jazz would only apply to the measure of the metronomic beat" and "if applied to writing would only aply [*sic*] to the metrical aspect of versification." In contrast to such an alleged reduction of "breath-measuring" to metre, Kerouac stresses its importance for improvisation: the "effort to improvise the melody line" in jazz corresponds to "breath-separations of the expostulated speech line" in writing, that is, "phrases improvising the story line" in "a poem or a story." Thus, for Kerouac, breath-measure not only pertains to form but also to content.

54. The idea that breath is relevant for measuring free verse was expressed earlier. For example, Amy Lowell suggests translating the French term *vers libre* as "cadenced verse" and defines cadence as "a rhythmic curve, containing one or more stressed accents, and corresponding roughly to the necessity of breathing" (141) in her investigation of "Some Musical Analogies in Modern Poetry" from 1920.

55. The German poet Rainer Maria Gerhard joined that conversation in 1952 in the course of his attempt to introduce new avant-garde poetry from America to the German-speaking world. His formulations, written when he already knew Olson's "Projective Verse," recall what Martin Buber and Franz Rosenzweig in the late 1920s designate as structural "Atemeinheiten" (units of breath). Gerhard states that modern verse is "eine Sache des Atems, also des Sprechens, des Ohrs" 'a matter of breath, that is, of speaking, of the ear'—here the references to "Projective Verse" are obvious. Then, Buber and Rosenzweig's vocabulary enters the description: "In contrast to earlier times, the new unit is a unit of breath [Einheit des Atems]" (*Umkreisung* 122; my translation).

56. It is interesting that Ginsberg mentions the "mind-break" earlier than the "breath-stop." In 1954, he notes, "Lines measured according to conceptual content" and "Principles of thought-rhythm" (*Journals Mid-Fifties* 30).

57. Kerouac's "History of the Theory of Breath" is a very good example: "rhetorical breathings" as measure are part of a larger discussion that then dominates the essay in the end and breath in particular is no longer mentioned. Rather, Kerouac focuses on "the emancipation of spontaneous vernacular American English," "grammatical syntactical + socio-political prohibitions" versus "free expressions of the mind."

58. Such an emphasis on voice was repeatedly articulated. See for example a letter to Don Allen in 1957: "the crude glad (if-you-wish-Carlylean) personal quavering sound of my own voice which took me so long (15 years of writing) to find and tap and only after removing all that literary and grammatically-inhibited and unenlightened debris" (*Selected Letters* 15).

59. While the influence of Black music on the Beat Generation is obvious, the way in which the Beats theorized breath, especially in terms of "breath-unit = thought unit," is inconsistent with the jazz or blues rhythms that Ginsberg calls the "new breath" (*Spontaneous Mind* 146).

60. A very good example is a lecture Baraka gave on speech, rhythm, sound, and music at the Naropa Institute in the 1980s: even though the topic would invite to do so, he never mentions breath. Instead of breath, he continuously refers to the heart when he discusses rhythm and its rootedness in the human body: the heart, as "rhythm-keeper," is what keeps humans alive and connects the body to poetry and song ("Amiri Baraka Class on Speech, Rhythm, Sound, and Music").

61. This conflation ultimately allows Ginsberg to argue against an aesthetics of genius. Understood as breath, inspiration does not only occur to chosen ones, it is available for everyone: "The ideal idea of spirit—spiritual—actually relates to the

breath. And if you take the word "spirit" to relate to the physical breath, then you've got something you can work with, literally, without bullshit, without being a faggot aesthetician, you can actually just have real spirit, meaning breath. You don't have to worry about the validity of your discussion of inspiration. You can do it with ordinary mind. You can have inspiration with ordinary mind in the sense that there is such a thing as inspiration (or unobstructed breath, in this case, or breathing)" (*Expansive Poetics*). In a writing class, he contradicts Robert Duncan who tells the students that they are not taking a "magician's workshop"—"Inspiration. You can't learn that, nobody can teach it to you, you either feel it or you don't"—by claiming, "I think you can teach inspiration. . . . Taking it literally, inspiration being a matter of breath, you can teach breathing" (*Allen Verbatim* 109).

62. In a lecture titled "Mind, Mouth, and Page," Ginsberg presents his theory as an elucidation of "Projective Verse" (which is, in fact, a rather free interpretation of Olson's text): "if read aloud, the rhythmic breathing will turn you on and give you a buzz, because you're reproducing the poet's inspiration and exhalation. . . . Here, Olson is saying you can also get the poet's mind, the energy of the poet's mind."

63. The idea that breath might last over centuries has fascinated writers continually: Charles Olson evokes it in one of his earliest recorded references to breath in 1949, when he writes that "words contain the breath (which was the original meaning of *spiritus* (spirare: to breathe) of generations of men" (*Notes for a Lecture on Corrado Cagli*) and Sam Kean bases the title of his book *Caesar's Last Breath* on it: "our breaths entangle us with the historical past. Some molecules in your next breath might well be emissaries from 9/11 or the fall of the Berlin Wall. . . . And if we extend our imagination far enough in space and time, we can conjure up some fascinating scenarios. For instance, is it possible that your next breath—this one, right here—might include some of the same air that Julius Caesar exhaled when he died?" (1) Even though some molecules we inhale might have been around for a very long time and might have gone through another person's body via breath, the thought that we share the "same breath" with past generations is, as Olson's note suggests, more indebted to the etymology of breath than to its material constitution.

64. The text was published under various titles, but only in smaller journals: as "Power and Weakness in Poetry" in *Poetry Project Newsletter*, no. 80 (Feb. 22, 1981): 8–9; and in *Amanda Blue*, vol. 2, no. 1 (Sept.–Oct. 1981): 15–16; and as "Wherein Lies the Power of the Poet" in *Relations*, no. 1 (Oct. 1981): 38–39. I will quote from Ginsberg's unpaginated typescript based on the original transcription of the lecture in Belgrade that is held in the archive at Stanford University (*Power and Weakness of Poetry*).

65. At times, Ginsberg mixes phallic and vaginal imagery when talking about inspiration. "And the physical sensation of inspiration, of poetic inspiration, is that the spine is straight, and that the body feels like a hollow tube, or thinking reed . . . , a big hollow column of air" (*Naropa Workshop*). Consequently, the "hollow tube"

does not necessarily refer to a woman's body; it may also point to orifices that are not gender-specific, such as the mouth or anus.

66. Steps in that direction have been taken, for example by Mossin, Duncan, and Katz. By contrasting Olson and Jack Spicer, whose poetics he clearly favors, Katz specifically focuses on a "resistance to a certain reading of projective verse: one that anchors the poetic fact in breath, itself grounding both the integrity of the line and the singularity of the voice, and views proprioception as closeness to the primal given of the body as presence." The reservations he has about a poetics of breath and the danger of reverting to phonocentrism are plausible; however, when he suggests that the process of "breath implies cyclic completion and wholeness" (81), Katz reproduces a certain understanding of breath that has as little to do with Olson's poetics as it has with the physiological process of respiration.

67. At the Charles Olson Research Collection, these drafts are separated into two folders: the first draft, which Olson sent to Frances Boldereff and Robert Creeley, is titled "Projected Verse (Early Draft): Photocopy of Typescript, 1950" in the research aid, but as this title is clearly misspelled, I refer to it as "Projective Verse: Early Draft, February 1950." All other drafts are collected in a single folder titled "Projective Verse: Early Draft: Photocopy, February–July 1950"; I will reference individual drafts from that folder with the tag "Projective Verse: Early Drafts, February–July 1950."

68. On July 10, Olson claimed to have completed a final version, after a "five hr run on it" (205).

69. In a letter to Chad Walsh in 1967, Olson explicitly distinguishes his own writing practice from "Ginzy's latest, or later work (example, Wichita Vortex Sutra)" (*Selected Letters* 388), and, even though he generally thinks highly of Kerouac's writing, he calls the "Essentials of Spontaneous Prose" a "disease of the single horizontal line, non-interrupted spilling of the self" (qtd. in Maud 168).

70. Generally, breath is more predominant in the later drafts than in the first version, where it only occurs in the following instances: "where breath has its beginning"—a passage that originally stood in the beginning of the essay and was then moved to the very end; "breath has a double meaning which latin has not yet lost"; and in the context of typewriter-notations that should "indicate exactly the breath, the pauses"—with respect to the typewriter, all references to breath that can be found in the printed versions are already there in the first draft.

71. The dominance of the voice in the earlier versions could be related to a prominent source in in these versions that Olson then decided to cut out later: in the earliest draft of "Projective Verse," Olson quotes extensively from an entry on "music" in the *Encyclopædia Britannica*—the quotes he inserts to expand on the "lost secrets of the voice" focus on the structure of ancient Greek music, which "represents an organization of the *rise* and *fall of the voice* as elaborate and artistic as the organization of the verse"; "Thus the rhythm of classical Greek music seems to have been *entirely identical with that of verse*" ("Projective Verse: Early Draft").

What interests Olson about voice overlaps with what interests him about breath: that elements of oral speech lead to a rhythmical, musical structuring of language.

72. Across Olson's work, the status of the voice and orality remains contradictory. Olson is not always consistent in how he uses the terms. There is, however, a strong tendency to be hesitant about addressing orality in the sense of speaking out loud. In a polemic comment in a letter to Robin Blaser in 1957, Olson states: "I jump with yr identifying breath with texture. It gives me all I ever wanted to protest against stupid oral verse and voice!" (*Selected Letters* 243). Olson may have become aware that "voice," even designated as "silent," may immediately be linked to what he calls "stupid oral verse"—using breath instead did not help with regard to the reception of "Projective Verse," which is often considered as a manifesto for oral poetry. That Olson no longer referred to breath in his attempt to write a second part of the essay in the late 1950s may well be related to his awareness of such readings of "Projective Verse."

73. It can be assumed that this notion of breath in the notes written in 1954 coincides with what Olson has in mind when he mentions that the typewriter allows to "indicate exactly the breath, the pauses" ("Projective Verse" 22) in a poem's written notation.

74. In "Projective Verse," one sentence specifically invites reading Olson in line with Ginsberg's and Kerouac's suggestion to end a line or unit when one runs out of breath: "And the line comes (I swear it) from the breath, from the breathing of the man who writes, at the moment that he writes, and thus is, it is here that, the daily work, the WORK, gets in, for only he, the man who writes, can declare, at every moment, the line its metric and its ending—where its breathing, shall come to, termination" (19). However, claiming that the breath of the writer "declares" where the breathing of the line comes to termination does not necessarily mean that the end of a line coincides with the author's breath-stop.

75. The implication of silent voicing is much more obvious in the earliest draft: there, the typewriter is described as a "machine now available to the poet to record the inner voice exactly, and the steps which it shall be necessary to take in order that projective verse may be given PROJECTION" ("Projective Verse: Early Drafts").

76. Similar problems emerge when Olson mentions that the "manuscript," that is, print and writing, implies a "removal of verse from its producer and reproducer, the voice" and it is suggested that in print, verse is removed "from its place of origin and its destination," namely, breath (22). Whereas breath is identified with the place of "origin" and "destination" here, the famous line "the HEART, by way of the BREATH, to the LINE" (19) rather suggests that breath indicates a direction toward a destination, in this case a realized part of the poem, the line. In this respect, the tensions cannot be resolved: Olson certainly flirts with the idea of breath as a physiological origin of the poem; this, however, stands in contrast

with other claims about projective verse. I rather focus on the latter so as to offer an alternative to the more dominant reception of "Projective Verse."

77. Olson specifically stresses the importance of the relation between things when he discusses how the phonetic system of a specific language affects literary composition and claims that "any practicing American poet would [hail? hear?] Sapir when he says that it is even doubtful if the innate sonority of a phonetic system—in other words sound—counts for as much, as esthetic determinant, as the *relations between sounds*" ("Verse [notes]").

78. The sentence in Projective Verse II is: "there is no form until the poem creates its own"; there is no prior discourse in the "non-Euclidian world . . . no statement or rule—by which the poem rests" (17).

79. This includes the partly incorrect etymology of "is," "not," and "be," in a quote from Fenollosa's *The Chinese Written Character as a Medium for Poetry* ("Projective Verse" 18). For a discussion of these etymologies and Olson's poetics see my article "Fishy Etymologies."

80. This passage anticipates later poetic reflections that employ vocabulary and ideas of Alfred North Whitehead's *Process and Reality*. The comment on breath and atoms in "Mouths Biting Empty Air" echoes in "Projective Verse II" when it is claimed that "flow (rhythm is rhein, to flow) . . . is leaped atomism, quanta jumping like nerves in fatigue"; "The syllable (the particle—the letter) is wave and particle, at once, either, each" (*The Principle of Measure in Composition by Field: Projective Verse II*, 34).

81. For a discussion of breath and particularity in Olson's work see the chapter "Administering Poetic Breath for the People: Charles Olson and Amiri Baraka" in Lisa Siraganian's book *Modernism's Other Work*.

82. There is no proof that Olson already knew Sapir's book when he wrote "Projective Verse"—the first reference to it I could find in the archive is from 1955. However, Sapir's reflections go hand in hand with the assumption that the poet has to be obedient to the prosodic structure of language ("Projective Verse" 18). In an unpublished prose piece from 1955, Olson explicitly refers to Sapir's discussion of phonetic and rhythmic particularities of specific languages in order to expand on the observation that the "American language has a particular set of esthetic factors which it does not completely share with any other language" (Verse [notes]).

83. "Probably nothing better illustrates the formal dependence of literature on language than the prosodic aspect of poetry" (211). "To summarize, Latin and Greek verse depends on the principle of contrasting weights; English verse, on the principle of contrasting stresses; French verse, on the principles of number and echo; Chinese verse, on the principles of number, echo, and contrasting pitches" (246).

84. For example, the demand to obey "the whole (hate that fucking word) every particle by every other particle" during the writing process, a "precision work [*sic*] that requires forty hrs a day" (*Charles Olson and Frances Boldereff* 362).

85. This is one of the passages in which Olson's poetics of breath strongly resonates with Paul Celan's, which will be discussed in the fifth chapter. Even though Celan and Olson roughly at the same time both developed a poetics of breathing, they most probably did not engage with the other's writings. This was confirmed to me by Klaus Reichert, who was Celan's editor and Olson's translator into German. In an email, Reichert told me that he mentioned Olson to Celan and vice versa but neither showed much interest in the poetic "coconspirator" on the other side of the Atlantic. A selection of Celan and Olson's poems do meet on paper, in volume 4, no. 2 of the literary journal *Sulfur*.

86. The projective poem thus assimilates "life, that discontinuous bitch" (*Charles Olson and Frances Boldereff* 122). The *Encyclopædia Britannica*, which Olson calls "my source" in the earliest version of "Projective Verse," offers an interesting addition to this with respect to rhythm and the importance of pauses, which, as we have seen, Olson identifies with breath: "Pauses take an essential importance in the construction of modern rhythm, of the variety and vitality of which they are the basis. They are introduced for the purpose of relieving the monotony of successive equal groups of syllables" (277; emphasis added).

Notes to Chapter 3

1. "Stillstellen" literally means "putting to stillness."

2. I owe a lot to the three and a half pages Hart Nibbrig dedicates to "Breaths of a Summer's Day," and his reflections serve as a guide for mine.

3. On November 18, 1924, she makes a similar comment in her diary: "I believe it is getting the rhythm in writing that matters. Could I get my tomorrow mornings rhythm right—take the skip of my sentence at the right moment—I should reel it off" (*The Diary of Virginia Woolf* 2: 322).

4. In her comment on Woolf's reflection on rhythm in the letter to Vita Sackville-West, Emma Sutton observes that rhythm "is primary whilst words are secondary," it "precedes the act of 'writing'" and has a "generative . . . force" (177). This is precisely how I want to characterize the generative dimension of rhythm.

5. When it comes to details, the accuracy of Benveniste's observations are questionable. For my purposes, these details are not acutely relevant. With respect to the rhetoricians and Woolf's and Musil's texts, the rough notions of rhythm as flow and segmentation as Benveniste sketches them are sufficient to address the distinctions negotiated by the poetic positions in question.

6. Both "breaking" and "tumbling" are words that Woolf used in connection with waves: "the tumbling waves" (*Jacob's Room* 34); "The waves broke on the shore" (*The Waves* 228).

7. For example, Michael Golston, *Rhythm and Race in Modernist Poetry and Science: Pound, Yeats, Williams, and Modern Sciences of Rhythm*; Kirsty Martin,

Modernism and the Rhythms of Sympathy: Vernon Lee, Virginia Woolf, D. H. Lawrence; Ralf Konersmann and Dirk Westerkamp, editors, *Rhythmus und Moderne: Zeitschrift für Kulturphilosophie 2013*, vol. 1; Massimo Salgaro and Michele Vangi, editors, *Mythos Rhythmus: Wissenschaft, Kunst und Literatur um 1900*. The title of the literary magazine *Rhythm* (1911–1913), a publication that included contributions by Katherine Mansfield and D. H. Lawrence, shows the prominence of the term in the modernist period.

    8. "Tumble": "To roll about on the ground, or in the water or air; to wallow": a continuous, irregular movement (*Oxford English Dictionary* online).

    9. Cicero notes that in a "perpetual flow and ever-flowing loquacity, without any pauses" which "is to be thought rude and unpolished . . . there are no numbers; distinction, and strikes at equal with or often varied intervals, constitute numbers; which we may remark in the falling of drops of water, because they are distinguished by intervals, but which we can not observe in the rolling stream of a river" (III, XLVIII, 247).

    10. Hart Nibbrig stresses this when he introduces Musil's passage: in his argumentation, its words replace a silence, an interruption of the conversation (103).

    11. "Das Ganze bildet eine Forts. der Atemzüge = Bewegung vom Anfang u. mit ihm eine Einheit."

    12. I deliberately take up Agamben's animistic formulation and use the words "think" and "reflect" without intending to establish a smooth one-to-one correspondence between anima as mind and anima as vital principle. Of course, the words in the texts I am looking at do not engage in any kind of intentional thinking. But, they do, and not randomly so, trigger my thinking, they relate to my living body and mind and they do direct it back to their own nature as words. I am encouraged to react in a certain way. What makes me do so? If it is not only my projection on the words, it must be something in them. This assumption would consequently imply that they are not wholly inanimate after all. That they are involved in something—maybe something like reflection (in the sense of "casting back") or even thinking, provided we stop confining the term to intentional, cognitive processes that are limited to human beings.

    13. This is true for Woolf's and Musil's contemporary readers and also, to a great degree, for today's readers, even though there is a revival of oral reading practices at the present moment.

    14. At the same time, it has been claimed that they have already been pronounced orally by their author, Musil, who used to "read his writing over aloud." The translator of the "Posthumous Papers," Burton Pike, claims that this was the key to translate Musil into English: "Once the complex rhythms of his prose were understood as spoken rhythms, . . . , it was possible to more closely approximate the original. . . . Paying attention to the rhythm of Musil's German helped to capture both the music and the unremitting sense of urgency that mark the original" (*The Man without Qualities* 1773).

15. Staging something prelinguistic in language represents a paradox that corresponds to the contradiction Gelhard, Schmidt, and Schultz observe regarding the temporality of standstills/immobilizations: recurring to Derrida's *Given Time: I. Counterfeit Money*, they mention the impossible simultaneity of two temporalities, of two events that cannot happen at the same time (8).

16. Hart Nibbrig claims that Agathe's and Ulrich's reflective verbalizations only accelerate the moment's withdrawal (105).

17. In the English translation, the intrusion of the words is described less dramatically: "these few words dispersed the cloudy weight of silence and memory" (1130).

18. It is interesting that the word "rhythm" isn't mentioned explicitly in the German original: "Also waren ihre Gedanken zwar noch immer im Bannkreis des Blüten- und Totenzugs; aber sie bewegten sich nicht mehr mit ihm und auf seine stumm-feierliche Art, sondern Agathe dachte 'hin und her,' wie man es im Gegensatz zu dem Geisteszustand nennen könnte, worin das Leben 'tausend Jahre' ohne einen Flügelschlag währt" (1235).

19. Also Agathe's imagination of the mystical Millennium that is—at least on the surface—paralleled with the "dream of nature" (silence, etc.) makes use of a language of binaries in which "inner" and "outer" are distinguished linguistically, even though Agathe wants to convey that the separation between inner and outer is annihilated: "finally outer and inner will touch each other as if a wedge that had split the world had popped out!" (1329).

20. "hin und her" (1235).

21. Musil also tried out several variations for "Blütenschnee": "Es erleichterte ihr den Anblick des ohne Ziel seines Wegs ziehenden Blüten -schnees -schleiers -flaums" (V, 5, 202, November 1941).

22. Burton Pike stresses the special importance of the semicolon in Musil's prose in the afterword to his translation of *The Man without Qualities*: the "hallmark" of the German original "in the polished sections . . . is the cadence of clauses set off by semicolons. (Musil is the master of the semicolon!)" ("Translator's Afterword," 1773).

23. Here one can point out a parallel between the revolutions in the arts in the modernist period and revolutions of the natural sciences at the same time. The modernist obsession with flowing currents of smallest particles coincides with the discovery of the wave-particle dualism at the beginning of the twentieth century in the context of quantum physics.

24. Two typescript versions for "The Lady in the Looking-Glass" are recorded; they are archived at the Berg Collection (New York Public Library).

25. I use the terms "medium" and "mediality" in the broadest sense here, focusing on processes of transmission and the materiality of carriers.

26. It is interesting that breath does not tend to be identified as figuration of the medial, whereas messengers, for example, have extensively been discussed in German media studies (Krämer, "Medien, Boten, Spuren" 69–73; Krämer *Medium,*

Messenger, Transmission: An Approach to Media Philosophy). When Krämer mentions angels, prophets, poets, and apostles as medial figures, she does not refer to models of inspiration.

27. "Glanzlos" probably was the preferable adjective because of its sound.

28. The scholars I am referring to do not particularly focus on a specific medium or specific media technologies but pursue a philosophical approach to media and the phenomenon of mediality in general.

29. See also her explications in *Medium, Messenger, Transmission: An Approach to Media Philosophy* 31.

30. Krämer uses the same Blanchotian formula: in being present, the medium effects the presence of an absence (85). For an introduction to what Mersch designates as "negative media theory," see, for example, "Medialität und Undarstellbarkeit: Einleitung in eine 'negative' Medientheorie."

31. Mersch repeatedly refers to the "view from the side" (212), which, however, is only one possibility.

32. In the article quoted here, Mersch gives the example of anamorphoses (212–15).

33. "'Medial reflexivity' . . . is capable of paradoxical manoeuvres that show the mediality of the medium" (Mersch, "Tertium datur" 218).

34. For example, Winkler 215–16.

35. On circulation and media see Krämer, "Medien, Boten, Spuren" 80.

36. A narrative solution to this troubling scene is offered: the mirror image reveals the "true image" of Isabella Tyson: "She stood perfectly still. At once the looking-glass began to pour over her a light that seemed to fix her; that seemed like some acid to bite off the unessential and superficial and to leave only the truth" (68). This "truth" is that she "had no thoughts. She had no friends. She cared for nobody." Ironically, the supposed "truth" only reveals the social image of an elderly spinster—before, in the approach to Isabella Tyson that compensates the fact that little is known about her with "imagination," the wealthy, independent woman who traveled the world is considered to be "happy." So the "truth" uttered in the end is no final truth at all, it shifts like the inversion of "superficial" when the surface of the mirror "bites off" the "superficial . . . to only leave the truth" (66–68).

37. In "Medien, Boten, Spuren," Sybille Krämer characterizes media as nonpersonal (67).

38. For my investigation, I used material provided by Woolf Online, a project initiated by Julia Briggs and then carried out by Pamela L. Caughie, Nick Hayward, Mark Hussey, Peter Shillingsburg, and George K. Thiruvathukal.

39. I discussed Woolf's editing process of "Time Passes" in a different context in my article "Forces of Unworking in Virginia Woolf's 'Time Passes.'" Parts of the following pages coincide with the article.

40. The airs ask, "How long would they endure?" (138), and McNab asks, "How long shall it endure?" (143).

41. See *Woolf Online, An Electronic Edition and Commentary of Virginia Woolf's "Time Passes."* As there are only minor differences between the proofs and the printed version, I will concentrate on the holograph draft, the typescript, and the printed version.

42. The holograph draft has around 11,180 words, the typescript around 7,000 words, and the printed version around 5,750 words. See *Woolf Online: An Electronic Edition and Commentary of Virginia Woolf's "Time Passes."*

43. In the typescript, the sentence runs thus: "Here, one might say to those sliding lights on the ceiling, those grey airs of midnight that bend over the bed itself, here you can neither touch nor destroy" (4).

44. The passage continues as *follows*: "Flies wove a web in the sunny rooms; weeds that had grown close to the glass in the night tapped methodically at the window pane. When darkness fell, the stroke of the Lighthouse, which had laid itself with such authority upon the carpet in the darkness, tracing its pattern, came now in the softer light of spring mixed with moonlight gliding gently as if it laid its caress and lingered stealthily and looked and came lovingly again" (144). The airs are not explicitly mentioned here, whereas they are clearly identified as spies in the corresponding passage in the holograph draft and the typescript.

45. The following example suggests that the word "spy" seems to be deleted on purpose. In the typescript, we read: "the stray airs, spies, advance guards of great armies, blustered in" (6), and in the printed version: "those stray airs, advance guards of great armies, blustered in" (6).

46. The discussion of the air-spies is also part of my article "Forces of Unworking in Virginia Woolf's 'Time Passes.'"

47. This goes along with the following claim of Sybille Krämer: "As a core task of media, transference has to be understood as making perceptible what is not perceptible." "We understand the media's own materialisation and embodiment as an act of making the imperceptible perceptible" ("Medien, Boten, Spuren" 84).

48. The slightly odd image of a "wandering taper" fits into the depiction of writing by hand: "taper," no matter if it refers to a candle or a form whose width or thickness decreases toward one end, calls to mind the shape of a pen—the very writing instrument Woolf used for writing the draft.

49. Hart Nibbrig is one of the few who does not do so: with a chuckle he mentions how Musil researchers appreciatively gnaw at the idea of reading the scene as an analogy for the Other Condition (104) while admitting that Agathe and Ulrich themselves interpret it as an image for the Other Condition in retrospect (105).

50. See Gschwandtner; Smerilli 28, 233; and Wagner-Egelhaaf 195–215.

51. The Other Condition has been extensively discussed in terms of mysticism and unio mystica in Musil studies. In the unio mystica, men and God are unified, the difference between the mortal and immortal is overcome, as Harald Gschwandtner explains in his book dedicated to the "neo-mystic" in Musil's work

(17). The self dissolves and in Martina Wagner-Egelhaaf's terms becomes featureless, "without qualities" (200) or distinction—by merging with God and its surroundings, it ceases to be something of its own. Mysticism considers the unio mystica as something that escapes language, because representing God is always inadequate. Paradoxically, however, it is language's task to evoke what is unspeakable: the sudden, fleeting epiphany (Gschwandtner 19). Gschwandtner here refers to Ludwig Wittgenstein, Martin Buber, and Karl-Heinz Bohrer as well as to Wagner-Egelhaaf's and Schmitz-Eman's readings of Musil. The unio mystica thus circles around the unspeakable in the medium of the speakable, as Wagner-Egelhaaf puts it (197); mystics use language in order to reach the border of what can be said in language (205, quoting Walter Haug). Wagner-Egelhaaf, Gschwandtner, Arntzen, and Smerilli, who especially focuses on the relation between language and the body when discussing the Other Condition in his book *Moderne—Sprache—Körper: Analysen zum Verhältnis von Körpererfahrung und Sprachkritik in erzählenden Texten Robert Musils* provide attempts to elucidate how Musil adopts such mystic endeavors in a Modernist context and how the wordless experience of the Other Condition is articulated in his writing.

52. Arntzen, for example, notes that Agathe "experiences" the Other Condition when observing the parade of blossoms in his commentary to *The Man without Qualities* (387). In "Musil und die Mystik der Moderne," Wagner-Egelhaaf states that Musil conceptually tests experiences of the Other Condition in "Breaths of a Summer's Day" (206).

53. For example, Gschwandtner; Smerilli; Arntzen; Anders; and Schmitz-Emans 182–207.

54. For example, Arntzen; Anders; Grill.

55. The fleetingness and momentariness of the experience of both the Other Condition and unio mystica has been repeatedly addressed by Musil scholars: see Gschwandtner, esp. 104; Wagner-Egelhaaf, esp. 208; and Anders 166–76. Hart Nibbrig also stresses the fleetingness of the scene with the blossoms (106), but he deliberately does not discuss it in terms of the Other Condition (102).

56. Also: "good and evil simply fall away" (199).

57. There is no single English word that encompasses all meanings of "Gleichnis," which can mean "comparison," "metonymy," and "metaphor"—it has, for example, been translated as "figure of speech" or "metaphor" (1178–79). Musil himself does not use the term coherently.

58. For example: "It is in this condition that the image of each object becomes not a practical goal, but a wordless experience; and the descriptions . . . of the symbolic face of things and their awakening in the stillness of the image belong without a doubt in this context" ("Toward a New Aesthetic" 199). For an extensive reflection of "Gleichnis" in *The Man without Qualities* itself, see the chapter "The Two Trees of Life and a Proposal to Establishing a General Secretariat for Precision and Soul." In Musil studies, there is a tendency to predominantly concentrate on

"Gleichnis" or the image when it comes to the linguistic or aesthetic implications of the Other Condition (see Schnell; Grill; Arntzen 127; Smerelli 205; Wagner-Egelhaaf 207; and Anders 173).

59. The blossoms are mostly discussed with respect to Ulrich and Agathe. See, for example, Wagner-Egelhaaf; Arntzen, 387; and Fanta 525.

60. For a detailed account of Musil's work on the chapter, see Fanta, especially 518–26.

61. That is, after the wording had been polished by 1938 after a long process of trial and error and moved to the beginning of the chapter in 1941.

62. Lisa Siraganian's book *Modernism's Other Work: The Art Object's Political Life* is an attempt to counteract such an assumption: "Autonomy from the world was never, for the modernists, a failure of relation to it" (4). It is not surprising that breathing plays an important role in Siraganian's investigation of relationality in modernist art.

63. "Das gesprochenen Wort verliert seinen Eigensinn und gewinnt Nachbarsinn. Alle Versicherungen drücken nur ein einziges flutendes Erlebnis aus" (1084). In his reading of the passage, Smerilli argues that for Musil, words become transparent to many meanings; he links the dissolution of the word's boundaries to the idea of unio mystica. While Smerilli focuses on semantics and on meanings, on metaphor and analogy (233), I suggest an alternative reading that considers the material dimensions of words, especially their tonal qualities.

64. Agathe's amused, teasing suggestion to refer to the appetitive and non-appetitive passion as an "animal" and a "vegetable" disposition (1331) in a way already anticipates that the passion between Ulrich and Agathe has the capacity to exceed the human. Whereas Agathe's naming points to the passion of nonhuman organic beings, I want to go further and consider an eroticism of the inorganic.

65. "To joy is the crossing of the other. The other cuts across me, I cut across it. Each one is the other for the other—but also for the self" ("Shattered Love" 100).

66. Musil is aware of the inorganic material constituents of the human body, as the following sentence shows: "The legends of almost all peoples report that mankind came from the water and that the soul is a breath of air. Strange: science has determined that the human body consists almost entirely of water" (1453).

67. I want to retain the word "object" here because Ulrich uses it, even though according to W. J. T. Mitchell's distinction between "objects" and "things" in *What Do Pictures Want?*, "thing" as the object that became unfamiliar and Other would be the more appropriate term here.

68. Nancy distinguishes "sense" from "meaning"; it involves corporeal relations that disturb attributions of meaning. I here follow his explications in a lecture titled "Körpersinn—Sinnkörper" at the University of Basel in March 2014.

69. The earliest plans for the chapters were made in 1910.

70. See Walter Fanta's annotations in the *Klagenfurter Ausgabe*.

71. In the English translation, the exact correspondence of the word is not maintained, as "Atemzüge" is translated as "breaths" in "Breaths of a Summer's Day" and as "breathing" in the journey chapter.

72. In the German original, it is "the memory" rather than "their memory," which further supports my reading: "Ancona . . . stand in der Erinnerung fest" (1652).

73. Once more, the connection between the chapters is more marked if we consider the German original: the same word is used for the airstream, "Strom" and "Ströme" (in the plural), whereas in the English translation "stream" is used in "Breaths of a Summer's Day" and "current" in the journey chapter.

74. Walter Fanta does so when he points to the erotic connotation of the stream of blossoms and mentions that a drive ("Trieb") is operative in it (525). In a different context, flowers are explicitly related to erotic sensation: "erotische[] Zerstreutheit, die wie Blumenregen . . . fiel." ("erotic distraction, falling like a flower-rain"; my translation; 601).

75. In her article "Erotisch-poetisches Stillstellen in Robert Musils Mann ohne Eigenschaften" which focuses on the notion of still life, Tanja Schultz touches upon the eroticism of the inert body and standstills, focusing on another momentary pause in the last chapter drafts for *The Man without Qualities* (180).

76. Joachim Harst addresses the erotic dimensions of the materiality of words in his article on Musil's *Triëdere* and May Blecher's *Aus der unmittelbaren Unwirklichkeit*. Referring to Roland Barthes, he argues that in these texts, words become counter-words ("Widerworte") that enfold an eroticism in the play between their material presence as signifiers and the palpable absence of coherent meaning (468). Harst is interested in the erotic abandonment to the world of things observed in *The Confusions of Young Törless*, for example (472), and how this coincides with the moment when the difference between word and thing collapses (240) on a textual level.

77. The two positions are substantially different: Bennett contests the "assumption that matter is dull and passive" and inanimate with a notion of "vibrant matter" (1), thus giving a "voice to a vitality intrinsic to materiality" (3), a vitality that is mostly considered in terms of movement and agency. By contrast, Perniola stresses how passivity, inertia and the particularly inorganic nature of matter accounts for a sex appeal and enables an experience of "neutral sexuality" (14). It is interesting that at one point Bennett quotes Perniola and claims that "the 'sex appeal' of the inorganic, like a life, is another way to give voice to what I think of as a shimmering, potentially violent vitality intrinsic to matter" (61; emphasis added).

Notes to Chapter 4

1. What David Lloyd argues about breath in Beckett and Celan also applies to Beckett and Plath: "breath in both their works [serves] as a marker of the marginal presence of human being and as a reduction of the working of art to its minimal element" (180).

2. The poem has two explicit intertexts in which the scene being depicted is described as a failed suicide attempt: a passage in Plath's novel *The Bell Jar* and a remark on her personal life in one of her letters.

3. This goes hand in hand with Adam Michael Winstanley's study of breath in Beckett's *The Unnamable*. In his dissertation, "First Dirty, Then Make Clean': Samuel Beckett's Peristaltic Modernism, 1932–1958," he investigates respiration as contamination, drawing on Theodor W. Adorno's discussion of the "text's recurrent tropes of contamination, repulsion and waste" and Jean-Paul Sartre's reflections on the "'cleansing' (nettoyage) and 'curing' (guérison) of language" (182–83).

4. The parallels between the poem and the passage from the novel and an account of Plath's own suicide attempt have, for example, been pointed out and discussed by Peter J. Lowe in "'Full Fathom Five'. The Dead Father in Sylvia Plath's Seascapes." I want to draw attention to a few echoes between the poem and the novel: "Egg Rock" appears as "A big round grey rock, like the upper half of an egg" (*The Bell Jar* 149). "Behind him the hotdogs split and drizzled / On the public grills, and the ochreous salt flats, / Gas tanks, factory stacks" (*The Collected Poems* 115) is recalled in "A glassy haze rippled up from the fires in the grills and the heat on the road, and through the haze, as through a curtain of clear water, I could make out a smudgy skyline of gas tanks and factory stacks" and "A smoke seemed to be going from my nerves like the smoke from the grills and the sun-saturated road. The whole landscape—beach and headland and sea and rock—quavered in front of my eyes like a stage blackcloth." The last image is a particularly interesting adaptation: while the sun's scorching light lets everything recede to white in the poem, culminating in the self-referential blank paper, its effect in *The Bell Jar* is a black-out, expressed in an image pointing to another artform, the theatre. The "worms" and the verb "split" ("the hotdogs split") reappear in the novel, but in different contexts and locations: the body of Cal, the arranged date, who accompanies Esther in the water but then returns to the beach when he's exhausted "was bisected for a moment, like a white worm" (*The Bell Jar* 150–54).

5. At the end of the novel, the words are repeated again: "I took a deep breath and listened to the old brag of my heart. / I am, I am, I am" (*The Bell Jar* 233). Thus, a sense of foreboding overshadows Esther's recovery. Even though she is breathing fresher, healthier air now that "the bell jar, with its stifling distortions" (230) has lifted, the cardiovascular rhythm of the body keeps repeating the "old brag."

6. For a more detailed discussion of the I's uncanny role in Plath's poetry, see my article "Sprechen jenseits des Lebenden bei Sylvia Plath."

7. Krieger elucidates this claim as follows: "One of the fundamental problems of working with a printed text, as writer or as reader, is that each word is permanently located in a specific space, each is static and immobile, but none can have syntactic significance until process is introduced" (988).

8. While "I can't go" is a very conspicuous echo of *The Unnamable*, "I can't stay" most strongly recalls "I'll stay here." Together, the two instances add up to the reverse mirror image of the end of *The Unnamable*, "I can't go on, I'll go on" (*The Unnamable* 132–34).

9. I spare myself from adding the absurd footnote listing all occurrences of "I can't go" as well as "I," "can't" and "go" in *The Unnamable*.

10. The drafts of the poem are, to my knowledge, not archived.

11. The quotation from Beckett is from "Ceiling" (*Company / Ill Seen Ill Said / Worstward Ho / Stirrings Still* 130).

12. Connor assumes that this might be biographically motivated: "The young Beckett, whose psychosomatic crises of the early 1930s included spasms of breathlessness as well as paroxysms of palpitation, seems to have experienced air as an alien element, and to have sought relief from the occupation of breath in fantasies of absolute expiration" ("Beckett's Atmospheres" n.p.).

13. In his preface to *The Unnamable*, Connor traces this line of reception in Beckett studies in detail (xx).

14. "The Outside, the Night" was published in 1953, shortly after "Where Now? Who Now," and "Orpheus's Gaze" and "Inspiration, Lack of Inspiration" were published shortly before.

15. This may, on the one hand, not be surprising, as this space is beyond the lived-in world of beings and bodies. However, on the other hand, gazes and vocal sounds, especially when murmuring, do find their way into Blanchot's sometimes very palpable depictions of the inspirational domain in *The Space of Literature*. I discussed the sonic qualities of Blanchot's space of inspiration and the other night in "Aesthetic Autophony and the Night."

16. In his essay "Modernism and the Writing Hand," Steven Connor gives a brief reading of Malone's writing scene. He observes a syncopal movement of continuity and interruption that can be extended to the text as a whole: "The blindness and interruptedness of Malone's writing here is magnified in the text of *Malone Dies* itself, which presents an unbroken continuity, word following word (until the theatrical rifts which begin to open up visibly in the text toward the end), and yet is full of abrupt breakings off ('What a misfortune, the pencil must have slipped from my fingers, for I have only just succeeded in recovering it after forty-eight hours (see above) of intermittent efforts' *MD* [*Malone Dies*], 222)" n.p.

17. This is further substantiated by the fact that the effect of disrupted syntax and a coincidence of what is said and the words in front of future readers is perfected in the English translation. Even though the subordinate clause also rips the main clause apart in the original French, the verb is not as radically suspended as in the English version because it follows a repetition of the subject: "et l'air qui caresse mon respire à travers cahier . . . cet air n'est pas celui de cette avant-dernière demeure" (*Malone meurt*, MS-HRC-SB-7-4, 44r).

18. The manuscript, held by the Harry Ransom Center at the University of Texas at Austin, is reproduced from *Malone meurt/Malone Dies: A Digital Genetic Edition*.

19. What Van Hulle and Weller observe about the first draft of *The Unnamable*, "Most sentences appear to have been written fluently and without undue hesitation" (*The Making of Samuel Beckett's* L'Innommable / The Unnamable 120), to a great extent also applies to the first draft of *Malone Dies*.

20. This goes hand in hand with Dirk Van Hulle and Pim Verhulst's observation that "the manuscript invites an interesting 'who's who' game between the

writer and the character, and it is sometimes difficult to distinguish who is 'the author in the autograph, and who is writing about whom" (*The Making of Samuel Beckett's* Malone meur 26).

21. As in the fictional text, *Malone Meurt* is written in a notebook (*The Making of Samuel Beckett's* Malone meurt 35).

22. Van Hulle and Weller refuse to read the drafts in terms of a "reduction of being to language" (27) ascribed to Blanchot. However, what they outline as "unwording" clearly echoes "unworking." They pinpoint the "movement towards a radically new form of what might be termed unwriting" (21) in *The Unnamable*. As the novel is considered a stylistic radicalization of Beckett's prior work, it is well justified to—at least to some degree and as a first step—extend this claim to *Malone Dies*.

23. The writing scene is then echoed in the description of another body part: "For my arse for example, which can hardly be accused of being the end of anything, if my arse suddenly started to shit at the present moment, which God forbid, I firmly believe the lumps would fall out in Australia" (322). In *The Unnamable*, the comical analogy between the mouth and anus and their respective emissions is continued: "I once knew a doctor who held that scientifically speaking the latest breath could only issue from the fundament and this therefore, rather than the mouth, the orifice to which the family should present the mirror, before opening the will" (*The Unnamable* 56).

24. I take this expression from M. NourbeSe Philip who uses it to describe her own—substantially different—poetics of breathing in *Zong!*

25. William Hutchins opens his article on breath in Beckett's writing with the claim: "Whatever else Beckett's characters lack—limbs, mobility, sight, memory, or even life itself—They 'are' breath; that is, their existence is confirmed by (and their subsistence consists of) breath shaped into words" (Hutchins 85). While this observation is very convincing, the positive, affirmative terms "are breath," "their existence is confirmed by . . . breath shaped into words" are somewhat misleading. The Nancean perspective I pursue in the following offers a, to my mind, more adequate vocabulary.

26. It only does so in the English translation.

27. All manuscripts and drafts for the novel, held by the Harry Ransom Center, the University of Texas at Austin, are reproduced from *L'Innommable/The Unnamable: A Digital Genetic Edition*.

28. See Steven Connor's observation in "Beckett's Punctuation": "The adversary in Beckett's work up to the end of the 1950s is the 'mask' or 'veil' of 'grammar and style', and punctuation is a principal means of drilling through or decomposing that 'imperturbability' " (279). The words in quotation marks are quoted from *The Letters of Samuel Beckett I, 1929–1940*, edited by Martha Dow Fehsenfeld and Lois More Overbeck, 518.

29. Steven Connor argues that *How It Is* stages an "anaerobic or surd (= dumb, voiceless) condition" and thus does not involve a breathing rhythm: "We

are repeatedly told that the voice that is heard and transmitted in *How It Is* only heard 'when the panting stops', which seems to forbid reading the staccato phrases as a respiratory rhythm" ("Beckett's Punctuation" 279).

30. Referring back to James Williams's analysis of Beckett's punctuation, Connor describes such a tension as "the play that punctuation effects between connection and disconnection" ("Beckett's Punctuation" 274).

31. Adam Michael Winstanley, whose intriguing reading of breath in *The Unnamable* I can only hope to tie in with, comments on this passage as follows: "The imperative to 'go on' becomes an imperative to keep on breathing. . . . If breathing takes on the character of a reflexive compulsion . . . , there can be no final, decisive act of expiry, only an obligation to keep on expiring, to keep on producing contaminated air that will subsequently be forced back into the body" (195).

32. In his introduction to the novel, Steven Connor describes *The Unnamable* as "the maximum of minimality" (xxii).

33. See Derval Tubridy's argument: "The temporal distanciation between the body and the dramatic presentation necessary for the 'recorded vagitus' and the 'amplified recording' of the breath, dislocate, quite literally, the lived experience from its representation. Breath here exists at the moment of both anticipation of, and withdrawal from, presentation" (116).

34. In her poem "A Birthday Present," Sylvia Plath sketches a similar respirational scene in which an overload of inhaled material becomes deadly: "But my god, the clouds are like cotton. / Armies of them. They are carbon monoxide. // Sweetly, sweetly I breathe in, / Filling my veins with invisibles, with the million // Probable motes that tick the years off my life" (*The Collected Poems* 207).

35. *Breath* was first written in English. Using the Latin *vagire* when referring to the infant's birth cry marks an interruption in the otherwise simple language of the stage directions (see Lozier 247). That the list in the draft of *The Unnamable* echoes the most uncommon word in the stage directions of *Breath* makes the parallel quite pronounced.

36. This goes hand in hand with Ronan McDonald's observation, "The Unnamable reveals that all is generated by the spillage of words on the page" (103).

37. "Jedes einzelne Wort ist geschwängert von seiner eigenen Geschichte, jedes einzelne Wort trägt in sich eine endlose Entwicklung von Metapher zu Metapher."

38. The transcriptions of the "Psychology Notes" are taken from Matthew Feldman's thesis, "Sourcing Aporetics: An Empirical Study on Philosophical Influences in the Development of Samuel Beckett's Writing." I want to thank Matthew Feldman for sharing his work with me.

39. "Es wünscht sich selbst an den Ort zurück, wo es noch keinerlei Störungen von außen gab" (*Das Trauma der Geburt* 27). These reflections are an attempt to reformulate the Freudian death drive in—quite paradoxically—organic and libidinal terms.

40. In the English translation, the last breath disappears and becomes "giving up the ghost": "and giving up the ghost be born at last, to the sound perhaps of one of those hiccups which mar alas too often the solemnity of the passing" (*The Unnamable* 56).

41. The speaker then adds, "I was grievously mistaken in supposing that death in itself could be regarded as evidence, or even a strong presumption, in support of a preliminary life" (*The Unnamable* 56). Even though the "preliminary life" here also hints at a beyond in the sense of an inversed afterlife, Rank's primordial unity with the mother is also evoked in the context of the passage that plays on *The Trauma of Birth*.

42. What "they" refers to remains unclear in this passage where pronouns themselves act according to their linguistic function and primarily shift.

43. This mention of suffocation and breath brimming with literary references stands in contrast to that of another "creation" of the unnamable, the "head in the jar." The head in the jar is the most physical of all figures we encounter in the novel. He has a body that is deteriorating but still clearly there. When he addresses his fear of suffocation, he gives a physiological and medical account: "There is only one thing that worries me, and that is the prospect of being throttled if I should ever happen to shorten further. Asphyxia! I who was always the respiratory type, witness this thorax still mine, together with the abdomen. I who murmured, each time I breathed in, Here comes more oxygen, and each time I breathed out, There go the impurities, the blood is bright red again. The blue face! The obscene protrusion of the tongue!" (*The Unnamable* 45).

44. Fritz Mauthner touches on an unfathomable foundation of language, especially figural language, in *Beiträge zu einer Kritik der Sprache I*, a text Beckett studied thoroughly: "What in a primordial time forces us to make comparisons, to expand terms, or to name is . . . something nameless, something unconscious, a feeling. In this respect poetry and the origin of language have to coincide" (my translation).

45. The relations between *Breath* and Rank's *Trauma of Birth* are, for example, also pointed out by Lozier (245–46).

46. Connor's source is Tom Bishop and Raymond Federman's collected volume *Samuel Beckett in the Cahier* de l'Herne series.

47. We do not know whether Beckett sensed that this etymology is questionable. If we read his comment on Breath as an allusion to it, it is in any case striking that the whole play is built on a suspension: "a whole play, and life built out of a suspended interval" (Connor, "Beckett's Punctuation" 276 [going back to Bishop and Federman]; emphasis added).

48. Sozita Goudouna, for example, observes: "The evasion of figuration, the abeyance of the mimetic, and principally the reduction of duration in Breath are related facets of the technique of abstraction" (51).

49. A close look at the English version shows that even there the symmetry is not perfect. In her detailed word-by-word analysis of the stage directions, Claire

Lozier observes that "repetition is indeed never exact, and there are some changes and irregularities in the doublings which introduce disorder and disrupt the apparent organization." She concludes: "There is, then, an illusion of order and symmetry, rather than a real systematic organisation" (247).

50. For reasons that will unfold step by step in the following discussion, I refer to the humans at the center of Plath's "Paralytic" and "Tulips" as "patients" rather than "speakers" because, as it will turn out, they do not express themselves orally. "Patient" lends itself because the characters are hospitalized, and, more generally, because they are sketched as the opposite of agents.

51. Even though Plath was familiar with both Rank's and Freud's work, it is not certain whether she knew the specific texts in which these concepts are introduced, *The Trauma of Birth* and *Beyond the Pleasure Principle*. She certainly knew some of Freud's accounts of the intrauterine state. In her diary, she refers to "A return to the womb, Freud might have it" (*The Journals of Sylvia Plath* 92). She read *The Basic Writings of Sigmund Freud*, where "phantasies concerning the intra-uterine life, the sojourn in the mother's womb" (394) are addressed and the sentence that incited Rank's theory occurs: "The act of birth, moreover, is the first experience attended by anxiety, and is thus, the source and model of the affect of anxiety" (395). In this book, *Beyond the Pleasure Principle* is not included. However, according to Peter K. Steinberg's catalogue of Plath's library, she read *Mourning and Melancholia* from *A General Selection from the Works of Sigmund Freud*, which also contains *Beyond the Pleasure Principle*. She does not explicitly mention the text in either her diary or letters but once makes (a rather generic) reference to "the death urge" (*The Journals of Sylvia Plath* 234).

52. Going back to the very example Freud discusses in order to trace the origin of the sex drive back to the death drive, Rank discusses the splitting of the primeval unified beings in Plato's *Symposium* and mentions the "yearning for a lost state" (173), a "unio mystica, the being at one with the All" (176).

53. A discussion of the notion of wholeness in Plath's work and the problematic reception of Plath and her work in terms of wholeness can be found in Lisa Narbeshuber's book *Confessing Cultures. Politics and the Self in the Poetry of Sylvia Plath*, 6–8. She convincingly argues that "when Plath evokes images of 'wholeness,' she inevitably undercuts them" (8).

54. "The soft anonymous / Talkers: 'You all right?' "; "Photographs visit me— / My wife, dead and flat . . . / Two girls / As flat as she, who whisper 'We're your daughters" (*The Collected Poems* 266).

55. In a different context (discussing Charles Baudelaire's "Le Cygne" in his essay on apostrophe), Jonathan Culler discusses comparable acoustic/visual/semantic ambivalences of the letter O: "when it seeks something other than itself (eau), it finds only itself (O), which may also be nothing (O)" ("Apostrophe" 65).

56. I briefly touch on this point in "Sprechen jenseits des Lebenden bei Sylvia Plath" 349.

57. The way in which Hamlet's last breath and the utterance of Freud's child in *Beyond the Pleasure Principle* are textually depicted recalls one of the most conventional elements of poetry: apostrophe. Both utterances could be read as addresses to someone absent, or to absence itself, and they represent a "conjunction of mouth and happening," which Jonathan Culler defines as a major characteristic of apostrophe. Moreover, and I again refer to Culler's essay on apostrophe, "the pure O of undifferentiated voicing" ("Apostrophe" 62–63) punctures significant language in both Shakespeare's and Freud's text.

58. James Strachey translates "Zauderrhythmus" as "vacillating rhythm" (35), which fails to convey the sense of hesitating and being indecisive that the German "zaudern" implies.

59. Freud never explicitly makes that connection, even though his first and most widely known example of repetition compulsion contains a literary reference to breath. In the introduction of Strachey's English translation, Gregory Zilboorg compares repetition compulsion to physiological breath: "It is hardly necessary to go into more detail to observe that the compulsive element of which Freud speaks when he speaks of compulsive repetition is something that the individual is not conscious of, . . . and that it is just as or no more compulsive than breathing" (*Beyond the Pleasure Principle*, xiv).

60. In his essay on Proust, Beckett describes breath as dull habit: "Habit is the ballast that chains the dog to his vomit. Breathing is habit. Life is habit" (8).

61. Beckett's prominent source Fritz Mauthner comes up with a very palpable description of breathing as unconscious "mechanic habit": "The thoroughly vegetative memories like . . . breathing stick to the human. . . . Hours, days after the so-called death, . . . the ciliated epithelial tissue keeps working in the respiratory tract, like a subaltern after his master's death who keeps working for a little . . . air" (593; my translation).

62. It was written in March 1961 and published in the *New Yorker* in April 1962. A poetry editor from the New Yorker wrote "I have heard nothing but the most extravagant praise of TULIPS. Everyone I know thought it extraordinary. So do I" (*The Letters of Sylvia Plath* 2: 769).

63. In a passage parallel to the photographs of "wife" and "daughters" visiting the patient in "Paralytic," the one in "Tulips" notes "My husband and child smiling out of the family photo" (160).

64. For an analysis of smiling as a gesture that becomes an imperative for feminine subjects deprived of wilfulness see Ahmed (e.g., 58).

65. I consulted the drafts of "Tulips," a manuscript and a typescript, held at the Houghton Library at Harvard University. Unfortunately, I was unable to secure a permission to cite from them.

66. This confirms Laure de Nervaux-Gavoty's claim that colors "appear as autonomous entities" in Plath's work and that they "overflow[] all boundaries" (110–12).

67. See *The Letters of Sylvia Plath* 2: 626.

68. I cite a number of comments on Plath's recordings from (partly difficult to access) sources Kate Moses compiles in her well-researched article "Sylvia Plath's Voice, Annotated."

69. Plath repeatedly stresses the BBC's financial benefits, for example, "The BBC are the one organisation that pay excellently for poetry—$ 3 a minute for a reading, something like that" (*The Letters of Sylvia Plath* 2: 475); "Ted's income from the BBC this year has been as good as a salary" (532).

70. The sentence, "they are written for the ear, not the eye: they are poems written out loud" (*Ariel* 195) is from a script for the BBC broadcast "New Poems by Sylvia Plath," and "I've got to say them . . . I say them aloud" (Orr 170) is from a BBC interview with Peter Orr. Apart from these two well-known claims, there are no recorded comments by Plath on the specifically oral nature of the *Ariel* poems. The diaries from that time are lost/destroyed and other references to reading her own poetry aloud are not limited to the late poems. In fact, in the interview with Orr, it sounds a bit like a marketing strategy when Plath says that designing poetry to be read aloud was "something I didn't do in my earlier poems. For example, my first book, *The Colossus*, I can't read any of the poems aloud now. I didn't write them to be read aloud" (170). This plainly contradicts what she says about her earlier poetry before on numerous occasions: in a diary entry from 1957, she commands herself to "Say them [her poems] aloud always" (*The Journals of Sylvia Plath* 285). She also keeps telling her addressees to read aloud the new poems she shares in letters: "Perhaps if you read them aloud you will get more of them" (to Hans-Joachim Neupert about some new poems in 1949; *The Letters of Sylvia Plath* 1: 153); "Read aloud for word tones, for full effect" (to her mother about new poems in 1955; 882); "read aloud also" (to her mother in 1956 on "The Pursuit" 1133); "if you will read the poem out-loud (it's meant to be)" (to her mother in 1956 about "Channel Crossing" 1133); "Listen: here are two lyrics; they are meant to be said aloud" (to her mother in 1956 on "Ode to Ted" and "Song" 1167); "Read it aloud—for the sounds of it" (to her brother in 1958 about "Mussel-Hunter at Rock Harbour"; *The Letters of Sylvia Plath* 2: 244). That reading poetry out loud (generally, not only her own) was a common practice by her (and Hughes) is stressed throughout her letters and diaries.

71. A week before she committed suicide, Plath wrote to her mother: "I . . . have a chance for 3 weeks in May to be on the BBC Critics program at about $ 150 a week, a fantastic break I hope I can make good on" (*The Letters of Sylvia Plath* 2: 963).

72. See Plath, *The Spoken Word*, BBC recording.

73. This contrast becomes eminently clear if we compare the way Plath reads the first lines with the way she reads the last lines.

74. When commenting on Plath's late poetry, Alfred Alvarez gestures in this direction when he stresses the difference "between finger count and ear count. One

measures the movement by rules, the other catches the rhythm by the disturbance it creates. And she could only write poems out loud when she discovered her own speaking voice, that is, her identity" (qtd. in Moses 94). That he chooses to integrate the "disturbance" of rhythm into a narrative of self-discovery—Plath finding her voice and thus her identity—is a persistent tendency in Plath scholarship. Kate Moses, for example, postulates a vocal harmonization of writer and text in Plath's late recordings: "The poems and the poet, like the horse in Ariel and its rider, have become one, a driving force in the late recordings" (92). I would, on the contrary, argue that the tensions and opposing tendencies interacting in recordings like "Tulips" result in a "faltering rhythm" that unsettles any notion of unity and settled identity.

75. Plath composed several poems in syllabic verse, for example "Mussel-Hunter at Rock Harbour," which she explains to her brother by giving a textbook-definition: "measuring lines not by heavy & light stresses, but by the number of syllables." She further comments: "I find this form satisfactorily strict (a pattern varying the number of syllables in each line can be set up, as M. Moore does it) and yet it has a speaking illusion of freedom (which the measured stress doesn't have) as stresses vary freely" (*The Letters of Sylvia Plath* 2: 247).

76. These traits also appear throughout Plath's letters and journals. A very poetic description can be found in a diary entry from January 1958: "A small draft of deadly night air seeping through the white-painted metal slats of the venetian blinds sets me coughing, wheezing, with an ominous click and whistle deep in my lungs" (*The Journals of Sylvia Plath* 312). Plath frequently describes visible cold air and breath: "I rode home at 11:30 tonight, forcing great gulps of frosty air into my lungs" (153); "my breath hangs white in the air in frosty clouds!" (*The Letters of Sylvia Plath* 1: 977); "seeing my breath come out in frosty white puffs" (1057); "breath coming in great white clumps" (1103); "my breath comes out in great white puffs & tinkles in icicles to the floor" (*The Letters of Sylvia Plath* 2: 36); "my breath hangs in white puffs on the frigid air" (39). A number of these frozen breaths are part of Plath's depictions of the insufficiently heated buildings she lived in, which are not unrelated to her regular suffering from pneumonia, sinus infections, and severe colds. Plath also often uses images of freezing and paralysis when she addresses her mental health condition: "I am stymied, stuck, at a stasis. Some paralysis of the head has got me frozen" (1957; *The Journals of Sylvia Plath* 272); "Now to get out of the chill paralysis" (1957; 292); "Paralysis again. How I waste my days. I feel a terrific blocking and chilling go through me like anaesthesia" (1959; 522); "I am so numb . . . I am hollow as a zombie inside & without motion" (1962; *The Letters of Sylvia Plath* 2: 793); "What appals me is the return of my madness, my paralysis, my fear & vision of the worst—cowardly withdrawal, a mental hospital, lobotomies"; "Ted's leaving would be hard, but manageable. But there is this damned, self-induced freeze" (967–68). The last two passages are from the last letter in the collection, written to her former therapist, Ruth Beuscher, on February 4, 1963.

77. The Lilly Library catalogues the sheet as "**Stillborn** [poem]" and adds "Holograph draft of an untitled poem on verso" as further information on the item. All citations in the following paragraph are from this unpaginated sheet.

78. For a more detailed discussion of this performative contradiction, see my article "These Things Astonish Me beyond Words: Virginia Woolf, Sylvia Plath, William Carlos Williams."

79. I am citing the first line from the Lilly Library's catalogue of the Plath manuscripts, http://webapp1.dlib.indiana.edu/findingaids/view?doc.view=entire_text&docId=InU-Li-VAC4807. Unfortunately, I was unable to secure a permission to cite from the rest of the poem.

80. The qualities of what I designated as cold breath keep coming up in the passage: "Ice water seeped down my throat"; the slope is "a plane of whiteness" (93).

81. See, for example, Christina Sharpe in *In the Wake: On Blackness and Being*, drawing on Frantz Fanon and Eric Garner's last words "I can't breathe," which became a motto of the Black Lives Matter movement after Garner's violent death, esp. 108–12, 130; see also Sara Ahmed, *Living a Feminist Life* 219, 221, 245.

82. A possible reading would be to consider the move toward death as failure of the feminist fight and receding into whiteness as an act of making women invisible and their voices unwritten. At a closer look, many nuances of texts discussed in this chapter contradict such a generalized hypothesis, which would, as a starting point, assign a fixed meaning and place to whiteness and death—and this is strongly resisted by the texts. As compelling as readings of whiteness in Plath's hospital poems as an indicator of colonialism, homogeneity, conformity, or capitalism like Lisa Narbeshuber's are, they do not pay enough tribute to this gesture of Plath's work.

83. In the course of the novel, it becomes very clear that this fantasy of an omnipotent will is illusionary.

84. Sara Ahmed points out that happiness is derived from Middle English "hap, suggesting chance." When pitted against a teleological pursuit of happiness, the accidental quality of hap, allowing one to "let . . . oneself go" and attend to "breakable" things, becomes one of Ahmed's guideline for a feminist life (265–66).

85. Marianne Egeland devotes a whole subchapter of her book to that trajectory of Plath scholarship (201–7). Undoubtedly, Plath herself was interested in the psychological question of divided selves, which she frequently addressed in her diaries and elaborated on in her undergraduate thesis "The Magic Mirror. A Study of the Double in Two of Dostoevsky's Novels." It is still problematic to read either her work or her life in these terms. In her influential study *The Haunting of Sylvia Plath*, Jacqueline Rose questioned the teleological movement implied in reading Plath's poetry in terms of a true selfhood unfolding, and highlights the questionable role Ted Hughes played in promoting the "concept of an emergent true self" (103) when he framed the *Ariel* poems (144–49). Elisabeth Bronfen convincingly shows how the narrative of the divided-self led to a conflation of author and work:

"Hughes discusses her poems in relation to the way they fit his narrative about the old, false self, shattered to the point of being reduced to its essential core, repairs and renovates itself until reborn. . . . By postulating that the importance of her poems lies in registering this psychic development from falsity to authenticity, Ted Hughes . . . gave birth to what has continued to vortex all subsequent reading of Sylvia Plath's woks—namely, our inability to sever her psychic life from the body of writing she brought forth" (9). After years of Plath criticism and scholarship, this narrative still holds strong, as reviews of the just published second volume of Plath's letters show: in her *New York Times* review, tellingly titled "A Marriage Falters and Masks Fall Away," Parul Sehgal claims "We don't hear Plath but 'Sivvy'" (n.p.). In the *New Yorker*, Dan Chiasson writes "Plath monitored life from behind a façade of chipper enthusiasm. Her genius took shape hidden by this screen, and when it flowered, especially in 'Ariel,' the book of poems that she wrote in the months leading up to her suicide" (n.p.).

86. Marjorie Perloff's influential reading, "'A Ritual for Being Born Twice': Sylvia Plath's 'The Bell Jar'" links "the relationship of Esther's private psychosis to the larger social situation" (551). She draws on R. D. Laing's popular book on schizoid personalities, *The Divided Self*, where the splitting the self is described as a strategy "in order to live in an unlivable situation" (Laing qtd. in Perloff 518). Perloff then argues that "the division of Esther's self" is at the heart of the novel whose central action is "the attempt to heal the fracture between inner self and false-self system so that a real and viable identity can come into existence" (509).

87. Both types of self are undermined in her literary texts, which older and more recent Plath scholars confirm. To give two examples: Jacqueline Rose scrutinized the idea of a unified self in Plath's work while at the same time asking "How can woman assert themselves against social oppression . . . without propelling themselves beyond the bounds of identity, without abolishing identity itself?" (145–46), and Lisa Narbeshuber argues that "every notion of self seems to be under devastating scrutiny in Plath's late poetry" (12).

88. Plath's fashioning of self-images has been investigated extensively in Plath studies; to give only one example, Sally Bayley and Tracy Brain dedicate their collection of essays *Representing Sylvia Plath*, to "Plath's own paradoxical notions of self-presentation. The essays share an interest in what Plath's many poetic speakers hide, veil, and leave out, as well as what they say directly" ("Introduction" 1).

89. Marjorie Perloff traces the beginnings of a clearly male version of the Plath myth in these comments on *Ariel* but then seems to take a similar line when claiming "vengeance and rage found their outlet in a set of remarkable poems" (12).

90. For the sake of the rougher overview attempted here, I focus on those that have been discussed in most detail in the book and leave aside some that have only been touched on.

91. Beckett, for example, cites Keats's "Ode to the Nightingale" in "Dante and the Lobster" (88).

Notes to Chapter 5

1. Relations and resonances between Müller and Celan have been discussed previously. Müller herself repeatedly mentions that she is familiar with Celan's writing (e.g., *Mein Vaterland war ein Apfelkern* 38; *Der König verneigt sich und tötet* 27). Proximities between their poetics of breath and their use of compounds, especially "Atemschaukel" and "Atemwende," are touched on by Părău; Haines 127; Nannasch 298–99; Leipelt-Tsai 77–78; Hartwig; de Oliveira 103; Braun 47.

2. At least in "Daddy," this imagery is linked to breath: facing the Nazi-father, the speaker is "barely daring to breathe or Achoo" (*The Collected Poems* 222). His German language is described as "an engine, an engine / Chuffing me off like a Jew. / A Jew to Dachau, Auschwitz, Belsen" (223).

3. What Anja Lemke concludes about Celan's conception of poetry also applies to the poetic implications of Müller's Atemschaukel: "Poetry as caesura thus implies a possibility of commemorating a historical caesura without locating it in a historical scheme too soon and thus storing it in the save archive of memory as something past" (255; my translation).

4. See, for example, Schönfelder 33–34. In his harsh criticism of the dominant trauma theory following Cathy Caruth's influential work, Joshua Pederson sums up more recent research as follows: "Susan Brison notes, victims' textual narratives of trauma—which are possible according to [Richard] McNally—have healing power. Speaking trauma pulls it from the realm of painful obscurity and hastens the process of rehabilitation" (338).

5. For two recent discussions and overviews of Celan's treatment of breath in his notes and poetry, see David Lloyd's article, "Breath Crystals: A Vestigial Poetics of Breath in Beckett, Celan, and Arikha," and Antti Salminem's article, "On Breathroutes. Paul Celan's Poetics of Breathing."

6. "Gestalt, und zugleich auch . . . Atem, das heißt Richtung und Schicksal" (*Der Meridian* 3). The German original and Pierre Joris's translation have the same page numbers.

7. This has been observed and discussed by Anja Lemke: "In its experience of the abyss, Lenz's 'furchtbare[s] Verstummen" which also takes away our breath and word, already refers to the historical caesura of Auschwitz by taking up the Bremer Rede" (243; my translation).

8. For the sake of readability, I choose not to reproduce some of the typographical labels and special characters used for editorial annotations and so forth in *The Meridian: Final Version—Drafts—Materials* (for example, I decided to leave out the signs marking insertions). An exact reproduction of the notes and drafts with full editorial annotations is only given when relevant for the argument.

9. "Nobody can tell how long the breath pause—the hope [for an encounter with the 'totally other'] and the thought—will last" (8; translation modified). In his article "'Was auf der Lunge, das auf der Zunge': Paul Celans 'Offene Glottis'—

Trauma/U-topie," Thomas Böning stresses the poetic importance of the breathing pause and its relation to trauma, suffering, and death: he notices that in the context of the physiological breathing process, the interruption of the breathing pause indicates a moment when death invades life. "Moreover one has to consider that physiological inspiration is preceded by a breathing pause. For Celan, the poetic consequence is that poetic inspiration comes from the pain of death and that the poem therefore can be designated as 'that which literally *speaks-itself-to-death*' with respect to a poetic articulation drawing on expiration" (221; my translation).

10. On the precariousness of the Celan's dialogic notion of poetry and the temporal complexities it involves with regard to the message in a bottle, see Zanetti 70.

11. For a discussion of this movement of "hindurchgreifen," see Zanetti 64–65.

12. For a discussion of the different temporal implications of the image of the handshake and the message in a bottle see Zanetti 42.

13.

	Einatmen		inhale
Seelenatome		*soul atoms*	
	Ausatmen		exhale

Celan added this note in his copy of *Grundriß der Geschichte der Philosophie des Altertums*. It refers to the following passage: "Through inhalation, we take in soul atoms from the air, through exhalation we give them back to it, and life lasts as long as this process continues" (*La Bibliothèque philosophique* 20; my translation).

14. Celan read *Die Philosophie der Inder: Eine Einführung in ihre Geschichte und ihre Lehren*, where the following passages can be found: "Âtman is etymologically related to our word 'Atem' (is the essence of a person, what remains of the person) when one removes everything accidental, the 'true self' "; "According to this theory the single constituents of the deceased enter the corresponding elements of the world upon death (the breath merges with the wind, thought with the moon, the self with space etc.)" (*La Bibliothèque philosophique* 585; my translation).

15. Celan marks the following passages on breath in antiquity: "limitless breath" (*La Bibliothèque philosophique* 668; my translation); "Beyond the circle of fire there is the limitless or unbound air (πνεῦμα) from which the world draws its breath" (*La Bibliothèque philosophique* 670; my translation).

16. Especially in earlier Celan scholarship, there is a tendency to read "breath," along with references to its etymological history and its connotations, in a Christian and Jewish theological context, as something "Geistiges" or transcendent, either in a spiritual sense, or as the (necessarily concealed) "truth" of the word or the poem (see Herman Burger's reading of "Weggebeizt," esp. 137, or Gadamer's, esp. 110).

17. Salam Schocken criticized the fact that Celan's *Bremer Rede* represented an attempt to cover his Jewishness because it was not explicitly mentioned. In his defence, Celan wrote a letter to his son Gershom Schocken in which he stresses that Jewishness is a pneumatic matter, not a thematic one (Koelle 68).

18. The reference to a specifically contemporary poetry embeds the comments in the letter in a thematic complex established in *The Meridian* and the notes and drafts, where commemoration, silence, and breath are designated as characteristic of poetry "today": "Perhaps what's new in the poems written today is exactly this: theirs is the clearest attempt to remain mindful of such dates?" (8); "the poem today—shows . . . a strong tendency to fall silent" (32); "the poem today—it is a breathturn" (127).

19. Another prominent thinker of dialogism, Ferdinand Ebner, explicitly connects the relation between I and thou to language and breath in *Das Wort und die geistigen Realitäten. Pneumatologische Fragmente* (e.g., 17, 25). Even though it is not certain whether Celan read Ebner, some of his reflections, such as the fact that relation between I and thou "can never be understood psychologically but only pneumatically" (21; my translation), echo in Celan's writing.

20. See Celan's note: "'Atemeinheiten' (Buber); *Kolen*"; "'Breath-units' (Buber); *cola*" (109).

21. "Faithful Bible translation is an attempt to translate back into the oral, to reawaken the spoken word" (Buber, "The How and Why of Our Bible Translation" 212).

22. I use the sign "|" to mark insertions in the continuous text.

23. See Salminen's discussion of Celan's versus Rosenzweig's and Buber's notion of breath units: "In Celan breath is inscribed as a rhythmic pattern reminiscent of laughter, asthmatic attacks, gasps, and stutters" (120).

24. For a discussion of physiological speech production and breath in Celan's work, see Bönnig 217–44, esp. 218–24. Bönnig shows that in his poem "Offene Glottis," Celan refers to the process of voice formation as it is described in Hans Reichel and Adolf Bleichert's *Leitfaden der Physiologie des Menschen*, a book Celan read.

25. Also see "The poem is one person's language-become-shape, it has objectivity, presentness and presence; it stands into time. There is a lyric koine. And there is the poem as singular, breath-carried, heart- and sky-grey language in time" (55); "Poetry is heart-grey, breath-clouded *breath-marbled* [*atemdurchwachsene*] language in time" (110).

26. The status of the notes and drafts, which were not designed for publication, is a challenge for literary scholars. They display trains of thoughts, reflections, and arguments that Celan experimented with. It has to be acknowledged that the fragments do not result in a fully coherent, encompassing poetics and that such a poetics cannot be reconstructed by using the notes to fill gaps or elucidate cryptic passages of *The Meridian*. Concerning the material in question, I find it important to start from two assumptions: (1) we have, on the one hand, a textual cluster of notes and drafts, and on the other a painstakingly composed text. (2) Concerning the temporal relation between these texts, the notes, and drafts precede the formulated speech. However, it is impossible to tell why some reflections or threads were rejected and whether they represent arguments that Celan deliberately abandoned

during the writing process. When I concentrate on reflections and connections of topoi in the notes that no longer appear in the speech, I am interested in how some reflections are silenced and rendered invisible by being left out in the speech, within the sketch of a poetics in which silence assumes a central role.

27. A comparative look at the notes and what is not taken into the finished speech also allows us to see something that might easily be overlooked in the notes. Celan primarily refers to breath and not to breathing. In his published literary work, he rarely uses the verb "atmen." In two early poems where he does so, the idea of a purely vital and connecting breath is unsettled: "Erinnerung an Frankreich": "Wir waren tot und konnten atmen" ("We were dead and able to breathe"; *Mohn und Gedächtnis* 28; my translation); "Fernen": "gemeinsam / laß uns atmen den Schleier / der uns voreinander verbirgt" ("together / let us breathe the veil / that conceals us from each other"; *Von Schwelle zu Schwelle* 95; my translation). Here, breathing already breaks with biology: it is not presented as an organic process of or integral to the living human body. Such a detachment from the organic body and biology is more easily effected by the noun "breath," which can stand on its own in contrast to the verb requiring a subject.

28. David Wills argues in a similar direction when he claims that Celan understands "the I-distancing or pneumatic self-exile, a provisional respiratory expiration" as "the condition of possibility of the poetic odyssey." The "breathturn" implies "a sense of life that persists or survives in poetry because of, and not in spite of—indeed, that is enabled by—the very interruption of its naturality, the fact of its being traversed by a radical otherness, an otherness whose structure . . . cannot not include the non-natural, the prosthetic, the artificial, the inanimate" (142–44).

29. "Im Gedicht geschieht nicht Mitteilen, sondern *Sich*mitteilen" (*Der Meridian* 132). The English translation is "In the poem what happens is not communication, but *self*-communication" (*The Meridian* 132). Self-communication does not have the same implications as "sich-mitteilen," which implies to communicate with oneself, but also to be parted ("teilen" = to divide, split) in this process.

30. In *The Meridian*, one can find a clear differentiation between "I" and "person": the place of poetry, or, maybe rather the moment when poetry takes the route of art, is assumed to be the place "where the person was able to set himself free as an—estranged—I" (7). When it turns into a person set loose from a living body, the I becomes a stranger to itself. For a discussion of "Gedicht und Person" see Charles de Roche's chapter in *Monadologie des Gedichts: Benjamin, Heidegger, Celan* 189–93. De Roche argues that "the poem as I-search" and "the poem as the I's becoming-person" shift its "telos precisely to the speaking I's parting from its fictionally or empirically determined identity; a parting that is the prerequisite and performance of its emergence into a personal identity at the same time" (189; my translation).

31. Celan is skeptical of the word "Schicksal" (destiny), which, understood as a clearly predestined path, indeed would run counter to the precarious uncertain

paths he ascribes to poems: "'Fateful' [Schicksal]: a highly contestable word, I know; but let it function at least as an auxiliary word; as auxiliary word, for ex., for the description of this experience: that one has to emulate one's poem [daß man seinem Gedicht nachleben muß] . . . 'You have to go through here, life!'" (*The Meridian* 118).

32. Except in a few instances, Celan uses the word "Atemwege" in the plural. Exceptions are: "The route of poetry: the breathroute" (40) and "they know that your breath pauses here—they know that they tread on your breathroute—they throttle—Helpful you gill!" (*Mikrolithen* 33; my translation).

33. "Buber, I and Thou 137 '—until the great fright comes, and the holding of one's breath in the dark, and the readying silence': / for only at times it was unpleasant for him" (129).

34. "Die Angst verschlägt uns das Wort [Fear takes our breath away]"; *Was ist Metaphysik* 35; my translation); "Das Drohende kann sich deshalb auch nicht aus einer bestimmten Richtung her innerhalb der Nähe nähern, es ist schon 'da'—und doch nirgends, es ist so nah, daß es beengt und einem den Atem verschlägt—und doch nirgends [Therefore that which threatens cannot bring itself close from a definite direction within what is close by; it is already 'there', and yet nowhere; it is so close that it is oppressive and stifles one's breath, and yet it is nowhere]"; *Sein und Zeit* 186; *Being and Time* 231). That Celan quotes Heidegger here has been observed and discussed by Anja Lemke (249).

35. "es verschlägt dir den—*falschen*—Atem; du bist / an der Atemwende" (123).

36. "ein erratischer Sprachblock, schweigt es [das Gedicht] dich an. ~~Es wirft dir dein Gerede zurück: bis sich dir der Atem [. . .] wendet~~" (97; emphasis added).

37. This is not a chronologically linear line of influence: the edition Celan owned was published in 1962, that is, after he delivered and published the *Meridian* speech.

38. A very similar formulation occurs in the letter to Hans Bender: "Craft means handiwork, a matter of hands. And these hands must belong to one person, i.e., a unique, mortal soul searching for its way with its voice and dumbness. Only truthful hands write true poems. I cannot see any basic difference between a handshake and a poem" ("Letter to Hans Bender" 26).

39. In the speech, the "Meridian" is the only image that is said to be open to a "touch," and this is the only instance where touching is mentioned: "I believe I have just now touched it [the Meridian] again" (12).

40. Other related passages in *Corpus* are: "Writing is addressed (it addresses us) from a there to an out-there, in the right-here" (19); "bodies are existence, the very act of ex-istence, being" (19).

41. In two literary texts Celan worked on at approximately the same time, to be precise.

42. Beside his translations, an essay, and various commemorative references to Mandelstam's name in his poems, Celan dedicated *Die Niemandsrose* to Mandelstam: "Dem Andenken Ossip Mandelstamms" (*Die Niemandsrose*).

43. A brief discussion of breath and silence with respect to Celan and Mandelstam and Celan's translations of Mandelstam's poems can be found in Jürgen Lehmann's article "Atmen und Verstummen: Anmerkungen zu einem Motivkomplex bei Mandel'štam und Celan."

44. This is how the scene from Büchner's Lenz that Celan cites in *The Meridian* depicts art's Medusa's head. Lenz sees a group of young girls and ponders: "At times one wishes one were a Medusa's head in order to turn a group like this into stone, and call everybody over to have a look" (5).

45. In his essay "Zwischentextlichkeiten von Celans Gedicht *Zwölf Jahre* und *Auf Reisen*," Hans-Jost Frey discusses the necessity of words undergoing a process of petrification or congealment for the possibility of speaking and speaking-toward-an-other (145).

46. Admittedly, this is a simplified reading that does not dwell on the complexities of the poem as a whole. "Weggebeizt" is a much discussed poem in Celan studies and there are plenty of readings that do more justice to it than my brief comment. For a reading especially relevant in the context of breath and literature, see Lloyd 180–82.

47. I want to point out a more far-fetched resonance: in her poem "Wuthering Heights," Sylvia Plath too conjoins commemoration, breath and air, and stones: "Of people the air only / Remembers a few odd syllables. / It rehearses them moaningly: / Black stone, black stone" (*The Collected Poems* 168).

48. This translation is my own; it has the sole purpose of reproducing Celan's translation in English as literally as possible. For a freer official English translation of Mandelstam's poem see Mandelstam 34.

49. In German, "Hauch" and "Atem" both mean breath. "Hauch" would never be used in a medical or physiological context; its meanings reach from "whiff," "breeze," "odour" "atmosphere" to "tinge" and "nuance"—the notion of fleetingness is clearly more marked in "Hauch" than in "Atem." Often, the biblical pneuma or spiritus is translated as "Hauch."

50. I owe my thanks to Christian Zehnder for his help with the Russian terms.

51. With David Lloyd, who also discusses Celan's breathcrystal, one can argue that precisely for that reason, breath is a vestige (191). Drawing on Nancy, Lloyd writes: "The trace is not the image of the subject, but the mark of its passing. As such, it bears witness" (192).

52. Once more, there are resonances between Celan, or in this case Celan's translation of Mandelstam, and Sylvia Plath: "My mirror is clouding over— / A few more breaths, and it will reflect nothing at all. / The flowers and the faces whiten to a sheet. / I do not trust the spirit. It escapes like steam." (*The Collected Poems* 152).

53. Celan stresses that for him, touch does not imply a direct contact: After quoting Whitman, he adds "Only from by this touch—that is not a 'making contact'—comes the way to intimacy" (132). Celan's idea of a still physical intimacy

without direct contact anticipates Nancy's ideas of sense and touching, which has already been hinted at and will be discussed in more detail in the end of this chapter.

54. I follow the numbering suggested in *Die Gedichte aus dem Nachlaß* 368–69.

55. For convenience's sake, I will talk about the "first" and "second" version when referring to the two reading-texts. I will address the whole complex of typescripts as "Ricercar," even though, strictly speaking, typescripts C and D are untitled.

56. The following (to a large extent literal) translations are my own.

57. It is important to note that "gehen" in German means "to go" and "to walk."

58. Relations between Celan's poem, especially the occurrence of numerous self-citations therein, and the musical term "ricercar" were pointed out by the editors of *Die Gedichte aus dem Nachlaß* (368) and discussed by various scholars, for example, Gilda Encarnação, *Fremde Nähe. Das Dialogische als poetisches und poetologisches Prinzip bei Paul Celan* (142–44); Arno Barnert, *Mit dem fremden Wort. Poetisches Zitieren bei Paul Celan* (64).

59. "nachtdurchwachsen," to be precise.

60. Arno Barnert discusses this quote along with the musical implications of the word "ricercar" (64).

61. See Yvonne Al-Taie's observation (based on Derrida's essay on Celan "Poétique et politique du témoignage") that ellipses in Celan's work are a *coupure* in the sense of both the "interruption of the text's flow, and its bodily dimension of a wound, which it reveals and inscribes in the text" (my translation, book forthcoming). For a more extensive analysis of Celan's use of ellipses with respect to the unintelligibility see her book, *Poetik der Unverständlichkeit. Schreibweisen der obscuritas als epistemologische Herausforderung bei Johann Fischart, Johann Georg Hamann, Franz Kafka und Paul Celan*.

62. The term "mandeläugig" contains a part of Mandelstam's name, which complicates the expression.

63. See Christen 105.

64. This goes hand in hand with David Wills's argument about a "paradox that Celan seems to allow": "that unutterable horror speaks through its silence as well as through its mention. And I am suggesting that if the memory of the victims of Auschwitz lives on thanks to the turn of the breath out of itself, it is because there exists a conception of inanimate life—call it memory, or the archive—that survives beyond natural life" (149).

65. That quoting can be considered a commemoration practice in Celan's writing has been discussed in Celan studies. For example, Barnert points out Barbara Wiedemann's comment "Self-allusion . . . is an attempt to 'remain mindful of the dates'" (Wiedemann 234; my translation).

66. Breath plays a significant role in Kasper's reflections on the citations of Baudelaire in the camp: in an atmosphere of pesterous air, the recitation of poetry

both enables taking breath and is breath-taking ("Kata/strophisches Lesen. Baudelaire in Buchenwald" 125).

67. The lines about the mole seem to be based on an anecdote Celan deliberately withholds. Underneath the passage, there is another handwritten note: "thinking about what has been learned about moles from Mme Desmares" (*Gedichte aus dem Nachlaß* 369; my translation). Madame Desmares was a farmer at Moisville, where Celan's family had a holiday house.

68. In *The Sense of the World*, Jean-Luc Nancy mentions "the Germanic root sinno ('direction')" (76). Thomas Böning points out that Celan's use of "Sinn" draws on this Indo-Germanic root (223).

69. Celan's well-known harsh criticism of metaphors is related to his claim that poems and words are singularities that cannot be transferred or translated.

70. A similar argument can be made about the "Uhrzeiger": clearly, the word "Uhrzeigersinn" is evoked by the spatial proximity to "Sinn" in the same line and the reference to "Uhrzeigersinn" in the "Ansprache anlässlich der Entgegennahme des Literaturpreises der freien Hansestadt Bremen." "Uhrzeigersinn" is a clearly designated direction; for Nancy, "Uhrzeigersinn" is one of the rare instances where "sense" can be identified with reference and indicates an orientation—a clear orientation which runs counter to what "sense" implies otherwise: "In this sense, referential sense makes no more sense than the circular sense of the hands of a clock" (77). In "Ricercar," the orientation usually granted by "Uhrzeigersinn" is abandoned because the word "Uhrzeiger" is separated from "Sinn" (in contrast to the Bremer Rede, where "Sinn" and "Uhrzeigersinn" are identified): the "Uhrzeiger" floats freely, a detached hand of a clock, which no longer indicates a specific direction or time, which has lost its point of reference.

71. A relation between breath and name is also established in the poem "Hüttenfenster": "Something //—a breath? a name?—// roams the orphaned" (*Gesammelte Werke* 1: 278; my translation).

72. The word occurs in the poem "Engführung."

73. Different readings of "Ricercar" could be considered as "differential articulations of singularities that make sense in articulating themselves, along the edges of their articulations" (78).

74. It would be easier to inquire into, and maybe track, such a sense of singular-plurality if I recorded and published the entire process of my reading experience in the manner of T. J. Clark's experiment of revisiting and taking notes on two paintings by Poussin every day in the Getty Museum in 2000, which is documented in his book *The Sight of Death: An Experiment in Art Writing*. In his introductory comments on the experiment, Clark observes how the details emerging in repetitive viewing rupture a (violent) coherent reading and it becomes noticeable that something of the paintings radically withdraws: "astonishing things happen if one gives oneself over to the process of seeing again and again: aspects after aspect . . . seems to surface, . . . the larger order . . . breaks up, recristallyzes,

fragments again, persists like an afterimage. And slowly the question arises: What is it, fundamentally, I am returning to in this particular case?" (5) The specific temporality of repetitive viewing, as Clark describes it, ties in with the tension between petrification and temporal openness/transactuality that Celan's texts reflect: by revisiting the paintings, by writing on and on about them, one "throw[s] the image back into time" in order to avoid their immobilizing (8).

75. See for example Müller, *Mein Vaterland war ein Apfelkern* 198–200; Müller, "Gelber Mais und keine Zeit" 129.

76. All translations from "Immer derselbe Schnee und immer derselbe Onkel" are my own.

77. In the English translation, the title is changed to *The Hunger Angel*.

78. For literary scholars, this enigmatic word poses a challenge—there have been numerous attempts to approach it, be it in terms of trying to decrypt it or to follow associations of both "Atem" and "Schaukel": see Kory, Steinecke 29; Haupt-Cucuiu 116; Bergmann 224–225; Leipelt-Tsai 79; and Kormann 287. Bettina Bannasch observes that "Atemschaukel" stresses the processuality and interminability of an artistically rendered memory of the camp (298). My own approach focuses on precisely such processual aspects of the word.

79. Müller claims that she did not touch the drafts for the novel for almost a year after Pastior's death because "in the notes the whole person was here again" ("Ich glaube nicht an die Sprache" 48; my translation).

80. Such a circling around silence coincides with the way Müller characterizes the word "Atemschaukel" and the way it works in the novel. The rotating movement can also be traced back to "Schaukel" as such, which, according to the *Deutsches Wörterbuch von Jacob und Wilhelm Grimm*, refers to several kinds of apparatuses: the hanging seat swaying to and fro, the seesaw moving up and down, and the "Schaukelrad" or Russian swing circling around (online). Müller never specifies the particular kind of swing implied by "Atemschaukel," but many passages in the novel suggest both a rotating and a to-and-fro movement.

81. In a different context, I discussed the writing process of Atemschaukel in "'Die erfundenen Worte holen Luft': Zum Schaukeln und Schaufeln der Zeit bei Herta Müller."

82. Respiratory images do not play a central role in Pastior's notebooks.

83. All translations from *Mein Vaterland war ein Apfelkern* are my own.

84. All translations from "Lebensangst und Worthunger" are my own.

85. Some of the poetic reflections discussed here and in the following are not particularly about *Atemschaukel*, but they do give evidence to a continuous poetics she developed over years, which is central to the novel.

86. All translations from "Der Teufel sitzt im Spiegel" are my own.

87. There is a precise echo between "Die Ich-Person macht mit seiner Erinnerung, was sie wollte" (*Mein Vaterland war ein Apfelkern* 209) and what Müller writes about the straying qualities words in poetic images: "Sie verzerrten die Wahrnehmung

blitzschnell, machten aus ihr, was sie wollten [They distorted perception as quick as lighting and did with it whatever they wanted]" ("Immer derselbe Schnee" 96). This is echoed in the novel when Leo reflects on words which attack him in order to drag him back into the camp after he returned home: "Es gibt Wörter, die machen mit mir, was sie wollen" (*Atemschaukel* 232); "There are words that do whatever they want with me" (*The Hunger Angel* 221). Here, the continuity Müller establishes between her poetics, her accounts of the writing process, and what goes on in the novel Atemschaukel becomes eminently apparent.

88. The term is taken from Spyros Papapetros even though the context in which he introduces it his book *On the Animation of the Inorganic: Art, Architecture, and the Extension of Life* (20–21) is a completely different one.

89. In German, "Hase" is rabbit and "Weh" is woe.

90. In her *Paris Review* interview, Müller describes this mechanism of constructing a valid reality in words that first detaches itself from "actual" reality as follows: "I start with a reality, but I have to completely demolish this reality. And then I use language to create something completely different. And if I'm lucky, it comes back together and the new language comes close again to the reality" (n.p.).

91. In this sentence, the English translation significantly deviates from the German original—the one I give mirrors the parallels and symmetries established in the German version. In almost all instances where the word breath-swing occurs, the English translation is significantly different from the German: often, the translator attempts to integrate breath-swing in an image of Leo's breathing body (for example by translating "die [the] Atemschaukel" as "his" breath-swing), a gesture that is repeatedly resisted in Müller's text.

92. The option left open in the English translation, that "swing" in the "dizzying swing in the breath" (237) refers to the movement of swinging rather than the object "swing" is not given in the German original, where "Schaukel" clearly designates the object.

93. I discussed the disrupted temporality of a traumatic past invading the presence in terms of transactuality in "'Die erfundenen Worte holen Luft': Zum Schaukeln und Schaufeln der Zeit bei Herta Müller."

94. See, for example, the scene where the prisoners are forced to dig holes for planting trees in the middle of the winter, when the "earth was frozen hard as bone" (65).

95. See David Wills's *Inanimation*, especially his elucidation of the term in the introductory chapter.

96. For an overview of trauma theory, see, for example, Atkinson and Richardson 5–6 or Schönfelder 27–41.

97. For a criticism of theories stressing the traumatic amnesia and its unspeakable nature that embraces the possible therapeutic effect of narrating traumatic events, see, for example, Joshua Pederson's "Speak, Trauma: Toward a Revised Understanding of Literary Trauma Theory."

Notes to Chapter 6

1. See, for example, *Becoming the Iceman: Pushing Past Perceived Limits* or the many YouTube videos promoting the "Wim Hof method."

2. In his article "Feminist Breathing," Jean-Thomas Tremblay sketches a genealogy of feminist breathing since the 1970s (in which, as he intriguingly argues, "feminists train themselves to keep inhaling without the certainty that there will be a world to welcome their exhalation"), especially focusing on "indigenous and black feminisms" (94).

3. Górska is very careful not to idealize the potential resistance of breath, which "is not only a productive force." "Resistance is something that must not merely be glorified for the potentiality of change it offers. Resistance is also embedded in the painful, tormenting and exhausting practices of living in suffocating social power relations" (*Breathing Matters* 181). Panic attacks, for example, "are not alternatives in the ideational sense of desired ways of being. And, simultaneously, in their painfulness they break norms apart. These breaks are terrifying, but they also open potentialities of being otherwise. The political potentialities of anxious and panicky breathing are, therefore, not only optimistic or happy in themselves, or for the sake of being alternatives, but enactments of different directionalities" ("Feminist Politics of Breathing" 253).

4. For example, Butler in *Undoing Gender* (8, 31, 58, 219); Sharpe in *In the Wake: On Blackness and Being*, especially the chapter "The Weather"; and Ahmed in *Living a Feminist Life* (219, 221, 245).

5. "The struggle for a breathable life is the struggle for queers to have space to breathe. Having space to breathe, or being able to breathe freely is . . . an aspiration" (Ahmed's *The Promise of Happiness*, qtd. in Górska, "Feminist Politics of Breathing" 253); "This is the case in terms of not only air pollution and environmental toxicity but also breathing through the racist, gendered, classist, ableist, sexist, cis-, and heteronormative social norms of human subjectivity and struggling for nonhegemonic breathable life and existence" (255). Working outside the field of feminist criticism and gender studies and with a focus on literature, Franco Berardi addresses "our contemporary condition of breathlessness" in his book *Breathing: Chaos and Poetry*, arguing that "the metaphor of poetry" offers "the only line of escape from suffocation . . . only poetry, as the excess of semiotic exchange, can reactivate breathing" (10).

6. Irigaray asserts a feminine subject position that has predominantly been molded within and through male discourses in Western culture. "Theorized on masculine models" alone, "women's subjectivity and sexual specificity remain unarticulated," as Jean Marie Byrne puts it ("Breath of Awakening" 76). Irigaray's reflections on breath both attempt to resist male gender narratives and to create new feminine ones in which women do not only break out of phallocentric discourse, but "return" to their "original" state of being beyond linguistic mediation.

7. The "forgetting of breathing" (*Between East and West* 77) that Irigaray diagnoses in Western culture is then counteracted with a theory and aspired practice of the "feminine divine." Woman receives the divine with breath at birth but is urged not to remain faithful to her own breathing (2). Her task is thus "incarnating actively in herself the divinity received at birth" (4) and increasing the inherent divinity "through faithfulness and attention to her own breathing," a "cultivation of breath before and beyond any representation and discourse" (16).

8. See Kerouac's literary ejaculation, "Come from within, out—to relaxed and said," as well as the "mindflow": "sketching language is undisturbed flow from the mind." The "flow" echoes in the English translation of "The Laugh of the Medusa," going back to Cixous's own liquid images: "I, too, overflow [moi aussi je débrode]" (876; *Le Rire de la Méduse* 38); when they speak, women "overflow at the lips [sourdre aux lèvres qu'elle va deborder de ses écumes]" (887; *Le Rire de la Méduse* 58).

9. Once more I want to refer to Rebecca Comay's and Frank Ruda's intriguing study of Hegel's dashes and their discussion of the multiple functions of the dash and its linguist spectrum in German and English (esp. 54–55). Their analysis of dashes in Hegel's *Phenomenology of Spirit* and *Science of Logic* shows how the punctuation mark, informed by these conventional functions and the semantic implication of its name always also bears witness to its individual use by a particular writer in the context of a particular text; punctuation is like handwriting and breathing, always introducing variations in the necessarily adhered-to predetermined pattern, which is thus individuated.

10. For example, "If woman has always functioned 'within' the discourse of man, a signifier that has always referred back to the opposite signifier which annihilates its specific energy and diminishes or stifles its very different sounds, it is time for her to dislocate this 'within,' to explode it, turn it around, and seize it; to make it hers, containing it, *taking it in her own mouth, biting that tongue with her very own teeth* to invent for herself a language to get inside of (887; emphasis added).

11. For example, "woman must write woman. And man, man" (877).

12. Apart from the call to "write your self" in conjunction with her reference to breath, Cixous also highlights the importance of song for écriture féminine: "In women's speech, as in their writing, that element which never stops resonating . . . is the song" (881).

13. Heine, "Circulating Multitudes" 219–20.

14. In her *Queer Theory: An Introduction*, Annamarie Jagose gives an overview of the complicated history and relation of queerness and questions of identity (72–93, 96–100). For recent critiques of identity and subjectivity, and intriguing ways of thinking beyond these terms see, for example, Irving Goh's *The Reject*, Lee Edelman's *No Future*, or John Paul Ricco's work on queer neutrality from *The Logic of the Lure* to *The Decision between Us*.

15. Bersani does not make this relation explicit: he discusses breathing in the chapter "Receptivity and Being-In" and the notion of impersonal force in "Force in

Progress," which are in large part dedicated to the films *Boys Don't Cry* and *Melancholia*. However, the connection immediately suggests itself through the receptive bodies at the center in both chapters.

16. See the definition of "contraction" in *Oxford English Dictionary* online.

17. *Leaves of Grass* 451.

18. In later versions of *Leaves of Grass* these dashes are replaced by commas.

19. This is one of the characteristics that Comay and Ruda ascribe to the dash.

20. See Comay and Ruda: The dash "signals either a continuation or a definite rupture" (7).

21. As we have seen in the discussion of Whitman's *Leaves of Grass*, this "bar" can take the form of the dash: "My songs cease—I abandon them"; "I spring from the pages into your arms—decease calls me forth."

22. Edelman uses breath-imagery when he outlines a spiritualization that goes hand in hand with reproductive futurity and the queer negativity it is based on: "queerness exposes sexuality's inevitable coloration by the drive: its insistence on repetition, its stubborn denial of teleology, its resistance to determinations of meaning . . . and, above all, its rejection of spiritualization through marriage to reproductive futurism"; "Empty, excessive, and irreducible, it designates the letter, the formal element, the lifeless machinery responsible for animating the 'spirit' of futurity" (*No Future* 27).

Bibliography

Ackerley, Chris. "Samuel Beckett and Thomas à Kempis: The Roots of Quietism." *Samuel Beckett Today/Aujourd'hui*, no. 9 (2000): 81–92.
Agamben, Giorgio. *Homo Sacer: Sovereign Power and Bare Life*. Translated by Daniel Heller-Roazen. Stanford: Stanford University Press, 1998.
Agamben, Giorgio. *Idea of Prose*. Translated by Michael Sullivan and Sam Whitsitt. Albany: SUNY, 1995.
Agamben, Giorgio. *Potentialities*. Translated by Daniel Heller-Roazen. Stanford, CA: Stanford University Press, 1999.
Agamben, Giorgio. *The Use of Bodies*. Translated by Adam Kotsko. Stanford, CA: Stanford University Press, 2016.
Ahmed, Sara. *Living a Feminist Life*. Durham, NC, and London: Duke University Press, 2017.
Allison, Raphael. *Bodies on the Line: Performance and the Sixties Poetry Reading*. Iowa: University of Iowa Press, 2014.
Al-Taie, Yvonne. *Poetik der Unverständlichkeit. Schreibweisen der obscuritas als epistemologische Herausforderung bei Johann Fischart, Johann Georg Hamann, Franz Kafka und Paul Celan*. Paderborn: Wilhelm Fink, 2021.
Alvarez, Alfred. "The Blood Jet Is Poetry." *Time Magazine*, June 10, 1966. content.time.com/time/magazine/article/0,9171,942057,00.html.
Anaximenes. *Anaximenes aus Milet: Die Fragmente zu seiner Lehre*. Edited and translated by Georg Wöhrle, Stuttgart: Franz Steiner, 1993.
Andermatt, Verena Conley, and Goh, Irving, editors. *Nancy Now*. Cambridge: Polity Press, 2014.
Anders, Martin. *Präsenz zu denken . . . Die Entgrenzungen des Körperbegriffs und Lösungswege von Leibkonzeptionen bei Ernst Mach, Robert Musil und Paul Valéry*. St. Augustin: Gardez!, 2002.
Apel, Willi. "Ricercar(e)." *Harvard Dictionary of Music*. Cambridge, MA: Belknap Press of Harvard University Press, 1969, pp. 731–34.
Aristotle. *The "Art" of Rhetoric*. Edited and translated by John Henry Freese. London: William Heinemann, 1926.

Aristotle. *De Anima*. Edited and translated by R. D. Hicks. Cambridge: Cambridge University Press, 1907.
Aristotle. *On the Soul. Parva Naturalia. On Breath.* Translated by W. S. Hett. London: William Heinemann, 1964.
Arnold, Edward Vernon. *Roman Stoicism*. Freeport, NY: Books for Libraries Press, 1971.
Arntzen, Helmut. *Musil Kommentar zum Roman "Der Mann ohne Eigenschaften."* München: Winkler, 1982.
Artaud, Antonin. *The Theatre and Its Double*. Translated by Victor Corti. London: John Calder, 1985.
Atkinson, Meera, and Richardson, Michael, editors. *Traumatic Affect*. Newcastle: Cambridge Scholars Publishing, 2013.
Bailly, Jean-Christophe. "The Slightest Breath (On Living)." *The New Centennial Review*, vol. 10, no. 3 (Winter 2010): 1–11.
Balaev, Michelle, editor. *Contemporary Approaches in Literary Trauma Theory*. London: Palgrave Macmillan, 2014.
Bannasch, Bettina. "Das aufgesperrte Maul der Null." In *Herta Müller und das Glitzern im Satz: Eine Annäherung an Gegenwartsliteratur*, edited by Jens Christian Deeg and Martina Wernli. Würzburg: Königshausen & Neumann, 2016, pp. 297–318.
Baraka, Amiri. "Amiri Baraka Class on Speech, Rhythm, Sound, and Music." Recording. Naropa Poetics Audio Archives, 1985. archive.org/details/naropa_amiri_baraka_class_on_speech.
Baraka, Amiri. *Conversations with Amiri Baraka*. Edited by Charlie Reilly. Jackson: University Press of Mississippi, 1994.
Barnert, Arno. *Mit dem fremden Wort: Poetisches Zitieren bei Paul Celan*. Frankfurt am Main and Basel: Stroemfeld, 2007.
Barnes, Jonathan. *The Presocratic Philosophers*. London: Routledge, 1986.
Barthes, Roland. "The Grain of the Voice." In *The Sound Studies Reader*, edited by Jonathan Sterne. New York: Routledge, 2012, pp. 404–510.
Bates, Catherine. "Sonnets and *A Lover's Complaint*." In *The Oxford Handbook of Shakespeare*, edited by Arthur F. Kinney. Oxford: Oxford University Press, 2012, pp. 343–51.
Bayley, Sally, and Brain, Tracy. "Introduction: 'Purdah' and the Enigma of Representation." In *Representing Sylvia Plath*. Cambridge: Cambridge University Press, 2011, pp. 1–10.
Beckett, Samuel. "Breath." *Gambit. International Theatre Review*, vol. 4, no. 16 (1970): 8–9.
Beckett, Samuel. *Comment c'est*. Paris: Les Éditions de Minuit, 1961.
Beckett, Samuel. *Company / Ill Seen Ill Said / Worstward Ho / Stirrings Still*. Edited by Dirk Van Hulle. London: Faber & Faber, 2009.

Beckett, Samuel. "Dante and the Lobster." In *The Selected Works of Samuel Beckett. Volume IV: Poems, Short Fiction, Criticism*, edited by Paul Auster. New York: Grove Press, pp. 77–88.
Beckett, Samuel. *Disjecta: Miscellaneous Writings and a Dramatic Fragment*. Edited by Ruby Cohn. London: John Calder, 1983.
Beckett, Samuel. *How it Is*. Translated by the author. New York: Grove Press, 1964.
Beckett, Samuel. *The Letters of Samuel Beckett I, 1929–1940*. Edited by Martha Dow Fehsenfeld and Lois More Overbeck. Cambridge: Cambridge University Press, 2009.
Beckett, Samuel. *L'Innommable*. Paris: Les Éditions de Minuit, 1953.
Beckett, Samuel. *L'Innommable / The Unnamable: A Digital Genetic Edition*. The Beckett Digital Manuscript Project, module 2. Edited by Dirk Van Hulle, Shane Weller, and Vincent Neyt. Brussels: University Press Antwerp (ASP/UPA), 2013. www.beckettarchive.org. (c) The Estate of the Samuel Beckett.
Beckett, Samuel. "Malone Dies." *Molloy, Malone Dies and The Unnamable: Three Novels by Samuel Beckett*. New York: Grove Press, 1959, pp. 241–398.
Beckett, Samuel. *Malone Meurt*. Paris: Les Éditions de Minuit, 1951.
Beckett, Samuel. *Malone meurt / Malone Dies: A Digital Genetic Edition*. The Beckett Digital Manuscript Project, module 5. Edited by Dirk Van Hulle, Pim Verhulst, and Vincent Neyt. Brussels: University Press Antwerp (ASP/UPA), 2017. www.beckettarchive.org. (c) The Estate of the Samuel Beckett.
Beckett, Samuel. "Molloy." In *Molloy, Malone Dies and The Unnamable: Three Novels by Samuel Beckett*. New York: Grove Press, 1959, pp. 1–240.
Beckett, Samuel. *Proust*. New York: Grove Press, 1970.
Beckett, Samuel. "Psychology Notes." In "Sourcing Aporetics: An Empirical Study on Philosophical Influences in the Development of Samuel Beckett's Writing," PhD thesis. Transcribed by Matthew Feldman. 2004.
Beckett, Samuel. "Souffle." Holograph. Samuel Beckett Collection, University of Reading, Manuscripts: Drama BC MSS DRAMA/BRE, MS 1227/7/2/1. (c) The Estate of the Samuel Beckett.
Beckett, Samuel. *Souffle*. In *Comédie et actes divers*. Paris: Les Éditions de Minuit, 1972, pp. 135–37.
Beckett, Samuel. *Stories and Texts for Nothing*. New York: Grove Press, 1967.
Beckett, Samuel. *The Unnamable*. Edited by Steven Connor. London: Faber & Faber, 2010.
Beckett, Samuel. *Waiting for Godot*. London: Faber and Faber, 1965.
Belletto, Steven, editor. *Cambridge Companion to the Beats*. Cambridge: Cambridge University Press, 2017.
Benchetrit, Gila, et al. "Individuality of Breathing Patterns in Adults Assessed over Time." *Respiration Physiology*, no. 75 (1989): 199–210.
Benjamin, Walter. *Einbahnstrasse*. Berlin: Rowohlt, 1928.

Benjamin, Walter. *One-Way Street and Other Writings*. Translated by J. A. Underwood. London: NLB, 1979.

Bennett, Jane. *Vibrant Matter: A Political Ecology of Things*. Durham, NC, and London: Duke University Press, 2010.

Benso, Silvia. "The Breathing of the Air: Presocratic Echoes in Levinas." In *Levinas and the Ancients*, edited by Brian Schroeder and Silvia Benso. Bloomington: Indiana University Press, 2008, pp. 9–23.

Benveniste, Émile. "The Notion of 'Rhythm' in Its Linguistic Expression." In *Problems in General Linguistics*, translated by Mary Elizabeth Meek. Coral Gables: University of Miami Press, 1971, pp. 281–88.

Berardi, Franco "Bifo." *Breathing: Chaos and Poetry*. South Pasadena, CA: Semiotext(e) Intervention Series, 2018.

Bergmann, Christian. "Das Unsagbare sagen: Metapher, Symbol und Allegorie in Herta Müllers Roman 'Atemschaukel.'" *Muttersprache: Vierteljahresschrift für deutsche Sprache*, no. 3 (2011): 220–26.

Bernhard, Thomas. *Der Atem: Eine Entscheidung*. München: dtv, 2011.

Bersani, Leo. *Receptive Bodies*. Chicago: University of Chicago Press, 2018.

The Bible: Authorized King James Version. Edited by Robert Carroll and Stephen Prickett. Oxford: Oxford University Press, 2008.

Bishop, Tom, and Federman, Raymond. *Samuel Beckett*. Paris: Editions de L'Herne, 1976.

Blanchot, Maurice. *L'Espace littéraire*. Paris: Gallimard, 1955.

Blanchot, Maurice. *The Space of Literature*. Translated by Ann Smock. Lincoln: University of Nebraska Press, 1989.

Blanchot, Maurice. "Where Now? Who Now?" In *On Beckett. Essays and Criticism*, edited by S. E. Gontarski. London and New York: Anthem Press, 2012, pp. 111–17.

Böning, Thomas. "'Was auf der Lunge, das auf der Zunge.' Paul Celans 'Offene Glottis'—Trauma/U-topie." In *Schmerz und Erinnerung*, edited by Roland Borgards. München: Wilhelm Fink, 2005, pp. 217–44.

Brain, Tracy. *The Other Sylvia Plath*. Harlow: Pearson Education, 2001.

Braun, Michael. "Die Erfindung der Erinnerung: Herta Müllers *Atemschaukel*." In *Gegenwartsliteratur. Ein germanistisches Jahrbuch: A German Studies Yearbook*, no. 10, 2011, pp. 33–53.

Brinkley, Douglas, editor. *Windblown World: The Journals of Jack Kerouac 1947–1954*. London: Viking Penguin, 2004.

Bronfen, Elisabeth. *Sylvia Plath*. Horndon: Northcote House, 2004.

Buber, Martin. "From the Beginnings of Our Bible Translation." In *Scripture and Translation*, translated by Everett Fox and Lawrence Rosenwald. Bloomington and Indianapolis: Indiana University Press, 1994, pp. 176–83.

Buber, Martin. "The How and Why of Our Bible Translation." In *Scripture and Translation*, translated by Everett Fox and Lawrence Rosenwald. Bloomington and Indianapolis: Indiana University Press, 1994, pp. 205–19.

Buber, Martin. *I and Thou*. Translated by Ronald Gregor Smith. New York: Scribner, 1958.
Buber, Martin. *Ich und Du*. Heidelberg: Lambert Schneider, 1977.
Buber, Martin. "On Translating the Praisings." In *Scripture and Translation*, translated by Everett Fox and Lawrence Rosenwald. Bloomington and Indianapolis: Indiana University Press, 1994, pp. 90–98.
Buber, Martin. "On Word Choice in Translating the Bible." In *Scripture and Translation*, translated by Everett Fox and Lawrence Rosenwald. Bloomington and Indianapolis: Indiana University Press, 1994, pp. 73–89.
Buber, Martin. "A Translation of the Bible." In *Scripture and Translation*, translated by Everett Fox and Lawrence Rosenwald. Bloomington and Indianapolis: Indiana University Press, 1994, pp. 166–71.
Buckley, Jeff. *Grace*. New York: Columbia Records, 1994.
Burger, Hermann. *Paul Celan. Auf der Suche nach der verlorenen Sprache*. Zürich and München: Artemis, 1974.
Butler, Judith. *Undoing Gender*. New York and London: Routledge, 2004.
Byrne, Jean Marie. "Breath of Awakening: Nonduality, Breathing and Sexual Difference." In *Breathing with Luce Irigaray*, edited by Lenart Škof and Emily A. Holmes. London: Bloomsbury Academic, 2013, pp. 67–82.
Caruth, Cathy. *Trauma: Explorations in Memory*. Baltimore and London: Johns Hopkins University Press, 1995.
Caughie, Pamela L., et al., editors. *Woolf Online*. www.woolfonline.com.
Celan, Paul. "Ansprache anlässlich der Entgegennahme des Literaturpreises der freien Hansestadt Bremen." In *Gesammelte Werke in fünf Bänden. Dritter Band. Gedichte III, Prosa, Reden*. Edited by Beda Allemann and Stefan Reichert. Frankfurt am Main: Suhrkamp, 1983, pp. 185–86.
Celan, Paul. *Der Meridian: Endfassung—Entwürfe—Materialien*. Edited by Bernhard Böschenstein and Heino Schmull. Frankfurt am Main: Suhrkamp, 1999.
Celan, Paul. *Die Gedichte*. In *Kommentierte Gesamtausgabe in einem Band*, edited by Barbara Wiedemann. Frankfurt am Main: Suhrkamp, 2003.
Celan, Paul. *Die Gedichte aus dem Nachlaß*, edited by Bertrand Badiou, Jean-Claude Rambach, and Barbara Wiedemann. Frankfurt am Main: Suhrkamp, 1997.
Celan, Paul. *Die Niemandsrose*. Frankfurt am Main: S. Fischer, 1965.
Celan, Paul. *Gesammelte Werke in fünf Bänden. Erster Band. Gedichte I*, edited by Beda Allemann and Stefan Reichert. Frankfurt am Main: Suhrkamp, 1983.
Celan, Paul. *Gesammelte Werke in fünf Bänden. Zweiter Band. Gedichte II*, edited by Beda Allemann and Stefan Reichert. Frankfurt am Main: Suhrkamp, 1983.
Celan, Paul. *Gesammelte Werke in fünf Bänden. Dritter Band. Gedichte III, Prosa, Reden*, edited by Beda Allemann and Stefan Reichert. Frankfurt am Main: Suhrkamp, 1983.
Celan, Paul. *Gesammelte Werke in fünf Bänden. Fünfter Band. Übertragungen II*, edited by Beda Allemann and Stefan Reichert. Frankfurt am Main: Suhrkamp, 1983.

Celan, Paul. *La Bibliothèque philosophique: Die philosophische Bibliothek*. Edited by Alexandra Richter, Patrik Alac and Bertrand Badiou. Paris: Éditions Rue d'Ulm, 2004.

Celan, Paul. "Letter to Hans Bender." In *Paul Celan: Collected Prose*, translated by Rosmary Waldrop. New York: Sheep Meadow Press, 1986, pp. 25–26.

Celan, Paul. *The Meridian: Final Version—Drafts—Materials*. Translated by Pierre Joris. Stanford, CA: Stanford University Press, 2011.

Celan, Paul. *Mikrolithen sinds, Steinchen: Die Prosa aus dem Nachlaß*. Edited by Barbara Wiedmann and Bertrand Badiou. Frankfurt am Main: Suhrkamp, 2005.

Celan, Paul. *Selected Poems and Prose of Paul Celan*. Translated by John Felstiner. New York and London: W. W. Norton, 2001, p. 247.

Celan, Paul. "Speech on the Occasion of Receiving the Literature Prize of the Free Hanseatic City of Bremen." In *Selected Poems and Prose of Paul Celan*, translated by John Felstiner. New York and London: W. W. Norton, 2001, pp. 295–96.

Celan, Paul. "Voices." In *Selected Poems and Prose of Paul Celan*, translated by John Felstiner. New York and London: W. W. Norton, 2001, pp. 88–93.

Celan, Paul. *Werke. Historisch-Kritische Ausgabe I. Band 11*. Edited by Holger Gehle and Thomas Schneider. Frankfurt am Main: Suhrkamp, 2006.

Chiasson, Dan. "The Girl That Things Happen To." *New Yorker*, Nov. 5, 2018. www.newyorker.com/magazine/2018/11/05/sylvia-plaths-last-letters.

Chion, Michel. *Film, a Sound Art*. Translated by Claudia Gorbman. New York: Columbia University Press, 2009.

Christen, Felix. "Celans Humanismuskritik." *Celan-Perspektiven*, no. 1 (2019): 97–106.

Cicero. *De Oratore libri tres*. Edited by August S. Wilkins. Hildesheim: Georg Olms, 1990.

Cicero. *Oratory and Orators*. Translated and edited by J. S. Watson. New York: Harper & Brothers, 1875.

Cixous, Hélène. "Hélène Cixous at the NYS Writers Institute in 2007." YouTube, Aug. 11, 2011. www.youtube.com/watch?v=evT0gGJ5Oms.

Cixous, Hélène. *Le Rire de la Méduse et autres ironies*. Paris: Galilée, 2010.

Cixous, Hélène. "The Laugh of the Medusa." Translated by Keith Cohen and Paula Cohen. *Signs*, vol. 1, no. 4 (Summer 1976): 875–93.

Cixous, Hélène. "Medusas 'Changeance': Ein Interview mit Hélène Cixous." In *Das Lachen der Medusa zusammen mit aktuellen Beiträgen*, edited by Esther Hutfless, Gertrude Postl, and Elisabeth Schäfer. Wien: Passagen, 2013, pp. 181–91.

Cixous, Hélène, and Derrida, Jacques. "From the Word to Life: A Dialogue between Jacques Derrida and Hélène Cixous." *New Literary History*, vol. 37, no. 1 (Winter 2006): 1–13.

Clark, T. J. *The Sight of Death: An Experiment in Art Writing*. New Haven and London: Yale University Press, 2006.

Clément, Catherine. *Syncope: The Philosophy of Rupture*. Translated by Deirdre M. Mahoney and Sally O'Driscoll. Minneapolis: University of Minnesota Press, 1994.

Climent, James, editor. *Encyclopaedia of the Jazz Age. From the End of World War I to the Great Crash*. Volumes 1–2. London and New York: Routledge, 2015.
Cohn, Ruby. *A Beckett Canon*. Ann Arbor: The University of Michigan Press, 2001.
Comay, Rebecca, and Ruda, Frank. *The Dash—The Other Side of Absolute Knowing*. Cambridge, MA: MIT Press, 2018.
Connor, Steven. "Beckett's Atmospheres." Paper given at the After Beckett/Après Beckett conference, Sydney, January 2003. stevenconnor.com/atmospheres-2.html.
Connor, Steven. "Modernism and the Writing Hand." Expanded version of a paper given at the Modernism and the Technology of Writing conference in the Institute of English Studies, March 26, 1999. stevenconnor.com/modhand.html.
Connor, Steven. "Preface." In *The Unnamable*. London: Faber & Faber, 2010, pp. vii–xxiii.
Connor, Steven. "Was That a Point? Beckett's Punctuation." *The Edinburgh Companion to Samuel Beckett and the Arts*, edited by S. E. Gontarski. Edinburgh: Edinburgh University Press, 2014, pp. 269–81.
Crawley, Ashon T. *Blackpentecostal Breath: The Aesthetics of Possibility*. New York: Fordham University Press, 2017.
Crowther, Gail, and Steinberg, Peter K. *These Ghostly Archives: The Unearthing of Sylvia Plath*. Stroud: Fronthill Media, 2017.
Culler, Jonathan. "Apostrophe." *Diacritics*, vol. 7, no. 4 (Winter 1977): 59–69.
Culler, Jonathan. "The Closeness of Close Reading." *ADE Bulletin*, no. 149 (2010): 20–25.
Davidson, Michael. "'By ear, he sd': Audio-Tapes and Contemporary Criticism." *Credences*, vol. 1, no. 1 (1981): 105–20. www.audibleword.org/poetics/Davidson-By_Ear_He_Sd.htm.
Davidson, Michael. *Ghostlier Demarcations: Modern Poetry and the Material World*. Berkeley: University of California Press, 1997.
Dejours, Pierre. *Respiration*. New York: Oxford University Press, 1966.
Dejours, Pierre, et al. "Étude de la diversité des regimes ventilatoires chez l'homme." *Journal de Physiologie*, vol. 53 (1961): 320–21.
Deleuze, Gilles. *Essays Critical and Clinical*. Translated by Daniel W. Smith and Michael A. Greco. London and New York: Verso, 1998.
Deleuze, Gilles, and Guattari, Félix. *What Is Philosophy?* Translated by Hugh Tomlinson and Graham Burchell. New York: Columbia University Press, 1994.
Dellwo, Volker, Huckvale, Mark, and Ashby, Michael G. "How Is Individuality Expressed in Voice? An Introduction to Speech Production and Description for Speaker Classification." In *Speaker Classification I. Lecture Notes in Computer Science*, vol. 4343, edited by Christian Müller. Berlin and Heidelberg: Springer, 2007. https://doi.org/10.1007/978-3-540-74200-5_1.
de Nervaux-Gavoty, Laure. "Coming to Terms with Colour." In *Representing Sylvia Plath*, edited by Sally Bayley and Tracy Brain. Cambridge: Cambridge University Press, 2011, pp. 110–28.

de Oliveira, Claire. "Composition et décomposition: Les néologismes subversifs de *La Bascule du soufflé.*" In *Kann Literatur Zeuge sein? Poetische und politische Aspekte in Herta Müllers Werk. Jahrbuch für Internationale Germanistik.* Reihe A—Band 112, edited by Dorle Merchiers, Jacques Lajarrige, and Steffen Höhne, Bern: Peter Lang, 2014, pp. 99–108.

de Roche, Charles. *Monalodogie des Gedichts: Benjamin, Heidegger, Celan.* München: Wilhelm Fink, 2013.

Derrida, Jacques. "Edmond Jabès and the Question of the Book." In *Writing and Difference*, translated by Alan Bass. London and New York: Routledge, 2001, pp. 77–96.

Derrida, Jacques. *Heidegger: The Question of Being and History.* Translated by Geoffrey Bennington. Chicago: University of Chicago Press, 2016.

Derrida, Jacques. "La parole soufflée." In *Writing and Difference*, translated by Alan Bass. London and New York: Routledge, 2001, pp. 213–45.

Derrida, Jacques. "Violence and Metaphysics: An Essay on the Thought of Emmanuel Levinas." In *Writing and Difference*, translated by Alan Bass. London and New York: Routledge, 2001, pp. 97–192.

Derrida, Jacques. *Writing and Difference*, translated by Alan Bass. London and New York: Routledge, 2001.

Descartes, René. *The Philosophical Writings of Descartes. Volume 3: The Correspondence.* Translated by John Cottingham et al. Cambridge: Cambridge University Press, 1991.

Deutsches Wörterbuch von Jacob und Wilhelm Grimm. Leipzig 1854–1961. Leipzig: Hirzel, 1971. woerterbuchnetz.de.

Dolar, Mladen. *A Voice and Nothing More.* Cambridge, MA: MIT Press, 2006.

Drinker, Philip, and Shaw, Louis A. "An Apparatus for the Prolonged Administration of Artificial Respiration: I. A Design for Adults and Children." *JCI: The Journal of Clinical Investigation*, vol. 7, no. 2 (1929): 229–47.

Duncan, Joel. "Frank O'Hara Drives Charles Olson's Car." *Arizona Quarterly: A Journal of American Literature, Culture, and Theory*, vol. 72, no. 4 (2016): 77–103.

Duncan, Joel. "The Song in the Machine: Organic Forms of American Poetry," PhD thesis, University of Notre Dame. curate.nd.edu/show/2r36tx33n8n.

Dunn, Patrick. "'What If I Sang': The Intonation of Allen Ginsberg's Performances." *Style*, vol. 41, no. 1 (2007): 75–93.

Dünzl, Franz. *Pneuma: Funktionen des theologischen Begriffs in frühchristlicher Literatur.* Münster: Aschendorff, 2000.

Ebner, Ferdinand. *Das Wort und die geistigen Realitäten: Pneumatologische Fragmente.* Innsbruck: Brenner, 1921.

Edelman, Lee. "Against Survival: Queerness in a Time That's Out of Joint." *Shakespeare Quarterly*, vol. 62, no. 2 (Summer 2011): 148–69. https://doi: 10.1353/shq.2011.0015.

Edelman, Lee. *No Future: Queer Theory and the Death Drive.* Durham, NC, and London: Duke University Press, 2004.

Egeland, Marianne. *Claiming Sylvia Plath*. Newcastle: Cambridge Scholars Publishing, 2013.
Encarnação, Gilda. *Fremde Nähe. Das Dialogische als poetisches und poetologisches Prinzip bei Paul Celan*. Berlin: De Gruyter, 2007.
Encyclopædia Britannica. Volume 19. Cambridge: Cambridge University Press, 1911.
Fanta, Walter. *Die Entstehungsgeschichte des "Mann ohne Eigenschaften" von Robert Musil*, Wien: Böhlau, 2000.
Feldman, Matthew. " 'Agnostic Quietism' and Samuel Beckett's Early Development." In *Samuel Beckett: History, Memory, Archive*, edited by S. Kennedy and K. Weiss. New York: Palgrave Macmillan, 2009, pp. 183–200.
Felman, Shoshana. "Trauma and Pedagogy." In *Trauma: Explorations in Memory*, edited by Cathy Caruth. Baltimore and London: Johns Hopkins University Press, 1995, pp. 13–60.
Fenollosa, Ernest. "The Chinese Written Character as a Medium for Poetry." In *Instigations*, edited by Ezra Pound. New York: Boni and Liveright, 1920, pp. 357–88.
Fradenburg, L. O. Aranye. *Staying Alive: A Survival Manual for The Liberal Arts*. Edited by Eileen A. Joy. New York: punctum books, 2013.
Freud, Sigmund. *The Basic Writings of Sigmund Freud*. Edited and translated by A. A. Brill. New York: The Modern Library, Random House, 1938.
Freud, Sigmund. *Beyond the Pleasure Principle*. Edited and translated by James Strachey. New York and London: W. W. Norton, 1961.
Freud, Sigmund. *Psychopathology of Everyday Life*. Translated by A. A. Brill. London: T Fisher Unwin, 1928.
Frey, Hans-Jost. "Zwischentextlichkeiten von Celans Gedicht *Zwölf Jahre* und *Auf Reisen*." In *Paul Celan*, edited by Werner Hamacher and Winfried Menninghaus. Frankfurt am Main: Suhrkamp, 1988, pp. 139–55.
Gadamer, Hans-Georg. *Wer bin ich und wer bist Du? Ein Kommentar zu Celans Gedichtfolge "Atemkristall."* Frankfurt am Main: Suhrkamp, 1986.
Gaelic Dictionary, in Two Parts. London: Printed for James Duncan, Howell and Stewart, 1825.
Gelhard, Andreas, Schmidt, Ulf, and Schultz, Tanja. "Stillstellen: Einige Vorbemerkungen." In *Stillstellen: Medien, Aufzeichnung, Zeit*, edited by Andreas Gelhard, Ulf Schmidt, and Tanja Schultz. Schliengen: Edition Argus 2004, pp. 7–11.
Gerhardt, Rainer Maria. *Umkreisung: Das Gesamtwerk*, edited by Uwe Pörksen. Göttingen: Wallstein, 2007.
Ginsberg, Allen. "Albuquerque Auto Poesy Reading at Santa Fe College." Recording. 1966, Allen Ginsberg Papers, Special Collections, Stanford University, Box 66, Tape 66A1/045. Recording.
Ginsberg, Allen. "Allen Ginsberg: An Interview by Gary Pacernick." *American Poetry Review*, July/August 1997, pp. 23–27.
Ginsberg, Allen. "Allen Ginsberg Chants and Poems." Recording. London, August 1967, Iowa Digital Library. digital.lib.uiowa.edu/cdm/ref/collection/ictcs/id/26832.

Ginsberg, Allen. *Allen Verbatim: Lectures on Poetry, Politics, Consciousness*, edited by Gordon Ball. New York: McGraw-Hill, 1974.

Ginsberg, Allen. "Basic Poetics #14." Recording. 1980, February 28, Allen Ginsberg Papers, Special Collections, Stanford University, Cassette Box 14, Audiocassette, 80F2/027.

Ginsberg, Allen. "Basic Poetics #15." 1980, March 3, Allen Ginsberg Papers, Special Collections, Stanford University, Cassette Box 15, Audiocassette, 80F2/028. Recording.

Ginsberg, Allen. "Buddhism and Breathing—The Red Tin Begging Cup." Recording. Montreal, 1969, Allen Ginsberg Project.

Ginsberg, Allen. *Collected Poems 1947–1997*. New York: Harper & Row, 1984.

Ginsberg, Allen. *Expansive Poetics*. Recording, Course at Naropa Institute, 1981, Naropa University Audio Archive. cdm16621.contentdm.oclc.org/cdm/singleitem/collection/p16621coll1/id/1018/rec/13.

Ginsberg, Allen. *The Fall of America and Iron Horse [Draft]*. Allen Ginsberg Papers, Special Collections, Stanford University, Box 39, Folder 6.

Ginsberg, Allen. "Fourteen Steps for Revising Poetry." In *Deliberate Prose: Selected Essays 1952–1995*, edited by Bill Morgan. New York: HarperCollins, 2000, Part 6.

Ginsberg, Allen. "How *Kaddish* Happened." In *Deliberate Prose: Selected Essays 1952–1995*, edited by Bill Morgan. New York: HarperCollins, 2000, pp. 232–35.

Ginsberg, Allen. *Iron Horse*. Reading. Recording. Maryland Institute, Johns Hopkins University, Baltimorem 1967, April 11, Allen Ginsberg Papers, Special Collections, Stanford University, Box 377, Audiocassette 71A1/031.

Ginsberg, Allen. *Iron Horse [Draft]*, Allen Ginsberg Papers, Special Collections, Stanford University, Box 7.1, Folder 41.

Ginsberg, Allen. *Journals Mid-Fifties*, 1954–1958, edited by Gordon Ball. New York: HarperCollins, 1995.

Ginsberg, Allen. *The Letters of Allen Ginsberg*. Edited by Bill Morgan. Philadelphia: Da Capo Press, 2008.

Ginsberg, Allen. *Mind, Mouth, and Page*. Recording. Naropa Institute Lecture, 1975, Allen Ginsberg Project.

Ginsberg, Allen. *Naropa Workshop, Part 1*. Recording. 1983, May 2, Allen Ginsberg Papers, Special Collections, Stanford University, Cassette Box 26, Audiocassette, 83F2/037.

Ginsberg, Allen: "Notes for *Howl* and Other Poems." In *The New American Poetry 1945–1960*, edited by Donald M. Allen. Berkeley: University of California Press, 1999, pp. 414–20.

Ginsberg, Allen. *Power and Weakness of Poetry*. Speech delivered to Serbian Writers conference, 1980, Allen Ginsberg Papers, Special Collections, Stanford University, Box 67, Folder 16. Transcript.

Ginsberg, Allen. "Some Metamorphoses of Personal Prosody." In *Deliberate Prose: Selected Essays 1952–1995*, edited by Bill Morgan. New York: HarperCollins, 2000, pp. 258–59.

Ginsberg, Allen. *Spiritual Poetics II*. Recording. Lecture at the Naropa University, July 31, 1974, Naropa Poetics Audio Archives. archive.org/details/ Allen_Ginsberg_class_Spiritual_Poetics_part_2_July_1974_74P002.
Ginsberg, Allen. *Spontaneous Mind: Selected Interviews 1958–1996*. Edited by David Carter. New York: HarperCollins, 2001.
Ginsberg, Allen. Untitled [*Iron Horse*, Recording of Composition]. Recording. Allen Ginsberg Papers, Special Collections, Stanford University Box 67, Tape 66A1/053.
Goh, Irving. *The Reject: Community, Politics, and Religion after the Subject*. New York: Fordham University Press, 2014.
Golston, Michael. *Rhythm and Race in Modernist Poetry and Science. Pound, Yeats, Williams, and Modern Sciences of Rhythm*. New York: Columbia University Press, 2007.
Gontarski, Stanley E., and Ackerley, Chris J. " 'The Knowing Non-Exister': Thirteen Ways of Reading Texts for Nothing." In *A Companion to Samuel Beckett*, edited by Stanley E. Gontarski. Chichester, Maldenn and Oxford: Wiley-Blackwell, 2010, pp. 289–95.
Górska, Magdalena. *Breathing Matters: Feminist Intersectional Politics of Vulnerability*. Linköping Studies in Arts and Science No. 683. Linköping, 2016.
Górska, Magdalena. "Feminist Politics of Breathing." In *Atmospheres of Breathing*, edited by Lenart Škof and Petri Berndtson. Albany: SUNY, 2018, pp. 247–59.
Goudouna, Sozita. *Beckett's Breath: Anti-theatricality and the Visual Arts*. Edinburgh: Edinburgh University Press, 2018.
Greenblatt, Stephen, editor. *The Norton Shakespeare*. New York: W. W. Norton, 1997.
Greene, Roland, et al., editors. *The Princeton Encyclopedia of Poetry and Poetics*. Princeton: Princeton University Press, 2012.
Grill, Genese. *The World as Metaphor in Robert Musil's* The Man Without Qualities: *Possibility as Reality*. Rochester, NY: Camden House 2012.
Grosjean, François, and Collins, Maryann. "Breathing, Pausing and Reading." *Phonetica*, no. 36 (1979): 98–114.
Gschwandtner, Harald. *Ekstatisches Erleben: Neomystische Konstellationen bei Robert Musil*. München: Wilhelm Fink, 2013.
Guggenheim, Peggy. *Out of This Century: The Informal Memoirs of Peggy Guggenheim*. New York: Dial Press, 1946.
Guthrie, W. K. C. *A History of Greek Philosophy. The Earlier Presocratics and the Pythagoreans*. Cambridge: Cambridge University Press, 1962.
Hahm, David E. *The Origins of Stoic Cosmology*. Columbus: Ohio State University Press, 1977.
Haines, Brigid. "Return from the Archipelago: Herta Müller's Atemschaukel as Soft Memory." In *Herta Müller*, edited by Brigid Haines and Lyn Marven. Oxford: Oxford University Press, 2013, pp. 118–35.
Harst, Joachim. "Gegenstände, Widerworte: Erotik von Wahrnehmung und Sprache bei Robert Musil und Max Blecher." *Germanisch-romanische Monatsschrift*, vol. 57, no. 4 (2007): 465–85.

Hart Nibbrig, Cristiaan Lucas. "Ver-rückte Augenblicke: Vom Atmen der Texte." In *Rhythmus: Spuren eines Wechselspiels in Künsten und Wissenschaften*, edited by Barbara Naumann. Würzburg: Königshausen and Neumann, 2005, pp. 93–108.

Hartwig, Ina. "Der Held heißt Hungerengel." *Frankfurter Rundschau*, Oct. 12, 2009. www.fr-online.de/kultur/shortlist-deutscher-buchpreis-der-held-heisst-hungerengel,1472786,2965066.html.

Haupt-Cucuiu, Herta. "Herta Müllers 'Diskurs des Alleinseins'—Eine Stilbeschreibung und eine (späte) Antwort auf Iris Radischs Verriss der *Atemschaukel*." In *Interkulturelle Erkundungen. Leben, Schreiben und Lernen in zwei Kulturen, Teil 1*, edited by Andrea Benedek et al. Frankfurt am Main: Peter Lang, 2012, pp. 109–18.

Heidegger, Martin. *Being and Time*. Translated by John Macquarrie and Edward Robinson. Oxford: Blackwell, 2006.

Heidegger, Martin. *Was ist Metaphysik?* Frankfurt am Main: Vittorio Klostermann, 1998.

Heine, Stefanie. "Aesthetic Autophony and the Night." *Angelaki*, vol. 23, no. 3 (58–74). https://doi: 10.1080/0969725X.2018.1473927.

Heine, Stefanie. "Animi velut respirant. Rhythm and Breathing Pauses in Ancient Rhetoric, Virginia Woolf and Robert Musil." *Comparative Literature*, vol. 69, no. 4 (2017): 355–69. https://doi: 10.1215/00104124-4260409.

Heine, Stefanie. "Breathing Machines. Inspiration and Interdependence in Contemporary Art Installations." In *Die Kunst der Rezeption*, edited by Marc Caduff, Stefanie Heine, and Michael Steiner. Bielefeld: Aisthesis, 2014, pp. 69–85.

Heine, Stefanie. "Circulating Multitudes: From Antiquity to Cell Theory." *Walt Whitman Quarterly Review*, vol. 35 (2018): 219–44. https://doi: 10.13008/0737-0679.2288.

Heine, Stefanie. " 'Die erfundenen Wörter holen Luft': Zum Schaukeln und Schaufeln der Zeit bei Herta Müller." In *Transaktualität: Ästhetische Dauerhaftigkeit und Flüchtigkeit*, edited by Stefanie Heine and Sandro Zanetti. Paderborn: Wilhelm Fink, 2017, pp. 249–59.

Heine, Stefanie. "Ebb and Flow. Breath-Writing from Ancient Rhetoric to Jack Kerouac and Allen Ginsberg." In *Reading Breath in Literature*, edited by Arthur Rose et al. Cham: Palgrave Pivot, 2019, pp. 91–112. https://doi: 10.1007/978-3-319-99948-7_5.

Heine, Stefanie. "First Thought, Best Thought: Improvisation bei Jack Kerouac und Allen Ginsberg." In *Improvisation und Invention: Momente, Modelle, Medien*, edited by Sandro Zanetti. Zürich: Diaphanes, 2014, pp. 245–59.

Heine, Stefanie. "Fishy Etymologies: Sprachgeschichtliche Irrwege bei Charles Olson." *Colloquium Helveticum*, vol. 46 (2017): 131–43.

Heine, Stefanie. "Forces of Unworking in Virginia Woolf's 'Time Passes.' " *Textual Cultures*, vol. 12, no. 1 (2019): 120–36. https://doi: 10.14434/textual.v12i1.27150.

Heine, Stefanie. "Sprechen jenseits des Lebenden bei Sylvia Plath." In *Lyrikologie. Band 1: Wer spricht das Gedicht?* Edited by Claudia Hillebrandt et al. München: de Gruyter, 2018, pp. 340–51. https://doi: 10.1515/9783110520521-018.
Heine, Stefanie. "These Things Astonish Me beyond Words: Virginia Woolf, Sylvia Plath, William Carlos Williams." *Figurationen*, no. 2 (2013): 28–44.
Heine, Stefanie, and Zanetti, Sandro, editors. *Transaktualität: Ästhetische Dauerhaftigkeit und Flüchtigkeit*. Paderborn: Wilhelm Fink, 2017.
Henke, Suzette A. *Shattered Subjects: Trauma in Women's Life-Writing*. New York: St. Martin's Press, 1998.
Herren, Graley. "A Womb with a View: *Film* as Regression Fantasy." In *The Edinburgh Companion to Samuel Beckett and the Arts*, edited by S. E. Gontarski. Edinburgh: Edinburgh University Press, 2014, pp. 237–50.
Hof, Wim, and Rosales, Justin. *Becoming the Iceman: Pushing Past Perceived Limits*. Minneapolis, MN: Mill City Press, 2012.
Honold, Alexander. "Der singende Text. Klanglichkeit als literarische Performanzqualität." In *Literatur intermedial: Paradigmenbildung zwischen 1918 und 1968*, edited by Wolf Gerhard Schmidt and Thorsten Valk. Berlin and New York: de Gruyter, 2009, pp. 187–207.
Houston, Keith. *Shady Characters: The Secret Life of Punctuation, Symbols, and Other Typographical Marks*. New York: Norton, 2014.
Hrebeniak, Michael. "Jazz and the Beat Generation." In *The Cambridge Companion to the Beats*, edited by Steven Belletto. Cambridge: Cambridge University Press, 2017, pp. 250–64.
Hutchins, William. "Abated Drama: Samuel Beckett's Unbated 'Breath.'" *Ariel: A Review of International English Literature*, vol. 17, no. 1 (1986): 85–94.
I Heard There Was a Secret Chord. Participatory artwork by Mouna Andraos and Melissa Mongiat at the exhibition, "Une brèche en toute chose /A Crack in Everything." Musée d'Art Contemporain de Montréal and online. asecretchord.com/en.
The Interlinear Hebrew-Aramaic Old Testament. Volume 1. Edited by Jay P. Green. Peabody: Hendrickson, 2014.
The Interlinear Hebrew-Aramaic Old Testament. Volume 2. Edited by Jay P. Green, Peabody: Hendrickson, 2014.
The Interlinear Hebrew-Aramaic Old Testament. Volume 3. Edited by Jay P. Green, Peabody: Hendrickson, 2014.
Inwood, Brad, editor. *The Cambridge Companion to the Stoics*. Cambridge: Cambridge University Press, 2003.
Inwood, Brad, and Gerson, Lloyd P., editors. *The Stoics Reader: Selected Writings and Testimonia*. Indianapolis and Cambridge: Hackett Publishing Company, 2008.
Irigaray, Luce. *Between East and West: From Singularity to Community*. New York: Columbia University Press, 2002.
Irigaray, Luce. *Die Zeit des Atems. The Age of Breath. L'epoca del respire. Le temps du soufflé*. Rüsselheim: Christel Göttert, 1999.

Irigaray, Luce. *The Forgetting of Air in Martin Heidegger.* Austin: The University of Texas Press, 1999.

Jagose, Annamarie. *Queer Theory: An Introduction.* New York: New York University Press, 1996.

Jakobson, Roman. "Linguistics and Poetics." In *Language in Literature*, edited by Krystyna Pomorska and Stephen Rudy. Cambridge, MA, and London: The Belknap Press of Harvard University Press, 1987, pp. 62–94.

Jones, Norman L. *The Ins and Outs of Breathing.* Bloomington, IN: iUniverse, 2011.

Kasper, Judith. *Der traumatisierte Raum: Insistenz, Inschrift, Montage bei Freud, Levi, Kertész, Sebald und Dante.* Berlin: de Gruyter, 2016.

Kasper, Judith. "Kata/strophisches Lesen. Baudelaire in Buchenwald." In *Unfälle der Sprache: Literarische und philologische Erkundungen der Katastrophe*, edited by Ottmar Ette and Judith Kasper. Wien: Turia+Kant, pp. 117–30.

Katz, Daniel. "From Olson's Breath to Spicer's Gait: Spacing, Placing, Phonemes." In *Contemporary Olson*, edited by David Herd. Manchester: Manchester University Press, 2015, pp. 78–88.

Kaye, P., Young, H., and O'Sullivan, I. "Metal Fume Fever: A Case Report and Review of the Literature." *Emergency Medicine Journal*, vol. 19, no. 3 (2002): 268–69.

Kean, Sam. *Caesar's Last Breath: Decoding the Secrets of the Air around Us.* New York: Little, Brown and Company, 2017.

Kerouac, Jack. "The Art of Fiction No. 41." *Paris Review*, no. 43 (1968). www.theparisreview.org/interviews/4260/the-art-of-fiction-no-41-jack-kerouac.

Kerouac, Jack. "Dialogues in Great Books." In *Empty Phantoms: Interviews and Encounters with Jack Kerouac*, edited by Paul Maher. New York: Thunder's Mouth Press, 2005, pp. 184–202.

Kerouac, Jack. "Essentials of Spontaneous Prose." In *The Portable Beat Reader*, edited by Ann Charters. New York: Viking, 1992, pp. 57–58.

Kerouac, Jack. "History of the Theory of Breath as a Separator of Statements in Spontaneous Writing by Jack Kerouac." Berg Collection, New York Public Library, 12.39.

Kerouac, Jack. *Holograph notebook [The / Spiral / Composition / Book].* 1944, Berg Collection, New York Public Library, 53.3.

Kerouac, Jack. "I Know I Am August." In *Atop an Underwood. Early Stories and Other Writings*, edited by Paul Marion. New York: Penguin Books, 1999, pp. 41–43.

Kerouac, Jack. "Letters to Myself." Photocopied typed letter, unsigned, Nov. 21, 1960, Berg Collection, New York Public Library, 12.9, C1, f.8.

Kerouac, Jack. "New York Nite Club—." In *Atop an Underwood: Early Stories and Other Writings*, edited by Paul Marion. New York: Penguin Books, 1999, pp. 61–62.

Kerouac, Jack. "A Play I Want to Write." In *Atop an Underwood: Early Stories and Other Writings*, edited by Paul Marion. New York: Penguin Books, 1999, pp. 28–29.

Kerouac, Jack. "Rasping Smoke in a Dry Throat." Typescript, revised, 1940, Berg Collection, New York Public Library, B1, f.4, 4.5.
Kerouac, Jack. "The Repetoire [sic] of Modern Ideas." Holograph draft. Berg Collection, New York Public Library, 43.4.
Kerouac, Jack. "Se dur pour mue parle l'Angla [sic] parse je toujour parle le Francais Canadien." Typescript fragment, revised, Berg Collection, New York Public Library, A1, f.23, 1.24.
Kerouac, Jack. *Selected Letters, 1940–1956*. Edited by Ann Charters. New York: Viking Penguin, 1995.
Kerouac, Jack. *Selected Letters, 1957–1969*. Edited by Ann Charters. New York: Viking Penguin, 1999.
Kerouac, Jack. "Supreme Reality." Holograph notes. 1943, Berg Collection, New York Public Library, B11, f.33, 7.56.
Kerouac, Jack. "There's Something about a Cigar." In *Atop an Underwood: Early Stories and Other Writings*, edited by Paul Marion. New York: Penguin Books, 1999, pp. 66–71.
Kerouac, Jack. Typescript fragment. Berg Collection, New York Public Library, 16.21, D2, f.31.
Kerouac, Jack. "Various Notes, Fragments and Scraps." Berg Collection, New York Public Library, A6, f.23, 3.40.
Kerouac, Jack. "Writing for Yourself." Typescript essay, revised. September 29, 1950, Berg Collection, New York Public Library, 42.2.
Kirk, Geoffrey, Raven, John, and Schofield, Malcolm, editors. *The Presocratic Philosophers: A Critical History with a Selection of Texts*. Cambridge: Cambridge University Press, 1983.
Kittler, Friedrich A. *Gramophone, Film, Typewriter*. Translated by Geoffrey Winthrop-Young and Michael Wutz. Stanford, CA: Stanford University Press, 1999.
Kleinberg-Levin, David Michael. *Before the Voice of Reason: Echoes of Responsibility in Merleau-Ponty's Ecology and Levinas's Ethics*. Albany: SUNY, 2008.
Knowlson, James. *Damned to Fame: The Life of Samuel Beckett*. London: Bloomsbury, 1996.
Koelle, Lydia. *Paul Celans pneumatisches Judentum. Gott-Rede und menschliche Existenz nach der Shoah*. Mainz: Matthias Grünewald, 1997.
Konersmann, Ralf, and Westerkamp, Dirk, editors. *Rhythmus und Moderne: Zeitschrift für Kulturphilosophie*, no. 1. Hamburg: Felix Meiner, 2013.
Kormann, Eva. "Wie viel Sprachekunst verträgt die Darstellung des Schreckens?" In *Herta Müller und das Glitzern im Satz: Eine Annäherung an Gegenwartsliteratur*, edited by Jens Christian Deeg und Martina Wernli. Würzburg: Königshausen & Neumann, 2016, pp. 279–96.
Kory, Beate Petra. "Herta Müllers Sprachpantomime Atemschaukel. Ein Annäherungsversuch an die Zentralmetapher des Romans." *Temeswarer Beiträge zur Germanistik*, no. 10 (2013): 59–67.

Krämer, Sybille. "Medien, Boten, Spuren. Wenig mehr als ein Literaturbericht." In *Was ist ein Medium?*, edited by Stefan Münker and Alexander Roesler. Frankfurt am Main: Suhrkamp, 2008, pp. 65–90.

Krämer, Sybille. *Medium, Bote, Übertragung: Kleine Metaphysik der Medialität*. Frankfurt am Main: Suhrkamp, 2008.

Krämer, Sybille. *Medium, Messenger, Transmission: An Approach to Media Philosophy*. Amsterdam: Amsterdam University Press, 2015.

Krieger, Elliot. "Samuel Beckett's Texts for Nothing: Explication and Exposition." *MLN*, vol. 92, no. 5 (Dec. 1977): 987–1000.

LaCapra, Dominick. *Writing History, Writing Trauma*. Baltimore: Johns Hopkins University Press, 2001.

Lavoisier, Antoine Laurent, and Séguin, Armand. "Premier mémoire sur la respiration des animaux." In *Mémoires sur le respiration et la transpiration des animaux*. Paris: Gauthiers-Villars, 1920, pp. 31–51.

Lehmann, Jürgen. "Atmen und Verstummen. Anmerkungen zu einem Motivkomplex bei Mandel'štam und Celan." *Paul Celan. "Atemwende": Materialien*, edited by Gerhard Buhr and Roland Reuß. Würzburg: Königshausen & Neumann, 1991, pp. 187–99.

Leipelt-Tsai, Monika. *Spalten—Herta Müllers Textologie zwischen Psychoanalyse und Kulturtheorie*. Frankfurt am Main: Peter Lang, 2015.

Lemke, Anja. "Dichtung als Zäsur—Zum Zusammenhang von Sprache, Tod und Geschichte in Celans Büchnerpreisrede und Heideggers Hölderlin-Deutung." In *"In die Höhe fallen." Grenzgänge zwischen Literatur und* Philosophie, edited by Anja Lemke and Martin Schierbaum. Würzburg: Königshausen and Neumann, 2000, pp. 233–70.

Levinas, Emmanuel. *Otherwise Than Being or Beyond Essence*. Pittsburgh: Duquesne University Press, 1988.

Lewis, Charlton T., and Short, Charles. *A Latin Dictionary*. Oxford: Clarendon Press, 1879. www.perseus.tufts.edu.

Liddell, Henry George, and Scott, Robert. *A Greek-English Lexicon*. Oxford: Clarendon Press. 1940. www.perseus.tufts.edu.

Light, Allan. *The Holy or the Broken: Leonard Cohen, Jeff Buckley & the Unlikely Ascent of "Hallelujah."* New York: Atria Books, 2012.

Littré, Émile. *Dictionnaire de la langue française. Tome 3*. Paris: L. Hachette, 1873–1874.

Littré, Émile. *Dictionnaire de la langue française. Tome 4*. Paris: L. Hachette, 1873–1874.

Lloyd, David. "Breath Crystals. A Vestigial Poetics of Breath in Beckett, Celan, and Arikha." *Samuel Beckett Today / Aujourd'hui*, no. 30 (2018): 179–95.

Lowe, Peter J. "'Full Fathom Five': The Dead Father in Sylvia Plath's Seascapes." *Texas Studies in Literature and Language*, vol. 49, no. 1 (Spring 2007): 21–44.

Lowell, Amy. "Some Musical Analogies in Modern Poetry." *The Musical Quarterly*, vol. 6, no. 1 (1920): 127–57.
Lowell, Robert. "Foreword." In *Ariel: Poems by Sylvia Plath*. New York: Harper and Row, 1961, pp. vii–ix.
Lozier, Claire. "'Breath' as 'Vanitas': Beckett's Debt to a Baroque Genre." *Samuel Beckett Today / Aujourd'hui*, vol. 22 (2010): 241–51.
Lutze, Ernst. *Die Germanischen Übersetzungen von Spiritus und Pneuma: Ein Beitrag zur Frühgeschichte des Wortes "Geist."* Bonn: Rheinische Friedrich Wilhelms-Universität, 1960.
Mackey, Nathaniel. "Breath and Precarity. The Inaugural Robert Creeley Lecture in Poetry and Poetics." In *Poetics and Precarity*, edited by Myung Mi Kim and Cristanne Miller. Albany: SUNY: 2018, pp. 1–30.
Mandelstam, Osip. *Complete Poetry of Osip Emilevich Mandelstam*. Translated by Burton Raffel and Alla Burago. Albany: SUNY, 1973.
Martin, Kirsty. *Modernism and the Rhythms of Sympathy. Vernon Lee, Virginia Woolf, D.H. Lawrence*. Oxford: Oxford University Press, 2013.
Martínez, Roberto Sanchiño, and Schlesier, Renate. "Die Subversivität der Inspiration. Einleitung." *Zeitschrift für Ästhetik und allgemeine Kunstwissenschaft*, vol. 51, no. 1 (2006): 43–44.
Martinez-Lozano Sinues, Pablo, Kohler, Malcom, and Zenobi, Renato. "Human Breath Analysis May Support the Existence of Individual Metabolic Phenotypes." *PLoS ONE*, vol. 8, no. 4 (2013). https://doi:10.1371/journal.pone.0059909.
Maud, Ralph. *Charles Olson's Reading: A Biography*. Carbondale: Southern Illinois University Press, 1996.
Mauthner, Fritz. *Beiträge zu einer Kritik der Sprache: Erster Band: Zur Sprache und zur Psychologie*. Stuttgart und Berlin: J. G. Cotta'sche Buchhandlung, 1921.
McDonald, Rónán. "Prose Works." In *The Cambridge Introduction to Samuel Beckett*. Cambridge: Cambridge University Press, 2007, pp. 71–115.
McDonald, Rónán. *The Cambridge Introduction to Samuel Beckett*. Cambridge University Press, 2006.
McKirahan, Richard D. *Philosophy before Socrates: An Introduction with Texts and Commentary*. Indianapolis and Cambridge: Hackett Publishing Company 1994.
McLuhan, Marshall. *Understanding Media: The Extensions of Man*. Cambridge, MA: The MIT Press, 1994.
Menge, Hermann. *Langenscheidts Grosswörterbuch Griechisch: Teil I, Griechisch–Deutsch*. Berlin, München, and Zürich: Langenscheidt, 1967.
Mersch, Dieter. "Medialität und Undarstellbarkeit: Einleitung in eine 'negative' Medientheorie." In *Performativität und Medialität*, edited by Sybille Krämer. München: Wilhelm Fink, 2004, pp. 75–96.
Mersch, Dieter. "Tertium datur: Introduction to a Negative Media Theory." *Revista MATRIZes*, vol. 7, no. 1 (2013): 207–22.

Michel, François-Bernard. *Le Souffle coupé: Respirer et écrire*. Paris: Gallimard, 1984.
Middleton, Peter. *Distant Reading: Performance, Readership, and Consumption in Contemporary Poetry*. Tuscaloosa: University of Alabama Press, 2005.
Moorjani, Angela. "Beckett's Devious Deictics." In *Rethinking Beckett: A Collection of Critical Essays*, edited by Lance St. John Butler and Robin J. Davis. Basingstoke: McMillan, 1990, pp. 20–30.
Mortenson, Eric. "Allen Ginsberg and Beat Poetry." In *The Cambridge Companion to the Beats*, edited by Steven Belletto. Cambridge: Cambridge University Press, 2017, pp. 77–91.
Moses, Kate. "Sylvia Plath's Voice, Annotated." In *The Unravelling Archive: Essays on Sylvia Plath*, edited by Anita Helle. Ann Arbor: University of Michigan Press, 2007, pp. 89–114.
Mossin, Andrew. "'In Thicket': Charles Olson, Frances Boldereff, Robert Creeley and the Crisis of Masculinity at Mid-Century." In *Olson's Prose*, edited by Gary Grieve-Carlson. Newcastle: Cambridge Scholars Publishing, 2007, pp. 16–46.
Moten, Fred. *The Universal Machine*. Durham, NC, and London: Duke University Press, 2018.
Müller, Herta. "The Art of Fiction No. 225." *Paris Review*, no. 210 (2014). https://www.theparisreview.org/interviews/6328/the-art-of-fiction-no-225-herta-muller.
Müller, Herta. *Atemschaukel*. Frankfurt am Main: S. Fischer, 2011.
Müller, Herta. *Der König verneigt sich und tötet*. Frankfurt am Main: Hanser, 2003.
Müller, Herta. "Der Mensch ist bequem, gleichgültig, denkfaul." *Profil*, Sept. 14, 2009.
Müller, Herta. *Der Teufel sitzt im Spiegel: Wie Wahrnehmung sich erfindet*. Berlin: Rotbuch, 1991.
Müller, Herta. "Gelber Mais und keine Zeit." In *Immer derselbe Schnee und immer derselbe Onkel*. München: Carl Hanser, 2011, pp. 125–45.
Müller, Herta. *The Hunger Angel*. Translated by Philip Boehm. New York: Metropolitan Books, 2012.
Müller, Herta. *Ich glaube nicht an die Sprache: Herta Müller im Gespräch mit Renata Schmidtkunz*. Klagenfurt: Wieser, 2009.
Müller, Herta. "Immer derselbe Schnee und immer derselbe Onkel." In *Immer derselbe Schnee und immer derselbe Onkel*. München: Carl Hanser, 2011, pp. 96–109.
Müller, Herta. *Lebensangst und Worthunger: Im Gespräch mit Michael Lentz*. Leipziger Poetikvorlesung, 2009. Frankfurt am Main: Suhrkamp, 2010.
Müller, Herta. *Mein Vaterland war ein Apfelkern: Ein Gespräch mit Angelika Klammer*. München: Carl Hanser, 2014.
Müller, Herta, and Pastior, Oskar. "Vom Hungerengel eins zwei drei." *die horen: Zeitschrift für Literatur, Kunst und Kritik*, no. 3 (2005): 123–34.
Münker, Stefan, and Roesler, Alexander. "Vorwort." In *Was ist ein Medium?*, edited by Stefan Münker and Alexander Roesler. Frankfurt am Main: Suhrkamp, 2008, pp. 7–12.

Murray, Penelope. "Poetic Inspiration in Early Greece." In *Oxford Readings in Ancient Literary Criticism*, edited by Andrew Laird. Oxford: Oxford University Press, 2006, pp. 37–61.

Musil, Robert. *Der Mann ohne Eigenschaften*. Hamburg: Rohwolt, 1952.

Musil, Robert. *Klagenfurter Ausgabe, kommentierte Edition sämtlicher Werke, Briefe und nachgelassener Schriften, mit Transkriptionen und Faksimiles aller Handschriften*, edited by Klaus Amann, Walter Fanta, and Karl Corino. Universität Klagenfurt: Robert-Musil-Institut, 2009.

Musil, Robert. *The Man without Qualities: Into the Millennium / From the Posthumous Papers*. Translated by Burton Pike. New York: Alfred A. Knopf, 1995.

Musil, Robert. "Toward a New Aesthetic." In *Precision and Soul: Essays and Addresses*, edited and translated by Burton Pike and David S. Luft, Chicago: University of Chicago Press, 1990, pp. 193–208.

Nahm, Milton C., editor. *Selections from Early Greek Philosophy*. New York: Appleton-Century-Crofts and Meredith Publishing, 1964.

Nancy, Jean-Luc. *Being Singular Plural*. Translated by Robert Richardson and Anne O'Byrne. Stanford, CA: Stanford University Press, 2000.

Nancy, Jean-Luc. *Corpus*. Translated by Richard A. Rand. New York: Fordham University Press, 2008.

Nancy, Jean-Luc. *The Discourse of the Syncope: Logodaedalus*. Translated by Saul Anton. Stanford, CA: Stanford University Press, 2008.

Nancy, Jean-Luc. *Ego Sum: Corpus, Anima, Fabula*. Translated by Marie-Eve Morin. New York: Fordham University Press, 2016.

Nancy, Jean-Luc. *Expectation: Philosophy, Literature*. Edited by Ginette Michaud, translated by Robert Bononno. New York: Fordham University Press, 2018.

Nancy, Jean-Luc. "Exscription." Translated by Katherine Lydon. *Yale French Studies*, no. 78, On Bataille, 1990, pp. 47–65.

Nancy, Jean-Luc. *Le Sens du monde*. Paris: Éditions Galilée, 1993.

Nancy, Jean-Luc. "Literary Communism." In *The Inoperative Community*, translated and edited by Peter Connor. Minneapolis: University of Minnesota Press, 1991, pp. 71–81.

Nancy, Jean-Luc. *The Sense of the World*. Translated by Jeffrey S. Librett. Minneapolis and London: University of Minnesota Press, 1997.

Nancy, Jean-Luc. "Shattered Love." In *The Inoperative Community*, translated and edited by Peter Connor. Minneapolis: University of Minnesota Press, 1991, pp. 82–109.

Nancy, Jean-Luc. ". . . would have to be a novel . . ." In *Expectation: Philosophy, Literature*, translated by Robert Bononno. New York: Fordham University Press, 2018, pp. 57–62.

Nannasch, Bettina. "Das aufgesperrte Maul der Null." In *Herta Müller und das Glitzern im Satz. Eine Annäherung an Gegenwartsliteratur*, edited by Jens

Christian Deeg and Martina Wernli. Würzburg: Königshausen and Neumann, 2016, pp. 297–318.

Narbeshuber, Lisa. *Confessing Cultures: Politics and the Self in the Poetry of Sylvia Plath*. Victoria: ELS Editions, 2009.

Nietzsche, Friedrich. *Philosophy in the Tragic Age of the Greeks*. Translated by Marianne Cowan. Washington, DC: Regnery, 1962.

Nixon, Mark. *Samuel Beckett's German Diaries* 1936–1937. London: Continuum, 2011.

Nowell Smith, David. *On Voice in Poetry: The Work of Animation*. London: Palgrave Macmillan, 2015.

Olson, Charles. "II/A Long Time to Fill the Wells." March 1958–November 1958, Charles Olson Research Collection at the University of Connecticut, prose no. 7.

Olson, Charles. "The Cave." Typescript. 1953, Charles Olson Research Collection at the University of Connecticut, prose no. 255.

Olson, Charles. *Charles Olson and Frances Boldereff: A Modern Correspondence*. Edited by Ralph Maud and Sharon Thesen. Hanover and London: Wesleyan University Press, 1999.

Olson, Charles. *Charles Olson & Robert Creeley: The Complete Correspondence*. Volume 1. Edited by George F. Butterick. Santa Barbara, CA: Black Sparrow Press, 1980.

Olson, Charles. *Charles Olson & Robert Creeley: The Complete Correspondence*. Volume 10. Edited by Richard Blevins. Santa Rosa, CA: Black Sparrow Press, 1996.

Olson, Charles. "Equal, That Is, to the Real Itself." In *Collected Prose*, edited by Donald Allen and Benjamin Friedlander. Berkeley: University of California Press, 1997, pp. 120–25.

Olson, Charles. "Form, No More Than Means, Is Caused." Typescript. 1954, Charles Olson Research Collection at the University of Connecticut, prose no. 81.

Olson, Charles. "Mouths Biting Empty Air." Typescript. October 27, 1946, Charles Olson Research Collection at the University of Connecticut, prose no. 15.

Olson, Charles. "A New Short Ars Poetica, A Litle Boke." Typescript. ca. 1955–1956, Charles Olson Research Collection at the University of Connecticut, prose no. 89.

Olson, Charles. *Notes for a Lecture on Corrado Cagli and the 4th Dimension*. Typescript. Ca. December 15, 1949, Charles Olson Research Collection at the University of Connecticut, prose no. 31.

Olson, Charles. "Notes on Language ['Base Texts . . .']." Typescript. Ca. October 1951, Charles Olson Research Collection at the University of Connecticut, prose no. 41.

Orr, Peter, editor. *The Poet Speaks: Interviews with Poets Conducted by Hilary Morrish, Peter Orr, John Press and Ian Scott-Kilvert*. London: Routledge & Kegan Paul, 1966.

Olson, Charles. *The Principle of Measure in Composition by Field: Projective Verse II*. Edited by Joshua Hoeynck. Tucson: Chax Press, 2010.

Olson, Charles. "Projective Verse." In *Selected Writings*, edited by Robert Creeley. New York: New Directions, 1966, pp. 15–26.

Olson, Charles. "Projective Verse: Early Draft." February 1950, Charles Olson Research Collection at the University of Connecticut.

Olson, Charles. "Projective Verse: Early Drafts." February–July 1950, Charles Olson Research Collection at the University of Connecticut.

Olson, Charles. "Pun as the True Meaning as Well as of Rhyme." Typescript. 1964, Charles Olson Research Collection at the University of Connecticut.

Olson, Charles. "Quantity in Verse and Shakespeare's Late Work." Holograph/typescript. April 1956, Charles Olson Research Collection at the University of Connecticut, prose no. 280.

Olson, Charles. *Selected Letters*. Edited by Ralph Maud. Berkeley: University of California Press, 2000.

Olson, Charles. *Shakespeare Essays: Notes and Fragments*. Holograph/typescript. 1954, Charles Olson Research Collection at the University of Connecticut, prose no. 271.

Olson, Charles. *Verse (notes)*. Typescript, November 1955, Charles Olson Research Collection at the University of Connecticut.

Oxford English Dictionary. Oxford: Oxford University Press, June 2017. www.oed.com.

Papapetros, Spyros. *On the Animation of the Inorganic: Art, Architecture, and the Extension of Life*. Chicago: University of Chicago Press, 2012.

Părău, Cristina Rita. " 'Atemwende'—'Atemschaukel': Paul Celan und Herta Müller: Differenzen und Homologien." In *Interkulturelle Erkundungen: Leben, Schreiben und Lernen in zwei Kulturen: Teil 1*, edited by Andrea Benedek et al. Frankfurt am Main: Peter Lang, 2012, pp. 373–86.

Partridge, Eric. *A Dictionary of Slang and Unconventional English*, edited by Paul Beale. Abingdon: Routledge 2000.

Pearson, Drew. "Washington Merry-Go Round." Jan. 7, 1956, American University Digital Research Archive. auislandora.wrlc.org/islandora/object/pearson%3A19641#page/1/mode/1up.

Pederson, Joshua. "Speak, Trauma: Toward a Revised Understanding of Literary Trauma Theory." *Narrative*, vol. 22, no. 3 (Oct. 2014): 333–53.

Perloff, Marjorie G. " 'A Ritual for Being Born Twice': Sylvia Plath's 'The Bell Jar.' " *Contemporary Literature*, vol. 13, no. 4 (Autumn 1972): 507–22.

Perloff, Majorie. "The Two Ariels: The (Re)making Of The Sylvia Plath Canon." *American Poetry Review*, vol. 13, no. 6 (Nov./Dec. 1984): 10–18.

Perniola, Mario. *The Sex Appeal of the Inorganic*. Translated by *Massimo Verdicchio*. New York and London: Continuum, 2004.

Philip, M. NourbeSe. "The Ga(s)p." In *Poetics and Precarity*, edited by Myung Mi Kim and Cristanne Miller. Albany: SUNY, 2016, pp. 31–40.

Piperno, Daniel. *Histoire du soufflé: Respiration dans l'antiquité occidentale*. Paris: Imothep, 1998.

Plath, Sylvia. *Ariel: The Restored Edition*. New York: HarperCollins, 2004.

Plath, Sylvia. *The Bell Jar*. London: Faber & Faber, 1966.
Plath, Sylvia. *The Collected Poems*. Edited by Ted Hughes. New York: Harper & Row, 1981.
Plath, Sylvia. *The Journals of Sylvia Plath, 1950–1962*. Edited by Karen V. Kukil. London: Faber & Faber, 2000.
Plath, Sylvia. *The Letters of Sylvia Plath. Volume 1: 1940–1956*. Edited by Peter K. Steinberg and Karen V. Kukil. London: Faber & Faber, 2017.
Plath, Sylvia. *The Letters of Sylvia Plath. Volume 2: 1956–1963*. Edited by Peter K. Steinberg and Karen V. Kukil. New York: HarperCollins, 2018.
Plath, Sylvia. *The Magic Mirror: A Study of the Double in Two of Dostoevsky's Novels*. Rhiwargor, Llanwddyn, and Powys: Embers Hardpress, 1989.
Plath, Sylvia. *The Spoken Word*. London: British Library, 2010. Audio CD.
Plath, Sylvia. "Tulips, Drafts." Sylvia Plath papers for Sickroom Tulips. MS Am 1780.
Pott, August Friedrich. *Etymologische Forschungen auf dem Gebiete der indogermanischen Sprachen*. Lemgo: Meyersche Hofbuchhandlung, 1833.
Pott, Hans-Georg. "Anderer Zustand / Ausnahmezustand." In *Terror und Erlösung: Robert Musil und der Gewaltdiskurs der Zwischenkriegszeit*, edited by Hans Feger, Hans-Georg Pott, and Norbert Christian Wolf. München: Wilhelm Fink, 2009, pp. 141–67.
Poulet, Georges. "Phenomenology of Reading." *New Literary History*, vol. 1, no. 1 (Oct. 1969): 53–68.
Povinelli, Elizabeth A. *Geontologies: A Requiem to Late Liberalism*. Durham, NC: Duke University Press, 2016.
Quintilian. *Institutio Oratia*. Translated by H. E. Butler. Cambridge, MA: Harvard University Press, 1943.
Quintilian. *Quintilian's Institutes of Oratory: or, Education of an Orator in Twelve Books. Volume 2*. Translated John Selby Watson. London: Bohn's Classical Library, 1856.
Rancière, Jacques. "Literary Communities." In *The Common Growl: Towards a Poetics of Precarious Community*, edited by Thomas Claviez. New York: Fordham University Press, 2016, pp. 93–110.
Randel, Don Michael. "Ricercar, ricercare." *The Harvard Concise Dictionary of Music and Musicians*. Cambridge, MA: Harvard University Press, pp. 561–62.
Rank, Otto. *Das Trauma der Geburt und seine Bedeutung für die Psychoanalyse*. Leipzig, Wien and Zürich: Internationaler Psychoanalytischer Verlag, 1924.
Rank, Otto. *The Trauma of Birth*. London: Kegan Paul, Trench, Trubner & Co; New York: Harcourt, Brace and Company, 1929.
Reich, Wilhelm. *The Function of the Orgasm: The Discovery of the Orgone*. Volume 1. Translated by Vincent R. Carfagno. London: Souvenir Press, 1983.
Reichel, Hans, and Bleichert, Adolf. *Leitfaden der Physiologie des Menschen*. Stuttgart: Enke, 1996.

Renan, Ernest. *De l'origine du langage*. Paris: Michel Lévy Frères, Libraries Éditeurs, 1964.
Ricco, John Paul. *The Decision between Us: Art and Ethics in the Time of Scenes*. Chicago: University of Chicago Press, 2014.
Ricco, John Paul. *The Logic of the Lure*. Chicago: University of Chicago Press, 2002.
Rix, Helmut, editor. *Lexikon der indogermanischen Verben*. Wiesbaden: Ludwig Reichert Verlag, 2001.
Robertson, Lisa. *Nilling: Prose Essays on Noise, Pornography, The Codex, Melancholy, Lucretius, Folds, Cities and Related Aporias*. Toronto: Bookthug, 2012.
Rose, Arthur. "Combat Breathing in Salman Rushdie's *The Moor's Last Sigh*." In *Reading Breath in Literature*, edited by Arthur Rose et al. Cham: Palgrave Pivot, 2018, pp. 113–34.
Rose, Arthur. "Introduction: Reading Breath in Literature." In *Reading Breath in Literature*, edited by Arthur Rose et al. Cham: Palgrave Pivot, 2019, pp. 1–16.
Rose, Jacqueline. *The Haunting of Sylvia Plath*. London: Virago, 1996.
Rosenzweig, Franz. "Scripture and Word." In *Scripture and Translation*, translated by Everett Fox and Lawrence Rosenwald. Bloomington and Indianapolis: Indiana University Press, 1994, pp. 40–46.
Rothman, Ellen K., et al. "Boston Doctors Use First Iron Lung." *Mass Moments*, Oct. 12, 1928. www.massmoments.org/moment-details/boston-doctors-use-first-iron-lung.html.
Salgaro, Massimo, and Michele Vangi, editors. *Mythos Rhythmus. Wissenschaft, Kunst und Literatur um 1900*. Stuttgart: Franz Steiner Verlag, 2015.
Salminem, Antti. "On Breathroutes. Paul Celan's Poetics of Breathing." *Partial Answers: Journal of Literature and the History of Ideas*, vol. 12, no. 1 (Jan. 2014): 107–26.
Sapir, Edward. *Language, an Introduction to the Study of Speech*. New York: Harcourt, Brace and Company, 1921.
Saussy, Haun. *The Ethnography of Rhythm: Orality and Its Technologies*. New York: Fordham University Press, 2016.
Schlesier, Renate. "Künstlerische Kreation und religiöse Erfahrung. Verwendungsgeschichtliche Anmerkungen zum Begriff der Inspiration." *Ästhetische Erfahrung im Zeichen der Entgrenzung der Künste: Epistemische, ästhetische und religiöse Formen von Erfahrungen im Vergleich: Sonderheft des Jahrgangs 2004 der Zeitschrift für Ästhetik und Allgemeine Kunstwissenschaft*, edited by Gert Mattenklott. Hamburg: Felix Meiner, 2004, pp. 177–94.
Schmitz-Emans, Monika. "Sprachspiel und 'Unsagbares'—Zu verwandten Motiven in Robert Musils Sprachreflexion und der Spätphilosophie Wittgensteins." *Musil-Forum*, vol. 19, no. 20 (1993–94): 182–207.
Schnell, Rebekka. *Natures mortes: Zur Arbeit des Bildes bei Proust, Musil, W.G. Sebald und Claude Simon*. Paderborn: Wilhelm Fink 2016.

Scholes, Percy A. "Ricercare." In *The Oxford Companion to Music*. London: Oxford University Press, 1970, p. 876.

Schönfelder, Christa. *Wounds and Words: Childhood and Family Trauma in Romantic and Postmodern Fiction*. Bielefeld: Transcript Verlag, 2013.

Schultz, Tanja. "Erotisch-poetisches Stillstellen in Robert Musils Mann ohne Eigenschaften." In *Stillstellen: Medien, Aufzeichnung, Zeit*, edited by Andreas Gelhard, Ulf Schmidt, and Tanja Schulz. Schliengen: Edition Argu,s 2004, pp. 180–88.

Sedgwick, Eve Kosofsky. *Tendencies*. Durham, NC: Duke University Press, 1993.

Sehgal, Parul. "In New Volume of Sylvia Plath's Letters, a Marriage Falters and Masks Fall Away." *New York Times*, Oct. 24, 2018.

Shakespeare, William. *Shakespeare's Comedies, Histories, and Tragedies, a Reproduction in Facsimile of the First Folio Edition 1623*, edited by Sydney Lee. Oxford: Clarendon Press, 1902.

Sharpe, Christina. *In the Wake: On Blackness and Being*. Durham, NC, and London: Duke University Press, 2016.

Shaw, Lytle. *Narrowcast: Poetry and Audio Research*. Stanford. CA: Stanford University Press, 2018.

Siraganian, Lisa. *Modernism's Other Work: The Art Object's Political Life*. Oxford: Oxford University Press, 2012.

Škof, Lenart. *Breath of Proximity: Intersubjectivity, Ethics and Peace*. Heidelberg, New York, and London: Springer, 2015.

Slonim, Balfour. *Respiratory Physiology*. Saint Louis: Mosby, 1976.

Sloterdijk, Peter. *Bubbles: Spheres 1*. South Pasedenam CA: Semiotext(e), 2011.

Smerilli, Filippo. *Moderne—Sprache—Körper: Analysen zum Verhältnis von Körpererfahrung und Sprachkritik in erzählenden Texten Robert Musils*. Göttingen: V&R unipress, 2009.

Söffner, Jan. *Metaphern und Morphomata*. Paderborn: Wilhelm Fink, 2015.

Steinberg, Peter K. "Catalogue of Sylvia Plath's Library." www.librarything.com/catalog/SylviaPlathLibrary.

Steinecke, Hartmut. "Herta Müller: *Atemschaukel*. Ein Roman vom 'Nullpunkt der Existenz.'" *Gegenwartsliteratur: Ein germanistisches Jahrbuch. A German Studies Yearbook*, no. 10 (2011): 14–32.

Stewart, Garrett. *Reading Voices: Literature and the Phonotext*. Berkeley: University of California Press, 1990.

Sutton, Emma. "'Putting Words on the Backs of Rhythm': Woolf, 'Street Music,' and *The Voyage Out*." *Paragraph*, vol. 33, no. 2 (2010): 176–96.

Tremblay, Jean-Thomas. "Breath: Image and Sound, an Introduction." *New Review of Film and Television Studies*, vol. 16, no. 2 (2018): 93–97. https://doi: 10.1080/17400309.2018.1444458.

Tremblay, Jean-Thomas. "Feminist Breathing." *differences: A Journal of Feminist Cultural Studies*, vol. 30, no. 3 (2019): 92–117. https://doi: 10.1215/10407391-7974016 .

Trigilio, Tony. *Allen Ginsberg's Buddhist Poetics*. Carbondale: Southern Illinois University Press, 2007.
Tubridy, Derval. "Beckett's Spectral Silence: Breath and the Sublime." *Limit{e} Beckett*, vol. 1, no. 1 (Autumn 2010): 102–22.
Van Hulle, Dirk, and Verhulst, Pim. *The Making of Samuel Beckett's* Malone meurt / Malone Dies. London: Bloomsbury, 2017.
Van Hulle, Dirk, and Weller, Shane. *The Making of Samuel Beckett's* L'Innommable / The Unnamable. London: Bloomsbury, 2014.
Vendler, Helen. *The Art of Shakespeare's Sonnets*. Cambridge, MA, and London: Belknap Press of Harvard University Press, 1997.
Wagner-Egelhaaf, Martina. "Musil und die Mystik der Moderne." In *Ästhetische und religiöse Erfahrungen der Jahrhundertwenden II: Um 1900*, edited by Wolfgang Braungart, Gotthard Fuchs, and Manfred Koch. Paderborn: Ferdinand Schöningh, 1998, pp. 195–215.
Wall, Duncan. *The Ordinary Acrobat: A Journey into the Wondrous World of the Circus, Past and Present*. New York: Alfred A. Knopf, 2013.
Waters, William. *Poetry's Touch On Lyric Address*. Ithaca, NY, and London: Cornell University Press, 2003.
Weinkauf, Wolfgang, ed. *Die Philosophie der Stoa: Ausgewählte Texte*. Stuttgart: Reclam, 2001.
Wesling, Donald. *The Chances of Rhyme: Device and Modernity*. Berkeley: University of California Press, 1980.
Whalen-Bridge, John. "Buddhism and the Beats." In *The Cambridge Companion to the Beats*, edited by Steven Belletto. Cambridge: Cambridge University Press, 2017, pp. 225–39.
White, Michael J. "Stoic Natural Philosophy (Physics and Cosmology)." In *The Cambridge Companion to the Stoics*, edited by Brad Inwood. Cambridge: Cambridge University Press, 2003, pp. 124–52.
Whitman, Walt. *Leaves of Grass*. Philadelphia: David McKay, 1891–92.
Wiedemann, Barbara. " 'für die Anfänge zeugt'—Paul Celans Frühwerk in der 'Atemwende.' " In *Paul Celan, "Atemwende": Materialien*, edited by Gerhard Buhr and Roland Reuß. Würzburg: Königshausen & Neumann, 1991, pp. 225–34.
Wills, David. *Inanimation: Theories of Inorganic Life*. Minneapolis: University of Minnesota Press, 2016.
Winkler, Hartmut. "Zeichenmaschinen: Oder warum die semiotische Dimension für eine Definition der Medien unerlässlich ist." In *Was ist ein Medium?*, edited by Stefan Münker and Alexander Roesler. Frankfurt am Main: Suhrkamp, 2008, pp. 211–21.
Winstanley, Adam Michael. " 'First Dirty, Then Make Clean': Samuel Beckett's Peristaltic Modernism, 1932–1958," PhD thesis, University of York, Department of English and Related Literature, 2013. core.ac.uk/download/pdf/14343764.pdf.

Witmer, Robert. "Blow." *The New Grove Dictionary of Jazz*, edited by Barry Kernfeld, Grove Music Online. Oxford Music Online. Oxford University Press. www.oxfordmusiconline.com.myaccess.library.utoronto.ca/subscriber/article/grove/music/J047600?q=blow+jazz&search=quick&pos=9&_start=1#firsthit.

Wöhrle, Georg, editor and translator. *Anaximenes aus Milet. Die Fragmente zu seiner Lehre*. Stuttgart: Franz Steiner, 1993.

Wolff, Christoph. "Ricercar." In *Handwörterbuch der musikalischen Terminologie: Ordner V: P–Se*, edited by Albrecht Riethmüller. Stuttgart: Franz Steiner, 1972, pp. 1–9.

Woolf, Virginia. *The Diary of Virginia Woolf. Volume 2: 1920–1924*. London: Hogarth Press, 1978.

Woolf, Virginia. *The Diary of Virginia Woolf. Volume 3: 1925–1930*. London: Hogarth Press, 1980.

Woolf, Virginia. Draft of "Time Passes." Holograph ms., Berg Collection, New York Public Library. *Woolf Online*, edited by Pamela L. Caughie et al. www.woolfonline.com.

Woolf, Virginia. *Jacob's Room*. London: Penguin Books, 1992.

Woolf, Virginia. "The Lady in the Looking-Glass: A Reflection." In *The Mark on the Wall and Other Short Fiction*, edited by David Bradshaw. Oxford: Oxford University Press, 2001, pp. 63–68.

Woolf, Virginia. "The Lady in the Looking-Glass." Typescript with the author's ms. corrections. May 28, 1929. Berg Collection, New York Public Library.

Woolf, Virginia. *The Letters of Virginia Woolf. Volume 3: 1923–1928. A Change of Perspective*. London: Hogarth Press, 1977.

Woolf, Virginia. Manuscript Box [Haunted house, A]: "The Lady in the Looking-Glass." Later typescript with the author's ms. corrections. n.d. Berg Collection, New York Public Library.

Woolf, Virginia. "Modern Fiction." In *The Essays of Virginia Woolf. Volume 4: 1925–1928*. London: Hogarth Press, 1984, pp. 157–65.

Woolf, Virginia. Outline for *To the Lighthouse*. Holograph ms. Berg Collection, New York Public Library. *Woolf Online*, edited by Pamela L. Caughie et al. www.woolfonline.com.

Woolf, Virginia. *To the Lighthouse*. London: Penguin Classics, 2000.

Woolf, Virginia. Typescript of "Time Passes." *Woolf Online*, edited by Pamela L. Caughie et al. www.woolfonline.com.

Woolf, Virginia. *The Waves*. London: Penguin Books, 2000.

Wright, Rosemary. *Introducing Greek Philosophy*. New York: Routledge, 2014. Zanetti, Sandro. *"Zeitoffen": Zur Chronographie Paul Celans*. München: Wilhelm Fink, 2006.

Zukofsky, Louis. *A Test of Poetry*. Brooklyn: Objectivist Press, 1948.

Index

Ackerley, Chris, 237
affect(s), 160–69; free-floating, 168; of sensations, 167; transition to, 165; validity of, 165
Agamben, Giorgio, 25, 35, 115, 125, 127, 193, 222, 236, 301, 309n12
The Age of Breath (Irigaray), 19, 22
Ahmed, Sara, 309, 365n81, 365n84
air, 8; Anaximenes, 18–19; function as traces, 149; mediating textual, 147–43; as primary substances, 17–19; and soul, 9
Allen, Don, 61
Allison, Raphael, 50, 76
Al-Taie, Yvonne, 373n61
Alvarez, Alfred, 363n74
Anaximenes, 7–10, 17; air, 18–19; inside and outside, notions of, 9–12
anima, 7, 124, 127
animate, 12–16; respirational intertwining of, 12
anxiety, 91–108, 200; blocking inbreaths and outbreaths, 95; defense mechanism against, 95; eliminating conditions of, 95; Kerouac's inspiration, 96–97; leads to "symbol formation," 203
Ariel (Plath), 224, 237–38, 239

Aristotle, 10, 52, 57–63, 94, 131, 136, 222; account of respiration, 12; rhythm for composition, 122
Artaud, Antonin, 29, 82
Atemschaukel (Müller), 241, 278–99, 302, 320; attack Leo in, 295; meta-term in, 293; movements of "Atemschaukel," 286–93; mutability of words in, 284–85; occurrence of "Atemschaukel," 290–91; *parole soufflée*, effect of, 284–85; production of, 280–82; qualities of "Atemschaukel," 289–90; role shoveling plays in, 292
"Atemzüge," 163
Atop an Underwood (Kerouac), 85

"bad machinery," 74
Bailly, Jean-Christophe, 10, 15, 33
Baraka, Amiri, 99, 100–1
Barnes, Jonathan, 8
The Basic Writings of Sigmund Freud (Freud), 361n51
Bates, Catherine, 40
Baudelaire, Charles, 361n55
Bayley, Sally, 366n88
Beat and Black Mountain: movement, 97; poets, 100; schools, 97; writers, 45, 51, 52, 338n10

Beckett, Samuel, 43, 45, 46, 47, 171–208, 305; account of automatic writing, 182; adaptations of Rank's theory, 201; autonomous blowing of air, 182–83; being and breathing, 187; biblical "breath of life," 203; creative process, 183; interview with Israel Schenker, 194–95; *Malone Dies*, 177–78, 184; *Malone meurt*, 181, 183, 184; organic-inorganic assemblages, 173; organic theories of language formation, 204; "original separation," 186; parallels with Blanchot, 177, 179; Peristaltic Modernism, 356n3; "Psychology Notes," 205–6; respirational "words like smoke," 171, 172; respiratory texts, 239; "sovereign passivity," 182; *Texts for Nothing*, 171, 172; transform language, aspiration to, 195; writing scene, 182. See also *The Unnamable*

Beckett's Breath (Goudouna), 195

Before the Voice of Reason (Kleinberg-Levin), 20

Being Singular Plural (Nancy), 35

The Bell Jar (Plath), 174–75, 230–38, 355n2; death drive, figurations of, 233–34; engagement with breath, 235–36; Esther's flight in, 232–33; feminist impulses in, 237; parallels with *Ariel*, 232; protagonist, 230; respiratory atmosphere, 233; transgression shatters boundaries, 231; tubercular condition in, 230

Bender, Hans, 371n38

Benjamin, Walter, 43

Bennett, Jane, 16

Benveniste, Émile, 121, 122, 123, 130; original meaning of rhythm, 136

Berardi, Franco, 377n5

Bersani, Leo, 33, 318, 379n15

Besetzbarkeit (occupiability), 302

Beyond the Pleasure Principle (Freud), 211, 213–18, 221, 361n51, 362n57

"bisexuality," 316

Bishop, Tom, 360n46

Blackpentecostal Breath (Crawley), 34

Blanchot, Maurice, 177–80, 319; automatic writing, conception of, 182–83; dead hand, 186; essay on *The Unnamable*, 178–79; inspiration as "sterile prolixity," 198; space of inspiration, 187

blowing, 57–58

Bodies on the Line (Allison), 50

body, 185–93; and ego, 187–88; exscribed, 190, 192; inorganic, 193; language as, 190; organic, 193; writing, 186–87

Boldereff, Frances, 98

Böning, Thomas, 368n9

Brain, Tracy, 366n88

breath, 1–3; Anaximenes's notion on, 7–10; animating quality of, 13; audible, 1; biblical image of, 13–14; contiguities of, 153; gendered framings of, 306–7; as generative, formative, and constitutive principle, 16–32; and intersectionality, 307–10; and language, 22–28; life-giving instances and, 12–13; and liminality, 6–7; literary depictions of, 2–6; in literature, 1–2; movement of breath, 9; related terms, 5–7; shift in, 137–38; syncopal literary, 5; "vibrant matter," 16

Breath (Beckett), 195–97, 201, 204–8, 238

breathing, 1; in literature, 2; movement of, 3; as physiological process, 2, 3, 5; poetic, conceptual framework for, 3–4, 5; prelinguistic, 22–23; primordial wholeness of, imaginations of, 19–22; rhythm of, 4

Breathing: Chaos and Poetry (Berrardi), 377n5
Breathing Matters (Górska), 34, 307
"breathing space," 261
"breathing their skin," 322
breath in nostrils, 199–208; *Deckerinnerung*, 203; in *The Trauma of Birth*, 202–3
breath-measure, 97–100; literal and figural, 102–3; oral compositional acts, 46–47; during writing process, 54
Breath of Proximity (Škof), 34
breath-pause, 54, 55, 58, 59, 60, 62; in ancient rhetoric revisited, 123–25; coherent segments of speech, 52–53
breath-rifts, 280–82
breathroutes: continuous, 251–52; interrupted, 252–57
breath-soul, 9, 11
breath-stop, 67, 70; ancient origins of, 51–55; measure of, 53; natural speech pauses, 55; and thought-division, 52
breathturn, 252
Bremer Rede (Celan), 246
brép, 6
Brison, Susan, 367n4
broken breaths, 101–8
Bronfen, Elisabeth, 365n85
Bubbles (Sloterdijk), 33
Buber, Martin, 249–51
Butler, Judith, 309
Byrne, Jean Marie, 377n6

Caruth, Cathy, 297–99, 367n4
Cassady, Neal, 99–100
Celan, Paul, 17, 43, 45, 46, 47, 241–78, 305, 367n1; "Atemwege," 371n32; continuous breathroutes, 251–52; criticism of metaphors, 374n69; dialogic notion of poetry, 368n10; inspiration—conspiration, 255–57; interrupted breathroutes, 252–57; Jewishness, 248; Mandelstam's poems, translation of, 259–78; notes, essays, and speeches, breath in, 242–47; notes and drafts, 369n26; "Offene Glottis," 367n9; poetics of breathing, backgrounds of, 247–51; poetry and translations, breath in, 257–59; response to Adorno's claim, 243–44; "Schicksal" (destiny), 370n31
cellular respiration, 15
Chion, Michel, 12, 318
Chrysippus, 19
Cicero, 52, 53, 131, 136; breathing pause, 123; rhythm for composition, 122
cigar, 86–87
Cixous, Hélène, 310–17; bisexuality, 315–16; *écriture féminine*, 313; feminist project, 312; figure of woman sketched by, 314; influence of Derrida's *La parole soufflée*, 314; "sexual opposition," 315–16; "voler," 313–14; *vs*. Kerouac, 311–13; writing practice in terms of breathing, 314
Clark, T. J., 374n74
Clément, Bruno, 184
Clément, Catherine, 4, 27
cold breath, 227–30
Comay, Rebecca, 59, 378n9
commas, 61, 71, 192, 193
compositio, 134
composition, breathing and, 51–63; breath-stop, ancient origins of, 51–55; Ginsberg and Quintilian, 55–57; Kerouac and Aristotle, 57–63; physical breath, 82; respiratory, 135–38
Connor, Steven, 178, 357n12, 357n13, 359n32; *How It Is*, 358n29; "Modernism and the Writing

Connor, Steven *(continued)*
  Hand," 357n16; "Beckett's
  Punctuation," 358n28
consonant, 252
continuous breathroutes, 251–52
coptein, 77
Corpus (Nancy), 186, 190, 258,
  371n40
cosmic *pneuma*, 19
Crawley, Ashon T., 34
Creeley, Robert, 98, 113
Crowther, Gail, 224
Culler, Jonathan, 216

Daniel, Samuel, 104, 105
dash, 61
The Dash (Comay), 59
Davidson, Michael, 50, 63, 64, 77
De Anima (Aristotle), 222
death, 12–16, 40
The Decision between Us (Ricco), 319
Deckerinnerung (Freud), 203
Deleuze, Gilles, 6
De l'origine du langage (Renan), 31
de Nervaux-Gavoty, Laure, 362n66
de Roche, Charles, 370n30
Derrida, Jacques, 7, 8, 20, 29, 314, 315
The Discourse of the Syncope (Nancy), 4
Dolar, Mladen, 24, 25, 27, 28
Drinker, Philip, 209
Duncan, Joel, 76

ebb and flow, 51–63
Eberhart, Richard, 98
Ebner, Ferdinand, 369n19
ecstatic breath, 230–36
Egeland, Marianne, 365n85
ego, 188
Einbahnstrasse (Benjamin), 43
escapist fantasy, 232
Essays Critical and Clinical (Deleuze), 6

exhalation, 1, 2, 17, 26, 38, 72,
  75; air, 5; audible, 68–69; dashes
  and, 51; irregular rhythms of,
  85; movement of breathing, 3;
  orgiastic, 94; rhythm of breathing
  and, 15; sexual climax and, 93–94;
  during smoking, 88; syncopnea, 4;
  unrestricted flow, 93

The Fall of America (Ginsberg), 66, 69,
  80, 82, 84
"false" breath, 256
"faltering rhythm," 217
Fanon, Frantz, 365n81
Federman, Raymond, 360n46
Feldman, Matthew, 359n36
Felman, Shoshana, 297
feminism, 308–9
figurative language: movement of,
  145; processual, 143–47; and
  respirational-medial processes, 147
*The Forgetting of Air in Martin
  Heidegger* (Irigaray), 20
formative rhythm, 131–35
Fradenburg, L. O. Aranye, 2
Freud, Sigmund, 203, 211, 212, 213,
  215, 217, 218, 221, 231, 361n52,
  361n58
Frey, Hans-Jost, 372n45
"*fügen*" ("placing," "joining"), 134
The Function of the Orgasm (Reich),
  93, 94

Garner, Eric, 365n81
Gelhard, Andreas, 119
gendering, of breath, 237–39
generative caesurae, text-internal,
  125–31
generative rhythm, 127, 131;
  prelinguistic quality of, 137–38
Ginsberg, Allen, 43, 45–48, 50–59,
  97–100, 311, 324; audio recordings,

analysis of, 327–28; compositional processes, 85; *Fall of America*, 69; human-machine interaction, 77; inspirational transmission, 102; "Iron Horse," 67–84; Kerouac's accusation, 97; lecture on "Poetry, Politics and Consciousness" in 1974, 75; "Love Poem on Theme by Whitman," 321, 323; "paradoxical attitude," 76; physical breath, 72; pneumatic queering, 323; poetic reflections on breath, 63; "power" of inspirational weakness, 101–8; "prophetic" voice, 64; recorded breath, 66–85; reproduction of breath via media technology, 65; respiratory poetics, 64; respiratory rhythm, 121
God's breath, 13–14
Gontarski, Stanley, 237
"good nature," 74
Górska, Magdalena, 34, 307, 308; argues for "breathable" conditions for minorities, 309–10; "materially-discursive" by, 308; potential resistance of breath, 377n3
Goudouna, Sozita, 195, 360n48
grammatical subject, 187
"grand apnoea," 195, 201, 204
groan(s): of iron tons, 83–84; of wheels, 83
Guggenheim, Peggy, 200

"Halsweh," 284
Hamlet (Shakespeare), 60
Harry Ransom Center, 358n27
"Hasoweh," 284
"Hauchschrift, Handschrift," 264–67
The Haunting of Sylvia Plath (Rose), 365n85
Herren, Graley, 200, 204
"Herzschaufel," 291–92
Hippolytus, 17–18

Histoire du souffle (Piperno), 14
Hollander, John, 98
Homo Maximus (Swedenborg), 256
Honold, Alexander, 168
Howl (Ginsberg), 56, 68, 70
Hughes, Ted, 224, 365n85
human-machine interaction, 77
The Hunger Angel (Müller), 375n77
Hutchins, William, 358n25

"immortal breath," 105–8
"I'm the partition," 189–94; being outside and inside, 192–93; in *The Unnamable*, 190–93
inanimate, 12–16; respiratory intertwining of, 12
inanimation, 16
Inanimation (Wills), 376n95
"inclusive metawriting," 168
inhalation, 2, 17, 38, 72, 75, 83, 94; air, 5; audible, 68–69; breath of strangers, 35; breath outside, desire for, 12; dashes and, 51; and flow of sound, 26; irregular rhythms of, 85; movement of breathing, 3; rhythm of breathing and, 15; during smoking, 88; syncopnea, 4; "taking a breath," 55; of toxic fumes, 89
inhalation-exhalation, 207, 208
inside, 10–12
inspiration, 28–32, 86, 91–108; anxiety, 96; Ginsberg's reflection on, 103–4; grants transactual quality to poetry, 106; immortality and, 104–5; inspirational transmission, 102; Kerouac's complicated relation to, 96; Kerouac's reservations about, 91–92; meaning, 30; physiological, 30; poetic, 30, 91–92; *Poetics of Breathing*, 30–31, 32; respiratory, 30–31, 32, 38; rethinking, 30; "souffler" refers to, 97; structural

inspiration *(continued)*
  implications of, 29–30; transcendent implications of, 29
inspirational transmission, 102
inspiration anxiety, 96–97
inspiration—conspiration, 255–57
"inspiration-expiration," 207
interdependence, 32–43
interrupted breathroutes, 252–57
intersectionality, 307–10
In the Wake (Sharpe), 365n81, 377n4
invisible breaths, 140
Irigaray, Luce, 19, 20, 22, 310–11, 315, 334n32, 377n6, 378n7
"Iron Horse" (Ginsberg), 67–84; "better" functions, 70, 73; at Johns Hopkins University in April 1967, 70; reading in London (1967), 72; recorded breaths on original tapes of, 74–75; and respiratory imagery, 78; smoking cigarettes, 78–79

Jagose, Annamarie, 378n14
Jakobson, Roman, 133
Joris, Pierre, 367n6

Kerouac, Jack, 43, 45–48, 50–55, 57–63, 311–13; accuses Ginsberg, 97; "Essentials of Spontaneous Prose," 98, 312; image of breath, deployment of, 92–93; literary ejaculation, 378n8; poetic reflections on breath, 63; "Rasping Smoke in a Dry Throat," 85–91; repression, 91–101; reservations about inspiration, 91–92; respiratory poetics, 64; respiratory rhythm, 121; *On the Road*, 86; *The Subterraneans*, 86; typewriter fantasies, 65, 85–91
Kittler, Friedrich, 63, 64, 65

Klagenfurter Ausgabe (Musil), 132, 134
Kleinberg-Levin, David Michael, 19, 20–22, 23, 24, 26, 33, 34
Krämer, Sybille, 140, 141, 142, 145
Krieger, Elliot, 175, 356n7

Lacan, Jacques, 23
LaCapra, Dominick, 297, 299
Laing, R. D., 366n86
language: liberating, 49; self-reflexive, 155, 159
language, breath and, 22–28, 32–33; development of speech, 23–24; prelinguistic breathing, 22–23; voice and rhythm, 24–28
Language: An Introduction to the Study of Speech (Sapir), 114
"language infiltration," 75
Leaves of Grass (Whitman), 90, 323, 324–25, 379n18, 379n21
Lemke, Anja, 367n3, 367n7
Lentz, Michael, 281
Le souffle coupé (Michel), 24
Levinas, Emmanuel, 33–34
life, 12–16; breathing and, 12; depends on soul or *pneuma*, 12–13; identify breath with, 13; respiratory maintenance of, 15; warmth, 12
Lilly Library catalogues, 365n77, 365n79
liminality, breath's, 6–7, 142
Lloyd, David, 15, 205, 355n1, 367n5, 372n51
Lord, Sterling, 59
loss, 298–300
Lowe, Peter J., 356n4

"macché," 204
machines, 66, 75–78; industrial, 78; tape recorder, 63–66, 75; typewriter, 65; writing, 65

Malone Dies (Beckett), 177–78, 185, 187, 238; final version of, 184; "l'air qui respire" in, 186; movement of air, 178; syncopnea in, 177, 181, 188

Malone Meurt (Beckett), 181, 183, 324, 358n21; breath in manuscript of, 324; process of body's exscription, 186; writing scene in, 184

Malone's writing scene, 189, 192

Mandelstam's poems, translation by Celan, 259–78; handwritten breath-seas, 274–76; "Hauchschrift, Handschrift," 264–67; pneumatically touchable poem I, 263–76; pneumatically touchable poem II, 276–78; preliminarity, 267–69; repetition, variation, and citation, 269–73; "Ricercar," 267–78

The Man without Qualities (Musil), 117–19, 320; "Breaths of a Summer's Day," 117–18, 153, 154, 163–64; drafts and notes for, 158–59; erotic connotations of breath in, 160–62; "Holy Discourse," 154; Other Condition, 153–60; Ulrich and Agathe travel to Italy in, 162–65; Ulrich's and Agathe's bodies, 165–69

materiality, 46; acoustic, 125; of concrete media, 141; of language, 142; literature's, 119; words', 152

"materially-discursive," 308

Mauthner, Fritz, 360n44, 362n61

McDonald, Rónán, 237, 359n36

McLuhan, Marshall, 85

mediality, 31; contiguities of, 153; and invisibility, 139–43; mediating textual airs, 147–43; mediation, representation, and figurative language, 143–47; pneumatic, 144; respiratory, 138–39; staging breaths, 119; withdrawal of, 142; words reflect, 127

media technology, 65

medusa-likeness, 254

Mein Vaterland (Müller), 292

The Meridian (Celan), 244, 259, 260, 367n8, 369n26, 372n44; breath presented as interruption, 245–46; continuous breathroutes, 251–52; "I" and "person" in, 370n30; interrupted breathroutes, 252–57; notes and drafts for, 257; reflections in, 247

Mersch, Dieter, 140–43, 146

meta-pherein, 145, 146

Michel, François-Bernard, 24

Middleton, Peter, 37, 45

mind-break, 55, 56–57, 343n56

mindflow, 57

modern literature, 43–45

Molloy (Beckett), 196

"monolithic chauvinism," 107, 108

Moorjani, Angela, 200

Moses, Kate, 363n68

motion, breath in, 83

"moving breath," 83

Müller, Herta, 43, 45, 46, 47, 241–42, 278–97, 303, 367n1; balance and delirium, 286–93; breathing words, poetic implications of, 282–86; breath-rifts, 280–82; comments on word, 279; discussion of breath in metatexts, 296–97; haunting the readers, 293–97; image of tyrannical words, 294–95; interview with Michael Lentz, 281–82; *parole soufflée*, effect of, 282–86; Pastior's death, 279–80; phobic animation, 282–86. See also *Atemschaukel*

"multiple machinery," 76

Musil, Robert, 43, 45, 46, 47, 117–22, 145–46, 162, 198; air and

Musil, Robert *(continued)*
  water as media, 141; approaches to antiquity, 121; "Atemzüge," 163; breathing pauses by, 125; breaths of natural world, 171; collocations of breath and intervals, 127–28; formative rhythm in writing process, 131–35; generative rhythm, 129–31; *Klagenfurter Ausgabe*, 132, 134; medium and mediality, 153; respiratory intervals, 126; on rhythm, 121; rhythm for composition, 136; silence/sound and movement/standstill, treatments of, 128–29. See also *The Man without Qualities*

Nancy, Jean-Luc, 4, 7, 35–38, 40; arguement on body, 187–88; *Being Singular Plural*, 35; body's relation to outside, 11; *Ego Sum*, 188; existence outside oneself, 20; on inspiration, 29; notion of soul, 10, 11; "original separation," 186; *The Sense of the World*, 374n68
Narbeshuber, Lisa, 361n53, 366n87
Nibbrig, Christiaan Hart, 120, 139
No Future (Edelman), 326
nonanimate noise, 223
"non-duality," 21
Nowell Smith, David, 26
"nutritive soul," 222

O'Hara, Frank, 76
Olson, Charles, 45, 49–50, 76, 101, 108–15, 311; breath as silent propellant, 112; breathing patterns and rhythm of languages, 114–15; human breathing patterns, 114; poetics of breath, 112–14; "Projective Verse," 97–98, 100, 103, 108, 109–15; reflections on breathing, 117; rhythm of languages, 114–15
On the Road (Kerouac), 86, 100
On Voice in Poetry: The Work of Animation (Nowell Smith), 26
orgasm, 93–94; reflex, 95
"original unity," 20
"Other Condition," 153–60; articulation of, 154; as image or metaphor, 156; in *The Man without Qualities*, 153–54, 155; Musil's notion of, 158; mystical unity of, 160; normal condition *vs.*, 155; references to breath, 156; self-reflexive language, 155, 159; *unio mystica*, 157; utopian, 158
Otherwise Than Being (Levinas), 33–34
outside, 10–12; breath, desire for, 12; dependence of body, 15; exposure to, 15

Papapetros, Spyros, 44, 376n88
"Paralytic" (Plath), 208–23, 228, 230, 231, 233, 238; Brain's views, 210–11; "dead eggs" in, 213–15; historical iron lungs in, 209; mechanical respirator, rhythm of, 210; Pearson's views on, 209–10; "o," 216–17; Rankian topos resonating in, 210–13; resonances with *Beyond the Pleasure Principle*, 213–18; respiratory environment, 212, 214; transition from unicellular to multicellular constitution, 216
Pastior, Oskar, 279–80, 281, 283, 285, 292
Pearson, Drew, 209
Pederson, Joshua, 367n4, 376n97
Perloff, Marjorie, 366n86, 366n89
Perniola, Mario, 167–68
"phallocentric tradition," 310
"phases," 207

Phenomenology of Spirit (Hegel), 378n9
Philip, M. NourbeSe, 358n24
Philolaus of Croton, 12
physical breath, 6, 11, 44, 50, 51, 58, 66, 72, 82, 83
Piperno, Daniel, 14
Plath, Sylvia, 43, 45, 46, 47, 171–76, 208–36, 305; "A Birthday Present," 359n34; *Ariel*, 224, 237–38; BBC's financial benefits, 363n69; breath beyond death, 173–74; cold breath, 227–30; emotional distance mentioned by, 176; engagement with breath, 235–36; gender in respiratory poetics of, 237–39; holocaust imagery, 241; literary breath thwarts, 236; "My god the iron lung," 208–18; organic-inorganic assemblages, 173; poems in syllabic verse, 364n75; relation of body to writing, 175–76; respiratory images, 234–35; suicide attempt, 356n4; "Suicide off Egg Rock," 171, 172, 176; "Tulips," 218–28. See also *The Bell Jar*; "Paralytic"
Plato, 18
pneuma, 5–6, 7–10, 20, 44, 127, 166, 249; Anaximenes's analogy, 9–10; cosmic, 19; identification of, 12–13; as primary substances, 17–19; and respiration, 13; Stoic, 19; as wind and breath, 9–10
pneumatic mediality, 144
pneumatic potentiality, 230–36
pneumatic queering, 323
pneumatic singularities, 36
poetic breathing, 3–4
Poetics of Breathing, 16, 30–31, 32, 34, 38, 45, 46, 305–6, 307, 318
Poulet, Georges, 38, 42, 43
Pound, Ezra, 50
Povinelli, Elizabeth A., 12, 33

Power and Weakness of Poetry (Ginsberg), 106
preliminarity, 267–69
prelinguistic breathing, 22–23, 24
"prophetic" voice, 64
psyche, 7, 201

queer breath, 317
"queer negativity," 326
"queer resistance," 326
queer syncopnea, 317
Queer Theory: An Introduction (Jagose), 378n14
"quiet breath," 239
Quintilian, 52, 131, 136; breathing pause, 123–25; description of pause, 127; rhythm for composition, 122

Raleigh, Walter, Sir, 103
Rancière, Jacques, 36
Rank, Otto, 199–206; "biological basis," 204–5; desperate birth, 201; and Genesis, 202–3; primal trauma, outline of, 203; "symbol formation," 204
Receptive Bodies (Bersani), 33, 318
Recherche (Proust), 60
recorded breath, Ginsberg's, 66–85; audible inhalations and exhalations, 68; breath-stops during composition, 70; changes made during revision, 81–82; *The Fall of America*, 66, 69; "Iron Horse," 67–84; "Meadowgold Butter," 82–83; mind-break and breath-stop, 66–67; nonrespirational pause markers, 80; revised and rearranged version, 80–81
"reduced respiration," 95
Reich, Wilhelm, 92–95
Renan, Ernest, 31
representation, 143–47

Representing Sylvia Plath (Bayley), 366n88
repression, 91–101
respiration, 1; Aristotle's account of, 12; cellular, 15; chemical aspects of, 95; literary depictions of, 2; modern literary, analysis of, 3; reduced, 95; temporality of, 32
respirational *écriture féminine*, 310–17
respirational inspiration, 30, 32, 38
respirational singularity, 35
respirational writing scenes, 63–66
respiratory gender-turns, 300–3
respiratory inhibition, 95
respiratory language, 32
respiratory mediality, 138–39, 138–53
respiratory rhythm, 121; generative impact of, 136
rhetorike techne, 53
rhythm, 24–28, 102–7, 113–14; "animi velut respirant," 120–38; archetypal, 103, 104; breathing pause, 123–25; domain of potentiality, 121; emotion objectified outside as, 105; flow and segmentation, 120–23; formative, 131–35; of inhalation and exhalation, 85; intertextual network, 121; natural voice, 100; respiratory, 121, 136; respiratory articulation, 105; respiratory composition, 135–38; rhetorical exhalation, 92; text and, 120; text-internal generative caesurae, 125–31; transference of, 49–50; in Woolf's writing process, 120–22
"Ricercar," 267–78; breathroutes, 273; divisions and interruptions in, 278; earlier version of, 272; first line of, 273; graphical linguistic counterpoints, 274; "Kola," "Atem," and "Sinn," 275–76; self-citation in, 271–72; setting of sense in, 276–77; typescript E of, 277–78; unnamed names in, 277
Robertson, Lisa, 27, 35, 37
Rose, Arthur, 205, 340n29
Rose, Jacqueline, 365n85, 366n87
Rosenzweig, Franz, 249, 251
Ruda, Frank, 378n9

Sackville-West, Vita, 120
Sapir, Edward, 114
Saussy, Haun, 37, 39
Schenker, Israel, 194
Schmidt, Ulf, 119
Schocken, Salam, 368n17
Schultz, Tanja, 119
Science of Logic (Hegel), 378n9
Sedgwick, Eve Kosofsky, 317
The Sense of the World (Nancy), 374n68
sensual aspects of words, 44
"sex economy," 93
sexual climax, 93–94
Shakespeare, William, 38, 40, 60, 104
shared-separation, 36–38
Sharpe, Christina, 309, 365n81
shattered selves, 230–36
Shaw, Louis Agassiz, 209
Shaw, Lytle, 79
Shelley, 101–3, 104, 104, 106
The Sight of Death (Clark), 374n74
silent consonant, 252
silent propellant, 108–15; composition's, 110; voice as, 111
singularities, 35–36; pneumatic, 36; respirational, 35
Škof, Lenart, 34
Sloterdijk, Peter, 33
Smith, David Novell, 318
"smoke-cathedrals," 81
smoke/smoking, 63–66, 86–91; cigar, 86–87; cigarettes, 78–79, 86, 87,

88; exhaled, status of, 89–90; respirational movement of, 88
Sonnet 81 (Shakespeare), 38–39, 41
soul, 8, 9; identification of, 12–13; notion of, 10; and physical breath, 11; semantic connection of breathing to, 28
The Space of Literature (Blanchot), 357n15
speech: development of, breath and, 23–24; empirical bodily dimension of, 27–28; nonsemantic aspects of, 27
spirit, 101
spiritus, 5–6, 7
Steinberg, Peter, 224
Stephensen, Wen, 224
"sterile prolixity," 177, 178, 183, 198
Stewart, Garrett, 50
Strachey, James, 362n58
The Subterraneans (Kerouac), 86, 100
suffocation, 199–208, 360n43; at birth, 204; conjunction of birth and, 200–1
"Suicide off Egg Rock" (Plath), 171, 172; breathing-and-beating machine in, 174
Swedenborg, Emanuel, 256, 290
syncopal literary breath, 5
syncopnea, 3–5, 77, 305; definition of, 3–4; inspirational, 177; movement of, 188; rhythms of, 4
System of Dante's Hell (Baraka), 101

tape recorder, 63–66
"technicule," 205
A Test of Poetry (Zukofsky), 104, 105
text-internal generative caesurae, 125–31
Texts for Nothing (Beckett), 171, 172, 195, 237; force of language in, 175; "haggard vulture face," 173

The Theatre and Its Double (Artaud), 29
To the Lighthouse (Woolf), 117, 148–53; composition of, 120; harmonious acoustic flow, 134; preliminary versions of, 148; "Time Passes," 118–19
transactual relationality, 32–43
trauma, 297–300
The Trauma of Birth (Rank), 199–202, 204, 205–6, 360n41, 361n51
Tremblay, Jean-Thomas, 306, 377n2
Tubridy, Derval, 359n33
"Tulips" (Plath), 218–28; "bound verse" *vs.* vivid free verse, 226–27; iambic pentameter, 225–26; images in printed version, 220–21; inversion created in, 221–22; mobility and warmth in, 222; modes of breathing in, 220; monotonous respiration in, 219; patient in, 219; produced as written and spoken text, 223–25; sonic atmosphere of, 219–20; *vs. De Anima*, 222–23; *vs.* "Paralytic," 218–20; zone of indetermination in, 225
typewriter, 63–66; fantasies, 85–91

Undoing Gender (Butler), 377n4
The Unnamable (Beckett), 174, 187, 193–99, 196, 201, 238, 356n9; "breath of life" in, 204; conspicuous echo of, 356n8; failing breath marks, 193–94; frames, Beckett's comment on, 195; "I'm the partition," 190–93; mouth in, 188; revisions in, 183–85
The Use of Bodies (Agamben), 35

Van Hulle, Dirk, 183–84, 191, 357n19, 357n20, 358n22; disappearance of commas, 193
Vendler, Helen, 41

Verhulst, Pim, 357n20
vigorous release sign, 61
vigorous space dash, 60
"vital energy," 94–95
voice, 24–28; "prophetic," 64
A Voice and Nothing More (Dolar), 24
vulnerability, of respiring body, 106–7

Waiting for Godot (Beckett), 195
Wallon, Henri, 21
The Waves (Woolf), 120
weakness, 106–7
"Weggebeizt," 372n46
Weller, Shane, 183–84, 191, 357n19, 358n22; disappearance of commas, 193
Whitman, Walt, 30, 50, 76, 90, 167, 263, 316, 323, 324, 326
Williams, James, 359n30
Williams, William Carlos, 50
Wills, David, 16, 17, 31, 168–69, 370n28, 373n64, 376n95
wind, 7–10
Winstanley, Adam Michael, 356n3, 359n31

Woolf, Virginia, 43, 45, 46, 47, 145, 146, 305; approaches to antiquity, 121; breathing pauses by, 125; breaths of natural world, 171; collocations of breath and intervals, 127–28; handwriting, 152–53; letter to Sackville-West, 120; *To the Lighthouse*, 117, 118–19, 134, 148–53; notion of unworking, 183; "permit effects of media reflection," 142; "profound" rhythm, 137; respiratory intervals, 126; rhythm for composition, 135–36; rhythmical force described by, 121–22; rhythm in writing of, 120–23; silence/sound and movement/standstill, treatments of, 128–29; "Time Passes," 163; writing process, 131–35, 147
writing: formative movement, 121; intertextual network, 121

Zanetti, Sandro, 267, 368n10
"Zauderrhythmus," 217
Zehnder, Christian, 372n50
Zilboorg, Gregory, 362n58
Zukofsky, Louis, 104, 105

www.ingramcontent.com/pod-product-compliance
Lightning Source LLC
Chambersburg PA
CBHW020257240426

43673CB00039B/626